## ADVANCE PRAISE

"Whiteness is the socio–political default. To disrupt whiteness, it must be exposed. This collection, curated by visionary Dr. Ken Hardy, brilliantly and accessibly takes up this weighty task. This is a revelatory and essential new work, clear-eyed and instructive, yet also deeply personal and eloquent. Oh, that it may be required reading for anyone in human services!"

–**Robin DiAngelo, PhD**, author of *White Fragility* and *Nice Racism*

"Seething and triggering, yet brilliantly analytical and refreshingly timely. This book should become a national treasure, because it makes visible the ubiquitous tyranny of whiteness, the effects of which occupy the minds and bodies of People of Color and to a more detrimental degree, Black People. Dr. Hardy and the other contributors speak a fiery truth to the centrality of whiteness in a way that has yet to be done. This book activates our duty as people of whiteness and People of Color to use simple, salient, and profound remedies to increase racial sensitivity and to create a path toward more constructive cross-racial conversations."

–**Michelle Cromwell, PhD**, author of *Racism: The Challenge of Dismantling Lies in the Dilemma of Definition*

"Dr. Kenneth Hardy's book, *The Enduring, Invisible, and Ubiquitous Centrality of Whiteness*, is shocking, provocative, clear, inspiring, and personal. It is deeply touching as well as disturbing in a most blessed way, and it absolutely achieves its purpose: the demystification of whiteness. Hardy has brought together a strong, broad, clear and very astute group of authors to help challenge us on this topic, which is so essential to our very survival. This is the book we have been needing to help us work together to cultivate a society where multiple ideologies can coexist without domination, marginalization, annihilation, or indoctrination."

–**Monica McGoldrick, PhD**, Director of the Multicultural Family Institute in Highland Park, NJ, author of *Genograms*

# THE ENDURING, INVISIBLE, AND UBIQUITOUS CENTRALITY OF WHITENESS

# THE ENDURING, INVISIBLE, AND UBIQUITOUS CENTRALITY OF WHITENESS

KENNETH V. HARDY PHD, EDITOR

W. W. NORTON & COMPANY
*Independent Publishers Since 1923*

This book is intended as a general information resource for professionals practicing in the field of psychotherapy and mental health. It is not a substitute for appropriate training or clinical supervision. Standards of clinical practice and protocol change over time. No technique or recommendation is guaranteed to be safe or effective in all circumstances, and neither the publisher nor the author(s) can guarantee the complete accuracy, efficacy, or appropriateness of any particular recommendation in every respect.

The names and identifying details of patients and certain other people described in this book have been changed, and some patients and situations described are composites. Any URLs displayed in this book link or refer to websites that existed as of press time. The publisher is not responsible for, and should not be deemed to endorse or recommend, any website, app, or other content that it did not create. The author, also, is not responsible for any third-party material.

Printed in the United States of America
First Edition

For information about permission to reproduce selections from this book, write to
Permissions, W. W. Norton & Company, Inc., 500 Fifth Avenue, New York, NY 10110
For information about special discounts for bulk purchases, please contact
W. W. Norton Special Sales at specialsales@wwnorton.com or 800-233-4830

Manufacturing by Lakeside Book Company
Book design by Daniel Lagin
Production manager: Katelyn MacKenzie

Library of Congress Cataloging-in-Publication Data

Names: Hardy, Kenneth V., editor.
Title: The enduring, invisible, and ubiquitous centrality of whiteness : implications for clinical practice and beyond / Kenneth V. Hardy.
Description: New York, NY : W. W. Norton & Company, [2022] | Series: A Norton professional book | Includes bibliographical references and index.
Identifiers: LCCN 2021038683 | ISBN 9781324016908 (paperback) | ISBN 9781324016915 (epub)
Subjects: LCSH: Whites--Race identity--United States. | Race relations. | Racism--United States--Psychological aspects. | African Americans--United States. | Race discrimination--United States.
Classification: LCC HT1575 .E54 2022 | DDC 305.809--dc23/eng/20211021
LC record available at https://lccn.loc.gov/2021038683

W. W. Norton & Company, Inc., 500 Fifth Avenue, New York, N.Y. 10110
www.wwnorton.com

W. W. Norton & Company Ltd., 15 Carlisle Street, London W1D 3BS

1 2 3 4 5 6 7 8 9 0

*To my beloved parents, both children of the old South, who saw more than they were probably ever able to say, experienced more than they were ever allowed to acknowledge, and felt more than they were ever allowed to express. Dad, I hope you are lying still spiritually, trusting and finding peace and solace in knowing that I am saying all that you could never say. And to my mother, for whom no sacrifice was ever too great for you to make for any of your children, I am aware that it has been your sacrifices that have been the incubator for my successes. On your shoulders, I will always stand.*

# Contents

# Note on Capitalization

There is an ongoing debate within journalistic and writing communities regarding the capitalization of the "B" and "w" when referring to Black and white people, respectively. Throughout the book, all references to Black people, as a racial group with a distinct and shared history of oppression, have been capitalized, while the lowercase "w" has been used in references to white people, except in Chapter 20. The author of Chapter 20 specifically requested the use of the uppercase "W" when referring to white people to establish compliance with the common parlance used in racial justice movement work. This accommodation was made for Chapter 20, and it was important to note the exception and the rationale here.

# Acknowledgments

No project of this magnitude is ever remotely possible without the dedicated contributions of many. I would first like to extend my warm and sincere gratitude to all of the authors for conscientiously devoting your time, energy, passion, and wisdom to this important project. I thank each of you for your patience and endurance during the tedious moments of this process, especially those requiring incessant tweaks, when one more tweak was almost always followed by yet another "final" request. Thank you for keeping this project high on your list of priorities as many of you balanced writing with working remotely from home, providing home schooling, and being emotionally overwhelmed by unprecedented racial unrest and protests, a white nationalist insurrection of the US government in the nation's capital, and a deadly global pandemic that claimed hundreds of thousands of US lives in less than one year, and we are still counting. Through it all, each of you stayed the course on this journey and I am grateful. I am also eternally grateful to Dhara Mehta Desai, one of the most loyal, hardworking, and conscientious staff members that anyone could ever hope to work with closely. Dhara, thank you for your willingness to have your fingerprints all over every segment of this project. There is simply no way the process would have gone as smoothly as it did without the involvement of your steady hand along the way. I would also like to express gratitude to the staff at Norton for the dedicated guidance and support you extended to me throughout this process. Thank you, Mariah Eppes and Olivia Guarnieri, for your responsiveness and acute attention to all the details that help make a project like this successful. I would also like to extend a very special thank you to Deborah Malmud for your unrelenting patience and generosity of spirit. I really appreciate your editorial brilliance and your ability to deliver straight talk that is positively challenging and instrumental in unlocking hidden potential. I have grown immensely from my collaboration with you and I eagerly look forward to our next venture together.

And finally, to my beloved family. Any words I commit to paper at this point would significantly fall short in expressing the depth of the heartfelt gratitude and love I feel for you. Thank you for your patience, commitment, and all the ways in which each of you inspire and sustain me. I am passionately and eternally grateful for your unrelenting support, embrace, and unconditional love. Thank you for all the sacrifices you have made to help fertilize my opportunities, not just with this project, but throughout my career. I hope this project is one that you can welcome and clasp with a sense of pride. To the next generation of Hardys, it is my hope that this book might in some small way pave the path for you to inherit a world that is more racially just, equitable, and embracing of your Blackness and humanity. Hopefully, you will not have to spend much of your precious lives, as so many did before you, trying to find ways to replenish your souls of all that was denied or violently stolen by the consequences of living in a racially oppressive society.

# Preface

KENNETH V. HARDY, PHD

There are moments when I think that there is a bit of irony, if not hypocrisy, involved in my quest to talk about, let alone devote a book to, whiteness. After all, I live my life as a Black man, and thus so much of what I have to say about whiteness will very likely not be received as trustworthy because it is through my *tainted eyes* as a member of the racially subjugated. For this reason, I have often wished that I could actually be white for a brief moment to enhance the credibility of my critique of whiteness.

I am not entirely sure I believe in an afterlife in the religious sense. However, just in case it exists, I have often entertained a wish to live my next life as a white person. For this reason, I have made my respectful request by prayer, email, fax, text, and Twitter that following my untimely death (whenever it is, it will be untimely for me), next time I wish to return to the planet as a white man! I don't want my motivation or intent to return to the planet as a white person to be misconstrued. For the record, I absolutely, unequivocally love being Black, and there is no sign of this changing. Although living life while Black has been replete with hardships, agonies, countless inequities, and, to paraphrase the iconic Black poet Langston Hughes (1994) in his poem "Mother to son," "ain't been no crystal stairs" (p. 30), I would not exchange it to be white. Being Black, from my perspective, has imbued me with a certain degree of humility. It has introduced me to the softer side of humanity as well as given me more than a glimpse of the side that is rough around the edges. It has taught and helped me to live with rejection, scorn, and taught me what it means to be the symbol of universal hatred and disdain by whites, by other People of Color who share in the struggle but want no part of being Black, and even by some of our brothers and sisters from our motherland who also think of us as a despised other.

My desire to come back white has nothing to do with a desire to be authentically white or to disavow my Blackness. Instead, it has more to do with an unrelenting curiosity I have as one who has lived life along the margins. It is the educator and scholar in me that wishes to return as a white man. The desire emanates from a curiosity to know what it is like to be at the center . . . to treat stepping on the bodies of others and crushing their hearts, souls, and spirits as a contact sport . . . to be in a position to place premature expiration dates on the dreams, hopes, and ambitions of others as if it were an inalienable right . . . to know what it is like to leave my fingerprint and footprint on everything I touch and everywhere I stand and to claim it as mine with impunity. I want to know what it is to live a wholesome and well-integrated moral life and balance that with knowing that I never have to say "I'm sorry" for anything . . . not slavery, not murder, not land stealing, nor all that I reject in others then later claim as mine through cultural appropriation. These are the curiosities that fuel my desire to be white.

Admittedly, my sardonic and often times very public self-proclaimed desire to return to the planet as a white man always masks a legitimate deep-seated rage that lives full-time inside of me about the life-threatening inequities that some of us are forced to endure. My curiosity about whiteness intensified a few years ago, at the most unpredictable and inconvenient time, as an unexpected blessing and gift was bestowed upon me. I had the opportunity to sit nightly for several months with my then ailing father as he metaphorically walked slowly through *the valley of the shadow of his death.* As my father's health and overall functioning continued to decline steadily, we were confronted with the inevitable difficult decision about whether to place him in a nursing facility. The pragmatics of the matter made this an easy decision. Theoretically he would get the medical care he needed from those more imminently prepared and trained to do so than from novice, untrained family members. Racially, we thought as a family that our contemplation of placing him in an institution made no sense and would be a personal affront to him, his life, and the sense of dignity that he had spent his entire life and early stages of death fighting to obtain. For him, as is the case with most People of Color, dignity was never a birthright; instead it had to be relentlessly fought for, even begged for at times. As a family, it was clear that our independent and collective concerns about race, and more specifically about his Blackness in a context of whiteness, was of far greater concern than the prima facie reassurance we had about him receiving good medical care at a facility. We felt a sense of shame and disappointment that we even considered the possibility of placing him in the care of an institution that would most likely respond more quickly to his Blackness than to his elevating blood pressure. Even as we maneuvered to position and prepare ourselves for the inevitable, we were all distracted by the daunting reality that in life, near death, and in death there is a stark differential value attached to Black and white lives. As a family, there was not a single one of us who could convince ourselves, let alone each other, that my dad would receive the treatment and care that he deserved, not just as a patient but also, and in some ways equally as important, as a Black man. His entire life was one in which white people *looked* at him but could rarely see or experience anything they regarded as intimately and innately human. From his formative days as a child in Florida, he was entangled in a lifelong struggle, fighting for what most whites take for granted, to be seen and treated as a respectable human being. Given this reality, one that doesn't uniquely belong to my father but to most People of Color, how could we expect that, during one of his most fragile moments in life, whites would treat him any better than had been the case during the more robust moments of his life? We made the racially just decision to keep my father at home, and we, his children, would provide 24-hour around-the-clock care for him with my mom also playing a key but minimal role, largely due to her health.

Due to the flexibility of my schedule as an academician, I cared for my father from 8 p.m. to 7 a.m. the following morning on a daily basis. It was during this time, especially in the middle of the night and early morning hours, that I found myself trapped in my thoughts about life and death in black and white. I remember thinking about the fact that death is a certainty and no one of us escapes it. I was sure this was true of my white friends and colleagues, and yet I was equally certain that they did not have to balance their experiences and moments of grief and loss with tussling with dynamics of race, racial oppression, and the negative imposition of whiteness. For whites, whiteness is an asset, a protective factor, a universally accepted, recognizable, valuable resource that can always be relied upon. The universal and abiding power accorded to whiteness is usually the metaphorical kryptonite for those of us who are not white.

During my nights of sitting in the darkness with my father, there was always a glaring bright light cast on the enduring, invisible, and ubiquitous centrality of whiteness that was hard to ignore. My nocturnal obsessions about whiteness were further ignited by the mental confusion and terrified emotional outbursts that my father intermittently experienced throughout most nights. On more than one occasion, I found myself fruitlessly trying to comfort and stabilize him while he was in a hallucinatory-like state. It was remarkably noticeable that the centerpiece of his mental confusion was *always*, without a single exception, about race and ultimately his relationship as a Black man with white men. Night after night, I occupied a front row seat, teary-eyed and stunned, battling a complex array of emotions that ranged from sadness and guilt to despair and rage as I witnessed his emotionally compelling exchanges with white men. "YOU will NOT disrespect me in front of my son; do you hear me? I am not going to let you or no other damn white man disrespect me in front of my son! You can do to me whatever you want, but you WILL NOT disrespect me," he stated repeatedly and passionately one night. These episodes were common. The intensity, sense of resolve, and rage he spoke with as he had these ongoing conversations with white men while on his dying bed will forever be etched in the walls of my memory. So will the deep emotion I experienced during these moments.

The final days with my father had afforded me a sacred space and time to reflect not only on our relationship but also on the ways in which whiteness was frequently at the core of it as well. I will never know whether his resistance to being "disrespected in the presence of his son" during his state of mental confusion that one summer night was totally induced by his ailing condition or whether it was residue from a previous real-life experience. However, I do know that white people and whiteness did impact how he parented. It affects how most People of Color, and especially Black parents, parent. It was white people and whiteness that were the impetuses for "the talk" that my parents gave me during my childhood long before I knew anything about the intricacies and complexities of race relationships in the United States of America. Whiteness and white people were at the center of the parental admonitions repeatedly given to me: "do not ever trust white people" or that "they will tolerate you, especially if they need or want something from you, but don't be mistaken, they will ALWAYS stick together!"

I later realized that it was my father's death that gave birth to a heightened and infinitely more nuanced awareness about whiteness that was both emerging and erupting inside of me. I began to think about the ubiquity of whiteness and how every microtissue of the lives of People of Color is profoundly shaped by whiteness, from conception to death, and that most white people either are oblivious to, ignore, or deny this daunting reality. I began to think about how it is common for People of Color to discuss the imposition and devastating effects of whiteness on our lives among ourselves and within Communities of Color, but rarely to and in the presence of white people with full honesty and authenticity. Unfortunately, the rules of racial engagement and the inability of some whites to confront racism makes it virtually impossible to have authentically honest cross-racial conversations, especially those involving any critique of whiteness. It has been the incessant stream of realizations and reflections about the ubiquity of whiteness and its effects on Black, Brown, and, quite frankly, white lives that have fueled the inspiration for this book. Among my many emerging epiphanies about whiteness was the realization that I don't have to be white to edit this book. As a Black man who has lived his entire life under the tyranny of white occupation and wears the intergenerational scars of it, who better than I to produce an anthology devoted to an exploration and exposé of whiteness?

The purpose of this book, in short, is to offer a demystification of whiteness. In a sense, it is more about whiteness as an ideology or worldview than it is about white people, although there is some entanglement of the two that is inextricable. One aim of this book is to explicitly name whiteness rather than continue to treat it as an invisible, often unnamed referent that ensures whites an abdication of racial responsibility and impunity for racial transgressions. This book is organized and structured to intentionally offer some challenge to dominant (white) discourses about what constitutes scholarship, knowledge, and who and what constitutes a scholar. A diverse group of authors—in terms of age, race, class, sexual orientation, ethnicity, religion, geography, gender, and career paths, just to name a few—has been invited to provide an understanding, analysis, and deconstruction of whiteness through the prism of how and where they stand in the world. Too often, white, heterosexual, cisgender males produce "objective scholarship," where their social location as white and male is strewn throughout the pages they type without any acknowledgment that their position could be a factor in what they see, say, and write. Rather than participate as expert, objective, detached, report-from-the-sidelines professionals, the authors invited to write for this book were encouraged to locate themselves within the context of their chapters to make explicit how their respective contexts do in fact contribute to the formation of their respective realities. In this regard, the book also makes an earnest attempt to uplift the voices of People of Color by creating space for them to tell their seldom publicly shared stories about their slights, struggles, and efforts to cope and survive in what author Gene Cash (Chapter 14) refers to as "a sea of whiteness."

In the second section of the book, psychologist and family therapist David Trimble, a long-time educator and antiracist advocate, offers a candid and insightful analysis of whiteness as a disease that not only creates havoc on the lives of People of Color but also injures the souls of white people. Lane Arye (Chapter 4) offers a further deconstruction of whiteness by acknowledging its omnipresence and the many ways it is reinforced by what he describes as a "vicious cycle of white centrality." If we are ever to make significant strides in our cross-racial relationships, being mindful of and attentive to the vicious centrality of whiteness is imperative. Unlike Arye and Trimble, Jeff Mangram, an educator, lives on the other side of the centrality of whiteness as a Black man. In his chapter, "The Elephant Is the Room: The Art and Peril of Navigating Whiteness," Mangram invites the reader to join him as he provides a painful and eloquent description of walking on a tightrope as he attempts to navigate *the art and peril* of being a Black man in predominantly- and all-white spaces. According to Mangram, whiteness is not merely *the elephant in the room*, it is so much bigger and pervasive. Thus, he argues it is the Elephant, that is, whiteness, that *is* the room!

Section III is devoted to examining whiteness as an intersectional issue. This dynamic is often a very challenging one for many who possess both salient privileged and subjugated identities. For example, there is often a major source of racial tension between some white-identified Jews and People of Color. On the one hand, the protracted history of the oppression of Jews around the world, as is the case with other ethnic and religiously persecuted groups, has been instrumental in promoting sensitivity to the suffering of People of Color. This acute understanding has promoted a solidarity with the racial plight of People of Color that extends over decades. Yet, despite the shared experiences of being the recipients of sociocultural victimization, genocide, and slavery, many Jews benefit from the privileges of whiteness and their proximity to it, while simultaneously only seeing themselves as subjugated. The Jewish experience of suffering, one that Epstein and Kliman acknowledge in their chapters, obscured their ability to be intimately acquainted with their dominant privileged identity as white. Ken Epstein and Jodie Kliman, in their respective chapters, discuss in very poignant and incisive ways the intersectional dynamics and tensions of being Jewish and white. The complexities inherent in these conflicting identities are illustrated by Epstein, who is white and grew up in New York but never consciously thought about it much until well into adulthood, and Kliman (Chapter 5), who grew up in Brooklyn, New York, not thinking of herself as white as a child, but who mostly identifies as such now.

Ovita Williams, a Jamaican-born Black woman, provides the introductory chapter to Section IV of the book, *Cross-Racial Encounters and Relationships*. In her chapter, "Herding Cats: The Burdensome and Exhausting Task of Negotiating Whiteness," Williams highlights the goals of this section as she describes her ongoing struggles and the inner turmoil she often experiences in her relationships with white women—struggles that, according to Williams, manifest in both her personal and professional relationships, even with white women she considers friends and mentors. Irene In Hee Sung, in her chapter "Silenced by Whiteness: A Personal Account," reports how her voice as a Korean-American psychiatrist was powerfully and implicitly silenced by whiteness during medical school training, her residency, and later in her professional life. Her chapter chronicles her enduring struggle to empower her voice in white spaces and with white people, even those with whom she has long-term intimate relationships. Ana Hernandez, a Dominican Afro-Latina, paints a powerful portrait of whiteness for the reader through the eyes of the Black immigrant experience. The brushing up against and the bruising that she has experienced from whiteness has been exacted by those who are phenotypically white as well as some who are ideologically white People of Color. Taiwanese-born Liang-Ying Chou also provides an analysis of whiteness through the lens of an immigrant, not one who is demonized and maligned for having Black skin, like Hernandez, but who instead is confined and defined by the *golden handcuffs* of being a *model minority*. Chou makes a compelling case for why seemingly innocent acts, such as assigning white, European names to Asians to supplant their birth names, are all part of a process to "whiten" Asians. Gene Cash, although born in a different era and on a different side of the world than Chou, also shared Chou's experiences of being pressured to be white. Given his European name at birth, the pressures to be white that he describes in his chapter extended well beyond the name he was given. Cash takes the reader on a journey through his life, characterized by moments where he eschewed his Blackness, struggled to reclaim it, and even temporarily surrendered to the ideology of whiteness as a tactic for survival. In her chapter, "Shunning the Shame of Being Black in a World of Whiteness," Cynthia Chestnut echoes many of the same underlying pressures that both Chou and Cash allude to in their respective chapters. Chestnut, like Chou, had to grapple with the intersections of race and gender. The white woman has always been the prototype for beauty, not only in the United States but around the globe. Historically, Women of Color have been harshly criticized for their "failure" to adhere to white notions of beauty, be it to the size and shape of one's eyes, hair texture, skin complexion, or overall physique. Chestnut's chapter is a celebration of the hard emotional psychological work she devoted over the course of her life to find her beauty within as a "dark-skinned big Black girl" (Chapter 8). Each chapter in this section underscores the potent and deleterious effects that whiteness has on the self-esteem and the social–emotional development of People of Color starting at a very early age. Chou and Chestnut also point out how gender and sexism compound these issues for women. Despite the widespread effects of whiteness and the ways in which it permeates virtually all our major institutions, it is rarely a point of inquiry or interrogation. Whiteness is both relational and structural and it is essential that the interlocking of the two are effectively addressed.

The chapters in Section V examine the phenomenon of *white spaces* and how the ideology of whiteness is deeply embedded and manifested in institutional structures. Robin Nuzum offers a brilliant and compelling analysis of white spaces and how whiteness permeates much of our existence without recognition or scrutiny. Nuzum (Chapter 17) argues that

> the embeddedness of White supremacy ideology within the master narratives of American life is a matter of crucial scholarly interest and engagement. Meanwhile these narratives remain rather protectively ensconced in the actual lives of white Americans who have not explored or done the difficult work of unearthing and interrogating the racial and racist dimensions of their governing ideas. (pp. 312–313)

Her chapter raises a number of often unexamined issues underpinning white supremacist ideology and the maintenance of it. Carlin Quinn draws on her work as a practicing therapist to examine the toxic trends of whiteness and how it is infused within the worldview and work of white practitioners as well as within our notions about healing. Christiana Awosan (Chapter 16), a university professor, provides a critical insider's view of what she describes and experiences as toxic whiteness in academia. Niki Berkowitz, who has devoted her career to working in the trenches of community mental health, describes how the centrality of whiteness contributes to the systemic underserving of racially marginalized populations. Jen Leland, like Berkowitz, has a long and dedicated history of working in community-based organizations. Leland's chapter centers around her work in child welfare and the juvenile justice system. Quinn, Berkowitz, and Leland, all white, recall how developing a keener understanding of their whiteness was a prelude to even beginning to question how it negatively affected the lives of Clients of Color or how the systems in which they were employed were steeped in an impenetrable culture of whiteness. Toby Bobes, a clinician, educator, and supervisor, also realized that her efforts to address race and diversity in the classroom and in supervision were often hampered by her unfamiliarity with her whiteness. In her chapter, "Getting Acquainted With My White Self," Bobes describes how her lifelong commitment to Self of the Therapist work had only in recent years led her to think of and explore herself as a white person. It is difficult to imagine how white people committed to dismantling whiteness in institutional structures can do so effectively if they have not identified or explored their whiteness. Thus, embracing and critiquing one's whiteness is the first barrier that any aspiring white antiracist must eclipse in order to do the work with integrity and efficacy.

Mary Pender Greene, a Black antiracist trainer, offers a comprehensive array of strategies for anyone interested in becoming an antiracist organizational leader. Bonnie Cushing and Hinda Winawer join Mary Pender Greene as contributors to Section VI, which is devoted to exploring the landscape of antiracist work. Cushing's chapter, "From Illness Toward Wellness: Transmuting Individual Consciousness," draws from her work as an antiracist advocate, trainer, and clinical social worker. She reminds us that the work of "becoming" an antiracist advocate involves more than skill acquisition; there is a spiritual dimension to the work that involves a transformation of self. Winawer's chapter chronicles her personal and ongoing journey of wrestling with the personal, spiritual, and personal transformation dimensions of becoming a white antiracist. All the authors in this section assert that, in one way or another, the work of the white antiracist involves a lifelong commitment and must focus on both who we are and what we do.

The final collection of chapters under Section VII is devoted to programs, approaches, and strategies for addressing and/or dismantling whiteness. Alana Tappin, a Black woman, and cotrainer Robin Schlenger, a white woman, are cocreators of The Shame Resiliency Model, a program designed to help whites overcome the race-related feelings of shame that often get activated in antiracism and white accountability work. Their chapter explains how shame is often a major deterrent to white people challenging and overcoming internalized white supremacy. This chapter presents a model for helping white people overcome shame-based barriers. The chapter by Cristina Combs similarly introduces a model for working directly and specifically with white people. The Recovery from White Conditioning Model is a twelve-step program. According to Combs (Chapter 26), this

> derivative work based on the twelve steps of Alcoholics Anonymous (AA), is rooted in accountability and love. It involves us white people working, within our community, to transform violent legacies of whiteness into healthier, white, antiracist community . . . and it requires having the courage to start with ourselves. (p. 507)

Tim Baima (Chapter 28) advocates self-love as a type of transformative love that whites need to develop as a key element to combat the "addiction to domination disorder" (McGoldrick & Hardy, 2019, p. 10) that he asserts is embedded in what Combs (Chapter 26) refers to as white conditioning. Baima sends a clear warning to whites that remaining addicted to domination reinforces reliance on oppression practices that undermine healing. We frequently end up relying on this instrument of oppression, even in our efforts to advance healing and justice. His chapter is an impassioned plea for whites to relinquish their dependency on domination and learn to invest in the power of transformative love as a viable alternative. Michael Boucher, a white antiracist clinician who has devoted his life and career to working in nonprofit community-based organizations, continues the aim and spirit of this section by offering a vision in his chapter of what nonracist clinical work could look like when whiteness is decentered. According to Boucher (Chapter 25), the ways in which we conceptualize and practice clinical work "needs to more urgently disrupt and interrupt racially oppressive practices that result in deadly consequences for People of Color" (p. 493); this, he asserts, requires widespread behavior modification and the decentering of white supremacy in clinical practice and institutions. Keith Alford shares Boucher's desire to decenter whiteness in therapy and provides a model for doing so with Black men. Alford (Chapter 24) provides a model of therapy that highlights what he refers to as an Africentric approach that takes into consideration the unique race-related struggles Black men encounter in their daily efforts to mediate the effects of whiteness.

It is my hope that the collection of insightful and provocative chapters assembled in this book will help to elevate the significance of thoughtfully and persistently including whiteness in our broader discourses about race. When whiteness remains unnamed, unacknowledged, and unaddressed, it constructs an impenetrable wall-less prison around the lives of People of

Color. While it remains an unnamed, unacknowledged, and unidentified coconspirator in the destruction of Black and Brown lives, those who are most maligned, most victimized, and intergenerationally targeted are left with the burden of blame for their suffering. We cannot achieve the ideals that so many of us crave and many have died for as long as the issue of race is considered a People of Color problem. If we are ever to be able to achieve the ideals of racial fairness, justice, and equity, it will require all of us, regardless of racial background, to see, appreciate, and embrace our shared humanity. The group of authors invited to contribute chapters to this book, while far from perfect or as inclusive as I had initially and ideally hoped, may be a flawed example of where and how we might start as well as what striving for inclusivity might possibly look like. Everyone has a story to tell that deserves to be told, listened to, heard, and validated. Not all data have to be quantified or packaged and presented through sophisticated statistical tools. The stories of our lives, and the life notes that accompany them, acknowledge what unites us as well as what divides us and can be powerful data if given the space to be respectfully shared and honored. White people must be willing to break their silence regarding whiteness and its long-term, pervasive, and deleterious effects on the lives of People of Color and all of humanity. White people must be forthright and engage in a gut-wrenching truth-telling about their whiteness, their complicity with the centrality of whiteness, and what they pledge regarding dismantling the prevailing racial order.

People of Color must also be actively engaged in the dismantling of mechanisms that help maintain and support the centrality of whiteness. To this end, People of Color must be diligent in naming whiteness in the presence of whites and while in white spaces. Even when whites ignore, deny, or rebuff these efforts, doing so with commitment and resolve still paves the way for the liberation of our enchained souls. As People of Color, we need not follow the path of my beloved father, who carried the millions of petite piercings of whiteness that severely wounded him to his death bed. My dad used the final breaths of his life to tell his version of what it was like to live a life stolen by white supremacy and the centrality of whiteness. I am grateful that he told his story and didn't take it to his grave. I am grateful that I had the opportunity to listen to all of them during our final and waning moments sitting in the dark. I am grateful that I listened attentively with dignity, grace, humility, and great pain to his story. Now all of you know his story and that which has given birth to this book.

## References

*Hughes, L. (1994).* The collected poems of Langston Hughes *(A. Rampersad, Ed.). Vintage Books.*

*McGoldrick, M., & Hardy, K. V. (2019). The power of naming. In M. McGoldrick & K. V. Hardy (Eds.),* Re-visioning family therapy: Addressing diversity in clinical practice *(3rd ed., pp. 3–27). The Guilford Press.*

# SECTION I

# INTRODUCTION

CHAPTER 1

# The Centrality of Whiteness

KENNETH V. HARDY, PHD

Speaking openly and honestly about race within racially integrated spaces is never easy; it is often marred by discomfort, defensiveness, coded language, and avoidance. These conversations become even more difficult when naming whiteness, especially in the presence of white people. I was reminded of this challenge during a workshop I was conducting on the topic of race. Within the first hour of my day-long presentation, a self-proclaimed racially woke, benevolent white male participant felt inspired to offer me a piece of unsolicited and sage advice about being Black and how to be a better version of it. Obviously triggered by a comment I made about the historical and systemic racial oppression of Black people and other People of Color by whites throughout history, Walter, a clinician from a local clinic, assertively waved his right hand to capture my attention. I acknowledged his raised hand and invited him to speak. He politely thanked me and then reminded me: "You said that we could be honest with you today, right?" I replied: "Yes, absolutely!" He then promised, as his breathing dramatically shifted, and his voice tone became louder as he spoke, "Okay I am going to be totally honest with you!" He continued: "I want to challenge your excuse about Black people being oppressed, because the last time I checked, there was nobody holding Black people back. *It* is out there for anyone who wants it badly enough. I honestly think, in all due respect to you, Dr. Hardy, I think it is people like you who are oppressing yourselves by blaming others for your hardships. I think you and other Black people would be better off if you didn't look in the past so much! That is one of your biggest problems; you keep looking to the past, looking for someone to blame other than yourselves. I think you and other Black people would be better off if you were more like other minority groups who you never hear complain. This is why they own and run things, they don't run around obsessed with the past and looking for others to blame. So, my advice to you is that I think it is time for you to look in the mirror!" The room was eerily quiet, although the intensity was palpable and the troubled and agitated facial expressions worn by many of the People of Color as well as some whites exposed the inner turmoil that many in the room were experiencing. Despite the silence, it was clear there was a wide range of emotions that permeated the auditorium. I thanked Walter for his courageous disclosure. I also indicated to him that in some ways his comments made sense to me, when viewed through his eyes as a white male. I further acknowledged that it was not surprising to me that we would see the phenomenon of race and racial oppression differently because we live in, essentially, two different worlds. And finally, I confessed to Walter that I didn't think that he, as a white person, could teach me anything about being Black because I have lived every day of my life with an unrelenting consciousness and acute awareness about what it means to be a *racialized being* impacted by a white supremacist ideology.

The exchange between Walter and me further increased the emotional temperature in the room. Although it was just a little more than an hour into the workshop, the room felt tense and virtually everyone seemed anxious as they wondered what would happen next. The stifling tension in the air was never overtly acknowledged but was hard to ignore. This is what customarily happens when there are earnest attempts to have meaningful conversations about race that move beyond our usual cautiousness and exchanges of hyperpolite platitudes. The fact that the conversation explicitly named and centered whiteness didn't make it any easier to have. I made a similar process comment during the workshop about what tends to happen when attempts are made to talk about race in cross-racial settings and white accountability is a focus. This comment was a perfect segue and opportunity for me to return to my workshop notes. This portion of the workshop was centered around the identification of ten tasks that white people must execute in order to participate in substantive and progressive conversations about race. This material was based on the PAST (the **P**rivileged **A**nd **S**ubjugated **T**asks) model that I developed and has been widely published (Hardy, 2016). The model essentially explicates tasks that both whites, as members of a privileged group, and People of Color, as a subjugated group, must execute in order to enhance the chances of having more viable and sustainable conversations about race.

I introduced and discussed the first three tasks in detail. However, before I could fully introduce the fourth, I heard a loud baritone-like voice from the back of the room: "DR. HARDY! DR. HARDY! . . . DR HARDY!" In a loud and extremely agitated tone, dripping in condemnation, a white male, Michael, from the rear of the auditorium stood up and stated: "I am really struggling with this workshop! What is the endgame here? . . . I need to know if this is what we will be listening to all day today. If it is . . . I need you to explain yourself. No more than 90 minutes ago, I heard you tell Walter over there that he couldn't teach you how to be Black because he wasn't Black, yet for the last 30 to 45 minutes you have done nothing other than lecture us about how we can be better white people. I resent this, and I guess what I really need to know from you, sir, is whether this is a function of your hypocrisy or your arrogance. If neither I, nor Walter, or any other white person in this auditorium can't teach you anything about being Black, WHAT the hell qualifies you, sir, to teach us white people about being white? This is either your arrogance or your ignorance and I guess I just need to know which is it? So, what is it sir?"

The attempt to openly discuss race and whiteness in an uncharacteristically straightforward and uncensored way was beginning to take its emotional toll. A bevy of hands immediately were raised in response to Michael's comment. It was not immediately clear to me whether it was his poorly veiled anger coupled with his confrontational style or his uncensored words that triggered reactions from every corner of the large auditorium. I deliberately avoided inviting anyone else into the conversation at this critical juncture because I was not convinced that it could or would be constructive. Emotions were just too high, and I had not completed my discussion of the strategies for conducting progressive conversations about race. I did, however, attempt to address the important question that had been raised about my potential hypocrisy and/or arrogance. I acknowledged that it was possible that it could have been either, neither, or both, depending on one's perspective. However, I didn't believe that Walter's implied self-proclaimed expertise on Blackness and his advice-giving to me and other Black people was even remotely comparable to my expertise and advice-giving to whites about whiteness. This analysis was greeted by a sense of intrigue by many and moans, groans, and eye-rolling by others.

## Living in Separate Worlds

It remains a shocking, painful, and irrefutable reality that even over a decade into the twenty-first century, People of Color and white people share the same soil, Earth, and planet and live in two distinctive and staunchly different worlds. The question posed to me during the workshop regarding my potential hypocrisy and/or arrogance was rooted in a false equivalency. Walter, like most white people, has the luxury of living his entire life and NEVER having to think about what it means to be white or the *burden* of thinking about what it means to be Black in a white-dominated world. It is possible for him to live his life virtually void of any meaningful and substantive interactions with People of Color and Blacks in particular. Thus, where would his knowledge base and expertise on Blackness come from? Even if he lived his entire life in a Black community, he would have done so as white man in a white dominated society in which there is no corner of existence where white is not privileged—not even in a Black community!

## A Self-Proclaimed Expert on Whiteness

At the risk of sounding and appearing arrogant, I do consider myself an expert on whiteness and white people. Unlike Walter, Michael, and many other whites, I am deeply credentialed in the phenomenology, psychology, and epistemology of whiteness. My prolific credentials in the study of whiteness and the unofficial participant–observer qualitative research that I have conducted throughout much of my life imbue me with the insight, experience, and ability to offer advice to white people about whiteness. Intergenerationally speaking, I was introduced to whiteness from the day of my birth. I am the first-born son of two children of the Old

South, the place where singer Billie Holiday (1939) lamented, "Southern trees bear a strange fruit," where the lynching and torture of Black people were treated as sport and where separate but equal was never intended to be equal, only separate. I am the progeny of parents who never overcame the trauma of living in the Deep South, one of whom carried the scars of racial degradation to his grave and the other who lives with the scars and open wounds today as these words appear on my computer screen. The racial trauma they experienced growing up in the South significantly informed their approach to parenting their Black children. Thus, I knew whiteness and the viciousness of it long before I ever directly interacted with anyone white. I was introduced to whiteness during childhood as I, standing next to my dad, witnessed more times than I care to remember and times that were too painful to forget as he was disrespected by white men and his humanity was assaulted without regard for either of us. No, it was not the type of disrespect that the child of Philando Castile witnessed from his car seat as his father was murdered by a cop during a routine traffic stop. I also don't imagine that it was comparable to the disrespect that the children of Eric Garner or George Floyd experienced as they watched their respective fathers choked to death at the hands of callous, racially insensitive police who found it hard to see any thread of humanity embedded in those men's Blackness. No, I didn't experience these levels of disrespect, but what I did experience belongs in this conversation because of the spiritual death it caused. Whiteness has been an integral part of my life for my entire life.

It is because of whiteness that I have known since approximately age 4 that I was Black. I had to know because my parents knew that my life depended on me knowing. Through their eyes, as prisoners of whiteness themselves, my knowing I was Black was a guardrail. It helped me to know and navigate what the boundaries were for Black people living in a society where one can rely on being constantly surveilled, policed, and targeted. I had to know I was Black so that I would at least have an intellectual understanding of the barrage of indignities that would come my way over the course of my life. It was meant to be a vaccine, attempting to inoculate me from the many times I or someone close to me would be called nigger, stupid, thuggish, or criminal. Understanding my Blackness was considered paramount to understanding whiteness. The understanding was designed to provide a pathway to making sense out of the nonsensical aspects of life that I had not yet experienced, but undoubtedly would, such as discrimination, hatred, and bigotry. It would help to explain why my great-grandmother, the granddaughter of a slave, was not allowed to attend school in South Carolina and was then harshly criticized for being "stupid." For all these reasons and a myriad of others, I have known for much of my life that I was Black and have been reminded incessantly of the differences between Black and white in our society. As a middle-aged Black man, I have lived under the armpits and tyranny of whiteness my entire life. I wonder, at what age did Walter, Michael, or the other white workshop participants become aware that they were white?

My education in whiteness has been a lifelong endeavor. After all, People of Color must absolutely know what is important to white people, not only to succeed, but to survive as well; the reverse is not true. My vast knowledge of whiteness has been obtained over decades and has occurred in all facets of my life. For my undergraduate education, I attended a predominantly white institution where I was the only Student of Color in my classes. All of the professors were white, all of the theories I was exposed to were white-driven, all of the audio-visuals used were of white people, and the entire administration was white. My Blackness stood out to me, as I am sure it did to others, but it was never acknowledged. My master's and doctoral degree educational experiences were replicas of that undergraduate experience, except I also had to complete clinical practica and internships where I would be supervised by white supervisors. Interestingly enough, while the clients were often predictably and disproportionately poor People of Color, there was never a single reference to race nor any attention given to how it might be a critical clinical factor to consider. I also completed two post-doctoral training programs that continued the immersion and indoctrination into whiteness that started at birth and continued well into my advanced educational experiences—never once having a Black person or Person of Color as a mentor, professor, or supervisor, and no one ever acknowledging that this could be an impediment. Instead, the pure and exclusive whiteness of my education was considered another credential that helped to fortify the value of my doctorate. I was duly certified as a *well-trained and qualified Person of Color*. As I confessed back in 2008 during my quiet self-reflective moments, even I had to admit that I had been trained to be a better-than-average white therapist (Wyatt, 2008).

I didn't take the time to ask Walter or Michael how many Black educators, teachers, professors, or clinical supervisors they had during their training. It would have been interesting to know what Black, Brown, or nonwhite theoreticians had been instrumental in shaping their worldviews or theories of therapy. I suspect the exact same number I had been exposed to academically: none! Admittedly, attending college and having formal education experiences are an important but small component of our overall learning journey in life. My uneducated great-grandmother was a testament to this point. While she was deemed stupid by some, she was one of the most brilliant thinkers and philosophers I have ever met. The knowledge and lessons she imparted to me about life, living, humanity, and inhumanity have been life changing. While my entire higher educational experience was obscenely skewed toward and replete with whiteness, in my civilian life I was immersed in a Black community, surrounded by members of my tribe that helped me stay centered and grounded as much as possible. Even this was challenging and had to be fought for because even in "Black spaces," whiteness is often a persistent and imposing force of infiltration, indoctrination, and sabotage. It is pervasive and ubiquitous.

To be a Person of Color, and especially Black, in the United States is to live a protracted life under a form of metaphorical white occupation. It is for this reason that I think it is in many ways more important, or at the very least just as important, to discuss and critique whiteness as it is to talk about white people. Whiteness is a pervasive and dominant ideology that is enduring, invisible, and ubiquitous. Despite its centrality, it is rarely named, acknowledged, or concretized. People of Color suffocate from it, and its invisibility smothers accountability. It is the phenomenon that leads the Walters of the world to conclude that the plight of Black people is of their own making and that *it* is out there to be roped in by those who have the motivation, will, and drive to "go get *it*." According to this view, those who don't get *it* are at fault for simply failing to work hard enough or lacking in motivation, drive, and focus. The Walters of the world are not only blinded by the invisibility of their whiteness but also by the invisibility of it in the broader society. Consequently, they also can't see the *white-constructed invisible fences*, barriers, walls, and *ways of being* that aggressively encroach on the lives of Black and Brown people over the course of a lifetime. The inability to see these and other structural barriers allows many whites to overendow the saliency of white-dominated values, such as personal responsibility and rugged individualism.

## The Ubiquitous Centrality of Whiteness

The centrality of whiteness is a weighty, exhausting burden that People of Color live with across the life cycle. It requires that People of Color, as a matter of survival, be consumed with and obsessively preoccupied with white people. It ensures that white people and, by extension, whiteness, occupies a full-time dwelling in the heads and psyches of countless numbers of People of Color. My life has been no exception. This is one of the fundamental reasons why I believe I am an expert on whiteness and infinitely qualified to dispense cogent knowledge and wisdom to whites. I have, by necessity, carefully studied, analyzed, and critiqued whiteness my entire life. In a sense, who better to discuss the phenomenology and centrality of whiteness than he who represents those who have spent a lifetime living under the tyranny and occupation of whiteness? The sad truth is that there is no dimension of the lives of People of Color that isn't profoundly shaped by the nuances and pervasiveness of whiteness. So many of us spend a lifetime worrying about what whites think, say, do . . . or how we will ultimately be judged, accepted, or rejected by them.

Whiteness is weaved throughout our lives, lifestyles, and even styles. For example, it dictates who and what is considered attractive and who/what isn't. It dictates what hair texture is considered good or bad, what hairstyles are acceptable and which are too ethnic, what language accents are exotic and which are too primitive. Whiteness dictates what is deemed *the standard* as well is what is considered *aberrant, pathological,* and *undesirable.* Thus, People of Color's preoccupation with whiteness is borne out of living under the occupation of whiteness. Historically, as well as contemporarily, People of Color have been the incessant targets of white people's scorn, criticism, rejection, and objectification. For centuries, the racial dynamic and climate in the United States has been one whereby white people have historically performed the role of hunter while Blacks and other racially oppressed groups have been *occupied* and relegated to the position of the hunted. As People of Color, our sense of freedom, humanity, and dignity has been disrupted, and often canceled, by the centrality of whiteness.

The centrality of whiteness and its philosophical underpinnings do not require one to be phenotypically white in order to subscribe to the prevailing worldview. People of Color can and do often become major purveyors of the centrality of whiteness. In fact, the acquiescence of People of Color to the centrality of whiteness is a mandated precursor for surviving in the white world. It is as lethal as it is invisible. It infects the souls of each of us. It blinds the vision of the white liberal, fuels the venom of the white conservative, and validates the lack of worth and assaulted sense of self (Hardy, 2013) of many People of Color. The assaulted sense of self is an invisible wound of racialized trauma. It profoundly shapes how one views oneself and how they believe they are perceived by others. The following vignette is a poignant illustration of the wound:

## TOO DARK

I was conducting a racial sensitivity training with a small group of senior executives for a large organization on the West Coast. I started the training by asking each of the twenty participants to introduce themselves by their name and by their race, stating what significance the latter had on their lives. The only Black person in the group, Lester, went last and stated: "I have been struggling with your question about race . . . I am African American but I can't think of any significance it has in my life." I continued to push him a little for more in hopes of getting him to connect to some area of significance, but my efforts proved futile. Lester seemed relieved but appeared troubled throughout the remainder of the day-long training.

Two weeks later, at the second of the four-day training sessions, I started the training by asking if there were any residuals from the first session. Before I could finish formulating the question, Lester blurted out: "I have something I need to say . . . I lied last session when I said I couldn't think of any significance that being Black has for me. . . . As everyone here can see, I am a dark-skinned Black man, and I have grown up hating my complexion . . . sometimes even hated being Black. . . . Being Black has stolen my life from

> me. Black people judge you and white people judge you. Race is always present in my life. I know this will sound crazy to everybody here . . . I grew up loving watermelon. . . . It is one of my favorite foods AND I will NEVER eat watermelon at work or in public (especially around white people). NEVER . . . even this morning when I was getting fruit salad from the breakfast table, I made sure I didn't take the watermelon." When I asked him why, he simply stated, in a soft voice, slightly above a whisper, with his eyes and head lowering: "IMAGES!" After a few seconds of silence that felt like hours, I repeated quizzically: "Images?" The tears began to flow as he shared: "I have vivid memories from my childhood of the television images of the caricature of the super dark Black man with huge platypus-type lips devouring a slice of watermelon accompanied by uncivilized and beast-like sounds. This is what I think of when I eat watermelon in the presence of white people. I fantasize that this is how they perceive me. It makes me angry, and it hurts to have your life stolen just because of the color your skin." With his head lowered onto the table, Lester continued to cry while hitting his clenched fist on the table and repeatedly stating: "It's not fair . . . it's not fair!"

It would be tempting, but admittedly shortsighted, to blame Lester for his shortcomings, to blame him for his emotional hang-ups and hypersensitivity. Yet, this is how the centrality of whiteness works in our society. Lester has been well socialized and indoctrinated in a world that has taught him that his dark skin, even among other Black people, is unattractive, problematic, and inferior. The childhood cartoons that he watched for entertainment were not just action-packed mini stories designed to capture the imagination of the young, they were also inundated with race-related messages that conveyed how society viewed Black people. The innocent, nonracialized-on-the-surface amusement left him with indelible racial scars that assaulted his sense of self and ultimately interfered with how he showed up at his job as an ivy-league educated senior executive. His stellar credentials, while impressive, were an impotent salve for soothing the deep wounds inflicted by racial trauma and the centrality of whiteness.

Lester's struggles were emblematic of those suffered by many People of Color attempting to navigate the enduring, invisible, and ubiquitous centrality of whiteness, although their struggles may not be directly attributable to the same issues. One of the many complexities of whiteness is that it is so much more than a phenotype, it's a philosophy, an epistemology . . . a way of thinking about the world. It is synonymous with what is *right, standard, normal,* and above all . . . what is *human.* Perhaps this is why when whites commit heinous crimes, we, as a society, are almost always allowed to see their humanity. We are immediately schooled about their hardships as well as their redeemable qualities. This is in stark contrast to Black and other People of Color who are almost immediately presumed guilty until proven innocent while all aspects of their lives are demonized, in spite of their guilt or innocence. Murder victims Michael Brown, Ahmaud Arbery, Breonna Taylor, George Floyd, Trayvon Martin, Walter Scott, Freddie Gray, Eric Garner, and a long list of others, too many to cite here, were demonized and to varying degrees blamed for their senseless and untimely deaths. The centrality of whiteness often has a way of demonizing People of Color while concomitantly sanitizing the transgressions of whites even when they are culpable. During the early days of January 2021, the world watched incredulously as white domestic terrorists attacked the halls of Congress, and despite their flagrant acts of malice and mayhem, they were granted considerable latitude to do whatever they wanted to do, with minimal resistance. Some of us were reminded that when peaceful Black protesters marched months earlier in support of racial equality, they were greeted by a battalion of law enforcement in full riot gear, wielding batons, bombing crowds with tear gas, and robustly arresting protesters. The blatant broadcasting of these stark inequities is yet another reminder of the centrality and supremacy of whiteness.

Whiteness is not only dominant but dominating as well. Across the racial divide as well as within circles of racial allies, it is the one factor upon which we all understand and agree—those of us who are Black, Asian, Latinx-Hispanic, Indigenous, and white can find common ground—that WHITENESS is at the center. It is to be revered, emulated, emboldened, and embraced by each of us regardless of our hue, circumstance, or other dimensions of our identities.

The dominating force of whiteness is evidenced by the fact that its centrality is not relegated to white faces but also becomes inculcated in all of our institutions and thus contributes to the formation of *white places*. When whiteness becomes centralized, discreetly and cleverly codified, it becomes encrypted into the fabric of what it means to be an American, a good institution or organization, even a good person. The essence of white places is that the inclusion of People of Color does not disrupt the poignancy or the ubiquity of the centrality of whiteness. Furthermore, it is a place where "qualified minorities" are recruited, valued, and embraced, as long as they subscribe to and perpetuate the centrality of whiteness, never naming it, always deferring to it, and never risking or threatening to be one's authentic racial self. It is a place where People of Color can survive but rarely thrive, especially if they are too emotional, not appropriately measured and constrained in showing passion or any feelings that can be misconstrued as anger.

While the presence of white faces is *not* a prerequisite for creating and sustaining white places, many, nevertheless, are inundated with white people. Interestingly, the preponderance of whites comprising *a place* rarely generates more than cursory curiosity, if any at all, regarding how whiteness potentially informs the establishment of rules, regulations, protocols, and standards of practice. On the other hand, the centrality of whiteness ensures that whites are virtually always emotionally safe and comfortable with regard to race, and many "rules" and standard operating procedures are unwittingly designed to deliver these amenities. In the rare instances where whites fail to comprise the numerical majority and/or function as the framers of the rules, either feelings of discomfort are quickly transformed into claims of "not feeling safe" or more concrete ground rules are demanded. To deny or dismiss the racialization of whiteness and the sense of superiority and supremacy that is associated with it serves to perpetuate the status quo. The invisibility and denial of whiteness help to promulgate the notion that race is a People of Color's issue and that whiteness is not an issue at all.

Another salient feature of the centrality of whiteness is that it often legitimizes whites supporting other whites without any recognition or declaration that it has anything to do with race. When whites are simultaneously the *makers*, *appliers*, and *enforcers* of the "rules," the "standard operating procedures," and the "selection criteria," whiteness is often seamlessly baked into the cake of these processes while they are concurrently purported to be fair, equitable, and color-blind. Thus, when someone is either selected or rejected based on the established criteria, of which white people and whiteness have been the major architects, it is often believed to be an indisputable truth that "race had nothing to do with it." In fact, as it is commonly noted: "this decision was based on the policy!" This dynamic is further exemplified by white leaders' fervent proclamation that selection decisions will not be based on race but on who constitutes the best qualified candidate that represents the greatest fit. This process is often proudly heralded as one that is a derivative of a larger commitment to fairness, equity, and objectivity. The pervasive and potentially influential, implicit biases associated with whiteness remain invisible, unacknowledged, and thus never factored into the calculus of the selection process. When one is operating from a framework of objectivity and color blindness, there is little motivation to (self) interrogate the potential role and unintended consequences of one's whiteness in a selection process. I have been a member of a countless number of minority fellowship committees, graduate school admissions committees, employment panels, and other such entities, where viable Black and Brown applicants have been denied access and opportunity "NOT on the basis of race," but rather because of their misalignment with a policy or because they lacked the proper ill-defined or vaguely defined "fit factor." The criterion of "fit" was rarely, if ever, operationally defined and thus was nearly impossible to deconstruct or ascertain how it might have negatively affected Applicants of Color being considered by predominantly white evaluators.

The potency of the centrality of whiteness is in part derived from and reinforced by the fact that it is often invisible, unnamed, and virtually impossible to talk about, especially in cross-racial settings. McGoldrick and Hardy (2019) warn about "the problems of naming" (p. 8) and of not naming. The politics and privilege of naming and not naming are virtually always aligned with those who have power. Too often, People of Color and progressive whites are reluctant to name whiteness because it is frequently met with resistance, resentment, and defensiveness. The ensuing attempted conversations almost always erupt into rapid escalation, blaming, and ultimately polarization and cutoff. On the other hand, many whites are wholly oblivious to whiteness, especially the intricacies of it, and thus find it difficult to discuss that which is far removed from their consciousness. Thus, silence reigns and *white silence is violence* (Thum-Gerber, 2020).

Seeing and naming the ubiquity and centrality of whiteness is no small or simple task. It requires us to recognize the insidious ways in which whiteness is seamlessly integrated into the microfibers and fabric of who we believe we are and who we aspire to be as Americans (or as I prefer to say *United Statesians*). Some of the subtle and not so subtle ways whiteness is concretized and reinforced while remaining invisible and unnamed are implicated in the following core ideological principles and values that undergird our everyday interactions:

1. *Anglocentrism*—This is an overarching worldview that advances the notion, implicitly and explicitly, that (Western) European, particularly English, history, values, knowledge, and ways of being are not only "normal" but superior to all others, thereby helping to produce and justify Europe's dominant position in the world (Hobson, 2012). *Exceptionalism* is a by-product and integral component of Anglocentrism and the two concepts are virtually inextricable. I separate them here solely for the purposes of illustration, definition, and punctuation.

2. *Exceptionalism*—This guiding principle is a hallmark of Anglocentrism, which is predicated on notions of supremacy, and is often expressed as European exceptionalism. *White supremacy* and *European exceptionalism* are essentially synonyms. The governing ideology of former US President Donald Trump was his passionate belief in what he termed "America First." It is not surprising that Trump's adherence to this value culminated in two defining aspects of his presidency: (1) widespread strained relationships with many long-standing foreign allies, and (2) the rise and overt expression of white nationalism and racial divisiveness. Exceptionalism is based on a belief in one's inherent superiority. It is our nation's belief in exceptionalism, even if/when Trumpism is repudiated, that blinds us to the multitudinous ways in which People of Color are marginalized while whites consistently and permanently occupy the center. If not for our belief in exceptionalism, that is, white supremacy, how do we, as a nation, explain the conspicuous absence of significant numbers of People of Color from

corporate board rooms, high levels of government, the US presidency, and the high courts? What explanations do we give ourselves, as a nation, to justify the lack of representation of a single Person of Color on any of our monetary currency? One could surmise that the reason these issues are so blatantly on display in wide open spaces for us all to see without questioning or scrutiny is because they are affirmations of what is believed and practiced but rarely overtly stated: whites are central and regarded as superior. Our collective failure to question the overrepresentation of whites in our systems is a testament to our comfortable and harmonious coexistence with the principle of exceptionalism.

3. *Dualism and Dichotomous Thinking*—This form of thinking is needed to support an orientation toward exceptionalism. It is a form of segregated thinking based on either/or dichotomies. Whereas dualistic thinking divides the world into *either* this *or* that, relational thinking usually advocates a *both/and* orientation. Dualistic and dichotomous thinking is closely linked to both exceptionalism and hierarchical thinking. It is difficult to create and support that which is deemed exceptional without segregation . . . in our thinking as well as in our deeds.

4. *Hierarchical View of the World*—This approach to the world was not created by white people, nor is it limited to them; however, it is nonetheless a central organizing principle associated with whiteness. Dichotomous thinking is used to divide the world into this *or* that, and the hierarchical perspective is used to arrange the world in accordance with the values of exceptionalism. This gives rise, for example, to the belief systems that espouse the assumption that white is better than Black, light is better than dark, book knowledge (based on intellectualism) is better than experience-based knowledge, and so forth. The orientation toward a hierarchical view of the world also assigns differential value among whites. Thus, white people who were Jewish, Irish, or Italian were historically considered not as white or not as "good" as white Anglo-Saxon Protestants. The nascent trend among white people to differentiate the "good, woke white" from the "racist, bad white"

is another example of the application of this principle. This is the same principle that creates and supports the often-destructive hierarchy among People of Color, where those who are white-like, white-identified, and very light complexioned enjoy proximity to whiteness and are assigned benefits that are not made available to those with less proximity to whiteness, and Black people are assigned to the bottom of the racial/complexion hierarchy. None of these structural arrangements would be sustainable without the confluence of hierarchical thinking/being that is rooted in exceptionalism and dualism.

5. *Objectivity*—This principle refers to the ability to observe and/or act free of bias. Declarations and proclamations of objectivity are often entangled in the web of whiteness. Objectivity posits and is based on the belief that knowledge is based on observable facts and not on feelings or opinions. When one is convinced of one's objectivity, there is little motivation to engage in a process of self-interrogation or to consider how one's unexamined subjectivity may in fact mask or obscure objectivity or, ultimately, taint what one sees. For example, many whites often express fear that People of Color in positions of power will extend preferential treatment to their counterparts because of their presumed shared experiences and subjectivity (bias) while simultaneously adhering to the unalterable belief that their decisions, as whites, vis-à-vis People of Color as well as other whites, are based on objectivity.

6. *The Universality of Truth and Reality*—This organizing principle is very closely aligned with objectivity and asserts that "truth" and "reality" are universal phenomena. Embedded in this worldview is the belief that there is one only (objective) truth and that all other views are maligned by subjectivity and the absence of concrete measurable facts. Unfortunately, all too often it is those who possess the greatest power and privilege who are positioned to determine what constitutes "reality," "truth," and "objectivity." The belief in the universality of truth, as in the case with objectivity, rejects the notion that context and reality are richly intertwined. In fact, they are commonly viewed as two separate independent phenomena. When this principle is inter-

spersed with the others listed in this section, it easily culminates in the promulgation of the view that the white way is the right way, and this is treated as an objective, independent, universal reality.

7. *Stoicism*—This organizing principle promotes and values self-control and personal fortitude, especially during times of great stress and duress. It values clear thinking over feelings, especially as a means to ensure "objectivity" and the ability to be an unbiased and reasonable thinker. The white dominant society's commitment to principles of stoicism usually has a significant impact on what is considered "professional" and what constitutes the appropriate markers of "professionalism." The relational gulf that often exists between many People of Color and whites is often fueled by the former wanting the latter to show more emotions and the latter feeling stifled by the emotional intensity of the former. These differences, especially in the workplace, often culminate in People of Color being reprimanded by whites for being "too emotional" and/or "not professional enough," while whites are often perceived by their Colleagues of Color as cold, distant, cunning, and feelingless. All of this usually occurs without the centrality of whiteness or the values attached to stoicism ever constituting a point of inquiry or scrutiny.

8. *Intellectualism*—This principle refers to an ideological stance and approach that perceive thinking and feeling through a dichotomous, dualistic lens, with a higher value attached to the former. As in the case with Anglocentrism and exceptionalism, intellectualism and stoicism are so intricately interwoven that it almost belies the need for a separate discussion. However, I separate them here to explicitly magnify the connection. It is virtually impossible to maintain an appropriate level of stoicism if one is too emotional. On the other hand, when one's ability to remain stoic is compromised, according to these rules of engagement, so is one's level of objectivity and the ability to think clearly. Within this framework, intellectualism and cognition are generally considered assets, symbols of self-control and professionalism, while affect, and particularly too much of it, is considered a liability and, in some cases, an undisputed sign of weakness. Once again, it is

of little wonder that more often than not People of Color, particularly in white places, are considered too emotional, too subjective (e.g., too focused on race), and to exhibit questionable professional ethos, at best. There is absolutely no necessity or urgency to use the word "race" in discussions or critiques based on this or any of the other ideological concepts described in this section because the invisibility and centrality of whiteness are intricately embedded and remain unnamed.

9. *Individualism*—This belief places a high premium on the values, freedom, and rights of the individual. Thus, the *me* always takes precedence over the *we*. This principle contributed heavily to the staggering coronavirus infection rates experienced by the United States during the COVID-19 pandemic. There were an exorbitant number of US citizens who refused to adhere to the safety protocols outlined for combating the virus because they believed the measures impinged on their individual freedom and liberty. Consequently, from their point of view, maintaining their respective individual freedom took precedence over contributing to the safety of the masses.

10. *The Schism Between Product and Process*—One of the many artifacts of either/or, dualistic thinking and a hierarchical view of the world is the creation of a rigid schism between product and process. The elevated significance and priority attached to *product* contributes to the formation of a cultural value that consistently reinforces a mentality that affirms "the end justifies the means." Relationships and decision-making are often considered through a pragmatic, social exchange, transactional lens. Thus, the disproportionate attention devoted to *product* often leaves very little room for the valuing of *process*, which tends to emphasize attending to relational dynamics and the emotional currents embedded in them. The privileging of *product* over *process* is consistent with the promulgation of and preferences for stoicism. A focus on *process*, it is often feared, would require too much emotion, too much personal reflection, and ultimately a compromise of objectivity and personal fortitude. *Product* is important and, understandably, should be a critical dimension of any relationship (especially in the workplace). It should always receive acute attention; however, it

is the rigid schism between it and *process* and the elevation of it over *process* that is exceedingly problematic.

The *product/process* schism is replete throughout white-dominated spaces and is often a source of underlying cross-racial tension. I am reminded of Michael's irate question of me during the workshop that I described earlier in this chapter. His question, "What is the endgame here?" was essentially a question about *product* and an implicit critique of the *process* that, at the time, was heavily centered on interrogating whiteness. Coming from a workshop participant, his question was completely legitimate, and I was also hopeful, as I often am about these issues, that he could have tolerated a greater degree of tension and ambiguity between *product* and *process*.

Many community mental health centers provide an excellent example of how the aggressive and narrowly focused push for *product* over *process* can have unintended negative consequences for lower-income and racially oppressed clients. In an effort to comply with funding sources and accrediting, regulatory, and other governing bodies, many community mental health centers have stringent quotas that have to be met in terms of number of therapy sessions allowed, how many clients have to be seen in a week, and the type of information that should be obtained and comprehensively documented in relatively short periods of time. These product-oriented foci, because they are germane for funding and ultimately survival of the organization, usually take priority over more process-oriented issues. Thus, Clients of Color, for example, who have long-standing, generalized mistrust toward white people and institutions, are seldom granted a space to metabolize these issues of mistrust and suspicion that are deeply rooted in a long history of racial discrimination and trauma. When therapy is limited to 8–10 sessions and critical information must be obtained quickly, there is little time to build a trusting relationship or to meaningfully explore toxic issues, such as race, the whiteness of the therapist, whether the Therapist of Color is a sellout, or why it is hard for the client to invest in a process that feels dehumanizing and structured for the convenience of the therapist/system. The lack of attention to process inevitably contributes to high rates of client attrition (behavior that is narrowly construed as "resistant"), breached treatment goals, and low levels of client and therapist satisfaction. Above all, this dynamic contributes robustly to the systemic poor and unfulfilling services routinely delivered to racially oppressed and traumatized clients.

These ten ideological principles, while discussed here individually for convenience, are complexly and intricately intertwined in ways that are invisible, undetectable, and extraordinarily difficult to dismantle. It is the synergistic interplay of these dynamics that helps to fortify the centrality of whiteness while also ensuring its invisibility. These principles are often extolled as universal core values that constitute the pillars of best practices and are rarely, if ever, recognized for what they really represent: the instruments for reinforcing the centrality of whiteness and the reification of a prevailing white supremacist ideology. Their delicate and sophisticated entanglement creates a fortress around the centrality of whiteness that makes it hard to see and even harder to dismantle. Consequently, they must be at the center of all efforts to deconstruct and interrogate whiteness. Because these principles are so deeply and seamlessly embedded in both our individual psyches and our institutional structures, it is imperative that we remain unwavering in our resolve and commitment to challenging them, and in so doing we will de facto inevitably confront the enduring, invisible, and ubiquitous centrality of whiteness.

Here are some beginning measures that we can implement to expose and challenge the centrality of whiteness by naming it and making it visible:

1. *Give White Children the (Race) Talk*—Children of Color, and especially Black children, are given *the talk* early in life. *The talk* is essentially a talk about race that introduces them to the racialized dimension of their broader complex identity. It is a way to assist Children of Color to think critically about who they are racially and what they can reasonably expect as they interact in a world where the significance of race is often denied but is always in full operation. The widespread implementation of *the talk* in white families would ensure that we would have a future generation of white people who would in fact know that they are white. This would enable them, early on in life, to think critically about what it means to be white, how their lives are shaped by

it, and how it affects the everyday lives of those who are not. It would then no longer be possible, for example, for a little white Catholic boy to know that he was Catholic, know that he was boy, but not know that he was white.

2. *Know Thy (White) Self as a Racialized Being*—Paramount to challenging and dismantling the centrality of whiteness is the important task of developing a keen awareness of one's whiteness and, ultimately, one's sense of self as a racialized being. Before white parents can effectively introduce their children to whiteness and conduct *the talk*, they have to know and have explored their own racial background and sense of self racially. People of Color, by necessity, must know that they are People of Color in order to survive in a white-dominated society. If there is ever a lapse in knowledge, memory, or judgment about this important detail, white society has a plethora of practices and systems in place to remind People of Color about their designated standing in the white world in which they live. In contrast, it is possible for many white people to live much of their lives virtually never having to think about themselves as a racialized being. Many are consciously aware that People of Color are People of Color, but they rarely think of themselves racially in a significant and meaningful way. Hence, as noted earlier in this chapter, being white is intricately enmeshed with being American, human, and/or just a person. As long as whiteness remains deracialized for and by whites, it never has to be explored, understood, or implicated in the suffering, domination, and oppression of others who are not white. There can be complete abdication of responsibility and accountability for the intended and unintended actions they take to ensure the supremacy of whiteness, while also confining People of Color to prisons of systemic subjugation. If the centrality of whiteness is to be seriously challenged and dismantled, it will be critical for white people to become highly conscious of themselves as racialized beings. This involves nothing less than owning whiteness as a critical dimension of their complex identity, as well as making a concerted effort to comprehensively understand the anatomy of white culture, its history, as well as the issues of pride and shame that are attached to it. Racial sensitivity for white people is an

important and effective strategy for helping whites develop a deeper sense of their whiteness; however, efforts to do so should not be limited to training initiatives only. It is equally important, perhaps even more so, for whites to increase their active participation in personal and professional interactions and relationships that are not exclusively white and where they are the racial minority.

3. *Interrogate Self Before the Critiquing of Other*—It is critically important for whites to develop a strong *self in relationship to other* (SIRO) perspective as a precursor to participating in meaningful cross-racial conversations. As a matter of principle, white people, regardless of position, should refrain from offering ANY critical feedback to a Person of Color until they have conducted a thorough racially based self-interrogation. This process involves the white person actively considering how their impending opinion about, feedback to, or critique of a Person of Color may be informed by whiteness or how their whiteness influences how the message is delivered and potentially received. This process is not intended to shield People of Color from receiving critical feedback or to suppress authentic cross-racial discourse. It is, however, intended to disabuse whites of the mistaken notion that they can provide feedback *solely* from their position as a supervisor, colleague, fellow human being, or some other deracialized position. It is an invitation for whites to be in relationship with their whiteness as a prerequisite to cross-racial engagement. Once this process is completed, the white person should, ideally, enter the conversation by self-identifying as white, as noted in the next recommendation.

4. *Name, Claim, and Locate Whiteness in Conversations*—Because whiteness is virtually always an invisible referent, its significance, pervasiveness, and overall influence is seldom, if ever, exposed. As a preliminary step toward disentangling whiteness from what it means to be human, objective, and the sole proprietor of universal truths, it is critical for whites to preface all comments, opinions, and disclosures by referencing their whiteness. Thus, the use of prefatory comments such as "As a white person . . . ," "The part of me that is white is wondering what the endgame is here," or "I am wondering

how our whiteness is informing our positions here" can be helpful and transformative. It probably seems trite to offer such a minute and mundane remedy for such a colossal issue, but it is a means to making the invisible visible and increasing racial sensitivity. Despite the simplicity of this strategy, it is often met with resistance from some white people. I encountered such resistance when a white psychiatrist admonished me that my suggestion that he verbally acknowledge his whiteness in his clinical work was the "dumbest recommendation that [he had] ever heard from a so-called education person." He went on to assert: "Why in the hell do I need say I am white when it is obvious that I am white and you know that I am white? This makes absolutely no sense to me." My reply was simple: "Yes, you know you are white; I know you are white; but if I were your Black client, I would want and need to know that you knew you were white. This is the reason for the racial self-acknowledgment."

5. *Design and Promote Institutional Interventions that Name Whiteness*— The development and implementation of institutional interventions designed to name whiteness is essential to promoting change and a new world order. The following is a sample of institutional interventions that could be implemented:
   - Adopt the term *historically white institutions* to refer to colleges and universities that historically practiced racial segregation, either overtly or covertly. Predominantly white colleges and universities (PDWCU) that promulgate an exclusively or heavily Anglocentric approach to teaching and learning would be referred to as such and would self-identify using this PDWCU moniker.
   - Overtly develop and adopt a curriculum for White Studies to be offered alongside African American, Black, Chicano, Asian, and Women's Studies curricula.
   - In addition to the likes of queer, feminist, and critical race theories, white theory could also be overtly acknowledged. Doing so would pave the way for the official acknowledgment of the discipline of white psychology as a sibling to Black psychology, which was originally created because of the exclusionary and narrow focus of white psychology.
   - In addition to the Association of Black Social Workers, the Association

of Latino Social Workers, the Association of Black Psychologists, and the host of other racially identified organizations, those that perpetuate the centrality of whiteness could be referred to as the National Association of White Social Workers, the White American Psychological Association, or since "American" often translates into "white," the White Psychological Association, and the White Association for Marriage and Family Therapy, just to cite a few.

6. *Adopt a White Acknowledgment Statement Protocol*—The white acknowledgment statement protocol is a standard operating principle to be employed in meetings where there is not a critical mass of People of Color and therefore the representation of those in attendance is greatly skewed toward white people. It requires the convener of the meeting to publicly acknowledge at the outset that the space is essentially a white space, and everyone is invited to seriously consider and be mindful of how this dynamic might shape the meeting, its process, and the participation of those who are underrepresented. This is an accountability and acknowledgment measure that names whiteness and makes explicit the potential it holds to shape the dynamics of the meeting. Developing a protocol of this type is not intended to be a gimmick nor an act of political correctness; instead, the intent is for systems and organizations to be proactive in creating and implementing accountability measures to acknowledge the centrality of whiteness. It is important to keep in mind that the phenomenon of whiteness as an ideological framework is an extraordinarily complex one. It is possible for whiteness to be operative even when there are no white people present or, although rarely the case, for it to be absent even when only whites are present. Since whiteness is a worldview and a deeply entrenched organizing principle, it is not necessarily singularly defined by the presence of white people, although this is a critical dimension of it. These nuances are important to consider when making decisions about the development and invocation of a white acknowledgment statement protocol.

7. *Avoid Using Heart-Warming Coded Deracialized Language*—This recommendation is closely related to the forthcoming one regarding the elimination of white euphemisms; however, it requires a more

nuanced examination due to its unique relevancy to white people. It is rare for many whites to overtly name whiteness, and the underlying reasons for their not doing so are usually different from those of many People of Color. As it has been stated throughout this chapter, many whites tend to be oblivious of their whiteness, what it means, how it dominates people and places, or why it needs to be a point of discussion. It is difficult for many whites to say anything about that which their eyes have not been trained to see. Thus, when whites refer to a "lack of diversity," "being more inclusive," or "striving to be a more multicultural organization," none of these phrases overtly addresses whiteness or its centrality. Unfortunately, the wish to be more diverse or multicultural is not exactly a commitment to dismantle whiteness. Thus, "increasing diversity" and "becoming more multicultural and inclusive" are wonderful heartwarming sentiments that effectively circumvent having the more challenging, tense, and provocative conversations about decentering and challenging the centrality of whiteness. Making whiteness the focal point of conversations and initiatives is imperative if substantive change is the goal.

8. *Resist the Creation and Recruitment of Good Mainstream Minorities*—The culture of many predominantly white institutions, particularly where whiteness has not been recognized or critiqued, implicitly demands that People of Color relinquish or suppress major parts of who they are racially in exchange for and in the interest of becoming a part of "the (white) team." To achieve any modicum of success and upward mobility in these spaces, it is frequently both the unspoken demand of the institution and the belief of People of Color that People of Color must often compromise who they authentically are racially and become *white-like* and in some cases *white-lite*. The former is a tactic where one mimics aspects of whiteness, while white-lite is a process that requires the internalization of whiteness. In many cases, People of Color must deny, defy, and/or suppress any racial trait, attribute, or characteristic that might engender discomfort in whites because it is unfamiliar, too ethnic, or "not professional enough." The good effective mainstream minority (GEMM; Hardy, 2008) is often the product of this larger and pervasive organizational cultural process. The GEMM not only cognitively under-

stands what is required to appear white-like or white-lite, but is also able to demonstrate mastery of it. The GEMM understands that having a healthy, feigned, racially neutral relationship with whites is transactional. There are benefits to be obtained by not being or appearing too closely identified with one's authentic racial identity. The presence of a masterful GEMM provides white people with two of their most desired and coveted reassurances: (1) personal comfort because the GEMM "are so easy to talk to"; and (2) freedom from guilt and worry about being racist. After all, the presence of the GEMM is a measurable affirmation of a commitment to diversity and racial inclusion. The other salient performative function the GEMM affords to whites is a racially safe sounding board to reassure them that they are good white people and that their difficulties engaging other more angry, obstreperous, and hard to engage People of Color is understandable. The hiring and/or cultivation of a GEMM is a win–win proposition for most whites and white spaces. It allows for the diversification of the group on the one hand and the perpetuation of the centrality of whiteness on the other. Given the origins and evolution of the GEMM, whites should not rely solely on them for feedback to gauge their progress in appropriately and effectively challenging the pervasive centrality of whiteness. This is not to suggest that all People of Color are GEMMs nor that it would be inappropriate or ineffectual for whites to consult with People of Color about race and issues of whiteness. Since acquiescence, appeasement, and a conscious avoidance of authentically addressing race constitute some of the core requirements for becoming a GEMM, these behaviors cannot be casually cast aside in the interest of providing honest feedback to whites when they think they want it. The GEMM, as a matter of survival, success, and institutional culture, has been rewarded for telling white people what they want to hear, not necessarily what they need to hear. Challenging the centrality of whiteness requires whites to eliminate the conditions that necessitate, mandate, and incentivize People of Color becoming GEMMs as one of the few viable pathways to achieving professional advancement and success. Whites must also resist soliciting input, solace, and feedback about other cross-racial interactions from GEMMs or other People of Color with whom they feel comfortable talking about race. In fact, it can be more growth producing when feedback is solicited from a Person of Color with whom the white person feels the least comfortable and deems more challenging to engage in a racial conversation. On the other hand, People of Color must find affiliative strategies for engaging with other People of Color who are GEMMs or who are being actively recruited to become one. Popular feel-good tactics, such as People of Color questioning the GEMMs' Blackness, Asianness, Latinxness, or Indigenousness, are often emotionally cathartic but serve no other viable purpose than to reinforce, recreate, and calcify the centrality of whiteness. Thus, People of Color discovering ways to actively engage GEMMs in a healthy process of racial interrogation is of paramount importance.

9. *Challenge Racial Trauma and Avoid Using White Euphemisms*—Historically, People of Color, and especially Black people, have been terrorized and traumatized by white people. One of the keys to surviving the choking grip of racial trauma and oppression has been to be acutely mindful of the potential harm that an emotionally reactive and dysregulated white person can impose on the well-being of People of Color. This recognition has created a trauma-based *survival reflex* in many People of Color that is often activated when in the presence of whites. The reflex often provokes caution and is usually expressed as a trepidation of candidly and uninhibitedly naming whiteness in the presence of whites. This trauma reflex often propels People of Color to use oblique and indirect language when describing or referring to whiteness. Phrases such as "the dominant group," "people of other cultures and ethnicities," "other people," and "we don't have much diversity" are all euphemistic references to whites and whiteness. Even the commonly used reference: "*There are not many people who look like me* in my clinical practice" is coded to avoid saying white. The absence or dearth of "people who look like me" is an indirect, presumably safe, and obscure way of acknowledging that white people are in abundance. While these white euphemisms allow for some degree of momentary comfort and safety, they perpetuate the harmful practice of ensuring the continued mystification of whiteness and all the assaults that accompany it. Acting on this recommendation will be challenging and anxiety-producing for some People of Color; however,

it will also offer multiple invaluable benefits. Not only will it expose the centrality of whiteness, but it will also offer an opportunity to struggle with and overcome an invisible wound of racial trauma.

10. *Cease and Desist Taking Care of White People*—People of Color and white people are similarly socialized to participate in a kind of symbiotic relationship that has the caretaking of whites by People of Color as its major predicate. It has been commonplace throughout the history of race relationships in the United States for People of Color to be the mandated and designated caretakers of white people, even while People of Color are maligned as inferior, stupid, and lazy. For example, Black and Brown women serving as nannies for white children, some of whom are authors in this book, have been an integral part of our complicated cross-racial history. People of Color have been racially socialized to take care of whites, and whites have been racially socialized to desire, expect, and feel entitled to it. Whether providing lawn care, serving as secretaries, office administrators, and custodians, or being the only high-powered, well-placed executive, the expectation is the same: People of Color are expected to sacrifice their needs and well-being to be available to place the physical, emotional, and psychological needs of whites above theirs, both personally and professionally. Thus, the centerpiece of racial caretaking rests on the premise that People of Color, as a matter of common practice, are expected to suppress, ignore, and minimize their needs while elevating the significance of the needs of white people. The manifestations of racial caretaking can be physical, emotional, or relational. *Physical* racial caretaking involves performing physical tasks for the benefit of white people, while *emotional* racial caretaking involves offering emotional comfort and support to a white person while simultaneously suppressing one's feelings. A Person of Color offering unconditional comfort to a white person following their perpetration of a painful racial microaggression in which the focus is on the purity of the perpetrator's intentions rather than the hurt experienced by the Person of Color would be a common example of this manifestation. An example of *relational* racial caretaking can be observed during an interaction wherein a Person of Color—usually unconsciously—accosts, reprimands, or confronts another Person

of Color who is behaving in ways that make white people feel either uncomfortable or "unsafe." The interaction quickly shifts from an intense cross-racial interaction to one between two People of Color, with the white person observing. The racial caretaking relationship is a stable one where the rules of engagement are as clear as they are implicit and unspoken. Nevertheless, it is a dysfunctional relationship that helps to support the centrality of whiteness. As anxiety-producing and fear-provoking as it is, it is absolutely imperative that People of Color become more cognizant of this dysfunctional symbiotic relationship and begin to develop strategies that help foster a healthier relationship. It is important for People of Color to retire from the business of taking care of white people. The strategies that perpetuate this business are sophisticated and often unconscious, thus it is not a simple undertaking. The first crucial step is to recognize that the tendency to rescue, save, and caretake white people is a response to racialized trauma. Next, it is important to make a conscious and concerted effort to disrupt these tendencies. This is usually most effectively achieved when People of Color can work supportively and collaboratively together as a holding community that offers unlimited patience, understanding, and support. It is also important for People of Color to draw a critical distinction between "taking care of whites" and expressing "care about whites." One is a trauma-induced reflex; the other is a sentiment nestled in our shared humanity. *Caring about* is a process based on mutuality, equality, reciprocity, and accountability, while *taking care of* relies heavily on inequality, exploitation, and emotional suppression. It is also incumbent on whites to identify their needs and tendency to lure, reward, manipulate, and coerce People of Color into caretaking roles that perpetuate the centrality of whiteness, even when it may not be the intention or desired outcome.

## Conclusion

It will be difficult, if not impossible, for us to create a more equitable and racially just world so long as we cling fervently to the vestiges of the centrality of whiteness and white supremacy. It is imperative that each of us, in and throughout all stations of life, make the ideology and centrality of whiteness visible. We have to exercise the resounding crime-prevention message developed by the NYC Metropolitan Transportation Authority and the US Transportation Security Administration: "If you see something, say something" (MTA, 2002, para. 2; United States Department of Homeland Security, 2010). Our continued silence should not be a choice nor an option. All of our institutions, large and small, clinical and nonclinical, must make a solid commitment to a tenacious, systemic, and ongoing interrogation of whiteness. It is imperative that the interrogation take place at both the individual as well as the institutional levels. Spaces must be created to incorporate, explore, and honor other ways of being that reflect the cultural and racial values for each of us who are not, nor care to be, white, but who are often coerced into being battered, beleaguered, and compromised facsimiles of it. Our collective task will then be to sort out and work together to authentically cultivate a multiracial society where multiple ideologies can coexist without relying on overly used and too often tested and failed tools of human degradation: domination, marginalization, annihilation, and indoctrination.

**KENNETH V. HARDY, PHD,** is a Clinical and Organizational Consultant at the Eikenberg Institute for Relationships in New York, New York, where he also serves as director. He provides racially focused trauma informed training, executive coaching, and consultation to a diverse network of individuals and organizations throughout the United States and abroad. He is a former professor of family therapy at both Drexel University in Philadelphia, Pennsylvania, and Syracuse University in Syracuse, New York, and has also served as the director of Children, Families, and Trauma at the Ackerman Institute for the Family in New York, New York. He is the author of: *Culturally Sensitive Supervision: Diverse Perspectives and Practical Applications*; *Promoting Culturally Sensitive Supervision: A Manual for Practitioners*; *Revisioning Family Therapy: Addressing Diversity in Clinical Practice*; and *Teens Who Hurt: Clinical Interventions to Break the Cycle of Adolescent Violence*. In addition to his consultation work, Dr. Hardy is a frequent conference speaker and has also appeared on ABC's 20/20, NBC's Dateline, PBS, and the Oprah Winfrey Show.

## References

*Hardy, K. V. (2008). On becoming a GEMM therapist: Work harder, be smarter, and never discuss race. In M. McGoldrick & K. V. Hardy (Eds.),* Re-visioning family therapy: Race, culture, and gender in clinical practice *(2nd ed., pp. 461–468). Guilford Press.*

*Hardy, K. V. (2013). Healing the hidden wounds of racial trauma.* Reclaiming Children and Youth, *22(1), 24–28.*

*Hardy, K. V. (2016). Antiracist approaches for shaping theoretical and practice paradigms. In M. Pender Greene & A. Siskin (Eds.),* Anti-racist strategies for the health and human services *(pp. 125–139). Oxford University Press.*

*Hobson, J. M. (2012). The Eurocentric conception of world politics: Western international theory, 1760–2010.* Cambridge University Press. *https://doi.org/10.1017/CBO9781139096829*

*Holiday, B. (1939). Strange fruit [Song]. Commodore Records.*

*McGoldrick, M., & Hardy, K. V. (2019). The power of naming. In M. McGoldrick & K. V. Hardy (Eds.),* Re-visioning family therapy: Addressing diversity in clinical practice *(3rd ed., pp. 3–27). Guilford Press.*

*MTA. (2002).* MTA security campaign. *https://www.mta.info/mta-security-campaign*

*Thum-Gerber, H. (2020, June 19).* White silence is violence. *Anti-racism digital library. https://sacred.omeka.net/items/show/315*

*United States Department of Homeland Security. (2010).* If you see something, say something. *https://www.dhs.gov/sites/default/files/publications/SeeSay-Overview508_1.pdf*

*Wyatt, R. C. (2008, June).* Kenneth V. Hardy on multiculturalism and psychotherapy *[Interview]. Psychotherapy.net. https://www.psychotherapy.net/interview/kenneth-hardy*

# SECTION II

# REFLECTIONS ON THE CENTRALITY OF WHITENESS

**CHAPTER 2**

# The Elephant Is the Room

## The Art and Peril of Navigating Whiteness

JEFFERY A. MANGRAM, PHD

As a Black* man in the United States, to navigate whiteness is to constantly dilute and restore my humanity on a daily basis. "Navigating" whiteness is a series of strategic and tactical mental dispositions, identity performances, and discursive choices I have learned to employ to ensure peaceful coexistence with white people. I call these behaviors "the performances of survival." These performances can be deployed within a continuum ranging from obeisance to conflict depending on context. Situational context determined the utility and the degree of which performance I deployed. While necessary, such behaviors are tinged with a deteriorating effect on the mind, body, and spirit. Whites reward me for being the "black" man that is palatable to them. What follows is a description of the pervasiveness of whiteness, of the strategies and tactics I enacted to navigate whiteness, of the effects navigating whiteness has had on my professional and personal life, and of how I have managed to better protect myself and my family from the ideology of whiteness.

---

* Like Grinner (2004), I capitalize the word "Black" and not "white" because I, too, want "to disrupt the relations of power within this binary construction" (Grinner, 2004, footnote p. 205). When I do not capitalize the word "black," those are instances in which I was enacting a black performance that I believed white people preferred.

## Whiteness Is Ideological

In the US context, whiteness is an ideological state that grants privileges and immunities to those whom whites deem worthy (Feagin, 2013; Omi & Winant, 2015). Like the double helix structure of a DNA molecule, this ideology is both prescriptive and descriptive. Prescriptive ideology is a systematic body of ideas articulated to mislead, distract, or justify a set of real conditions. For instance, I know the idea of "whiteness" is not a biological reality, but I observe white people every day, and as a society we organize our lives around this false idea as though it is real. By descriptive ideology, I mean a systematic body of ideas that present a particular worldview or perspective. Descriptive ideology is unspoken. It is, period. As Nealon and Giroux (2012) aptly state, it "is what you think *before* you think or act—what thinking and action silently take for granted" (p. 99). For instance, I often ask my students to tell me what images come to mind when I say the words "CEO of a Fortune 500 company." Even before I ask about gender or race, I ask about height. Did anyone conjure in their minds someone less than six feet? Not once has someone answered in the affirmative. Height is assumed. And because we are socialized to believe CEOs of Fortune 500 companies in the United States are tall, it is not surprising when this is borne out in reality (Barth & Wagner, 2017).

Because the governing institutions within the United States protect and promote a whiteness ideology, it is ubiquitous in all aspects of life in the United States. Educational, religious, political, legal, and social institutions are complicit in the enactment of whiteness. US society rewards those who abide by the standards of whiteness. Historically and contemporaneously, Black people have challenged the enshrinement of whiteness within institutions. From slave rebellions to the Civil Rights movement of the 1960s, from the Black Power movement to the Black Lives Matter movement, Black people have resisted and have called for institutional reforms. These institutions have proven flexible and resilient enough to sustain the demands of Black protests and challenges. I mention this because it is institutions who promulgate whiteness as an ideology. Thus, I not only navigate white people, I also navigate the institutions that produce their ideology.

For me, navigating whiteness means recognizing the breadth and depth of this ideology. For instance, having taught for 28 years at the secondary and higher educational levels, I understand that whiteness as an ideology was taught to me as a youngster, informed the way I was trained to be a social studies teacher and eventually college professor. It informs how I interact with my students, how I engage with my colleagues, and how I behave in social situations.

Additionally, navigating white people and the ideology of whiteness is perilous. On the one hand, there are whites who are aware of this ideology and are attempting to resist it. On the other hand, there are whites who are oblivious to whiteness as an ideology. Interacting with whites is to attempt to determine which is which and in what contexts. I have to determine if this white person is an ally or a danger or both. Even when I believe I am with a white ally, I also have to pay attention to the context because the ally may not break with white solidarity in certain situations. This constant monitoring of my safety and threat is tiring. Because I believe my very existence depends on this monitoring, I do not have the luxury of disengaging.

## Navigating Whiteness: Performances of Survival

Because the United States is a segregated society, I mainly interact with white people in the workplace. The majority of my interactions with white people occur in the educational space in which I work. It is in this professional space that I used to (and still do at times) enact performances of survival. Again, the performative strategies and tactics are designed to protect my sense of self from white people while also ingratiating myself with them because I fear their retribution could imperil my life or livelihood. These performances were mutual and interlocking, were interchangeable, and were enacted to varying degrees depending on the situation. I can categorize and classify these performances of survival with clarity presently because I have had time to reflect on them. When I was performing them in the past, many of the acts were unconscious responses to the environment, which I deemed hostile. At other times, I was aware of this. In either case, I was not aware of the physical nor psychological toll such hyperawareness and vigilance would have on me. I want to describe four of these performances of survival strategies: (1) the affable black man; (2) feigning agreement/hiding my perspective; (3) silencing race; and (4) self-effacement. In each of the performative states, I will explain first the strategy and then the tactics I used to attain my ends.

### *The Affable Black Man*

The strategy behind the affable black man was to lessen the fear white people have of Black men. I had to put whites at ease, especially white women, because of the historical stereotypes of the black brute out to physically assail them. The strategy conveyed: "I am here to support you. I am not a threat."

The three tactics I employed in this performance were: the happy-go-lucky black man, gratuitous acknowledgment of accomplishments, and body positioning. First, I knew that I had to be positive, upbeat, and happy at all times in order to allay white fears. I needed them to believe my experience in their presence was a pleasant one. I smiled in front of white people until my jaw hurt. Even when not humorous, I laughed at their jokes. I fell right into the happy-go-lucky black man stereotype. Second, I consciously and consistently applauded my colleagues' scholarship, teaching, and presentations. I did this in order to relieve any threat of being in competition with them for resources or notoriety. In fact, I thought their scholarship was, at best, ordinary and banal. But I would never speak critically of it. Thirdly, I paid keen attention to how I physically positioned myself in relation to white people. I never wanted them to feel physically threatened. In fact, I was very conscious of how close I stood to them, especially women, and what I did with my hands. Again, the goal was to present a persona of the affable black man. I am not a threat.

### *Feigning Agreement/Hiding My Perspective*

From my perspective, white people tend to be professionally threatened by confident Black people. Thus, I performed feigning agreement as I engaged my white colleagues. Agreeing even when I did not believe in the idea or project became my modus operandi. I went along to get along, even when I thought I had good ideas to share. Disagreement was not an option. And in those rare moments when I did disagree, I would use opaque language that obscured my objections. Agreement was the goal.

I did not offer my perspective because maintaining a collegial relationship was more important than giving constructive feedback. Taking care of white people's feelings and intellectual confidence was my priority. There is no other way to say it: my fear of making white people mad at me overrode my desire to share with them my worldview. Indeed, the aforementioned strategies and tactics complemented the silence I imposed on myself around racial issues.

### *Silencing Race*

How did I use silence as a performance of survival? Very simply: I did not say anything when it came to racial issues. And when I did say something, I used words that would hide my thoughts. I did not even know I was doing this. Avoiding saying or participating in anything that would trouble the racial equilibrium was the strategy. I colluded with whites in the conspiracy of silence around racial issues. To be clear, I colluded with white solidarity and white supremacy. At both the secondary level and in higher education, I personally watched the unequal and unfair treatment of Black students, and, in most instances, said nothing. Again, the goal was to keep the peace because I did not want white rage to turn on me. I often used discursive moves to hide my silence. In fact, I would use words to hide my thoughts. How so? I often asked questions about a matter instead of saying what I thought. I made intense realities around race into intellectual propositions to be debated. The Black experience, my experience, was an abstraction to be puzzled over. While I did not admonish other Blacks about speaking out about racism, I did not support nor disagree with their claims. I stayed neutral. I stayed silent.

### *Self-Effacement*

I performed self-effacement in front of white people to downplay my self-assurance. The strategy was straightforward: Do not let white people know how much confidence I have in myself. Additionally, do not do anything to prick the insecurities of white people in such a way that they would take offense and vengeance against me. The tactics I performed here were: (1) surprise at success; and (2) feigning of self-doubt.

To enact surprise at my accomplishments, I often downplayed any notoriety I received. In front of white people, I would sarcastically say something like, "They chose me for this award?" or "They must have the wrong person," chuckle, chuckle. The affable black man would appear, and my sense of who I was would disappear. Especially in meetings, I would say things like, "I am not sure how to proceed here" or "I need your help" even when I saw clear solutions to the matter. This tactic could be confusing to me because at times I did need my colleagues' assistance. So, I had to remember which colleagues I used this strategy on and which I did not. I had to be careful here: I could not overwhelm whites with too many of my problems. Their needs came before mine. Unwittingly, I was losing my self in these enactments. Indeed, I was effacing me in order to keep white attention at bay.

### *The Toll*

Enacting these performances of survival impacted my sense of identity and had an impact on my family and friends. First, because I expended so much time and energy on these inauthentic performances, I became the performances. Over time, I could not separate myself from the performances when I was outside of the venue of white people. The affable man showed up in my relationships with my family. I feigned agreement in my social relationships with friends. I was silent about racial issues when they arose in my children's education or as my children engaged in after-school activities. I was self-effacing over my children's accomplishments. Second, I could not reconcile being rewarded for the performance of being the black man palatable to white people with my emerging need to be me and not a performer of me. White people spoke glowingly about me. No one disliked me. So what was the problem? To articulate my reality was to undo and lose the rewards of colluding with whiteness and white supremacy. Third, once I realized what was happening, I took responsibility and began to change. Here is the rub: In some instances, my colleagues, friends, and family members yearned for the performative me instead of who I was becoming. That hurt because now I realized I was reacting to larger socio-historical-political forces. I realized that I had moved away from the values of Black pride and Black dignity and Black integrity that my parents and grandparents had so deeply and beautifully implanted in me. I had let down my family, my people, in order to ingratiate myself with whiteness. So, how did I come to realize this?

## Embracing Rage—An Awakening

Until someone gave me feedback regarding these behaviors and explained to me why I was enacting them as well as the problematic nature of them, I continued to enact them. While cliché, the notion that you cannot be what you do not see resonates with me. I needed to see a contemporary Black man who could speak to these issues. I had seen Malcolm X, the Reverend Dr. Martin Luther King Jr., Reverend Al Sharpton, and many others, but I saw them from afar, on documentaries and the news. It is one thing to see mediated images of these men, it is another to have them come into your space and speak unspeakable things in your presence and in the presence of white people. In 2005, Dr. Kenneth V. Hardy entered my life and did just that.

Dr. Hardy conducted a diversity workshop at a local school where I taught. At the workshop, he introduced concepts such as multidimensional view of the self, dominant and subordinate identities, whiteness, and privilege. He spoke the unspeakable in front of white people: he named their whiteness in the room, he spoke about racial trauma, he spoke about internalized devaluation of Black people's experience, he spoke about the assaulted sense of self, he spoke about internalized voicelessness, and he spoke about Black rage. He spoke my experience! And he gave me ways to understand what had and what was happening to me. But something he pointed out to me in a smaller workshop changed me forever.

At a follow-up workshop two weeks later with 12 attendants in a small conference room, Dr. Hardy and I were the only Black people present. The group was discussing how to better enact diversity initiatives at the school. There was the usual give and take in the conversation, and I participated and performed accordingly. However, Dr. Hardy noticed not the content of what I was saying, but how I was saying it. I did not use declarative statements but rather I asked questions instead. In quite an even tone, he said, "I notice when you speak you ask questions and do not give your opinion" (K. V. Hardy, personal communication, October 2005). He then slammed his hands on the table and quite forcefully said, "Either you are a coward, or you are crazy, or you are in a context in which you do not trust the people in the room. But you are at the table, and you must speak and have a right to speak!" (K. V. Hardy, personal communication, October 2005). For me, time stood still. He outed me. He saw through my performance. He exposed me in front of all those white people! His eyes never left me. "You are right," I responded. But "right" about what? Was I crazy or a coward, or did I not trust the people in the room? Indeed, I would spend the next two years attempting to answer all three of those questions.

I suspect Dr. Hardy understood my plight because Blackness is his plight too. He understood my behavior because he understood his behavior. He awakened a reservoir of rage in me that I would have to embrace and master because that, at some level, had always been a part of me and I had been of afraid of its power to propel me to new heights, or destructiveness if not used properly. I had to have a reckoning with myself. And I did.

### *Struggle and Progress*

Motivated by Dr. Hardy's comments, I began deep introspective work to understand why I did not advocate for myself while in the same moment performing behaviors that undermined me, in particular, and Black people in general. In due time, I recognized the relationship between racial trauma and whiteness as an ideology. I recognized how institutional power was implicated in this process. I recognized how institutions created, perpetuated, and protected whiteness. I recognized the interpersonal violence and microaggressions that I was experiencing in my interactions with whites and others. I recognized the psychic and emotional healing that I needed because of these destructive interactions. As Hardy (2013) states, "racial oppression is a traumatic form of interpersonal violence which can lacerate the spirit, scar the soul, and puncture the psyche" (p. 25). Lacerate. Scar. Puncture. I avoided connecting the historical and contemporaneous trauma that Black people experience at the hands of white people because it was too painful for me. In order to mature, I learned to acknowledge these truths.

In acknowledging the perniciousness and implications of whiteness as an ideology, I became able to name and explain Black devaluation and disrespect that I had endured in the larger society. That acknowledgment was integral to my growth because it created space within my mind to begin reclaiming and restoring my voice. I had to restore my ability to advocate for myself. I took small steps and had to learn to modulate the tonality and projection of my voice. I was using a new language and, accordingly, my behavior began to change. For instance, I began using declarative statements, I advocated for my perspective, and I disagreed with white people in meetings. I was filled with angst and fear because I was now making white people uncomfortable. I now understood where that fear emanated from: historically and contemporaneously, Blacks who disagreed with whites could be killed. Still, I disagreed with them and I was not smiling anymore. I changed and people noticed. While I cannot elaborate because of space limitations, I engaged my rage and used it in productive ways around my teaching and advocacy of Black people in general and Black children in particular. Because I found clarity in what mattered to me, I was able to jettison what did not, which allowed me to institute news ways of navigating the ideology of whiteness.

## Navigating Whiteness: Clarity and Hope

Navigating whiteness is an ongoing process for me. It is an iterative, not linear, process. I pay close attention to my behaviors, reflecting on when I deviate from my integrity. I seek consistency. I seek to align my words, feelings, and actions. I now engage white people from a more intimate and genuine racial stance. Indeed, some of the ways I do this include, but are not limited to, the following: (1) naming whiteness and acknowledging the power differential; (2) stopping the caretaking of white people; and (3) modeling courageous conversations.

### *Naming Whiteness*

The power of whiteness in the United States is in its ubiquity and invisibility. Whiteness is everywhere and nowhere. Thus, I name it. I illuminate it. I challenge it. I try to dispel the power of whiteness by acknowledging its presence and the meanings it has for me. In some instances, this acknowledgment triggers white fragility, as whites become defensive, angry, and agitated (DiAngelo, 2018). Now that I understand racial identity theory, I am not surprised by these reactions. When white people respond in this manner, I encourage them to explore their reactions in relation to their understanding of white racial identity formation (Cross, 1991; Helms, 1990). While I listen empathically, I still hold white people accountable to engage in this work.

*Stop Caretaking of White People*

I no longer caretake white people. Grasping the idea that Black people were socialized to take care of white people was such a hard concept to accept that I have had to disrupt my mentality to change my behavior. If truth be told, I am still struggling with it. But, because I am aware of it, I can disrupt the behavior. While I am respectful to all people, I no longer let white people's angst trigger my need to emotionally or physically care for them. I often watch this caretaking occur and I point it out and explain what could be happening. For example, white women's tears no longer intimidate me. When white women sometimes cry in meetings or workshops regarding issues of race, I gently attempt to explain the historical and political significance those tears have had *on Black people*. I then encourage the group to continue moving forward.

*Model Courageous Conversational Behavior*

Now as I navigate whiteness, I model courageous conversational behaviors. First, I speak clearly and simply about matters of race. I do not use my language to obscure the subject matter. I speak not to change white people but rather to remind myself that in speaking there is liberation of the spirit, liberation of the soul. Second, I listen empathically. The power of the ideology of whiteness is that most white people do not comprehend how these forces have socialized them to be in the world. To undo years of socialization and to act in new ways takes time, effort, and support from others. Thirdly, I take risks in conversations around race. I attempt to challenge myself to speak in the session or meeting those words that some of us are thinking but will not say. My hope is that such behavior will become contagious and habitual.

## The Elephant Is the Room

The elephant (whiteness) is not *in* the room. Whiteness, in the context of the United States, IS THE ROOM. I relocate the metaphor to reveal that whiteness as an ideology is so much more complex and deeply rooted in every aspect of life in the United States. Whiteness dominates. That does not mean hopelessness is my fate nor the fate of Black people nor that social justice and equity cannot be achieved. What it does mean is that in order to change the situation, I must acknowledge reality as clearly and as accurately as I can. Then act accordingly. Act with a sense of integrity, act with a sense of purpose, act with a sense for justice. Act like a Black man.

**JEFFERY A. MANGRAM, PHD,** is an associate professor and coordinator of social studies education in the Syracuse University School of Education. His scholarly interests revolve around diversity education, media education, urban education, teacher education, and high leverage practices in the classroom. He also directs the Charles Hayden Summer College Program, in which rising high school seniors of Color spend a six-week summer residency program at Syracuse University, where they take college courses for credit. Mangram's work is featured in such publications as *Theory and Research in Social Education* and the *Journal of Social Studies Research*. The International Society for Social Studies named Dr. Mangram Outstanding Faculty Member in 2011. He has been a principal or coprincipal investigator on approximately $1.1 million in grants. He earned his undergraduate degree (policy studies/political science), master's degree (social studies education), and PhD (teaching and curriculum) from Syracuse University.

## References

*Barth, I., & Wagner, A. L. (2017). Physical appearance as invisible discrimination. In J. F. Chanlat & M. F. Özbligin, M. F. (Eds.),* Management and diversity: Thematic approaches *(International perspectives on equality, diversity, and inclusion, Vol. 4, pp. 127–146). Emerald Publishing Limited. https://doi.org/10.1108/S2051-233320160000004008*

*Cross, W. (1991).* Shades of black: Diversity in African-American identity. *Temple University Press.*

*DiAngelo, R. J. (2018).* White fragility: Why it's so hard for white people to talk about racism. *Beacon Press.*

*Feagin, J. R. (2013).* The white racial frame: Centuries of racial framing and counter-framing *(2nd ed.). Routledge.*

*Grinner, L. A. (2004). Hip-hop sees no color: An exploration of privilege and power in "Save the Last Dance." In R. A. Lind (Ed.),* Race/gender/media: Considering diversity across audiences, content, and producers *(p. 205). Pearson.*

*Hardy, K. V. (2013). Healing the hidden wounds of racial trauma.* Reclaiming Children and Youth, *22, 24–28.*

*Helms, J. E. (1990).* Black and white racial identity: Theory, research, and practice. *Greenwood Press.*

*Nealon, J. T., & Giroux, S. S. (2012).* The theory toolbox: Critical concepts for the humanities, arts, and social sciences *(2nd ed). Rowman & Littlefield.*

*Omi, M., & Winant, H. (2015).* Racial formation in the United States *(3rd ed). Routledge.*

## CHAPTER 3

# Whiteness as a Disease of the Soul

## Shame, Rage, Guilt, Self-Absorption, and Ignorance

DAVID TRIMBLE, PHD

CENTER FOR MULTICULTURAL TRAINING IN PSYCHOLOGY,
BOSTON MEDICAL CENTER

This chapter offers an exploration of whiteness, particularly its psychological operations and spiritual afflictions. It is grounded in my life experience as a 75-year-old white, heterosexual, cisgender man, a veteran of the Civil Rights movement as a voter registration volunteer in the 1964 Mississippi Freedom Summer. I witnessed, and participated in, unconscious performances of whiteness that ruptured the civil rights coalition of the 1960s. As an antiracist activist for more than five decades, I live with the spiritual afflictions of my whiteness. I recognize that healing this disease of the soul lies not within me, but in the solidarity of a movement to dismantle racism. A psychologist and psychotherapist strongly committed to integrating an inclusive spiritual approach into healing practice (Trimble, 2018), I hope that my perspective may be useful for mindful antiracist practice. Addressed particularly to my white readers, this chapter is intended for all readers engaged in struggles for social justice. What wisdom I may have to share emerges primarily from what I have learned from others.

I do not pretend that the problem of racism is reducible to whiteness, but I do believe that the problem of whiteness, if not addressed, undermines and disrupts multiracial solidarity in the struggle for racial justice. When my white peers and I are oblivious to the effects of our assumptions, words, and actions on others, particularly People of Color, we obstruct the formation of a durable coalition to dismantle racism. White people need to get out of others' and our own way as we struggle alongside People of Color to transform established white spaces into multicultural communities capable of flourishing in a twenty-first-century world.

Exploration of the psychological and spiritual maladies of whiteness is a messy, confusing, and uncomfortable process to start with. The deeper we go, the closer we get to feelings of fear, anger, confusion, hurt, and deep sorrow. The world that all of us share, white people and People of Color alike, is organized by the dominant discourse of white supremacy. One way that discourse serves us white people is by protecting us from the emotional pain intrinsic to racial oppression. That protection is withheld from all others.

We cannot escape our whiteness. If we are committed to dismantling the system, we must uncover painful emotional truths and must recognize how readily we can lapse into ignorance. No matter how long, how seriously, how open-heartedly we examine ourselves, we have to accept that we can never claim to have "solved" this problem of whiteness. We must maintain clear-minded awareness of our ongoing enactments of this spiritual malady. I invite you to join me in this messy, confusing, painful journey, and I offer you the prospect of spiritual healing in the solidarity of a multiracial struggle for justice.

White people committed to solidarity with People of Color must take responsibility for certain obligations. We must accept the leadership of People of Color. We must listen deeply and *believe* them when they recount their experiences, particularly their experiences of our actions, our utterances, and our demeanor as we engage with them. We must use the power embedded in our racial social location to challenge, subvert, and disrupt the racial status quo. We must work for concrete reparation of damages from the thefts of land, liberty, and labor, stolen from generations of Native Americans and African Americans, as well as of damages from ongoing subjugation and exploitation of those and other Groups of Color. We must struggle for that reparation with full recognition that the wealth of white America is built on those damages. We must acknowledge our complicity in, and the benefits we receive from, white privilege. We must recognize our internalization of the dominant discourse of race, whether we name it white supremacy, "proracist ideology," or, simply, racism. We must earn, by our actions, permission to serve as open-hearted witnesses to the testimonies of those who suffer domination by our racial group in a racist society.

We do not measure up to our responsibility. We either don't recognize our obligations or fall well short of meeting them. The failure to engage in solidarity between white people and People of Color assures the perpetuation of racism. Because of the pervasive and pernicious influence of racism in US society, the persistence of this failure corrupts all efforts toward social justice.

This chapter seeks to make sense of white people's failure—including my own—to engage in true solidarity and shared responsibility for healing and social transformation. It seeks a path toward effective multiracial solidarity in the struggle to dismantle racism. In it, I challenge the reader, specifically, the white reader, to engage in a messy, painful process of self-examination. Writing this chapter has challenged me to go deeper into that process myself. My exploration of the phenomenology of white racism is premised on the assumption that none of us in our racist society can free ourselves, as individuals, from internalizing the dominant discourses of white supremacy. This chapter offers a spiritual lens, one that I hope affords a reasonable prospect of redemption.

## Whiteness as the Embodiment of White Supremacy

Whiteness is a social location and a state of mind constructed in relation to that location. When one is perceived by others to embody the quality of whiteness, one is granted a social position that affords power and privilege. The dominant discourse of white supremacy secures that social position by orchestrating operations of power at relational, institutional, and cultural levels. The daunting task of dismantling racism requires deconstruction of that dominant discourse, particularly as it is internalized by those who see themselves, and are seen by others, as white.

A discourse is "a system of statements, practices, and institutional structures that share common values" (Hare-Mustin, 1994, p. 1). White supremacy is a pervasive dominant discourse that defines whiteness as normal and preferred in all ways. It includes ideology, customs, cultural media, including art, print, other media, and institutional structures, including laws and police to enforce them. It suppresses and marginalizes alternative discourses that might challenge it. It highlights phenomena that work for the powerful while obscuring those that support the subjugated. Examples of other pervasive dominant discourses in US society include sexism, heteronormativity, and ageism.

The primary way that dominant discourses maintain social control is through their internalization by members of a society. Internalization does not constitute agreement or cooperation. In one way or another, all members of US society internalize the dominant discourse of white supremacy. A society organized by the discourse of white supremacy operates as a constant threat to the lives of People of Color. Their existential survival requires daily struggles with the messages of devaluation at the core of white supremacy, particularly as the messages invade their interior psychological space. For example, the toxic internal psychological effects of microaggressions (Sue et al., 2007) contribute to well-documented chronic health conditions that are contributing to the disproportionate death rate from COVID-19 among People of Color (Moore, 2020).

I invite the reader to examine the discourse of white supremacy as it is internalized by white people. My goal is to make these internalizing processes visible to white people, including myself. Although whiteness is intrinsically a moral and spiritual affliction, it also affords us wealth and power at the expense of People of Color, and we are, in this way, its beneficiaries. One way this discourse assures our comfort is by making itself invisible to us at the same time that it is visible to the People of Color who are victimized by our acts of whiteness.

## White Supremacy as Internalized by Those Who Embody Whiteness

White supremacy makes whiteness the normal, default state of being. We experience our whiteness as "just the way things are." We accept the values of white supremacy as universal human values and so do not interrogate them to expose their grounding in Eurocentric, individualistic, capitalistic values. Normalizing whiteness thus spares us the discomfort of conscious reflection on the inherent injustice embedded in our social location. We may not even be conscious of our whiteness until we encounter those who do not embody it. We automatically experience them as Other, as abnormal, as less valuable, as exotic, as lacking, etc.

In organizations, we accept as truisms a set of values grounded in white supremacy and yet are mystified when our organizations fail to retain People of Color despite our recruitment practices, intended to "diversify" our predominantly white organizations. The antiracism group Dismantling Racism Works has articulated some of those white values, as follows (Okun, 2020): perfectionism, sense of urgency, defensiveness, quantity valued over quality, worship of the written word, paternalism, either/or thinking, power hoarding, fear of open conflict, individualism, progress defined as bigger or more, objectivity, and right to comfort.

The world is arranged materially, socially, and culturally for our benefit, at the expense of everyone else. The invisibility of these arrangements assures our comfort with them. While invisible to us, they are starkly visible to members of targeted and subjugated groups. When we are called out for our performances of whiteness, we activate protective mechanisms, including microaggressions (and not-so-micro-aggressions), to silence those who call us to be accountable. We thereby keep these processes invisible, if only to ourselves.

### *Three Forms of Internalized White Supremacy*

What follows are three manifestations of white supremacy, each of which white people, including those of us who strive for racial justice and solidarity, enact and internalize. I continue to discover myself operating from all three positions. As internalized white supremacy, they are the three voices of racial bigotry, color blindness, and aspiration to racial sensitivity. We tend to be unconscious of these internalizations, particularly our internalized inner voice of racial bigotry. To meet our obligations for successful solidarity with People of Color, we have to tolerate the emotional discomfort that accompanies full conscious awareness of these internalizations, which I describe herein.

#### **Racial Bigotry**

The origins of racial bigotry in the form of anti-Black racism can be traced to fifteenth century Europe (Kendi, 2016). Bigotry manifests in contemptuous, hateful stereotypes of People of Color and in explicit white nationalism that argues for the intrinsic genetic, moral, and intellectual superiority of the white race. White people who denounce racial bigotry would prefer to restrict the term *white supremacy* to bigotry as a way to deny our own internalized racism. However, even the most progressive whites among us can be pulled into racially bigoted thought, which lurks opportunistically in the recesses of all our consciousnesses.

Through the middle of the twentieth century, the bigoted form of white supremacy was dominant in white speech, institutions, and culture. Following the achievements of the mid-twentieth-century Civil Rights movement, including the dismantling of legal apartheid in the United States, explicitly bigoted utterances became unacceptable in polite white society. Bigotry has not disappeared and is particularly lethal. It is manifest in mass shootings, hateful and murderous mass assemblies, and in the informal subcultures of police departments whose members reinforce each other's brutal and contemptuous stereotypes of People of Color as animals whose lives are not worthy of being valued. The lethality of this bigoted police subculture is manifest in the stream of police murders of African Americans that has flowed uninterruptedly from the time of slave patrols to the present in which it is now manifest to general public awareness. Lynching, the ritualized murder of African Americans by white private citizens as a public event, persisted well into the twentieth century. Without the ceremonial trappings of ritualized public events, lynching of African Americans by white citizens continues in the present, as in the cases of James Byrd, Trayvon Martin, Ahmaud Arbery, Breonna Taylor, and so many others, including many Black women whose deaths have received less public attention.

**Color Blindness**

Many white people prefer to maintain the illusion that race doesn't matter, which supports the comfortable invisibility (to us) of white supremacy. All white people engage in this fiction at least some of the time: "We are all just human beings," we insist. This allows us to maintain the illusion that white supremacy is the sole province of the bigoted and relieves us of our obligation to confront and dismantle racism. We are blind to our implicit white-normalizing perspective. Critical deconstruction of the "we" who are "all just human beings" makes it visible that "we" are very much like white people, after all, with others invited to the table—our table—so long as they approximate the trappings of whiteness.

We can't address our obligations to dismantle racism when we hold the illusion that we don't see color. It is a thin illusion, full of contradictions. When we are color blind, we may congratulate ourselves for having voted for Obama, only to vote for Trump because he "speaks his mind."

It is not uncommon for either the bigot or the color blind to introduce a white supremacist utterance with the claim, "I am not a racist . . ."

**Aspiration to Racial Sensitivity**

Kenneth Hardy defines racial sensitivity as the "determination to recognize the ways in which race and racism shape reality" (Hardy & Laszloffy, 2008, p. 227). If we want to understand why we white people fail to meet our obligations, we must recognize that determination alone is not enough. I include myself among those white people who *aspire* to racial sensitivity (as "seekers"), often with moderate success, but not deeply or consistently enough for reliable solidarity with People of Color in the project of dismantling racism. We seekers are particularly vulnerable to self-congratulation when we delude ourselves into believing that we "get it"; that we are "woke." We often talk the talk as a way of hiding from ourselves the internalized racism that obstructs sincere efforts to walk the walk.

We thus avoid coming to terms with the painful reality that, from our social location as white people, we cannot step out of our whiteness, with its attendant internalization of white supremacy. It is impossible for us to see ourselves through the eyes of People of Color, eyes in which our unconscious racism is obvious.

Why is it so difficult for us to recognize our internalized white supremacy? Over the course of five and a half decades of confronting this issue, personally and in my profession, organizations, and society, I have come to understand two sets of obstacles, one relational and one psychological.

## Relational Obstacles to Recognizing Our Racism

Certain patterns of engagement between people obscure evidence of internalized white supremacy. They serve the comfort of white people by hiding signs of our racism from ourselves. People of Color may unconsciously collude with these patterns to protect themselves from painful direct awareness, potentially increasing their vulnerability to real relational injury.

### *Microaggression*

Microaggressions are everyday insults, dismissals, and devaluations by members of privileged groups (e.g., whites, males, US-born people, or heterosexuals) toward members of targeted groups (e.g., People of Color, women, immigrants, sexual and/or gender minorities) (Pierce, 1995; Sue et al., 2007). They are mostly invisible to their perpetrators, usually clearly visible but sometimes ambiguous to the people whom they target. Racial microaggressions sustain privilege and marginalization through common, everyday relational practices. Their toxic effects are manifold and pernicious, fostering internalization of white supremacy and undermining confidence and self-esteem in People of Color. The ambiguity of these encounters contributes to health disparities (Duru et al., 2012; Hall & Fields, 2015; Moore, 2020), as microaggressions stimulate a constant state of vigilance in their victims, with attendant chronic physiological arousal and exhaustion. When targeted by a microaggression, one is faced with the choice of either calling it out or absorbing it, with little likelihood either way of authentic relational engagement.

Despite our commitment to "recognize the ways in which race and racism shape reality" (Hardy & Laszloffy, 2008, p. 227), seekers, embedded as we are in our whiteness, are still liable to perpetrate microaggressions unwittingly. I know from painful personal experience that I, a dedicated seeker, can and do engage in harmful microaggressions, even against People of Color whom I love and respect. It is a cruel paradox of the struggle for racial justice, and for the solidarity between People of Color and white people necessary for that struggle, that we white seekers often need feedback, not only from white allies but also from People of Color, to see our own offenses. This places undue relational and psychological demands on victims, given the risk of failure in any venture to call a white perpetrator to account for a racial microaggression. Perpetrators may angrily deny that there was a microaggression, invalidating victims' perceptions and perhaps provoking confusion and uncertainty, given the ambiguity intrinsic to some microaggressions. Should victims' anger rise in response to the denial, motivating them to redouble their efforts to show perpetrators what they have done, they may be silenced by the perpetrator's adamant refusal to see what is so visible to their victims. The physiological arousal associated with this dynamic of provocation, silencing, frustration, and futility feeds vulnerability to cardiovascular and other diseases (Hall & Fields, 2015).

Perhaps perpetrators may not deny the feedback but react instead with such a strong display of painful emotion as to stimulate a caretaking response from victims, who wind up coming to the aid of the person who hurt them rather than attending to their own injury. White perpetrators also have the option of withdrawing into the white world, choosing to interact solely with other white people in one or more of a multitude of available segregated white social spaces.

Responsible seekers live intentionally in multiracial social spaces and cultivate relationships with Neighbors, Colleagues, Friends, and Comrades of Color. They are racially literate enough to be aware of their liability to commit microaggressions, to respond with open minds and hearts when their microaggressions are challenged, and to recognize the relational risks and costs to the People of Color who call them out for their microaggressions. They demonstrate over time that they have *earned*, by their consistently antiracist practice, the trust of People of Color who take the risks and do the work of calling them out.

Such a community for me and for my wife, Jodie Kliman, is the Boston Institute for Culturally Affirming Practices (or BICAP), a multiracial, multicultural group of professional colleagues. We have become comrades and trusted friends over more than two decades of self-reflective exploration of the operations of power, particularly in our own processes of relational injury and repair with each other (BICAP, 2017). Although there is room in our group for us to explore our emotions of distress when we learn how we have hurt people whom we love, we all acknowledge the priority of the victim's experience of injury over the distress of the person who has caused hurt. Without questioning, we afford the victim power over the choice and timing of repair, from naming the injury through the sequence of acknowledgment, validation, apology, and forgiveness (Hardy & Laszloffy, 2002, p. 94). For the apology to be acceptable, it must include commitment to targeted action, with meaningful follow-through (K. V. Hardy, personal communication, November 17, 2020).

I have been working consciously and systematically for over five decades to dismantle my own internalized white supremacy. I take and have taken many risks as I persist in antiracist activism. I live and work in a multiracial world. For all that, I have come to accept that I will always be a seeker and can never legitimately claim to recognize, consistently and in all circumstances, the ways in which race and racism shape reality. In my search for a deeper understanding of my internalized white supremacy, I have come to discern the insidious process of microentitlement (Kliman et al., 2019).

*Microentitlement*

Microentitlement is a process of affirming and reinforcing white privilege and dominance. Like microaggressions, microentitlements may occur without the parties' awareness of the process and can manifest at cultural, social, relational, and psychological levels. At the cultural and social levels, the dominant discourse of the United States normalizes my white life and otherizes the lives, cultures, and bodies of People of Color. I can choose to live wherever I can afford, and my access to educational and occupational opportunities is not questioned, as it likely would be for a Person of Color. The intersection of my gender and racial identities (Kliman, 2010) affords me confidence that I will be respected and deferred to in public and private spaces. Because all members of US society internalize, in some manner or other, the dominant discourse of white supremacy, I may get caught up in a dance of deference with People of Color, whose engagement with me is shaped by ancestral habits of survival in the white-dominated world.

I have committed myself to recognizing moments of microentitlement and moving to undo them when I see them. Despite my determination, I miss these moments more often than I catch them. Moments of microaggression toward People of Color may at the same time be moments of microentitlement for white people. In the face of "minor" microaggressions from white people, People of Color may choose to let the moment pass. Perhaps they are not sure if they misunderstood, or perhaps they decide not to take on the risk and cost of calling the microaggression out. The silence of People of Color in the face of microaggressions not only harms them but also serves as a microentitlement for white people, who are protected from awareness of their performances of privilege.

I believe that the invisibility of white privilege from the perspective of its beneficiaries is partially sustained by white people's failure to recognize and acknowledge moments of microaggression and microentitlement as they occur. Invisibility results from collusive avoidance of difficult relational moments. As noted earlier with microaggressions, challenging white people in instances of microentitlement comes with the risk of evoking their emotionally defensive reactions. As visible as our microaggressions and microentitlements may be to People of Color, their efforts to bring them to our attention can be risky or costly and always involve work. This pattern is intrinsically unpleasant. Given the implicit power that white people can access, ranging from economic retaliation to the ultimate recourse of mobilizing protective responses from police, the pattern is potentially lethal.

## Psychological Obstacles to Recognizing Our Racism

At times, I have volunteered to facilitate or cofacilitate difficult conversations about race, with exclusively white groups and with mixed groups, with People of Color and white people. I have also challenged, or witnessed the challenging of, white people for their racist acts or utterances. With my psychologist's eye, I have discerned a characteristic sequence of emotions, psychological operations, and avoidant behavior that often manifests when white people are challenged for their racism.

### *The Dynamic of Shame, Rage, Guilt, Self-Absorption, and Ignorance*

#### Shame

Unless we are committed to explicit white nationalist ideology, when we become aware of our enactments of internalized white supremacy, we experience them as violations of conventional notions of right and wrong. We see that we do wrong when confronted with our unwitting assumptions of privilege and superiority, our mistreatment of others, or the unfairness of advantages granted us based on our skin color. This awareness stimulates feelings of shame. At tolerable levels, shame is a salutary social emotion. When our actions evoke the utterance, "You should be ashamed," from others, it affords a powerful incentive for us to cease the actions for which we are being shamed. Beyond tolerable levels, however, shame is an overwhelming and paralyzing emotional state. If we can't tolerate the shame, we may shift into emotions of rage or guilt or use denial and escape into the psychological comfort of unconscious whiteness. As we do so, we lose the opportunity to observe, recognize, and transform our enactment of racist discourse. Consider a naïve white person, with little prior experience around People of Color, using the phrase, "you people," never having learned that the phrase is particularly offensive to People of Color. When called out, that person might feel a bit ashamed learning about the effect of their words on others. This mild discomfort might serve to change the person's use of language in the future. A stronger emotion of shame might lead further into the dynamic sequence.

**Rage**

We may obliterate our painful emotion of shame by reacting with intense anger and indignation. We may shift from painful emotions over how we are seen to aggressive emotions, rooted in the impulse to thrust aside perceived obstacles to our well-being (Panskepp, 1998). We treat them as adversaries; our "How dare you!" stance makes our assumption of entitlement obvious to people who have called us out. Giving in to our rage carries implicit assumptions of superiority. We are communicating that we care little for the opinion of someone before whom we are exhibiting a loss of emotional self-regulation. Our indignation includes the message, whether or not it is overt, "Who do you think you are? Do you know who *I am*?"

**Guilt**

Perhaps we recognize that our rage is out of control and relationally offensive or that we are trying to use rage to fight off shame over our enactment of whiteness. We may respond to this awareness by feeling guilty. Alternatively, we may transform the shame directly into feeling guilty. Shifting from rage into shame or into guilt contributes to relational breach. When I feel shame, I feel emotional pain about how I am seen by the other. When I feel guilty, I feel emotional pain about how I see myself. These emotions are ultimately about me, not the other.

**Self-Absorption**

Unless we are mindful of the dynamic and we have built our capacity to tolerate painful emotional states, we are at risk of retreating inward to tend to our emotional wounds. By this step in the dynamic sequence, it is very difficult to restore dialogue. We can be captured by our internal monologues, retreating from dialogical engagement (Kamya & Trimble, 2002). The opportunity for dialogue may be further obscured by our emotional display of distress, perhaps evoking caretaking responses from the very people who have confronted us for our hurtful enactments of white supremacy.

**Ignorance**

If we are unable to tolerate the pain of the dynamic, we, as white people, have the option to retreat into ignorance. We can settle into denial. We can withdraw from multiracial social spaces into a white world that implicitly congratulates itself for "not being racist," that assures the invisibility of white privilege and white supremacy, a world whose color blindness reinforces the delusional "normality" of whiteness.

### *Overcoming the Obstacles to Recognizing Our Racism: Developing "Thick Skin"*

Hardy (2016) advises white people committed to antiracist practice to develop "thick skin" (pp. 131–132). Recognizing the discomfort white people experience when challenged for their whiteness, Hardy counsels against defensive efforts to withdraw or to escalate and against tactics, including rebuttal and retribution, that shut down dialogue. As I understand it, "thick skin" is a metaphor for the capacity to tolerate relational and emotional distress without disintegrating and while remaining present in difficult conversation. In my efforts to develop this capacity, I have to balance inner awareness with relational engagement. I need to be mindful of my inner voices of the bigot, the color blind, and the seeker. I need to recognize, and to regulate, my emotional reactions to these inner voices and to the people who are challenging me for my racism. My inner work must be diligent enough to be effective without drawing me into self-absorption. I must, simultaneously, be fully and authentically engaged in relationship with people who activate, and perhaps directly challenge, my enactments of white supremacy. It is a difficult dance, and I often stumble, hurting or offending others as I do. One way that I am able to go on in the face of these personal limitations is to draw on my spirituality.

## Whiteness as a Disease of the Soul

What are the implications of this dynamic of shame, rage, guilt, self-absorption, and ignorance for effective solidarity between People of Color and white people in the struggle to dismantle racist injustice? I argue that we white people must be conscious of unpleasant psychological and emotional realities about ourselves if we are to be fully relationally present with our Comrades of Color in the struggle. It is critically important, however, that we do not allow this consciousness to be paralyzing.

It is also very important that we do not allow emerging awareness of our enactments of racism to lead us into practices of self-silencing. McWhorter (2020) has called out as racist the white practice of making rules against saying things that might offend People of Color. Second-guessing ourselves inhibits our capacity to be fully and authentically present in relationship. It is a monologic practice that obstructs genuine dialogue (Kamya & Trimble, 2002; Seikkula & Trimble, 2005).

Painful as it is to hold it in my awareness, I accept that my racism will manifest as I engage in relationship with People of Color—and that I am responsible for those manifestations. The paradox is that, although I am willing to take responsibility for these enactments, I can only do so in relational space with others. Full accountability is possible only when I have earned enough trust from friends, colleagues, and comrades for them to expect me to be responsive and responsible when they call on me to take responsibility. I strive by my conduct to make their relational risk, if they choose to take it, worthwhile. It is a cruel and, I think, inescapable paradox that, as a white man, I hurt the people I love in the course of our righteous struggle together for social justice.

I choose the words "disease of the soul" to acknowledge the intrinsic evil of my racism but also to assert that the remedy for the evil includes spiritual practice. The Abrahamic religions of Judaism, Christianity, and Islam acknowledge that the capacity for evil is intrinsic to the human condition. Raised as a Christian, but a convert to Judaism, I am familiar with the ideas of original sin, in the former, and of *yetzer hara* (the intention to do evil, balanced in the soul with *yetzer tov*, the intention to do good), in the latter. Although I am aware of the differences between them, these ideas of human limitation to me appear to bear similarities with the idea of sin in Islam (Dogan, 2014). In all three traditions, we are obliged to engage with our limitations in order to transcend them. From my limited experience, it appears that all human spiritual and religious traditions acknowledge our limitations as intrinsic to the human condition while also challenging us to transform ourselves.

In a three-year dialogue among a group of family therapists with a diverse range of spiritual and religious beliefs (Trimble, 2018), we entered sacred space, a Bakhtinian "space between" (Trimble et. al., 2018, p. 132), from which flowed unique understandings and a shared experience of intimacy that we referred to as "nameless but achingly familiar sensations" (p. 127). Each member of this racially and religiously diverse group was deeply grounded in their particular faith practice. Among us, we embodied traditions grounded in Asian, European, Indigenous American, and African cultures. The impulse behind the assembling of this group was the opposite of color blindness. Our differences were integral to our project. We were seeking to respond to the dilemma of human spirituality at an historical moment when the planet is at risk of collapse from the activities of its dominant species—from war, environmental degradation, or both. On the one hand, a global culture grounded in respect for the universality of human spirituality could potentially support strategies to save the planet. On the other hand, much of human history has been marked by murderous warfare over religious beliefs and practices. We sought, in our dialogue with each other, to address the strains between the universal and the particular in human spirituality.

Over the course of the conversation, we found certain words that to us embodied human qualities, practices, and experiences common to spirituality, that were beyond the particularities of distinct faiths. They included community, compassion, courage, generosity, grace, gratitude, hope, humility, intimacy, love, mindfulness, openness, remorse, respect, responsibility, reverence, seeking, shame (!), stillness, struggle, suffering, transformation, virtue, vision, voice, and yearning. As I make sense of my personal struggle to address my internalization of white supremacy, I find myself drawing on the spiritual truths embodied in those words.

Looking at it as a spiritual affliction, I see that whiteness, with its roots in colonialism and chattel slavery (Kendi, 2016), consistently leads me into ethically indefensible actions and spiritually destructive emotional states. I recognize that my affliction with whiteness is inescapable as long as I live in a society that affords me disproportionate power and wealth, whose dominant discourse assures me micro- and macroentitlements, that obscures my racial macroaggressions, and that makes my microaggressions invisible to me as I perform them. Antiracism must therefore be part of my personal spiritual practice, as my traditions call on me to temper destructive emotions, to acknowledge my moral failings as aspects of my human nature, and to cultivate practices of truthfulness, compassion, courage, steadfastness, humility, and other spiritual virtues.

In this context, the feeling of shame can be a salutary emotion, in the right dose, signaling my transgression to me without overwhelming me. Rage can be tempered into righteous indignation, best directed at organizations or institutions rather than at individuals. Remorse, embodying its imperative of relational accountability and restoration, can supplant the self-absorption of guilt. Relational engagement can counter individual self-absorption. When confronted for ignoring my racist practices and attitudes, I can recognize and modulate my reflexive emotional reactivity and listen intently to what others tell me.

## Implications for Therapy, Education, and Training

In interviews with clinicians and academics, including Shani Dowd, Gonzalo Bacigalupe, Richard Pinderhughes, and me, assembled in a William James College video on facilitating difficult conversations about race in the classroom (Alhadi et al., 2015), each respondent made the independent observation that the process is "messy." Perhaps this chapter provides some illumination of the mess that immerses us when we take on the challenge of engaging with antiracist practice. The therapist, teacher, or leader who takes on difficult conversations about race needs to have a high level of tolerance for confusion, for unpleasant feelings, and for experiences of failure. There is no way that any of us can expect to be comfortable as we struggle in solidarity to dismantle racism. The following suggestions may be helpful for white people who take on this challenge:

### *Spiritual Grounding*

Whether or not one has formally adopted a faith practice, it helps to have a perspective that embraces experience beyond the boundaries of the self. Through a lens that sees whiteness as a disease of the soul, we can envision healing through the cultivation of spiritual qualities. It takes humility to accept our failures and limitations, including our inevitable internalization, reproduction, and enactment of the very white supremacy that we are struggling to dismantle. Practices of meditation and cultivation of inner peace can help us to modulate the strong emotions of shame, rage, and guilt. Critical awareness of the ego as a spiritual impediment can help us to resist self-absorption and invite us to discard any illusion that we can succeed by ourselves. We must draw on generosity and compassion as we engage authentically with fellow sufferers, open-hearted and broken-hearted together. We must draw on a persistence ultimately grounded in faith, whatever form that faith may take for each of us. My persistence in this messy and painful struggle is grounded in the words of sages in my religious tradition: "You are not required to complete the work, but you are not free to abandon it" (*Pirké Avot*, 1997, 2:16).

### *Attend to How You Are Seen*

This chapter has focused exclusively on whiteness as a disease of the soul for white people, but this is only a partial deconstruction of the spiritual toxicity of the dominant discourse of white supremacy and of its inescapable internalization in its different manifestations by everyone of all races in a racist society. I will not presume to tell People of Color how to teach, train, lead, or heal. Although my suggestions are directed to people who identify and/or are identified by others as white, I hope that a Reader of Color may find some value in them.

The developmental state of our own racial identity (Helms, 1990), our progress on the antiracist journey, and how others may, based on our appearance to them, identify us racially powerfully influence our opportunities and obstacles as we seek to teach, train, heal, or lead. As we track our own reflective awareness of our whiteness, it is important not to assume that we know how we are seen by others in the room. When teaching from a culturally sensitive perspective, we need to maintain an attitude of open curiosity about how others' responses are shaped by their perceptions of us.

### *Attend to Your Internal Voices*

Although there are some topics that we may prefer to learn about by jumping right into teaching about them, this is not the case with facilitating difficult conversations about race. We need to have done enough work to be able to recognize the inner voices of the bigot, the color blind, and the seeker of racial sensitivity. It is particularly important that the latter voice not blind us by the flattery of self-congratulation. Seekers, by definition, never arrive; seekers who consider themselves "woke" can be harmful to the process. We should be poised to listen to the inner voices with curiosity about what they may be indicating about how we are reacting to what is going on in the room, balancing inner listening with a firm intention not to let the voices interfere with the work of facilitating the process unfolding in the room.

### *Avoid Reducing Racism to Either the Social or the Psychological*

It is important to maintain a "both/and" rather than an "either/or" perspective on racism. Racism is a powerful social and institutional system of exploitation and oppression with a specific history, embodied in customary practices and in formal policies that distinguish groups from each other and that afford one group privilege over the other (Kendi, 2019). Racism is also a psychological phenomenon, explored in its form as whiteness in this chapter. The social and psychological phenomena intersect in racism's relational forms, as manifest in microaggression and microentitlement, in decisions employers make about hiring, in police perceptions of persons as "suspicious," in teachers' responses to student behavior, etc.

It is important not to reduce racism to either its social or its psychological manifestations. If one teaches a group of white people about the historical and current social outrages of racism exclusively, they may come away insufficiently aware of the real social consequences of their internalization of white supremacy. If one teaches a group of white people about racism solely as a psychological phenomenon, they may feel that their obligation is solely to transform themselves psychologically. This is not only impossible, given the power of macro- and microentitlements to shape psychological experience, it also relieves them of their obligation to struggle in solidarity with People of Color to dismantle racist customs and policies.

### *Attend to Who Is in the Room*

The process and the prospects for the conversation depend on whether everyone in the room identifies as white, everyone identifies as of Color, or the group is mixed. It is important both to acknowledge intersectionality (Kliman, 2010) and to emphasize that the topic at hand is, specifically, race. White participants may invoke other dimensions of difference and power, such as gender, class, ethnicity, or ability, to avoid the specific emotional discomforts embodied in conversations about race.

#### Groups In Which All Participants Are White

One major advantage of all-white groups is that it may be more possible to deal with the emotional pain of whiteness as a disease of the soul when participants' enactments of white supremacy are not also injuring People of Color in the room. Mutual compassion can build solidarity so that participants can examine internalized racism and commit to antiracist practices. If the group has not assembled voluntarily, however, it can be very difficult to arrive at this state of mutual support. This can be the case when an employer or a consent agreement has made participation mandatory. The facilitator can be confronted with the full force of the dynamic of shame, rage, guilt, self-absorption, and retreat into ignorance. Such situations require us to reach deeply into ourselves to afford transparent, fully embodied personal presence in order to shift the group conversation out of constricted monologues and into open dialogue (Seikkula & Trimble, 2005). This calls for a determination to maintain a thick skin and an open heart, with a spiritual attitude of humility.

My experience leading voluntarily assembled exclusively white groups is that it helps, during the initial orientation, to state explicitly that each person in the room, regardless of where they are on their antiracist journey, can learn from the others. It was with such an attitude that I could listen deeply, in an exclusively white group, to participants who were for the first time discovering and facing the voice of their inner bigot. Although I had for years tracked the voice of my own internal bigot, I had been treating this internal conversation as a shameful personal secret. Seeing how powerfully this conflict was obstructing white people's antiracist progress, I recognized how important it was to be explicit about it as an inescapable aspect of whiteness and to be transparent about my own personal struggle with it.

**Racially Heterogeneous Groups**

As with groups of any composition, the leader should hold with compassion the painful emotions that will emerge and not collude with resistance to the deep conversation that intrinsically and inevitably provokes those painful emotions. It is important during the initial orientation to clarify the distinction between "safety" and emotional discomfort and to be explicit that difficult conversations about race are intrinsically and inevitably uncomfortable. The leader should prepare to work swiftly through impasses where that distinction is not clear. For example, white participants may interpret being called out for microaggression as verbal assault. Distressed by calls to examine their performances of racial privilege, they may act from their privilege to demand that the group soothe their distress and affirm them as "good people" (DiAngelo, 2018).

The leader can draw on principles of antiracist practice using the Privileged and Subjugated Task (PAST) model developed by Hardy (2016), which locates white participants in the privileged position and People of Color in the subjugated position. The leader might include these principles in the initial orientation or articulate them as illustrations emerge in the group conversation. Tasks of the privileged include the following: Differentiate between intentions and consequences, and always start with an acknowledgment of the latter (the leader focuses the conversation on the consequences experienced by the subjugated person). Avoid overt and covert negation of subjugated conversations and disclosures (the leader counters negation of the voices of Participants of Color by practicing the art and skill of validation). Avoid the reactive reflexes of relational retrenchment, rebuttal, and retribution (the leader encourages white participants to develop the thick skin necessary to contain reactive reflexes—to notice and respond to, rather than suppress, relational challenges). Avoid the issuance of prescriptions (the leader encourages white participants to offer vulnerable disclosures about themselves rather than suggesting to People of Color how to think, feel, or act). Avoid presuming to speak from a knowledgeable, neutral, objective, expert position (the leader insists that white participants always locate their racial selves in the conversation).

The tasks of the subjugated include the following: Challenge silence and voicelessness (the leader encourages Participants of Color to take the risk of making one more statement than they are comfortable making and to embed "I" messages—e.g., "I think, I feel, I wish"—in all their statements). Regulate and rechannel rage (the leader encourages Participants of Color to use rage as an energy source to foster and reinforce voice and self-advocacy, to resolve to stay engaged in difficult conversations, to attack ideas, not people). Engage in a process of exhaling (the leader encourages Participants of Color to focus on being coherent and communicating accordingly, to say what they mean and mean what they say). Cease and desist from caretaking of the privileged (the leader encourages Participants of Color to stay intimately engaged while granting uninterrupted emotional space for white participants to experience, explore, and understand the complex thoughts and feelings that the conversation is likely to provoke: "Be caring without caretaking"). Maintain investment in the conversation (the leader encourages Participants of Color to speak from the core of their thoughts, feelings, and experience, while refraining from analyzing the white "other").

When possible, it is better for a multiracial pair or team of leaders to collaborate in facilitating difficult conversations about race. No matter how far white leaders may have traveled on their personal antiracist journey, they are never free of the spiritual disease of whiteness that can affect their judgments, perceptions, and actions. They can rely on their Coleaders of Color to call them out for their unconscious errors. Their comrades can rely on them to "draw fire" from indignant resistance by white participants. Collaborative leadership must be grounded in familiar, trusting relationships, making it natural for the Leader of Color to challenge their white collaborator and for the white leader to respond to challenges with curiosity and open-hearted humility. Such exchanges between leaders may provide participants with useful models for addressing power, disagreement, or alternative perspectives across racial differences.

### Groups with White Leaders, When All, or Most, Participants Are People of Color

It would be presumptuous for a white person to take on such a leadership role in difficult conversations about race when all or nearly all the participants are People of Color. The power embodied in the role of leader and the obstacles that whiteness places in the way of accurate perception of one's performance of racism create unacceptable risks of relational injury and toxic group processes.

Systemic racism, however, produces segregated schools in which white people teach, train, or lead groups in which they might be the only white person. Antiracist training settings that primarily serve Students of Color may demonstrate their commitment to multiculturalism by hiring a minority of white faculty members to assure a multiracial educational experience.

Antiracist white teachers in such settings must be vigilant about the risks of doing harm from their positions. They should provide formal opportunities for collective critical feedback from the group about their performance along with assurance that the students' feedback will not put them at risk of retaliation, such as in future evaluations or recommendations. Although the collective format provides some protection from abuse of the leader's power, Students of Color may have had experiences that make them realistically skeptical of assurances of safety. White leaders should themselves be skeptical, because all that they can assure are their good intentions. Their whiteness can blind them to consequences they may unwittingly impose on students for their criticisms.

Serious commitment to antiracism in such a situation requires that white teachers live antiracist lives, embedded in multiracial networks of personal and professional relationships. They need to have established trusting relationships, relationships accustomed to difficult conversations about race, in which their Friends and Colleagues of Color expect that they will be heard. Particularly in the workplace, white teachers' practices need to be fully transparent and open to colleagues' observations, criticisms, and suggestions. Students need to be assured that they can turn to other faculty with their concerns and that those faculty will engage directly with the teacher about whom the students have expressed concern, relieving students of responsibility for the corrective feedback that needs to come from colleagues.

There is no escaping the cruel paradox that white people's antiracist practice requires the engagement of People of Color, adding another challenge to the many challenges that People of Color endure living in a white supremacist world. With an awareness of this paradox, a demonstrated lifetime commitment to dismantling racism, and self-compassion for the spiritual affliction of whiteness, white people can build solidarity with People of Color in the struggle. Through processes of rupture and repair, relationships across racial differences do, over time, become stronger in the broken places.

**DAVID TRIMBLE, PHD,** a veteran of the Civil Rights Movement of the 1960s, and the father of children with English, Scots-Irish, Nipmuc, Narragansett, and West African ancestors, has throughout his professional career been closely affiliated with the Center for Multicultural Training in Psychology at Boston Medical Center, where he teaches the Multicultural Family Therapy Seminar. He is the editor of *Engaging with Spirituality in Family Therapy: Meeting in Sacred Space* (Springer, 2018). He has a clinical psychology practice in Brookline, Massachusetts.

## References

*Alhadi, F., Tannenbaum, S., & Kliman, J. (2015, March 18).* Facilitating conversations on multiculturalism and social justice *[Video]. Youtube. https://www.youtube.com/watch?v=q709-YvjDN8*

*Boston Institute for Culturally Affirming Practices (BICAP). (2017). Deconstructing power to build connection: The importance of dialogue. In E. Pinderhughes, V. Jackson, & P. Romney (Eds.),* Understanding power: An imperative for human services *(pp. 195–218). National Associaton of Social Workers Press.*

*DiAngelo, R. (2018).* White fragility: Why it's so hard for white people to talk about racism. *Beacon Press.*

*Dogan, R. (2014). Nature of man in Islam.* The International Journal of Religion and Spirituality in Society, *4(3), 27–39.*

*Duru, O. K., Harawa, N. T., Kermah, D., & Norris, K. C. (2012). Allostatic load burden and racial disparities in mortality.* Journal of the National Medical Association, *104, 89–95.*

*Hall, J. M., & Fields, B. (2015). "It's killing us!" Narratives of Black adults about microaggression experiences and related health stress.* Global Qualitative Nursing Research, *2, 1–14. https://doi.org/10.1177/2333393615591569*

*Hardy, K. V. (2016). Anti-racist approaches for shaping theoretical and practice paradigms. In M. Pender-Greene & A. Siskin (Eds.),* Anti-racist strategies for the health and human services *(pp. 125–139). Oxford University Press.*

*Hardy, K. V., & Laszloffy, T. A. (2002). Couple therapy using a multicultural perspective. In A. Gurman & N. Jacobson (Eds.),* Clinical Handbook of Couple Therapy *(pp. 569–593). Guilford.*

*Hardy, K. V., & Laszloffy, T. A. (2008). The dynamics of a pro-racist ideology. In M. McGoldrick & K. V. Hardy (Eds.),* Revisioning family therapy: Race, culture, and gender in clinical practice *(2nd ed., pp. 235–237). Guilford.*

*Hare-Mustin, R. (1994).* Discourses in the mirrored room: A postmodern analysis of therapy. Family Process, *33, 19–35.*

*Helms, J. E. (Ed.). (1990).* Black and White racial identity: Theory, research, and practice. *Greenwood Press.*

*Kamya, H., & Trimble, D. (2002). Response to injury: Toward ethical construction of the other.* Journal of Systemic Therapies, *21, 19–27.*

*Kendi, I. X. (2016).* Stamped from the beginning: The definitive history of racist ideas in America. *Bold Type Books.*

*Kendi, I. X. (2019).* How to be an antiracist. *One World.*

*Kliman, J. (2010, Winter). Intersections of social privilege and marginalization: A visual teaching tool.* AFTA Monograph Series, *39–48.*

*Kliman, J., Winawer, H., & Trimble, D. (2019). The inevitable whiteness of being (White): Whiteness and intersectionality in family therapy practice and training. In M. McGoldrick & K. V. Hardy (Eds.),* Re-visioning family therapy: Addressing diversity in clinical practice *(3rd ed., pp. 236–250). Guilford Press.*

*McWhorter, J. (2020, July 15). The dehumanizing condescension of white fragility.* The Atlantic. *https://www.theatlantic.com/ideas/archive/2020/07/dehumanizing-condescension-white-fragility/614146/*

*Moore, D. (2020, August 27). New study confirms staggering racial disparities in COVID-19 cases in Massachusetts.* The Boston Globe. *https://www.bostonglobe.com/2020/08/27/nation/new-study-finds-staggering-racial-disparities-covid-19-cases-massachusetts/?s_campaign=breakingnews:newsletter*

*Okun, T. (2020, July 10).* White supremacy culture. *DRWORKSBOOK. https://collectiveliberation.org/wp-content/uploads/2013/01/White_Supremacy_Culture_Okun.pdf*

*Panskepp, J. (1998). Affective neuroscience: The foundations of human and animal emotions. Oxford University Press.*

*Pierce, C. (1995). Stress analogs of racism and sexism: Terrorism, torture, and disaster. In C. Willie, P. Reiker, B. Kramer, & P. Brown (Eds.),* Mental Health, Racism, and Sexism *(pp. 277–293). Routledge.*

*Pirké avot:* Wisdom of the Jewish sages *(C. Stern, Ed.). (1997). Ktav Publishing House, Inc.*

*Seikkula, J., & Trimble, D. (2005). Healing elements of therapeutic conversation: Dialogue as an embodiment of love.* Family Process, *44, 461–475.*

*Sue, D. W., Capodilupo, C. M., Torino, G. C., Bucceri, J. M., Holder, A. M. B., Nadal, K. L., & Esquili, M. (2007). Racial microaggressions in everyday life: Implications for clinical practice.* American Psychologist, *62, 271–286.*

*Trimble, D. (2018). From the margins to the center: Generative possibilities in multicultural*

*dialogue on spirituality. In D. Trimble (Ed.),* Engaging with spirituality in family therapy: Meeting in sacred space *(pp. 1–13). American Family Therapy Academy.*
*Trimble, D., Abu-Baker, K., Arora, K., Bava, S., Hines, P., Kamya, H., King, J., Longo-Lockspeiser, L., & Robbins, R. A. (2018). A conversation in sacred space. In D. Trimble (Ed.),* Engaging with spirituality in family therapy: Meeting in sacred space *(pp. 123–140). American Family Therapy Academy.*

## CHAPTER 4

# The Vicious Cycle of White Centrality

LANE ARYE, PHD

This chapter focuses on white centrality to highlight how the centering of white people and whiteness, externally and internally, with or without our awareness, pushes Black, Indigenous, and People of Color (BIPOC) to the margins of society, of relationships, and of white people's priorities, with disastrous results. It will critically and comprehensively explore how the centrality of whiteness affects our daily lives and cross-racial relationships.

My lived experiences as a white man in the United States will illustrate the benefits I receive from how the world centers whiteness. I will demonstrate how the centrality of whiteness lives in me and how it impacts my relationships with BIPOC. The serious consequences of this will become clear. Finally, I will offer suggestions about what whites, like me, can do to challenge whiteness in the interest of contributing to a more racially just society.

It is my hope that white readers will see reflections of themselves in these personal stories that reflect universal patterns. There is a risk you might dismiss the larger points because your story is not the same as mine. We white people are socialized to see ourselves as individuals (DiAngelo, 2018). If you find yourself discounting what I am saying because our backgrounds are different or judging my hurtful mistake as something you would never do, please take a breath, look at yourself with compassion, and be open to the possibility that this lives in you too.

BIPOC readers, I imagine you already know more about this topic than I do, from your own lived experience. I hope that this chapter will validate some of your experiences and that it will be refreshing to hear a white man talk directly about issues that are often denied or remain unspoken between us. The risk is that, in my attempts to deconstruct whiteness, I may reveal my racially based blind spots and reinforce my own centrality. Part of me wants to stay safe by staying silent, but that maintains the status quo, which ultimately hurts BIPOC and the efforts to contribute to the creation of a more racially equitable world.

## The Centrality of Whiteness

Society favors white people in countless ways. This shapes how white people see themselves, BIPOC, and the world. That, in turn, impacts how white people interact with BIPOC, and how BIPOC are treated in the world. The society that benefits white people is, in this way, strengthened, creating a vicious cycle.

The term *white centrality* describes how white people and whiteness itself are at the center, considered normal, get the focus, and create the social norms everyone is expected to live by. BIPOC are pushed to the margins, considered "other," put down, seen through the lens of whiteness, and are demonized, avoided, or ignored. White centrality is intimately connected to *white supremacy*, the conscious or unconscious assumption that white people and whiteness are superior, as are the behaviors and systems that stem from that assumption. I see white centrality and white supremacy as two sides of the same coin; however it lands, whiteness always wins. One did not create the other. Rather, they were both created by the power that white people and whiteness have held historically and still hold in the world. Whites, through the centrality of whiteness, decide what is seen as superior and inferior, what is highlighted or ignored, and how different groups are treated. White centrality and white supremacy both emerge from that power, and their effects concretize that power. Yet another vicious cycle.

## The Cycle

White centrality has outer and inner manifestations. On the outside, society centers whiteness through laws, policies, institutional structures, and systems. Racially speaking, whiteness largely determines whose voices are heard and who is seen and in what way. All of this is invisible to most white people. These outer manifestations of white centrality seep into us. (They seep into everyone, but when I use the word "us," I mean white people like me.)

The inner aspects of white centrality are even harder for us to notice. We are imbued with the sense that whiteness is the norm and the ideal. We see ourselves as people, rarely locating ourselves racially. Not noticing the privileges of whiteness nor its centrality, we take them for granted and feel we deserve them.

Internalized white centrality turns back outward. It impacts how we relate to BIPOC. It impacts how we feel and respond when they express their upset or rage or when they do not see our good intent. This in turn impacts BIPOC; and those impacts have emotional, physical, relational, and practical consequences.

The outer and inner aspects of white centrality reinforce one another. This hurts BIPOC and white people. As I write this, the streets of most major cities are boiling over with expressions of grief and rage at the killings of unarmed Black people in this country, injustice created and perpetuated by white centrality. This is urgent, not academic. People's lives are at stake every day.

## Outer White Centrality—How the World Centers Me as a White Person

I grew up hearing that my dad was the son of poor immigrants. Starting with nothing, he worked hard and was smart, so he succeeded. I did not notice the current of privilege at his back. DiAngelo (2012) defines privilege as "rights, benefits and resources that are purported to be shared by all but are only consistently available to the dominant group" (p. 52). She says privilege is like a current pushing in the direction we are swimming. We do not notice the current is helping us nor that it is pushing *against* people who do not share that privilege. But they notice it.

My father *did* work hard and *was* smart. He also had a current at his back, a system of structural advantages designed to help white people. My father was a veteran of WWII, so the GI Bill, available only to white people, paid for his law school (Blakemore, 2019). He bought a house in the suburbs using a Federal Housing Authority loan, which were offered only to white people. And because of redlining, only white people could buy homes in those suburbs (Gross & Rothstein, 2017). In our neighborhood, the police were friendly. My friends and I were never stopped, frisked, arrested, beaten, or shot. When my father died, my brothers and I inherited that house. In this way (and many others) I benefited from the current at my father's back, at my back. Yes, I worked my tail off to get a PhD, but I also had unfair advantages that put me in that position. Laws and structural advantages for white people, and disadvantages for BIPOC, center white people like me and push BIPOC to the margins of economic, professional, and housing opportunity.

Outer white centrality—the structural and systemic centering of white people in our society—has serious ramifications. In 2016, the median wealth of white households in the United States was more than 10 times greater than the median wealth of Black households and 8 times greater than the median wealth of Latinx households. A good job does not close this gap. And, incredibly, "blacks *with* [emphasis added] at least a college degree still had about 30 percent less wealth than whites *without* [emphasis added] a college degree" (Hanks et al., 2018, para. 32).

One result of socially engineered segregation based on race was that I grew up with white people all around me. No one ever mentioned the unfair advantages of whiteness. In my high school in the 1970s, we spent a year studying the Civil Rights movement. None of my teachers, all of whom were white, mentioned that racial inequity and oppression were still happening or that they were present in the very fact that there were no BIPOC in our classes. Interestingly, I never noticed this or thought it odd or considered the ways in which it may have been a detriment to my education as well as to my growth and development as a human being.

## White Centrality Seeps Inside—How I Learned to Center Myself and My Whiteness

Everywhere I looked I was reflected—in film, television, books, and the news. I was told some people were beautiful, brilliant, powerful, or worth listening to; they were all white. As far as I knew, the stories I read or watched or heard were everyone's stories. My experiences must be the same as everyone's experiences. I had internalized a white pattern called *universalism* (DiAngelo, 2012). No one ever mentioned we were white. Other races were named. That is a Black neighborhood. That is an Asian woman. But we were just people. The norm.

Because I did not notice the current of privilege, the message I got was that we worked hard, were smart, and deserved what we had. The corollary message was that BIPOC must not work as hard or be as intelligent or worthy because they did not have as much. In this way I internalized another pattern, *white superiority and dominance.* This happens when those of us in the dominant group are socialized to see our higher status as natural and deserved (DiAngelo, 2012). Whether conscious or unconscious, this is white supremacy. Of course my family hated overt white supremacists like the Klan and the Nazis. We were the good people who believed that everyone is equal and deserves equal rights.

When driving to the city and passing through neighborhoods filled with people who did not look like us, though, my parents reflexively locked the car doors. I got the message then that BIPOC were dangerous. I heard their schools and neighborhoods were "bad" and I felt sorry for them. We gave money to "lift them up." I knew *we are all equal. They are just like us. Everybody is.* I never questioned the incongruity between our stated values and the implicit messages. The system that put us at the center was rooted inside me.

I internalized white superiority and dominance in other ways. I was told I lived in a good neighborhood and went to a good school. (No one told me that "good" was code for "white and no BIPOC.") My teachers valued my ideas, and I was rewarded for speaking up. Around the dinner table, our family would debate issues of the day. Our parents would cut down our opinions but applaud us when our arguments were clear and convincing. I learned that I am free to speak up and will be rewarded when I do it well.

I learned that I should think my ideas are important and do my best to eviscerate other people's ideas.

After learning so much from Robin DiAngelo's book *What Does It Mean to Be White,* I was thrilled to attend a workshop with her. I participated in the ways I was raised to: I listened, took copious notes, and asked what I thought were probing and challenging questions. Yet, as is often the case, my intentions as a white male were very different from my impact. Robin gave me feedback that she found my questions, tone, and body language aggressive, and that the impact of my engagement was actually domination and superiority. I was horrified and defensive. But I spent all night taking in her feedback and came to see the truth in it. Luckily, she had taught us a powerful model of repair, and I prepared myself to practice it with her. The next day, I requested permission, as she had guided us to do, and was touched that she granted me the opportunity. I explained what I had come to see about my behavior and apologized. She accepted and said she felt closure and was ready to move on. She shared that she found it both rare and powerful to receive a repair from a white man.

That night over dinner, moved and grateful for teachings that had become so personal, I told my wife and kids about the experience. While we were doing the dishes, my wife told me I had dominated the dinner table conversation! Even in sharing what I had learned about my internalized dominance, I continued to manifest it. Conditioned patterns run deep. I will not be free of them in my lifetime, but I am committed to continually unearthing and addressing them and being accountable for their impact. (In this example, male centrality was in the foreground. Peggy McIntosh [1988] delineates correspondences between white privilege and male privilege.)

## What Stews Inside, Leaks Out

The cycle continues. What is outside, seeps in. What stews inside, leaks out. One of the myriad ways internalized white centrality gets externalized again is in our interactions with BIPOC. Here are a few hurtful examples to show how this plays out. I would rather show you a curated version of myself that you might like and respect. But society already does that, and these stories are more instructive.

During a workshop about race, I was having lunch with a Latinx man. He made a comment that conflicted with something I had learned and taught about. I cited my source and, basically, contradicted him. He soon made a polite excuse and got up from the table. I did not think anything of it. I later learned he is an eminent psychologist, widely quoted in the national media. This led me to examine what I had done. I realized my racial conditioning had been in control. I would not have said so at the time, but I felt superior to him, more educated and smarter, although I clearly was not. Like in my childhood, there was a disconnect between my stated conscious values and the implicit messages in my head/gut that white people, like me, are the teachers, professors, and experts who know—not a Latinx like him. I had been indoctrinated while driving through Spanish Harlem with doors locked as my liberal mother bemoaned bad schools and lack of a decent education. I do not want to admit this to myself, much less to you. But when I don't, it operates underground, unquestioned, hurting BIPOC and hurting me.

My freedom to jump in with my idea centered my knowledge over his and pushed him to the margin and literally away from the table. I did not know why he left; he did not say. Maybe I was the tenth white person who had recently disregarded him despite his genius and accomplishments. As is often the case with white people, I did not even know I had disrespected him. I was too busy centering myself and showing what I thought I knew. Since I am centered by the world, I did not have to notice or be concerned with whether I'd hurt or angered him. If I had not heard he was an esteemed psychologist, I may never have thought about it again. That night, though, I reflected on my actions and the next day asked if I could repair with him. He confirmed my analysis of our interaction and said something I have heard from many BIPOC; it costs them too much energy to educate white people about what we have done. Without feedback, we stay in our bubble, not realizing there is a problem. This is a loss for me and many white people who lose chances for relationships and lose opportunities to know the experience of BIPOC. Talking over him deprived me of an opportunity to learn and benefit from his wisdom, all because the white centrality and supremacy around me had seeped inside and leaked back out onto him.

I attended another workshop about race, this one taught by Amy, a masterful national presenter who is an Asian American woman. Having been to her seminars before, I was excited. On the third afternoon, during time for questions, I asked the burning one I had come with. I described the racial difficulties of an organization I was working with. Amy began outlining different considerations and approaches. Remember, I needed her supervision and had waited for this opportunity. She clearly was not finished with her analysis or suggestions. But instead of hearing her out, I interrupted her to say, "I have done those things," and went on to describe all the good work on racism I had already accomplished with this organization. Eventually, I realized I was *broadcasting my racial credentials*, another typical white pattern. I apologized, but the damage had been done. Amy was no longer analyzing the problem I had presented. Instead, she looked at me with eyes that seemed to say, "This guy does not get it."

During a break she gave me the gift of her feedback. My attempt to convince her that I am an exceptional white person had the opposite effect. It convinced her I valued my reputation more than her wisdom or authority. She had not centered me as I was used to being centered by the world. My question, she said, was part of her workshop; she had been outlining different possibilities for the benefit of all the participants before giving her advice to me. Too busy centering my own needs, I had not seen hers nor the needs of other students. My conscious need was to get help from her. My unconscious need was for her, and everyone present, to see me racially as I saw myself. It backfired. Instead, she and the other BIPOC there saw me clearly, as a white person in the grips of *white fragility*. When I experienced racial stress (by not feeling sufficiently centered and valued in a conversation about race), I had a defensive response (to center myself and try to prove my value). For a moment, this worked like DiAngelo (2018) describes, "to reinstate white racial equilibrium . . . return our racial comfort, and maintain our dominance in the racial hierarchy" (p. 2). As often happens, though, it also shut down the conversation.

I am sad to say that was not the only time my white fragility has led me to, reflexively and unconsciously, attempt to recruit a BIPOC to restore my racial comfort. I do not remember the details that prompted me to apologize to John, a Black friend. But I remember that after my attempted repair, I asked him, "Was that okay?" He was furious, saying that this question was much worse than my original comment. My implicit communication was really, "Do you think I am okay? Help me feel better about myself!"

DiAngelo calls this *seeking absolution*. We grow up with the white belief that *racist = bad* and *not racist = good*, a pattern DiAngelo (2018) calls a false binary. When I realized my original comment to John was racist, I felt I was bad. My conscious intent was to relieve John's pain by apologizing. Asking if my apology was ok, though, gave John the job of making me feel better. He told me later that he was already working overtime managing his own feelings in that racially fraught interaction. Indirectly asking him to manage mine added to his burden, which I did not see because I was centering my own experience. Moreover, my request *ignored historical context*. Black people have been forced to take care of and do the work of white people in this country for hundreds of years. I pulled on him to take care of me rather than taking care of myself. My initial racial hurtfulness had filled me with shame. My racial socialization had filled me with entitlement that granted me the right to ask John to fix it. It also made me unaware there was anything wrong with that. Astonishingly, it also gave me, for a fleeting moment, the self-satisfied feeling that I was a good, antiracist white man because I had apologized to him. Not surprisingly, this interaction weakened John's racial trust in me.

These stories illustrate some of the dynamics that white people tend to fall into with BIPOC. They also show how cross-racial relationships, trust, and opportunities for learning can suffer as a result. It is important, though, to not get stuck in the trap of thinking that this means white people are bad or that there is something wrong with us. The ways we often think about, feel about, and interact (or do not interact) with BIPOC stem directly from our inevitable internalization of society's racist conditioning. Additionally, as the last vignette shows, thinking we are bad because we have internalized that conditioning is one of the unhelpful patterns we have been taught. What is our alternative? As Shakil Choudhury (2015) suggests in *Deep Diversity*, "Self-compassion helps us observe ourselves with curiosity rather than judgement. It is the salve to lessen the painful sting of our mistakes so we do not beat ourselves up. Yet it still holds us accountable" (p. 45). Self-compassion helps us be kind to ourselves so we can learn, grow, and work to make things better.

## The Snake Bites Its Tail—The Cycle Perpetuates Itself

Society's centering of whiteness seeps inside white people. When internalized white centrality leaks out, it is harmful to BIPOC. As we will see, these leaks also intensify racial inequities, perpetuating the cycle.

Internalized racial socialization contributes to microaggressions that are invariably hurtful. Derald Wing Sue et al. (2007) assert, "Racial microaggressions are brief and commonplace daily verbal, behavioral, or environmental indignities, whether intentional or unintentional, that communicate hostile, derogatory, or negative racial slights and insults toward people of color [*sic*]" (p. 271).

Dr. Roberto Montenegro (2016), a sociologist, physician, and psychiatrist, researches the impact of microaggressions on mental and physical health. He studies what the repeated experience of discrimination does to people's bodies. He describes the night he went to a fancy restaurant with his wife to celebrate completing his dissertation. After dinner, as they waited for a valet to get their car, a white woman stepped out of a Jaguar and gave Dr. Montenegro her keys, mistaking him for the valet. Before his car arrived, another white woman did the same thing. "I was at the pinnacle of my celebration, and with one swift action, I was dismissed. I was made invisible. I was negated" (Montenegro, 2016, p. 2071). The same kind of thing happens when he is doing rounds in the hospital. Although he is dressed in his white MD coat, white people often mistake him for the janitor or interpreter.

Dr. Montenegro says that every time this happens, his face turns red and his heart pounds. Stress hormones, like adrenaline and cortisol, course through his body. While helpful for fight or flight, these hormones harm the body when released continuously. Research has found that the stress of racism leads to chronic low-grade inflammation that puts BIPOC at risk for heart disease, sleep problems, and asthma (Bichell, 2017). This, combined with inequitable access to health care, contributes to inequitable health outcomes, including lower life expectancies for BIPOC. During the 2020 COVID-19 pandemic, the death rate for Black people in the United States was two times higher than for white people (The Covid Racial Data Tracker, 2020).

How can such stark injustice occur? It is a dangerous combination of outer and inner white centrality. On the outside are systemic inequities such as the racial bias that was discovered in the federal government's formula for distributing COVID-19 aid to hospitals (Ross, 2020) and the racial bias in commercial algorithms the US health care system uses to guide health decisions (Obermeyer et al., 2019). Internalized white centrality is evidenced, for instance, by widespread false beliefs that Black bodies are more resistant to injury than white bodies and feel less pain. These are the same persistent myths that were used to justify slavery. Stemming from the dehumanizing, racist ideas that Africans are like animals, and "legitimized" by torturous "medical experiments" in the eighteenth and nineteenth centuries, these baseless and false claims include the assertions that Black people have thicker skin or fewer nerve endings (Villarosa, 2019). According to a 2016 study, at least one such belief was held by 73% of whites surveyed and by a staggering 50% of medical students surveyed. The researchers found that this contributes to the well-documented practice of doctors offering and prescribing pain medicine to Black patients at a much lower rate than to white patients (Hoffman et al., 2016). When health care workers have internalized (conscious or unconscious) racist beliefs like this, it is no wonder that Black people are denied coronavirus testing or ICU beds (Garber, 2020). Their distress and concerns are simply not believed, especially since they are thought to possess a higher threshold for injury and pain.

Racial socialization influences mental health care as well. A review of empirical research on race and the diagnosis of psychotic disorders spanning a 24-year period found an unmistakable and widespread pattern (Schwartz, 2014). Black consumers of mental health services were diagnosed with psychotic disorders three to four times more often than white consumers. Latinx consumers were, similarly, diagnosed three times more often than white consumers.

It seems implausible that Black and Latinx people are biologically that much more prone to psychosis; so why this imbalance? Kenneth V. Hardy (2013) provides us a clue when asserting that the trauma of racism (including lifetimes of degradation and devaluation) push BIPOC into rage. I think this is often diagnosed as personal pathology rather than societal pathology. Unconscious racial bias also influences other psychiatric diagnoses.

As Fadus et al. (2019) have shown, Black and Latinx youth who should (and would if white) get a diagnosis of ADHD are often given diagnoses of disruptive behavior disorders like oppositional defiant disorder or conduct disorder. An ADHD diagnosis can open up access to medication, therapy, and services, while diagnoses of disruptive behavior disorder can "put ethnic and racial minority children at risk for perpetuating the disparities which currently exist in the medical, educational, and juvenile justice systems" (Fadus et al., 2019, para. 2). The study's authors continue, "Individual biases, whether they are implicit or explicit, can lead to systemic biases and structural racism as a whole" (Fadus et al., 2019, para. 15). As objective as clinicians try to be (whether white or BIPOC), they may see patients through a subjective lens, one tinted by racial socialization and white centrality. Those tinted lenses contribute to systemic biases and structural racism. And this phenomenon (of internalized racial socialization leaking out in hurtful ways that contribute to damaging systemic problems) does not stop with health care.

Researchers from the Yale Child Study Center showed videos of preschoolers interacting to preschool teachers. The teachers were asked to identify potentially challenging behavior. (The children were actors, and there was no challenging behavior in the videos!) Eye-scan technology found that when looking for bad behavior, the teachers looked at Black children, especially Black boys, more than at white children. According to the US Department of Education (2016), Black children are 3.6 times more likely to be suspended from preschool than white children. As the lead researcher in the Yale study told National Public Radio, "If you look for something in one place, that's the only place you can typically find it" (Turner, 2016, para. 24).

We see that internalized white centrality reinforces and amplifies external racial inequity. Microaggressions, or what Ibram X. Kendi (2019, p. 47) calls "racist abuse," contribute to inequitable health outcomes. The white gaze influences who is diagnosed with psychosis or disruptive behavior disorders and who is suspended from preschool. It must also impact how teachers view older Kids of Color, leading to more suspensions and the involvement of law enforcement (euphemistically called school resource officers). This supports the school to prison pipeline, contributing to huge racial disparities in incarceration, tearing apart BIPOC families, creating hiring difficulties, hindering voting rights, and contributing to the already immense wealth gap. These in turn feed the internalization of white superiority and centrality, as well as the false story that BIPOC are inferior and dangerous. This contributes to police and white people shooting unarmed BIPOC "in self-defense." And since Black people supposedly do not feel pain, they must be shot again and again to be subdued. The cycle is endless, with devastating consequences. I am reminded of Yeats (1921/1997):

> Turning and turning in the widening gyre
> The falcon cannot hear the falconer;
> Things fall apart; the centre cannot hold;
> Mere anarchy is loosed upon the world,
> The blood-dimmed tide is loosed, and everywhere
> The ceremony of innocence is drowned (p. 91)

And I contribute to it. When I unknowingly center whiteness, I center my gaze. Like white people who look at Dr. Montenegro and see a valet or janitor, it becomes easy for me to see BIPOC as I think they are (or who I have been conditioned to think they are) rather than as they really are. If I think a BIPOC is too angry or reactive, too sensitive, extreme, or aggressive, that is where my analysis of the situation often stops. Racial conditioning taught me that they are the problem. I do not consider my role in their anger, that I may have put them down in some way I did not notice, that my taking the center pushed them to the margin. If they react, my white reflex is to judge them. *Their subjective reaction is clearly out of balance with what is objectively happening.* Since I usually do not position myself racially or historically, though, I do not remember that my one-sided conditioning means I am anything but objective. Since people with power are mostly white, my story will likely be supported. The system is on my side.

On one hand, I broadcast my racial credentials (describing the good work I have done on racism) in order to present the best version of myself. On the other, I was socialized to see BIPOC as dangerous and inferior. That means I get to show the world all that is good about me, while I also get to see what is wrong, inferior, and broken in others. Since this is all unconscious, I often do not notice it, much less think about how it informs my interactions with BIPOC. Considering my position of power as a therapist, teacher, supervisor, and facilitator, this becomes even more potentially harmful. These have been distressing truths to acknowledge. When I pathologize, dismiss, doubt, discount, or contradict the experience of BIPOC or try to convince them I am a good white person (or that they are to blame) when they tell me I have been hurtful, I unwittingly contribute to a system that carves years off their lives. What impact does this have on me?

Like many of you, I consider myself to be a good person. I commit my life to helping people, to being the best (imperfect) father I can be, to resolving conflicts and healing wounds. It is heart-rending to face the evidence presented here that my conditioning has led me to play a part in harm and injustice committed on a massive scale. I strive to be compassionate and kind, but the system I unthinkingly contribute to is anything but that. It is painful to sit with that dissonance. Even now, the impulse is strong to dissociate and return to my comfortable white world where I do not have to think about my part in the subjugation of BIPOC. But, like an addict who sees the devastation his addiction has wrought, it feels unthinkable for me to go back to my old ways, yet easy to drift back into unconsciousness.

I imagine some white readers thinking, "Give yourself a break!" I do not feel, though, that I am being hard on myself. Nor, as one of my friends suggested, am I taking responsibility for all the pain of racism. I am, however, looking at my part, and this can be painful. It is what Resmaa Menakem (2017) calls *clean pain*, as opposed to the *dirty pain* that comes from avoiding and denying. "Experiencing clean pain enables us to engage our integrity and tap into our body's inherent resilience and coherence. . . . Paradoxically, only by walking into our pain or discomfort—experiencing it, moving through it, and metabolizing it—can we grow" (Menakem, 2017, p. 20). At the same time, it is not helpful to add to our pain by shaming ourselves. Shame shuts us down and makes us unavailable. Self-compassion opens us up and helps us "focus our attention long enough to learn about and unlearn some bad habits" (Choudhury, 2015, p. 45). We are not responsible for the self-perpetuating system of white centrality. We inherited it and we inhale it with each breath. We are not powerless, though, and we can make changes in our awareness, our sensitivity, our actions, and our circles of influence. Here are some ways to begin.

## What Can We Do Differently?

We can interrupt white centrality anywhere in the cycle. We can learn to notice and question the racist messages society sends us. We can ask ourselves and our kids why there are only white people on that TV show; why BIPOC are portrayed in stereotypical ways; why most of our neighbors look like us; or how and why we made the choice to live around only other white people. We can tell our kids how we feel about all that, how we contribute to and benefit from it, and how much we lose because of it. Maybe they can grow up with eyes open to how they are being conditioned, with hearts open to how it impacts BIPOC and all of us.

We can learn about patterns of whiteness and be honest about how they live in us. Honesty is the hard part. It takes self-awareness, courage, humility, and vulnerability to admit these things to ourselves. We need to learn to not fear our mistakes, so we can grow in our relationship to race.

Once we start noticing white centrality, we can interrupt it in ourselves and in other white people, whether or not BIPOC are present. But let us not think we are better than white people who are being unconscious or hurtful. What we see in them is probably something we ourselves have done in some way or will do later. As Arnold Mindell (2002) says, "You today and me tomorrow" (p. 36). This reminder brings compassion for them and for ourselves, which can help us support each other to do the work and appreciate how we are growing while also holding each other accountable.

In conversations with BIPOC, we can pause and observe ourselves. Does what we want to say come from a pattern of whiteness? Will it have a negative impact, no matter our intent? Are we speaking first? Thinking our ideas are best? Taking lots of airtime? This does not mean we should silence ourselves, which can also center us (and seem dismissive). If we are normally quiet because we do not want to mess up or are just naturally introverted, we can choose to take a risk.

When we speak, we can practice humility. The lived experience of BIPOC is more informed than our preconceptions or the books we have read about race. They have had to face, think about, and manage racism every day of their lives, and we are relative newcomers to even considering it. We can center their experience and knowing instead of ours. And, as K. V. Hardy (personal communication, January 20, 2018) advises, "Run it through your heart before it comes out of your mouth."

If we talk about ourselves, we can show our vulnerability. We can talk about our failures, not just our shining moments. By locating ourselves racially in the conversation, we send a message that race is our issue, not just theirs. BIPOC are often the only ones showing pain and emotion about racism. What is *our* pain about racism?

In the inevitable times we are hurtful, we can repair. Of course, we will misstep, but it is what we do after that is important. I love the three powerful models of repair from Ijeoma Oluo (2018, pp. 220–223), Lee Mun Wah (Lee, 2013), and Robin DiAngelo (2018, pp. 145–146). (Oluo's passage addresses what to do if we have been called racist, but I find it is helpful also as a frame for racial repair.) All three writers suggest we focus on the impact we have had without mentioning our good intentions. They invite us to reflect on our words and actions and to discern our biases and how we reinforced racism. All three emphasize the importance of listening to what the other person has to say about the incident and about our impact on them. They all find it vital that we use what we learn from the interaction to change our behavior and attitudes as we move forward in our lives. Ijeoma Oluo (2018) reminds us that, as white people, we can never understand what it is like to be continually impacted by racism. She says that although we may feel hurt by what happened, so does the other person; this is not the moment to express our own pain nor to deny or invalidate theirs. Lee Mun Wah (Lee, 2013) invites us to express our feelings about what we've done. Seeing the apology as bigger than one specific relationship, he suggests we share what we've learned with others and continue the conversation with the groups we have impacted. Robin DiAngelo (2018) recommends that, before a repair, we should process our own reactions with another white person who will listen, hold us accountable, and help us get clear about what we've done. She encourages us to ask the BIPOC if they are willing to meet and to be open to hearing *no*. If they agree and we repair, she suggests we commit to doing better without making promises we can't keep about never doing it again.

If BIPOC give us feedback, we can receive it as a gift, an act of generosity, and be open to learning and growing from it. Feedback may not come wrapped in a ribbon. It might come with rage. Hardy differentiates anger, which he calls "an emotion connected to immediate experiences" (Hardy, 2013, para. 10) from rage. "Rage can be a deep-seated emotional response to experiences of degradation and devaluation. Rage builds over time as a result of cumulative suppressed emotions precipitated by voicelessness" (Hardy, 2013, para. 10). Knowing the difference can evoke our compassion as well as the realization that our judgement and fear only contribute to the problem. When BIPOC express rage, even toward us, we can regulate our own emotions in order to hold and hear their rage without dismissing, arguing, pathologizing, or retreating into white fragility. If we get scared, we can give ourselves compassion while also remembering who is truly in danger. Historically and to this day, an uncomfortable, scared, or angry white person can cause BIPOC to be suspended from school, fired from work, arrested, lynched, or killed.

Calming ourselves when we feel racial discomfort requires our own inner work. Rage (and all racial stress) can trigger our own trauma. When we are dysregulated, we are most likely to hurt others. We can work with our trauma, recognize its telltale signals in our bodies, learn and practice ways to calm and regulate ourselves, and practice these during racial conversations (Menakem, 2017).

Being connected to our deepest self, through dreamwork, trauma work, self-inquiry, meditation, prayer, or whatever works for us, helps foster what Mindell (1995) calls psychological and spiritual rank, or personal power. We need personal power to not crumble or be defensive when someone tells us we have been hurtful, to not turn to self-hatred or dissociation when we see how we contribute to racism. It is counterintuitive. Although as white people we are given considerable power in the world, we need to develop a different kind of power if we are to have the fortitude to sit in the fire and transform ourselves and the world.

It is helpful to avoid personalizing issues. Something hurtful we say to a BIPOC is like one raindrop; it reminds them of the rainstorm that has been pouring on them their entire life. If we focus on our shame about the raindrop, we center ourselves and pull away from them. If we focus on how we feel about the rainstorm, this makes a bridge between us and those being rained on (C. Kutz, personal communication, January 8, 2018).

As we have seen, white racial conditioning often leads to racial patterns that can, without our awareness or intention, create empathic failure, invalidation, negation, defensiveness, disrespect, and disconnection. These outcomes are the opposite of what therapists and supervisors, or faculty in therapeutic training programs, want for their clients, supervisees, students, and colleagues. Luckily, we can apply the principles discussed in this chapter to decenter whiteness in our work.

We can notice if we start to think that BIPOC clients, students, supervisees, or faculty members are too angry, complaining too much, too sensitive, or seeing perceived slights that we think are not there. We can remember that our racial perception is likely limited because we have been socialized to not notice race and we have not been sensitized by repeated racial humiliation and degradation in overt and subtle forms. If we dismiss, doubt, or invalidate their concerns, that is itself a racial harm, particularly coming from someone in a position of power or, in the case of a therapist, from someone entrusted to be caring and supportive.

If our client, supervisee, student, or colleague seems to not trust us, we can avoid thinking of this as resistance, defiance, or an unwillingness to learn or relate. We can consider that our way of being in the session, class, supervision, or faculty meeting may contribute to their mistrust and that their experience with white people until now may not have always engendered trust. Instead of believing our own interpretations, we can explore together whatever signals we notice and inquire what might be behind them. Locating ourselves racially in the relationship and leading with humility and curiosity will likely engender more trust, respect, and "progress" in the therapeutic, training, supervisory, or collegial relationship.

When we are practicing, teaching, and supervising in institutions, we can notice how our BIPOC colleagues are being treated. We can remember that microaggressions can be manifestations of structural racism and can also contribute to structural racism. If we turn away from those things when we notice or hear about them, we contribute to a culture of racial harm. We can instead decide to contribute, in our own little corner of the world, to a more racially just and, I would say, kind and heart-centered culture. This might mean speaking up when we notice racially problematic behaviors, interactions, or interpretations, whether they come from someone else or from ourselves. This might happen when BIPOC are in the room or not. We may have access to spaces where BIPOC are not present, whether by chance or due to structural discrimination in the workplace. Speaking up there is equally, if not more, important. Of course, this is risky. We may be branded as troublemakers or told that we misunderstood what was happening or that we cannot take a joke. Our access to those spaces might be jeopardized, and our relationships might be strained. These potential, serious consequences can perhaps help us empathize with the position of our BIPOC clients, supervisees, students, and colleagues, who are faced with these choices every day. We can take courage from the possibility that speaking up ourselves might lighten their load a bit. All of this is part of advocating for an organization that is antiracist, not just in words but also in deeds. This includes hiring, retaining, and promoting BIPOC clinicians, faculty, and leaders, and creating a culture where they feel respected, valued, and heard, and where they are not the only ones speaking about racism and how it inevitably arises among us.

The centrality of whiteness is deeply ingrained and will not disappear, despite our best efforts. But we can recognize and control it and learn racial sensitivity. This includes noticing our centrality and its impacts on BIPOC. With practice, we can notice it before it expresses itself in our words or actions. This stops the cycle, one moment at a time.

We will make mistakes, be hurtful, fall on our faces, be called out, get defensive, and repair. It is important to foster resilience. We can take inspiration from Nelson Mandela, who said in the documentary, Mandela (Gibson & Menell, 1996), “Do not judge me by my successes, judge me by how many times I fell down and got back up again.”

## Acknowledgment

I want to express my deep gratitude and indebtedness to my friend and colleague Bill Say. He is a brilliant trainer and facilitator who is a Korean Japanese American. He gave me permission to say this. With patience and, perhaps more importantly, impatience, Bill has helped me many times to see my white centrality and how it impacts him and our relationship. I have been asked to write this chapter partly because of all I have learned from him. I benefit from the courage and generosity he continually exhibits when he calls me out and calls me in. This is not our isolated experience; white people learn and benefit in uncountable ways from the brilliance, courage, and pain of BIPOC. This chapter is one attempt to pay this forward.

**LANE ARYE, PHD,** is a senior trainer of Processwork (developed by Arnold Mindell) and a founding faculty member of the Process Work Institute in Portland, Oregon. Whether teaching, working in private practice, facilitating community and organizational conflicts, or learning and training alongside social justice groups, Lane partners with people to help create more inner and outer freedom, inclusion, and wholeness. He co-led a six-year UN-funded project in the Balkans that brought together Serbs, Croats, and Muslims after the war to work on ethnic tension, post-war trauma, and building sustainable community. He facilitated conflicts between high-caste and low-caste Hindus, between the British and the Irish, and between white and Aboriginal Australians Down Under. Lane has been deeply researching whiteness, and leading groups for white people about race, resilience, and repair. Lane lives in the San Francisco Bay Area with his wife and two teenagers, who grow his heart every day.

## References

*Bichell, R. E. (Reporter). (2017, November 11). Scientists start to tease out the subtler ways racism hurts health [Radio broadcast].* NPR. *https://www.npr.org/sections/health-shots/2017/11/11/562623815/scientists-start-to-tease-out-the-subtler-ways-racism-hurts-health*

*Blakemore, E. (2019, September 30). How the GI Bill's promise was denied to a million black WWII veterans.* HISTORY. *https://www.history.com/news/gi-bill-black-wwii-veterans-benefits*

*Choudhury, S. (2015). Deep diversity: Overcoming us vs. them. Between the Lines.*

The COVID Racial Data Tracker. *(2020). The COVID Tracking Project. Retrieved December 1, 2020, from https://covidtracking.com/race/*

*DiAngelo, R. (2012).* What does it mean to be white? Developing white racial literacy. *Peter Lang Inc., International Academic Publishers.*

*DiAngelo, R. (2018).* White fragility: Why it's so hard for white people to talk about racism. *Beacon Press.*

*Fadus, M. C., Ginsburg, K. R., Sobowale, K., Halliday-Boykins, C. A., Bryant, B. E., Gray,*

*K. M., & Squeglia, L. M. (2019). Unconscious bias and the diagnosis of disruptive behavior disorders and ADHD in African American and Hispanic youth.* Academic Psychiatry, *44(1), 95–102. https://doi.org/10.1007/s40596-019-01127-6*

*Garber, J. (2020, April 2).* How racial bias is impacting coronavirus care. *Lown Institute. https://lowninstitute.org/how-bias-is-impacting-coronavirus-care/*

*Gibson, A., & Menell, J. (Directors). (1996). Mandela [Motion picture]. South Africa, USA: MGM.*

*Gross, T., & Rothstein, R. (2017, May 3).* A "forgotten history" of how the US government segregated America *[Radio broadcast]. In Fresh Air. NPR.*

*Hanks, A., Solomon, D., & Weller, C. E. (2018, February 21).* Systematic inequality: How America's structural racism helped create the Black-white wealth gap. *Center for American Progress. https://www.americanprogress.org/issues/race/reports/2018/02/21/447051/systematic-inequality/*

*Hardy, K. V. (2013). Healing the hidden wounds of racial trauma.* Reclaiming Children and Youth, *22(1), 24–28. https://static1.squarespace.com/static/545cdfcce4b0a64725b9f65a/t/54da3451e4b0ac9bd1d1cd30/1423586385564/Healing.pdf*

*Hardy, K. V. (2016). Anti-racist approaches for shaping theoretical and practice paradigms. In A. J. Carten, A. B. Siskind, & M. Pender Greene (Eds.),* Strategies for deconstructing racism in the health and human services *(pp. 125–139). Oxford University Press.*

*Hoffman, K. M., Trawalter, S., Axt, J. R., & Oliver, M. N. (2016). Racial bias in pain assessment and treatment recommendations, and false beliefs about biological differences between blacks and whites.* Proceedings of the National Academy of Sciences, *113(16), 4296–4301. https://doi.org/10.1073/pnas.1516047113*

*Kendi, I. X. (2019).* How to be an antiracist. *One World.*

*Lee, M. W. (2013, July). In search of a real apology [Handout from resources]. StirFry Seminars & Consulting. http://www.stirfryseminars.com/resources/handouts/Topic-2-03.pdf*

*McIntosh, P. (1988). White privilege and male privilege: A personal account of coming to see correspondences through work in women's studies. In M. Anderson, & P. Hill Collins (Eds.),* Race, class, and gender: An anthology *(pp. 94–105). Wadsworth.*

*Menakem, R. (2017).* My grandmother's hands: Racialized trauma and the pathway to mending our hearts and bodies. *Central Recovery Press.*

*Mindell, A. (1995).* Sitting in the fire: Large group transformation using conflict and diversity. *Lao Tse Press.*

*Mindell, A. (2002).* The deep democracy of open forums: Practical steps to conflict prevention and resolution for the family, workplace, and world. *Hampton Roads Publishing.*

*Montenegro, R. E. (2016).* My name is not *"interpreter." Journal of the American Medical Association, 315(19), 2071–2072. https://doi.org/10.1001/jama.2016.1249*

*Obermeyer, Z., Powers, B., Vogeli, C., & Mullainathan, S. (2019). Dissecting racial bias in an algorithm used to manage the health of populations.* Science, *366(6464), 447–453. https://doi.org/10.1126/science.aax2342*

*Oluo, I. (2018).* So you want to talk about race. *Seal Press.*

*Ross, C. (2020, August 7). Study finds racial bias in the government's formula for distributing Covid-19 aid to hospitals.* STAT. *https://www.statnews.com/2020/08/07/racial-bias-in-government-covid19-hospital-aid-formula/*

*Schwartz, R. C. (2014). Racial disparities in psychotic disorder diagnosis: A review of empirical literature.* World Journal of Psychiatry, 4(4), *133. https://doi.org/10.5498/wjp.v4.i4.133*

*Sue, D. W., Capodilupo, C. M., Torino, G. C., Bucceri, J. M., Holder, A. M. B., Nadal, K. L., & Esquilin, M. (2007). Racial microaggressions in everyday life: Implications for clinical practice.* American Psychologist, *62(4), 271–286. https://doi.org/10.1037/0003-066x.62.4.271*

*Turner, C. (Reporter). (2016, September 28). Bias isn't just a police problem, it's a preschool problem [Radio broadcast]. In Morning Edition.* NPR. *https://www.npr.org/sections/ed/2016/09/28/495488716/bias-isnt-just-a-police-problem-its-a-preschool-problem*

*US Department of Education. Office for Civil Rights. (2016). 2013–2014 Civil rights data collection: Key data highlights on equity and opportunity gaps in our nation's public schools. https://www2.ed.gov/about/offices/list/ocr/docs/2013–14-first-look.pdf*

*Villarosa, L. (2019, August 14). How false beliefs in physical racial difference still live in medicine today.* The New York Times Company. *https://www.nytimes.com/interactive/2019/08/14/magazine/racial-differences-doctors.html*

*Yeats, W. B. (1997). The second coming. In E. Larrissy (Ed.),* W. B. Yeats *(pp. 91–92). Oxford University Press. (Original work published 1921)*

# SECTION III

# WHITENESS AND ISSUES OF IDENTITY AND INTERSECTIONALITY

## CHAPTER 5

# Whiteness, Intersectionality, and the Contradictions of White Jewish Identity

JODIE KLIMAN, PHD

WILLIAM JAMES COLLEGE

This chapter speaks to several challenging questions Dr. Kenneth V. Hardy posed to me about the complex relationship between Jews and whiteness. First, he asked me to discuss "why the deconstruction of race and Jewishness is relevant, if not critical, to the dismantling of whiteness" (K. V. Hardy, personal communication, June 30, 2020). That question alone could fill volumes; but next he asked me to address, as a Jewish woman who (now) identifies as white, the tensions that regularly emerge in conversations on race between Black and Brown people and Jews as well as their very different ways of making sense of those tensions. The second question triggered emotional reactions for me and reminded me of several historical explanations, which I share below.

I hope this chapter can be healing and informative for all readers while also helping me clarify my emotionally fraught responses to these important questions. I hope that it is healing and informative for my fellow white Jews who may struggle with acknowledging our recently gained privilege even as we navigate the sequelae of a long history of oppression and collective danger. I hope that this chapter helps my fellow white Jews be accountable for how our increased racial privilege can create the unwanted capacity to hurt people, including those we love, who do not share our privilege.

I also hope this chapter will be affirming and healing to Jews of Color, whose very existence is too easily overlooked by white Jews and non-Jews of Color, alike. It may also be beneficial to those non-Jews of Color who may not have considered how othering Jews intensifies our *shared* vulnerability to the very same white Christian supremacists who target People of Color. Our shared targeting by avowed white Christian supremacists on the radical right and by more subtle, pervasive forms of systemic prejudice and unintentionally internalized white (and Christian) supremacy presents a strong argument for deep solidarity between marginalized groups. Alas, that solidarity among the oppressed is hard to come by, particularly when white Jews do not recognize their internalized white supremacy or when Christians of Color do not recognize their internalized Christian supremacy.

## Are Jews White?

### *Are European Jews White?*

First, are Jews white?* The best answer I can give is: yes and no; and it depends, for most but not all of us. I will write later in this chapter about the very different experiences of those Jews who are undeniably People of Color and cannot be identified as white by any standard. Am I personally white? I am an American Jewish woman whose ancestors came from pre-Soviet Ukraine (by way of Greece and probably Spain before that), Lithuania, and Germany. Like most Jews, I undoubtedly have ancient Middle Eastern or North African roots admixed with more recent European ones. When "white" today generally means "of European ancestry," am I white? My ancestors, denied European citizenship, were never acknowledged as European while in Europe, neither before nor after the "invention" of race. They were seen as a "foreign race." In their long, embattled sojourn, official government papers identified them as both racially and nationally Jewish. So, am I even European, despite the impact of centuries on that continent? Am I white, despite not always having been perceived as white in my own youth in the United States?

---

* I refer to whiteness, and to race in general, not as a scientific categorization but as a shifting and insidious social construct with enormous power to define and determine lived experience.

As for myself, yes, I acknowledge whiteness in today's US context, along with the responsibilities for racial self-examination, accountability, and repair that come with that complex, ambivalent, and layered identity. Since my teen years in the Civil Rights, antiwar, and feminist movements, I have acknowledged my whiteness because of the privilege and protection that appearing, and being, more or less white affords me. Yet I simultaneously feel the painful call of my recent and ancient forebears to remember their suffering as Jews and my personal vulnerability to the latest wave of violent anti-Semitism. Like the Inquisition and the Holocaust, this new, unsubtle wave of anti-Semitism uses the language of race, and not religion alone, against Jews. Yet since most anti-Semitism is more subtle and insidious and more religiously than racially based than we see among avowed and proud white Christian supremacists, my whiteness needs to be acknowledged. From my radically multiracial graduate school cohort, I learned about the importance of that acknowledgment, despite my religious and ethnic—and my people's historically racialized—marginalization. I learned still more upon joining a multiracial family and starting to coparent Children of Color in my late 20s.

I finished writing this chapter shortly after an organized mob of avowed and proud white Christian supremacists stormed the halls of Congress in a terrifying insurrection, armed with weapons, confederate flags, nooses, and T-shirts emblazoned with "Camp Auschwitz" and "6MWE" ("six million wasn't enough"). They openly threatened our elected officials (especially Jewish, Black, Muslim, Hindu, Catholic, and Indigenous members of Congress) as well as Blacks, Jews, and Immigrants of Color in general. Most Republican Congress members excused the then-President's explicit incitement of that lethal insurrection. I feel personal and collective vulnerability because the virulently white and Christian supremacist movement that this insurrection and its apologists represent is flourishing. It puts Jews, all People of Color, and immigrants and Muslims of all races in their crosshairs. Synagogues, Black churches, and mosques are all targets, as are Asians, who, like Jews, are viewed as outsiders and are being assaulted in growing numbers. I fear for my Jewish congregation just as I fear for my stepchildren, who walk in the world as People of Color.

I am recognized as white. Unlike Orthodox and Hasidic Jews, I am not immediately recognizable as Jewish. I am not forced to live in walled-off

Jewish ghettos and to wear clothing marking me as not-Christian, like my ancestors in Europe. Neither am I as recognizable nor as vulnerable to hate crimes as those who are visibly Jewish or Black, Brown, Asian, Indigenous, or, especially, LGBT People of Color. So, I acknowledge my racial privilege out of accountability to and solidarity with People of Color, especially my Loved Ones of Color. I will interrogate the ambivalence with which I do so in these pages.

The ambivalence comes from my loyalty to all Jews killed and traumatically bereaved through genocide, particularly to my great-grandmother's parents, siblings, and cousins, the Yaneshevskys and Korotovskys, killed in a pogrom when my grandmother was a child. I attribute their deaths to both religious and racial hatred of what was then (if not now) called the "Jewish race" or the "Hebrew race." It also comes from the murdered loved ones of the chosen "aunts" and "uncles," some with numbers tattooed on their forearms, of my childhood. They were targeted for explicitly racial reasons when Hitler began the "Final Solution" to rid Europe of the "Jewish race," which he repeatedly associated with Black people.[1]

My current white racial privilege is real. Categorizing Jews as white, however, requires problematizing racism and relating it to religious hatred through history's shifting racial lenses. Since the Roman Emperor Constantine vilified Jews in the third century for crucifying and rejecting Jesus as the messiah,[2] through centuries of brutally anti-Semitic crusades and pogroms, onto the Inquisition, and culminating in the Holocaust, Jews have faced oppression, official discrimination, and mass murder throughout Christendom (Carroll, 2002). This vilification was purely religious and tribal before race emerged as a construct, centuries later. The Roman Empire's vilification of Jews for the Crucifixion whitewashed the Empire's responsibility for both the Crucifixion and Jews' oppression under Roman rule. This whitewashing might be compared to the Confederate whitewashing of the brutality of slavery with narratives of happy slaves, the concept of whites' God-given responsibility to "civilize" dark-skinned peoples, and the valiant championing of states' rights.

Although this ancient othering of Jews was originally based on religion (and, before Constantine, on tribe), it shifted toward a racialized othering just as the new concept of race emerged in the mid-fifteenth century.[3]

Jewishness was first racialized when the Spanish and Portuguese Inquisitions, starting in the fourteenth century, forced Jews (and then Muslims) to "choose" between forced conversion to Catholicism, exile, or being tortured to death (Schama, 2013, 2017). Inquisition authorities doubted the true Christianity of Jews (and later, Muslims) forcibly converted to Catholicism (not without reason, since some resisted, practicing Judaism secretly for generations). This suspicion extended for generations, even for "New Christians" who gave all appearances of observant Catholicism. Thus, Jews, converted or not, were marked not just as religiously evil for their creed that rejected Jesus but as racially inferior based on their tainted and evil Jewish blood (Carroll, 2002; Schama, 2013, 2017). New Christians and their descendants were called *marranos* (Spanish for "swine"). The "one drop of blood" rule was first applied not in the American South but in fifteenth-century Spain (Kivel, 1998; Schama, 2017).

While it may seem puzzling because it maps poorly onto current constructions of race, this fifteenth- and sixteenth-century racialization radically changed Jewish experience and identity, first in Iberia and then throughout Europe. This inconsistent racial labeling closely twinned Europeanness (and hence whiteness) with Christianity. Sometimes it categorized Jews with Blacks, and sometimes with Asians; periodically, Jews were categorized at the bottom of the white part of the hierarchy, with an asterisk. Jews (and Muslims) in Iberia differed in appearance from Europeans, having "swarthy" phenotypes as Middle Eastern and North African transplants. They were "not of Europe," by citizenship, culture, nor physical appearance.

Into the twentieth century, even most Ashkenazi Jews maintained Middle Eastern, North African, and Sephardi[4] cultural roots, despite having lived (largely apart from Europeans) in Europe (Siegel-Itzkovich, 2006). In addition to the bonds of common religious practice, in large measure these cultural roots were maintained by travel. Jewish merchants,[5] having Hebrew literacy in common with the Jews of the Middle East and North Africa, traveled back and forth, sharing evolving customs and knowledge. Pre-Inquisition Spain, during the Golden Age of Muslim rule, was a uniquely fertile meeting place of Muslim, Jewish, and Christian cultural knowledge that Ashkenazi merchants and scholars regularly visited and brought back to their local communities (Schama, 2013).

Iberian Jews' (and Muslims') racialization spread to all of Europe and then to the Americas. In the English colonies and the early United States, white supremacy, the belief in a natural racial hierarchy with Europeans at its apex, was an explicitly white and *Christian* supremacy that had equated whiteness with Christianity from the time that race was first invented to justify racism.

Although whiteness and Christianity are more subtly and insidiously conflated today than during the Inquisition-era in Spain, the founding of the United States, or the Third Reich, the predominant form of white supremacy in the United States today remains white *Christian* supremacy. The religious aspect of this conflation is most visible to non-Christians, just as white supremacy is most visible to People of Color. Although most Jews whose ancestors came from Europe to the United States identify and are identified as racially white, strands of a racist form of anti-Semitism survive among Christians, both white and of Color, and in Jews' sense of vulnerability. Again, I distinguish between the systematic tainting of consciousness through normalized, supremacist whiteness and Christianity and the explicitly *avowed* and *proud* white Christian supremacy of groups like those that overran the US Capitol preceding the 2021 presidential inauguration. I believe that racial as well as religious animus still feeds part of the prejudice against Jews on the part of both white Christians and Christians of Color in the United States, but for different reasons, discussed below.

Some eighteenth-century racial hierarchies categorized Jews as Mongoloid; others placed them precariously on whiteness' lowest rung (Painter, 2011). Jews were widely regarded as between "not-quite-white" and barely white in the 1950s and 1960s (Barrett & Roediger, 1997; Brodkin, 1998), when I was growing up. In my parents' youth, Jews were regularly assaulted and harassed in organized hate crimes incited by propaganda by anti-Semitic demagogues, such as radio personality Father Coughlin (Greenberg, 2018). I first encountered anti-Semitism at age four or five on the Maryland Naval Base where we, and no other Jewish children, lived when my father was drafted. The gentile children's parents did not let them play with me but surely taught them the names their children called me as they roller-skated past me: "Dirty Jew! Kike!" I learned what that meant from watching my mother's face when I asked why they called me that. I never did learn to roller-skate.

The racial othering of Jewishness continues quietly today in white "polite society," and much more dangerously in proudly white Christian supremacist circles. The threat is not subtle. According to Arango (2020), the most recent year for which statistics are available at this writing, more hate crimes were reported in 2019 than any year since 2008—the year President Obama was elected. In 2019 a total of 1,943 hate crimes were reported; 1,930 of them were against Blacks (12% of the US population). Five hundred twenty-five hate crimes were reported against Latinx people (18.3% of the US population), including the 2019 Walmart shooting in El Paso that killed 22 Mexicans and Mexican Americans. A disproportionately higher 953 hate crimes were reported against Jews (only 2% of the US population) and Jewish institutions in 2019. That is a 7% increase from 835 in 2018, which included 11 lives taken at the Tree of Life synagogue in Pittsburgh (Arango, 2020). Like Jews, Asians are often reviled as foreign threats; just as Jews were falsely blamed for earlier plagues, Asians have been blamed for COVID-19. Hate crimes against Asians went up 146% in 16 major US cities between 2019 and 2020 (the year the COVID-19 pandemic began) (Center for the Study of Hate and Extremism, 2021). All these numbers are vastly underreported, as only 2,172 of the 15,000 local law enforcement agencies report hate crimes to the FBI (Arango, 2020).

Journalist Emma Green (2016) spoke to a racial aspect of anti-Jewish animus in puzzling over whether Jews are white, positing:

> On the extreme right, Jews are seen as impure—a faux-white race that has tainted America. And on the extreme left, Jews are seen as part of a white-majority establishment that seeks to dominate people of color [sic]. Taken together, these attacks raise an interesting question: Are Jews white? (para. 3)

Green reported that of the many angry reader reactions she got to this question from non-Jews on left and right, the most chilling was from David Duke, former Imperial Grand Wizard of the Ku Klux Klan, who wrote, simply and in all caps, "No—JEWS ARE NOT WHITE!" (Green, 2016). I admit to feeling fear about owning my white privilege when I see statements like that made by such threatening sources as David Duke. All the more reason to stand fast. I must acknowledge both the vulnerability to the newly empowered white Christian supremacist right that I share with People of Color and the racial protection and invisibility my olive skin confers. For the latter reason, I must stay mindful that my ability to go unnoticed risks my unintentional complicity with systemic racism. As mutual targets of hatred, we are easily divided. We must stand together, or we will all fall.

As the extreme right has strengthened recently, with its virulently anti-Black, anti-Semitic, and anti-immigrant threats and violence conjoined, *am* I still white after all? Here I must say to People of Color: "Yes, I am white—I recognize my unearned racial privilege and I will always stand in solidarity with you from that position, informed and inspired by my religious, and once-racial, marginalization." Yet to the David Dukes and insurrectionist mobs, like the one that recently besieged Congress with explicit threats to Blacks and Jews alike, I say: "I resist you, who define both nonwhites and non-Christians as less than human. I stand in deep solidarity with everyone you hate. We must resist you together." This is a complex position to hold, but Jewish experience has always been complex.

### *Jews' Racial Heterogeneity in the United States and Worldwide*

The clearest reason not to automatically categorize all Jews as white is that 12–15% of US Jews are Black, Brown, Asian, Indigenous, and racially mixed (Kelman et al., 2019). Some People of Color have ancient Jewish ancestries on one or both sides of their families. Others were adopted into otherwise white, Jewish families. Still others are Jewish Converts of Color and their progeny. This figure can be expected to rise in the coming generations, since there are more younger Jews of Color than older ones. Jews of Color's experiences in the United States will be addressed later in this chapter.

Most Jews worldwide are Ashkenazim, with proximate European backgrounds (and, in most cases, older roots in the Middle East and North Africa). In Israel, however, in which about 75% of the population is Jewish, 52% of the Jews are Mizrahim (Middle Eastern, North African, and South Asian Jews) and Sephardim. Another 1% are Ethiopian Jews, whose Jewish ancestry goes back thousands of years (Centre for Israel and Jewish Affairs, 2015) and who face harsh racial discrimination in Israel. Most of the balance are Ashkenazim. While it is the case that the Ashkenazim have disproportionate power in Israel, and that Israel is often misperceived as a European culture surrounded by the Middle East, it is a distinctly Middle Eastern culture.

## Jewish Intersectional Identity's Challenges for Interracial Dialogue

Experience is constructed at the meeting place of many identities. We are intersectional beings with many defining domains of identity, each carrying relative privilege or marginalization, which may shift with time and context (Kliman, 2005, 2010; Watts-Jones, 2010). Intersectional thinking, however, poses risks for engaging with racial accountability because people so readily focus on their subjugated or marginalized identities, overlooking their privilege. We white Jews may reflexively focus on our Jewishness in the face of anti-Semitism, overlooking or even denying the impact of our privileged identities, particularly in relation to race. Too often, people with privilege in any domain draw on that privilege without awareness, in ways that harm those without privilege in that same domain (Hardy, 2016; Kliman, 2010). Schraub (2019) argued that, "what whiteness 'does' to Jewishness is act as an accelerant for certain forms of antisemitic [sic] marginalization even as it ratifies a racialized hierarchy within the Jewish community" (p. 379).

The dynamics of focusing on one's marginalized identities while acting on one's privilege (Hardy, 2016; Kliman, et al., 2021) is key to understanding common sticking points in conversations about race between Jews and People of Color. White Jews can be pulled into inner or spoken monologues about their legacy trauma, shutting out or dismissing the pain of their Interlocutors of Color. This reflexive response throws sand into the gears of what might otherwise become intersubjective, dialogical, and healing interracial conversations, oriented both toward finding common ground and addressing accountability around important differences.

Internal and spoken monologues about the long collective trauma of Jewish historical oppression and our own families' particular experiences of racialized oppression and loss can separate white Jews from our conversational partners' painful legacy traumas. It can also separate our Interlocutors of Color from our pain; with their pain unheard, they are unlikely to feel solidarity with ours. At the same time, People of Color may engage in parallel inner and spoken monologues about their own historical collective oppression in ways that silence and invalidate Jewish narratives about Christian supremacy, including, but not limited to, Christians of Color.

This process operates both psychologically and societally for all concerned. My focus, however, is on its operations for white Jews with current racial privilege and traumatic individual, family, and collective memories. We can cause harm from that position. When we invalidate the pain that we cause another person by arguing that we too know oppression (Kliman et al., 2019), we further the damage. For instance, if a Jew commits an unintended microaggression in an interracial dialogue, and a Person of Color argues that Jews have to acknowledge their white privilege but then further ascribes unrealistic political power and influence to Jews,[6] the static created by Jewish collective, intergenerational legacy trauma around such false accusations can interfere with the Jewish person's accountability for the original conversational injury.

Channeling our parents', grandparents', and other ancestors' oppression activates our invisible loyalties (Boszormenyi-Nagy et al., 1991) to them and to the legacy trauma they left us. These very personal invisible loyalties contribute to our difficulty in seeing our current racial privilege. An old photograph on my wall shows my great-grandmother Blume's parents, sister, and sister's family; all were slaughtered in a 1912 Ukrainian pogrom, as were her other siblings and their entire *shtetl* (Jewish ghetto). My grandmother told me that upon getting the news of the pogrom, weeks after losing a second child to illness, her mother went mute for months. My grandmother was four at the time. She also told me that her parents and uncle had been scrimping on garment workers' wages to save money to bring their relatives here to the United States, desperately hoping to keep them safe. When my father, who as a child lived with his parents and his grandparents, asked about that side of the family, he was met with silence. (The story finally emerged when I did my first genogram.)

My great-grandmother's grief was enormous but also silent and therefore mystifying. Yet the horror of their deaths was never lost. Nor was my family's urgency to protect loved ones and others against such horrors, a desperation my great-grandmother (who lived until I was 17) and my grandmother mutely passed on to my father and then to me. That picture on my wall shows my great-grandmother's sister's striking resemblance to me in my youth; my great-great-grandmother resembles my grandmother (her granddaughter) in old age. That family resemblance captures me each time I see it; it feels like some of my own blood was shed with theirs. They live in me, inspiring my commitment to today's refugees.

When faced with so massive an intergenerational trauma, we can go silent, as my great-grandmother and so many others did. Alternatively, we can overload ourselves and others with uncensored stories of such pain, as some Holocaust survivors did with their children, or we can mix silence with terrifying and confusing snippets of terror and warning (Weingarten, 2003). The message I received, long before I knew how my Yaneshevsky and Korotovsky kin had died, was that we could never, *ever*, do enough to protect the vulnerable because the outcome could be too terrible.

I believe that African Americans transmit a similar legacy regarding the horrors of the Middle Passage, slavery, and Jim Crow—a collective pain too great to pass on to children, but impossible *not* to pass on (Hardy, 2007). Native Americans pass on such a legacy as well, from exterminations, land theft, and the cultural genocide of boarding schools (Hartmann et al., 2019). These legacies involve not only invisible loyalties (Boszormenyi-Nagy et al., 1991) but silenced or dysregulated ones screaming to be heard, demanding that we honor (all) our dead.

It can be profoundly confusing to us, as white Jews, to feel oppression in our bones and yet have much privilege. It is surely also confusing to those with whom we engage. In a chapter I coauthored as part of the Boston Institute for Culturally Affirming Practices (2019), my friend, Roxana Llerena-Quinn, wrote with love and hurt about a moment when I had equated my ancestral pain over my great-grandparents' refugee experience with her personal experience of arriving, without her family, in the United States as an adolescent Peruvian political refugee. However understandable, my reflexive protection of the memory of my dead ancestors, triggered in that moment by invisible loyalties to my great-grandmother's devastating loss, jostled aside Roxana's direct and immediate pain as a teenaged refugee. Thankfully, once she named the injury, our trusting and accountable relationship allowed me to take in her pain and respond with compassion, acknowledgment, validation, and regret.

Legacy trauma does not obstruct meaningful interracial dialogue alone. Hardy and Laszloffy (1998) likened internalizing proracist ideology to living or working in a sick building; regardless of our beliefs and values, we still breathe in that poisonous air. Racism and white supremacy cannot be *avoided*, only *resisted*. I add anti-Semitic ideology to their argument, since I believe that racism and anti-Semitism are the shared and sturdy spawn of the white Christian supremacy that fueled early capitalism, organized race-based slave trafficking, and the genocide of Indigenous people, Jews, and many others. Both continue as the uneasy foundation of US society.

Since both racism and anti-Semitism are pervasively internalized in white Christian supremacist society, they also obstruct true dialogue, even between People of Color and Jews who actively resist them. While many Jews feel kinship with People of Color (others, alas, do not), we are still tainted by racist ideologies. And while some non-Jewish People of Color similarly feel a kinship to Jews (and others, alas, do not), they inevitably internalize anti-Semitic ideologies. Both toxins play out in our encounters with each other.

A long history of what seemed in my youth to be a natural solidarity between Blacks and Jews frayed badly in the late 1960s. Jews, the vast majority of white civil rights activists of that era, contributed to that fraying in part by enacting white privilege. As the Civil Rights movement birthed Black nationalism (including a few explicitly anti-Jewish versions) and Afrocentrism, and was less welcoming of white allies, the solidarity frayed further.

As European Jews have slowly "become" white over the last three generations (Brodkin, 1998), we have internalized white supremacy, in general, and anti-Black prejudice, in particular, despite our historical fraternity with Blacks and Immigrants of Color. Immigrant Jews and their descendants assimilated into US society, becoming white, or sort of white, by shedding the obvious Jewishness of Orthodox or Hasidic religious garb and traditions. US-style racism accompanied this shift. These partially assimilated Jews reassured themselves and their children of their new place in society with the message, "the Christians may still hate us, but at least we aren't Black." I read that shameful sentiment in two ways: first, as internalized white supremacist discourse, and second, as comfort in knowing that we are no longer as vulnerable as we were in Europe's Jewish ghettos or as our Counterparts of Color remain.

Conversely, while Black people tended to be less anti-Semitic than other non-Jews during the early civil rights era, more expressions of anti-Semitism have emerged among Blacks and other People of Color in recent years than among whites who reject overtly white Christian supremacist beliefs. I believe this change partly relates to the whitening (with accompanying induction into unconscious white supremacy) of most US Jews and the Christianity (with its accompanying anti-Semitism) of most Black Americans. Recent propaganda that falsely claims that Jews were major players in the African slave trade[7] may add to Black anti-Semitism. Other unfounded Jewish conspiracy theories[8] have contributed to that anti-Semitic strain as well.

A recent argument equating Jewishness and Zionism presents Israeli Jews as Europeans colonizing the Palestinians (not as refugees from the Nazis; Joffe, 2017). Like many progressive American Jews, I strongly disavow and protest Israeli policy, which I see as oppressing Palestinians in Palestine and in Israel, including the displacing of some two million Palestinians when Israel was established in 1948. Ironically, many Palestinian homes that were left vacant in 1948, when Palestinians were forced to flee war believing they would soon return, were given to Jews who had also been forcibly expelled over the twentieth century, including from Yemen, Syria, Egypt, Libya, Iraq, and Iran, where they had lived for millennia (Basri, 2002).

### *Jews of Color*

The clearest reason to question whether Jews are necessarily white is that some Jews, including 12–15% of US Jews, are People of Color by anyone's definition (Kaye/Kantrowitz, 2007; Kelman et al., 2019). Over half of Israeli Jews are Sephardim (Iberian Jews) and Mizrahim (Middle Eastern and North African Jews descended from those never exiled from Israel/Palestine and those expelled from Arab countries, Iran, and North Africa throughout the twentieth century). Arab Jews, like dark-skinned people in the United States and Europe, face racial discrimination in Israel, as do South Asian, African, and especially Ethiopian Jews. Ethiopian Jews, descended from ancient Israel's King Solomon and Ethiopia's Queen of Sheba, were long denied *aliyah*, the right to immigrate to Israel with the full citizenship automatically granted to all Jews, and they still face overt racial discrimination today. Israel is currently embroiled in controversy over refusing *aliyah* to the Abayudayah (Ugandans whose ancestors converted as a village to Conservative Judaism a century ago; Maltz, 2018). Israel's Orthodox rabbinate controls whose conversion meets Israeli standards; they would not question the Judaism of practicing Jews four or five generations post-conversion who are not Black.

The first Jews in the colonial United States were Sephardim expelled from Inquisition-era Spain and Portugal (Schama, 2017). Jewish communities go back centuries in India, China, Uganda, Latin America, and the Caribbean, and millennia in Ethiopia and North Africa. Their members are generally racially indistinguishable from those in their surrounding communities. Jews of Color are Jews by birth and by heritage, as are Jews born to mixed marriages between Jews (of any race) and Partners of Color (Jewish or otherwise). In the United States, some People of Color are adopted into otherwise white, Jewish families. Increasingly, some are converts to Judaism (Kaye/Kantrowitz, 2007; Kelman et al., 2019). In the United States, Jews of Color face discrimination primarily as People of Color and secondarily as religiously Jewish.

Some Latinx people whose ancestors fled the Inquisition to Spain's American colonies and lost track of their Judaism after they came to the Americas have reclaimed their Jewish roots and formally converted to Judaism (De Sedas, 2018). Some Latinx converts discover that their beloved family rituals were originally Jewish. For instance, my late sister-in-law, a Puerto Rican with distinctly African and Taino features and whose family practiced Catholicism and Santería, converted to Judaism after marrying my brother. In studying for conversion, she discovered that her family's special Friday night candle-lit dinners, covering mirrors when in mourning, and last name, Perez, were all of Jewish origin.

Most Jews of Color face intersectional othering and outsider status in both their Jewish communities and their racial and ethnic communities. Neither community is likely to believe they are really Jewish. Jews of Color regularly meet with painful microaggressions when white Jews interrogate their Judaism with pointed questions about their path to or knowledge about Judaism—even when they were born Jewish. De Sedas (2018), in her study of Latinx converts to Judaism, quoted one woman as saying:

> Being Latina in the Jewish community can be really hard. . . . People always assume I converted. . . . The implication of that is, "Oh, you can't be Latina and Jewish." I find it so offensive because there are so many Jews in Latin America. . . . There are lots of Jews there who did not convert. . . . White Jews in Jewish communities can be incredibly racist and not even realize it. I don't like being the angry Latina in the room who's yelling at people for their racism . . . but I feel like it's almost like I have to push more or something or I have to put more emphasis on my Latina identity because I'm the only person in the room thinking about issues that relate to the Latino community. (p. 70)

At the same time, Gentiles of Color may have trouble believing that Jews of Color could have grown up Jewish, let alone *chosen* Judaism. Moreover, Jews of Color are painfully exposed to racist talk among Jews and anti-Semitic talk from non-Jews of Color. Intersectionality for Jews of Color, regardless of gender, means, as Crenshaw (1989) described for Women of Color, double discrimination and double othering.

Questioning the Jewishness of People of Color occurs because most American Jews, after being deemed white in their own or their parents' lifetimes, normalize whiteness. It also occurs because many People of Color in the United States, like white Christians, normalize Christianity. Unlike white Christians, however, some tend to see Jews not only as white, but as *very* white; in keeping with stereotype, they are assumed to be economically exploitative.

I am ashamed to admit that I also assumed that virtually all American Jews (if not Israeli Jews) were white until well into my adult life (despite dating two multiracial Jews in my teens!). I did much of my early clinical work in Spanish, when I had racially ambiguous curly-to-kinky black hair; I still have olive skin. Some of my Latinx clients in the South Bronx and in Brooklyn, assuming that I was *Nuyoriqueña* (a New York-born Puerto Rican), would chastise me (or my mother) for not knowing certain words or foods. When I corrected them, saying, "*pero no soy Puertorriqueña; soy judía*" ("but I'm not Puerto Rican; I'm Jewish"), a few teased me about trying to "pass" as a member of a higher-status minority group. Their response confounded me at the time, but brought home my racial privilege, lest I had any doubt.

Why didn't I realize that *of course* I could be Puerto Rican *and* Jewish? Or that saying, "No, I'm Jewish" when mistaken for Black or racially mixed was not a sufficient identifier? I knew that a visitor seeking a synagogue in Guatemala, Uganda, Ethiopia, India, Jamaica, or Israel would find many dark-skinned Jews worshipping on Shabbat. When my own politically progressive synagogue began attracting significant numbers of Jews of Color by birth, adoption, and conversion, some white congregants assumed they were non-Jewish guests, not worshippers. Perhaps they—and I—didn't see the obvious because US Jews who have become white *don't have* to think about race because we are white. Our marginalization lies with Judaism as a religion and Jewishness as an ethnicity and no longer with race. Though still pained by the European dehumanization and massacring of Jews, we now can "forget" about race and ignore Jewry's racial rainbow.

### *Identifying as a White, Jewish Woman: My Intersectional Journey*

I am a white, straight, cisgender, Jewish woman in my late 60s. I married into a multiracial and multifaith family with far more racial and class privilege than my multiracial stepchildren, while still feeling my legacy trauma as a Jew. The normative anti-Semitism of my postwar childhood qualified and sometimes negated my whiteness, as did the painfully recent Holocaust, which some of my parents' closest friends had survived. Jewishness had defined my grandparents as not-white for most of their lives. Anti-Semitism rendered my great-grandparents and all Jews in the pre-Soviet Russian Empire stateless. They were stamped as "Jews" by both nationality and race there and were unwelcome here as not-quite-white. Anti-Semitism justified, even glorified, their extinction by frequent pogroms like the one that killed my great-grandmother's family.

As a child, I knew I was Jewish by ethnicity and religion, but my racial identification seemed slippery and confusing. In my multiracial, multiclass, unofficially segregated suburban New York community, I understood that I was white—more or less. I had more "rights," in the language of the day, than my Black peers (I knew few Latinos or Asians then). I had far more than Southern Blacks but less than my white Christian peers. Yet white Christians periodically made me anxious, for reasons I did not understand, by politely calling me a member of "the Hebrew race."

My family's racial privilege diminished, however briefly, each year during the summer as my family, the three of us with racially ambiguous appearances, drove south from New York to visit relatives in Jim Crow Florida. En route, we literally and figuratively lost some whiteness to the sun and some to the South's different racial categorizations. Our changed condition played out again on our drive back home, our presunscreen skins darkened, unprotected from skin cancer and from segregated rest stops, water fountains, and motels along Georgia's country roads. What should we do when my father, brother, and I were mistaken for Black? What should we do when we were recognized as Jewish? Over the years, I grasped that I was almost-white at home but almost-Black in the South.

Each year, I understood more about my parents' racial calculations south (or just north) of the Mason-Dixon line: which motels do we stop in, where and how do we eat, use the bathroom, and gas up? They took those calculations in solidarity with Black people (my father having been a civil rights activist in 1940s Ohio and Kentucky), but also with our own safety and dignity in mind.

After spending my teens in the (northern) civil rights, anti-Vietnam war, and second-wave feminist movements, I acknowledged my whiteness in my early 20s, in solidarity with graduate school Classmates of Color who did not carry my white-skin privilege through life. (I had the good fortune to attend a doctoral program whose [short-lived] radical affirmative action quota required half of incoming students to be of Color and half to be female, when psychology was overwhelmingly white and male.) I felt my racial privilege most keenly in discussions with classmates who could never "pass" as white with a police officer or a bank officer and whose lives were not reflected in class materials. Perhaps this was easier for me to do in the 1970s, when overt anti-Semitism was receding, during a respite between my postwar youth and recent years.

I recognized my whiteness (and class privilege) at a deeper, more personal level on becoming the stepmother of two beloved (now middle-aged) children whose father is white and whose late mother was Black and Native American. Their parents raised them as Black, but both identify as multiracial. When their father and I adopted a light-skinned infant (whose African roots we correctly suspected and whose Native roots we discovered years later), our worries for him were necessarily very different than for his siblings. He chose to identify as multiracial at age six, thinking that since his family was multiracial, so was he.

I have written elsewhere (Kliman, 1994) about injuring my new teenaged stepson shortly after joining his family by channeling generations of Jewish adults challenging the thinking of children as bright as he was, in the service of honing their intellectual skills, in keeping with Talmudic and later secular Jewish tradition. To my horror, I learned that I had made him feel stupid. He received my questions, which I saw as a mark of (Jewish) intellectual respect, as evidence that I didn't respect his intelligence, congruent with the messages given to Black and Indigenous children. I had been raised by my parents (but not always by schools, because I was a girl) to believe that my ideas were worth sharing and should be respected. That was not the message he got.

If I could get a re-do on that mistake, which shadowed our relationship for several years, I would have listened more, asked fewer questions, and wondered what impact my questions could have on my Stepson of Color and our new relationship. I would not have jumped in so quickly with the intellectual jousting that I'd thrived on growing up. I would coach my younger self to recognize how the easy confidence of my white privilege and educational privilege, combined with the Jewishly confident feistiness of my younger years, could be hurtful to a child whose poor Black and Indigenous maternal family had no college experience.

### *Final Thoughts*

I return to Dr. Hardy's provocative question: "Why is deconstructing race and Jewishness relevant, if not critical, to the dismantling of whiteness?" Jews who are white or perceived as white are racially confusing to others. We can be confused ourselves. Most of us have acquired racial privilege but still carry familial and collective scars of previously racialized oppression and chronic religious marginalization. Non-Jews of Color can view us as especially white, perhaps informed by memories of Jewish small business owners who kept their businesses, but not their homes, in once-Jewish working-class neighborhoods that transitioned to Black ones or informed by anti-Semitic conspiracy theories about Jewish world domination. White Jews may feel strong kinship with People of Color yet still operate with all the privilege and prejudice of our whiteness. Our collective story, since biblical days, involves being singled out for both a unique spiritual mission and a unique experience of oppression (neither of which I, personally, believe is unique). That story can contribute to the "oppression Olympics," serving our relationships with People of Color poorly. Yet when we purposefully couple our long experience of oppression with the social influence that our newfound privilege provides, white Jews and Jews of Color can and must engage in deep solidarity and true dialogue with our non-Jewish Brothers and Sisters of Color.

**JODIE KLIMAN, PHD,** a social–clinical psychologist, is a professor of clinical psychology at William James College's Clinical PsyD Program in Newton, Massachusetts. Her clinical work, research, and publications focus on intersectionality in family therapy and training relationships; social constructionist and culturally responsive approaches to family therapy; clinical work with immigrants and refugees; and family and collective trauma. Her current research involves a computerized visual representation of individuals' intersectional domains of privilege and marginalization, to be used in training, supervision, and research, based on her "Intersections of social privilege and marginalization: A visual teaching tool." She publishes and trains on intersectionality, systems approaches to disaster and war, and network therapy and has edited a monograph, *Working in War Zones, Near and Far: Oscillations of Despair and Hope* (2005). She is a founding member of the Boston Institute for Culturally Accountable Practices and has a private practice in Brookline, Massachusetts.

## Notes

1. With anxiety, I quote Hitler (1969), whose hateful propaganda will surely remind the reader of the Confederacy and the KKK:

    With satanic joy in his face, the black-haired Jewish youth lurks in wait for the unsuspecting girl whom he defiles with his blood, thus stealing her from her people. With every means he tries to destroy the racial foundations of the peo-

> ple he has set out to subjugate. Just as he himself systematically ruins women and girls, he does not shrink back from pulling down the blood barriers for others, even on a large scale. It was and it is Jews who bring the Negroes into the Rhineland, always with the same secret thought and clear aim of ruining the hated white race by the necessarily resulting bastardization, throwing it down from its cultural and political height, and himself rising to be its master. (para. 19)

2. Carroll (2002) argued that this vilification changed the foundation of Christianity from Jesus's (Jewish) social gospels to Jesus's torturous crucifixion and death. It also took the blood from the death of Jesus off the hands of the Roman empire (which had previously systematically killed Jewish baby boys in response to rumors of the birth of a new prince of the Jews, hence Mary and Joseph's flight to Egypt) and placed it on Jewish hands. This political sleight of hand rendered the newly Christian Roman Empire blameless in the Crucifixion, justifying massacres of Jews. Constantine placed the crucifix on the swords Roman soldiers used to slaughter Jews and Muslims.
3. Portugal's Prince Henry the Navigator "invented" race and racial hierarchy in the mid-fifteenth century to justify the lucrative emerging Portuguese slave trade out of West Africa (Kendi, 2019). For millennia before, people whose tribes or nation-states were conquered had been enslaved as human spoils or because of their desperate poverty (Painter, 2011). The new race-based European slave trade of Africans fueled and was fueled by early capitalism (Kendi, 2019).
4. Ashkenazim are Jews from Western, Central, and Eastern Europe, though most are originally Middle Eastern. The Sephardim are originally Middle Eastern/North African Jews who spent several centuries before the Inquisition in Spain and Portugal. Most of those who survived the Inquisition scattered to the Mediterranean, the Netherlands, and the Americas.
5. Jews were disproportionately merchants, money-lenders, and rent collectors for gentile landlords because European governments did not allow them to own land or enter trades. A few were wealthy; most were not.
6. The first attribution must be addressed respectfully and compassionately by the Jewish member of the conversation. The latter attributions, however, must be challenged. Accusations of secret Jewish plots to dominate national economies, governments, and other institutions have long been used to justify Jewish oppression and fueled by invented propaganda screeds like the 1903 Russian "discovery" of the *Protocol of the Elders of Zion*, which outlined a vast Jewish global conspiracy to dominate the world (Zipperstein, 2020). Still influential, this publication continued a long line of anti-Semitic conspiracy theories, including: that the Jews' crucified Jesus; that Jews kidnap, torture, and murder Christian children to put their blood in Passover matzoh(!); and that Jewish witchcraft causes crop failures, droughts, and plagues that were falsely believed not to affect Jews. These theories fueled centuries of pogroms, especially at Easter. Unfortunately, some People of Color today believe the Jewish world domination conspiracy theories.
7. The Nation of Islam's (1991) *The Secret Relationship Between Blacks and Jews* claimed that Jewish financiers bankrolled most of the slave trade and were slave traders and holders in great numbers. However, historians widely agree that Sephardic Jews participating in the Atlantic slave accounted for about two percent of that brutal industry (Steele, 1995), a shameful enough figure.

8. Jews are widely believed to exert stunning financial and political domination worldwide (however do we organize ourselves to do that?). Moreover, a common conspiracy theory term, "cabal," derives from the *Kabbalah*, the Hebrew religious text offering mystical interpretations of the *Torah*, the Hebrew Bible, according to *A Dictionary of Etymology of the English Language: And of English Synonyms and Paronymes* (Oswald, 2010). It seems the very act of discerning spiritual meaning Jewishly is to engage in conspiracy.

## References


*Arango, T. (2020, November 6). Hate crimes in the US rose to highest level in more than a decade in 2019.* The New York Times. *https://www.nytimes.com/2020/11/16/us/hate-crime-rate.htmll*

*Barrett, J. R., & Roediger, D. (1997). Inbetween peoples: Race, nationality, and the "new immigrant" working class.* Journal of American Ethnic History, 16*(3), 3–44.*

*Basri, C. (2002). The Jewish refugees from Arab countries: An examination of legal rights—A case study of the human rights violations of Iraqi Jews.* Fordham International Law Journal, 26*(3), 654–720.*

*Boston Institute for Culturally Affirming Practice. (2019). Deconstructing power to build connection: The importance of dialogue. In E. Pinderhughes, V. Jackson, & P. Romney (Eds.),* Understanding power: An imperative for human services *(pp. 195–218). National Association of Social Workers.*

*Boszormenyi-Nagy, I., Grunebaum, J., & Ulrich, D. (1991). Contextual therapy. In A. Gurman & D. Kniskern (Eds.),* Handbook of family therapy *(Vol. 2, pp. 200–238). Brunner/Mazel.*

*Brodkin, K. (1998).* How the Jews became white folks and what that says about race in America. *Rutgers University Press.*

*Carroll, J. (2002).* Constantine's sword: The church and the Jews: A history. *Mariner Books.*

*Center for the Study of Hate and Extremism. (2021).* Report to the nation: Anti-Asian prejudice and hate crime. *Author. Retrieved from https://www.csusb.edu/sites/default/files/Report%20to%20the%20Nation%20-%20Anti-Asian%20Hate%202020%20Final%20Draft%20-%20As%20of%20Apr%2030%202021%206%20PM%20corrected.pdf*

*Centre for Israel and Jewish Affairs (CIJA). (2015, August 14). Demographics of Israel. https://cijaarchive.ca/resource/israel-the-basics/demographics-of-israel/*

*Crenshaw, K. (1989). Demarginalizing the intersection of race and sex: A black feminist critique of antidiscrimination doctrine, feminist theory, and antiracist politics.* University of Chicago Legal Forum, 140, *139–167.*

*De Sedas, M. (2018).* Latinos who convert to Judaism: An exploration of the intersection of ethnic and religious identities *(Publication No. 10812329) [Doctoral dissertation, William James College]. ProQuest.*

*Green, E. (2016, December 5). Are Jews white?* The Atlantic. *https://www.theatlantic.com/politics/archive/2016/12/are-jews-white/509453/*

*Greenberg, D. (2018, November 2). America's forgotten pogroms.* Politico Magazine. *https://www.politico.com/magazine/story/2018/11/02/americas-forgotten-pogroms-222181*

*Hardy, K. V. (2007).* The psychological residuals of slavery *[Film]. Psychotherapy.net.*

*Hardy, K. V. (2016). Anti-racist approaches for shaping theoretical and practice paradigms.*

*In M. Pender-Greene & A. Siskin (Eds.),* Anti-racist strategies for the health and human services. *Oxford University Press.*

*Hardy, K. V., & Laszloffy, T. (1998, May).* Dynamics of pro-racist ideology *[Keynote Address]. The Annual Culture Conference, Family Institute of New Jersey, New Brunswick, NJ, United States.*

*Hartmann, W., Wendt, W., Burrage, R., Pomerville, A., & Gone, J. (2019). American Indian historical trauma: Anti-colonial prescriptions for healing, resilience and survivance.* American Psychologist, 74*(1), 6–19. https://doi.org/10.1037/amp0000326*

*Hitler, A. (1969). Extracts from* Mein kampf *by Adolf Hitler [Class notes]. https://www.wm.edu/offices/auxiliary/osher/course-info/classnotes/fall2017/Schilling_Holocaust-Extracts-from-Mein-Kampf-Ideology.pdf*

*Joffe, A. (2017, September 3).* Palestinian settler-colonialism. *The Begin-Sadat center for strategic studies. https://besacenter.org/perspectives-papers/palestinians-settlers-colonialism/*

*Kaye/Kantrowitz, M. (2007).* The colors of Jews: Racial politics and radical diasporism. *Indiana University Press.*

*Kelman, A., Tapper, A., Fonseca, I., & Saperstein, A. (2019).* Counting inconsistencies: An analysis of American Jewish population studies, with a focus on Jews of color. *The Jews of Color Field Building Initiative, Stanford Graduate School of Education, University of San Francisco. https://jewsofcolorfieldbuilding.org/wp-content/uploads/2019/05/Counting-Inconsistencies-052119.pdf*

*Kendi, I. X. (2019).* How to be an anti-racist. *One Word Press.*

*Kivel, P. (1998, Spring).* I'm not white, I'm Jewish: Standing as Jews in the fight for racial justice *[Conference Talk]. What is White Conference, University of California-Riverside, Riverside, CA, United States. http://paulkivel.com/wp-content/uploads/2015/07/imnotwhiteimjewish.pdf*

*Kliman, J. (1994). The interweaving of gender, class, and race in family therapy. In M. P. Mirkin (Ed.),* Women in context: Toward a feminist reconstruction of psychotherapy *(pp. 25–47). Guilford Press.*

*Kliman, J. (2005). Many differences, many voices. In M. P. Mirkin, K. L. Suyemoto, & B. F. Okun (Eds.),* Psychotherapy with women: Exploring diverse contexts and identities *(pp. 42–63). Guilford Press.*

*Kliman, J. (2010, Winter). Intersections of social privilege and marginalization: A visual teaching tool.* AFTA Monograph Series, *39–48.*

*Kliman, J., Moní, Y., Dzilala, F., Eisner, M. & Higuera, A. (2021). The Social Matrix: A tool for visualizing intersectional identity. Author. Retrieved from https://www.socialmatrixdiagram.org*

*Kliman, J., Winawer, H., & Trimble, D. (2019). The inevitable whiteness of being (white): Whiteness and intersectionality in family therapy practice and training. In M. McGoldrick & K. V. Hardy (Eds.),* Re-visioning family therapy: Addressing diversity in clinical practice *(3rd ed., pp. 236–250). Guilford Press.*

*Maltz, J. (2018, May 31).* Exclusive: Israel rules not to recognize Ugandan Jewish community. *Haaretz. https://www.haaretz.com/israel-news/.premium-exclusive-israel-rules-not-to-recognize-ugandan-jewish-community-1.6137079*

*Nation of Islam. (1991).* The secret relationship between blacks and Jews *(Vol. 1).*

*Oswald, J. (2010).* A dictionary of etymology of the English language: And of English synonyms and paronymes. *Kessinger Publishing.*

*Painter, N. I. (2011).* The history of white people. *W. W. Norton & Company.*

*Schama, S. (2013).* The story of the Jews: Finding the words *(Vol. 1). HarperCollins.*
*Schama, S. (2017).* The story of the Jews: Belonging *(Vol. 2). HarperCollins.*
*Schraub, D. (2019). White Jews: An intersectional approach.* AJC Review, 43*(2), 379–407. https://doi.org/10.1017/S0364009419000461*
*Siegel-Itzkovich, J. (2006). Gene tests show that two fifths of Ashkenazi Jews are descended from four women.* British Journal of Medicine, 332*(140). https//doi.org/10.1136/bmj.332.7534.140-a*
*Steele, B. (1995, March 2). Jews were never dominant in the slave trade, Pitt historian says.* University of Pittsburgh Times. *https://www.utimes.pitt.edu/archives/?p=4321*
*Watts-Jones, T. D. (2010). Location of self: Opening the door to dialogue on intersectionality in the therapy process.* Family Process, 49*(3), 409–420.*
*Weingarten, K. (2003).* Common shock: Witnessing violence every day—How we are harmed, how we can heal. *Dutton.*
*Zipperstein, S. J. (2020, August 25). The conspiracy theory to rule them all: What explains the strange, long life of* The Protocols of the Elders of Zion? The Atlantic. *https://www.theatlantic.com/politics/archive/2020/08/conspiracy-theory-rule-them-all/615550/*

## CHAPTER 6

# The Landscape and the Mirror

## The Duality of Being White and Jewish

KEN EPSTEIN, PHD, LCSW

Since being invited to write a chapter about my Jewish and white identities, I have struggled to understand what I have to contribute. For as long as I can remember, I have known that I was Jewish. My journey to recognizing my whiteness has been much less clear. Growing up at the intersection of white and Jewish identities has informed my views toward anti-Semitism and the ways Jewish people have been marginalized, brutalized, and murdered. Yet it has prevented me from metabolizing the ways in which being white helped me gain access to the privileges embedded in white supremacy—the same white supremacy that tattooed identification numbers on the forearms of Jewish prisoners in Auschwitz, which made it difficult for me to deeply consider and understand the similarities and differences to the branding of African and Indigenous peoples who were colonized, enslaved, murdered, and marginalized.

On the advice of a trusted colleague, I connected with a younger white Jewish woman who has spent considerable time thinking and working in the space of being white and Jewish. She was so articulate and thoughtful, I asked if she should write this chapter instead of me. Without pause, she said that my confusion and hesitancy were the very reason that I needed to write this. It is from this confusion that I began to make sense of the ways in which I have been socialized as a Jew and as a white man as well as the impact this has had on my clinical and leadership career.

This exploration of cultural, racial, and professional identity has been inspired by participation in numerous conversations with mixed race health care professionals in which one or more phenotypically white-appearing participants has stated that they did not identify as white and stated their racial identification as Jewish. In some incidences, I have witnessed Jewish participants, when pressed about their whiteness by a Person of Color, react by stating that this line of questioning was anti-Semitic. My immediate response has been to reject their responses as unprocessed and problematic. However, internally I understand the perceived challenges and dangers of integrating and not integrating these two identities in the United States. There are also ramifications for nonwhite-appearing Jews when white-appearing Jews denounce whiteness as their racial identity.

I will try to traverse the landscape of Jewish history as victims of unthinkable atrocities, our experiences with modern day anti-Semitism, and our complicity in maintaining and sustaining white supremacy in the United States. Concurrently, I will look into the mirror and explore how this has shaped my own personal and professional identity. I hope this will be helpful for all clinicians and leaders in the healing professions as we sort through the ways whiteness is operationalized and impacts the way we think, react, and practice.

## The Landscape: Being Jewish and White

> At first glance it might seem strange that the attitude of the anti-Semite can be equated with that of the negrophobe. It was my philosophy teacher from the Antilles who reminded me one day: "When you hear someone insulting the Jews, pay attention; he is talking about you." And I believed at the time he was universally right, meaning that I was responsible in my body and soul for the fate reserved for my brother. Since then, I have understood that what he meant quite simply was that the anti-Semite is inevitably a negrophobe. (Fanon, 2008, p. 101)

As with all immigrants to the United States, the Jewish experience is not a monolithic story. We arrived in the United States at different times, took different paths, represented different social classes, had different skin colors, spoke different languages, and brought with us different levels of acculturation. My Jewish grandparents, like other ethnic groups, learned to live with an array of contradictions. Jewish immigrants came to the United States with shared experiences of escaping oppression and continuing a historical pattern of acculturation, only to become disenfranchised in their adopted country.

Survival of the Jewish identity required becoming a part of the fabric of our adopted country while at the same time maintaining a cultural connection to Judaism as both a religion and an ethnic identity (Brodkin, 1998). Jewish immigration to the United States was seen as an opportunity to be safe, to build a community, and to become part of the growth of this nation, planting seeds for the generations to come. While my great-grandparents thought they were integrating seamlessly into the fabric of American society, they spoke mostly Yiddish and lived in isolated Jewish communities.

The acculturation process of generations of Jewish immigrants from dangerous and fervently anti-Semitic places contributed to the duality of holding together as a people by proclaiming Jewishness as a race and managing integration into the white caste system embedded in the United States's power structure. The generational acculturation process involved speaking less Yiddish; moving out of the tenements; accumulating resources, employment, access to housing, loans, and college education; and pursuing professional opportunities (Goldstein, 2006).

Karen Brodkin (1998) describes the construction of the Jewish American ethno-racial identity as "a kind of double vision that comes from racial middleness: of an experience of marginality vis-à-vis whiteness, and an experience of whiteness and belonging vis-à-vis blackness" (p. 2). White Jewish descendants of European immigrants have had a historical double bind, characterized as being othered by the construction of a white Nordic caste system that considered Semitic races mongrels, worthy of destruction, as well as benefactors of admission to the white privilege system (Brodkin, 1998; Wilkerson, 2020).

The complexity of these interwoven identities has been the subject of much debate and dialogue. How do we white Jews simultaneously understand the near destruction of our people, culminating in the Holocaust, and our membership and privileges associated with whiteness? Ironically, white Jews have benefited from a white caste system in the United States after being nearly annihilated by an Aryan caste system in Germany.

> A caste system is an artificial construction, a fixed and embedded ranking of human value that sets the presumed supremacy of one group against the presumed inferiority of other groups on the basis of ancestry and often immutable traits, traits that would be neutral in the abstract but are ascribed life-and-death meaning in a hierarchy favoring the dominant caste whose forebears designed it. (Wilkerson, 2020, p. 17)

Three caste systems are most notable, including the system in India, Nazi Germany, and the race-based system in the United States (Wilkerson, 2020). Hitler himself was an inspired student of the United States's history of the destruction of Native American culture and sovereignty and the enslavement and racist policies toward Black people (Wilkerson, 2020). White Jewish immigrants faced an unholy dilemma between the construction of identity through victimhood borne of religious persecution and the acculturation and socialization of white supremacy in the United States (Goldstein, 2006). White Jews' identities, then, have been greatly defined by annihilation and assimilation.

The white Jewish experience, and the experience of African Americans and Native Americans, has been profoundly impacted by a social order built on supremacy and annihilation. Yet the Jewish journey in the United States was borne of choice, and our affiliation has been defined by our whiteness. The Black experience was defined by enslavement and being subject to a caste system defined by skin color. There was and is no choice afforded. My skin color has offered me the privilege of claiming a Jewish identity and benefiting from my white identity. This is different from what Du bois (1897) described as the dichotomy of a Black man living in a white dominant culture as a "double consciousness" (pp. 10–11). Survival is based on a double life, characterized not by choice but by the necessity of being seen and treated as the "other" while struggling to maintain one's self worth and stature.

Jewish socialization established that we are, similarly to People of Color, a resilient people that cannot be wiped out, and, at the same time, whose very existence has been threatened or almost extinguished. We have learned to be suspicious of the white Anglo-Saxon power structure and competition to achieve status and recognition. Therefore, our subjugation has shaped us. This historical link to adversity and resilience formed our collective need for social justice and healing. However, in order to maintain the narrative of Jewish exceptionalism, we were forced to deny or ignore our contribution to and inclusion in white supremacy in the United States.

## The Mirror: What Is Hidden in the Family Genogram

> The things other people have put into my head, at any rate, do not fit together nicely, are often useless and ugly, are out of proportion with one another, are out of proportion with life as it really is outside my head. (Vonnegut, 2009, p. 5)

Identity can be biologically determined and socially constructed. Much of the way we internalize who we are is a product of our own life story and our socialization in the context of our personal, professional, and family stories. Our family stories constitute what is known and passed on and can be a subjective tableau with which to embrace or whitewash history. The genogram, first developed in the 1980s, is a way of eliciting family history, patterns, strengths, and secrets through stories, relationships, and culture (McGoldrick et al., 2008). I will briefly discuss a few examples from my relational family history and explore what happens when I analyze my genogram through white- and Jewish-colored glasses.

As I map my own family history, my external experience of being an activist Jewish person and my internal structures of whiteness and privilege collide. What I could readily see in others was more obscured when I looked inside myself . . . because it was hidden in plain sight. How do I carry my pride around my Jewish heritage and my shame, guilt, and rage around my acculturated whiteness?

My family immigration history followed a typical Jewish progression; my Eastern European great-grandparents settled in New York's lower east side and later moved to Brooklyn to raise their children and grandchildren.

Generationally, we progressed from laborers to business owners to professionals. Each generation became more educated, thus increasing our upward mobility. While Jewish people were restricted from clubs, communities, civic institutions, and colleges, my grandparents and my parents were able to "break through," purchase property, and immerse themselves in a community. My parents and grandparents would talk about how our Jewish network in the community shared workarounds and loopholes with each other.

However, there was no discussion about the explicit access to property acquisition afforded by our whiteness. A colleague told me a story about how their grandfather was able to acquire property through word of mouth at the temple. Later, they learned that the property they acquired had been taken from a Japanese family that had been interned during World War II. While we were able to attain property, redlining policies restricted Black and Brown citizens from realizing the "American Dream" of owning property and accumulating wealth (Alexander, 2012). This is how communities were kept segregated (homogenous). I can only imagine that Jewish admittance to the "white home ownership club" was recognized by our Black and Brown neighbors who were denied access and left without the same upward mobility options.

Outside of work and community, family life was centered around the temple as well as on pursuing leisure activities. Both sets of my grandparents belonged to golf clubs that were almost exclusively Jewish. The only People of Color I remember seeing worked for the club as service personnel. Ironically, these golf clubs were located in larger communities that were not open to Jewish or Black residents. My grandparents disdained the Gentile gold club that was segregated, yet did not recognize or acknowledge that their own club excluded People of Color. Perversely, there was a pride in belonging to a club communicating our status. That our leisure represented an attained privilege was unspoken. This is but one example of the American "caste" system in action.

In 1960, when I was two years old, we moved to a Long Island town that was "open" to Jews and thus overwhelmingly white and Jewish. There were virtually no People of Color in my neighborhood. My parents bought a house there because the streets were safe, the schools were good, there was space to play, and there were ample resources. We were afforded the opportunity to acculturate in white space while simultaneously living in Jewish space to which Black and Brown people's access was restricted, except for work.

Amanda began working for our family when we moved to Long Island. Amanda was African American, the granddaughter of descendants who had been enslaved. She worked for our family a few days a week as a domestic employee for over four decades. She was a mother, a grandmother, and a foster mother. In her community she was considered an elder, revered in her church, a matriarch of her family, and a leader. Amanda would often refer to me as her "white baby," and no doubt she was the central moral authority, caretaker, and emotional connection in my childhood. Amanda referred to my parents as Mr. and Mrs. Epstein even though she was older than them. I always used Amanda's first name in speaking to her.

During the many years in which my dad disappeared into his work and my mom suffered immobilizing depression and anxiety, Amanda provided stability and nurturing. I played with her grandchildren and foster children. At the age of 10, on April 5, 1968, the day after Martin Luther King Jr. was shot, Amanda explained what had happened and I remember crying with her. Once when I was 12, I broke three fingers playing basketball. Amanda took me to the emergency room, where they refused to treat me because she was not my mom. I remember her pleading with the hospital staff to no avail. This would have been different if she was white.

My parents always made a point of telling me how well they treated her. They gave her gifts and insisted that she was family, yet when she worked on holidays she did not sit with the family at mealtimes. Meanwhile, I remember hearing my extended family referring to Black people as *schvartzes*, a derogatory Yiddish word for Black people. To this day I struggle to integrate my love for Amanda and my family's embedded racism.

My Jewish self was nourished in Hebrew school and by family rituals and holidays. My white self was educated in predominantly white public schools composed of Jewish or Christian students. My Jewish education taught me about social justice, self-determination, breaking the cycle of poverty, and achievements related to the fortitude and grit of Jews as well as about the historical discrimination of Jews. It prepared me to question the status quo and resist oppression.

I was more subtly socialized in white exceptionalism at school and from my family. I learned American history, which erased our country's original sins of slavery, the brutal colonialization of Native Americans, Jim Crow, and redlining, the discriminatory practice of denying resources to Black and Brown people. Most painfully, I was not helped to understand that white Jews' ascent was not solely a result of our grit and determination, that our inclusion in being white allowed us to benefit from white privilege.

Being a child in the 1960s and 1970s, I was exposed to the social unrest in the United States and the world but was distanced from its epicenter. In high school, college, and culminating in graduate school, I became increasingly politicized and began a lifelong path to understand and fight inequity and injustice. This path ultimately brought me to be involved in intellectual, political, and social pursuits, challenging the status quo and rejecting what I had been taught. I was literally waking up and seeing the world differently.

At the same time, my unprocessed socialized whiteness drew me to numbing and increasingly risky behaviors. It was like two parts of myself were operating independently without an internal discussion or an external moderator. My rejection of my middle-class whiteness allowed me to critique where I came from, but it did not provide the space for self-interrogation to recognize the contradictions between my internal and external self. At home, my family connected with our subjugation alignment with Black and Brown Americans while continuing our own embodiment of whiteness.

During my adult life I have learned about *the talk* that generations of African American parents have felt compelled to give their children to keep them safe, to keep them alive. Kenya Young (2020), an executive at National Public Radio, reflects on *the talk* she has given over and over again to her three Black children when they wanted to go to the park: "Don't wear your hood. Don't put your hands up. Don't make a lot of moves. Tell them your mother works for NPR" (June 28, 2020). My mom and dad never gave me that kind of talk; they told me to get out of the house and be sure to be home for dinner. I now realize that because I was a white child, they didn't need to give me *the talk*. My safety and well-being are integral parts of the *benefits package* that comes with being white.

My father, now deceased, and my mother have both experienced dementia and Alzheimer's. Their illnesses have offered an opportunity to get an unfiltered view of their long-term memory, their compassion, and their vulnerability as they emotionally reviewed their lives. We have visited the neighborhoods they grew up in and reminisced about their lives, connecting injustices they experienced with stories of resilience. My dad continuously wanted to know about all of the experiences of everyone he met regarding their immigration, family, and culture. In the midst of the pandemic, my mom requested that her caregiver take her to the Black Lives Matter protest outside her apartment. As each of their filters loosened, both of my parents made outwardly racist statements and pronouncements. These included calling some of their Caregivers of Color "lazy" or "stupid," demanding service, and/or expressing superiority. Their dementia has helped me to look in the mirror and grieve and rage about the painful collision of my Jewish and white identities.

## Recognition and Repair: Implications for the Healing Professions

> Learning about the abandonment of moral principles or healthcare professionals and scientists, their societies and academic institutions, to a murderous ideology yields fundamental concerns and global implications. . . . Could the Holocaust, one of the greatest evils ever perpetrated on humankind, have occurred without the complicity of physicians, their societies and the scientific community? (Reis et al., 2019, p. 1)

On May 25, 2020, the world bore witness to the murder of George Floyd in Minnesota. While there have been too many graphic videos and stories documenting the brutality of police violence against Black men and women, this particular episode struck a chord and triggered a racial reckoning across America. Anti-Black racism does not manifest exclusively through police violence, it is witnessed and sustained among health care workers, clinicians, and clinical leaders.

The issues of health disparities, access to health care, differential treatment, and embedded racist policies have been documented, discussed, and problem solved for generations. Yet the health disparities in almost all health and wellness outcomes between Black Americans and white Americans persists. Anti-Black racism is built into the bricks and mortar of most every institution in America; the indoctrination of white supremacy, the hidden part of our training, practice, and family lives, is the foundation of this racism.

Engaging as a white Jewish clinician and leader has required me to recognize and acknowledge the landscape of racism, beginning with the ways my training and practices have contributed to harm. The work requires the active and persistent repair of the impact on clients, coworkers, and organizations, continually reconciling the inequalities of antiracist practices and policies. How can we in the helping profession resist the powerful forces of white supremacy that maintains whiteness as an operating system and resists change? To do this I need to interrogate the landscape and mirror of my training and career.

### *Recognition*

> There is a strength, a power even, in understanding brokenness, because embracing our brokenness creates a need and desire for mercy, and perhaps a corresponding need to show mercy. When you experience mercy, you learn things that are hard to learn otherwise. You see things you can't otherwise see; you hear things you can't otherwise hear. You begin to recognize the humanity that resides in each of us. (Stevenson, 2014, p. 290)

My education, practice, supervision, mentoring, and theoretical orientation was shaped by white Jewish professors, theorists, supervisors, and leaders as my career developed. It was as though I was part of a brotherhood of social justice Jews. How did we all end up doing this particular line of work? How did our work inform my Jewish, white, and professional identities? Over the years, these individuals helped me heal, find meaning, shape my career, and provide individual, organizational, and systemic ways to understand and address adversity and mental wellness. I benefited from a consistent investigation of therapeutic interventions that incorporated the understanding and impacts of poverty, discrimination, violence, and racism on child development and family functioning. While there was genuine concern and caring in our work, we lacked a sustained approach to consider the ways in which our work could be harmful. The same influences that inspired me to thrive in becoming a healer also limited my qualifications to work with Black and Brown children and families.

I started my career working in specialized school and residential settings for children and youth that served primarily Black and Brown clients and that were staffed and led by a majority of white staff. The children and youth were disproportionately removed from their homes, medicated, labeled with externalizing diagnoses, segregated in schools, and incarcerated in juvenile detention facilities. It was common practice to use physical restraint, restrict family access, and treat the young people in facilities outside of their neighborhood, sometimes hours away from family. This is the space I entered as I began to learn and grow as a social worker.

*Repair*

> We need a powerful sense of determination to banish the ugly blemish of racism scarring the image of America. We can, of course, try to temporize, negotiate small, inadequate changes and prolong the timetable of freedom in the hope that the narcotics of delay will dull the pain of progress. (King, 1963/2000, p. 122)

Repair begins with listening and ensuring others feel heard. Such a practice impacts both the listener and the teller. When I conducted interviews with Holocaust survivors in college, Irma Birnbaum (personal communication, October 1978) shared a painful story about being a child and escaping as the rest of her family perished. But she assured me that telling her story was "liberating," and it's important to note that repair is not a one-way street. For me, listening to Ms. Birnbaum affirmed my Jewish identity and began my own healing process. The act of listening to these stories helped me interrogate my self-medicating as a coping response to my suburban numbness. Yet in the United States, the wounds of racism are silenced, which promotes the voicelessness that Dr. Kenneth Hardy (2013) says "erodes the ability to defend against a barrage of unwelcomed and unjustified negative, debilitating messages" (p. 26). Voicelessness and bias are built into health care and are directly associated with adverse events and outcomes (Ofri, 2020; Snowden, 2003; Washington, 2006). In what ways did my training and supervision help me understand how I could help repair the wounds of racism and give voice to the voiceless?

Hardy (2013) reminds us that the impact of "racial oppression is a traumatic form of interpersonal violence which can lacerate the spirit, scar the soul, and puncture the psyche" (p. 2). Repair, then, is about giving voice to the inequities and brutality and needs to be structured into our leadership and practice. The Kinship Support Network (Cohon & Cooper, 1999) in San Francisco was started after a doctor and a nurse at San Francisco General Hospital listened to the stories of African American grandmothers who were foisted into the role of raising their grandchildren. Their stories were mixed with a devastating analysis of the impact of white supremacy on their lives and their spirits as they did whatever they could to protect their families from destruction. Speaking their truth was essential to their healing. Their repair required sacred and trusted space outside of a white dominated place.

For me, recognition has been able to hold the impact of connection of Jewish mentors and realize the lack of influence and direction I received from Black and Brown supervisors and directors. There should have been obligatory training in "unpacking the invisible knapsack of white privilege" (McIntosh, 2019, p. 220) and facing the wounds and ruptures of my white helping-class oblivion before I began working with Black and Brown children. This means training programs, organizations, and service systems need to go beyond training staff in competencies, biases, and humility, and provide context for facilitated multiracial conversations where whiteness is interrogated relative to our practices, our policies, and our procedures.

To repair the racial wounds of white professional dominance, I have had to learn that my loud social justice Jewish voice needed to quiet down to see the disruptiveness of my white male silence. Too often, I see something and then say something later, privately, protecting the discomfort of another white person (and my own discomfort) while allowing the discomfort for a Person of Color to persist. I recall failing to speak up when a white physician leader in a meeting insulted a Physician of Color by disparaging the work required in her community of non-native English speakers. How many times have I failed to stand up and speak out? How many times have I spoken too much? How often have I backed away from a problem for fear of disrupting? How often did I see and use my Jewish identity as a protective shield from my distress or dominance of my whiteness? The answer is, too frequently to make any denial of my complicity credible.

Interrogating myself includes apologizing when I falter and having the courage to speak to other white staff when a microaggression or macroaggression has taken place. Repair begins with adopting the belief that everything I do as a clinician and leader needs to be seen through the lens of anti-Black racism and to be questioned, which could mean risking the comfort of my status or position within and outside of the organization I work. This includes actively identifying and resisting institutional forms of racism in our diagnoses, evidence, practices, policies, and procedures. Recognizing ways the status quo of whiteness has created harm and taking the necessary steps to repair that harm are the bedrock for being qualified to work toward systemic change.

## A Cautionary Tale: Beware of Quick Fixes

> It is not freedom from conditions, but it is freedom to take a stand toward the conditions. (Frankl, 1962, p. 153)

My life is not a blueprint nor a proclamation of the Jewish and white experience in the United States. This chapter is my attempt to understand how my two identities have impacted the ways in which I see the world and act professionally. Looking in the mirror and understanding the landscape does not exonerate me nor eliminate me from working in the healing professions. Ultimately, it is how I integrate these identities and recognize my limitations that define my qualifications to serve effectively.

This, then, is a cautionary tale full of facts to dispute, experiences to reinterpret, and conclusions to question. Clearly, I must learn to embrace the joy, pride, and certainty as well as the confusion, dissonance, and discomfort as I traverse my Jewish and white identity. Without continuous reflection and readjustment, I will address the problems with universal solutions, standard practices, compliance, fairness, risk mitigation, and efficiency and implement them in a system that is deeply biased and flawed.

Years ago, while I was an agency director, an African American employee was disciplined by their Latinx supervisor after a complaint about their productivity. The staff member resisted the disciplinary action and made a very strident case that the accusations and proposed consequences were unfair. Over the three decades I have served as a director and clinical leader, very few staff have been suspended, and none were given as much time as this person. I read through the infraction and the appeal. I discussed the situation with my supervisor, who was Black, and the human resources person, who was Latinx. My recommendation was to reduce the suspension to a warning. I was told that while this was my decision, it was not good practice to contradict the supervisor. I went forward with the reduction. The employee was angry that the discipline had not been removed entirely, the supervisor felt I undermined them, and the HR administrator told me I set a bad precedent. My act potentially softened the degree of harm but did not touch the system of harm that is built around racist policies.

## Final Thoughts

I arrived early for a racial awareness conversation with Dr. Kenneth Hardy. A white woman who I did not know arrived a few minutes later. We said hello to each other and acknowledged our earliness. She explained, "I'm German; the trains always run on time," unaware that this reference would trigger my immediate association with the trains deployed to deport European Jews to Nazi death camps. I smiled and said nothing. Rage swallowed my being and impeded my focus. I have reflected on that moment often. My Jewish self responded automatically with a visceral reaction and consideration of the near destruction of the Jews by the hands of Nazi Germany. She, on the other hand, was connecting with my whiteness. She was unable to see my Jewishness, and I failed to afford her that opportunity. Metabolizing my whiteness means I need to afford Black and Brown people's grief and rage the opportunity not to be silenced, misdirected, or disregarded. I need to have "double vision."

Racialized trauma is transmitted and sustained in the context of relationships and therefore must be healed in relationships. Lieberman et al. (2015) wrote that to start healing from trauma we must "speak the unspeakable" (p. 14). To this I would add we must hear the unhearable and ultimately do the undoable. For me this has meant holding and loving my Jewish and white identities and endeavoring to get to a place of uncomfortable armistice, negotiating the richness of my Jewish culture and resisting erasing the impacts and privileges of my whiteness.

Looking in the mirror and across the landscape in health care requires that we understand the ways embedded whiteness in practices, procedures, and policies creates and sustains inequity.

If my wiser older self could consult with my younger self, I would offer three lessons. First, look at your family genogram through many lenses and specifically center the impact of anti-Black racism and whiteness; embracing our subjugated and privileged identities means we connect with more humility and more authenticity. Second, curiosity opens doors, and certainty closes them; we need to ask ourselves and those we work with what has happened rather than what is wrong. Finally, for those of us that have benefited from white privilege, we need to recognize our collective accountability for the pain and rage of Black and Brown people and to consistently marshal the courage to disrupt the proliferation of the status quo.

**KEN EPSTEIN, PHD, LCSW,** is the principal of P.R.E.P for Change Consulting (kenepstein.org), helping organizations promote and achieve culture change by implementing and sustaining relational organizational practices. He also serves as a leadership coach for Trauma Transformed (traumatransformed.org). Dr. Epstein has worked within family and youth service programs since 1981 in clinical and administrative positions at nonprofit, university, and government agencies. Most recently, he retired from his behavioral health director position at the San Francisco Department of Children, Youth and Their Families. In this capacity he developed and led the vision and implementation of Trauma Informed Systems, which has become an organizational promising practice. Beginning in 1990, Dr. Epstein has specialized in developing, supervising, teaching, and practicing couples and family therapy. He is the founding director of the Intensive Family Model Clinic that he replicated at University of California, San Francisco, where he currently serves on the clinical faculty in the department of psychiatry.

## References

*Alexander, M. (2012).* The new Jim Crow: Mass incarceration in the age of colorblindness *(Rev. ed.). New Press.*

*Brodkin, K. (1998).* How Jews became white folks and what that says about race in America. *Rutgers University Press.*

*Cohon, J. D., & Cooper, B. A. (1999). Kinship support network: Edgewood's program model and client characteristics.* Children and Youth Services Review, 21*(4), 311–338. https://doi.org/10.1016/S0190-7409(99)00023-7*

*Du Bois, W. E. B. (1897).* Strivings of the Negro people. *Atlantic Monthly Company.*

*Fanon, F. (2008).* Black skin, white masks. *Grove Press.*

*Frankl, V. E. (1962).* Man's search for meaning: An introduction to logotherapy. *Beacon Press.*

*Goldstein, E. L. (2006).* The price of whiteness: Jews, race, and American identity. *Princeton University Press.*

*Hardy, K. V. (2013). Healing the hidden wounds of racial trauma.* Reclaiming Children and Youth, 22*(1), 24–28.*

*King, M. L., Jr. (2000).* Why we can't wait. *Penguin. (Original work published 1963)*

*Lieberman, A. F., Ippen, C. G., & Van Horn, P. (2015).* Don't hit my mommy! A manual for child-parent psychotherapy with young children exposed to violence and other trauma. *Zero to Three Press.*

*McGoldrick, M., Gerson, R., & Petry, S. S. (2008).* Genograms: Assessment and intervention. *W. W. Norton & Company.*

*McIntosh, P. (2019). White privilege and male privilege: A personal account of coming to see correspondences through work in women's studies. In M. McGoldrick & K. V. Hardy (Eds.),* Re-visioning family therapy: Addressing diversity in clinical practice *(3rd ed., pp. 215–225). Guilford Press.*

*Morales, A. L. (2002, April).* Red sea. *Aurora Levins Morales. http://www.auroralevinsmorales.com/red-sea.html*

*Ofri, D. (2020).* When we do harm: A doctor confronts medical error. *Beacon Press.*

*Reis, S. P., Wald, H. S., & Weindling, P. (2019). The Holocaust, medicine and becoming a physician: The crucial role of education.* Israel Journal of Health Policy Research, 8*(55), 1–5. https://doi.org/10.1186/s13584-019-0327-3*

*Snowden, L. R. (2003). Bias in mental health assessment and intervention: Theory and evidence.* American Journal of Public Health, 93*(2), 239–243. https://doi.org/10.2105/ajph.93.2.239*

*Stevenson, B. (2014).* Just mercy: A story of justice and redemption. *Spiegel & Grau.*

*Vonnegut, K. (2009).* Breakfast of champions: A novel. *Dial Press.*

*Washington, H. A. (2006).* Medical apartheid: The dark history of medical experimentation on black Americans from colonial times to the present. *Doubleday.*

*Wilkerson, I. (2020).* Caste: The origins of our discontents. *Random House.*

*Young, K. (2020, June 28).* It's been a minute *[Radio broadcast]. NPR.*

# CHAPTER 7

# Getting Acquainted with My White Self

TOBY BOBES, PHD

My core perspectives and philosophical stance about teaching, supervision, diversity, and social justice have evolved over my 40 years as a therapist, supervisor, teacher, and author. My personal experiences and cultural history inform the principles, practices, biases, and assumptions of my personal and professional life. I am a white, financially privileged, Jewish, heterosexual woman. I grew up in a middle-class family. I was educated in mostly white educational and training institutions; thus, my perceptions and worldviews are both informed and limited by my educational experiences. I am 81 years old and able-bodied. I am a proud mother of three adult children and grandmother of four. During the process of writing this chapter, my husband of 58 years, Norman, passed away. I am deeply saddened. I am in the throes of grief with the peaks and valleys that come with the tremendous loss of my life partner and best friend.

Since my husband passed, I have begun to reflect deeply and viscerally upon other losses in my life as well, including the disavowal of my white self. This process began when I was a young girl, from the moment I had the ability to comprehend who I was. As I reflect on my life, it has been rather recently that I have begun to critically consider how I internalized messages of superiority and entitlement throughout a significant portion of my life. I have vivid memories of seemingly innocent and benign messages offered by my parents as they strongly encouraged me to select friends who were "like me" and cautioned that I should be fearful of anyone who was different from me. I grieve now for the pain and suffering of People of Color and for my contribution to their ongoing subjugation and oppression. While steeped in the racial inequities of the Deep South, in Atlanta, Georgia, I was part of society's silence in keeping race, and especially whiteness, invisible and unspoken. Until recently, my view of what it meant to be white had been a cognitive and intellectual process. Now my visceral experience of grief is a catalyst that opens up another level of knowing and expands my comprehension of what it means to be white.

I am at the age and stage of life where I have begun to reflect on my life as if looking through the rearview mirror. I have enjoyed an invigorating and insightful career as a clinician, author, and university professor. Throughout my life and career, I was keenly aware of many of these aspects of my life and how they both informed and enriched my life. I am also white, an identity I have lived with all my life but never consciously thought about in a critical way until I was 50 years old, and even then, not with in-depth self-examination. I never thought about how my whiteness defined or contributed to my life and impacted the relationships I have enjoyed. I never allowed myself to imagine what it would feel like if one of my children wanted to date or marry a person who wasn't white. As I think about my life over time, I am now forced to think about what implicit or explicit messages Norm and I offered our children about being white and how they should interact with those who were not white. What messages did we teach them by failing to teach and remind them that they were white? They knew they were Jewish, a fact that was important to us as a family. We did talk about race from time to time, and about "those people," but we never talked about what it meant to be white. I am genuinely reflecting on how it could be that someone like myself, a self-proclaimed and committed advocate for social justice with a visceral understanding of suffering, lived such a fulfilling life free from serious contemplation of my whiteness. For most of my life, my whiteness had never been named and remained very much invisible; thus, it was nearly impossible to critique or even acknowledge.

## A Story About My Other Mother

Ruby Stanton was an African American woman my family had hired as a housekeeper. Ruby was very special to me. She didn't just prepare meals and clean for our family; she also played a very valuable and instrumental role in parenting me and my sister. She was like a second mother. Ruby was the only person in my family with whom I felt comfortable and safe. Interestingly, neither as a child nor during much of my adult life did I spend much time wondering about Ruby, her family, her life, or about her in any context other than the services that she provided for my family and for me. This is a by-product of whiteness. As whites, it is easy to dismiss the humanity of Blacks and other People of Color. I am ashamed to admit that, as whites, it is commonplace for us to see People of Color in very utilitarian ways. That is, by the services they provide for us. I turned to Ruby for comfort, and she gave generously of her love and care to me and to my sister. I still ponder whether Ruby's own family was deprived of her love and attention when she spent so much time focusing on the needs of our family. As Monica McGoldrick (2008) wrote about her own similar personal experiences, "It is painful to realize that my love and benefit have meant someone else's loss and deprivation and that the two are intertwined" (p. 106).

I shared this story during a two-and-a-half-day racial sensitivity training that was facilitated by Ken Hardy. The group was comprised of thirty-three people in all: Black, Brown, and white. My disclosures to the group triggered painful memories and experiences for some African American participants who resonated deeply and identified with my story. They were the symbolic daughters of Ruby. Some were the daughters of mothers who had left them alone during the dawn of many mornings to provide care for families like mine. While I shared my warm, endearing, and nostalgic reflections about my second mother, Ruby, some of these women were reminded of an enduring, deeply seated, nameless pain, rooted in the trauma of racial subjugation and oppression. I experienced, in that moment, their suffering and anguish, which was inextricably connected to my benefit and entitlement. I came to realize more deeply and viscerally my participation in privilege. Many other participants responded emotionally to the stories that were shared.

As I take a critical and retrospective view of my life, pivotal poignant moments such as the one just described are crucial to learning, especially for whites who, like me, lived a life mostly oblivious to my whiteness. We need to seek out opportunities such as racial sensitivity trainings that offer group experiences in which whiteness is named in a relational context and in which participants venture outside of their comfort zones as they struggle with naming their white selves.

In this chapter, I will discuss the problem of not naming whiteness and some of the processes by which we avoid naming it. But first, I take a closer look at my social location with respect to the dimensions of race and class.

## A Personal Account of Race and Class

I cannot write about myself as a white person without also discussing my class. For me, race and class are inextricably interwoven and connected. Throughout my life, I have felt and still feel entitled to many advantages I enjoy based on the color of my skin and my financial privilege. My life is comfortable because of my easy and immediate access to resources such as my bank accounts and credit card. This immediate access is because of both my whiteness and my financial privilege. I say that I want an integrated community in my quest for racial equity, inclusion, and social justice. And yet, I have chosen to live in a community that is segregated along the dimensions of race and class. My values and my actions do not mesh. I am not proud of this, yet I want to hold on to my comforts and, ultimately, my privilege. It is painful when I speak with People of Color and experience in those moments what I feel deeply inside myself—my advantages, entitlements, and benefits that mean someone else is deprived and disadvantaged. At the core and foundation of this location of my race and class is the essence of my sense of belonging *and* how it excludes the People of Color who do not hold the advantages to which I feel entitled, based on the color of my skin and class and my financial privilege.

What can I do about this marked discrepancy between who I am and what I do? For starters, I am acknowledging who I really am and taking actions to bridge the gap between my being and doing. Writing and teaching are ways that I take responsibility for the power and privilege that I hold as a professional. And yet, as I look in the mirror, I ask myself: What else am I willing to do to bridge the gap? What, if anything, am I willing to give up? How much discomfort am I willing to tolerate in the continuing self-examination required in becoming more transparent? I am still grappling with these questions, or maybe, in all honesty, it is the answers to these questions that I fear or am reluctant to admit.

## Why Do We Avoid Naming Whiteness?

White people avoid feeling shame, pain, guilt, and discomfort by not naming whiteness, and we are terrified of facing the worst in ourselves. Ijeoma Oluo (2019) asserts, "you have to try to adjust to the feelings of shame and pain that come from being confronted with your own racism. You have to get over the fear of facing the worst in yourself" (p. 224). I have avoided naming whiteness to protect myself from feeling the shame, pain, and discomfort of looking at my racism. Naming whiteness means acknowledging how I contribute to the harm and suffering of People of Color. By not naming whiteness and by avoiding conversations about race, whites put the burden squarely on the shoulders of People of Color (Oluo, 2019).

For whites, there is a continual seduction to maintaining white solidarity and with it a thick wall of apathy and numbness that engulfs our consciousness (Quinn, Chapter 15). Quinn notes that "our hearts have been systematically and strategically desensitized to feeling the harm and suffering we inflict on Bodies of Culture" (Chapter 15, p. 265). Our educational institutions created, perpetuated, and protected whiteness (Mangram, Chapter 2). I taught for many years in educational institutions, and I experienced first-hand the thick wall of apathy that surrounded our learning community, thus maintaining white equilibrium. In faculty meetings, race and whiteness were rarely named. My white colleagues' silence, complicity, and oblivion to whiteness were pervasive. I, too, was complicit by not naming whiteness and how it blinds us, as whites, from seeing just how unfair and harmful it is to People of Color when racial ruptures in the classroom are left unattended and racial empathy is missing. I have heard colleagues suggest that racial ruptures emanate from "complicated interactions" and "problem students," suggesting that these difficult interactions are dynamics of certain students who are simply disruptive, having nothing to do with race. This is an example in which faculty and others in predominantly white educational communities fail to incorporate culturally accountable practices and tend to pathologize the behaviors of some students. I believe that our educational systems must offer racial sensitivity trainings to educators and trainers to promote both individual racial transformation as well as to advance critical changes in pedagogy and program development. In my experience, "Experiential Teaching and Learning is the hallmark of supervision and training designed to promote cultural sensitivity" (Hardy & Bobes, 2016, p. viii). When some groups are treated inequitably in educational systems, it is an ethical mandate to incorporate culturally accountable practices throughout systems. Change does not occur in isolation but at all levels of the system (Mock & Cho, 2020).

I am heartened by the cracks we are making in the thick wall of apathy in our learning communities. My white colleagues and I are developing courage in naming whiteness and venturing out to participate more fully in conversations about race. While I am happy with the signs of progress, I am also saddened because I can only imagine the gravity of damage that has been done to Students of Color over the years while we, as a faculty, struggled to find our racial selves. In many ways it is too little, too late. However, knowing that I am in community with other whites struggling to venture out beyond our comfort zones, I am hopeful that the more practice we have in talking about race, the more we will be able to welcome discomfort with an unrelenting commitment to remain curious.

I hope that the next generation of white professors and clinical supervisors can and will learn from the mistakes, transgressions, and microaggressions of those of us who lived our lives oblivious to our whiteness while luxuriating in it. I hope they will be bold and relentlessly self-reflective and self-interrogating and seize every moment to name, deconstruct, and actively challenge whiteness. I hope they will see early on what took me a lifetime to see, that they will recognize all of the sophisticated and robustly rewarding ways that we as whites are socialized and recruited to be complicit with white supremacy. I hope that they will see the acute suffering borne out of racial inequity and act before being asked to do so . . . not because it is politically correct, fashionable, or evidence of being woke, but because it is the ethical, moral, and humanist thing to do.

It is never too late to stand up and fight for racial and social justice; in fact, it is an ethical imperative. The locus of change resides with white people (DiAngelo, 2018). Education, learning, and activism are lifelong processes. It is an endless endeavor to challenge whiteness, yet we must. For me, the passion and excitement about learning is generated relationally, and our strength is in community and through our combined commitment to challenge whiteness.

## Closing Reflections

I am humbled by the task of naming whiteness and pledge to do so now in ways that I failed to do in the past. Although it is a daunting task, it is central to our collective survival. I remain hopeful that as whites share their stories of race and use their power responsibly, they will begin to name their whiteness, a powerful instrument of change. As we work alongside each other in sharing our stories about race, we have the opportunity to create "a community eager to name whiteness, celebrate Blackness, and, in a world still governed by systems of racial oppression, begin to see that there's another way" (Brown, 2020, p. 23). Naming whiteness enables us to move forward with the courage to engage more fully in relational risk-taking and authentic conversations about race. It is only when whites join together in critical self-examination that we can take our next steps toward racial equity, inclusion, and social justice.

The time is now for us to develop a proficiency in talking about race, name the whiteness in the room, and make it explicit. We need to look at how racism contributes to relational suffering. This chapter is an invitation for white people to join together in becoming activists and to work toward creating a sense of belonging and a place that we can all call home. It is never too late to start.

**Acknowledgment:** I wish to thank you, Kenneth Hardy, for your unwavering support, vision, and guidance that have been inspirational to me. I am deeply grateful for your generosity of time and wisdom in collaborating with me on my chapter.

**TOBY BOBES, PHD,** is a licensed marriage and family therapist with 28 years of experience teaching graduate-level courses and 18 years of experience in clinical supervision. Dr. Bobes has taught many supervision courses, and she is a CAMFT certified supervisor. Her career includes 28 years in private practice. Dr. Bobes is coauthor of two books focusing on couple and family work and coeditor of two books that focus on promoting cultural sensitivity in supervision and training. She has taught at Pacifica Graduate Institute and Antioch University, Santa Barbara, California.

## References

*Brown, A. C. (2020).* I'm still here: Black dignity in a world made for whiteness. *Virago Press.*

*DiAngelo, R. (2018).* White fragility: Why it's so hard for white people to talk about racism. *Beacon Press.*

*Hardy, K. V., & Bobes, T. (2016). Preface. In K. V. Hardy & T. Bobes (Eds.),* Culturally sensitive supervision and training: Diverse perspectives and practical applications *(pp. vii–viii). Routledge.*

*McGoldrick, M. (2008). Finding a place called "home." In M. McGoldrick & K. V. Hardy (Eds.),* Re-visioning family therapy: Race, culture, and gender in clinical practice *(2nd ed., pp. 97–113). Guilford Press.*

*Mock, M. R., & Cho, L. (2020, May/June). Cultural humility and responsiveness in family therapy.* The Therapist Magazine of the California Association of Marriage and Family Therapists, 32*(3), 10–16.*

*Oluo, I. (2019).* So you want to talk about race. *Seal Press.*

## CHAPTER 8

# Shunning the Shame of Being Black in a World of Whiteness

CYNTHIA CHESTNUT, PHD

CAPELLA UNIVERSITY

As a preacher's kid (PK), I grew up in a proud Black family, yet there was so much shame about skin color and being raised, during my elementary years, in the Projects, representing a poor socioeconomic status. I learned early what it meant to have shame about where you come from and who and what you are. I learned that I was supposed to be ashamed and not share my upbringing; the fear was that others, especially white people, would use it against me. "Assimilate as much as you can" was the subliminal message. I was told repeatedly that "education would be my freedom" and it would strengthen my voice and position in life. Education did help, but the biggest disappointment was the ethos, movement, or nature of whiteness as a very dominant force. I needed to learn to not receive, internalize, and welcome projections that defined me on the basis of being Black.

When I think of my journey of confronting whiteness, I have to think critically about my journey in discovering what it means to be Black. For some reason, the nuances of both of these processes are somewhat vague. However, I can say it has been a slow and evolutionary process and that even today, at 40 plus years of working through it, I am still evolving in this discovery. I was a child of the 1960s who was assigned to be among the first sets of Black children to desegregate a majority-white elementary school, and I do know that this experience was critical in the development of my racial identity. It was one of the first and most memorable personal experiences that informed me, in a very painful way, about the realities of what it meant to Black. It also shattered every idealistic notion that I might have had about the equality of the races. The messaging that accompanied desegregation was: "The white schools were better and only smart Black kids would be privileged to go to a white school." I didn't understand concretely what was wrong with the all-Black school I attended in my neighborhood; I just knew it was not as good as a white school. I am now amazed at how much I looked at during my early years but didn't see. For example, I also didn't realize the messages I internalized from seeing more white people than Black people on the black-and-white TV that was a fixture in our family's living room. I now realize that virtually all of the programs we watched as a family created, cultivated, and reinforced stereotypical messages about whiteness and Blackness.

Being a preacher's kid, I was taught and believed in the value of fairness and justice. These values were also reinforced in school by the songs we sang in assembly meetings about our American flag, songs about the importance of being a proud American and the importance of being a good Christian American. I didn't realize, at the time, that even these songs and the patriotic sentiment that was being strongly espoused was a deeply racialized, white affirming, anti-Black message. I never questioned or struggled with the contradiction of being a proud American and extolling the values of fairness and justice as a descendant of slavery. This was just one of many underlying reasons why I so desperately wanted to be treated like white people: because they appeared to be special people. That was the message I had internalized.

I knew that I sensed that white people were better than Black people, and I didn't know how or why I believed this. I just did. My life was inundated with messages of white superiority and Black inferiority. There was no dimension of my life devoid of these powerful messages. As a "PK" (preacher's kid), even my faith and religious practice were heavily saturated in whiteness. As a child, I didn't question it or think twice about it. I routinely prayed and worshipped images of a "white Jesus" in the pictures and on the stained-glass windows at my church. These messages gave me strong and subliminal messages about adoring the beauty, majesty, and deity of whiteness. It appeared that everything that was good, godly, and that had value, like Jesus, was white. I also knew that I could never be white; and unfortunately, I felt less than. In my efforts to assimilate into whiteness, I lightened my skin, especially when acne would give me dark spots. I straightened my hair with a hot comb and permed it to be as straight as it could be. I learned to hate and be ashamed of my hair texture, no matter what length it grew to, at a very early age. My efforts to shun the shame of being Black also created many hurdles for me to overcome. The issue of race seemed so complicated and fraught with struggle and confusion. In grade school and in middle school, Black female peers chided me and often wanted to fight. I felt intimidated by them and never quite understood why I was singled out. They constantly accused me of either "acting like I was white" or of thinking I was "better than Black girls." I was fighting racial battles that I didn't even have the ability to completely understand. Years later, and now that issues of race and whiteness are clearer to me, I still question what my Black classmates were saying and seeing. Maybe they saw a young girl who looked very much like them but didn't act like them, therefore they thought and projected that I didn't want to be associated with them. I *was* ashamed of them and how they represented Blackness, which also made me feel ashamed of being a Black girl who looked like them. After all, why would anybody want to be Black and inherit a position of inferiority as a second- or third-class citizen in comparison to being white? Any negative behavior we show is associated with being Black, poor, and ignorant. So, I thought that getting comfortable in my Blackness would be tantamount to asking for a life of inferiority.

These incessant struggles with race, skin color, and racial identity experiences were major influences in my formative years and significantly shaped my perceptions of being Black and what this meant. I realized that I could never be perceived separately from my skin color. I struggled with the reality that I could not be anyone other than what and how white people saw me to be as a Black person. I had to accept, despite my wishes to the contrary, that white people could or would only see me the way they thought of all Black people: less than and inferior. I learned that being a dark-skinned Black girl with kinky hair placed me at the bottom of the racial hierarchy and that the darker you are, the worse your life will be. I learned a powerful and enduring life lesson: lighter skin is good; white is better and best!

My struggles with my racial identity and private wishes to have lighter skin and straighter hair nagged and nabbed me throughout my adolescence and into adulthood. To embrace the hierarchy of whiteness, to be a lighter Black girl who straightened her hair to move freely was the beauty image I could settle with. It wasn't until young adulthood that I began to recognize out loud the grief associated with being different and deemed inferior, which led me to pursue my journey of self-discovery and self-love. It became important for me to engage in a process of self-acceptance and self-love. I had to discover ways to love and accept all parts of myself. I had spent my entire adolescence and much of my adulthood not appreciating and accepting myself. To love and accept myself, I had to develop a compassionate and intimate relationship with my dark skin, my hair, my body, and my intelligence; my early days of integrating into white schools had started the process that stripped me of my Black identity for much of my early life. My adolescence and adult life reinforced the negative internalization associated with being a second-class Black person in competition with lightness and whiteness. My life began to feel more anchored once I resigned from self-hate and began to proudly embrace my Blackness. My process of self-discovery tended to go reasonably well. My entry into the professional (white) world of work perpetuated familiar haunts and anxieties.

To my surprise, I didn't realize until much later in my adult life that, while working at my first professional job in my twenties, I made a conscious decision to closely study my boss, who was a very tall, slender, white, Christian man who would teach me how to survive and advance in my professional life. Why did I choose him? At the time I really didn't know, but I knew that he was organizationally above all the rest of us who worked at the agency; 98% of us were Black, 1% were Hispanic, and he was the only white person. He was also the white person who attended all of the executive meetings, where 95% of the leaders in this large national company were white. The other 5% were People of Color. As strange as it may seem, at the time I didn't realize I was once again lured by the appeal of whiteness. I saw him as a beacon of power and powerfulness. I wanted to make life better for myself, and I knew intuitively that doing so would require me to be a facsimile of him. I knew that I would need to be mindful of negative stereotypical ideas and of appearances that appeared Black or associated with Black behavior; failing to do so would significantly reduce my chances of being a "better me." This white man became my example of what it meant to be not only a good Christian but a powerful influential leader as well. He was educated, an executive, a leader, a family man, and, most of all, he represented a good white man that would show me how to conduct myself to get the attention I needed to demonstrate that I could assimilate. He would teach me how to behave in ways that would blind others to my differences, even though my Black skin was ever present. Once again, the wishes from my elementary school days were haunting me: I wanted to be treated like them! I wanted access to what I saw as the privileged places, conversations, and entitlements they appeared to have. I needed to conform my looks, making sure my hair, makeup, and clothes conformed to the cultural workplace values. The validation I received made me think I was on the right track toward being successful. I was recognized as a model employee. I felt accepted because they saw me as one of their own, although I was a different color. My Christian upbringing was my main cultural orientation, more so than being Black. It was very difficult for me to differentiate my Black identity from the trauma I internalized in not fully accepting myself. My ignorance was in not knowing the extent of my self-hate and in my inability to articulate the assets and beauty of my Blackness. This became even clearer to me once I left that company to work for a hospital where a Black female colleague told me I wasn't Black enough. I was stunned because that message was familiar. I thought I was a progressive young professional Black woman at this stage of my life, yet I am still not Black enough. What did this mean? I didn't even understand the internal conflict that roared inside of me. I am Black, yet I am baffled and offended when I am accused of and bullied for not being Black enough. This is a narrow glimpse of what it is like to constantly have to wrestle with the complexities of race and to negotiate Blackness in a white supremacist society.

One might say my journey was about finding and forming my Black identity. However, it was more complicated and multifaceted than simply focusing on my Blackness. I needed not only to find ways to embrace all the parts of being Black that I associated with inferiority and ultimately rejection but also to simultaneously recognize how I associated whiteness and all the dimensions associated with it as not just better, but superior.

In the workplace, the more I associated whiteness with positive connotations, such as being good and better, the more I internalized it while simultaneously rejecting my dark skin and kinky hair and anything else that made me quintessentially Black. The subjugation of Blackness made sense to me. The world I exist in within this country has a well-established racial hierarchy that always situates white at the top and Black at the bottom. If I, and others like me, fail to demonstrate that we are white enough to belong, our abilities will likely be ignored and we risk being left behind. These racialized rules of engagement are subliminally expressed, and yet they are quite clear and virtually universal. Being white or whit*ish* meant that I had to be certain that my words were enunciated clearly, with good grammar and no accent. It meant I was to blend in and not allow myself to be associated with negative stereotypes associated with being "ghetto," which is often code for "too Black." There was no one standing over me saying: You are too Black and your hair is not quite what we expected. The messages were more nuanced and subtle. The nucleus of the conversations was never overtly about race or my Blackness, but about "professionalism" instead. These powerful, subtle, and clear messages shaped me professionally in ways that were so deeply engrained that they remained securely buried well beneath my consciousness for quite some time. Constantly brushing up against other professional Black women who often informed me, again and again, that I wasn't Black enough continued to expose my disavowed Black self, who was swimming in a sea of self-hatred. I had a thirst, hunger, and desperation to discover and become acquainted with my authentic Black self, to be bold enough to fully embrace the beautiful Black woman that I was, and yet it was difficult to do.

In ways that are hard to admit, I know that I was fully distracted by whiteness. I felt I was constantly being judged by the color of my skin, the texture of my hair, and whether I perpetuated stereotypical ideas of Blackness. I constantly questioned my role as a Black professional and whether I had been hired to serve some ulterior motive for whites. Am I supposed to serve as a compliant vessel that is a voice on their behalf? At times I felt I was being used, in my professional role, as the "token" Black who would sometimes tune into racial issues as they became apparent and was expected to redirect the focus onto the similarities of our diverse team. It was always welcomed and appreciated when I pointed out the similarities of the group and remained silent about race. I now realize how the tactic of fitting in by noting similarities was also quite destructive, dismissive, and insensitive regarding race. While my actions often facilitated opening up conversations about our common ground, it also shut out people who may have wanted or needed to be engaged and heard regarding racial differences. I also realize that another integral part of my unspoken duty as the Black professional was to manage the temperament, anger, and perceived "hostile communication" expressed by other Blacks regarding racial concerns. My conviction and stance on issues of race were, "I must modify who I am to help white people become comfortable with me and other Black people. I have to sacrifice myself and always be a team player. I must not complain about race and must make sure I see both ways so that I am not tainted about race." It was my "duty" to ensure that People of Color were nonthreatening, verbally and nonverbally, and I refrained from communicating in ways that white people would misunderstand, misinterpret, or ultimately feel threatened by. It was my job to keep People of Color in line, to protect everyone's image, my image, and to ensure white people's comfort. This is what it meant to display high levels of professionalism, even if it cost you your soul and assaulted your sense of self. I had to admit that I felt commissioned to keeping the People of Color in line. Whiteness is powerful, seductive, cunning, and manipulative. When it is presented as the ultimate of the ultimate, it is difficult to rebuff it, especially when it simultaneously marginalizes all other ways of being. I am still discovering how to differentiate and recognize my internal processes to be more transparent and honest with myself and recover from my racial trauma and complicity with whiteness.

I can see so clearly now the ways in which my complicity with whiteness extended to virtually every activity I participated in as a professional. Early in my professional career, I embraced a universal theoretical position that espoused focusing on similarities and not being distracted by differences. I had been trained to believe that focusing on similarities and operating from what Hardy (2020) refers to as the "*theoretical myth of sameness*" would make me an effective clinician, equipping me to work with and serve anyone. Recognizing that *we are all human* would enable me to be just and fair while operating within an established set of rules, policies, and practices that applied equally to everyone's actions. This meant that if I participated in interviewing and hiring, candidates needed to be a good fit with regard to values along with the skills, training, and education they had. The principle within itself seemed to be fair and to be the right position to take, but what I didn't realize was that there were so many other variables to consider, like what were the demographics of the population served by the agency? Are we hiring people from the community to match the population? I originally didn't consider the importance of race and culture because the agencies I represented didn't acknowledge these factors. I was inattentive to culture, although I did at least think about race. Again, the leadership at the institutions where I was employed consistently had mostly white people in executive level positions over People of Color, which seemed the norm that was accepted and not questioned. These messages told me that being white gained you opportunity, leadership, and wealth. Therefore, although I am a Person of Color with enough education and training to work in a leadership role, I had to work twice as hard to prove it and secure the mentorships to hone my skills and abilities to function accordingly. I noticed that I wasn't included in some conversations and that the white staff appeared to associate more frequently with people who looked more like them. It made me question myself, wondering if something was wrong with me. I noticed white people receiving mentorships and support that wasn't offered to me. I, along with the other Black people, continued to question myself and my abilities. It appeared that white people were getting opportunities that People of Color weren't getting. There were many times I questioned my ability: Was there something about me, or does my race and image have something to do not only with me not getting certain opportunities but other Black people as well? It couldn't be that there were no, or not enough, qualified People of Color. In retrospect, it was easier for me to question myself than it was to interrogate whiteness.

My continued "Self of the Therapist" work as a clinician has placed me on a path not only of questioning myself but also interrogating all of the powerful forces that impinge on me and the work I do with clients. I have been on a steady path of what Hardy (2018) refers to as *self-discovery designed to promote self-recovery*. I have been actively engaged in a process of understanding the deleterious, infectious, and pervasive effects that whiteness has had on me as a Black woman. Being in healing spaces with racially aware People of Color and self-interrogating white colleagues has been powerfully healing, racially affirming, and transformative. I have been warmly held as I have attended to the numbing effects of the racial trauma that I had surrendered to, but also suppressed for years. Being free to explore and deconstruct whiteness in a comprehensive and uninhibited way has also granted me the freedom to release myself and my soul from the racially subjugated thoughts, feelings, behaviors, and messages that aligned to keep me stuck in a place of self-hatred. I no longer aspire to be lighter or to embrace whiteness because I no longer accept the lies that I have been fed. To really know myself, my history, and who I am has been liberating. My journey is not over, nor is it even close to being complete. However, the only reason I was able to write this chapter is because I have discovered the depth and greatness of my Blackness. After all these years, I love me and finally accept who I am.

Listening to the echoes of the voices that told me I wasn't Black enough, I realized that I needed to understand that perception I held. I needed to know how to communicate to myself and others who honor my values on being authentic and transparent without fear, with racial awareness. It is my aim and desire as a clinician to maintain consciousness of myself and recognize that even while I am in my roles, everything I do matters! In the context of serving, how I conduct myself is a message and a model. It's important for me to be grounded in my own truth, so that what I do truly represents who I am.

I embrace subscription to the eight C's Schwartz & Brennan (2013) describe in being "self-led," evidenced by being *curious* about living this life; having *courage* to face my truth no matter how bad it is; giving *compassion* to myself and others; attending to my own intersectionality and the *connectedness* of my parts; walking in *confidence* even if I feel insecure; searching for *clarity* without fear of the emotions I will experience; pursuing *calmness* to restore my peace to live in the amazing resilience that keeps me whole; and, finally, being open to *creatively* recognizing the endless possibilities of change while never resigning my hope that healing is possible.

**CYNTHIA CHESTNUT, PHD,** is an approved supervisor and clinical fellow for the American Association for Marriage and Family Therapy. She is a postgraduate alumnus of Penn Council for Relationships and has a PhD in couple and family therapy. She has served couples and families for over 20 years as a therapist, supervisor, and cofounder of a marriage and family therapy community-based program in Philadelphia. Dr. Chestnut has also led a research team studying the five largest family shelters in the city of Philadelphia to understand recidivism of homeless families in city-contracted shelters. She presently serves as an intervention director under Philadelphia's Child Welfare Initiative Community Umbrella Agencies 1 and 7, serving districts 22 and 25; manages a private practice; and serves as a part-time faculty member at Capella University and adjunct faculty at Wilmington University.

## References

*Hardy, K. V. (2018). The self of the therapist in epistemological context: A multicultural relational perspective.* The Journal of Family Psychotherapy, *29(1), 17–29. https://doi.org/10.1080/08975353.2018.1416211*

*Hardy, K. V. (2020, October 17–November 21).* Uncovering racial trauma: Racially sensitive therapy for clients of color *[8-week online training]. Greater Malden Behavioral Health / BMHA INC. / Eikenberg Academy for Social Justice, New York, NY, United States.*

*Schwartz, J., & Brennan, B. (2013).* There's a part of me. . . . *Trailheads Press.*

# SECTION IV

# CROSS-RACIAL ENCOUNTERS AND RELATIONSHIPS

## CHAPTER 9

# Herding Cats

## The Burdensome and Exhausting Task of Negotiating Whiteness

OVITA F. WILLIAMS, PHD

In the last several years, it occurred to me there were key moments in my life related to success that have been heavily influenced by white people, white women in particular. This realization left me curious about how this could be, and I write this chapter as a way of exploring my connections with white people and the ways in which I have been influenced, encouraged, and supported to succeed with the aid of white women. It is a complex relationship, but also one in which I am both comforted and bewildered, confused and grateful, angry and hopeful. White people have both positively influenced and harmed me, and I have been conflicted in these relationships as I have become more active in antiracist work and aware of the centrality of whiteness. I have been both positively influenced as well as harmed by white people in my pursuit of higher education, in my profession as a social worker, and in my academic role in social work education. This chapter will explore my personal and professional relationships with white people and their whiteness, including lessons learned in my experiences navigating the centrality of whiteness.

## Centrality of Whiteness

Centrality of whiteness refers to the way in which my very existence in life is defined and shaped by white people's decisions about me, from grade school all the way through my career. My success, the place that I am in life, is heavily influenced by negotiating these spaces and being beholden to white folks' decisions about what I can have and what I cannot have, who I can be and who I cannot be. Don't get me wrong, I stand on my own two feet and have worked hard to achieve what I have: my degrees, my job, my financial stability, and my achievements. I am clear about the effort I put out in order to be independent and self-sufficient. However, making it through a world where white people control the doors that open and close or the granting or denying of access is heavily influenced by the determinations of non-Black people. Sadly, due to discrimination and oppression, Black people have not had the power to determine if I was capable enough to move up or gain public acknowledgment and respect. Unfortunately, these decisions were always influenced ultimately by whiteness. Would I be where I am today if it weren't for white people deciding that they felt I was capable enough, good enough, smart enough, able enough to be allowed through the door? That door remains locked unless its opening is decided by the privileges that come with white racial identity, people in positions of power and decision-making about Black lives. My access to opportunities, advancements, and the ability to earn a living are dependent on white people. This realization has left me almost immobile because I had not, until recently, felt the enormous reality of this fact.

Along this journey of realizing that the centrality of whiteness has been all-consuming to the way I lived and functioned, I began to think about the impact. Did I have to give up my Blackness to be accepted and enter spaces of success, awards, and accolades? My Blackness is always the center of my existence, how I am identified, how my family lived; but I have inevitably had to step back, hold my tongue, dress a certain way, straighten my hair, and be educated in compliance with the dictates of the dominant and imposing white culture.

I learned a number of valuable, yet problematic, lessons about being Black in the midst of whiteness. What follows are seven key lessons and examples from my personal experiences as I make sense of the impact of racism.

## Early Years

Politeness and discipline were exemplified throughout my earlier education years by my Caribbean parents, who in the late 1960s left their home for the shores of the United States. Speaking respectfully to my primary school teachers, who were mostly white, was expected in my household. Immigrating meant fitting in—not standing out for bad behavior. It meant being an upstanding citizen. Leaving Guyana as young parents, mom and dad knew opportunities would be limited if they did not take the leap of faith to establish a better life for their children. Education was emphasized at home as a way out, as a way to make money, and as a way to be respected and show respect. Growing up Black and Caribbean in the United States meant that there were messages ingrained in my head about toeing the line, remaining quiet unless spoken to, adjusting my gaze, and observing my manners. Bringing home bad grades or negative report cards about rude behavior or absences were not allowed and I received severe consequences if I did.

My schools, from kindergarten through high school, were all within walking distance of our home. During the two brief years I spent in a predominantly Black middle school, corporal punishment was the norm—traditional West Indian parenting carried over to the school—and it was common to witness a child or two on the public auditorium stage being punished with licks for being disrespectful, fighting, or some other offense deemed inappropriate.

### *Lesson #1: Act right and white folks will raise you up and reward you with gifts*

The first time I recall a white person taking interest in me and my education was in junior high school, when Mr. S, a white man, treated me as his favorite. I came to realize good grades and good behavior meant accolades and limited scrutiny. I was rewarded for being the good Black kid in a neighborhood in which the statistics were against us in the 1970s and early 1980s. My parents felt honored, and they awarded me with ice cream cake and small change for my good behavior and proper educational endeavors. My success was their success. My good citizenship awards and medals from city government honors and pats on my parents' backs from grade-school teachers meant that they had made the right decision to leave their homeland. My father beamed with pride each year we graduated from somewhere, and to this day he proudly inquires about my doctoral studies, sharing my success with his friends on Facebook. His father was a high-seated educator in Guyana, which was colonized by the British, and I know my grandfather would have been proud of me.

As I graduated from middle school, Mr. S rewarded me for my good behavior by giving me a token, a gift, a perfume I had never heard of before, Elizabeth Arden's *Blue Grass Mist*. This sweet-smelling fragrance was intoxicating, and I wanted more. Some may consider it inappropriate for a grown white man to give a young Black girl such an intimate gift. I didn't realize or consider it anything at the time. Years later, I recall the perfume as a symbol saying, *I kept in line; I must have made him comfortable enough; I behaved myself.* It felt nice, and my parents were proud of me reaching these heights. After all, they did come to the United States with hopes of us succeeding in this foreign land of plenty. If it meant making sure I acted the part, and I did, that meant they had succeeded.

### *Lesson #2: Act right, get good grades, and white folks will hand you the key to success and help you get there*

In high school, I achieved the number three status in my class, nearly making salutatorian but good enough to capture the white gaze once again. Our guidance counselor, a white woman, was favorably drawn to my academic prowess and encouraged me to attend college. My parents would be made proud yet again during these adolescent years when I behaved myself and kept on the narrow ledge toward success. I didn't even think about cutting school and going to hooky parties. My quiet, diminutive, white counselor introduced me to colleges and universities beyond my understanding, beyond my scope of realization and consideration. First, I had no idea how I would pay for college, and second, would my strict, family-oriented West Indian parents let me leave home? She asked me if I had heard of Brown, Columbia, Vassar, Dartmouth. I hadn't. She made me believe I could go to these places, and she walked me through the maze of applying mostly to predominantly white institutions. I noticed her interest did not extend to other kids, the youth who misbehaved or, maybe, to her did not seem motivated. Although my mom was not thrilled about me going far away, she was pleased I had conducted myself in such a way that I reached another milestone: going off to college. My guidance counselor encouraged me, said I was capable, and made me believe I could achieve success by going to a "good" college.

*Lesson #3: To reach success, you can hold on to your Black identity and keep it quiet, as long as you also play the part of whiteness and white culture*

One summer, I was invited out to the University of Southern California as part of a special program for high school Students of Color interested in science and math. A Black woman doctor was our mentor, and she took me under her wing that summer, escorting me to the Compton hair salons to get my Janet Jackson, 1980s, *When I Think of You* hairstyle on point. I saw my first and only Roberta Flack concert and ate In-N-Out Burger and sushi for the first time. She also took me to the Polo Store on Rodeo Drive, and I stayed at her beautiful Beverly Hills home where she pointed out the stars' homes. I was exposed to a whole other life, a life I questioned whether I could ever have. Maybe her message was that I could also have this life, or maybe she was pointing out the duality of Blackness, the *double consciousness* associated with being Black, as W. E. B. Du Bois (1903) discusses. Astutely sharing an inevitable phenomenon, my summer mentor silently explained this sense of two-ness, a balancing act of living in the glory of my beautiful Black body while having to restrain this joy at times to simultaneously act and fit into the ideals of white cultural norms. Du Bois (1903) noted over a hundred years ago that balancing this *double self* is about trying to maintain both worlds, being both Black and being American (white America specifically). Maintaining or combining both ways of being is tremendously arduous and impossible without losing oneself and, ultimately, the opportunities to succeed. I would forever have my life in two different worlds—in my Blackness, my Black West Indian pride and simultaneously in a world of white privilege and whiteness. But would I ever have full access if I didn't know how to balance these identities carefully and act the part by exemplifying more conventional approaches dictated by white dominance?

To me, negotiating the centrality of whiteness was holding both my deep Guyanese, Afro-Caribbean upbringing while sitting in white places as an obedient observer and allowing myself to engage and comfort white people around me. The seeds were sown. The message was clear. I was taught to respect all adults regardless of race. Knowing my place and succeeding in higher education meant being professional and espousing white supremacy culture (Okun, 2001) while staying true to my Guyanese heritage. This foundation, I believe, led to how I maneuvered and even "coped" with white people along my journey.

## Adult Years

Vassar, the first predominantly white space I encountered, was an interesting experience. On that predominantly white campus, the Black Student Union was my salvation; it was a place to awaken my Black revolutionary insights. Living with the centrality of whiteness at a predominantly white institution (PWI) for Black students means finding your place, fitting in, or maybe dropping out.

### *Lesson #4: Be Black and proud, but cautiously avoid too much activism; strike a balance and toe the line or you might lose everything*

During my first semester, when I was on the verge of leaving school, I called home to mom and asked her if I had made the right decision. I was clearly not smart enough. Though I was an A student with a passion for English in high school, I was now pulling a C average with poor grades in English. The white students around me seemed to know English better than me, write better than me, and receive constant praise for their writing from the white professors. I almost sank. I, as a young Black college student, almost let the centrality of whiteness at a PWI take me down. I can't recall what my mother said or how I pulled myself together to keep going, but I decided to stay in school. For me, the supports included sitting with my Black friends at lunch, celebrating Kwanzaa, and holding building-takeovers, demanding the improvement of the school's treatment of Black students. These coping strategies, along with befriending the other forty Black students, played a part in my making it through the vast maze of whiteness around me. Yet, even then, I was not as involved in the racism fight and protests as my Black peers who took front row, planned, hit the media, sieged the main building, and were threatened with never graduating and receiving their degrees. No, I was on the periphery, always knowing the risks were too great. In retrospect, I was afraid of not making it, not being accepted fully by the dominant white culture if I didn't maintain some part of the status quo.

*Lesson #5: To make it, your life depends on the decisions white people make about your ability to be successful and on them giving you their permission or not*

My job acquisitions and promotions were directly impacted by the decisions of white people, who had my professional career hanging by a thin thread, and by their perception of me. Black people are beholden to white people inviting us to the table and caring enough or recognizing enough of our abilities and qualifications to promote us. That is power; it is also a sad reality. As People of Color, we know this; we are hyperaware that in the spaces we want to enter, our success will be strictly dependent on white people making a decision about our ability to succeed and to make it up the ladder. We could be kicked down that ladder just as quickly as we were allowed a leg up.

White people decided to take a chance and hire me or invite me to take part in projects, trainings, workshops, and publishing. It surprises me and I am conflicted that it was white women who hired me for significant career jumps. At these critical moments, I had the bittersweet sense of wanting to accept the offers to run a program, teach a class, facilitate a workshop, or write a piece, feeling honored and excited about entering through the proverbial door of success or gaining a seat at the table. These offered advancements would bring me increased visibility and disposable income, helping me to do things I never could have done on my own or with help from any sort of anticipated family wealth or inheritance to support my economic stability. With these invitations from white people, I was able to buy my first home, send my daughter to college, get a car, travel, and start a consulting business. A conflicting decision: to turn away these offers because they were extended by white people who, by the nature of their racial identity, were racist, would leave me and my daughter way behind, forever relegated to always playing catch up to my white colleagues in life and in the professional world. Taking the benevolent handouts from white counterparts meant I could move ahead, maybe faster than if I rambled along solely on my resources as a Black woman, already affected by a long history of racial discrimination and inequality. One does not have to look far to view the manner in which racism produces detrimental disparities between Black and white people in wealth, income, and longevity, even among those with the same access to education. For example, in the United States, 72% of white people own their own homes, a sure sign of wealth, compared to 43% of Black families (Vega, 2016). A fear of being just another statistic may have been one rationale for my acceptance of the opportunities offered to me along the way, especially when analyzed through a lens of historical white supremacy and racialization of success.

On the flip side, when I wasn't promoted professionally, it was a direct decision made by white people and people who have closer proximity to whiteness than I will ever have. Even with established leadership examples and positive evaluations and favorable relationships with people I supervised, the times I was not promoted were because of decisions made by white people about my future. At one of my jobs, two white colleagues went by themselves and planned out how they would create a whole unit and, oh, by the way, give me a supervisor role. Throwing me a dog bone! I was glad and felt they must have known what they were doing. Looking back, their whiteness and their privilege gave them credibility and assured them they would be able to make the case to the directors to create a department. I have unforgiveable and unforgettable deeply rooted shame now to think how I acquiesced and thanked them for at least bestowing me a title, though very little power. After years of excellent work as a supervisor, clinician, and community planner at the same agency, the decision by white supervisors to promote me to codirector (not director) with a white woman who came *after* me, was hurtful. I stood up for myself then, but no one cared, no one listened, and, short of making allegations of discrimination to Human Resources, I settled.

My dreams and success were thwarted yet again at another job during a humiliating exercise of parading me in front of my colleagues through an intensive interview process, even after years of excellent reviews, to finally tell me I wasn't good enough. After two years of being an acting leader, my hopes of a promotion were crushed with a decision made by white men and, even more hurtful, non-Black People of Color, leaving me angered and confused. Demoralized, devastated, I almost did not rise from this last racialized episode. How many times must I experience doors slamming in my face before there is one ounce of recognition of the assault and injustice?

*Lesson #6: If white people really like you and see potential, they will help you, even invite you into their circle; it is conditional: just be a "good" Black person*

White women helped me achieve success in my career as a social worker, from professors to advisors to mentors, colleagues, and friends. Along the path, they gave me advice, offered me jobs and board memberships, and invited me to collaborate with them on projects. I visited homes, became part of families, was offered extended weekend stays in houses (by myself with full access), and generally was accepted as part of their world. White women wrote my recommendations for the PhD program I attended and were some of my biggest champions. How do I make sense of this as a Black woman? Interestingly, they were liberal, white, some of them Jewish, women with an extensive history in social work. They were human rights activists and feminists and even would call themselves antiracist white women.

There was a certain sort of white person I seemed to attract in my life, those who have an awareness of Black bodies as devalued, mistreated, and who would get behind advocating against racism, maybe attend a few protests, steep themselves in antiracist work, and show up as fighting for that cause. Danger was not a feeling I experienced with these white women who seemed to have seen something in me and to be comfortable with me. Negotiating these relationships has been a double-edged sword. I have both benefited and felt guilty to be receiving the sort of open doors these relationships have afforded me. I had no expectations; it just seemed to be the natural flow of our conversations and gatherings. I was safe, I felt safe myself around them, and maybe I am seen as a "safe" Black person. But what is an unsafe Black person to these white women? What would I have to do or say to create discomfort and be excluded from these white spaces? I didn't grow up as they did, I didn't have access to a house or two, or long partnerships built on combined wealth, or colonialist roots in this country.

I attempted to maintain my Black identity in these relationships, to show up as my authentic self. Honestly speaking, I often had to wear a mask, take cues from topics of conversations, observe mannerisms, and follow their lead to decide what version of me needed to be present. Again, the double consciousness. I am not sure if speaking with my Caribbean Patwa in their midst, blasting Cardi B on the car radio on a ride to the beach, sharing the journey of my locs during a conversation on hair, laughing about a recent episode of *black-ish* (Anderson et al., 2014), or sharing commentary about the previous evening's BET Awards would in any way be understood or appreciated as a major part of my experience, my world.

### *Lesson #7: You can only go so far with negotiating whiteness without falling apart*

These earlier lessons laid the foundation for what was to come, how I was making sense of my connections with white people, particularly women. White women would offer me a way of navigating the waters, showing me friendship as acceptance of my Blackness. Did I see them as good white people who were not out to harm me, but who liked me and truly wanted to offer their wisdom and guidance? Lately, understanding whiteness and white guilt, I wonder if their investing in me, a Black woman, might be a form of *credentialing* (DiAngelo, 2019). How did/do I make white women feel comfortable? Do I speak their language, do I avert my eyes, do I laugh at their jokes? Am I appeasing the parts of them they would never acknowledge as truly racist? Did my demeanor say, "It is ok, I don't blame you for years of hate and violence"? Is it the quiet way I offer guidance through their white racial journey of awakening without blaming or calling them out? Wrapped up with my upbringing to be respectful and nice was also my natural inclination to be liked and accepted. Possibly, these characteristics allowed for the easiness that white people feel around me.

Losing these white women as a significant part of my life is an interesting scenario to ponder. I go to white women for family advice, career advice—I trust they know how to work systems. They must have insight into navigating these spaces. They have given me some tools, some access, and mentorship. They know about my family, my love stories, my hopes and dreams, and they kept pushing me to succeed all the way through.

In my recent search for a new therapist I decided it was essential that the person be a Woman of Color, preferably Black. All my prior therapists have been white, mostly white women. Race never came up; racism was never addressed. If I tried to discuss my lack of job promotion through the experience of being Black and a woman, it still was never discussed. The therapist's response was more of a cursory, "That must be hard." Drained by the balancing act of being Black in the United States in white spaces and taking care of the emotions of white people, I am exhausted, and seeking a Therapist of Color has been necessary; maybe the centrality of whiteness around me and in me has taken its toll. Negotiating white spaces and acting the part and being respectful has caught up with me. At this time in my life, when I am facilitating antiracist work, seeking a Black therapist feels necessary. The exhaustion of trying to make sense of racism and to be antiracist when white people have been both helpful and harmful is tiresome. I am feeling burned out, always on alert, never having my guard fully down among white people.

## Present Moment

After a time of relative, eerily quiet racial unrest, but by no means ended in the United States. I woke up to the news that Ahmaud Arbery, while taking a jog, was stalked by two white men, driving in a truck, who shot him to death. It took several months for these white men to be arrested, and then the case was eventually presented to the Grand Jury. I immediately thought, "Here we go again" and was angered, riled toward disbelief and disgust. Brother George Floyd is murdered. That morning, the news hit me like a boulder. I felt something I don't allow myself to feel too often: deep anger toward white people, possibly even toward the very white liberals who found me good enough to be a friend. I questioned all white people in my life. Have I misjudged? Was I now realizing I was depending on them all my life and then they went and did this to me? Betrayal and conflict. Then, white women started to call me, one after the other. What was this new kind of white woman's guilt? *I am sorry* and *how are you* felt empty. Why were white women who know I am committed to creating space for conversations on race and our identities now calling me to "check in" after George Floyd was killed? It seems their own guilt at being a support but not really making a change was driving their own hopelessness and disbelief. "What can I do? What should I do? I don't want to burden you, but . . ." It happened to my daughter too; a beautiful young Black woman navigating white people in her younger generation of Instagram, Tik Tok, and Facebook. She was going mad, and I saw her start to crumble.

With clearer vision and an ability to deeply examine the sum of these lessons, I can move forward. Voicing what lies beneath the ways in which the centrality of whiteness has affected me in my personal and professional worlds brings light to a consciousness, a self-awareness to do what is necessary to disengage from these lessons and to resolve my own complacency. I am left with an urgency to be my authentic self, to be vocal, to hold white people accountable for understanding how the devastation of their unspoken and sometimes subtle messages preserve racial inequities.

### *Self-Assessment and Reckoning*

Why does all this matter? Recently, Lesley Lokko resigned as dean of the School of Architecture at City College in New York City citing a "profound act of self-preservation" (Flaherty, 2020, para. 6) after months of exposure to lack of empathy for Black women and to structural racism that impacted her ability to do the job. Sharing my story is about preserving my sanity. No matter how much I hate to admit it, I have a deep awareness of the power white people hold over whether or not I am able to achieve or advance or have power. I have chosen to navigate these spaces, which leaves me questioning my purpose. Have I been silent, quiet, accepting of the open arms of white people who are satisfied with me and what I am? Am I selling out, holding back, acquiescing, assimilating? Have I internalized messages about being the good Black person, being a version of Blackness that feels safe for white people to want to support me? "How have I chosen to navigate whiteness?" is a curious mental game that fills me with mixed emotions.

I love my Blackness; my Black is *my* Black. My deeply Afro-Caribbean roots have never left me, and neither will I shed these roots. I have been surviving.

My attempt is to unmask the daily negotiation of white spaces, which feels like herding cats, a metaphor that implies impossibility and sheer uselessness. White people need to improve their cross-racial interactions with Black people, which will include deconstructing the centrality of their whiteness in all aspects of their thinking and being.

I hope Black people will be honest and have the courage to hold white people accountable and to define healing from racial trauma in our own ways. I am not sure we can fully rid ourselves or our destiny from the puppetry of whiteness. However, I am finding the dance we do causes harm. I don't believe People of Color should learn "how to deal" with white people, but in essence that is what many of us have done. I have learned how to maneuver, speak to, tolerate, ignore, ask permission, and seek the advice of white people. The landmine can explode at any given time and leave us without access to resources or traumatized or . . . dead. So, I have had to figure out how to be, how to think because my very survival depends on my doing so. But I don't want dependency anymore, I want ownership.

My own healing, accompanied by the amplification of my voice, has come through my antiracist work. Being an antiracist educator and facilitator gives me a platform, a vehicle to elucidate for white people how they impact Black people and all People of Color. In the past twelve years, my work has included developing group processes that include practicing critical dialogue related to race, gender, sexual identity, and our intersecting identities. Inviting people together into a room of mixed racial company is incredible because there is no hiding, there is no getting away. It was a white woman who initially invited me to learn how to facilitate group dialogue, building people's capacity to practice these complicated conversations with one another. The workshops are remarkable to me in that people can change, can immediately see themselves as maintaining white supremacy structures and racist, sexist, heteronormative ways of thinking and being. The privileges across multiple identities, simultaneous with the nonprivilege across their subjugated identities, becomes blatantly obvious (Hardy, 2016; Tatum, 2000).

### *Curiosity and Growth*

As I get older and feel more established, my voice is unwavering as I attempt to be heard, to be understood, and to speak up for myself and Black people. I am centering Black mentors who have been there for me and seeking Black therapists and decision-makers who will be there for me and for one another. Recently, a Black colleague pushed for my promotion and invited me to pursue an opportunity. How liberating and joyful I felt for recognition to come from one of us.

What do the white people in my life see me as? How do they associate my Blackness with how they treat me? Do they see my color? Are they really wondering about how I see the world or how I see them? Are they ready to disengage with the centrality of their whiteness, to step back and allow for the necessity of liberation? These are the conversations I want to have, toward truly uprooting racism once and for all.

**OVITA F. WILLIAMS, PHD, LCSW-R,** is a clinical social worker specializing in intimate partner violence, racial equity, and forensic social work. Dr. Williams is an associate director of field education at Columbia School of Social Work and an adjunct assistant professor at Silberman School of Social Work. Previous positions include director of clinical services at the Kings County District Attorney's Office and family therapist at the Children's Aid Society. Her recent collaborative book, *Learning to Teach, Teaching to Learn: A Guide for Social Work Field Education*, 3rd edition, was published by CSWE Press in 2019. Dr. Williams facilitates interactive workshops on creating space for critical dialogues around race, gender, sexual orientation, and intersecting identities. Dr. Williams completed her doctoral studies at the City University of New York Graduate Center. Her dissertation offered a critical perspective of worker stress, vicarious trauma, and structural racism for district attorney–based social workers.

## References

*Anderson, A., Barris, K., Dobbins, E. B., Fishburne, L., & Sugland, H. (Executive Producers). (2014–present).* black-ish *[TV series]. Wilmore Films; Artists First; Cinema Gypsy Productions; ABC Signature.*

*DiAngelo, R. (2019, June 7–8).* Nothing to add: Silence as a function of White fragility *[Conference presentation]. Soul Work: Overcoming Voicelessness: The Power of (y)OUR Voice!, Stamford, CT, United States.*

*Du Bois, W. E. B. (1903).* The souls of Black folk. *A. C. McClurg & Co.*

*Flaherty, C. (2020, October 13).* "A profound act of self-preservation." *Inside higher ed. https://www.insidehighered.com/news/2020/10/13/spitzer-architecture-dean-quits-profound-act-self-preservation*

*Hardy, K. V. (2016). Antiracist approaches for shaping theoretical and practice paradigms. In A. J. Carten, A. B. Siskind, & M. P. Greene (Eds.),* Strategies for deconstructing racism in the health and human services *(pp. 125–139). Oxford University Press.*

*Okun, T. (2001).* White supremacy culture. *DRWORKSBOOK. https://www.dismantlingracism.org/uploads/4/3/5/7/43579015/okun_-_white_sup_culture.pdf*

*Tatum, B. D. (2000). The complexity of identity: "Who am I?" In M. Adams, W. J. Blumenfeld, C. Castaneda, H. W. Hackman, M. L. Peters, & X. Zuniga (Eds.),* Readings for diversity and social justice *(3rd ed., pp. 6–9). Routledge.*

*Vega, T. (2016, June 27). Blacks still far behind whites in wealth and income. CNN Business. https://money.cnn.com/2016/06/27/news/economy/racial-wealth-gap-blacks-whites/*

CHAPTER 10

# Finding My Voice as a Black Immigrant

## Reclaiming Self in a Sea of Whiteness

HUGO KAMYA, PHD

I was born in Uganda. I am an immigrant who lived through the days of brutal tyrannical military regimes following the political colonial patronage of Britain. I am also a cisgender, heterosexual Black man, a psychologist, a social worker with training in pastoral ministry, spirituality, and theology. I was raised Christian. My parents have a Catholic background, which they passed on to their children. My mother had eleven children, with two sets of twins, affording her a special status in the family and the community. She was known first as *Nalongo,* a name given to a mother of twins, then as *Nabalongo* (*Twice Nalongo*) when she had another set of twins.

This chapter offers a personal exploration of my journey as an immigrant in the United States. It highlights my journey to find my voice in the context of Uganda's colonial history, oppression, and imperialistic patronage by Britain. The journey into finding my voice has been painstaking. It has made me question aspects of my identity. While in some cases it has allowed me to speak loudly about my sense of self, at other times it has come crashing down on me, leaving me unable to speak. Even in the most revered places of academia, I have had to struggle to name who I am. Reclaiming my self in a sea of whiteness is about survival and listening even more intently to the words of Audre Lorde (1997), because "we were never meant to survive" (p. 255). This chapter explores various spaces that inhabit my life: Black, African, immigrant, academic, raising Children of Color. I examine how I have navigated self in various spaces and, ultimately, in a sea of whiteness. I examine how whiteness continues to envelop key experiences in my self-understanding. In order to find my voice, those spaces need to be reclaimed. This chapter expresses the beliefs that have informed my journey as it has evolved over time, from my humble beginnings in Uganda, my immigration journey to Kenya and to the United States, through higher education, to academia and being a professional mental health provider.

## Humble Beginnings

A little mud house was the place we called home during my childhood years in Uganda. I can vividly remember the tiny rooms where we slept and cared for each other. There was a living room that had only three chairs. We felt a lot of shame when guests came to our home and we had to welcome them in this small place without furniture. Where would company sit? Could we even welcome company? What would the neighbors say? How could we belong? This little house had a crack, which always reminded me that at any time it could fall crashing down on us. It also reminded me that burglars could invade our home and kill us. I was always terrified when it rained. I was afraid the structure was going to crash down on us. There was no lock on the only door to our house. While the door was our way into the house, it was also our only way out. It was secured by a simple nail to keep it closed at night.

There were only two bedrooms: one where my parents slept with the youngest of my siblings and another where the rest of the children slept. Later, my father added two other rooms, separated by a corridor. One room was claimed by my brother Joseph, whose anger and explosive temper made it difficult for us to stay in the same room with him; the second room became a small pantry, but my older brother, Henry, and I claimed an end part of it, where we slept on one bed. The corridor was claimed by my older sister. It was a tight squeeze. I can recall how bedtime was always about finding beddings and sorting out small places of comfort to enjoy a good night's sleep. It was not easy. There were only four beds for the entire family.

And there were other creatures who inhabited the house. Mice roamed in our little mud house as they sought food remnants. We had no running water; and my brother and I, who slept in one corner of the pantry, we felt these mice as they ran all over our feet and faces at night. There were times when they could not find any food remnants and our feet became the next best thing for them. They chewed on our feet, which made walking to school barefoot another painful experience. Yes, we were poor! We had very little, in terms of material goods. My parents had worked hard to raise us and to send us to school. My father believed in the value of an education, and he was very proud that he had a high school diploma and trained as an accountant.

My parents valued school and hard work. Even with the little we had, we excelled in school. Most importantly, we had each other. Both my parents were hard workers. My father worked as an accountant for a large British oil company. As was the case with other workers, their labor was exploited by the company. They lacked fair wages. Even with his accounting skills, my father was given menial tasks, often doing errands for the British employers. I recall going to my father's workplace and noting that one of his tasks was to deliver tea to his bosses during tea breaks twice a day. While his bosses had tea and cookies, there was none for him. Who were these white folks who had tea breaks but could not offer anything to the Black employees who worked so diligently under them? Why did they have to work for the white folks? What if they quit their jobs? Nevertheless, I loved visiting my father at his workplace. The manicured offices, the many magazines that decorated them, and the clean bathrooms all made me wonder about the privileges that were outside my reach.

Growing up, we encountered many white missionaries. We saw them as "saviors," a message they communicated. Near my home, missionaries ran the schools and the churches we attended. We did menial jobs like cleaning their shoes, washing their cars, and serving as altar boys. At such a young age, I began to look at white missionaries as truly God's special people to whom we owed everything we could do for them. Jesus was painted as white, and the Biblical message was delivered as essentially white. In fact,

I believed that nothing could come closer to the divine if it were not white. This narrative seems to have been scripted in me from a very early stage of my life. No one questioned it. And it was reinforced by the priests, who reminded us about the generosity of their presence in Africa. So often, I would hear them talk about their countries of origin and all that they could get back home that Africa could not provide. I, for my part, decided that I would learn as much as I could from the situation that was doled out to me.

We begged from the white missionaries, as our mother was overworked cleaning their rooms and did daily chores for them. She deeply struggled to feed us and clothe us. We were dressed in rags. She never gave up. When I was 10, a close friend of my dad's decided to pay for my tuition. I was so delighted he offered to do that because I had been worried that my hopes to continue school would be shattered. However, he also told me that once I completed seventh grade, his assistance would end. This always hung over me, as I knew that there was not going to be a future beyond elementary education. Just as I was finishing my elementary school, a white missionary priest offered to sponsor me in high school. While this was welcome news, I also knew it came with all kinds of conditions and reservations on my part. I did not realize until much later how much my survival was once again sold out to a white man who called the shots on it. I ended up in a high school 50 miles away from home. It was a boarding school, a minor seminary. At this school, I was greeted by boys my age, all who professed their dying wish to become priests. As I look back, I think about what I wished for and whether those wishes were just mine or if they were impressed on me, and how I could find my voice in that inevitable situation of my life. Did I really want to be a priest? Could I even think of priesthood? Whose interests and voices was I listening to?

All the instructors at this minor seminary were white missionaries, many of whom had left their countries of origin and reminded us on many occasions of the sacrifice they made to come to Africa. They told us about Europe and the different countries they had lived in. The missionaries made us feel that we owed them our benevolence. These white men lived in separate quarters, above the manicured offices we cleaned. They had bread and bacon every morning for breakfast, a morning tea break, a three-course meal for lunch, an afternoon tea, and an elaborate dinner. The aroma of their food lingered in our nostrils every day. We wished to have a bite of their meals. Every week, these white priests selected students from among us to clean their lunchroom and do their dishes. Every one of us wished for the opportunity to do the cleaning. It was everyone's dream to be selected to clean up after the priests. Those who were selected feasted on the remnants of white priests' meals.

Our meals were different. The cooks made a paste from crushed corn or cassava that was served with pinto or black beans. Because the beans were stocked for months, they soon became a breeding ground for bean weevils. Bean weevils produce larvae that are small, whitish, legless, and C-shaped. They feed inside dried beans and peas. The bean weevils and larvae would end up in our cooked meals. The white missionaries would remind us that they were actually good protein. We did not contradict them. Our white teachers, the white missionaries, served us meals that they chose not to eat. Their message did not match their actions.

As I reflect on my early teen years, I can say that white missionaries had a great influence on my current social location. The missionaries told us who we were supposed to be. Our self-understanding could be captured only through their lenses. We felt we had nothing to contribute to our existence. The interactions the missionaries had with us were couched in a religiosity of faith. Prayer, mass, and daily devotions marked our time in the seminary. Our social location as young people aspiring to the priesthood precluded us from interrogating these experiences. As Hardy (2019) writes, "socio-cultural oppression, for many, is an integral aspect of culture. . . an umbrella term that refers to experiences of domination-induced marginalization that results in the subjugation of a person or group based on social location" (p. 135). These experiences of domination can have deleterious effects on the groups on the receiving end. Groups that are often seen as outsiders endure various levels of discrimination. Collins (2000) notes that such discrimination is fueled by the power to name and to define. We learned what we were supposed to be, and we believed it. We also learned not to question it. In fact, some of the messages were delivered with religious and powerful images of divine retribution on those who challenged them. But one cannot ignore colonialism and its impacts on Africa. Colonial administrators and European missionaries not only "condemned everything African in culture—African names, music, dance, art, religion, marriage, the system of inheritance—and completely discouraged the teaching of all these things in their schools and college" (Boahen, 1987, p. 107) but also brought with them views that disparaged some social identities.

## Colonialism and Africa

The arrival of missionaries in Uganda coincided with the arrival of colonists. Our religious seminary training was colored by colonial vestiges of Europe. While some people have argued the positive impacts of colonialism on Africa, many more have underscored its negative impacts. It oppressed and exploited Ugandans. History books note that the first three decades of the colonial era in Africa introduced far more violence, instability, anarchy, and loss of lives than any other period. Missionary work and colonialism went hand in hand. There were many wars of occupation following the repression of African opposition and resistance. Similarly, colonialism afforded more opportunities for men than for women, especially in the labor markets and literacy (Boahen, 1987).

The power to define and name is evident in the creation of nation states. Although the resulting peace and nation states of Africa are seen as positive impacts of colonialism, the layout of the boundaries of these nation states also split certain groups and clans, which led to new wars among the peoples of Africa. The boundaries were arbitrarily drawn from the armchairs of these imperial powers in what has been referred to as the "Scramble for Africa," also called the "Partition of Africa," "conquest of Africa," or the "race for Africa." This was the invasion, occupation, division, and colonization of African territory by European powers. These emerging, artificial creations resulted in far greater problems by dividing groups and creating wars between groups. Today, there are multiethnic groups in different nation states.

The exploitation that colonialism unleashed on Africa has been documented to include the looting of natural resources out of African states for use by the European powers. Some states had more natural resources with greater economic potentialities than others. Some states were landlocked, while others enjoyed long coastlines, affording some states more opportunities for international trade (Boahen, 1987).

Colonialism delayed the maturity and development of African states on many different fronts. Colonialism placed many Africans in a subservient role, one in which they lost control of their destiny, one in which they lost control of planning their development, of managing their own affairs, of the opportunity to savor their successes or to learn from their mistakes without an overpowering colonial master who dictated the mind of the African. This colonization of the mind (Thiong'o, 1986) has had far-reaching effects on many Africans.

The psychological impact of colonialism on Africans has had serious negative effects. Racialized trauma has been the hallmark of a colonial mentality created in the minds of Africans. Many Africans resorted to the condemnation of Africa's traditional goods, favoring imported goods instead. This reinforced the "white as good" mentality. Colonialism focused on building a strong work ethic but did not help Africans develop a sense of responsibility and motivation. Most Africans were driven by consumption in the here and now as opposed to looking to the future. Finally, colonialism sowed feelings of inferiority and a loss of human dignity among Africans. This was an outcome of the constant denigration and humiliation that Europeans put Africans through. This inferiority complex pervaded African lives for generations. Colonialism appears to have done far more harm than good. Colonial powers extracted more from Africa on material and psychological levels than they were able to give to Africa. Much of what the colonists provided suited themselves more than it helped Africans. The exploitation, the wasted opportunities, and the humiliation of Africans did great harm. The colonial period in Africa was "an interlude that radically changed the direction and momentum of African history" (Boahen, 1987, p. 109). The legacy of colonialism and the birth of Africa's neocolonialism will continue to influence the peoples of Africa for many years to come. Internalized oppression and bias will continue to define the ways most Africans see themselves. Negative images of Africa's new elite or leadership continue to constitute the ways that the rest of the world views Africans on the world scene.

This colonial mentality permeated my training and my choices. As I look back, I notice the influence of white instructors on our thinking. We saw the world through the eyes of the British, our colonial masters. We read British books and sang British songs. We read European history and read British literature. Anything not English was devalued. The dedicated effort to brainwash our minds could be felt very deeply. Later, even as we sang songs in our vernaculars, they still had a European melody. It was an experiment designed to look, feel, sound, and taste British. English was taught as the official language, and no effort was made to teach local languages beyond elementary school. This was the air we breathed.

The French missionaries arrived in Uganda two years after the British. They, too, brought with them religion. The French arrived and competed against the British in Uganda. As did the British with English, the French enforced the teaching of French in school. Indeed, we, the Africans, became the fighting ground for the imperial powers that ruled Africa as we sought to learn French and English, an arena that cemented the French–British rivalry in schools and in other places of influence. Looking back, I can feel, with deep emotions, the frustration and the struggle we had learning French. Our introduction to French was in high school, whereas English was taught early in elementary school. I detest the fact that the British never made any effort to nor encouraged the teaching of the local languages in schools, thus shutting off locals from the very lifeline to their culture. There were even other languages, like Swahili, that had the potential of becoming the *lingua franca* for Africa. How come the missionaries did not want us to learn or to read and write in our vernacular tongues? It baffles me that the missionaries made every effort to learn local languages with detail to syntax and grammar, yet no formal teaching was dedicated to teaching of the local languages to native speakers. This stance characterizes one form of colonization of the mind.

My life was profoundly shaped by the narrative of Uganda as a "colony" of Britain. Growing up in a postcolonial country, I struggled to understand the "benevolence" of Uganda's colonial masters and their sanitized oppression. In my country, colonialism found other names that helped make its presence seem justified. Uganda was a "protectorate" rather than a "colony" of Britain.

Religion and strong cultural traditions of harmony and preservation of life grounded me in the need to build understanding. As a member of the largest tribe in my country, I felt a sense of power that was overshadowed by the helplessness I felt throughout postcolonial Uganda. This enabled me to understand the powerlessness embedded in retaliatory discourses. Perhaps even more pressing for me was the anger I intensely felt as I struggled to construct "the other" in those who oppressed my family. Although this anger gave me a means to deal with my pain, I could not live consumed by my anger, and I chose not to, instead solidifying my faith and hope, especially in the face of struggle and pain. The crack in the window became a metaphor for the mud hut crack. It became a metaphor through which I felt a sense of hope and deliverance.

The tyrannical regime of Idi Amin unleashed a sense of despair for many Ugandans. The murder and death of over 800,000 people in Amin's brutal eight-year rule left an indelible mark on the country. Amin was the creation of the British. He was elevated through army ranks even though he had very little education. History books report how Amin ascended to power, with the support of the British, in a coup that toppled Milton Obote, Uganda's ruler who had fallen out of Britain's favor (Kyemba, 1977). There were many disappearances, including members of my family, simply because one belonged to a tribe that was in disfavor. In fact, in Amin's final year of his rule, he had become a megalomaniac, consumed by paranoia of any challenge to his power. This paranoia extended not only to his enemies but also to his friends and close family members. He presented a charming self that would both entertain and also rebuff, sometimes to deadly ends. We would read in the papers or hear on national television about prominent people who disappeared without a trace. Amin felt threatened by anyone with an education. University students were particularly targeted. I remember the fate of many university students. I cannot believe I survived the squad of marauding soldiers that sought to kill university students.

The day the military stormed Makerere University was the day I decided I needed to leave my country. I made a conscious decision to flee the terror in my country. In my brain, I weighed the danger of escaping against the danger of staying. There were no easy answers. We all desperately feared for our lives. What was most painful is that most white people continued to live luxurious lives in Uganda. Many of them enjoyed free movement throughout the country without being stopped by Amin's pillaging soldiers.

## My Escape

I traveled at night, hitching rides from strangers and walking on foot as I crossed into Kenya with very few belongings. The journey across the border would not allow me to carry much, for fear of detection but also for the uncertainty that lay ahead.

My journey brought me to Uganda's neighbor, Kenya. There, I began to put my life together. I breathed a sigh of relief because I had just escaped the grip of a prowling dictatorial regime, but I was immediately plunged into something new and unfamiliar. I could not speak Swahili, the language used in Kenya. Being male, I became a suspect again in Kenya. The first people I encountered wondered whether I had been a collaborator with the regime in Uganda.

As I found my footing in Kenya, I began to evaluate my life. I did menial jobs. I looked forward, hoping that things would change in Uganda. I began school after I secured my academic records. There were a lot of people who needed to be convinced that I was who I said I was. As the war raged in Uganda, it became harder to stay in Kenya. Many Ugandans were again suspects. We were all suspects. With more people escaping Uganda, Kenya put Ugandans under great surveillance. One such program was the so-called "*Kipandilisho,*" a Swahili term that referred to being "documented." All Ugandans had to carry a large 4 x 6 identity card that had to be stamped regularly to authenticate one's legal status.

Leaving Kenya and traveling to the United States brought mixed feelings. On the one hand, there was excitement in coming to a country that was previously presented to me as embracing diversity. But on the other, the move brought back old images and feelings of alienation. I would need to assert myself, to prove myself every step along the way. Many things I had taken for granted did not matter. I found myself in a place where I needed to name who I was.

I was reliving the trauma I was leaving behind. It colored my perception of my new home. I met several people whose story was different from my story but who nonetheless suffered from the effects of general exposure to the devastation of wars. I spoke a language that I thought was English, but my pronunciation raised eyebrows and people often made comments about my accent.

My skin color caused more curiosity and more questions from those around me. Growing up in Uganda, we learned about race and racism in America. No exposure prepared me to face the racism in the United States. Over the years, I learned about this cancerous disease that fuels the life blood of America, indeed, what Jones (2000) has described as

> a system of structuring opportunity and assigning value based on the social interpretation of how one looks, a system that unfairly disadvantages some individuals and communities, unfairly advantages other individuals and communities, and saps the strength of the whole society through the waste of human resources. (p. 1213)

Arriving in the United States, I learned firsthand about the sense of powerlessness that has been the life story of many African Americans. I have noticed how much this sense of powerlessness is rooted in the wounds of colonialism and racism, often reflected in feelings of inferiority, anger, and mistrust. Like most African Americans, I, too, have experienced racial discrimination in subtle ways. I have witnessed many indignities in my life. First, I was confronted with the challenges that face all new immigrants. How was I going to make it in a new country? How would my family react to the changes that were about to happen in me? Out here, who would be on my side? Was I giving up too much in return for so little? More importantly, how is it possible that I escaped while most of my family did not? These vexing questions stayed with me.

Navigating my emerging voice in white spaces, in the context of structural and internalized oppression, was not easy. I soon learned that I needed to find my voice. I decided I would build on everything that had sustained me from my childhood. Spirituality has been a major force in my life, and it has anchored me through many challenges. Some of the most painful moments of hurt have come from people I respected and valued for their wisdom and for what I believed they stood for. They have disappointed me. My greatest hurt has come from my interactions with colleagues in the United States. To a certain extent, the colonial hurt in Uganda pales in comparison to the hurt I have experienced since arriving in this country.

Despite the hurts I have experienced, a number of white people have reached out to me, helping me put down roots in the United States. I recall, for example, how Henri Nouwen was instrumental in launching my life as a student at Harvard. Shortly after arriving in the United States, I was admitted to Harvard Divinity School. I could not afford to go to the school. I remember sitting outside on the steps of Andover Hall at Harvard to attend an informational session. As I sat on the steps, I noticed ants that seemed to move aimlessly from one step to another. I thought about how minute their lives were, but also what mattered to them. Lost in thought, I wondered about what it feels like to be an ant. I wondered if there was any organization in their life. I imagined myself to be an ant, and I asked myself questions that, for a moment, gave me a sense of satisfaction about where I was located in my life. Did the ants care about what lay in the future for them? Who was going to step on them and crush them? How much did it matter if someone disrupted their course? These questions led to another journey of self-inquiry. Did anyone care that I had left my home, my family? How did family members react to my being away from home? What history did I share, or not share, with them anymore?

Out of nowhere, a man, perhaps in his sixties, joined me on the steps where I sat. He asked me what I was doing and where I had come from, the latter a question I had now heard asked differently by people who scoffed at my immigrant status. I told him I had just arrived from Uganda and was working at L'Arche, a home for mentally ill persons in Syracuse, New York. "How do you like your work at L'Arche?" he asked. I was surprised that he showed interest in me and was asking me about my work. I told him about L'Arche and what I was learning about the simplicity of life and the spirituality of care, love, and hospitality.

Our conversation then turned to books. He asked what books I was reading. I mentioned a few books on my list. They included some books by a spiritual author, Henri Nouwen, whose commitment to hospitality, ministry, and woundedness had appealed to me a great deal. At some point, I stopped and asked about his interest in my taste for books. He replied, "Well, I am Henri Nouwen." I took a step back and looked at the man who called himself *Henri Nouwen*. I could not believe that it was the man whose books I had been reading and whom I admired greatly. He looked at me intently with kindness. He talked about his wish to work with L'Arche and the invitation to hospitality. He believed that people who struggle with mental illness invite us to look at our own woundedness. As he talked, he revealed a sharpness of mind, an openness of self, and a heart that was immensely generous. As we chatted on those steps, I felt that he communicated a depth of presence. At one point, he asked me: "Young man, you look sad. What is going on?"

"I have been accepted at Harvard but cannot accept the offer because I cannot afford it," I told him.

"Is this something you really want?" he asked.

"Yes, it is. . . . And I am also afraid this will never happen for me," I told him.

That moment brought back strong memories of childhood when we lacked the means to support ourselves. Shame and pain engulfed me. I felt so vulnerable, as I felt I was begging for help. So, I looked away and waited for him to express his disappointment for me and move back to the conversation on his books and/or about L'Arche. I reveled in the excitement of meeting an author and talking to him about his books.

"Well," he said at this point, "I will give it to you."

For a moment, I could not believe what I was hearing. To meet an author who I admired and then be told that he would sponsor my education was baffling. I thanked him and sat back to think about how the invisible hand of God was writing and rewriting my life through this man. His support launched my career. It also gave me some trust in the whiteness that had let me down.

Henri Nouwen's support through graduate school opened doors into academia. I obtained a master of divinity degree at Harvard University, a master of social work degree at Boston College, and a PhD in clinical psychology from Boston University. I felt that my dream to get a university education had been achieved. I had started on the long road of academia. But I had not imagined what would ensue. As an assistant professor at Boston College, I entered a cutthroat world no one had ever prepared me for. Publish or perish pressures and many other challenges marked the beginning of my quest for tenure. It was a white world again. Black and Brown faculty had to work twice as hard to prove themselves. Many of my white colleagues, on the other hand, enjoyed all kinds of support, none of which I could access. There were many times when I would coteach with white colleagues but the white colleague would be the only one recognized. And there were times when I would ask a question and students would directly respond to my white colleague. Perhaps even more painful was the total lack of acknowledgment on the part of my colleagues, who would carry forward with the class discussion without noting that dissonance. These assaults were rampant. On several occasions, I, even as a PhD and having gained tenure, sat through academic meetings where I made points that were dismissed or ignored until they were echoed by a white colleague. The painful wounds of erasure could be felt so deeply, especially as my colleagues did not seem to consider, or even notice, the impact of this form of aggression on me or on our relationship. My anger grew as I watched my white colleagues witness what was going on and not come to the rescue of the situation. Blitz and Greene (2006) warn against this collusion with racism. It is endemic, unchecked, and etched into so many aspects of our lives. I have experienced overt racism and microaggressions, for example, standing in conference hallways where other attendees have assumed that I wasn't "with" my group of white colleagues. I have felt uneasy, unsafe, and reminded that I didn't fully belong.

Academia has many facets to it. I wanted so much to succeed. I loved teaching, doing research, and mentoring students. I know I got in the game. It was playing hardball. Committee meetings, curricular development, research, and more. My deep interest in the lives of Africans who have immigrated to the United States fueled my research on African immigrants in the United States. I wanted to learn more about what sustains them and what guides their sense of hope amid the challenges they face. I posed questions. I wanted to explore African narratives in the context of their migration within the United States. I watched as my colleagues easily got small grants to jump-start their academic careers and compared it to how much I had to keep justifying the value of the research I was proposing. I also watched as my white colleagues were appointed to administrative positions, bypassing me with offers.

Later on, following the events of 9/11, a white colleague and I wrote an article deconstructing the events of 9/11. We both wanted to understand how collectively we choose to respond to any forms of injury and how we understand those who choose to harm us. We both saw it as embarking on a journey seeking to understand the importance of moving from monologic to dialogic discourse. In writing this article after the events of 9/11, we sought to explore alternatives to cycles of violence. We proposed the importance of finding emotional reconnection between victim and victimizer and the connection of victim with witnessing audiences. We proposed the importance of finding humanizing and caring ways that do not get mired in retaliatory discourse. Retaliation embodies the language of reaction rather than action. While this article was at the core of building humanizing relationships, it also revealed deep issues that underlie academia.

At the time of writing our response to injury, we struggled on issues of authorship. Who was going to be listed as lead author on the article? My colleague had assumed he was going to be listed as lead author. I felt we had both made equal contributions to the writing of the article, and the issue of lead authorship had not crossed my mind, as I later told my colleague. The more he pushed for lead authorship on our manuscript, the more I felt *otherized* in the very piece of work where we sought to debunk othering practices through the unpacking of monologic and dialogic discourse. At the time, I did not know how deeply affected I was by the discussion that ensued. I have vivid memories of withdrawing into my shell and questioning my competence. A strong feeling about my sense of belonging overwhelmed me. Did I matter? What did I deserve? Who am I? I doubted myself. This nagging feeling blew in my face when my white colleague told me, on yet another occasion, something that for me translated into what I perceived as his devaluing of me. On one occasion, I confronted him about being fully honest about how he experienced me. He told me about his ongoing internal conversation with his "inner voices of the bigot, the color blind, and the failed seeker of racial sensitivity." He described to me about how this voice happens, sometimes; that the sight of my very dark, African skin can activate his racist stereotypes, and how he is always monitoring and containing these inner voices to keep them from intruding fully into his inner life and bursting into his words and actions in a relationship. With deep sadness, I shared with him that his internal process of monitoring and containing his racism is an obstacle to our experiencing deeper intimacy with each other.

Although my colleague and I are trained as psychologists, I noticed that he felt that his educational acumen was far greater than I could ever contribute to our learning spaces. So, for years, we sat in meetings in which I worried about how he received my ideas. Did he value my contributions, or did he pretend to value my contributions? Most frustrating about all of this is how much I allowed myself such denigration. I did not speak out. My voice was silenced by the very person with whom I thought I shared a deep connection.

This devaluation left an indelible mark in my self-perception and sense of self. I have questioned myself about my own sense of belonging. I have worried about what I can achieve. I worry that I will never be able to measure up. This is a worry that takes over my life, as does never feeling that I am being seen. And the more I felt I was not being seen, the more I felt like I was shrinking. Because I am Black, very black, I began to believe the stereotype about myself. The suspicions about myself grew so strong that I began to believe them. Steele (1999) describes stereotype threat that affects one's intellectual performance. My mind went through all kinds of responses about what I could do to remove these self-observations. So, I asked myself, "Am I good enough? Can I measure up?" I thought about my humble beginnings and the colonial vestiges that characterized my upbringing. This was happening before my very eyes.

My pain, the feeling of deep subjugation, further hurled my voice in silence as I contemplated my white colleague's intentions. I have wondered about the privilege to claim no ill-intent by white bodies, which is often not afforded to Persons of Color or Black bodies. Thinking about my conversations with some white colleagues, I cannot help but wonder how some of my colleagues selectively attend to those aspects that connect to their experiences but choose to leave out of experiences that intimately affected Persons of Color or Black bodies. How does that happen? Whose story matters?

In seeking to find my voice, I have also struggled with ways in which some white people seek out People of Color. At times, there appears to be a nagging wish to connect or to associate with People of Color, a form of association that affords them credentials to comfortably belong in the malaise of racism.

In my choice to find and use my voice, I have decided to confront the white malaise that often characterizes such relationships. I have listened with deep scrutiny when white bodies invite me to engage in conversations which are about their own self-interests. As I seek my voice, the question "who am I?" is resoundingly loud for me. I look for authentic conversations that speak truth without compromising integrity and about moving relationships forward.

As I think about my relationship with my white colleague, who has come to represent the oppression of white spaces, I keep asking myself questions. Why did I allow myself to be subject to this denigration? Who was I pleasing? Whose performances was I playing into? How much did I betray my humble beginnings and allow myself to wallow in the sea and whims of whiteness?

My family has been a place to develop my voice. I fell in love with a white woman, whom I married, and we started a family. We became parents of two biracial children. I made white friends who I felt accepted me for who I am and with whom I felt safe, and I moved into a diverse community that, on the surface, felt welcoming of diversity. Being married to a white woman highlights the complexities that characterize my narrative. As parents, we are intentional about engaging in conversations about race. We have made a conscious effort not only to notice what is happening but to focus on what we can do about racial justice. I have challenged my white partner to pay attention to the burden People of Color carry against many competing demands. She, on her part, has been cognizant about the trap of credentialing that our relationship affords her. We have both asked ourselves how we engage competing voices to find our own. I have come to appreciate the importance of my partner's not speaking for me but speaking out against white racism. The same message I have passed on to my daughters, as I have underscored the weight of whiteness that they live through. I have shared with them the system of anti-Blackness that pervades our lives as Black people. Together, we have talked about having a Black father and a white mother. I have struggled with what it means to raise Children of Color with a white mother. My children have taught me far more than I could have imagined. I have listened to the pain they have endured in a predominantly white school. Together, we have talked about what it means to grow up Black in a sea of whiteness. A recent conversation I had with my daughter showed the depth of her thoughts. She wrote to me:

> There is no remedy for racism. There is nothing a mother can do to protect her son from the police when he leaves the house. There is nothing a father can do to make his daughter more white, like the popular girls. There is nothing society can do to erase the systemic racism that has occurred for over 300 years. But what we can do

> together as a collective is empathize, unify, collaborate, understand, and strive for better. Better for the Black boys who are more likely to be suspended than their white peers, better for the Black girls who have to wear their hair a certain way so they are respected. Better for the lives lost, Trayvon Martin, Breonna Taylor, Ahmaud Arbery, George Floyd, and countless others. Better for the opportunities missed, passed up, ignored because of skin color. As an African American female, in a world full of white people, I oftentimes don't know who I am and who society wants me to be. Should I be the angry Black woman the world depicts me to be? Because I can be that. Because I am angry. Or should I be the "you're black but you sound white" kind of person who has a few more opportunities than a darker skinned girl . . . but always wonders if I am filling a quota or if it is because of my merits. There are so many different boxes I can fit into, and this is the case for many Black and Brown people. But we often do not fit into the boxes that society deems to be "best" or "worthy" and all the while we are striving to convince ourselves that we are important. When Black and Brown children walk into the school building that I am a counselor at I have made it a promise to tell them each day that they belong, they matter, and I think highly of them. I think a lot about who lifted me up when I was a little brown [*sic*] girl in a sea of whiteness. (S. Kamya, personal communication, November 18, 2020)

The experiences of Black and Brown people are captured by the words of my daughter. We have explored what keeps us together and the challenges of the forces we have to overcome. I have wondered about the varying levels of physical, psychological, emotional, and spiritual/religious rootlessness my family has had to go through. How do my children make sense of who they are? How do they embrace what they see unfolding before their eyes today? My daughter captures the fear that engulfs them as they share in the very experiences that have characterized the lives of many Black and Brown people. Their struggles through school and the disdain they have had to deal with has been painful to watch.

Even though I have lived in a progressive neighborhood and was surrounded by white allies, all the memories of the whites in my growing-up years came back to me in droves. The body remembers vividly and viscerally even after decades. The tendency to always be on the alert has been carved into my neural pathways. I can sense when my antenna goes up in my interactions with whites. This is a response to racial trauma. I have sought spaces where I do not have to be hypervigilant, places where I can finally breathe.

As I watch my children grow, I remain appreciative of the collective struggles we all share as Black people in the United States. I see moments in which our human condition as Blacks creates a connection. I imagined that I, as an African born in Africa, lived a very different life compared to African Americans, born in the United States. I know the forces leading to my immigration in the United States differ profoundly from the forcible removal and enslavement of these Blacks' African ancestors, as do the respective social and psychological consequences of those forces and actions. Sometimes I have questioned my place among my African American brothers and sisters. I have come to the realization that there are bonds in the history we all share.

The colonial politics in Africa created structures of oppression similar to the scaffolding that supports racism in America. Writing about how oppression occurs, Young (2000) identifies five concepts: exploitation, marginalization, powerlessness, cultural imperialism, and violence. Tourse et al. (2018) assert that these pillars are the very mechanisms that stabilize the scaffolding and help perpetuate racism. Just as the enslavement of Black bodies exploited the labor of a subordinate group at the hands of a dominant group, white colonial power exploited African bodies and the natural resources of their land.

Just as African Americans have been marginalized in education and labor markets, the colonial powers that occupied African countries denied educational opportunities, exacerbating the exploitation of Africans in their own lands. Another area of marginalization is denying Africans access to their local languages, thus erasing these languages. In the United States, this marginalization can be seen in the ways Children of Color are relegated to substandard schools (Tourse et al., 2018).

Writing on powerlessness, Tourse et al. (2018) state that "powerlessness is the inability to influence the forces that shape one's life and is the result of how labor, resources, and influence are distributed" (p. 11). Just like the enslavement of Africans forced them into extreme powerlessness and denied African Americans access to labor, resources, and influence, so the occupation of African countries by European colonial powers disempowered many African countries. Indeed, just like in the United States, European colonialism was promoted as the norm and culture. This cultural imperialism, sometimes doled out as violence, continues to pervade and shackle many Communities of Color.

These linkages have helped me embrace the drive to survive. They remind me of the importance of holding hands with my African American brothers and sisters. I have witnessed the violence that African Americans have lived through, the legacy of their historical trauma. I work in institutions that do not respect me or value my contributions. I have embraced my own struggles, and I seek the commonalities I have with African Americans, knowing that their struggle is also my struggle.

Experiences of domination have deleterious effects on people. Systems of oppression serve as "a means to assist those with power (the socially dominant group) in maintaining and legitimizing their existence by suppressing the individual group, and institutional free will of others [the socially subordinate groups]" (Tourse et al., 2018, p. 10). Tourse et al. (2018) propose *scaffolding* as a social construction metaphor, which maintains oppressive structures upon which exploitation, marginalization, powerlessness, cultural imperialism, and violence rest.

Tourse et al. (2018) build on the work of Young (2000), who states that "oppression refers to the vast and deep injustices some groups suffer as a consequence of often unconscious assumptions and reaction of well-meaning people in ordinary interactions, media and cultural stereotypes and structural features of bureaucratic hierarchies and market mechanisms" (p. 36).

I have wondered how I continue to find my voice and how I keep speaking, remembering Audre Lorde's (1997) words that "we were never meant to survive" (p. 255). I see finding my voice as a moment of self-preservation. One of the things I keep noticing about racism is that it is present in white liberal "performing" spaces. As Black bodies, we keep looking for a system that is accountable. We live in hierarchical structures of violence, where the challenge to speak truth to power looms all the time. We may not get any answers. We may not expect anything, but we must keep agitating. My conversations with my white colleagues have helped me to dig deep in recognizing white performative presences. So, in seeking to find my voice, I have made it a personal accountability practice to call out and call in white people into these very important conversations. I would like to hold white people accountable for their performative selves.

In looking for and exercising my voice, I am learning how to show kindness to myself. It is exhausting to live in these spaces. I need to find a place to process my vulnerability. I realize that this place is sometimes a draining place. I know that when I am drained, I cannot do anything for myself or others. I need to step back and say that it is OK, that I do not need to perform for white spaces. I am learning to set better boundaries. I keep seeking affirming places where my voice can be heard. I need to keep finding meaningful places and spaces that add to my "pot and stew." I have so much to offer and do not need the blessing of the structures that historically shut us down. Walking away with our heads held high is just as important. Finding my voice allows me to challenge performative white spaces, including academia, that continue to hold Black and Brown bodies into oppressive spaces. When white people around me dismiss me in different ways, I doubt myself and I stop speaking up. I cannot continue spending energy making mental calculations about the pros and cons of speaking up versus keeping quiet. I continue to value what whiteness has afforded but also challenge what whiteness has denied. My hope is that my children will be able to name and navigate layers of oppression, power, and privilege as they wade through the scaffolding of whiteness.

**HUGO KAMYA, PHD,** is Professor and the Social Work Alumni Fund Endowed Chair at Simmons University, where he teaches clinical practice and trauma, family, spirituality, group work, and narrative therapies. Originally from Uganda, Dr. Kamya studied at Harvard University, Boston College, and Boston University and trained in social work, psychology, and theology. His work has focused on immigrant populations and international efforts to assess the social service needs of people affected by HIV/AIDS and transactional sex. He continues to consult for and develop collaborative partnerships with agencies and organizations, and presents nationally and internationally on multicultural, diversity, racial justice, and cultural sensitivity issues. He collaborates in *Caring Across Communities*, a project of community-based services for refugees and immigrants that examines social, cultural, and human capital toward family functioning and well-being. He is the American Family Therapy Academy recipient for the 2003 Distinguished Contribution to Social and Economic Justice Award. In 2014, Dr. Kamya was accepted into the Fulbright Specialist Roster Program. Dr. Kamya is founding member of the Boston Institute for Culturally Affirming Practices (BICAP).

## References


*Blitz, L., & Greene, M. (2006).* Racism and racial identity: Reflections on urban practice in mental health and social services. *Routledge.*

*Boahen, A. A. (1987).* African perspectives on colonialism. *Johns Hopkins University Press.*

*Collins, P. H. (2000). Toward a new version: Race, class, and gender as categories of analysis and connection. In M. Adams, W. J. Blumenfeld, C. Castaneda, H. W. Hackman, M. L. Peters, & X. Zúniga (Eds.),* Readings for diversity and social justice: An anthology on racism, anti-Semitism, sexism, heterosexism, ableism, and classism *(pp. 457–463). Routledge.*

*Hardy, K. (2019). Toward a psychology of the oppressed. In K. V. Hardy & M. McGoldrick (Eds.),* Revisioning family therapy: Race, culture and gender in clinical practice *(3rd ed., pp. 133–148). Guilford Press.*

*Jones, C. (2000). Levels of racism: A theoretical framework and a gardener's tale.* American Journal of Public Health, 90, *1212–1215.*

*Kamya, H., & Trimble, D. (2002). Response to injury: Toward ethical construction of the other.* Journal of Systemic Therapies, 21, *19–27.*

*Kyemba, H. (1977).* State of blood: The inside story of Idi Amin. *Ace Books.*

*Lorde, A. (1997).* The collected poems of Audre Lorde. *W. W. Norton & Company.*

*Steele, C. M. (1999, August). Thin ice: Stereotype threat and black college students.* The Atlantic. *https://www.theatlantic.com/magazine/archive/1999/08/thin-ice-stereotype-threat-and-black-college-students/304663/*

*Thiong'o, N. W. (1986).* Decolonising the mind: The politics of language in African Literature. *J. Currey.*

*Tourse, R. W. C., Hamilton-Mason, J., & Wewiorski, N. J. (2018).* Systemic racism in the United States: Scaffolding as social construction. *Springer.*

*Young, I. M. (2000). Five faces of oppression. In M. Adams, W. J. Blumenfeld, C. Castaneda, H. W. Hackman, M. L. Peters, & X. Zúniga (Eds.),* Readings for diversity and social justice: An anthology on racism, anti-Semitism, sexism, heterosexism, ableism, and classism *(pp. 35–49). Routledge.*

## CHAPTER 11

# Encountering Whiteness and the Marginalizing Effects of the Model Minority

LIANG-YING CHOU, PHD

The year 2020, more than any other that I am aware of, gave the United States an opportunity to examine its racial ideology and culture. The COVID-19 pandemic, which was racialized and referred to as the "China virus" by the race baiting, divisive former US President Donald Trump, the brutal murder of George Floyd and related Black Lives Matter movements, and the election of the first Black-South Asian vice president all occurred with race looming in both the backdrop and the forefront. All of these issues have forced me to think more critically about myself racially, especially here in the United States.

The United States as a land of freedom and opportunity was imprinted in me since I was a young girl. Growing up in a small nuclear family in Taiwan and watching my extended family spread their wings to the United States, I always dreamed I would eventually come to the United States and live a better life here. I remember listening to my mother talking about Elvis Presley, Audrey Hepburn, Elizabeth Taylor, Marilyn Monroe, and the Kennedys and learning about proper etiquette from the movie *The Nun's Story* (Zinnemann, 1959). From a very early age, I began to dream about living in the United States.

## As Easy as Iris

To make my dream come true, while I was in Taiwan I took extra classes at the language institute to enhance my English-speaking skills. I was excited to meet teachers from the United States. Little did I know, in my first class I would be faced with a name change. My teacher, a young white man, told me that my Taiwanese birth name is long and difficult to pronounce and no one would remember it and that, since I was learning English, it would be better for me to immerse into the culture by adopting an English name. I was given the name Iris, as it is short, simple, and easy to remember. My first impression was that "Iris" was truly easy to spell, but I did not feel like an "Iris." Although I had no idea about the origin of the name or what it meant, I welcomed the change as a good student and envisioned future acceptance into US culture. "Life is as easy as Iris," my language teacher humorously told me. I later looked at the dictionary and found out that iris is a popular purple flower. I told myself that since I like flowers and I like purple, Iris would be a suitable name and that I would blend into the United States smoothly. If worse comes to worst, I could change to another name.

Years later, I was admitted into a graduate program in the United States. Overjoyed, I arrived at the dream land and began a short stay with a host family, an elderly white Catholic couple. The first question I was asked when meeting my host at the airport was "What is your American name?" I was confident and feeling well prepared as I answered them, "Iris." My host family seemed to be pleased and had no trouble remembering me as Iris. I felt good and believed that my language teacher taught me well. The host family helped me settle and be ready for school life. They introduced me to their daily routines, religious rituals, family members, photo albums, and family legacies. I was Iris, with no questions asked. The host family helped me make a smooth transition into this new country by offering me valuable tips and advice. My white socialization had begun in full force.

It was overwhelming to study in a different language and to situate myself in the classroom culture. I was shy and self-conscious. The lively classroom discussions and constant interactions with professors were intimidating; they were different than the classroom cultures that I was familiar with in Taiwan. In a conversation with my classmates after we had explored genograms, I was asked about my birth name and why I decided to use the name Iris. It took me by surprise, and yet I realized how much I appreciated their curiosity. I began to tell them the stories about my birth name and its meanings. My classmates could tell how proud I was of my name and the deep connection I have with it and my family. They put in effort to pronounce my name and made sure they got it right. When I told them about the reason why I used the name Iris, they were shocked and laughed at the nonsense that my language teacher told me. My classmates did not think that using a name like Iris would make me better remembered. I could sense the irritated undertone in my classmates' statements. It seemed to them that my language teacher was too lazy to learn my name or to show respect for me and my culture.

This was the beginning of my reflection on experiences with my name and the desire to be accepted into US society. At this point, I did not know enough to understand the ways in which US culture and white culture were synonymous. I recalled my host family's nonreaction to my American name and the eagerness from my classmates to perfect the pronunciation of my birth name. The contrast made me wonder. Before I departed from the host family, I prepared a meal for them with some of my favorite dishes from home. We had a nice conversation about food and dining traditions. However, there was no question of or mentioning my birth name or family or culture. From that moment on, Iris became history. Without hesitation, I took back my birth name and made everyone learn it. Since then, whenever I have been asked if I use "an American name," my answer has always been "No."

Did my journey to the United States go "as easy as Iris"? Not exactly. The experience with my name gave me a snapshot of what I should expect and what I should be prepared to accept as the norm. The hidden message, that life would be easier if I changed the parts of me that set me apart from the white culture, became clearer. This message was alarming. It revealed the deeply rooted hierarchy among racial and cultural groups. Also, it exposed what the immigration experience entails. How many immigrants show up to the host culture and intentionally dismantle themselves to assimilate? Looking around, how many Asians, not just in the United States but around the world, adopt or are given European or Christian biblical names? I began to ponder what the initial motivation is for them, and what this behavior says about the influence of Western culture as well as of the power and approval of white representation.

## Smile and Don't Rock the Boat

A few years later, I started working in academia. Comments about my looks often preceded any feedback I would receive on my professional skills. An elderly white male colleague advised me on how to better manage the office/classroom climate as a young beginning professor. I was told that I dressed too dark, too uptight and serious, and that I should use lighter dress colors, be more easygoing, and smile more, especially since I have a "beautiful smile." I perceived these comments as friendly social interactions until one day I showed up dressed in a pair of jeans and a T-shirt and then was told that I looked "like a student" by an older white female colleague. I was puzzled by the comment because I was following the advice I had been given "to loosen up and not appear so uptight and serious." I did not understand why I was perceived this way by her when other white colleagues in my age group dressed the same way and were viewed as relaxed and down-to-earth. An older Asian female colleague with seniority in ranking later came to me in private. She advised me not to wear jeans in the office as it would make me look unprofessional. I was told to be extremely careful with how I dress, speak, and act if I want to climb the ladder, because I would not be held to the same standards as our white colleagues. I was not surprised by this advice because I was aware of how Asians have historically been treated in the US workforce, and yet I was disappointed because I had hoped that my character and skills alone were enough for me to be valued.

I also noticed that when I spoke up and expressed my opinions firmly in meetings, I was often perceived as reactive and aggressive. However, I would be seen as resistant, passive-aggressive, detached, and noncooperative if I kept my mouth shut. I observed that these same behaviors would be seen as opinionated, sharp, standing up for herself, reserved, or wise when demonstrated by young white female colleagues. I questioned whether the ways in which I communicated were misleading. How come I seemed to have more "attitude" issues than white female colleagues? I tried to learn and imitate the ways white female colleagues behaved at work. In the end,

I realized that no matter what I did, I would not be seen or treated exactly the same way as my white colleagues. It was not about age, how I dressed, or what I said, it was the "skin suit" that I wore and that I couldn't and did not want to remove, literally or symbolically. It became very clear to me that my actions differed dramatically from the popular US stereotypes of Asians.

The racial dynamics and impressions in academia replicate those of the general society. I was often reminded by some colleagues to not take things that appeared racially inequitable "personally," especially when encountering white colleagues. I was cautioned by another Asian female colleague that "we Asians should be the master of harmony and know how to maneuver in the system among different groups/perspectives. Remember, we are the model minority." I was not sure whether there was sarcasm in this statement. Perhaps the statement was meant to lighten up my mood. I did not find it funny nor intelligent. Was I supposed to be Zen like? Was I supposed to be "like water," "not rock the boat," and "smile" through it?

If the model minority statement was intended to be sarcastic, it reflected complex underlying messages. It confirmed that the concept of model minority is projected on to and is internalized by many within the Asian population. According to the model minority myth, Asian Americans are perceived to be hypercompliant, to achieve a higher degree of socioeconomic success, and to serve as role models to other racial minority groups. Many Asians tend to pridefully pressure themselves to meet the perceptions of the model minority and to believe that they are "better" than other racial minority groups and are immune to racism. Unfortunately, this belief is certainly not reflected in the way Asians are treated in all areas of US society. Not only do Asian Americans experience racism and discrimination, but they are also plagued by the myth that they enjoy the same (racial) privileges as whites. The pervasive model minority messages were inescapable. As an immigrant, I felt constant pressure to play by model minority rules. I was beginning to experience confusion about who I was, who I wanted to be, who I needed to be, and who I should be. I continuously wondered: "Do I have to play this model minority role? What will happen if I don't? How do I survive, and how do I get along with other Asian colleagues, if I don't? Why was I perceived as taking things personally? Why didn't other Asians get accused of taking things personally? Was I imagining all of this?" I also wondered what was it that allowed other

Asian colleagues to remain calm and emotionally detached while I was often overcome with emotions.

Advice like "pick your fights" and "don't rock the boat" seemed noble and wise at first glance. However, I wondered what this advice was actually suggesting about the system, myself, and what I represent. How did the messages I received indicate my future relationship with the workplace and with the people who gave me the advice? What did the message tell me about the equality of all members of the workplace? When my behaviors strayed from the stereotypes, the discomfort of my white colleagues was expected. However, it was the strong and consistent encouragement to fit into and adopt the model minority role from other Asian colleagues that saddened me the most. It is too familiar for People of Color to be advised about the benefits of being silent and to be asked to participate in their marginalization by removing themselves from the center and stepping to the margin. Silence, obedience, and working hard are traits to be rewarded, as these characteristics do not pose threats to whites. Nothing rang louder in my ears at this point than the information on becoming a good effective mainstream minority (GEMM) family therapist (Hardy, 2008).

The essence of becoming a GEMM therapist is the same as being a model minority. This essence is a deeply rooted toxicity with a huge component of false hope. The delusional sense of safety from keeping quiet and the delusional sense of loyalty to the privileged group continue to promote the privileged. One of the privileges of being privileged is having the option to ignore the effects of oppression. People who don't see or hear don't relate. The efforts, coming from the model minority, to conspire with the stance of the white group only amplify the effects of domination and oppression. They further reinforce the separation, loneliness, misunderstanding, and ruptures in the relationship.

## Is There Something Wrong with Me?

I noticed that I seek advice less and less frequently as the years go by. This change is not due to confidence in my own decision-making, rather it is a result of not being willing to hear feedback that contains underlying messages about my deficiencies as an Asian. "You are nice looking, you have a sweet voice and beautiful smile; if you just play your cards wisely, your life can be much easier." "You are an Asian woman! White men love you. Use that!" "Why aren't you like other Asian women? Be softer and say yes more. Doors always open wide to sweet, nice Asian ladies." I always feel insulted by statements like these. It is unclear to me whether the advice is a rejection of me as a woman, as an Asian, or as an Asian woman. The underlying message, regardless of the motivation or intent, is that "a better version of you is needed, and you can best achieve it by being more of a model minority," more white-ish.

I continued to receive the message that I was not living up to the stereotype and that I was not using my racial/cultural assets to my advantage. I noticed that being both a woman and an Asian is perceived as inferior. If I were to take on the submissive role that is expected of Asian women, I would be seen as safer, trustworthy, and more acceptable. If I appeared to match the stereotypes, I would present no threats and no surprises and would be easier "to handle." My intelligence seems to be less important than the attitude I carry toward other races, particularly white people. Being myself, without caring to be what I was expected to be, seems to be a major cause for all of the difficulties I have faced in life. Is there something wrong with me?

Maybe if I were to surrender and follow the expectations placed on me by the white majority, I could feel more welcomed and secure. However, is it true that the "grass is greener on the other side"? As I want for my hair to be wavy, my eyelashes to be longer and curlier, my eyes to be bigger, and my nose to be higher, I wonder if any white women wish they could look like me. I doubt that any would want to have my nose or eyes or anything other than my straight black hair, which seems to be attractive to white women. I know some other racial groups might want to have "Asian genes" so that they could look youthful longer, but I believe that no one really wants to have Asian genes because the Asian race is portrayed as physically "weaker"—note who was the first to be killed off at the fighting arena in the movie *The Hunger Games* (Ross, 2012).

When it comes to martial arts, white people worship Bruce Lee and consider themselves inclusive and multicultural. However, I wonder if Bruce Lee would be as well-known and embraced as he has been if he didn't have a white name and wasn't married to a white woman. When white people want to prove themselves to be diverse and open-minded by stating that they "love Japanese animations," or "love Chinese food," do they know these statements have often been laughed at in Asian communities?

I admit that I am cynical when it comes to racial encounters. People have asked me, "Don't you want to be whiter?" "Come on, do you really think being darker is prettier?" Among all these racial judgments, the saddest ones would be the rejections coming from other Asians. I recall being approached by an Asian company for a potential training job in Asia. After providing my information and qualifications, I did not hear back from them for a long time. When I followed up, I learned that they had offered the job to a white trainer who had less expertise than me but was older and is associated with a well-known religious school in the United States. The company told me that their higher administration wanted someone who has more "authority" and their staff did not see the benefit of hiring an Asian person from the United States when they could find Asian experts in their own country. For overseas experts, they preferred to have white people. This rejection was crushing and hurtful to me; it felt like the most devastating form of betrayal, that which is handed out by my own people.

To gain a different perspective, I shared this experience with an acquaintance, a white male immigrant from Russia, who has done frequent business in Asia. He told me that this phenomenon of preference for white professionals over Asians is well established in Asian countries. He then told me that people in his own country would be more "inclusive" and welcoming of their own people. He asked me a question and offered me a solution: "Why don't you partner with a white colleague? People would value you more. Give people what they want." I appreciated his effort to comfort me, but I did not like the underlying message in his statements. The ideas of "I am not enough," "something is wrong with me," and "let white people save me" appeared repeatedly. It was disturbing. Once again, the message was clear that, as an Asian, I am lacking and deficient without a white person, preferably a man, standing next to me to legitimize not just my credentials but my humanity as well.

The various encounters I have described throughout this chapter all share a common thread, which is the continuous positioning of whiteness at the center and the corresponding assignment of Asians and other People of Color to the margins. Is this the kind of culture that we want to foster in our society? When I further reflected on what whiteness means to me, I recognized that when I say white, I don't mean the color, the race, or a certain complexion. Whiteness is an attitude: one of domination, superiority, control, and rule. Whiteness is a position: one that demands and is assigned authority, power, and privilege. As a white person, you don't have to change your name unless you wish to do so, you do not have to be restricted to what you can do or not do, or where you go or can't go. Unfortunately, for all who are not white, having the luxury to do as they please without care or worry is not an option. Being white means you have the freedom to just be human, an individual!

There are still a few curious and unsettled voices in my head that continuously question whether I would be more accepted if I had kept the name Iris and whether I would be more warmly embraced if I kept myself silent and surrendered to the model minority stereotypes. I wonder, too, if I were to say these thoughts to others, especially white people, would I be seen as a crazy, emotionally troubled, self-sabotaging Asian? I believe the answer would be yes, for now. Only when the experience of Asian people is understood and embraced can the dynamics between Asian and white people be experienced differently. White people have to understand and develop sensitivity to the widespread effects of whiteness on Asians and other Communities of Color.

What can we do to change the marginalized effects within Asian communities? We need to unlearn the disapproval of self and question the elevation of whiteness. As Asians, we need to shift perspectives and create a kinder narrative about ourselves. How do we begin to change the dominant narrative? Principles from the narrative family therapy approach (White & Epston, 1990) would provide a useful guide to help us search for the essence of our experiences. Questioning "reality," challenging our perceptions, deconstructing our experiences, hearing the other side of stories, and placing value on the voices of the marginalized are essential tasks. Patience and acceptance with oneself contributes to a solid foundation from which we can reach out to understand ourself and others.

## Summary

The phenomenon of the model minority, regardless of its intentions, is a harmful and restrictive conceptualization of Asians. It is a tool of the oppressor that demonstrates its power to name and define the experiences of others in a way that can be deceptively incarcerating. When we, as Asians, subscribe to the dictates of the model minority myth, we essentially participate in our own objectification and oppression. It also pits us against other racial minority groups who are named and defined by the same white dominated power structure but in less favorable and less endearing ways. Should anyone be surprised when there is tension and conflict between us and them, given the ways in which our respective groups have been defined?

Change of relationship requires change in perspectives. Li et al. (2020) introduce three of Zen's stages of enlightenment to describe the evolving nature of consciousness in our perception of relationships. Our consciousness progresses from an initial stage of believing what we see, to not believing what we see, and eventually to believing what we see with clear realization. To restructure the Asian–white relationship, we need to foster a process in which we move from seeing each other's reality without interpretation, to questioning the realities, and finally to reaching a clear realization that transcends the perceived relationship and to a systemic wholeness. The following is a list of twelve tips and practices that will be helpful for Asians and whites to implement as preliminary steps toward liberating the former from the shackles of the model minority myth.

### *Twelve Practice Tips for Asians*

Overcoming the internalization of the model minority is not a simple task. At its core, it will require Asians to be in a constant state of self-examination. The following steps are designed to assist with this lifelong learning process:

1. Practice not apologizing for who you are and for your cultural traditions.

2. Practice slowing down the process by staying in the moment and observing body sensations during difficult dialogues, especially those about race.

3. Practice self-love by increasing admiration of self and people who look like you through identifying areas of appreciation.

4. Practice self-care by achieving #3 and giving yourself time and space to process your experiences, feelings, thoughts, hopes, and dreams as an Asian person.

5. Practice acknowledging and appreciating your uniqueness without marginalizing others.

6. Practice taking up space physically and mentally.

7. Practice gaining awareness of the expectations you perceive others have of you as an Asian.

8. Practice voicing your reality and your individual narratives without accommodating the expectations of whites or changing any aspect of your narratives to fit into white culture.

9. Practice paying attention to how you behave similarly and differently to various racial groups.

10. Practice acknowledging other racial minorities without comparing or competing against them.

11. Practice acknowledging the experience of racial victimization from a social-cultural perspective while avoiding adopting a victim mentality.

12. Practice holding whites accountable for race-related microaggressions and slights that have been committed against you.

*Twelve Practice Tips for Whites*

It is equally important, perhaps even more so, for whites to take important steps to redefine their relationships with Asians in a way that is not predicated on dehumanizing stereotypes, such as the model minority myth. Here are steps that whites are strongly recommended to practice:

1. Practice putting yourself in environments that are unfamiliar and tolerating the discomfort caused by unfamiliarity.

2. Practice holding a curious and nonjudgmental stance in learning about unfamiliar racial/cultural norms.

3. Practice investing the time and enduring the discomfort involved in learning how to accurately pronounce Asian/non-European names.

4. Practice discipline, commitment, and respect by avoiding assigning Anglo names to Asians unless they ask for one.

5. Practice holding a curious stance in understanding the reasons why Asians might ask for Anglo names.

6. Practice self-examination and self-exploration to get in touch with how you feel and see yourself when interacting with Asians.

7. Practice slowing down the process by staying in the moment and observing body sensations during difficult dialogues.

8. Practice creating space for others in dialogues and actively listening to unfamiliar stories without giving suggestions.

9. Practice gaining insights on how your existence impacts others, especially on the psychological level.

10. Practice holding a curious stance during all interactions without the need of knowing or jumping to conclusions.

11. Practice acknowledgment and awareness of whiteness and its contribution to the dominant narratives in relationships.

12. Practice steady and continual examination of potentially deeply rooted exoticizing beliefs you harbor, especially those that are gendered, towards Asians.

As a relationship therapist, I believe that everything is about relationships. This does not mean that we have to chase and please others. I believe relationships are about having the awareness of who we are in relation to others, how we stand with others, how we are embraced by others, and what we are creating together with others. Tell our stories, Asian stories! The power of storytelling is not about self-expression or self-righteousness; it is about bringing awareness to the effect of our actions on others. It is important to allow the exposure of our positions in the system in hopes of shifting what is stuck and intentionally creating something different, the second order difference. If past methods for cultivating relationships between Asian and white Americans do not work, why would we continue the same approach? Why don't we find different voices and different solutions? Can we each commit ourself a little more to understanding each other and to creating a sense of home in our communities and in our nation? Attempting to put the aforementioned steps into action might just allow us to take a few steps closer to this ideal.

Keep in mind always the present you are constructing. It should be the future you want.

—WALKER, 1989, P. 236

**LIANG-YING CHOU, PHD,** is a family therapist and relationship coach. Born and raised in Taiwan, Dr. Chou is bilingual, fluent in English and Mandarin Chinese. Dr. Chou, a former assistant professor of marital and family therapy at Alliant International University in Irvine, California, has over ten years of experience teaching and supervising in accredited therapy programs. She works in private practice in New York and California. She concentrates on delivering services to diverse populations and the understanding of marginalized experiences. Her work, focusing on training and working with various Asian communities, has been presented in journals and major conferences nationally and internationally.

## References

*Hardy, K. V. (2008). Race, reality, and relationships: Implications for the re-visioning of family therapy. In M. McGoldrick & K. V. Hardy (Eds.),* Re-visioning family therapy: Race, culture, and gender in clinical practice *(2nd ed., pp. 76–84). Guilford Press.*

*Li, P.-F., Chou, L.-Y., Yang, I.-S., Chang, W.-N., & Kim, J.-H. (2020). Supervision with East Asian international supervisees: Unfolding unspoken complexities.* Journal of Systemic Therapies, 39*(4), 72–88.*

*Ross, G. (Director). (2012).* The hunger games *[Film]. Lionsgate Films.*

*Walker, A. (1989).* The temple of my familiar. *Harcourt.*

*White, M., & Epston, D. (1990).* Narrative means to therapeutic ends. *W. W. Norton & Company.*

*Zinnemann, F. (Director). (1959).* The nun's story *[Film]. Warner Bros.*

## CHAPTER 12

# Silenced by Whiteness

## A Personal Account

IRENE IN HEE SUNG, MD

I am a Korean American daughter of immigrants. These are not words that have flowed easily from my mouth in professional settings. In my medical training and through residency in psychiatry, these words were only relevant during those very few specific trainings on the impact of culture and race on the therapeutic process. Otherwise, they were put away, irrelevant to my practice. I was supposed to be either a blank slate or someone whose female gender, age, or "doctor" status would be used as material for patients' expressions of transference. Race was rarely mentioned.

In this chapter, I will explore the impact of whiteness on my identity as a professional and the parts of my life that were silenced and ultimately lost, even to me.

There were times in my psychiatry training when the impact of race on my work with patients became so blatant that I believed it could not be ignored. An example of this was in my second-year rotation at the VA hospital in San Francisco when a white male Vietnam veteran was admitted into urgent care, clearly in emotional distress, with his body shaking, fists clenched, and knuckles white. As the psychiatric resident-on-call, it was my duty to assess and stabilize the patient's symptoms. From the moment I walked into the room, he repeatedly described his distress as being due to the fact that he kept seeing "ornamentals." It took a few minutes to realize that he was referring to "Orientals" and that my presence was causing him further harm. I quickly refilled his medication, and he left the hospital. For the rest of the evening, I thought about his use of the word "ornamental." Was I simply an ornament, a decoration with little practical purpose? When describing the situation to my supervisor (a white man) the next morning, his assessment was that the use of this word was one of psychotic thinking and of little relevance, implying that any impact on me, a young Asian psychiatrist in training, was of little relevance as well. I had enough experience with white people to know that this was a sign to move on to the next subject. As a female, a resident, and an Asian, I knew there was absolutely no room for a discussion or a dissenting view. I used the only option that was available to me and one that I would, though I didn't know it at the time, use for much of my career: I remained silent. As a good model minority, I "decided" to move on.

## Model Minority Status Within Whiteness

Model minority. This is a term I have heard since I was young. This was the term to describe people like me (Asian people) in the United States. It was a term that set Asians apart from other People of Color and offered protection from the level of discrimination that other minorities endured. It allowed a path for Asian immigrants to reach the "American Dream." For my parents, this dream represented the socioeconomic success that would allow my future family and me physical comforts and financial security. This dream began with my Korean immigrant parents and their expectation that a higher socioeconomic status needed to be achieved and continued through my siblings and me, the first generation of our family to be born in the United States. I also believe they thought this status meant we would have the respect of "Americans," specifically, white Americans. To this day, I remember my father's words, "It is more important to be respected than to be liked."

I wonder if they understood that this pursuit would require me to embrace the model minority role—work harder, don't make waves, stay humble and quiet about your achievements, keep others around you comfortable. These are the qualities that would allow those in power—white people—to see my utility in a nonthreatening way. On this path, I gained the socioeconomic success of the American Dream by attending to my relationship with whiteness, which would dictate my success or survival and shape my interactions with others throughout my childhood, education, and early professional career. However, I remained acutely aware that, as demonstrated by events associated with the COVID-19 pandemic, being "model" does not assure respect nor imbue one with full protection from racist attacks (Lee & Yadav, 2020).

## Taejon: Whiteness in Korea

My relationship with whiteness did not start with me. It began in Taejon, a small Korean farming town, in the early 1930s, while Korea was under Japanese occupation. As a young child, my father had heard family stories of white people who would come to Korea to preach the teachings of Christianity, stories which were always coupled with the reminder that his family strictly adhered to the teachings of Confucius. Still, these reminders did not keep him from being curious about the Catholic church that he passed on his way to middle school each day. His very first glimpse of a white person was the priest of this church, the missionary—a tall, bearded man with big, round, blue eyes and a long, full, blond beard. I never thought, until later in my life, about what it must have meant for my father that his first glimpse of a white person was connected to deity.

The presence of the white man, however, was subsumed by an immediate threat. The Japanese rulers of their Korean colony were discriminating against, devaluing, and dehumanizing the Korean people. My parents, along with all Koreans at that time, faced a systematic wiping of Korean history including: making it illegal to teach Korean history or speak in the Korean language in schools; burning Korean historical documents and tearing down historical buildings, particularly palaces that represented Korean power; and removing native plant species, replacing them with those from Japan, thus changing the very landscape of Korea (Blakemore, 2018).

During the Second World War, my parents experienced additional oppression as high school students. Classroom education had all but disappeared, and students served as laborers; the girls would use their sewing skills to repair Japanese uniforms, and the boys would participate in hard labor, such as tarring airstrips for Japanese planes to land on. Any teaching that occurred was focused on promoting the Japanese government's propaganda. My parents were taught to fear Western influences and that the British, French, and Americans were trying to colonize Asia and would completely destroy the Korean way of life. Japan was supposedly protecting Korea from this fate, though one would question which would be worse: the severe oppression by Japan or colonization by the white men from the West. Would the white people destroy the Korean people and culture? What choice did Koreans have in the matter anyway? Communication was chaotic, and misinformation rampant. The only information Korean students received about the war from their teachers was that Japan was winning the war, all the way up until Emperor Hirohito announced the surrender of Japan on August 15, 1945. In Hirohito's address, Korea was not mentioned by name, and its liberation had to be inferred (Chee, 2020). My father remembers that day clearly, as well as the day the US soldiers marched into Taejon with trucks and tanks, several weeks later. They were many, well organized, and they gave away goods, such as chocolate and spam. To him, they represented abundance, power, and strength. Of equal significance is the fact that the Stalin-led Soviets, whose governments were modeled after their "white saviors," had arrived in the North, which set the stage for the partitioning of the Korean peninsula (National Archives, n.d.). While more benevolent in appearance, the US soldiers still had the markings of colonizers, and from my father's experience with the Japanese, it is the subjugated who need to adjust and to appease in order to survive.

## Collaborating with Whiteness: The Korean War

As a young doctor who just completed medical school, my father enlisted in the Korean Air Force and was sent to the front line, joining a Korean medical unit alongside medical staff from the United States. Upon arrival, he experienced mistrust from the Americans with whom he was working, and he found out they suspected that the Korean doctor from the prior tour of duty had stolen antibiotics from their unit.

The lead physician in the American medical unit was a white, Jewish man named Dr. G. My father spent an extensive amount of time speaking with Dr. G, presenting patient histories, diagnoses, and treatment plans, as well as passing on gifts that had been given to him from the local soldiers' families. My father believed that engaging Dr. G helped to build trust and led to true friendship. Dr. G freely shared his medical books and, together with my father, helped local Korean villagers who had fallen ill. This friendship led to an extension of my father's tour at the front line from the typical 6 months to almost 2 years, until the end of the war, in part because of his sense of duty for the South Korean cause and in part because Dr. G asked that he stay longer because the visibility of their growing friendship helped to minimize the discord between the Korean and American medical staff. This friendship also contributed to Dr. G's sponsoring my father's immigration to the United States for further medical training, for which he is eternally grateful.

It is still not clear to me whether this close relationship was built on utility or on true feelings of friendship. How much effort had Dr. G put into their relationship? What attempts had Dr. G made to speak Korean and understand the culture? Was the sponsorship to the United States a repayment for my father's added tour, or did he truly care for my father? Either way, hearing these stories as a young child reinforced the notion that a white man in your corner is invaluable, and it would be my responsibility, as the Person of Color, to build the trust of white men in power.

## Silenced by White Men

Over the years, my relationships with white male teachers have reinforced the silencing of any expression of individuality through resistance or feeling. This reinforcement played directly into the characteristics of the model minority that I was to embody. In fifth grade, my parents moved to a wealthy suburb on the outskirts of St. Paul, Minnesota. The elementary school I attended placed me in the classroom of Mr. P, a tall athletic white man in his 30s, who was popular among the students. I was new to the school and, largely due to historical redlining, the only Student of Color in our class. Each year, Mr. P held the tradition of giving birthday spankings to all his students in his class. Mr. P would approach this act playfully, often joking with students on the morning of their birthday that sometime during the day it would be their "turn." My birthday fell toward the end of the school year, which gave me an opportunity to observe closely how each student responded to his spanking. Some students ran around the classroom until he caught them before they submitted. One of my friends negotiated for getting a light spanking in return for standing quietly in front of him. There were others (mostly boys) who resisted, and he would forcibly bend them over his knee. I had the chance to choose who and how I would be in this moment. Playful? Submissive? Resistant? On the day of my "turn," I chose resistance. I would not allow him to spank me easily. I only recently remembered the rage that rose in me when he grabbed me on the day that I turned 11. When he got a hold of me, I did something that I hadn't done since I was a toddler. I bit him. My memory of the actual bite is somewhat fuzzy, but my memory of his response is not. I heard him say, "Oh, now you're really going to get it!" As I looked up while one of his legs held my bottom up and the other held my torso down, his face was red and angry, not playful as I had seen him with the other students. I remember the burn on my bottom and the tears in my eyes. What had I missed? Wasn't resistance an acceptable way to respond? Maybe just not for me. I remember my friend asked if I was OK. Not wanting to add humiliation to the pain, I brushed them off as tears of laughter. I learned my lesson: Do not resist; stay quiet.

Since then, I have remained quiet when I observed or experienced actions that degraded me as a professional. For example, twice in my adult professional life, I have been patted on the head by white men. Both were white male doctors, and both had an "isn't she cute" expression on their faces when they did it. One was the chief of surgery whose surgical rounds I attended as a senior medical student. The other was a psychiatrist who was chair of a national committee after I was introduced as an early career psychiatrist by my mentor. I have often wondered if there was something in me—my voice, my body, my actions—that encouraged this. As a young woman, I had never thought of my physical appearance as one of exoticism, as is often ascribed to Asian women. If anything, I thought I emanated the cute "china doll" look of Miyoshi Umeki, the housekeeper in *The Courtship of Eddie's Father* (Komack, 1969–1972), rather than the sexualized exoticism of Nancy Kwan in *Flower Drum Song* (Koster, 1961). Did this "china doll" look give them permission to touch me? Did I answer a question or make a joke in such a way that encouraged this? I honestly cannot recall what led to the seemingly playful, yet extraordinarily demeaning, pats on the head, but I do recall feeling that, somehow, I was responsible for the shock and dismay I felt for this public humiliation. I was in the early days of my career as a doctor, and I wondered how anyone could take me seriously. The second time was the last—from that point forward, I kept a close watch to keep my head out of the reach of white men and monitored myself to keep from doing or saying anything that could be construed as cute in their presence.

In my professional life, I valued my utility over my humanity and my productivity over my feelings, which were compartmentalized for "appropriate" settings—at home or with friends. I remained quiet in seminars unless I had the words to speak with a confident academic or clinical tone. For any required public speaking, I wrote my presentations out, word for word, and then practiced them for days until the words flowed smoothly from my mouth. If I didn't hear the praise "good job" or "good presentation" from my teachers or others, I would ruminate for weeks about how I could have made the presentation praiseworthy. This would be my only way to escape the feelings of humiliation, degradation, and pain. Today, I wonder if the words from my father "It is more important to be respected . . ." pushed me harder and if it made me question whether things along the way would provide me a path to achieve the respect component of the "American Dream."

## Understanding White Professionalism Through Professionals of Color

It took me some time to realize that the memories I have of my supervisory experiences with Professionals of Color had been drowned out by this fear of disapproval by white professionals. However, there is an early experience that I hold in stark contrast to much of my early training. In my first year as a doctor in training after medical school, I was placed on an Asian-focused inpatient psychiatric unit at San Francisco General Hospital. The lead psychiatrist for our clinical team was Dr. D, a small Vietnamese man who, prior to his immigration to the United States, had been trained as an infectious disease specialist. He sometimes mentioned his experience as a refugee "boat person," something he shared with some of the patients under his care. The United States did not fully accept his medical training in Vietnam, so Dr. D was required to start his career over when he arrived, and he began by volunteering on the very psychiatric ward that he led where I was his trainee. Rather than return to his infectious disease specialty, he chose to pursue his medical training in psychiatry. He was an astute clinician and generous teacher, often staying late with his trainees to teach about psychiatric assessments, diagnoses, and treatments. I will never forget the conversation we had late one evening after completing the hospital admission of a patient who had been suffering from mania and hallucinations. After the discussion about the patient and completion of admission orders, I had a quiet moment to complete my progress notes before heading home for the day. In this moment, Dr. D reflected on the importance of the field of psychiatry. He believed that this field helped us better understand people, explaining that it helped him understand his own parents better. It was this understanding that helped him love them more. I was moved by this statement. A psychiatrist sharing his own personal experience of love for his parents? This was one of the few times in training that I allowed myself to feel rather than just think.

He was my supervisor for one rotation—only 3 months. His ability to be vulnerable and show me his true self was so meaningful that it has stuck with me to this day. I understood that he was a person, not just a supervisor, doctor, or teacher. He saw me as a person, not just a trainee or student. He and other Professionals of Color whom I had the honor of learning from provided me a way to see that I was more than my utility. It provided a stark contrast to my experience of white professionalism, where objectivity, diagnosis, psychological formulation, and treatment planning were mainstays of the training. These were always discussed devoid of feeling because having feelings required analysis. Did they represent transference or countertransference? What in this patient's biology or past can be attributed to the behavior they are exhibiting and the feelings that are being expressed? What can we do to curb the dysfunction?

## My Own Dr. G

I have also had white supervisors and mentors who have helped me, who have supported my practice, who have connected me with colleagues, and for whom I hold great fondness. Yet what remains ever present is the embodiment of my experiences with whiteness and, in particular, white men. This complexity affects my working relationships to this day.

I have one such colleague, a Jewish man I met in the first year of my child and adolescent psychiatry fellowship. K was the lead social worker on the psychiatric inpatient unit and the teacher of our family therapy seminar. My approach to him at the time was similar to how I approached all white professional men—with vigilant deference; often silent and careful to review every word I was to speak in my head before I said them aloud. After I graduated, we kept in contact, sharing experiences as we both moved from the academic institution to community-based organizations; K's on the East Coast and mine in San Francisco. After his return to San Francisco several years later, we moved forward in roles with organizations that allowed us to work together more directly. Sometimes K was my superior and other times he was my subordinate. Throughout this time, our relationship strengthened. We frequently checked in with each other at the beginning or the end of our day to connect—sometimes to discuss work, sometimes to express frustration if something challenged us, and sometimes simply to say "hi." There are ways that I have relied on and felt gratitude for his help—to review a presentation I was to give or to be my sounding board before I made a difficult decision. I also believe this feeling is mutual and know that there are ways he has relied on me too. Our conversations always felt honest and true, even when we disagreed. Through our work, we have maintained a close, supportive friendship for over 25 years.

When I agreed to write this chapter, I did not anticipate that it would lead me to reflect on this particular relationship. Along with the parts of our relationship for which I hold immense joy and warmth, there are, still, ways in which K's privilege as a white man infuriates me. Upon reflection, I realized I have felt anger at his ability to walk into white spaces with ease, whereas I am not at ease in white spaces. I have felt jealous of the respect K commands when he speaks up in meetings and how effortless speaking up appears to be for him, while I struggle, searching for the "right thing to say."

I felt an urgency to share these feelings with K; and as I expected, true to our relationship, he was open to hearing what I had to say. By the time we were able to talk, I had several days to fully distill and imagine how the conversation would go. I imagined (and rehearsed) an honest expression of my anger and frustration. When we actually spoke, the conversation was very different. It began with gratitude, stating that our relationship has been an important one in my life and thanking him for helping me without expecting anything in return. Then, as I began to express my feelings about K's space in the world as a white man, I started censoring myself. My words came out as an explanation, justification devoid of feeling. In that moment, I wanted to take them back. I did not feel what I was saying, and I worried I was hurting him and/or our relationship in the process. So, I backed off. I expressed more gratitude, thanking him more than once for his willingness to hear me out.

Over the next few days, I ruminated over whether I truly felt any of the things I had said to him. I was having trouble connecting to any feelings, even sadness over the recent loss of a very close relative who unexpectedly passed away. One morning a few days later, I sat at my desk to write more of this chapter, still unable to access feeling; I texted him, "I'm really stuck." He called immediately and tears flowed from my eyes. In that moment, I was able to access all the feelings that had been pent up inside of me that I had stored away, those I was trying to express to him several days prior, and the disappointment that my self-censoring meant I still worried about how our relationship would be affected by this true expression.

I thought about my father. I wondered if his relationship with Dr. G held the same complexity of caring and oppression. It was the white leaders of USSR and USA who made the decision to divide Korea, which is the only reason the Korean War could even happen. Did my father's feelings about white people ever come into his relationship with Dr. G? Were they allowed to come up? Was he ever frustrated and/or exhausted that he was responsible for the burden of managing the relationship—to learn English, to stay at the front line longer? Did my father even recognize the complexity of their relationship; if so, was he ever able to communicate any of these feelings without fearing that he would lose Dr. G as a friend? Were his feelings also silenced?

## Lessons I Have Learned

It is difficult to distill 57 years of learning into a single chapter. Reconciling my experiences of being suppressed with those that supported my liberation (such as those with Dr. D) is much more nuanced and complicated than can be reflected in these few examples.

Reflecting on my most recent experience with my white friend has helped me realize that the compartmentalization of my feelings is so automatic that I will often fall into the familiar (yet ultimately painful) response of disconnecting what I am feeling behind words and explanations that have been rehearsed. It was as if the feelings were hidden not *by* me, but *from* me. In that moment, I began questioning myself, my feelings, my beliefs, and my own authenticity. It was not until I took time to reflect and review these things that I was able to bring forward what I have learned from Dr. D's expression of authentic feelings. This authentic expression requires continuous conscious awareness. When confronted with any perceived risk I will, if I am not paying attention, automatically shy away from the authentic feelings that accompany my thoughts, beliefs, and memories. It is not just the silencing of words, but the silencing of feeling that I continue to fight each day.

Obviously, I am still learning, even as I write this chapter, about the various ways in which my everyday life is organized by whiteness. Not surprisingly, the intricacies of sorting out whiteness on my sense of self is a daunting process that requires time and introspection. It is a process that I have been actively engaged in for quite some time, and I suspect this will continue. In the paragraphs that follow, I share a methodology for resisting the automaticity of compartmentalization so that my actions, thoughts, and memories can hold more authentic congruence with my feelings.

About 10 years ago, I attended a training on racial humility by Dr. Ken Hardy, who provided tools for recognizing the effects of racial dynamics within organizations. He called the method, "Seeing, Being, and Doing" (Hardy, 2012). In this method, rather than moving straight to action (doing), I would closely observe the racial interaction, event, or environment (seeing), and then reflect on who I was in relationship with: the interaction, the event, or the environment (being). In this way, the action (doing) I subsequently make becomes a choice rather than an unconscious reaction to previous experiences.

Almost a decade later, this model is still a powerful force in my life. I rely heavily on it to assist me in my ongoing journey to overcome my lifelong struggle with silence, especially in relationships with white people. I have adapted and modified it to include one additional step. Rather than applying it to organizations, I use it as a model for interpersonal and spiritual growth to help unmute my voice and maintain awareness of my feelings. The process involves four steps, drawing three of them from Hardy's (2012) work. The steps are as follows:

1. *Explore/Reflect:* For Professionals of Color, exploring one's relationship with whiteness is critical. The self-reflective questions we have to ask ourselves are: (a) How has whiteness affected our relationships with white people? With other People of Color? (b) How much of our interactions are automatic or reactive based on these experiences? White professionals must also engage in a process of critical self-examination and exploration. In so doing, white people must ask themselves, "What are the ways that I support structures and practices that mute the voices and suppress the feelings and voices of Professionals of Color?"

2. *See (Feel):* Pay close attention to feelings that arise, and do not allow them to be ignored or suppressed. Allow the feelings to be present and honored in the moment, even the painful ones; do not hide them away—they will not destroy you.

3. *Be:* Remember all of the parts of you (your history, your race, gender, family, etc.). Be yourself, not just your professional title, education, and/or skills. Do not let "white professionalism" dictate who you are or who you aspire to be.

4. *Do:* Then, choose which parts of your true self you want to bring forward. For example, it took me some time to understand that in my professional life, I could choose to share my life, my history, and my feelings with others. This choice is similar to the one Dr. D made as my supervisor, 30 years ago—a defining moment I will never forget. For the white professional: you can choose which parts of you to bring forward to dismantle the white supremacy that lives in our professional establishments that have routinely and historically silenced Clinicians of Color.

Lastly for my fellow Professionals of Color: be brave but also be gentle with yourself if you fall into old patterns of hiding—the strength of whiteness to silence is great, and it takes constant vigilance to combat. There will always be other opportunities to authentically feel and express. With collective courage, together we will allow ourselves, our true feelings, and our voices to be heard.

**IRENE IN HEE SUNG, MD,** recently retired from her position as chief medical officer of behavioral health for San Francisco's Department of Public Health, where she had worked for over 22 years. Since completing her training in child and adolescent psychiatry at University of California, San Francisco, in 1995, she has dedicated her career to community psychiatry, caring for underserved children and their families. In addition to her work in psychiatry, she served in leadership positions on a number of boards, including the Northern California Regional Organization of Child and Adolescent Psychiatrists and the San Francisco Drug Abuse Advisory Board. In the past seven years, she has focused on the impact of racial bias and how it surfaces in our interactions with others. This work has given her opportunities to discuss race issues in her trainings on leadership and participatory decision-making, a facilitation technique that encourages participants to hear all perspectives without judgment or bias.

## References

*Blakemore, E. (2018, February 27).* How Japan took control of Korea. *History. https://www.history.com/news/japan-colonization-korea*

*Chee, A. (2020, August 27).* My family's shrouded history is also a national one for Korea. *New York Times Magazine. https://www.nytimes.com/2020/08/27/magazine/korea-japanese-occupation-surrender-ww2.html*

*Hardy, K. V. (2012, August).* Racial sensitivity training. *San Francisco Department of Public Health, San Francisco, CA, United States.*

*Komack, J. (Producer). (1969–1972).* The courtship of Eddie's father *[TV series]. MGM Television.*

*Koster, H. (1961).* Flower drum song *[Film]. Ross Hunter Productions; Fields Productions.*

*Lee, J., & Yadav, M. (2020, May 21).* The rise of anti-Asian hate in the wake of covid-19. *Social sciences research council. https://items.ssrc.org/covid-19-and-the-social-sciences/the-rise-of-anti-asian-hate-in-the-wake-of-covid-19*

*National Archives. (n.d.).* US enters the Korean conflict. *https://www.archives.gov/education/lessons/korean-conflict*

## CHAPTER 13

# On Being White Through the Eyes of a Black Dominican

## America, the Land of the Free

ANA HERNANDEZ, PHD

The United States is a society that celebrates the accomplishments of individuals who traverse great obstacles, like poverty, abuse, and other injustices. Successfully overcoming hardships, while laudable, also comes with tremendous stress, anxiety, and mental anguish. The history of slavery in the Americas, not just the United States, is a story of overcoming great obstacles for Black people; however, once freed, the enslaved Africans never received mental health treatment for the trauma that they endured. In fact, they didn't receive anything, not finances, housing, medical care, land, or any other resource, from the dominant white majority who enslaved them (Mitchell, 2001). Individuals of other races often take pride in coming to the United States with "nothing" and somehow making it to the "top," which means obtaining high ranking positions, economic stability, housing, and access to resources. Black people are expected to do the same despite having greater obstacles. What often goes unacknowledged is that the United States, as a country, is a white space where Black, Latino, and Native Americans are not seen as part of the country, regardless of social location. Former President Barack Obama was an excellent example of this phenomenon. He had to prove that he was born in the United States, a validation proof that was never asked of any of the previous (white) presidents. What is also unacknowledged is that being at or on the "top" also means following a mandate to adhere to whiteness and white culture. If there is a top, there is a bottom, which is often a location relegated to our most vulnerable and marginalized population: the poor, immigrants, and Blacks. Being at the bottom in this country means being devalued, mistreated, and disrespected by the general population. These social hierarchies have serious implications for mental health. They are traumatic.

The fact that the United States can decide to own the title of "America" is an example of entitlement and de facto whiteness in action. North America is comprised of the United States of Mexico, the United States of America, and Canada. Yet Mexicans and Canadians are not typically thought of or referred to as "Americans." Costa Rica, Honduras, and Panama, among others, are in Central America, yet no one in these countries is allowed to consider themselves an "American," and they are all refused entry at the US border when seeking legal asylum. For South America, including Brazil and Chile, the same is true. Instead, the white people decided to create a term, *Latin America* (Phelan, 1968), to group all Spanish-speaking countries in the Western Hemisphere, even though there are different tribes, races, and ethnic identities. White people have this power to name and define an entire group of people. Everyone is expected to unquestionably accept it and forget that the white settlers came and stole this land from the Indigenous people who were already here. This, which emanates from the erasure of identity and the assault on a group's sense of safety and belongingness, is racial trauma.

Some of my earliest memories include my frequent visits to the Dominican Republic, the country of origin of my parents and grandparents, between the ages of 3 months and 5 years old. I was the first grandchild, on both sides of the family, and the first *American* born in the family. My mother was already pregnant with me when she arrived in Harlem, New York, at the age of 25. The courage it took to leave all that she knew behind in search of a better life, filled with opportunity, economic security, and progress for herself and the child in her womb, was a sign of tremendous faith. The hardships she endured as a Spanish-speaking, Black woman with minimal formal education was immense. She was unaware of the barriers she had to overcome due to structural racism, anti-Blackness, anti-immigrant sentiment, and sexism, and yet she still chose prosperity, freedom, and progress. This experience is not unique to her. Historically, slaves born in the Americas learned, from birth, how colonial society worked and how to best maneuver through that society in order to pursue freedom (Andrews, 2004). In some ways, she was doomed to endure the same hardships that she was persistently trying to escape back home, except that in the United States, they were subtle, covert, and at times misleading. The narrative of racism was shaped toward the African American experience.

## How a Latino Identity Erases Blackness

The stories of Black people from Central and South America and the Caribbean are often erased under the guise of forging a *Latino identity*. The story of how my family arrived can be misunderstood by many. Many Dominicans go to Puerto Rico via a boat as a means to get to the United States. This has caused tensions between Dominicans and Puerto Ricans that continue to this day. When I visit the Dominican Republic, I'm always exposed to the news, which tends to periodically give updates about the successes and failures of these boats. This is because the journey is quite dangerous. The boats are never secure, they are often overcrowded, and the ocean currents can be so strong and powerful that more often than not the boat is capsized, and all the people end up drowning, missing, or both. My mother's father fled the Dominican Republic via boat to Puerto Rico. My mother often tells me how hard it was for them to not have her dad around as the primary provider and how they had no way of communicating with him for over a year. During this time, they had difficulty getting enough food and other basic necessities. He made it to New York, but once there, he married a Dominican-American citizen, even though he was married through the church to my grandmother, who was back in the Dominican Republic. With this legal union, despite the heartbreak and turmoil he caused my grandmother and his children, he was able to successfully file a legal petition for his two oldest children to join him, my mother being one of them. As a result of my mother being here and having residency, she was able to petition for my father and my grandmother to legally come to the United States. My grandfather, a strong, dark-skinned Black man, was incredibly strategic. He was a warrior that thought beyond himself to his entire lineage: Los Solanos. Even in his death in 2008, both families attended his funeral and took turns saying their goodbyes. It was understood that, despite how it looked compared to the white Western Eurocentric family composition, where the ideal is having a two-parent home with 2.5 kids, he was the reason we were all here in the land of opportunity. This is a Black story too. When we Black people are not free, we are forced to be strategic, political, and visionary. Black people and People of Color are judged harshly by white America for certain decisions we make about our lives without realizing that we are forced under limiting conditions that create the necessary radical mobilization, sacrifice, and determination to be free, to be equal, and to ensure that our families suffer less than we have suffered. Whites sell us the myth of Black inferiority to justify the conditions we find ourselves in (Watson, 2013). White Europeans have secured a life of privilege for themselves and their race and have secured their lineage in this way, but they want this opportunity to be exclusive to them—and have disconnected from this reality.

## Family Bonds Between Two Nations

When I was 3 months old, my mother realized that she needed help with raising me in Harlem. She was living with her father's family in a small two-bedroom apartment and trying to finish college courses, while she waited for my father's travel visa to be approved so that he could come and help her make a life there. Thus, she made the difficult decision of sending me to live with my grandmother in Santo Domingo. My uncle, who brought me there on a plane, warned my grandmother: "Cuida bien a esta niña porque ella es Americana y si le pasa algo aqui, van a venir el militar a investigar" ("Take good care of this child because she is American. If something happens to her here, the United States military will come and investigate"). This set the stage for my grandmother to be overly protective of me and emotionally hypersensitive to my needs, often to the confusion of her sisters, who told her every time I fell and scratched my knee "You successfully raised five children into adulthood, stop overreacting!"

My family was acutely aware of the impact, privileges, and value of being born in the United States before I was aware of it myself. The value comes primarily from its white heritage, which is often unacknowledged and implicit. It comes from the value placed on the accomplishments of white people, not of the Native/Indigenous people or the African Americans. Implicitly, being American meant being white. In some ways, as a baby, and probably because I was born light-skinned, I was considered "white," and to this day my uncle jokingly refers to me as "white American" and not as a Dominican. The role of whiteness has impacted my identity and how others, even my own family, relate to me. I often wish that my specialness in my family was less about my proximity to whiteness as an American and more about my unique personality, style, and character. I learned early on that whiteness is defined by more than skin color, and it is cherished.

When I was in elementary school, I had to learn the mainstream course content plus learn English while in ESL classes. If this weren't enough, I also was learning deeply racial messages about my skin tone. I remember learning that there was something wrong with being my skin tone. I had internalized deeply rooted anti-Black sentiments. I wasn't aware of it, but I do remember going home and telling my mom that I wanted to rub my skin color off. I naively thought I could do this by using soap and water to scrub it off my arms. At 6 years old, I was already exposed to the dominant narrative about the inferiority of Blackness. This is an example of what it is like to be in a white space, where whiteness is glorified and Blackness is vilified. Despite growing up in the Bronx, New York, virtually all of my teachers were white men and women. At 6 years old, I had absorbed these negative sentiments, internalized them, and I believed them. I have spent years overcoming, unlearning, and externalizing these toxic messages.

When I was accepted into a predominantly white university, the University of Vermont, I was aware of the conditions. At the time, the University of Vermont was under the presidency of Daniel Mark Fogel, who had made a commitment to increase diversity at the institution. The University of Vermont partnered with several inner-city schools, and my school, Christopher Columbus High School, was one of them. I received a full scholarship due to having a high school grade point average of 85.00 or higher for four consecutive years. The scholarship was a combination of government assistance (Pell Grants) and a major scholarship called the Jonathan Levin Scholarship fund. Jonathan Levin was the son of the head of Time-Warner, Gerald M. Levin. Jonathan Levin was a 31-year-old high school English teacher at Taft High School in the Bronx. He was murdered on May 31, 1997, during a robbery by a student of his who considered him to be rich after discovering his identity and who his father was (Rohde, 1998). Jonathan Levin was committed to teaching in an underserved inner-city community, and as a result of his tragic death, the scholarship fund was started in his name. I would not be where I am academically if it hadn't been for government assistance and this scholarship fund that was meant to provide opportunities for people like me: people who would not have a lasting chance at higher education without someone thinking of us who are poor and marginalized. At the same time, I realized that this wealthy white man had such an influence on my journey by creating a path for my success in a way that I couldn't create for myself. I have depended on the United States government and white people for my livelihood my entire life. Some people will see this as testament that I should be grateful, and even I have struggled with this. The white savior is an important identity that white people enjoy and Black people and People of Color believe in. However, this is not the point. It is my belief that we need to restructure the conditions that create the need for a white savior. When these conditions are eradicated, Black people and People of Color will be free to reach their true purpose in life by their own means.

## Playing Catch Up

While I was in college, my social status was always painfully clear to me: poor and Black. I noticed that most of the student population was white as I walked around the beautiful campus in late August, a week before classes started. And as I walked down the hill toward the university bookstore, I saw long lines of mostly white students who were there to pick up their books for the semester. It suddenly dawned on me that these students had preordered *all* of their books, brand-new, and were picking them up. College books were between $50 and $200 each. I was shocked. I knew that I had to wait for my refund check, which would be processed after my scholarship money posted, and that almost always happened around at most two weeks *after* classes started. Also, most of the first-year students had completely moved into their dorm rooms with all of their computers, bedding, toiletries, TVs, microwaves, speakers, and everything that they needed to be comfortable and ready. All I had was the university brand bedding, a laptop that I'd had to take a loan out for—and which took me 3 years post-undergraduate school to pay off—and some basic toiletries. My TV, microwave, North Face coats, and books did not come until several semesters after my first. I realized that if I was going to survive, I had to make the system work for me. I applied, and was accepted, for an on-campus resident assistant position, which provided free room and board. For the remainder of my college career, I always received a substantial amount of money in my refund check because the part of the scholarship money that would have gone toward my room and board would now be refunded to me as cash that I could use for all of my living expenses. Like my grandfather and my mother, I had to be very strategic in order to survive. This is, in part, what it means to be poor and Black in America, "the land of the free."

As an Afro-Latina, I was 10 steps behind, and it took considerable effort to catch up to my white peers because of the confluence of my race and social class status. Most white students saw me as an affirmative action admission because of my skin color, even though I was working twice as hard as they were. I worked tirelessly because part of me wanted to prove that I really did belong there. Nevertheless, they just saw a Black person occupying space where there should have been another white person, and that alone was unacceptable in their eyes. I was never overtly told to "go back where you came from," but I felt the sentiment many times. I saw it in the way they looked at me, with looks that ranged from pity to disdain. I heard it in the tones of their voices that was never without an echo of superiority. Many of my friends reported incidents of racism on campus. My best friend, another Dominican, was attacked by a dog that belonged to a white woman. After fending off the dog, she was told by the white woman, "It's just that my dog is not used to seeing people like you." Another friend, a Haitian/Trinidadian woman who often wore baggy clothing and hoodies, was misidentified by the UVM police for a Black man who was sought after for reportedly stealing a laptop computer from a white college student. She was shoved to the ground by three white cops, handcuffed, and when they realized that the person they were looking for was a man and that she was a woman, she was let go. This incident led to a discussion between the ALANA (African, Latino, Asian, Native American) Center and the UVM police on a Saturday afternoon that lasted about 4 hours. Although conversations such as these continued to happen on campus, the incidents never stopped, which left me wondering if the white students were also having these conversations. As a community, we People of Color still had to show up to class, go to the library to do our homework, sit together in the cafeteria and eat lunch. There was an implicit message that we were not wanted on campus. Most of us were first-generation college students whose parents needed us to finish college against all odds.

We had to proceed with business as usual while drowning in a sea of emotional pain and this pain remained invisible.

This fueled rage that I often kept hidden, mostly because I was overly concerned with being perceived as an ungrateful angry Black person. When San Francisco 49ers football player Colin Kaepernick knelt during the national anthem in protest of police brutality and racial inequality in the United States, many white people I encountered made statements like, "He is a high-earning football player thanks to this country" and "We gave him a job so he should respect the flag and the nation." These expressions highlighted and reminded me of how white culture and the nation as a whole are oblivious to the struggles of Black people and judge us when we complain about it. The dominant narrative I get from white people in so many words is essentially "You are free and you have access to money and resources and education, so why are you complaining?" What they don't see is that Black people and People of Color are descendants of colonization and so are always 10 steps behind everyone else.

By the time I made it to graduate school, I had given up on white people. There were 10 students—Asian, Latino, Black, and white—in my graduating class at Syracuse University. Even though we were a diverse group, everyone was so white. They often made references to white music artists like The Fray or white movie stars like Ben Affleck. Though I am a dark-skinned Dominican, if I had followed their lead, I'd never have known about the soulful music of Ledesi or KEM. Luckily, I've stayed connected to my roots, so I know about the influence of Black Cuban woman Celia Cruz and Black Dominican merengue artist Kinito Mendez. Of course, I enjoyed the music of Amara La Negra before she became mainstream in the US market. My classmates were "white" because the system and their desire to succeed required them to be white! Being white means paying attention to white countries like Denmark and the United Kingdom. For example, when I'm in a "white" group and they talk about the great achievement of Switzerland having a woman president and how far behind the United States is for not having one. Yet, Brazil had a woman president, and Costa Rica had one too. The difference is that these are not white nations, therefore not in the minds of white people.

I remember a diversity class in which we were talking about race relations and I admitted that I had given up on white people and thus had no interest in having a racial dialogue in the class. The South Asian professor instructed me to look at all the white students in the class and tell them that. I followed her instructions and looked each of them in the eye and told them "I have given up on you." By the time I got to the last white person, the whole room was crying. This activity was so powerful that it propelled me to be honest and transparent. One of the white students, an older woman who was married with children, encouraged me to seek out a white professor who was no longer in the program but was known for facilitating racial dialogues and start our own group with that professor as a facilitator. We approached the professor at a conference and told her we were interested in her services and are willing to pay out of pocket. We motivated all of my class, except two students, to participate, and the group ran for two summers. By the end of the first summer, the director of the program, a white male, was not happy that we were doing this. He felt that it was unnecessary because the formal training we were getting was sufficient. The white classmate who had encouraged and inspired me to start the group was beginning to experience discomfort because of the director's disapproval. She ultimately decided to drop out of the group and didn't join the group for the second summer. She told me that she was concerned that the director's disapproval of the group could impact her grade or ability to graduate. Participation in the group should not have jeopardized our standing in the program because we were not violating any university or program policy and we were paying out of pocket. Even though three other white students continued to support the group and valued the racial dialogues, the behavior of this white woman who claimed to be—and initially had been—so supportive of racial conversations helped me realize that it will be futile to engage some white people around discussions about race. This triggered hopelessness and hurt in me because she had been so eager and supportive in the beginning, but when she became fearful, she stood and watched from the sidelines as the rest of us proceeded. I think it would have been ideal for us to continue the race conversations with that South Asian professor; however, it is very possible that she didn't feel like she could address these matters within her department, which was a predominantly white space, and that she did not have enough power and authority, even as a Brown professor, to do this. It is unfortunate that my only option was to seek out a white professor who was no longer connected to the program, and therefore had the freedom to do this work authentically, even though I had already given up on white people and had made that clear. This is an example of the pervasiveness of whiteness in the lives of Black people and People of Color. No matter how frustrated, angry, and hurt we are with white people, we still have to compose ourselves and show up to certain spaces for our own survival and livelihood.

## The Commodification of Black- and Brownness

As a Black Dominican, I knew I was a commodity in white spaces. As a Black person, I could provide leadership to diversity committees and take on Clients of Color at a higher rate than my white counterparts, who often struggled with understanding our issues. I also spoke Spanish and, as one of my white bosses told me, "We have had a very hard time finding *qualified* Latino people who speak Spanish in the Bronx." As a result, I was assigned all of the Spanish-speaking clients who needed therapy but otherwise wouldn't have access to it, due to the language barrier. I gladly took this on, because the Latino, Spanish-speaking community is also my community, as is the Black community, so I have always been professionally committed to these populations. However, it still concerned me that a "qualified" Latino was being sought and not found. What makes someone qualified is always their degree and license status and, of course, their mastery of the English language. Mastery of the English language is prioritized over mastery of the Spanish language, which is, in this case, more important since that is the primary language used to communicate with clients, whether you're a therapist, a social worker, or a psychiatrist. One of my white bosses at a mental health agency hired me only after we had a good, long conversation strictly in Spanish. I knew she was testing my Spanish proficiency. Apparently I passed, because I was hired, but I often wondered if she would have done this to a light-skinned Latina. I wondered this because, even though I passed her language test, at a meeting with a major NYC department, she introduced herself as a Latina and me as a person who speaks Spanish. This, too, shows how whiteness works. It glorifies proximity to whiteness and repudiates and demonizes Blackness. As a dark-skinned Afro-Latina, I am certain that she saw me as only Black, and thus not Latina. It was clear to me in that moment that she considered herself superior and a legitimate Latina because of her light skin. It was visible to everyone in the room that I was Black, so her introduction solidified the separation between Black and Latino and, essentially, between white (proximity) and Black. From her perspective, my Black skin negated my Latina identity; I was just someone who happened to speak Spanish, and she was Latina.

## Life Lessons

Based on my life experience, I find white people to be completely oblivious of their whiteness and influence around the world. Most of them even seem to lack a comprehensive understanding of their history. I often hope that white people will study their history and who they are as people. When I study white history, I see a lot of pain that is hard for me to fully understand and conceptualize because I am not white. My hope is that if whites focused on studying themselves and their experiences rather than studying everyone else, they might find what it is that leads the majority of them to develop such destructive systems that affect not only humanity but also animals and the planet. Whites have colonized every continent and have created a phenomenon in which nonwhites around the world want to be white, want to lighten their skin, and choose to disown their respective cultures. Once white people stop blaming others for this condition and start to take responsibility for what they have created, there may be hope for dissolving white supremacy.

As I interact with whites, it often appears to me that I know more about who they are than they know about themselves. When I introduce this notion in conversations, I experience defensiveness, emotional outrage, shutting down, anger, and condescension. I recall a white American woman with European ancestry who was a friend of mine telling me that I was "too smart" because I knew more about her German and Polish ancestral backgrounds than she did. Also, she continued to call the Dominican Republic a "third world country" when the appropriate term is that it is a *developing nation*. The Dominican Republic is actually one of the fastest growing economies in Latin America. This demonstrated to me that her knowledge of the Dominican Republic was quite limited and antiquated. She viewed the nation as less than, rather than one that has been recovering from the legacy of colonization started by her white ancestors. For this 37-year-old white woman, I was the first Black friend she had ever had. At the same time, she had a Black Lives Matter sign on her front porch, which I interpreted as her desire to "appear" in congruency with the movement for selfish reasons, like perhaps her property wouldn't get looted. I questioned whether she actually believed that Black lives actually matter. The inconsistency of her beliefs that her statements and actions conveyed to me was intolerable for me because it reminded me of the white friend and classmate from my master's graduate program that I described earlier. Cross-racial friendships, for many white people, have always seemed to be transactional and based on convenience. I have become exhausted with these types of relationships, so I ended the friendship. The pain of constantly having to deal with racism and white ignorance and insensitivity is exhausting. I no longer have the emotional-psychological bandwidth to interface with white spaces and white people and to continuously walk on eggshells and pretend to be interested in their platitudes about wanting things to change. As a people, we People of Color are dying daily, grasping for what is granted to white people as a birthright, an opportunity to breathe. I can't do it.

White people have a way of making me think that they are for me and in agreement with my vision and cause as a Black person, which includes freedom, until it gets too uncomfortable for them. This discomfort for white people is a product of the history of Black enslavement and Jim Crow that created massive inequalities in wealth and resources, resulting in Black people being totally dependent upon whites for their needs (Anderson, 2001). I do not believe that I can sustain a deep meaningful relationship with a white person because of this. I urge white people to go beyond academic book knowledge and social media to understand People of Color, in particular Black people. I encourage white people to engage in difficult conversations, whether in person, phone, or on video calls, with Black people that are important to them, and to be open to their vulnerabilities and pain within the context of your relationship with them. Being this vulnerable about my feelings toward white people is not an easy task, and it is possible that it is very difficult for some white people to read about. However, becoming sensitive to the vulnerabilities that often emerge during emotionally charged conversations and having the ability to encourage and tolerate discomfort and intensity is a crucial first step to intimacy and healing (Hardy & Bobes, 2016).

This has been my life, constantly working, constantly trying to think ahead and plan and strategize in order to survive and have access to what the world has to offer me. All the while, I watch white people just glide by effortlessly. I don't know if the playing field will ever get even; however, I know in my heart that I no longer feel the need to have white people truly "see" me. Instead, my energy has been focused on self-growth, self-healing, and serving the community that has repeatedly shown up for me, which includes Black people and Latinos. As I reflect on my journey and all that I have accomplished, I think about my preoccupation with whiteness and how I react to it all the time. I've learned several lessons on this journey:

1. Staying grounded in who you are and where you come from as a Person of Color is extremely valuable. Disconnecting from our cultural and racial groups out of deference to whiteness and trying to adopt values that do not serve us puts us, as Black people and People of Color, in a vulnerable position.

2. White supremacy is profitable. To have access to the American dream, Blacks have to make white people more comfortable with our very presence (Byrd & Tharps, 2001). When we relax our hair with chemicals or spend billions of dollars on hair and cosmetics "to become acceptable" by white standards, we are financially investing in our own oppression.

3. I don't trust that the same race that profited from our enslavement can be trusted to liberate us. Even mental health is hijacked by white supremacy so much that we continue to struggle with mental illness

to no avail. Self-hate leads to self-destructive behaviors, such as alcohol addiction and drug use/abuse. We cannot keep neglecting our body, mind, and spirit because, as a race, we die from illnesses medical practitioners label as treatable and preventable (Burrell, 2010).

4. We, as Communities of Color, need to have our own organizations and programs that service us. People from different races can be included as long as they understand that their needs are not always going to be the priority.

5. Black people are sometimes expected to "save the world." The logic is that because of all of the pain we have endured as a race, we should understand the pains of humanity. I think we need to attend to our pain and our humanity first and foremost.

6. The biggest threat to white supremacy is Black people from all around the world loving each other, connecting, procreating, strategizing, achieving, and succeeding independent of white people. I believe this will happen . . . one day.

I have shifted my work and energy toward people, like my grandfather, my mother, and my communities in the Dominican Republic and in the United States, who are trying to heal and liberate themselves from the mental stress, emotional turmoil, and economic pressures caused by the legacy of white supremacy. Unlike our beloved Dr. Martin Luther King Jr., who had a dream, I am rooted in a reality. It is a reality that constantly reminds me of all the obstacles we have faced as a race, and the necessity that we continue fighting. My tools of emancipation are my mental health training and experiences, and I will continue to use them to liberate myself and others for as long as I can breathe.

**ANA HERNANDEZ, PHD,** is committed to addressing social justice and mental health inequalities using a multicultural, systemic framework when providing mental health treatment to individuals, LGBTQ, couples, and Families of Color. Ana completed a doctorate in couple and family therapy at Drexel University and has designed research projects using a social justice approach. Ana is currently a supervisor at the Children's Services of Roxbury and has a private practice, Valiente Relational Healing, located in Boston, Massachusetts. Ana has published her work in journals, including *Contemporary Family Therapy* and *American Journal of Family Therapy*. She has coauthored two book chapters: (1) "Challenging Heterosexual and Cisgender Privilege in Clinical Supervision" in *Clinical Activities for Increasing Competence and Self-Awareness* (2014, Wiley and Sons) and (2) "Making the Invisible Visible: A Closer Look at Social Class in Supervision" in *Culturally Sensitive Supervision and Training: Diverse Perspectives and Practical Applications* (2016, Routledge).

## References

*Anderson, C. (2001).* PowerNomics: The national plan to empower Black America. *PowerNomics Corporation of America, Inc.*

*Andrews, G. R. (2004).* Afro-Latin America, 1800–2000. *Oxford University Press.*

*Burrell, T. (2010).* Brainwashed: Challenging the myth of Black inferiority. *SmileyBooks.*

*Byrd, A. D., & Tharps, L. L. (2001).* Hair story: Untangling the roots of Black hair in America. *MacMillan.*

*Hardy, K. V., & Bobes, T. (2016). Core competencies for executing culturally sensitive supervision and training. In K. H. Hardy and T. Bobes (Ed.).* Culturally Sensitive Supervision and Training: Diverse Perspectives and Practical Applications *(pp. 11–15). New York: Routledge*

*Mitchell, T. W. (2001). From reconstruction to deconstruction: Undermining Black landownership, political independence, and community through partition sales of tenancies in common.* Northwestern University Law Review, 95*(2), 505–580.*

*Phelan, J. L. (1968). Pan-Latinism, French intervention in México (1861–1867) and the genesis of the idea of Latin America. In J. A. Ortega Y Medina (Ed.),* Conciencia y autenticidad históricas: Escritos en homenaje a Edmundo O' Gorman *(pp. 279–298). Universidad Nacional Autonoma de Mexico.*

*Rohde, D. (1998, November 11). Jurors convict youth in killing of his teacher.* The New York Times. *https://www.nytimes.com/1998/11/11/nyregion/jurors-convict-youth-in-killing-of-his-teacher.html*

*Watson, M. F. (2013).* Facing the black shadow. *Marlene F. Watson.*

CHAPTER 14

# Drowning in the Sea of White Supremacy

## One Black Man's Journey to Breathe

GENE E. CASH JR., LCSW, LISW-S

COUNSELING ALLIANCE OF VIRGINIA

"Let's go. Hurry up; you are going to be late"; these are the words of our mother who was rushing us to get into the car. "You are going to be late, hurry up!" Getting up early on Saturday mornings, rushing to Oberlin College to participate in a cultural enrichment program, my mother put my sisters and me in every opportunity that arose. "You're going to be just as good as those white kids, and I am going to make sure of it. Now hurry up and get in there." We walked into a crowded room with cushions, chairs, couches, and pictures that reflected only white faces. It was a sea of whiteness. The white people were friendly and inviting, and there was not another single Person of Color involved in those programs. I remember feeling sheepish and uncomfortable. I never relaxed nor understood what we were there for, and I knew I had to be polite, "act right," and "not embarrass myself, my sisters, my mom, or other Black people." I was with my two older sisters, and I knew I was "safe" with them. At the end of each experience, we would receive our snack, and then we were free to go back home. Leaving that room was such a relief. I felt like I could relax, reclaim myself, and have fun again.

My mother, a strong Black woman, was raising three Black children in the civil rights and war on drugs eras, virtually as a single parent. My father, who grew up in the South in Oklahoma, was emotionally uninvolved in my upbringing and functioned as a peripheral parent. He was a Vietnam War Veteran who suffered from war-related PTSD and a mixture of debilitating familial and racial trauma that consumed his life. When I was five years old, I remember going to put my father's mother to rest in his hometown in Oklahoma. We were eating breakfast at a local restaurant that was apparently where my father worked prior to going away to war. The image that sticks with me is when the white owner came out and greeted my father with a warm hug and all the other workers came to say hello. My father appeared to be well respected. He was well dressed, with spit shined shoes, and looked happy and proud. I was so proud of my father and felt like he was "the man." As time passed, that image was slowly stripped away due to the tolls of structural and institutional racism upon him, America's "number one enemy." He was a strong Black man with pride and integrity who was ultimately defeated by the PTSD from Vietnam and the war on drugs. My father, who never used alcohol or any other substances prior to, or even during, Vietnam, came home with the stress of the world on his shoulders. Reintegrating and making a new life for himself and his family during New Jim Crow (Alexander, 2012) was taxing and debilitating. He turned to drugs and alcohol to cope with his depression, personal trauma, and trauma from the war. Moments when I saw my father as that strong Black and proud father coming home and bringing his family to his hometown occurred less and less frequently. My mother loved my father dearly, and she would share stories with me that later helped me understand how racialized hurt, hate, and dehumanization devoured my father as a Black man. My mother has painful memories of a racial event that occurred while I was still a baby in her belly. According to my mom, the story will forever be etched in her memory because she feared not only for her life but mine as well, long before I was born.

## Living with White Terror

My mom has told me about this incident countless times throughout my life. It still haunts her to this day! She often reminds me that, although I was in her belly, it is my story. One day while visiting my father's family down South, we were driving down a dirt road with my father's three brothers, who were younger than he, and my siblings. We were all happily making our travels back to the house. Though my mother was born in Mississippi—the Deep South—she was raised primarily in Missouri. So, because my maternal grandparents migrated North when she was young, neither she nor her children were accustomed to the overt, blatant racism and hateful acts that were commonplace in the Deep South. As my father was driving us home, a pickup truck filled with white men in it pulled up alongside us and began taunting, heckling, and calling us racial slurs as we drove. My mom says we were all terrified and worried for our lives. Then one of the white men threw a "bomb" into our car through the window. My father and uncles frantically fought to get the "bomb" out of the car as the car filled up with smoke. My mother thought we were all going to die. She cried and screamed for my father to get us out of there. My uncles eventually got the "bomb" out of the vehicle and it turned out to be a smoke bomb. My mother saw my father's rage as he slammed the pedal to the floor, seeking revenge on those racist white bigots who tried to "kill us." She never saw my father shy away or kneel to anyone in his life. After hearing the story, I revered my father as a "Black Superman." I later thought of him as a strong Black man determined to break the chains of white supremacy amid a system that was designed to kill him and all who look like him, including me. My father was unable to protect us nor get retribution. No police report, no searching for the assailants, no nothing! My mother says we went home and she told my father we were never going back to the Deep South again. My mother recalls no acknowledgment nor apologies from any local authorities regarding what had happened.

The rage from this indignity and others like it eventually and naturally turned inward within my family. It was safer this way. The trauma, pain, and blame had to be expressed in some form. Unfortunately, my father was blamed by my mother for not doing enough to protect and keep his family safe. There was no focus on the white men who physically and mentally terrorized us. For some reason, it often appeared that white people's hateful acts tended to become our fault. Victim blaming, especially toward Blacks, is deeply entrenched in white American culture. It seems that no matter how deeply victimized People of Color are by the misdeeds and racism of whites, People of Color are always treated as the culprits and are expected to fix the problem.

We never returned to Oklahoma as a family. My father's hometown is less than 2.5 hours away from Tulsa, Oklahoma, where one of the most heinous documented racist massacres against Black people in American history occurred. This unsolved crime against my family took me away from my heritage, which I am cut off from for the rest of my life. Cousins, aunts, uncles, grandparents, family, and friends; erased due to white supremacy being alive and well in America.

Both sides of my family of origin had strong roots in the South and were part of the migration north to seek jobs and the "American dream." My mother and father were in the automobile industry and suffered an unending onslaught of racial violence and abuse. Assimilation was the mode of survival for our family. My parents worked hard, and the message that was sold to them, which was then passed on to my siblings and I, was we had to work twice as hard in order to compete with white folks. We had to be this way if we were going to survive. "You are all going to college and have jobs just like the white folks. . . . You will not be working in a factory like slaves like your father and me." Now, much later in life, I must fight back tears and the deep emotion I feel when I think about how humiliating it must have been for my mother to liken her work to that of a slave and to endure all that came with it for the benefit of me and my siblings. My mother meant every word she said. "You are going to grow up and be somebody, and I will make sure of it. My kids will be able to compete with the white kids." So, being a young Black boy was inherently not good enough due to white supremacy and assimilationist ideologies. I had to be something other than Black, which was not good enough; this is something I learned early on. I had to search outside of myself into what I know now as the sea of white supremacy to find meaning and value in life.

The sea of white supremacy is closely related to what Hardy (Chapter 1) describes as "the enduring, invisible, and ubiquitous centrality of whiteness." It is a powerful and invisible force that often leaves People of Color feeling the stranglehold of degradation, marginalization, and outsider status from the moment we took our first breath in North America, and dehumanization and colonizing began. White supremacy believes that white people are superior to all other races and thus it is permissible to dominate them. According to Delgado and Stefancic (2017), white supremacy is a social system in which white people enjoy structural privilege over other ethnic groups on both a collective and an individual level, despite formal legal equality. When I envision the trans-Atlantic slave trade with millions of Africans stolen from their motherland, transported across the Atlantic Ocean, and sold into slavery for centuries, it makes me sick to my stomach. How could white people treat my ancestors and any other human beings so horribly? When I learned of the ways that Black people were beaten, tortured, and killed, I couldn't stop thinking about the story my mother told me about the visit to Oklahoma when our car was smoke bombed.

## Intergenerational Transmission of Racial Pain and Trauma

I am haunted by memories of my grandparents, aunts, and uncles reminiscing about how hot it was when they picked cotton in Mississippi during the Jim Crow days. I remember their stories of getting factory jobs up North or serving in the white man's military, fighting for a country that did not fight for them nor honor them as a whole human. How they had to shut up and be quiet and succumb to their internalized rage daily to survive and thrive in a world designed to hate and kill them. I imagine giving birth to a Black son was a proud and terrifying time for my parents and grandparents. I liken it to a metaphor in which they took me and threw me into the sea; I hit the water and sink, and then my instincts kick in, and I struggle to get to the surface, crying uncontrollably and gasping for air, and then another wave comes and takes me under. My mother jumps in frantically. She does not know how to swim but would die trying to save her baby. My father jumps in to rescue me and my mother, as he knows how to swim in the "sea." He has been swimming in the "sea" for a long time. So, he stabilizes my mother and me, and you might as well add my two sisters into the "sea" imagery as well. We, as a family, are treading water in the vast sea of white supremacy, floating along to survive without refuge in sight. Then another wave comes, and it is bigger and stronger and takes the entire family under again. As this continues to happen, we are swept out further and further to "sea." We have to learn how to swim, drink salty water, build a raft, and feed ourselves from this "sea" of white supremacy. This undertaking became all we knew, and it diminished my existence as a Black boy coming into the world. When my parents had me, they were already in the "sea" of whiteness! As I said earlier, our primary mode of survival, the boat we had to build, was assimilation. In other words, our survival was based on being as white as we needed to be in order to fit in and survive. From my parents' viewpoint, their teaching my siblings and me how to swim and stay alive in an unforgiving and relentless sea was necessary for our survival. The sea is in perpetual motion. There may be high tides and low tides, and we all know the tides and waves are coming. White supremacy in this world is in constant, unrelenting motion. It is something People of Color suffer from on a daily basis, constantly testing our internal fortitude and courage.

Living under the rule of whiteness and white supremacy suppresses the emotional and psychological growth of People of Color. Growing up in Ohio, we were close to the Great Lakes. Lake Erie was calm, shallow, and safe for us. We felt confident in that type of water. My first time going to the sea was when I moved to Charlottesville, Virginia, and my mentor, a white Jewish man named Dr. Steve Greenstein, exposed me further to the sea of white supremacy. He took me to his beach house in Corolla, North Carolina. Not only was the Atlantic Ocean huge, intimidating, and mesmerizing, so were the beach and town. It was white, and navigating that world as a Black man was a daily reminder that I did not belong or fit in with white people. "You are not supposed to be here" was the unspoken phrase that I often imagined hearing.

## Racial Socialization

I grew up in northeast Ohio in Oberlin, a small college town approximately 35 miles from Cleveland. Oberlin was well renowned for being the home of one of the first all-white colleges to admit Blacks in 1835 and then to admit women in 1837. The city was a strong proponent of abolishing slavery and a mainstay of the underground railroad, which was a systematic means of freeing slaves from the South. As a child, I remember being proud to grow up in a town that fought against slavery, yet I unknowingly lived in a sea of whiteness as the beacon all People of Color aspired to be—which engendered assimilation ideology and centralizing whiteness. This fostered less division among Blacks and whites in our small college town; however, we as Black people were still viewed as inferior. We were surrounded by white supremacist towns, or, as Loewen (2005) referred to them, sundown towns. These were towns where white people expressed a clear warning: if you were Black, you better not get caught in their town after the sun went down or your life would be in jeopardy. Towns like Wellington, 95.8% white, 1.2% Black (Wellington, 2013); LaGrange, 96.6% white, 0.4% Black (LaGrange, 2013); Amherst, over 92% white, 0.9% Black (United States Census Bureau, 2019a); Vermilion, 98.6% white, 0.1% Black (United States Census Bureau, 2019e), North Ridgeville, 93.3% white, 2.3% Black (United States Census Bureau, 2019d); and one town that my childhood friends and I will always remember: the village of Lodi, Ohio, over 97% white, 0.3% Black (United States Census Bureau, 2019c). We would travel to these small sundown towns in Ohio to play sports; ours was one of the only teams with predominately Black players on the team. We were all taught at an incredibly young age where the imperial wizard of the Ku Klux Klan (KKK) lived. We had to be no older than ten years old when we were told about the KKK and how Black members of the community had been harassed and subjected to police brutality in these small towns. The KKK was alive and well in the 1970s and late '80s in Ohio. When we played predominately white schools, we were called niggers, taunted by fans, treated unfairly by the referees, and always felt the other teams had an upper hand. We had to play twice as hard to win. It was the way of life for all Black people and People of Color growing up in my hometown. It was as normal as breathing air to accept whiteness as the only means of operating. I was so deeply steeped in whiteness that I used to call my mother a racist. I would attempt to convince her how "white people were not all that bad." However, with her wisdom and insight, she knew, from her lived experience, that white supremacy exists everywhere, and even this town that fought against slavery and promoted abolitionist ideologies was not truly inclusive of Black and Brown people.

We learned white people's truth about Harriet Tubman, Frederick Douglass, Crispus Attucks, and all the other abolitionists who fought against the insidious parts of America's racist history. As elementary, middle, and high school students, we would go every year to watch the college students arrive at the end of their walk of the slave trail from down south and get a huge reception at Finney Chapel and appreciation from the college and city in which they denounced slavery.

In elementary and middle school, most of my teachers were white, and our principal in middle school was a Black woman. The middle school principal and the high school assistant principal were both Black, and they were still the minority within the school system that was comprised of an all-white school board. There was no mention of Blackness or Afrocentrism for students attending public school. We had a multicultural group after school and, again, it was about all races and how they assimilated to the white world. No clear delineation for Black or Brown students to honor their true historical perspective.

Whiteness and white supremacy in academia and my world continued throughout high school, undergraduate, and postgraduate school. I rarely saw anyone who looked like me being successful outside of sports and entertainment. My maternal grandfather was the strongest male role model I had. He worked hard in the foundry, worked on cars at home, and eventually owned his own business. He was swimming in the sea of white supremacy and was making the way for us all. In my young eyes, white people could never "drown" my grandfather. Black male role models were hard to find while I was growing up. They were either drowning in the sea of white supremacy, fatigued from fighting all the waves (Jim Crow, War on Drugs, new Jim Crow [Alexander, 2012], mass incarceration, etc.) coming at them, or murdered by whiteness and white supremacy. I grew up believing, and perhaps even seeing, how white people truly feared Black people.

I grew up believing that I would be OK if I worked hard enough, presented myself *well enough*, and did not let white people see me struggle. I even believed that I could achieve whatever I wanted to. I heard in the back of my mind the words of my mother, "You will be able to compete, and I want you to have a job just like those white folks." The challenge of drowning in the sea of white supremacy is it's hard to get air into your lungs while being fully submerged in the sea of whiteness and white supremacist ideologies for long periods of time. Struggling to get to the top for a breath of air while being pulled back under was the challenge, especially in white institutions, of being a successful Black man in the sea of white supremacy. "The United States government played a key role in facilitating assimilation for some groups, forcing it on others, and blocking it still for others" (Fitzgerald, 2020, p. 194). Native Americans faced numerous attempts at forced assimilation to the point of genocide after the attempts of boarding schools and placing them on reservations. The Irish embraced assimilation to the dominant white mainstream culture and are considered white. Black people resisted, assimilated, and endured the Jim Crow era and the new

Jim Crow (Alexander, 2012) as white people continued to push institutional racism and, on some level, maintain a form of slavery.

Integrating from a "liberal" high school to a predominantly white college (a predominantly white institution, or PWI) in Northwest Ohio, I assimilated very well. I had many friends, white, Black, and Latino. I was befriended by three male peers when I was a freshman. One was a Black male representing Alpha Phi Alpha, a Black fraternity; one was a white male who worked for the university's recreation center as the intramural sports program leader; and one was a Latino male who worked for student government. All three were upperclassmen who introduced me to the college experience. The Alpha had me explore Greek life, the Black Student Union, and joining their mentoring program—Alpha Men of Tomorrow. Our relationship allowed me to become immersed in Black culture in a way I had never experienced growing up in my hometown. I experienced a new level of comfort when hanging with him on campus or going to parties and relating to someone who looked and sounded like me. I was navigating whiteness within an all-Black experience. The white male introduced me to intramural sports on campus. This evolved into my becoming an employee for the recreation department, which helped me pay for my tuition and living expenses. By the time I had gone off to college, our mother had become the primary financial provider for us. She was fortunate to maintain her job with a major automaker, and she supported us financially. We were not eligible for grants and did not have the means to pay for college. We acquired educational loans and worked while in college. Our parents instilled in us a drive to be hard workers. If you did not work, you were worthless. This line of thinking was a direct result of the stereotype of "the lazy, shiftless, Black looking for and relying on welfare" that was promulgated by white supremacist misinformation. It was important that we demonstrate that we were not lazy and working hard was one of the ways to do that. This forced Black people and People of Color to work twice as hard as white people. I became an umpire for softball and a referee for flag football and basketball. I eventually stepped into my white friend's position at the recreation center on a predominantly white campus of about 26,000 students. I enjoyed getting his position on campus at the PWI. I felt a sense of pride and sense of accomplishment as a young Black man. The Latino male was a member of a white fraternity and was well assimilated into the sea of whiteness/white supremacy. We could relate to one another on many levels. He taught me about networking and navigating white spaces on campus. He knew I was struggling academically and introduced me to his major, therapeutic recreation. He informed me that I could use recreation and sports with at-risk youth or people who suffered brain injuries or other illness. Changing my major from social work to therapeutic recreation eased my academic transition into college. I lacked the study skills to be successful in social work. My Latino friend worked for the student government as an on-campus security escort. He helped me get a second job with him in which we would safely walk other students to their cars or dorms at night. I was the only Black person working this job, and we were the only two People of Color acting as security escorts for the entire campus. It helped me to immerse myself even more into college life and (forced) assimilation. I would "kick it" at the Black Greek parties, I played street football with my boys, coached, and played on most, if not all, Black intramural basketball and flag football teams, and I played on a multiracial softball team. My assimilation occurred and I lived in the sea of whiteness without any true awareness. I was gradually pushed to assimilate and hide my Black self.

On campus at this PWI, racism truly stood out to me. Growing up in Oberlin and playing against teams from neighboring racist communities, racism was what we grew up with, expected, and learned to deal with. Being away from my hometown and being called a "nigger" by a random white male while walking to get dinner was mind-blowing. It was so out of context for me. I quickly had to weigh my choices. Do I knock this white dude out on campus and risk being expelled, locked up, or killed? Or do I let it go and continue getting my education? These were the choices I learned I had to navigate on a regular basis while being on a PWI campus.

The onslaught of racial violence and overt intimidation was pervasive in college. I was visiting a white high school classmate at Bowling Green State University in Bowling Green City, Ohio (86.9% white; United States Census Bureau, 2019b). While we were getting a late-night meal at a local restaurant, a white male bumped into me on the way out. I am a big guy, and it took me by surprise. I turned to my dude and said "What is up with your people down here?" Before he could respond, the white boy who bumped into me returned with two other white males, tapping on the window glass with a 2 x 4 piece of lumber, yelling for me to come outside.

It was a deafening realization of how some white people disliked me based on the color of my skin. So, I am not crazy, and I chose to send my white friend with my keys to grab the bats out of my trunk. Once we got our bats, we proceeded to go outside to the parking lot, and the white boys cowardly ran while calling me a nigger and my friend a nigger lover. Again, no police report, no apology, no protection, and no retribution. It was what Black people and People of Color had to deal with in white America. We were sure that if we called the police, we or I would become the target, and victim blaming would begin. The following scenario was etched in my head and nurtured my fear and anxiety if we actually called 911 and the police arrived: Officer: "What are you doing here?" Me: "Eating!" Officer: "What did you do to provoke them?" Me: "Be Black!" Officer: "Turn around and put your hands behind your back, BOY!!" My white friend watches. Any of those responses would be considered offensive and threatening to the white cops coming to the scene; so why compound the problem?

Based on the actions of these white people and the racist ones before them who attacked, tortured, and abused my family and friends, I have learned to always have some form of protection with me. As a Black man, I never feel safe and do not believe calling the police is a viable option. Doing so would NOT allow me to feel any safer. To this day, I keep something in my vehicle for protection that would not otherwise get me arrested, harassed, shot, or killed by the police. This strategy was taught to me by all the males in my family. My father carried a pipe, my grandfather and grandmother carried revolvers, a close family friend carried a gun, my uncle carried a knife, and my other uncle carried a gun. As Black men, we never felt safe in America and always felt the threat of violence from white supremacists and the fallout of institutional racism that plagued the marginalized and impoverished communities we would frequent. The need to protect ourselves and the ones we loved was constant. Unfortunately, today a cell phone in my hand can easily be mistaken for a weapon and get me killed. I could go on and share many more moments of how white supremacy, hate, racial abuse, trauma, and violence showed up in my life at a PWI—being the only Person of Color or Black person in the classroom, navigating group assignments with all-white classmates, sitting in staff meetings as the only or one of the few Blacks, being the only or one of the few People of Color in a leadership position. Yes, we may have held leadership positions, but they were very minuscule when compared to our white counterparts. While working at the recreation department and running the three major intramural team sports (football, basketball, and softball) on the PWI campus, I was the one designated to deal with all-Black teams and then the disrespectful and racist white teams. Was I put in those positions because of my size, my personality, or my race? Either way, I was doing much more heavy lifting than my white counterparts when it came to racism and racial conflict. It seemed that I could not show up, relax, and be comfortable and participate like my fellow white students. I had to navigate and check my surroundings continuously to feel safe. I felt like I could not make a mistake and that I had to be sure white people were comfortable.

## Confronting Internalized Whiteness

It is difficult, if not impossible, to swim in a sea of white supremacy as a Black person and not learn how to disavow one's Blackness. No one overtly tells you to hate yourself or Blackness; however, one learns incredibly early that there are handsome rewards for doing so. Two critical racist incidents stand out the most for me when reflecting on internalized whiteness and rejected Blackness. I will recount them next.

It was springtime my freshman year in college, and I, along with an all-white staff, was monitoring the spring softball games. Looking back, I was the only Black referee on the shift, and I was sitting with the all-white leadership for the games that day. The white males had their shirts off, taking in the sun, and I was hot as hell with my shirt on trying to stay cool because there was no shade in sight. They were talking about their summer plans and opportunities that awaited them postgraduation. They seemed free and unencumbered of a single worry in the world. I, on the other hand, was worried about my safety in the world as well as how I would afford the next semester. I was not able to relate to their sense of freedom. This was yet another time I was different and felt alone and on the outside. White people were on the ship in the sea of white supremacy, and I was treading water alongside of it, trying to keep up or benefit from the educational opportunity given to me. There were moments when I wished I had the freedom that I associated with being white.

There was another memorable moment that reminded me of the struggles, burdens, and challenges of being Black in a white world. During the fall of my junior year, I was heading to my car after a long day running the flag football intramural league (I was now in a leadership role), when I was approached by a group of Black players. Earlier that day, I had to forfeit their game due to their tardiness, which had extended beyond the allotted grace period. I remember feeling a strong presence coming up behind me as I was getting into my car. I turned around before getting into my car and there were Black men approaching me from behind. I must be honest, I was intimidated. What I remember most from the encounter was angrily being called an "Uncle Tom" and a "sellout" and being told I had better watch my back. In their eyes, I was whitewashed and I was aligned with the white man! "If you weren't so confused about who you are, you could have cut us some slack and given us more time," one of the men exclaimed. No physical blows were exchanged but the emotional and psychological ones landed clearly on the back of my head, on my face, and more importantly, in the heart of my soul. Was I wrong? Should I have not followed the rules to support my brothas who were dealing with the same struggles related to assimilation and anti-Blackness on a PWI campus as I? Should I have bent the rules the way I had often observed whites in power do for other whites? Would the same white power structure that routinely stretched the rules for other whites hold me to a different standard for stretching them? I was overcome with pain and confusion. I was reminded how I was not accepted by Blacks nor whites. My efforts to negotiate and tread water in the sea of white supremacy made me more palatable to whites while simultaneously less trustworthy to other Blacks. I was always too Black to really be fully embraced by white friends, classmates, and coworkers, and much too white to be fully trusted by Blacks, although we all faced the same challenges on and off campus. During my freshman and sophomore years, all my roommates were Black; but in my junior and senior years, all of them were white. Eventually, I lived on my own in predominantly white neighborhoods. I missed being with my Black roommates and felt torn as I continued to work on campus and helped them get jobs on campus. Slowly they all drifted away. My choices of roommates and where to live were all dictated by a pull toward whiteness. I continued my path of assimilation and internalizing whiteness. The more I grew at the university and embraced whiteness, the more I was perceived and accepted as the good effective mainstream minority—GEMM (Hardy, 2008). It was a sinking feeling, that day I was confronted about being "anti-Black," a perception I had never consciously considered. I never echoed those exact words to myself, but I couldn't solidly dismiss the notion either. *Did I sell them out? Was I an Uncle Tom working for the man?* These blows landed loudly and clearly. According to Martin (2010), "Blacks run the risk of being labeled a sell-out or they run the risk of being accused of 'acting white' if they gain or seek entry into the middle-class socioeconomic status" (p. 236). I was not white enough because I was still economically and socially behind my white classmates in achieving white American societal expectations. I was not Black enough to feel comfortable with people with my skin color when navigating my campus job. In her research, Martin (2010) continued to identify how economic prosperity became equated with whiteness, and economic insecurity with Blackness. She further explains how these ideologies are firmly rooted in the doctrine of white supremacy and Black inferiority and how this continues to exist today.

I did not understand why it was not possible for me to have the jobs I had and maintain racial solidarity with my people. The more I reflected on these issues, the more I began to realize that it wasn't my working for the recreation department that earned the ire of other Blacks, *but rather the race-related concessions that I had to make to be considered worthy of the job by the whites who had the power to judge and ultimately hire me.* These are some of the challenges inherent in negotiating the sea of white supremacy.

It was my senior year, and I was all set to graduate. I was enormously proud of myself; my family was proud of me and I was in a state of euphoria. I was finishing up my workday at the recreation center and had to deliver the timecards to the finance department. So, I jumped in a golf cart, raced across campus, and went up to share my good news with an older white female staff member. She and I had fostered a relatively good working relationship over time, and I wanted to share my good news with her about my new job. I said, "Good afternoon, Sue." She said, "Good afternoon." I said, "I wanted to let you know this is the last time I will be dropping off timecards, as I will be graduating this fall with my bachelor's degree in education and I got a job at a major faith-based hospital downtown." She said, "Congratulations, and good for you." I said, "Thank you," and then she said the unthinkable, which took all the wind out of my sails. She said, "So will you be an orderly?" My stomach dropped, and I could feel anger and rage come over me. I said no in a well-controlled manner, aggressively pushing down my hurt, anger, and disappointment to avoid making her feel uncomfortable or unsafe. "I will be a Therapeutic Recreational Specialist in the Adolescent Chemical Dependency Unit." She appeared shocked by my response. There was a pregnant pause, and the conversation was over. I left feeling dejected and angry. How could this person think I was going to college to become an orderly? In his song "No Vaseline," the famed rapper Ice Cube (1991) said, "Here's what 'they' think about you." This was evident by *my* misperception of Sue's whiteness. I thought Sue was an ally, and yet she had thoughts and beliefs that saw Black people as inferior. I am relatively certain that, through her eyes, she saw nothing wrong with the assumption that I would be an orderly. This notion fits a broader stereotype and perhaps even an implicit bias that many whites have about People of Color. My guess is that, at some unconscious level, she had internalized the white supremacist belief that it is the job of People of Color to take care of and serve white people.

My mother instilled in me that I could be whatever I wanted to be and that I would be able to compete with white folks. I can imagine what Sue's parents had taught her. The unfortunate truth of the matter is they both were operating out of the sea of white supremacy and the residual effects of slavery. When looking historically at white supremacy, white people have always believed they were better than all other races and cultures. Sue was clearly revealing that she could not fathom a Black man outside of the prescribed role of being a servant in that type of medical institution and that she struggled to conceive of Black people as having the capacity to be therapists, nurses, teachers, physicians, etc. I have learned from experience that white people tend to have a way of subtly and unconsciously exposing their private thoughts about the inferiority or second-class status of Black people. I felt the sting of this belief embedded in Sue's *innocent* curiosity about my new position. A major part of trying to breathe while drowning in a sea of white supremacy is always having to be on alert and prepared for both the overt and the covert manifestations of racism.

## My Evolving Black Identity

In May 2017, I took several of my staff, both Black and white, to attend a workshop entitled "Beyond Walking on Eggshells": How to Talk Effectively about Race (Hardy, 2017b). The timing of the workshop and my attendance at it were quite fortuitous as I was unsure what to expect. I was awaking to my identity as a Black man, and Hardy's lecture truly exposed me to a nonassimilated ideology that I knew existed but never felt the power to describe or own until that day. I watched him masterfully take on white people and whiteness in a clear and systematic way that made sense to me. I watched a man who undoubtedly had dealt with swimming in the sea of white supremacy and assimilation his entire life but who was also able to stand firm in his Black identity. I will never forget the moment that a white Jewish male participant stood up and challenged Hardy's belief that the Atlantic slave trade and the years of Jim Crow and the new Jim Crow that operates to this day were equal to, if not a greater suffering, than the Holocaust. It was the first time in my entire life that I witnessed a Black man truly denounce white superiority and white privilege with such grace, clarity, and resolve. It was done with such skill and conviction; it was liberating and validating all at the same time.

Attending the workshop triggered a bevy of old memories and forced me to revisit past racial slights, hurdles I had to overcome, as well as a host of missed opportunities to effectively confront white supremacy. I continued to reflect on my training as a therapeutic recreational specialist during my early twenties. I was so excited and loved being on that fantastic team to help mentally ill adolescents. I was one of three Black people on staff and one of four People of Color on a team of approximately thirty-five to forty clinicians, nurses, and doctors. I remember being surprised when I saw another Black professional on the unit. I was proud and in awe of their work as I was a young Black clinician, aspiring to be like them. It was common to see predominantly Black or People of Color on the housekeeping and food service staff. Even when it was in front of my eyes, I never knew I was swimming in the sea of white supremacy while working on this unit.

Housekeeping staff and I were always friendly, and I spoke with them regularly. It seemed like the senior housekeeping staff would always give me praise and encouragement while I was doing my job. Later I learned they were clear on how whiteness and white superiority was an institutional way of life at this faith-based hospital, and their hiring practices were geared toward Black and People of Color in subjugated and ancillary roles and white staff in managerial and privileged positions.

One intense and challenging day, a white, approximately 12-year-old male became aggressive and significantly dysregulated during a session I was leading. Panic buttons were hit, and all staff came to assist. We quickly engaged in nonviolent crisis prevention intervention and successfully escorted the young child to the seclusion room for safety and de-escalation. As always, we debriefed as a staff and made sure everyone was "physically" OK. I was young and excited and proud to be a part of the team. I felt like I was "home" and part of a healthy, tight-knit family unit caring for traumatized kids.

As a result of my waking up Black 25 years later coinciding with one of my coming-up-for-air in the sea of whiteness moments, I was able to process that experience from one of the tasks of the subjugated (Hardy, 2017a); a position that was liberating and allowed me to overcome learned voicelessness to the point of having a voice without centering whiteness or white people. Revisiting the whole incident 25 years later, I was taken aback by how being assimilated stripped me of who I was as a Black man. As I go forward in my career, I am now saying that I am a Black man with a voice with inalienable rights first and a therapist second.

That incident with the young man 25 years ago started from his refusal to follow my directions and escalated to verbal abuse, racial slurs, and property damage, which required him to be secluded.

The verbal abuse was directed at me, the session's leader. The client swore at me with extreme profanity and racial slurs—"nigger" and "porch monkey" are the two that remain in my memory today. It was not uncommon for white clients in our program to use racial slurs and spew hate and epithets at Black and Brown staff. I understood from the orientation and training processes that when a "mentally ill" person is in distress and crisis, you help them regain baseline functioning. I was identified as the person to support this client during his seclusion process (which placed more heavy lifting on me, with regard to race and stress, than it would have on my white colleagues had one of them been assigned to the task). Maybe this is what Sue meant when she wondered if I would "be an orderly," because in some ways that is what I was. During this seclusion process, the client called me those names for well over 90 minutes before he was able to de-escalate. Once matters settled down, the client and I debriefed the entire incident and found out what got him dysregulated. The client apologized for his behavior but not explicitly for calling me the racial slurs (until the next time he did it later in his treatment). The client was reintegrated back into the milieu, and we debriefed as a staff. I remember getting praise from white staff, who said they felt for me when the client was calling me those hateful names and who told me stories from the past and how typical this behavior was and that staff were expected to manage it. However, no one clearly stated that the behavior was not acceptable. This was how the institution managed the white supremacy and hate. They were just part of the "sea"; they were part of the culture. I can barely remember the client being held accountable. It was never suggested that he be removed from the program for his racialized threats and white supremacist comments and behavior nor that perhaps I be reassigned to another, less overtly racist client. I continued to treat this client up through his adolescence. He ultimately became a full-blown white supremacist gang member who eventually killed someone. The client's trauma and abandonment issues were clearly identified and on our radar. So was his racism. Still, his racialized hate was secondary, or tertiary, to our multidisciplinary treatment team.

As an assimilated and subjugated Black therapist, I did not have a voice to speak out on the racialized hate inflicted upon me, nor did I see it as wrong because I considered it to be part of my job. I did not have the words to articulate what I needed at that time. The acts of white supremacy and abuse were not discussed in my administrative or clinical supervision sessions nor our staff meetings; we went on, business as usual. The entire response, or lack thereof, was emblematic of what it is like to function as a Black person in a sea of white supremacy. The entire situation was treated as if it was just a "normal" event that happens, and Black and white people played their roles. I was the Black therapist doubling as a security guard, frantically trying to subdue a dysregulated white male while my white colleagues looked on admiringly. I was extolled for my "professionalism," which was code for not personalizing the countless number of times I was called "nigger" and "porch monkey" with disdain. At that moment, I was the good Black therapist who was able to remain clearheaded and focused while his dignity was used for target practice. This was the essence of the centrality of whiteness and what it means to be thrust into the sea of white supremacy. Whiteness was centered, and as the only Black clinician, I did not challenge or even express how unacceptable the white supremacist behavior was, as was my white colleagues' comfort with ignoring blatant acts of racism. Swimming in the sea of white supremacy continued, and my subjugation as a Black clinician and a Black person was perpetuated. Even more importantly, my centering of whiteness and making sure white people were comfortable or not challenged on their racist attitudes, values, and beliefs was engrained. The more I restrained myself from challenging my white colleagues, the more they revered me as a coworker. I was a GEMM, a good effective mainstream minority (Hardy, 2008), who fortified their comfort by sacrificing mine!

In 2019, I accepted an adjunct position in the Master's level Social Work program at a major university in Richmond, Virginia. I was qualified to teach this class: I had over 29 years of professional and clinical training; I owned and had been running two counseling agencies for the past 8.5 years, one in Charlottesville and one in Richmond, Virginia; and I was actively seeing clients and supervising clinicians for licensure in Virginia. However, my past trauma of swimming in the sea of white supremacy and my process of assimilation left me with significant self-doubt, anxiety, and a lack of faith that I was "good" enough or qualified for the position. Managing my subjugated self (Hardy, 2016) is an ongoing task that I carry in my life today. The micro- and macroaggressions, direct and indirect, that attacked my personhood wounded my self-confidence and perceived efficacy, even as a prominent Black businessman and Black clinician in my field. At times, my vision, insights, and clinical judgments were under scrutiny whenever I opened my mouth. When my thoughts were different than those of my white counterparts, I felt I needed their approval and had to justify my position, even when I was the supervisor or clinical director over the case.

Could this be solely my insecurity, or was I conditioned to center whiteness due to white supremacy and the centrality of whiteness? I would call my work unorthodox because it was not what a white person would do. It was not the "traditional" approach. I never considered how much "traditional" and "white" were so closely aligned in my mind. It was easy for me to assume, given my socialization as a Black person in a white world, that my approach to clinical work was deficient, even though it may have been more relevant to what clients needed than what they were receiving from white clinicians. All of this second-guessing of myself, my competency, and ultimately my professional worth left me feeling inept and ill-equipped to teach white master's-level students, even though my experience and credentials suggested otherwise.

The class was diverse, yet for many of my students, I was the first Black male professor they had in this program and, for some of them, in their entire life. I was proud to be my students' first Black male professor. When I went back for my master's, I knew only one Black male professor, and he appeared to be extremely assimilated. He was very strongly white-identified, a GEMM (Hardy, 2008). I withdrew immediately for fear he would mistreat me because I was Black. Yes, I feared a Black male professor because I imagined he would be twice as hard on his own. Intuitively, I knew that he knew that he would have to "prove" to white students and colleagues that he was "color-blind" and not partial to Black students. This is just one of multitudinous ways that the centrality of whiteness shapes and disrupts within-group relationships among Blacks and other People of Color. I know and understand this dynamic well. It is the dues you must pay as a Black professional to earn a membership card to the whiteness club. I know this dynamic painfully well. Sadly, I have done the same thing in my past to some of the Black clinicians in my clinical practice. The sea of white supremacy is insidious, and it is an ideology that teaches Blacks to turn on each other or be hard on each other to survive racism and white supremacy. I vowed to never again be the type of professor or clinical supervisor that used other People of Color to affirm my position and place with white people.

Although I reached a resolve about how I wanted and needed to cultivate my relationship with the Black students in the class I taught, I still experienced discomfort and insecurities with the white students. American history, my training, and traumatic racialized events had taught me that white people were right; if Blacks and People of Color did not comply, they were subject to death, metaphorically and/or physically. Modern-day white supremacy, or the new Jim Crow (Alexander, 2012), offers a set of rules, conditions, and consequences that white people do not have to contend with and that left me worried about how much cooperation I would garner from white students. I thoroughly enjoyed my place and role in training new master's-level social workers. However, the psychological stress was extremely high. In my subjugated mind as a Black professor, there was no space for error. If I upset a white student or colleague, my teaching career could be over as quickly as it started. This was a real-life fear that I carried the full two semesters.

While white students were the source of tremendous anxiety and uncertainty for me, I found comfort and a sense of deep purpose from my interactions with Black students. One Black female student in the program came to me after class and shared her thoughts of me being like a "unicorn" in her academic lifetime. She shared that, when she was at her previous PWI, there were no Black male professors in her program. She was excited to have me as her professor and appreciated me being a Black male. I was blessed to have her as my student for two semesters before COVID-19 put my teaching position on hold.

In the classroom, I challenged myself to take a clear stance on teaching my students about racial awareness and sensitivity—and the importance of dismantling white supremacy as it related to social work. One of my lectures during my very first semester included watching *When They See Us* (De Niro et al., 2019) as a class and processing it together to delineate social work competencies and ethics and (what we learned from this series) to clinical practice. This lecture encompassed four of the six core values of the National Association of Social Workers (NASW): social justice, dignity and worth, importance of human relationships, and integrity (NASW, 2017). The assignment raised considerable tension for the entire class. One could hypothesize that other professors did not discuss racism regularly in the classroom nor within cross-racial group settings. The tension in the room intensified the more I spoke of the series and how we would be dissecting white supremacy and how white supremacy was overtly and blatantly a factor in the lives of the six young Black children and their families depicted in this TV series. This lecture was overwhelmingly emotional for the students. Some students began to cry, while others became stoic and guarded. Talking about our racist American history as told through the eyes of *the prey* was a new paradigm for most of them. Students openly shared how this was an incredibly challenging lecture for them. White and some People of

Color stated they had seen previews but were scared to watch the content because of how it might impact them psychologically. The fear of the psychological impact was shared by Black, Brown, and white students alike. Some students, predominately the white ones, had never heard these families' stories, nor of the Netflix show (De Niro et al., 2019). The prospect of looking at this level of racial trauma and white supremacy was unsettling.

A white female student raised her hand after I shared what the lecture would be that evening and said, "Are we watching this?" I replied yes. "Is this all we are doing for the entire class tonight?" I replied yes, with my stomach dropping and anxiety building in my chest. She then shared how she had deliberately chosen not to watch *When They See Us* (De Niro et al., 2019) because it would be upsetting to her, and if she were not comfortable doing it alone, why would I expect her to do it in a room full of people? Hmm . . . I guess I was supposed to know that. I was taken aback by her tone and the strong sense of entitlement leveled toward me in front of the entire class. Would she have said this and been as outspoken if I was a white professor? Would she have spoken with the same tone of hostility and disgust to a white professor? My stomach dropped even further, and I realized I had to manage the anger, fear, and feelings of subjugation that I carry everywhere I go in this sea of white supremacy. I calmly let her know that this was the assignment for tonight, and if this was too much for her, she could choose to excuse herself without consequence. Oh no (Damn!), I immediately reflected that I had granted her an exception based, probably, on my discomfort. An exception with NO consequences! I had flashbacks to the Black team whose game I forfeited in college and how I insisted on stringently holding them to the rules. Was it actions like this that led them to think of me as an Uncle Tom, an undercover white man? She is actively living in her privilege, choosing what she engages in and what she does not, I reflected. The epitome of white fragility, supported by Black assimilation. A Person of Color would have never been granted an exception with so little resistance. After being distracted by a barrage of personal thoughts, I switched back to my professor's voice and stated this is what the lecture is for tonight. She huffed and picked up her belongings and left. As I continued with my other students and did my best to manage my anger and fear and complete the lecture, I knew in the back of my mind that I had just lost my adjunct teaching position. When class concluded, I immediately informed my teaching support person of the incident to cover my ass! I believed if I upset a white student, I would be terminated. I knew I was going to "drown" on this one.

The response from the university was minimal, and I continued to teach. However, I had this incident in my head for the rest of my time teaching, which was about seven more months. I was still sure I was inferior and not good enough to be teaching at a PWI, even after being asked to lead the second semester. The inferiority and psychological stress were constant. The critical thought that I always carried was, "If I were white, would I be demeaned or viewed as less than or incompetent?"

## Closing Thoughts

I had hoped to end this chapter with a list of brilliant, well-conceived, and effective strategies that could be deployed to counteract the widespread, deleterious effects of whiteness on the lives of People of Color. My wish was to offer a prescriptive manual for how to navigate, survive, and breathe while on the brink of drowning in a sea of white supremacy. Unfortunately, I have no such advice to offer at this point. To be honest, I am still trying to sort this out for myself, not only every day, but what often feels like every second. Every day seems to bring with it a new challenge, a new obstacle to overcome, and yet another self-reflection to consider. I am very much aware that, as a 51-year-old Black man who has been battling, struggling with, and terrorized by whiteness since I was in my mother's belly, this remains very much a work in progress. I am still deeply engaged in a process of finding ways to love myself in all of my Blackness, whether whites approve or disapprove. There are days that I master it, and others where I relapse. I take solace and comfort in knowing that survival is an integral part of the ancestral DNA of Black people, so I am hopeful.

This has been an exceedingly difficult, painful, yet healing chapter to write. I have opened my soul and put it all out on full display, not to satisfy some exhibitionistic impulse but rather to invite others who are also on the verge of drowning in the sea of white supremacy to know that you are NOT alone.

**GENE E. CASH JR., MA,** is the founder and CEO of the Counseling Alliance of Virginia (CAVA). CAVA strives to ensure that utmost professionalism and excellent mental health care is delivered consistently to the community they serve. While developing his craft over the past 29 years, he has worked in acute care, inpatient psychiatric and chemical dependency units, juvenile residential treatment, community-based wraparound services, private practice, and as an adjunct professor at Virginia Commonwealth University. After receiving his Master of Social Work from Ohio State University, he decided to increase his knowledge and skills in Structural Family Therapy by relocating to Charlottesville, Virginia, to train under his long-time mentor Dr. Steve Greenstein. The latter was a nationally recognized trainer in Structural Family Therapy and the former director of training at the Philadelphia Child Guidance Clinic in Philadelphia, Pennsylvania, under the direction of Dr. Salvador Minuchin, MD, the founder of Structural Family Therapy.

## References

*Alexander, M. (2012).* The new Jim Crow: Mass incarceration in the age of colorblindness *(Rev. ed.). The New Press.*

*Delgado, R., & Stefancic, J. (2017).* Critical race theory: An introduction *(3rd ed.). New York University Press.*

*De Niro, R., DuVernay, A., King, J., Rosenthal, J., Skoll, J., Welsh, B., Winfrey, O. (Executive Producers). (2019).* When they see us *[TV series]. ARRAY Filmworks; Forward Movement; Harpo Films; Participant; Tribeca Productions.*

*Fitzgerald, K. J. (2020).* Recognizing race and ethnicity: Power, privilege, and inequality *(3rd ed.). Routledge.*

*Hardy, K. V. (2008). On becoming a GEMM therapist: Work harder, be smarter, and* never *discuss race. In M. McGoldrick & K. V. Hardy (Eds.),* Re-visioning family therapy: Race, culture, and gender in clinical practice *(2nd ed., pp. 461–468). Guilford Press.*

*Hardy, K. V. (2016). Toward the development of a multicultural relational perspective in training and supervision. In K. V. Hardy & T. Bobes (Eds.),* Culturally sensitive supervision and training: Diverse perspectives and practical applications *(pp. 3–10). Routledge.*

*Hardy, K. V. (2017a). Essential skills for mastering context talk in supervision. In K. V. Hardy & T. Bobes (Eds.),* Promoting cultural sensitivity: A manual for practitioners *(pp. 55–58). Routledge.*

*Hardy, K. V. (2017b, May 19).* "Beyond walking on eggshells": Race inside and outside therapy *[Symposium workshop]. Virginia Society for Clinical Social Work – Pinkus-Schwartz Symposium, Virginia Commonwealth University, Richmond, VA, United States.*

*Ice Cube. (1991). No Vaseline [Song]. On* Death certificate. *Lynch Mob Records. Priority Records.*

*LaGrange, Ohio. (2013, January 7). In* Wikipedia. *https://en.wikipedia.org/w/index.php?title=LaGrange,_Ohio&oldid=531727429*

*Loewen, J. W. (2005).* Sundown towns: A hidden dimension of American racism. *The New Press.*

*Martin, L. L. (2010). Strategic assimilation or creation of symbolic blackness: Middle-class blacks in suburban contexts.* Journal of African American Studies, 14*(2), 234–246. https://doi.org/10.1007/S12111-008-9075-0*

*National Association of Social Workers. (2017).* Read the code of ethics. *https://www.socialworkers.org/About/Ethics/Code-of-Ethics/Code-of-Ethics-English*

*United States Census Bureau. (2019a).* Amherst city, Ohio. *https://www.census.gov/quickfacts/fact/table/amherstcityohio,US/PST045219*

*United States Census Bureau. (2019b).* Bowling Green city, Ohio. *https://www.census.gov/quickfacts/fact/table/bowlinggreencityohio/PST045219*

*United States Census Bureau. (2019c).* Lodi village, Ohio. *https://data.census.gov/cedsci/profile?g=1600000US3944604*

*United States Census Bureau. (2019d).* North Ridgeville city, Ohio. *https://www.census.gov/quickfacts/fact/table/northridgevillecityohio/PST045219*

*United States Census Bureau. (2019e).* Vermilion city, Ohio. *https://www.census.gov/quickfacts/fact/table/vermilioncityohio/PST045219*

*Wellington, Ohio. (2013, January 7). In* Wikipedia. *https://en.wikipedia.org/w/index.php?title=Wellington,_Ohio&oldid=531727320*

# SECTION V

# WHITENESS AND WHITE SPACES

## CHAPTER 15

# Toxic Trends of Whiteness

## Bridging the Relational Divide

CARLIN QUINN, LMFT

I am writing this chapter from Lisbon, Portugal: the land of the original colonizers of Turtle Island. Here, over 6 million kidnapped and enslaved African people, Bodies of Culture, were unwillingly indoctrinated into a social contract driven by the forces of exploitation and dominance. In this place, human beings were commodified and their motivations for "discovery" outweighed their value of human rights. An aspect of humanity was lost on this land and it has yet to be found. Something happened here, within the hearts of white European people (soon to become white Americans); a contagion of the soul developed and was exported across the ocean, passed down through families and generations, resulting in the culture of white communities today.

The current state of Western society—neo-Nazi terrorists called to the streets by a sitting US President; Black Lives Matter, now a global revolution, taking root in many white Western countries; COVID-19, a global pandemic, illuminating social inequities and preventing them from remaining in the collective unconscious; fascism rising globally; and white supremacy, as a term, concept, and system, being recognized in political discourse and policy, as a force to be contended with (finally)—we find ourselves being dizzyingly tossed about by a sour mix of hope and despair. I have been invited to write this chapter during a moment in history when white voices are rightfully being asked to quiet and the voices of Black, Indigenous, and other Peoples of Color, as activists, thinkers, scholars, and movement leaders, are finally being featured and called forward. I speak from my position, as a white, cisgender female, to my people and to the (disproportionately white) professional field I am a member of, with the hope that we, together, can be a part of collective healing; be wind at the backs of BIPOC/Bodies of Culture movement leaders rather than a smiling obstruction. Going forward, I will use the terms Bodies of Culture and People of Culture, terms created by Resmaa Menakem (2017), when referring to Black, Indigenous, and other Peoples of Color. The terms Bodies of Culture/People of Culture refer to Menakem's (2017) claim that bodies bear the trauma of the cultural context they are born into and that bodies hold the memory of the histories, stories, lineages, and connection to place, which were taken from Black, Indigenous, and other Peoples of Color by the system of white supremacy.

I believe that, as clinicians, part of our role in society is to tend to the health of our collective social fabric. As we work with the hearts and psyches of individuals, groups, communities, children, young adults, and elders across all social divides, we offer ourselves in service to healing. It is a large, complicated task that requires us, as individuals and as a collective, to engage in the never-ending pursuit of raising our consciousness related to the realities of culture and society. A fundamental issue we all face is that we have been formed and shaped by the same culture we endeavor to heal; we need many angles of perception and many different lenses to do our due diligence as clinicians, to become conscious of our blind spots and to remain humble and in service.

The topic of racial justice, as it relates to social equity and genuine healing, is massive. I think this is one reason why white clinicians continue to dodge the work required for true accountability. Given this book is geared toward the field of psychotherapy, I will be using terms and concepts of personal and collective trauma, the somatics of whiteness, and the concept of "fields" to illustrate my thinking and perceptions up to this point. I want to acknowledge that, due to the fact that I identify as a white, cisgender, able-bodied female, who was raised in the upper middle class and educated in all-white establishments, my thinking and perceptions are necessarily limited. What I am sharing comes from over a decade of study, personal research, stumblings, study, relational heartbreak, and my work as an equity facilitator, educator, coach, and psychotherapist.

As someone who has dedicated her life to racial healing and social equity, the more I engage this work, the less I have to say and the more I have to live. I feel conflicted about writing during this moment in time because so much has been written by People of Color that goes unread and unacknowledged by our field. I am also aware of the harmful history of "white words" and the power they have to harm, to disappoint, or to deter people from the real work. The work, as I have come to know it, is about forging a path *through* whiteness, practicing "a way" of being that is more about living than it is about speaking or concretizing anything as "certain" or "known." This work, with all its need for intellectual understanding, verbalization, and systemic dismantling, is ultimately a journey of deep rehumanization that stretches my heart beyond its capacity and humbles me every moment I allow it to. The "white word" has caused so much harm on our planet, wielding power thoughtlessly. I proceed with care, knowing we must continue to make conscious what is rendered invisible by the dominant culture.

As Ruth King (2018) states: "When whites are unaware of or disown whiteness and white group dominance, ignorance becomes harmful" (p. 38). Willful ignorance is the conscious decision to avoid becoming informed about something we know to be wrong/unjust because to become informed would require us to make undesirable/inconvenient decisions. In other words, *we* determine when and how *we* wish to be informed and at what level *we* wish to engage—often choosing to only engage in a way that does not unsettle our lives or challenge us too strongly. For white liberals, we will often engage in performative allyship on a superficial level, all the while maintaining our white comfort and control. This can look like making donations to racial equity organizations but doing nothing to change our lives or the culture around us; marching in the streets when another Black man is shot by police but driving by/ignoring when we see police pulling over a Black man in our neighborhood; posting antiracist material on social media but not interrupting microaggressions when they are happening right in front of us. As white people, we learn how to play the field without putting skin in the game, and this can be very harmful, confusing, and disorienting to the People of Color in our lives who wish to be able to build relationships of trust with us.

When we step out of willful ignorance and relinquish white control, we step into an enormous piece of work that is overwhelming to anyone with an open heart. The overwhelm is part of the initiation, at least it was for me. I often see whiteness as an octopus—it has its tentacles in absolutely everything; it is far reaching, slippery, and smart; and when it doesn't like something, it can cloud the space with its defenses and quickly escape interrogation. It takes huge effort and steadfast patience to gain a hold of such a complex force and to thread antiracist consciousness through and around it, to hold it firmly, and to guide it in a new direction, all the while fielding the ugliest parts of white culture: dominance, fragility, and our immature responses to the destabilization that comes with dismantling its power, potency, and authority. It is important for white people to know that our processes are messy and that they can be exhausting for the People of Culture in our lives. Even when we think we're doing alright, reading all the books, trying to figure out how to be good antiracist white people, we are still exhausting, messy, and harmful: we still create "work" for Bodies of Culture. As white therapists, we need to be acutely aware of the impact our personal process can have on our clients and how it can impact the transference and countertransference in the therapeutic relationship.

## Destabilization Is Necessary: It's How We Know We're Interrupting the Status Quo

Our world is organized in a racial hierarchy. Whether I am consciously experiencing it or not, I am always living a racialized, white experience, and therefore I am always responsible for dismantling my role in the racial hierarchy. This is one thing I wish to convey to my white community and also the clinical community: to engage in dismantling white supremacy, healing whiteness, and building an antiracist culture, there is little to no room for hypocrisy—we have to live the work in and outside of the consultation room, and we need to be willing to unravel, to share, and to be naked in our not knowing; only then do we access the possibility of becoming trustworthy white people. We *will* become destabilized; actually, we *must* become destabilized in order to crack the foundation of white supremacy, which was baked into our psychic and somatic core. It is hard to put this process into words because whiteness is an illness that we have always been stricken with, and its symptoms are multitudinous, multidimensional, and multifaceted. As Layla Saad (2020) says, "White supremacy is an evil. . . . It will feel like waking up to a virus that has been living inside you all these years that you never knew was there" (p. 19). Becoming conscious of our whiteness is a mental, physical, spiritual, emotional, energetic, and social process. It has taken me time to see how I, and we, have been strategically molded to be pawns on the chessboard of systemic racism. Our collective inability to engage authentically, consistently, and effectively with this work is part of what keeps the system thriving; therefore, what is required is a collective waking up process where we, as white people, focus on the individual and collective process of building antiracist culture, together.

This work is ultimately heart work. Healing internalized racism requires that we first get to know the heart infection that is white supremacy. The process of white people getting to know the nature of this infection tends to take years and, unless it is accompanied by conscious education and an antiracist community and is integrated into authentic relationships, our racist impact (on a systemic level) does not really change. Our hearts have been systematically and strategically desensitized to feeling the harm and suffering we inflict on Bodies of Culture. For years, I kept getting the feedback: "I see you engaging in antiracism study, but I cannot feel your heart. Where is your heart? Our children are dying, our communities are being poisoned, our people's humanity is being erased, and you say you care but I cannot feel you. Why isn't your heart breaking?" I became curious about this because it was true. Despite being a therapist and all my efforts to learn about systemic racism, there was a thick wall of intellect and numbness that would immediately appear when the work got real, such as when I engaged in real and emotionally intimate relationships with Bodies of Culture, receiving the truth of their painful experiences, or when I was asked to directly interrupt whiteness/racial harm in real life. The seduction of apathy was fast and unconscious. Not only did it support my emotional comfort, but it also functioned, very effectively, to maintain my security, power, and authority in any given situation. When I, as a white person, become overwhelmed, I always have an emotional and somatic escape route to keep me regulated; apathy and numbness are contagions that stand by in my system, ready to bring me back into white equilibrium the moment I allow them to. This happens quickly and unconsciously within the white psyche soma, and it requires us to slow down and become precise with our inner perception to see how and when it is at play. It is up to us to remedy this. Blow (2012) states,

> One doesn't have to operate with great malice to do great harm. The absence of empathy and understanding are sufficient. In fact, a man convinced of his virtue even in the midst of his vice is the worst kind of man. (para. 24)

The contagion of white apathy was born into Western European culture at the time of colonization and it has established itself as a foundational underpinning in the development of the white psyche. As white people, we can do harm, witness harm, and ignore harmful policies, laws, and practices (which erase the humanity of huge swaths of people in our society) while having little to no collective ability to feel or carry the weight of these injustices. We might give a moment of care to an unjust event, but our nervous systems and emotional bodies tend to go blank when it comes to carrying any sustained, authentic, felt response to the realities Bodies of Culture experience in our society. An example of this is the recent murder of George Floyd, which momentarily seemed to spark global involvement in the Black Liberation Movement. Weeks after Floyd's brutal murder by Officer Derek Chauvin, my organization (and every racial equity organization, speaker, facilitator, and coach that I know) was flooded with emails and requests for immediate work. Suddenly every white organization (who had likely been getting feedback for *years* that it lacked diversity and needed to get it together regarding equity and racial justice) was not only scrambling to publish some well-meaning Black Lives Matter (BLM) solidarity statement, but they were also ALL asking for training, workshops, consultations, and immediate quick fixes. And yet as I write this now, 6 months later, I can say the emails have waned, the attendance numbers have dropped, and most white people did not pick up the work. White apathy has cast its thick haze across the consciousness of the momentarily "woke," and put them back to sleep. White apathy is an epidemic; and until we, as clinicians, confront our susceptibility to this form of apathy, I believe we pose a threat to

Clients of Color because we lack access to the genuine empathy related to racial harm which aids healing.

## "Fields of Whiteness" in the Clinical World

After some time working with predominantly white groups—as a teacher, facilitator, clinician, student, and group member—and as a community consultant with (white) intentional communities in the United States and Europe, I started to observe a certain communal "cause and effect" related to whiteness, which resulted in an innate ability to create an energetic force field that functioned to preserve white space. This force field is unconsciously created through white bodies, white behaviors, white social agreements, and white relationships, and it seems to successfully protect white solidarity, white comfort, and white control. It also functions to, simultaneously, energetically "push out" Bodies of Culture who are attempting to join the space. "To understand the dynamics of racial group dominance and subordination, we must look at group habits of harm, rather than solely looking at individual acts or single incidents" (King, 2018, p. 37). I began to observe certain traits in myself and in my white peers that I call *the somatics of whiteness* and that seem to clearly contribute to the phenomenon of white social control.

The somatics of whiteness are the subtle (and sometimes not so subtle) ways our behaviors, energy, speech, relational styles, and general ways of being, as white people, create a seemingly impenetrable "field of whiteness" in daily life, which unconsciously functions as a closed system to protect white social control. The somatics of whiteness are driven by white superiority and an *entitlement to exist* that is inherent to the white body and reveals itself in the way we white people move through the world. This entitlement to exist is often accompanied by a *right to thrive*, which, unfortunately, can be at the expense of Bodies of Culture. When white people naturally have a right to thrive and don't advocate for and ally with those who do not carry that inherent right (because the system of white supremacy would be weakened if they did), then we end up being complicit in the system's hierarchy of worth.

This unseen, unnamed, unanalyzed field of whiteness is often what lands in Bodies of Culture as unsafe, threatening, or toxic. Since this phenomenon has yet to be understood and dismantled by the white collective, it can be impossible to speak to it without triggering white fragility and fears of losing access to social status and professional perks. I believe this is a major component contributing to the failure of many clinical training programs and organizations in their attempt to create cultures of equity. We cannot treat (in ourselves or in others) what we cannot see; we need to bring more dimensionality to our lens when we track the collective power of whiteness in group fields as well as in us as individuals.

Some somatics of whiteness that contribute to the creation of fields of whiteness:

- Physical entitlement to space—when we walk (or drive) through space, we go first, cut people off, and get frustrated when we need to wait in line, especially if we are pressed for time. Many white people literally *don't see* Bodies of Culture; they move about the world relating to and seeing white bodies only.
- White nepotism—we white people do not tend to think critically about our tendency to promote people who look, think, act, and feel "right" or "comfortable" to us.
- Holding anger in the body, communicating it passive-aggressively or energetically.
- Flat affect, lack of emotional availability, inability to be in authentic contact.
- Dishonest facial expressions—we do not show what we think or feel.
- Internalized superiority as it relates to thinking and speaking—beyond taking up space, we tend to believe our thoughts (and the way we think) are simply valid and right.
- Offering thoughts and opinions whenever we want, whether solicited or not.
- General belief that white consciousness is inherently a higher consciousness (more educated, proven, logical, right).
- Having a low window of tolerance when whiteness and power dynamics are being confronted.
- Being energetically irresponsible—when we feel anxious, afraid, or victimized, we transmit this energy into group fields and individual

relationships without consent or consciousness of impact [Resmaa Menakem (2017) refers to this as *dirty pain*].
- Setting group "norms" based on what feels "right" to white bodies and determining standards based on white Western colonial culture.
- Valuing and rewarding thought and verbal articulation over other forms of communication.
- Habitually creating spaces of hierarchy and linear power structures informed by patriarchy (and hence re-enforced by white supremacy).
- Verbally advocating for antiracist allyship without changing policy or being willing to interrogate and change group norms.
- Speed—white people tend to harness control by being fast. We maintain power by making quick decisions and not giving space to nonwhite perspectives or considering different ways of doing things.
- Hypersensitive nervous systems—we do not have inner resources to manage racial accountability. We often utilize dissociation, apathy, and numbness as our safety exit.
- Willful ignorance—we become easily overwhelmed by what we don't know and by how much is needed, and we choose to remain ignorant.
- Expectation that Bodies of Culture should and will assimilate into white culture—white is right.
- Apathy—our ability to carry on with "business as usual" when Black and Indigenous communities are taken over by grief in the face of police brutality. This allows us to preserve our energy and stay focused on our individual success and security.

In this attempt to illuminate some social and relational trends of whiteness, I also want to acknowledge that these behaviors tend to have more nuanced psychological underpinnings (in the white psyche) that require healing. This is where our personal ego structures and characterological defenses intersect with white socialization and where the work of healing becomes complex, nuanced, and, at times, very complicated. There is no "one size fits all" prescription for antiracism work, especially as it relates to healing whiteness. Many of the common defense patterns articulated by Dr. Robin DiAngelo (2018) in her book *White Fragility* can be found in the *Diagnostic and Statistical Manual* (*DSM*; American Psychiatric Association,

2013) under the list of personality traits of narcissism. As a collective, we (white people), are a narcissistic people and we have a low threshold for honest reflection that challenges our self-esteem and identification with being "good" people.

A consistent theme that shows up in my equity coaching is the overwhelming need for white people to do our own trauma healing before, and as, we engage in antiracism work. Learning to live antiracism has been the most powerful illuminator of every aspect of my ego that is still identified with superiority or subjugation. I have needed to develop compassion for myself and my fellow white people, realizing how much early life trauma handicaps us in being able to stand up with fierceness to systems of dominance. To be a reliable practitioner of antiracism, I need to have a place to go when my trauma gets hooked. The times I have failed the most at being an effective ally were the times that I got caught by my unhealed trauma and lost my ability to show up centered and heartfully engaged. While I was aware that I was in a trauma response related to my own personal wounding, I was *incapable* of untangling myself from it without therapeutic support. One classic example for me (and one I see in many white women who are climbing out of patriarchy) is how quickly my strong, caretaker structures (informed by patriarchy) can turn into white saviorism. For me personally, this plays out when I struggle to have healthy boundaries, overextend myself in cross-racial relationships, get overwhelmed by the level of pain or need that arises in the other person, then close my heart, shut down, and become emotionally unavailable to Bodies of Culture in my life. When this dynamic shows up within white relationships, it can be hurtful; but when it shows up in cross-racial relationships, it can be (and usually is) harmful—because when a Person of Color extends authentic relational trust to a white person, after the history of harm we carry, this trust is not only an act of vulnerability but an act that says "despite the history of our people, I see you are not your history and I am going to give you a chance to rewrite things." Each extension of relational trust between white people and People of Color is an opportunity to create a new story. However, if we, as white people, aren't able to hold the complex and painful experiences of Bodies of Culture as well as their joy, power, brilliance, and beauty, if we ourselves are not well enough to hold the impact our people have on Communities of Color, then we will continue to cause harm. We need to develop the lens through which we perceive our own whiteness so we can address it thoroughly, and from there we can begin to earn trust.

## Tracking Whiteness: Fields of Awareness

When establishing critical analysis in any area or topic, we are actively developing a new lens to see through. When looking through the lenses of different systems of oppression, any given incident can be read in different ways depending on which lens you have access to: the lens of patriarchy, of spirituality, or of whiteness. Each lens offers perspectives and nuances that are typically rendered invisible by the status quo. In this section, I will focus on what it means for white people to develop our racial lens as it specifically relates to whiteness. I use three different fields of awareness to do this: the internal/individual field, the relational/dyadic field, and the group/collective field.

### *Internal/Individual*

The individual field of awareness, similarly to how it is used in therapy, is our ability to perceive our internal racialized landscape. When we apply a practice of honest introspection through a racial lens, we are able to get to know certain characteristics of whiteness and observe how the socialization of dominance moves through our body, mind, and emotions. In any given moment, I can pause and ask myself, "How is whiteness revealing itself in my inner thoughts, reactions, movements, behaviors or narratives right now? How is dominance or superiority showing itself within my body, mind, and energy? What personal material is touched or triggered in this moment that might cloud my ability to track whiteness? Am I flooded, triggered, overwhelmed, resting in my privilege, fatigued, certain, or numb? Do I feel connected to my entire body, and am I able to be present to feelings and sensations? Is my heart open? Where is tightness, rigidity, or edge showing up inside of me? Am I connected to the wholeness and humanity of those I am engaging with right now?"

*Relational/Dyadic*

In the relational/dyadic field, we focus our lens on how whiteness and racial harm show up *between* people and in relationship. This lens is also subject to each individual's personal relational trauma, stemming from their life and childhood, as well as cultural trauma related to other systems of oppression. For example, patriarchy and whiteness often intersect here for me (as I am a woman, living in a society also ruled by patriarchy, who grew up surrounded by men in my family who were dominant and misogynistic). Because of this, I am less able to track my white dominance when I am triggered and experiencing subjugation related to patriarchy. To be with this complexity while still centering race, it is necessary to identify and track patterns of dominance in these relational fields, and then to apply race and gender analysis to help tease out how my whiteness may be showing up as a reaction to being identified with my subjugated self, which still contains my unhealed trauma.

Some questions I ask myself when tracking whiteness in my relationships are, "In what ways is whiteness showing up between me and the people I am with? Who is present at the tables I sit at and who is not present? If I am with a Person of Culture, how am I behaving? Do I feel relaxed and authentic or am I tight and performing? If I am with a white person, are we engaging in a way that perpetuates white solidarity and white comfort, that exercising privilege or apathy related to the injustices we are encountering in our time together (e.g., if we're enjoying an outdoor lunch at a cafe and a seemingly hungry person stands by the door asking for food, do we let this land in us, or do we ignore it?)? If I am upset or triggered, how am I treating the people I am with? Am I dominating the conversation—following whatever impulses I have to speak, interrupting, pontificating at my leisure—or am I falling silent when something racist occurs? Am I exhibiting behavior that communicates that I am entitled to space and to get what I want? If in conversation with a white male, is my relationship to internalized oppression as a woman keeping me from interrupting racism or standing up for equity? Am I able to stay connected to the other person's wholeness and humanity even if they are doing or saying something I don't like or that I disagree with? Am I emotionally available or am I numb?"

*Group/Collective*

The group/collective field is the social and energetic field that groups of people consciously or unconsciously create together. These groups have the power to influence individuals and larger social structures, such as access to resources and education. A group field creates its own culture which can, and often does, perpetuate the status quo (white supremacy) unless alternative approaches are consciously introduced and consistently applied. Many times, in predominantly white spaces, one can start to sense a field of whiteness emerging; over the years, these group fields have caused great harm to People of Culture, which results in these fields being unable to retain nonwhite group members over a long period of time. A field that may feel comfortable, nourishing, and engaging for white-bodied people can be experienced as suffocating, toxic, and oppressive for nonwhite bodies. If we are not addressing the influences of larger systems of oppression in group spaces, such as clinical training programs, it will be impossible to effect real change toward creating fields of equity.

As a racial group, white people must begin to see how whiteness moves between us to create impenetrable fields of control. White Western groups tend to carry forth trends that link back to colonialism—our relationship to time, to measured tone, to tidiness and not showing ourselves, to intellectualization and numbness, to certainty and dominance, to impersonal and often hyperstructured ways of coming together in sterile environments with clear agendas. We tend to feel comfortable within power hierarchies because they give us a sense of our security and show us our place, and we maintain an unspoken agreement that we will not challenge seats of power to the point where whiteness will be unseated from positions of control.

This white group field is one I have seen do the most harm to Bodies of Culture. I have played my part in the creation of these fields of whiteness and have been deeply challenged by the dismantling of them. It takes work to create fields of equity—the process requires each individual to take personal, relational, and collective responsibility for healing their relationship to dominance, subjugation, apathy, superiority, and whiteness. It challenges white people to embark on a deep and consistent excavation of our beings to unearth decades of socialization and conditioning and entitlement to existence, comfort, and power. In the following sections, I am going to break down how our relationship to trauma and to healing can provide a path forward in antiracist work for white people.

## The White Collective's Relationship to Trauma

The white Western collective community (in the United States and Europe) gained power by amputating aspects of our own humanity. It was a self-inflicted collective trauma in the name of power and control. Our communal fabric has been woven by threads tethered to systems of dominance. Every one of us was born into and unconsciously shaped by the systems of white supremacy, patriarchy, and capitalism; our self-image, our relationship to each other, and our innate entitlement to a right to thrive are all steered by the symptoms, conditions, and forces of these systems. One of the gifts of intersectionality and identity politics is that they give us frames and language for the systems that are rendered invisible by dominant culture. The untended, unhealed wounds of our collective past and present result in thick layers of unconscious behavior among white community members. These behaviors unconsciously perpetuate cultural practices that erase our connection to our own humanity (the ability to feel impact) and thereby function to erase the humanity of others (those being harmed). I believe the unhealed trauma of the white collective is at the root of where we (humanity) find ourselves today, politically (division, fascism, war), economically (the collapse of capitalism), and environmentally (the climate crisis).

It "is ultimately about the basic struggle we're all in, the struggle to be fully human and to see that others are fully human" (Kendi, 2019, p. 11). Something that sounds so reasonable and simple has proven to be incredibly complex and confronting for white people. Our struggle to be fully human requires us to face, feel, and process our collective past and present with uncompromised perception, fierce truth, and sustained effort. To do this work well, we need to have healed enough of our own personal trauma to be able to engage in a charged field without losing our shit. We need to develop the skills to settle our nervous systems and not allow our anxiety, harmful character traits, or defenses to land on and in Bodies of Culture.

This is where building antiracist culture interfaces with clinical work. Traumatic layers held within the collective of a people require a multifaceted approach to healing personally, relationally, and communally. As clinicians, it is safe to assume we enter this field to support healing on some level—whether personal, individual, communal, institutional, or systemic. We train in theories and modalities that have been grappling with "the human condition" for centuries. We develop the ability to think from multiple (white) perspectives, take in the stories of our clients, and extend our empathy, our compassion, and ourselves in service of healing so that our clients may find the relational care they need to be able to live dignified, whole, and healthy lives—to reclaim their dignity and humanity. But how then do we account for the impact our racial blind spots have on the psychological healing of our clients?

Part of what makes the clinical relationship so evocative as well as a catalyst for such profound change is that it has the ability to tap into the power dynamics experienced in early childhood and in society. When working with developmental trauma, we make ourselves available to the exploration and healing of the misuse and abuse of power, which usually results in defense structures inhibiting our clients' ability to live healthy, happy, and whole lives. As white clinicians, in cross-racial clinical relationships, we are also stepping into the possibility of an even more complex and nuanced relationship, with the potential to enact and evoke not only family power dynamics but also racial and social dynamics related to power and dominance. This has been one of my most humbling learnings as a white clinician and in my relationships with Black women. What I now realize in my racial healing journey is that my white body, psyche, and heart do not know how to naturally and genuinely engage in emotional intimacy with People of Culture, specifically with Black people. While my personal history and the story of my upbringing could explain why I might struggle with intimacy in interpersonal relationship, when I apply a racial lens to my inner field of awareness, I notice that there is a far more complex set of fears, projections, and inner barriers to my heart that arise when I am deepening in relationship with Black people, especially Black women. I have been socialized by a culture which is steeped in anti-Blackness. It has taken me years of inner perception, self-truth-telling, processing, and consciously practicing the teachings of Resmaa Menakem (2017), which aid my white body in learning how to "settle" in the presence of unfamiliar Black bodies.

As clinicians and as white people, we need to stop smiling and get real with how anti-Blackness shows up in our bones. It is not easy for me to admit that my socialization still shows up, at times, as a first response in my body or impulses. Part of living this work is that I continue to engage in a practice of seeing, deprogramming, and reprogramming my mind and nervous system away from anti-Blackness and toward a settled system with an open heart, and I am more emotionally available in intimate connection with People of Culture in my life. Although my racist socialization still appears in my tracking, it does not have the same power to unconsciously drive my actions because I have developed an observing ego with a racial lens, so I am able to stay more present and conscious of my internalized racism as it surfaces, or soon after the fact.

## Conclusion

> When white Americans build culture that is sane and loving, they will no longer feel a need to exclude People of Color from it. Ultimately, whiteness must transform race to culture. Once this has been achieved, it can begin to transform from culture into community. (Menakem, 2017, p. 273)

To build an antiracist culture, we must first admit, collectively, that we have a problem: as a people, we are at an infantile stage of development when it comes to living antiracism and embodying the skills which will support us in doing so. We have a long and profound path to walk before we are qualified for that task, yet systems of oppression place us at the cultural helm, holding all of the institutional power and decision-making authority. During the Trump presidency, we witnessed what it is like to have an infantile mentality sit in the most powerful seat in our nation. In some ways, Trump's presidency was an exaggerated but accurate reflection of what is so undeveloped in the white collective. While it is easy to "other" Donald Trump, and create a sense of separation between us, this does not serve me in taking the sobering reflection that his being elected is offering. It is confronting to accept that such a person was given the largest platform in the world to propagate racism. He is a US citizen, a product of our unhealed past, and his presidency has illuminated the ugly underbelly of a white supremacist nation. And while he was recently ousted from the presidency, the fact remains that 71 million Americans voted to reelect him.

As I sift through the articles, police reports, and the latest horrifying accounts of global white supremacy (in the last three days, another innocent Black man was killed by police in Philadelphia and seven Black children were killed in Cameroon), I realize just how much emotional intelligence is required to stay heartfully and wholly engaged in this work. My body and bones were not socialized to bear this sort of responsibility and complexity; in fact, white supremacy banks on my inability to stay with care, connection, empathy, and nuance related to the racial truths of the Western world. The more I see and get to know the rules of the white supremacist game, the more I can feel how deeply controlled my internal landscape is by its powerful narratives of entitlement, superiority, and dissociation.

But today I choose to engage. I am making a conscious decision to break with the comforts of white solidarity to use my voice, heart, mind, and body to do what is right and to reclaim the aspects of humanity my ancestors relinquished. Although I do not believe that we, as a collective professional body, should be tuning in to the voices of white people for guidance and insight, I do believe the clinical world is in rough shape when it comes to understanding how white-centered our theories, practices, and culture have been. In a time when the demand for mental health services is at an all-time high, we have an even greater ethical responsibility to dig deeper so we can serve better. However, my hope is that such an inspired effort not need a global pandemic for broad-scale mobilization. We have been irresponsible and neglectful as professionals with regard to creating equitable, inclusive, and diverse theoretical fields for far too long. It is up to us to push back the tide of the ocean of whiteness that floods our profession and to face how much we have to learn, to admit how harmful our ignorance has been, and to engage in living and practicing antiracism in our communities and consultation rooms. May we help pave a path forward for collective healing.

**CARLIN QUINN (SHE/HER), LMFT,** is a psychotherapist, facilitator, and antiracist coconspirator; she is the founder/director of Education for Racial Equity, a nonprofit organization aiming to support the liberation movement, end systemic racism, and bring about economic justice. In her facilitation and coaching work, Quinn uses a combination of critical race theory, psychodynamic theory, humanistic relational approaches, and somatic awareness to help unearth and address the complexities of whiteness, white supremacy, and racial trauma in the Western world of psychotherapy and our daily human interactions. As a community organizer and cultural activist, she is committed to being a part of the movement to create future cultures rooted in equity, compassion, and nonviolence. She currently makes home as a settler in Ohlone territory of the Muwekma Ohlone People, also known as Berkeley, California.

## References

*American Psychiatric Association. (2013).* Diagnostic and statistical manual of mental disorders *(5th ed.). American Psychiatric Association.*

*Blow, C. M. (2012, September 19). I know why the caged bird shrieks.* The New York Times. *https://campaignstops.blogs.nytimes.com/2012/09/19/blow-i-know-why-the-caged-bird-shrieks/*

*DiAngelo, R. (2018).* White fragility: Why it's so hard for white people to talk about racism. *Beacon Press.*

*Kendi, I. (2019).* How to be an antiracist. *Bodley Head.*

*King, R. (2018).* Mindful of race: Transforming racism from the inside out. *Sounds True.*

*Menakem, R. (2017).* My grandmother's hands: Racialized trauma and the pathway to mending our hearts and bodies. *Central Recovery Press.*

*Saad, L. F. (2020).* Me and white supremacy: How to recognise your privilege, combat racism and change the world. *Sourcebooks.*

## CHAPTER 16

# I Can't Breathe

## A Tale of Toxic Whiteness in Academia

CHRISTIANA IBILOLA AWOSAN, PHD, LMFT

One of the stories that I love hearing my parents share about me is of the day that I was born, January 2, 1981. The story goes as such: I was born one week after my father graduated, earning his bachelor's degree from Amadu Bello University (ABU) in Kaduna State, Zaria, Nigeria. The day I was born, my father was at the bookstore, purchasing a book. In my family, there was a long-standing narrative that I would be called to be a professor, not just because I physically resembled my father but because he was visiting a bookstore during my birth as well. This storyline proved to be accurate, and it never surprised me. Some of my earliest memories as a child were on the campus of ABU. Essentially, I grew up in academia. I have often joked that I started college at the age of 4. The adults in my life, my parents and uncle, alternated picking me up at the end of the school day from Laboratory Nursery School (the equivalent of kindergarten in the United States). I remember walking to my uncle's dormitory to hang out with him and his friends while we waited for my parents to finish their workday at 5 p.m. Other days, when my uncle was not able to pick me up, I hung out with my mother. One of the joys of my young, 4-year-old self was playing on the carpeted floor of my mother's spacious office in the beautiful Senate Building, in the Academic Office. However, most of my after-school time was spent with my father, either at his office in the Sociology Department or sitting among his students in the lecture halls and smaller classrooms where his courses were taught.

One of my earliest childhood memories is of my father teaching a classroom of about twenty students while I sat in the first row. Growing up, my siblings and I had the opportunity to know and experience the world of Black academia, where the art works at the campus museum and the books at the campus library were produced by African artists and authors. Virtually everyone on campus was Black, with the exception of a few white and South Asian faculty. In my early years, I never made anything of the fact that all these educators, administrators, staff, and students were Black. My siblings and I often spoke fondly of our early experiences on ABU campus, where Black brilliance was displayed and affirmed every day. It was a campus that held us and showed us that we belong; a place where we were able to see ourselves not only in the people who kept our kindergarten or elementary school campus clean, but also in our principals, teachers, and the university students who taught us; an institution where our parents' talents and hard work were acknowledged and respected.

All of this changed when we moved to the United States in 1994. We found ourselves in a land where "all men" were supposed to be "equal" regardless of their race—a country that offered hope and fulfillment of dreams, but the realization of these things often seems to depend on one's skin color. The United States of America promises education as "the great equalizer" for all races. However, my family's experiences of this declaration have been the opposite. In a land where whiteness is deified and seen as superior and Blackness is demonized and seen as inferior, my family and I, like many other Black families in this country, have experienced the numerous ways that the invisibility of whiteness creates interpersonal violence and the psychological trauma of dashed hopes and dreams.

My father left his teaching position at Amadu Bello University in 1991 to complete his doctoral degree at Northeastern University in Boston. Three years later, in 1994, when myself, my siblings, and my mother arrived in the United States, he was teaching full time at one of Massachusetts's largest public universities—University of Massachusetts, Dartmouth. Over the next 11 years, my father authored several articles and books and held an annual senior lecturer contract position at the university. Several times, he submitted his application for a tenure track position; he was always denied.

Even during my early days in Nigeria, I always experienced the passion and focus that he put into teaching and mentoring his students. I witnessed his tenacity and his joy for teaching and the ways that his students stayed after to engage with him. My father's devotion to his teaching and work as a professor did not wane when we moved to the United States. Night after night and early morning after early morning, I saw my father work and put time into preparing for lectures, grading, writing, and attending meetings. So, it was always a painful and frustrating experience when, with every submission of his application for a tenure track position, he was told that he needed to publish more. As his daughter, I can only imagine the amount of pain, frustration, and disappointment that my father experienced every time he applied and was turned down for the tenure position.

As one of the few Black faculty members at UMass Dartmouth and the only Black faculty in the Sociology Department, my father worked to create the African American studies program at the university. The university was not supportive of this endeavor, and they seemed not to want it to succeed. One of the painful incidents of my father's experience in academia was when he published his first book. The chair of the department, a white woman, expressed to him that he was "an asset to the department" and they were "happy to have him." However, weeks later, under the guise of a "peer-evaluation," the same chair, along with two other white faculty, showed up in his class without giving my father advance notice, and they peppered his students with questions that implied that he was a "poor instructor," according to two his students, one Black and one white. The Black student expressed to him that, in his three years at the university, he had never experienced an "instructor evaluation" like that. At the time, I was not aware that when white people compliment or say something nice about a Black person or a Person of Color, it is critical to be suspicious that this kind word may not be their true feelings toward you. Also, hearing about this experience quickly taught me that white people who hold positions of power in academia cannot be trusted, because they have different expectations for Black people compared to white people. Unfortunately, these requirements are not explicit, but Black people are supposed to know them in order to survive in white spaces. It appeared that my father's active engagement in the creation of and involvement in the African American Studies Program, as well as his dedication to meeting the requirements for a tenure-track position, was met with disdain by these white faculty members.

Year after year, I wondered how my father dealt with the disappointments and pain of going from being an esteemed professor in his homeland to, after all the hard work of obtaining his PhD in the United States, being devalued and having his work viewed as "less than and not good enough." My father is a very hopeful, faithful, and tenacious man. He came from a very poor family and left his home in Ilesha, Southwestern Nigeria, at the age of 14 for a chance at success in Zaria, Northern Nigeria. He practically raised himself. He lives his life with the motto, work hard and respect others, just like his mother taught him before he left home. "If you work hard enough and leave the rest to God, you can get anywhere" had been the story that guided his life from the age of 14. Unfortunately, it seemed that despite all the diligence, grit, credentials, and prayers he had, they were not enough to get the all-white search committee to see him as qualified for the tenure-track position. He applied and interviewed for another tenured track position within the department. The candidate who was offered the position was a white woman who had fewer publications than he had and was an ABD (all but dissertation), even though the job description explicitly indicated that ABD candidates would not be considered for the position. Having experienced yet another devaluation of his presence, qualifications, and work, my father spoke out to the chair about the dishonesty and racial inequality apparent in the search committee process. I was infuriated when I heard my father narrate the painful experience of arriving at his office one day to find his name tag removed from his office door, his office packed up, and a new person sitting in there. He was not given a new office until he made a complaint and was later asked to share a small office with another colleague. In this white space, his presence was denigrated and his contributions to the university were treated with contempt. One of the lessons I quickly learned when we moved to the United States was that when Black people challenge white people, there is often a consequence. Not surprisingly, the following semester, the chair refused to renew his contract for the next academic year. My father ended up suing the university for racial discrimination. After about three years of fighting the case alone, because it was practically impossible to find an affordable lawyer, he won. He received a small monetary compensation for damages, but no back pay or re-instatement of his position. However, this slight victory was not without the mental, emotional, and physical wounds that come with being undervalued and treated as "less than" in a white space. Witnessing my father's struggles with the stressors of racism and whiteness in academia, I became convinced that racism does not impact Black and Brown people mentally and emotionally only, it also has detrimental physical effects on our lives. I watched my father go from a man who hardly worried about his physical health to a man who was diagnosed with high-blood pressure at the height of the legal ordeal with the university.

## Whiteness as a Generational Weapon

Whiteness is everywhere, but most white people cannot see, name, and acknowledge it because of their deep-seated belief that they are objective: "just humans, with clear awareness conscious and no racial biases." This "white lie" blinds white people from seeing the ways their whiteness becomes a weapon that destroys the lives of Blacks, Indigenous, and People of Color (BIPOC). The invisibility of whiteness in white spaces, such as our educational, medical, justice, and religious institutions, hardens the generational stronghold and the continuation of white supremacy, whiteness, and racism in our society.

The use of whiteness is an unacknowledged weapon that allowed white settlers to plunder the land, lives, language, culture, and religious traditions and practices of Indigenous People. The oblivion to the weaponry of their whiteness made white colonizers believe that they had the right to obliterate empires on the continent of Africa, defining Africans as savages, as they, the white colonizers, looted her lands and raped and brutally enslaved her people. Whiteness is like a tear gas that has endangered the lives of Asians and other People of Color via tokenization and forced assimilation. The invisibility of whiteness is a toxic poison that continues to contaminate the air that we all breathe. Many white people are oblivious to the ways the invisibility of their whiteness impedes their ability to see, hear, and feel the impact of this toxin in all the spaces they occupy, while BIPOC continue to choke from it. If whiteness is a weapon, the usage of this weapon on BIPOC is racism, which is violence—white violence.

## Generational Impacts of White Violence

I have always carried the emotions of anguish and sadness regarding my father's mistreatment in white academia. It is very painful to see and feel the wounds of implicit racist beliefs from white people, some of whom viewed and treated my father as unqualified and devalued his intelligence because of his skin color. Such racist and brutal beliefs brought about interpersonal violent actions that derailed his hopes and dreams of being a tenured full professor. The agonizing racist experiences my father encountered in white academia showed me, his immigrant offspring, that one's qualifications, experiences, and credentials may not matter as much in white spaces. Or, at least, that for any of those elements to matter, one has to be overworked to the detriment of one's well-being. Over the years, I have witnessed and experienced this painful reality of being Black in the United States. It seems that regardless of one's educational attainment and experiences, one's skin color always seems to determine one's latitude in white spaces. Sadly, this has also been my siblings' and my experiences in white academia and corporate America in the United States. My parents often talked about the fact that they brought us to the United States to achieve our dreams. They did everything they could to prepare and equip us to be hardworking and passionate citizens of the world, but they cannot protect us from the ways in which the violence of white ideology and the practices that treat Black people as "less than" strive to choke out the hopes and dreams of Black people. Sadly, many Black families are unable to prevent the toxicity of whiteness from suffocating the lives that hold their hopes and dreams in the United States.

Soaking up my father's passion and talent for teaching at a young age gave me the confidence to realize my own love of teaching early in my academic career. However, as a master's student at Syracuse University, I began to fight against the thought that I could or would one day teach. I did not recognize that as a result of the mental and emotional trauma of my father's experiences in white academia, I completely closed myself off to the possibility of my being a professor. I remember trying to explain to my white professor and mentor, who was encouraging me to consider getting my PhD, why being a professor "was not my thing." "I will get my PhD, but being a professor is just too much work, too much pain, too much disappointment," I said, "definitely not my thing. I would rather just be a licensed marriage and family therapist." The Marriage and Family Therapy program at Syracuse allowed me to name and start to work through the emotional stress and trauma that whiteness has inflicted on me and my family. For two years, I witnessed the ways that the faculty members (one Black man, one South Asian woman, three white women, and one white man) not only engaged us, as students, in self-examination and interrogation of race and particularly whiteness, but also modeled this by their willingness to challenge whiteness themselves. After much self-reflection and many soul-searching conversations with family, friends, and professors on naming the anxiety and pain that I carry around my father's experiences in white academia, I decided to apply for my doctoral degree. Even then, I was not fully convinced that I would become a college professor nor work in academia.

## "White-Only" Leadership—The New "White Only" Sign

My exposure to Black leadership in Nigeria highlighted for me that white leadership is not the only way. At Syracuse University, as an undergraduate student, I was often one of a few Black students in my major science courses, and all my instructors in those courses were white professors. This experience of being "one of the few" Black students and of almost all professors being white was starkly different from my experience of majority Black teachers in Nigeria; even my high school in Boston had a diverse student body and diversity among faculty members. As an undergraduate Black student, the clear message I internalized was that white people are the only race trusted to hold positions of power and to make consequential decisions on the lives of generations of people. No one questions "white-only" leadership or is suspicious of their abuse or misuse of power. I often wondered if I, and many of my Black and Brown peers, have internalized this false toxic message about whiteness. Did our white classmates even notice this toxic poison of whiteness they were inhaling? Implicitly, the white-only standard of leadership and power communicates to white students that they can expect to see themselves in positions of leadership in any organizations in the workforce. And it overtly communicates to Students of Color that regardless of the degrees we work for at white institutions, we will rarely, if ever, see ourselves in positions of leadership, and we should not expect this in the workforce. I can only imagine what it feels like for white students to not have to worry or wonder as to whether their college degrees and the student loans that they have racked up to obtain these degrees will pay off in gaining their desired employment, promotions, and ascension to leadership positions in their chosen professions. The invisible white-only leadership in academia ripples into the larger society in which, even with similar levels of education, degrees, and experiences, Black college graduates are not hired or promoted at the same rate as white college graduates. Consequentially, this also reflects the dismal lack of representation of BIPOC and the overrepresentation of white people in leadership positions in many US companies and professional organizations.

Unfortunately, in many academic institutions, both white students and Students of Color are breathing in whiteness—the message that white leadership is the "only way, the norm, and the standard." The institutions that are tasked with preparing the next generation of professionals for the workforce are grooming students, implicitly and explicitly, to know and adhere to the racial order in society. Colleges and universities are socializing white students and BIPOC students to assimilate the age-old, single template of racial rule of engagement, in which white people are in the dominant position and Black, Indigenous, and People of Color are in the subjugated position (Hardy, 2020). The feverish need to hold on to white-only leadership and exclude BIPOC people from leadership explains the disdain Senator Mitch McConnell expressed regarding President Barack Obama's leadership when he boastfully proclaimed that his main goal was to make sure Obama was a one-term president. For eight years, McConnell and the Republican Party (majority white men and women) obstructed President Obama's efforts to achieve critical tasks for the nation (Obama, 2020). It is not surprising that eight years after the election of the first Black President in the United States, white men and women voted in large numbers for a racist and unqualified white man, Donald Trump, whose administration represented the ultimate white-only leadership and space. It appears that the United States' higher education system has done its job well in tacitly cultivating the consciousness of white Americans to believe that white representation of leadership is "the norm and the standard."

Such implicit messages of whiteness in leadership persist for white Americans on many college campuses in this nation. When we look at the makeup of the faculty members and nonacademic and nonadministrative staff, the majority of nontenured and tenured faculty members are white, while most adjunct professors are Black and People of Color. Similarly, the janitors, security men and women, cafeteria workers—the people who are essential to the day-to-day operations of keeping university campuses running—are majority Black and People of Color. Once again, what are the implicit and explicit racial messages that these racially shaped hierarchical structures communicate to the next generations of leaders and professionals? Daily, both inside and outside of their classrooms, students of all races are exposed to the toxic poison of whiteness. For white students, the toxin of whiteness clouds their ability to recognize the way that their white identity is taught as a defense for white superiority, instilling an internal sense of "I'm (white) better than and deserving" to be in this white space. And for Blacks, Indigenous, and Students of Color, this poison of whiteness suffocates their ability and efforts to fully see themselves as smart enough or deserving to be in a similar space as their white peers because they are consistently reminded that academia is a white-only space—a white-only space that proclaims that BIPOC students are "included." However, upon closer examination, one will notice that these students are only included in the way that a baker puts sprinkles on a vanilla cake—a white cake. The sprinkles do not change the fact that the cake is still vanilla—still white. A few BIPOC students on a majority white campus still makes it a white-only space because these students hardly see themselves represented in the curriculum, course readings, or in the faces of their instructors or administrators. White-only institutions mainly cater to white students and marginalize the realities and presence of BIPOC students.

## Pockets of Breathing Room—Still Not Enough!

At the time, I did not realize that I was attempting to correct the lack of acknowledgment of my Blackness in almost all my undergraduate classes. Throughout my undergraduate career at Syracuse University as a psychology (pre-med) major, I had one Black female professor, Dr. Catherine Cornwell. To gain further exposure to Black professors, I took some courses in the African American Studies department. I remember how surprised I was when I met another Black professor, Dr. Kenneth V. Hardy, in the Marriage and Family Therapy (MFT) program at Syracuse during the interview process for the master's program. I knew how great it felt to be seen and valued within Black academia from my experiences in select undergrad classes and in that master's program—places where my Blackness and experiences were represented and affirmed. Hence, when the opportunity came up for me to attend the Couple and Family Therapy doctoral program at Drexel University, which was chaired by a Black woman, and to be mentored by a Black man, I selected this program over the other two programs that accepted me. The other two programs in the Southeastern region of the country had a majority white faculty and one Black faculty, whom we'll call Dr. Mark Harris. Dr. Harris made sure to let me know during the interview that focusing both my research and clinical work on Black clients and racism should not be centered in the field of Marriage and Family Therapy. As the only Black candidate within the small group of interviewees assigned to him, I was filled with frustration and shame in hearing this Black professor implicitly endorse the notion and practice of "white universality" while he devalued Black experiences by singling out my research about why Black people don't come to therapy as "not good enough." In a way, he was warning me that as a Black person, I was going to have a hard enough time in white academia as it was, and that specifically devoting my research to race and racism was going to make my acceptance within the academy still more difficult. But even if that was his motivation, that day, I was reminded that one does not have to be white to espouse toxic ideology of whiteness towards Black people or in the presence of white people. Specifically, the experience allowed me to be attuned to the sad reality that even Black and People of Color in academia can embrace the practices of whiteness and be unaware of it.

Being well acquainted with the feelings of invisibility and of not belonging in majority white institutions, programs, and classrooms, I did not want to subject myself to four or more years of constant, unexamined ideology and practices of whiteness that devalue the lives, intelligence, and experiences of Black people. I knew if I attended either of those two programs in the Southeastern region of the country, the assaults of whiteness on my dignity, emotions, and intelligence would be relentlessly on display without much respite. I was not so naïve as to think that Drexel University, a majority white institution like Syracuse University, would embody less of the toxic assaults of whiteness. As a Black student, with both generational and personal traumatic experiences of whiteness in academia, I knew I needed a program that centered the experiences of Black people and People of Color and that interrogated whiteness. I knew this would be difficult to do in any majority white institution, even one with a majority Black faculty, because promulgating the ideas and practices of whiteness does not require any, or even a large number of, white people to prevail. In an attempt to disparage the Couple and Family Therapy program at Drexel for the fact that it had a large number of Black faculty and majority Black and Students of Color, it was labeled the Historically Black College and University (HBCU) of the MFT field. No one, however, referred to the Brigham Young University or the Virginia Tech MFT programs as the Historically White Colleges and Universities (HWCUs) of the MFT field. This exemplifies another form of the invisibility of white violence, in which white people are not able to recognize and name their whiteness, but are quick to recognize and negatively label Blackness, even though they swear that they "don't see color." I was proud to have attended the HBCU of the MFT field because it helped me continue to identify and experience the reality that it is possible for Black people to hold their own in white spaces, but not without the pain, stress, and trauma of whiteness.

I was able to work through the difficulties of not wanting to be a professor by seeing the ways in which my Black professors worked through violence of whiteness by effectively using their voices even when it was difficult. One pivotal moment that gave me an awareness of and reassurance that I may be finding my voice in white academia was when I presented my research on Black clients' experiences in therapy at our monthly "lunch and learn sessions." One of the white faculty was persistent, determined to let me know that Black clients' experiences with mental health services are no different from white clients' experiences. He insisted that "mental and emotional health issues are mental and emotional health issues. There are NO differences WHEN it comes to RACE about this." This was unlike the interaction with the faculty member during the doctoral interview I referred to earlier, where I did not say much in response to his denial of racism on the lives of Black clients. This time, I was able to access my voice because I was in an academic environment that encouraged me to scrutinize the effects of whiteness on Black lives, particularly within mental health services. I appreciated the fact that I had Black faculty members who modeled for me and my classmates, who were Black, People of Color, and white, the various ways to navigate the trauma of being a Person of Color in white academia. I also knew that there were more Black and Brown students who also needed someone like me to empower them and help them navigate the trauma of whiteness in academia. And for this reason, I began to fully embrace my decision to go into academia. Working with majority Black faculty, I realized that, at some point in our existence in white academia, we as People of Color will utilize one or all of the following three methods to attempt to survive in white spaces. First, some of us will use the tactic of "go along to get along." We will acquiesce to whiteness and fully embrace it in order to be accepted in white spaces. Second, some of us will put our head down and over-function in hopes that white people will change their distorted view of us and see our hard work, not just our skin color. And last, some of us will use our voice to challenge whiteness even though it may cost us. Regardless of the strategy we employ in our attempts to breathe through the toxic poison of whiteness in academia, it is crucial that we become mindful of the painful effects of this poison on our lives and career aspirations.

## The Fear of Not Breathing in White Academia

My decision to go to therapy to continue externalizing the anguish and fear that kept showing up for me around my father's experience in white academia came out of a difficult conversation I had with a Black female faculty mentor. While helping me process why I was stuck with my dissertation, she asked one question, "What would it feel like for you if you received tenure and your father didn't?" Words did not come out of my mouth; what did come out were tears from my eyes. These tears spoke of a little girl's admiration of her father's passion and brilliance for teaching. These tears were filled with my father's unrecognized hard work in white academia. And these tears held my own fears of the inescapable toxic effects of whiteness on my life and career. While working with my white therapist, who was strongly recommended by another Black clinician, I had several dialogues with him about his whiteness. We discussed his own introspective work on the influence of his whiteness on his clinical process. We explored how he would work with me as a Black woman whose fears and pain around whiteness seemed to be paralyzing me in completing my dissertation.

In therapy, I realized that the grief and sorrow that the violence of whiteness inflicted on my father and my family had grown into a mixture of guilt, rage, shame, and fear in me. When I was offered a full-time tenure track position, I thought of my father's hard work, his pain, and his disappointments around not obtaining a position like this. I felt rage and guilt. Rage with knowing that the violence of whiteness had not only stolen his achievements but robbed me as well. As his daughter, I had been robbed of the confidence to believe in the reality of my career aspirations. I asked myself "Why did I get to have this position and he didn't?" I felt shame because I knew how hard he worked to obtain his PhD and how much dedication he had put into his career. I also knew that he had been humiliated and devalued because of his skin color. My shame was also intertwined with a fear of disappointing my father.

In further processing all these emotions, the fear of me encountering the assault of whiteness as my father had done unmercifully brought about a transformative perspective in one of my conversations with my Black male dissertation chair. Sadly, white violence is vicious, and it is prevalent in academia; he helped me see that, even when I do experience the brutality of whiteness, my experience will be different from that of my father. He noted that my father's experience allowed me to be much more aware of how whiteness is embedded in academia and that the wisdom I gained from his struggles with the violence of whiteness will also help me to navigate my own encounters. In discussions with my father, I expressed how I feared that I would face racial discrimination and the imposition of whiteness on my career as he did. He said that he has similar fears but hopes and trusts that when that happens, I will make the best decision for myself. Even as I accepted my first full-time job offer in academia, the question lingered: When the violence of whiteness seeks to choke out my dreams and I can't breathe in academia, what will I do?

## A Challenge to White-Only Reality in the Classroom

As a Black professor with the experiences of teaching at five HWCUs' Marriage and Family Therapy (MFT) graduate programs as an adjunct and nontenured faculty member from 2012 to the present, I continue to witness white students' and Students of Color's differential internalization of the invisibility of whiteness on their college campuses and in their graduate training programs. Many Black students and Students of Color often tearfully express to me, with a blend of admiration and sadness, that I am the first Black professor they have had in their tenure in graduate school and, for some, throughout their entire education in the United States. On the other hand, it never fails that the minute I step into a classroom, some white students are quick to challenge my abilities and physical representation as their professor. In these instances, the white students are often not able to cognitively make sense of why they have a Black professor in the front of their classroom, because all their lives they have been taught subtly that the only person who should be in the front of their classroom is a white professor. This cognitive shock to the covert racialized message of "white-only teacher/professor" often turns into denigrating interactions, such as saying to me "Oh, you're the professor?" or Googling concepts on their phones while I lecture in real time, openly questioning my knowledge of the topic we are discussing. This is a form of interpersonal "white violence" in academia. In two classroom observation experiences, white students have challenged my teaching style and publicly complained about the ways I teach to the (white) department chairs and program directors.

At one family therapy graduate program, I was teaching a course in which the majority of the students were Black. All the white students expressed disapproval of me as their professor because I was "teaching differently." The white students interrogated me, with indignation in their voices, that "if the class was majority white" would I have structured and taught the class the way I was teaching it? Essentially, these white students were communicating that they wanted me to center whiteness—the racial order they were familiar with—"the norm." The very presence of my body as a Black female professor in the front of their classroom did not leave much room to center whiteness. Cognitively and emotionally, they were not able to make sense of the unfamiliar racial makeup of the classroom, in which the white students were the minority, the Black students were the majority, and the professor was a Black woman. For the entire semester, the white students expressed outrage, frustration, and sometimes even refused to complete assignments because they felt "unsafe." The white students indicated that they felt unsafe because my *experiential, affective, collectivist* pedagogical style of teaching was "not white enough." My teaching style is significantly informed by the Multicultural Relational Perspective (Hardy, 2016; Hardy & Laszloffy, 2002). This framework allows me to cultivate a collaborative, authentic learning community by actively and creatively engaging my students in critical exploration of themselves and the larger society within the course materials.

By complaining to the white program director and obstructing class exercises, these students fought against what they experienced as "different." They were unwilling to examine that the *different* they railed against was built on their acceptance of the invisibility of whiteness as the norm. This experience made it clear to me that, just as the Students of Color were expressing to me that I was their first Black professor, this was also likely true for some of my white students, and this is how they were letting me know. As a Black person, I can only imagine the mental torment white students must experience when they are confronted with the reality that their whiteness is not the norm, nor is it universal. This "white mental agony" is probably at the root of the defensiveness and indignant knee-jerk emotional reaction that white people exhibit when the false, suppressed belief in, and toxic poison of, whiteness as "superior and the standard" is challenged. For me, being in a position of power in the classroom as a Black professor seemed to create a space, physically and mentally, for my Black students and Students of Color to see themselves as "smart enough" because they can relate to me. Many of the white students seemed to see me as different, a deviation from what they were accustomed to in academia, and thus I did not belong in this position of power. No, they never expressed this directly, but I felt it intensely in many of our interactions. This is often how the institutionalization of whiteness works; the messages of disdain and disapproval are seldom directly expressed. As a Black professor, holding the joy of Black students and Students of Color seeing themselves in me and, at the same time, experiencing their sorrow as their white peers made it clear that they saw me—and them—as an "unequal other" was a painful experience.

## Fortification of White Spaces and Challenging Whiteness

Sadly, white students are not the only ones who view their BIPOC professors and peers as unequal others. A painful experience of devaluation of me and my work during a workshop at the American Family Therapy Academy (AFTA) annual conference, in front of attendees of diverse racial groups, still sits with me today.

Early in my career as a faculty member, I was excited to share my clinical knowledge and research on the work I had been doing with Black heterosexual couples. The workshop also featured a white man, in his mid-fifties and advanced in his career, who was presenting on his theoretical philosophy on couples in therapy. He presented his philosophy on "couples" with no mention of the contextual backgrounds of the couples he spoke about. Not surprisingly, we all knew, and he expected us to know, that he was referring to white couples. Why? Because we have been socialized and trained, in society as well as in the field of family therapy, that whiteness is virtually never named. There is an unspoken assumption that whiteness is "universal," and yet, we cannot name it. Sitting less than two feet apart from each other, in front of about twenty attendees, we completed our respective presentations and then moved into the question-and-answer portion of the workshop. Within a minute or two of the attendees directing their questions to me, out of the corner of my right eye, I noticed that my white copresenter was visibly upset. He began to shuffle his papers on the table, to fidget, and then proceeded to interrupt me as I spoke. With annoyance and agitation in his voice, he turned to me and said ". . . BUT you're only focused on BLACK couples. . . . Emotion is a universal experience. . . . There are no differences in working with white or African American couples!" I was not surprised by his "all couples are the same" statement because this universal ideology is the bedrock of many clinical theories and models.

As I attempted to engage him to examine the ways that his whiteness and white universality were predicated in his statements, he became even more agitated, interrupting more frequently, with a higher tone in his voice now, "You're NOT the only one who works with African American couples. . . . I've been doing this work with couples for years now." With the workshop attendees confused and my white, Jewish, female, former master's program professor sitting at the back of the room and having to raise her voice for him to hear her said, "Would you let Christiana F***ING speak! . . . Why are you so d*** upset?" He replied, "I don't know why she's getting ALL the questions. . . . She's NOT the expert on couple's therapy. . . . I've worked with AT LEAST TWO African American couples TOO! . . . Race doesn't matter! . . . Couples don't bring it up. Plus, NO one is asking about the work I presented on." I could not believe my ears nor my eyes, as I watched this grown man berate me and denigrate my work and personhood, all because he was not elevated and centered as the "expert of couple's therapy" based on this "universal" work on "white" couples. I cried uncontrollably for the remainder of that day. My tears gave voice to the trauma of the reality of being a Black woman in white spaces. This man's white mental agony and white violence toward me exposed the poison of whiteness that, no matter how hard I work, no matter the number of letters behind my name (i.e., PhD, LMFT), all of these do not matter, because what he saw was a Black person, a Black woman, who was an "unequal other . . . not qualified . . . and who lacked expertise," even as he professed that "race doesn't matter" and he "doesn't see color."

I appreciated my former professor speaking up for me, and I had not doubted that she would. It did not surprise me because on numerous occasions I had experienced her, a white woman, examining and interrogating her whiteness. In the interviewing process for prospective students, as well as in our classrooms and program meetings, I had observed her, along with the other faculty members, patiently and authentically create space for me and other students to name, examine, and challenge whiteness. Her response during my professional presentation was refreshing because she did not collude with whiteness. She confronted it right in that moment rather than waiting until after the incident was over and then telling me privately how that white man was racially insensitive, racist, and that I didn't deserve that. Sadly, this latter scenario has been the typical behavior of white people in my experience, particularly white women, when another white person racially assaults or invalidates me or another POC. It seems as if it is difficult for white people to publicly challenge other white people for their racist beliefs and acts toward BIPOC. My former professor once again modeled for me and others in the room that white people can make visible the violence of whiteness by making it explicit and interrupting the trauma of whiteness out in the open.

Under the guise of white objectivity, the universality of whiteness is rampant on college campuses and academic organizations. There is an incongruence between the philosophy and the practice of "diversity and inclusion," whereby the ultimate focus of those who are included, whose narratives are elevated, whose interests are protected, and whose comforts are centered, are those of white people. Whites subvert authentic racial diversity and inclusion when the pedagogical styles, research agendas, curricula, and procedural processes that center the experiences, perspectives, and work of Black and People of Color are excluded, vilified, viewed as deficient, and evaluated as "not good enough"—somehow missing the mark of the universal standard of whiteness. Essentially, when white-only curricula are taught, research and theoretical orientations that center whites and whiteness are presented, and the insistence on one right way—the "white way"—to do things is widespread. The passive yet deadly message that is perpetuated is that BIPOC faculty, staff, administrators, and students "don't belong here." The unspoken message of white universality is that the only people who belong in academic spaces are whites.

Unfortunately, white people are not the only ones who perpetuate the white universality of white ways of knowing, realities, narratives, emotions, culture, etc. Some Black people and People of Color embrace this view as well. There are indirect and direct ways that BIPOC promote the view that the only humans who are supposed to be seen and have inherent ownership to academic spaces are whites. Often, BIPOC's engage in these subtle collusions with whiteness as a coping mechanism for surviving the daily assaults of white violence in academia. However, the downside of placating whiteness by denying its viciousness is that it continues to give whiteness and white people more unearned power over the lives of Black and Brown people. I have met Black people and People of Color throughout my career in academia, as a student and as faculty, who have tried to convince me that my research/clinical focus on Black lives and racial issues would be a "dead end" to my career. The commentary conversation often goes like this: "Why do you want to do that? I don't want you to be pigeonholed as the Black diversity faculty. Good luck with that!" Essentially, this is the same thing Dr. Harris was indirectly conveying to me years ago during that doctoral interview: "White academia will not accept you. You already stand out as a Black person. Why do you want to bring more attention to yourself by focusing on race?" Painfully, these views create relational impasses among Black faculty and Faculty of Color that prevent us from associating with and supporting each other and our work. Being the only junior Black female faculty at my previous university, I attempted to connect with the only Black female full professor at the college for almost five years. However, she was only willing to meet with and mentor junior white male faculty members. The message I received from her consistent avoidance of me was, "This space belongs to white people, only a few of us—Black people—are allowed here."

White belonging, particularly in academia, is an internalized, unspoken reality that many white people and some BIPOC protect and defend without being conscious of it. The sense of whiteness and of being white subtly communicates to Black and People of Color, "You're not wanted here." Early in my academic career as a doctoral student, I often felt that I did not belong in academia; what has been referred to as "imposter syndrome" that many Black people and People of Color experience when in majority white spaces. Early in my faculty career, I began to realize that the feeling of not belonging in a white space was not accurately labeled. Labeling the sense of not belonging as an imposter syndrome seemed to decontextualize the imposition of whiteness on my physical presence and intelligence in a white space. This imposter syndrome is not a condition that I created, it is not a disease within me. It is the pattern and disorder of whiteness that have continuously reminded and burdened me, and others who look like me, that "we don't belong" in white spaces.

A vivid, traumatizing encounter that demonstrated that white belonging is real occurred when I sat in a writing group meeting, the only Black faculty in attendance, during the two years of continuous killings of Black men and women by white police officers in 2015 and 2016. One of the white male faculty members expressed, with pain and trepidation, his desire to discuss the killings of Blacks by white police officers with his students. I was aghast when the white female faculty, whose primary discipline was in sociology, expressed, "Our students are not thinking about that. . . . They are not even concerned about that." Immediately, I felt that I did not belong, I felt not seen and unwelcome in the group. I wondered whether the white female faculty noticed that she just excluded me and labeled the experiences of Black people who look like me as "not important" because "our students are not thinking about that." I questioned which of "our" students she was referring to—her white students? Or her Black students? I doubted I was included in the *"our* students," nor were the Black students who came to me, throughout the semesters, to process their emotions around the effects of white violence on their lives. In making such an insensitive, harmful remark in response to her white colleague's distress and attempt to broach the topic of race with his students, she reinforced the sense of white belonging. And she fortified the invisible white racial agreement contract that racism, particularly white violence on the lives of Black people, should not be identified or discussed openly. Unfortunately, the white male colleague conformed and reacted to the racial socialization of white belonging and the invisible white racial contract with silence, and he did not attempt to further challenge her statement. His compliance and silence solidified the notion and practice of white solidarity and maintained the invisibility of whiteness, even in a space that espoused diversity and inclusion. As their Black peer and colleague, I was left with the agonizing feeling that if her Black students' pain and suffering from white violence on their bodies does not matter, mine, the only Black person in their group, does not matter. I not only felt that I did not belong to the group, I also departed from the group with the overwhelming sense that, as the only Black faculty member in my department, one of only two at the college, and one of a small few at the university, I did not belong in this white space—the university itself.

This state of white belonging, though subtle, is entrenched in academia, particularly when it involves speaking about race and racism. Recently, a white colleague expressed, "It's uncomfortable for our students when we talk about race. . . . Why don't we just focus on inclusivity?" as we struggled to discuss ways to address antiracism awareness—the new trend of diversity and inclusion—on our college campus. There goes that word again: "our." As a Black person listening to this faculty's statement, what I heard was "our" white students do not feel comfortable with the topic of race, and it is paramount that we, as the faculty, be considerate of only our white students' comfort. It seemed to me that the white faculty did not even consider the possibility that our Black students and Students of Color are not just presently uncomfortable but also feel that their lives are literally threatened and in danger as the nation witnesses the killings of Black men and women by white men within months, sometimes within weeks, of each other. If universities and colleges are focused on inclusivity, it begs the question: if we do not want to discuss the presence of whiteness and white violence and its brutal effects on Black bodies and lives, what actually are we including? In essence, inclusivity indirectly means, do not talk about race, specifically white and whiteness because the effects of whiteness—racism—is the problem of Black people and not "ours"—whites. The implicit message then is: as long as white people are ignorant to the effects of the toxic poison of whiteness, comfortable with the polluted air of whiteness, and blind to the daily assaults of whiteness on BIPOC bodies, minds, and souls, this is acceptable and tolerable. The extreme focus on the comfort of our white students is stunting their capacity and capability as racial beings to examine and interrogate their whiteness and its violent effects on Black and Brown bodies and lives. The veiled proclamation of diversity and inclusion, usually a tokenization of one or two BIPOC, does not interrupt white belonging; in fact, it reifies white belonging and white silence while it moves us away from examining whiteness and its deadly effects. Unfortunately, not talking about whiteness keeps the next generation of white people in a place of not understanding the ways in which their whiteness perpetuates and maintains white dominance, even when there is the appearance of racial diversity and inclusion in white spaces.

## Confronting the Violence of Whiteness: Generational Trauma and Sacrifices

Refusal to see and name whiteness in white spaces, where diversity and inclusion, "social justice" and "antiracism" practices are performed, makes it difficult to dismantle racism and its generational effects. Relationally, it makes sense to me that if there are generations of whites who have been implicitly socialized not to see or have the words to name their whiteness, then there are also generations of People of Color who are impacted by the deadly effects of not naming whiteness. Sadly, I can relate to this generational trauma of whiteness in academia. After four years of impressive evaluations on my teaching, publications and services as an assistant professor, a white violence encounter with a white senior administrator turned my impressive evaluations and hard work into "lackluster" and "lazy."

At the height of the family separation trauma involving migrants from Central and South America under the Trump administration's racist and immoral policy, a few minutes into my two hours supervision class, the white administrator repeatedly peeped her head through the glass wall of my classroom to determine who was present in the room. A few minutes before the class ended, she asked her administrative assistant, a Woman of Color, to remove my students (one Black, one Latina and three whites) and me from the room. We were rushed out of the classroom in the middle of a student's clinical case consultation so that she and other white colleagues could have a meeting. That day, I had to finish supervision in the lounge as all the students expressed to me their sadness and frustration with the administrator for disrupting our class and eventually kicking us out of the room. My Black and Latina students in particular felt "disrespected" and expressed "We paid our tuition. Why did she have to treat us like we didn't belong here?" My Black student expressed the pain of witnessing me, as her Black professor, "dismissed and disrespected." I felt embarrassed, humiliated, and enraged. I decided to speak with the administrator. After I ended class, I walked into her office and expressed to her that her interaction with my students and me earlier was harmful, particularly coming from someone like herself who is white and in a position of power. I mentioned to her that I wonder about the type of message her actions conveyed to all of our students—BIPOC and whites. I expressed to her as a Black woman to a white woman, that her action towards me was humiliating and abusive. I requested of her that next time I would prefer that she come into the class and inquire about the time we were done rather than instructing her administrative assistant, another Woman of Color, to kick me out of my classroom in front of my students and colleagues. She then replied, with a tone of condescension, "I'm sorry, Christiana. I thought you were a student!" As if this was supposed to make everything better. Even in her inauthentic apology, she doubled down on her white violence towards me. I acknowledged her attempted apology and wondered even if I was a student, is this the way to treat a Black student? This administrator's engagement in and response to the white violence she perpetuated—racial assault, insult, invalidation and devaluation—was familiar to me. These types of interactions are common and they reinforce the invisibility of and silence about whiteness.

Knowing whiteness well, particularly when it is packaged as "inclusive, progressive, and liberal," I knew that my decision to use my voice that day was going to cost me. Often when whiteness is named and/or challenged, it is reasonable to expect retaliation, punishment, passive withdrawal, dismissal, intimidation, hostility, and defensiveness, both obvious and subtle. All of these I experienced in my professional interactions with the White administrator after the classroom incident. For example, although all my previous annual evaluations had been excellent, with 4-0 or 5-0 in support of my academic work, including teaching, publications, and service, in my next evaluation, she referred to my work as "lackluster," an accusation that she repeated in a larger meeting that included other faculty. She did not back up this charge with any specific critiques of my work. In addition, previously, she had agreed that the school would support my obtaining the AAMFT Approved Supervisor credential that I needed to be able to supervise students and teach clinical courses in the MFT program, which meant that the school would pay for me to take the required supervision, the supervision refresher course, and would grant me course releases (releasing me from certain teaching duties). Although I had regularly updated her on my progress, she knew that the process took 18 months, and I needed just one more semester of course release to complete the process of obtaining the credential, within weeks after the incident in the classroom, I was informed by the cochairs of the department, and not her, that she would no longer grant me the remaining course release.

Even more upsetting was her subsequent attack on the MFT program itself. A few months after the classroom incident, the administrator called me and the MFT faculty to a meeting. We had no idea what it was going to be about. For two hours, this same administrator and two of her colleagues attacked us about the state of the program. First they complained that enrollment was too low because the program didn't have as many students as a similar program at Drexel and other universities. Then they made the totally different argument that the program was in "academic distress," meaning that our students were not doing well, were not graduating, and were not getting licensed. They did not explain where they got the data on which they were basing these accusations. Since they had not given us any clue about the meeting agenda, we had not had any chance to prepare any response. It was a total ambush. It was especially unfair because we knew that at least two other programs in the department really did have low enrollment and they did not seem concerned about those programs. I did ask her why she had reduced the advertising budget for the program, which we could tell from looking at Google Ads and other metrics, since cutting the advertising certainly would tend to reduce enrollment. She insisted that she had not. But the most distressing part was when, in this already-hostile environment, another White administrator looked at me and said, in so many words, "I am not going to award tenure to any faculty member whose program is in "distress." Since I was the only non-tenured faculty member, and I was going to be applying for tenure and promotion in eight months, this comment clearly was a threat to me. At the end of the meeting, she told us that we needed to come back to them in a month with a plan to move forward and improve the various problems that they had identified.

I was aware that the marketing and recruitment are largely handled by the administration and university marketing department, not by professors. However, to appease their unfair white mandate, the program director and myself developed a presentation of some ideas to market the program and recruit more students. When we offered it to her and the other administrators at the second meeting, however, they did not even look at it. Another white male administrator from the finance department started right in on what he claimed were numbers showing low enrollment, again, compared to similar programs at Drexel and other schools. I had studied at Drexel, I was familiar with that program, and I knew that the numbers he was citing were not accurate. But when I said that and asked him directly where they were getting those numbers, they just doubled down. By this time, they were literally questioning the program's "viability." So we had gone from low enrollment, to academic distress, to viability—a huge jump and sadly, a familiar experience with whiteness for me as a Black woman, in which the "goal post" is always moving in efforts to consolidate power as white people and marginalize the efforts of BIPOC.

There was one last meeting that also went nowhere. At this meeting, I could no longer ignore the direct threat to my position. I said, I'm applying for tenure in eight months, this situation is putting me in limbo, and what do you want from me? I also pointed out that less than six months before these meetings, a white faculty member in the program had been promoted, apparently without any concern for the program's supposed "distress," and despite the fact that she had not even gotten her MFT license and an AAMFT Approved Supervisor credential, despite several years of promising that she would, and so was not even eligible to teach the clinical courses in the MFT program. The administrator did not answer, probably because she was so shocked that I brought up that fact. Finally, I said, we've presented a plan. You haven't looked at it. Let us know what you want us to do. But I got no answer. It seemed clear that they were not really interested in us actually solving the problems they were claiming to have.

After four years of me getting only positive feedback, this administrator's sudden criticism of my scholarship and performance, the abrupt withdrawal of the promise to support my AAMFT credential, the ambush at the initial meeting and the surprise attack on the MFT program, the direct threat to my tenure application (when a White faculty member who was not even licensed to teach in that same program had just been promoted), trying to put the burden on my program director and me to increase enrollment, the refusal to even look at the plan that we prepared, and the refusal to explain the numbers that they were using to claim that our program was in "distress," I experienced all of these as retaliation and punishment for making explicit her racial assault and disrespect of myself and my students. I felt dismissed, abused, unsafe and powerless. To me, it was unconscionable that my tenure prospects were being placed in jeopardy for these pretextual reasons. By that third meeting, I had already decided that instead of seeking tenure, I would resign, because I could not remain in such a toxic environment that was beginning to have a negative impact on my mental and physical health.

Despite having to go through this traumatic backlash, find another school, and add two more years to my tenure process, I don't regret calling out her whiteness and abuse of power that day. The daunting question of what I will do if I can't breathe in white academia because of the relentless violence of whiteness had finally arrived. I didn't want to be choked out by white violence nor allow its poison to destroy my dreams, so I decided to use my voice. For the sake of my humanity and dignity, confronting whiteness that day was bigger than my survival in the system. I'd rather define my worth than try to defend it to prove that I deserve to be a Black professor in white academia (Hardy, 2020). I thought about my parents' sacrifices. I thought about my father's years long experiences of racial assault and devaluation of his work and talent in white academia. I thought about the hard work that my mentors poured into me to use my voice in the face of whiteness and not sell my soul for tenure. I thought about the explicit and implicit message I would have conveyed to all my students if I remained silent in the face of whiteness and white violence. Yes, tenure is important. And at that moment, it was not important enough for me to let white violence remain unnamed and continue its cementation of generations of racial relational entrapment of white-dominance and Black-subjugation.

## Naming and Interrogating Whiteness: A Transformative Generational Shift Toward Racial Justice

Whiteness and its generational traumatic effects on the lives of Black and Brown people are not going to evaporate by a one-day or eight-week workshop on antiracism or diversity and inclusion training. White people, including boards of trustees, presidents, provosts, adjunct professors, nontenured professors, tenured professors, full professors, administrators, staff, and students, must be willing to recognize whiteness, name it, and interrupt the perpetuation of it in academia. If white people are truly invested in racial justice, now and for generations after, they have to be willing to face the ugliness and violence of whiteness, now and for generations ahead. White people must be willing to work assiduously to recognize, identify, and grapple with the contradictions and implicit messages of white dominance, "white objectivity," white universality, white norm, white belonging, white comfort, "white goodness," etc. that are entrenched in whiteness and white supremacy culture. White people must be willing to relinquish their tenacious, and often subtle, defense and protection of whiteness. White people must be willing to sit with and wrestle with the mental agony, shame, guilt, silence, isolation, resentment, and all other difficult emotions that accompany confronting and interrupting the brutality of their whiteness.

White people must be sincere and honest with themselves about interrogating whiteness in all spaces that they occupy, even when they are the only white person in that space. It is especially important for white people to look at their whiteness when everyone in the space is white. It is imperative that the active and earnest interrogation of whiteness start with each individual white person and then be extended to family and friendship circles; to neighborhoods; to schools; to places of play, work, worship, dining, organizations, and institutions; to the country and to the world. Interrogation of whiteness requires individual, interpersonal, institutional, and societal collaborative work. This work is not going to be completed in a few months, in a year, in a decade, or even in a generation. This is lifelong mind, spirit, and soul work that white people must be committed to for generations. Commitment to the work of identifying whiteness, grappling with it, naming it, and interrupting it is not just for the sake of Black and Brown lives, it is for our collective humanity. It is for the liberation from the bondage of inhaling, internalizing, and circulating the toxic poisons of white lies, white contradictions, and white violence. Doing this critical and difficult work is a powerful contribution to achieving racial justice in our society and in academia. For those who are invested in educating the next generation, here are a few soul-searching reflective questions that will help in the lifelong journey of developing the skills to truly interrogate whiteness in the service of a true racially equitable and just society and world:

1. What are the implicit messages that you received from your family, teachers, religious leaders, friends, etc. about your whiteness? In what ways are any of these implicit messages embedded with white lies and white contradictions?

2. In what ways have you internalized these implicit messages about whiteness? How have these internalized implicit messages about your whiteness informed how you show up in your relationships with other white people in your life? How do these messages inform how you view and interact with Black people, Indigenous people, and People of Color?

3. In what ways do you subtly engage with BIPOC colleagues, students, administrators, and staff from a position of white dominance, both in your thoughts and actions?

4. How do you participate in white objectivity and white universality and perpetuate white belonging in your curricula, pedagogical style, classroom, program, and/or and institution?

## Voices of BIPOC: A Necessity to Breathe in White Academia

The daily assaults of white violence in the white world of academia are not only exhaustive, they are also detrimental to the mental, emotional, spiritual, physical, professional, and financial well-being of BIPOC. The violence of whiteness triggers us to think, "we're not good enough or smart enough." It drains our energy, it consumes our time, it undermines our brilliance, and it chokes out our passion for the careers we've worked hard for. Many of us engage in silence to protect our energies and minds from the toxicity of whiteness, but it is difficult to escape the relentless racist assaults. Many of us over-function so that our white colleagues and students will approve of us and see us as more than "just a diversity hire." Yet, this, too, is futile, because no matter how much work we do, white people will often elevate a mediocre white faculty over an average BIPOC faculty, even more so for a Black faculty. Sadly, some of us wholeheartedly take on the role of the gatekeeper of white violence to avoid succumbing to the trauma of whiteness. This, like the other strategies, is meaningless because no matter how much we try to fit in with white people and exclude other BIPOC, white people will still treat us as not good enough and as if we don't belong in their circle.

As we, Black people, Indigenous people, and People of Color, strive to stay alive in academia and not be forced out by white obliviousness and the intentional and unintentional assaults on our souls, we must be willing to consider taking off the mask and the shield that we wear to defend and protect ourselves from the toxicity of whiteness. The violence of whiteness remains invisible when we do not name whiteness and its traumatic effects on us. The toxin of whiteness gains its strengths when we do not allow our voices to speak of the ravages and destructions of whiteness not only on our careers but on our souls as well. When we remain silent, over-function, and collude with whiteness, we inevitably allow white mental agony, white comfort, and white violence to frame our experiences, narratives, and well-being. Yes, using our voices in the world of whiteness in academia will come with struggles. And yet, a critical question still stands: What will we do when white violence seeks to stifle our voices, to smother the very life that gives breath to our hopes and dreams, and to put us in the forever, generational bondage of white-dominance and Black-subjugation? How will we use our voices to give breath to the recognition, financial stability, tenure, and promotion that we work hard for without losing our health, well-being, and souls to whiteness and white violence? Here are some soul-searching questions we can reflect on as we aim to breathe and reclaim our voices in white academia:

1. If you gave your voice the freedom to unleash itself, what would it utter about your experiences in white academia and with white violence?

2. As a Black faculty, Indigenous faculty, or Faculty of Color, what do you hope will define your presence, the use of your voice, and your work in white academia? How do these hopes represent the hard work, joy, and sacrifices your parents, families, and ancestors have experienced to get you where you are today in white academia? How could these hopes become a reality? What would this reality model to your BIPOC students and white students about the significance of using their voices to name whiteness and combat white violence?

3. In what ways have you, as a Black faculty, Indigenous faculty person, or Faculty of Color, denigrated, ignored, and isolated other BIPOC and their work in order to elevate yourself, to be "included," and to be a gatekeeper in white spaces, specifically white academia?

4. What steps do you need to take to allow yourself to fully breathe in white spaces?

**CHRISTIANA IBILOLA AWOSAN, PHD, LMFT,** is an assistant professor at Iona College in New Rochelle, New York, in the Marriage and Family Therapy program and an associate faculty with the Eikenberg Academy for Social Justice. She's also the founder of Ibisanmi Relational Health. Dr. Awosan conducts national and international trainings and seminars on issues related to understanding sociocultural trauma, such as racial trauma on the mental, emotional, and relational lives of People of Color. Her research focuses on diversity, inclusion, and social justice. She has published several book chapters and articles in peer-reviewed journals, including "Therapy with Heterosexual Black Couples through a Racial Lens" (2019, Guilford Press). She and her coauthors are also the recipients of the AAMFT 2020 Outstanding Research Publication Award for "Emotionally Focused Therapy: A culturally sensitive approach for African American heterosexual couples" (2019, *Journal of Family Psychotherapy*).

## References

*Hardy, K. V. (2016). Toward the development of a multicultural relational perspective in training and supervision. In K. V. Hardy & T. Bobes (Eds.),* Culturally sensitive supervision and training: Diverse perspective and practical applications *(pp. 3–15). Routledge.*

*Hardy, K. V. (2020, October 17–November 21).* Uncovering racial trauma: Racially sensitive therapy for clients of color *[8-week online training]. Greater Malden Behavioral Health / BMHA INC. / Eikenberg Academy for Social Justice, New York, NY, United States.*

*Hardy, K. V., & Laszloffy, T. A. (2002). Couple therapy using a multicultural perspective. In A. S. Gurman & N. S. Jacobson (Eds.),* Clinical handbook of couple therapy *(pp. 569–593). Guilford Press.*

*Obama, B. (2020).* A promised land. *Crown.*

## CHAPTER 17

# White Spaces, Empty Places

## Reflections on the Processes of White Supremacy

ROBIN NUZUM, MDIV, AM, MA

IN LOVING MEMORY OF DR. PATRICIA HILLIARD-NUNN

In his now iconic *Letter from a Birmingham Jail* of 1963, the Rev. Dr. Martin Luther King Jr. stated that he had almost come to the regrettable conclusion that the white moderate, not the KKKer, was the greatest impediment to Blacks achieving freedom (King, 1963). This past summer, well over sixty years later, a former Minneapolis mayor wrote in a *New York Times* opinion piece that as mayor she "saw how white liberals block change" (Hodges, 2020, p. 1). While there are a myriad of reasons and mechanisms through which well-meaning whites become impediments to real racial justice and equality, in this chapter I wish to explore the particular recalcitrance of predominately white spaces to becoming anything but white supremacist (often despite their stated goals or values that purport otherwise). I am especially interested in "voluntary" and civic spaces, such as spiritual organizations, academic conferences, reading groups, parenting groups (e.g., the PTA), and even, and especially, social justice groups designed for racial justice activism and advocacy. Often these predominately white spaces already have some moral imperative for inclusion and some ethic of justice, so why do they mostly fail to truly undo white supremacy within their own organizational bodies? I am purposely narrowing my focus to exclude large institutions of work, education, etc. that have broader bureaucratic structures and cultures.

I am one white, cisgender woman with a long history of engagement with antiracist work and ideas. My formation in racial and social justice work occurred in a quite singular and unique setting. The dominant theologies at the Christian seminary I attended as a young adult were liberation theology and the social gospel. These theologies present radical critiques of much contemporary Christian thought. The notion, for example, of God's preference for the poor and oppressed continues to illuminate the Gospel much more fully for some while provoking its repression by the powers that resist the radical reordering it requires. Liberation theology also places a heavy emphasis on action, not just thinking. (The famed action/reflection model.) In fact, this theology's methodology requires that thinking be based on specific types of active engagement. In some real sense, that is what I am doing here.

Though the seminary was a learning community and no single theology was required by us students, the space itself was a living crucible. Our theological education was a difficult and painful process for us students. Many students had their identities deconstructed but could not find an entry point to constructing a new identity. The calling out that occurs when bolstered by the great Judeo-Christian prophetic tradition and the calling in that comes from the authority of faith and belief are profound in their intensity. One's complicity in racism and other social structures of sin is harder to ignore and dodge when its undergirded by the ethics of a community, not just one's individual sense of what is just. I got in touch with profound white guilt, grief, and shame *in my body* during this Seminary tenure. I also gleaned, discerned, and learned—especially from my amazing professors (public intellectual and scholar Rev. Dr. Michael Eric Dyson and historian Rev. Dr. David Daniels)—the deep affinity and commonality that exist between the heavily stigmatized white people of the Appalachian region, the region of my birth and upbringing, and People of Color, despite the many obvious differences in our experiences. My fellow student and colleague, now the Rev. Michelle Hughes, remains my lifelong friend as well as a brilliant dialogue and accountability partner. (Michelle, who is now a leader on justice initiatives within the UCC serving as a conference minister, was then part of a very large cadre of seminarians at Chicago Theological Seminary whose home church was the acclaimed Afrocentric church on Chicago's south side, Trinity United

Church of Christ.) On a bookshelf in the room where I write this chapter is the button she gave me so many years ago that proclaims, "RACISM HURTS EVERYBODY."

My approach is heuristic, meaning I hope my reflections will spark reflections in the readers, especially with regard to their own locations and experiences within predominately white civic spaces. My primary object of inquiry is the white people who inhabit groups and organizations such as social justice groups, reading groups, academic conferences, and other varieties of voluntary and civic groups. I do not presume my analysis here applies to the People of Color who are also members of these social bodies. The questions of the group operations of white supremacy I am raising are complex in both etiology and manifestation across the many possible varieties of civic groups and organizations. Therefore, each particular organization requires additional work of specificity that can only be done by those with intimate knowledge of its dynamics. Still, I hope these thoughts can help facilitate that critical work.

For as long as Black people have been writing about or commenting upon racism in America, they have noted the white denial of the realities they have witnessed, endured, and described. In fact, a recent article by antiracism scholar Ibram X. Kendi (2018) is entitled "The Heartbeat of Racism is Denial." This erasure of acknowledgment is constitutive of the construction of white racial dominance over other races. It is *certainly* at work in any predominately white organization, from the past through to the present. Yet this denial requires a more rigorous look.

The "color-blind" type of denial ("I don't see color"), and "racism no longer exists" type of denial have been well theorized by many critical race theorists and are no doubt operative in these settings, but they do not fully account for or explicate the dynamics of the oppressive lingering of the ideology of white supremacy in these settings. These frameworks of denial are inadequate because many folks (or most folks, depending on the organization) already have some conscious acknowledgment of both race and racism. Yet they most sorely lack what Eddo-Lodge (2018) has called the "historical knowledge and political backdrop you need to anchor your opposition to racism" (p. xvii).

The embeddedness of white supremacy ideology within the master narratives of American life is a matter of crucial scholarly interest and engagement. Meanwhile these narratives remain rather protectively ensconced in the actual lives of white Americans who have not explored or done the difficult work of unearthing and interrogating the racial and racist dimensions of their governing ideas. Grand narratives of the Enlightenment, liberal democracy, humanism, and Christianity are fraught with racist underpinnings and assumptions that make them inadequate, in and of themselves, for deconstructing white supremacy in American life. In other words, the problem is endemic and far deeper than most white Americans believe, and the worldviews and discourses that inform white Americans' fundamental thought processes and behaviors are woefully inadequate for addressing the dislodging of white supremacy. (I am not in any way suggesting that these discourses are doomed and illegitimate, just that they have to be reprocessed and reimagined if they are to be employed in the service of dismantling racism and not perpetuating it. Others have held the opposite view that some of these discourses cannot be rehabilitated and their links to racial dominance are too intrinsic to be salvageable for a racially just social project. I respect and understand these positions and empathize deeply with the legitimate misgivings or even refusals, but I tend to disagree . . . mostly.) To be clear, I am suggesting that without an interrogation of the category of race from within the structures of these master narratives, white participants in civic spaces cannot gain real traction in being effectively antiracist. The explication of how this critical engagement unfolds is beyond my scope but is the subject of much important and available scholarly work. I can gesture toward a couple of examples to illustrate my position.

Charles Mills (as cited in Bouie, 2018) is a contemporary philosopher who has named the implicit "racial contract" (para. 5) undergirding the Enlightenment project:

> The Racial Contract establishes a racial polity, a racial state, and a racial juridical system, where the status of whites and nonwhites is clearly demarcated, whether by law or custom. And the purpose of this state . . . is specifically to maintain and reproduce this racial order, securing the privileges and advantages of the full white citizens and maintaining the subordination of nonwhites. (Charles Mills as cited in Bouie, 2018, para. 15)

The march of Enlightenment "progress" of European civilization was an imperialist one, which required the brutal subjugation of nonwhite subjects and the theft of their property. This reality undergirds how the modern category of "white" became the exemplar and carrier of both definitions of exclusionary property rights and social terror for nonwhites. Progress, then, for whom? This historical legacy of differences in notions of progress between white and nonwhite subjects warrants more careful scrutiny when thinking of the social goals of contemporary civic groups, etc.

I'll also briefly use the example of Christianity for illustration. I am purposively choosing examples of grand narratives that have at least some relationship to civic participation and betterment and intentionally leaving aside even more deleterious narratives, such as capitalism or capitalist expansion. I do so because I presume that when white folks join a civic, church, academic, or social justice grouping, they are relying on narratives that would indeed lead and engage them toward social change. The problem is, these narratives often receive even less scrutiny of their racist assumptions and are presumed to be adequate to inform antiracist work, justice work, or democratic inclusion. Tragically, they are *not adequate* unless and until *the category of race and racism* is the critical lens through which they are engaged and ultimately transformed.

Take for example the work of Black liberation theologian James Cone (2011). Following the lead of other liberation theology projects from Latin America and elsewhere, Dr. Cone began to apply this new methodology and to critique to the problem of race and racism in contemporary twentieth century theology and in America's ongoing refusal to confront its sordid and horrific racial reality. He noted the absolute dearth of attention from such prominent American theologians as Reinhold Neihbur to the ongoing historical problem that surrounded and informed his life as a Black man in the United States. While problems of justice and the redemption of society through the gospel project of the Kingdom of God were foregrounded in serious attention by these scholars/theologians, the place and signifiers of the social death of Black Americans to further that version of the Kingdom were woefully ignored. Cone (2011) asked the question (through decades of constructive theology work), "How could any theologian explain the meaning of Christian identity in America and fail to engage white supremacy, its primary negation?" (p. xvii). And yet time and time again, Christian white folks have relied on their conception of love (something like agape or inclusive love) to do work that such a concept cannot do or, in the case of the systemic evil of white supremacy, cannot undo. A far better term would be one I first learned at seminary: *justice love*. These refined and transfigured namings have profound effects both on how problems and goals are constructed as well as on their outcomes. They also help to finally begin to situate white people outside of their "manipulative suffocating blanket of power" (Eddo-Lodge, 2018, p. 92) that is white privilege. It is profoundly beyond time for this because, as W. E. B. Du Bois (as cited in Rabaka, 2006) noted over one hundred years ago, "Everything considered, the title to the universe claimed by white Folk is faulty" (p. 2).

Another powerful alchemical naming that is necessary is the problem of white *resistance*. This is a phenomenon as old, deep, and pernicious as white supremacy itself. Not all white people are resistant to merely naming racism and white supremacy, because as I noted initially, many white people ostensibly come to these organizations already doing so. Instead, the resistance I am referring to is the obstinate and enduring recalcitrance to engaging in processes or reflections (or challenging confrontations) that might actually disrupt and transform racism's hold on the group dynamic. As pedagogical scholar of justice, Zeus Leonardo (as cited in DiAngelo, 2018) notes, "for white racial hegemony to saturate everyday life, it has to be secured by a process of white domination, or those acts, decisions, and policies that white subjects perpetrate on people of color" (p. 64). I would add that these acts, decisions, and policies are also visited upon fellow whites who might also attempt to further an antiracist agenda for the group. DiAngelo (2018) states that "white fragility punishes the person giving feedback and presses them back into silence" (p. 125) while noting that the punishments are much more severe for People of Color. She notes that white people often define *respect* as no conflict and no real challenging of white supremacist patterns (DiAngelo, 2018, p. 127).

Indeed, Robin DiAngelo's (2018) recent best seller *White Fragility: Why It's so Hard for White People to Talk About Racism* is an extensive resource for elucidating the dynamics of white resistance to talking about racism. Importantly, she names that the resistance of liberal and progressive whites to engage antiracist content while feeling "beyond it" is an expression of white fragility, meaning "the result of the reduced psychosocial stamina that racial insulation inculcates" (DiAngelo, 2018, p. 101). I should also note that who is holding the *institutional authority* in the group (who is the leader; who funds the group; who has been there the longest; and other vectors of privilege, such as gender and class) greatly determines not only who can speak but, more importantly, who will actually be listened to and heeded during any confrontations made on race. Discursive strategies of ignoring and distancing from these challenges enacts what Peggy McIntosh (as cited in Applebaum, 2016) has referred to as the privileged person's "permission to escape" (para. 69) and, I would add, to stay white supremacist. Hytten and Warren (as cited in Applebaum, 2016) have clarified and named some of the tactics white people employ: "remaining silent, evading questions, resorting to the rhetoric of ignoring color, focusing on progress, victim blaming, and focusing on culture rather than race" (para. 69). Meanwhile, the enduring white privilege and power of the group can be traumatic and/or microaggressive to People of Color even as it appears as a "dull, grinding complacency" (Eddo-Lodge, 2018, p. 87).

Just as American and European grand narratives possess far deeper issues for critical race projects than might first meet the eye, white resistance to owning and dismantling its racism is, itself, grounded in and often hidden in a foundational way in a problematic and paradoxical *epistemology*. Epistemology, one will recall, is *how* we know what we know. After much scholarship theorizing how whiteness constructs its own invisibility, others have more fruitfully, I think, referred to it as a construction that is mostly unnamed or unspoken (Nottingham Contemporary, 2015). While some white ignorance is clearly designed to protect one's white "moral self-image" (Applebaum, 2016, para. 62), we must go further into what Jose Medina (as cited in Applebaum, 2016) has called an epistemology of "meta-ignorance" (para. 63). This is an

> active ignorance that operates at a meta-level and involves an ignorance of one's ignorance. To understand the ignorance of the privileged, Medina claims, we need to study not only the role of not knowing and not needing to know but, more significantly, *needing not to know*. (Applebaum, 2016, para. 63)

As Applebaum (2016) makes clear in her explication of how Medina frames needing not to know,

> The latter, according to Medina, is of particular significance because it not only fuels an active yet often unconscious epistemic obliviousness that persists "no matter what the evidence may be," but it also functions to protect privilege through systemically supported mechanisms of defense. (para. 63)

Understanding meta-ignorance helps us comprehend the deep white resistance to new knowledge about race. It also helps a white person learn to be humble in the face of assessing their own knowledge of racism's reach and grasp. Humility renders one open to feedback in never-before imagined ways. But the gateway is *through* one's meta-ignorance as a white person. These changes, over time, can transform a white person's stance from *needing not to know* to *needing to know*, precisely and thoroughly, how they can help dismantle white supremacy.

Yet the solution is not simply to educate whites to "give up" or denounce their white privilege. Racism is a structural, institutional, and political problem, not merely a personal one. And as scholars of white privilege pedagogy have noted, this pedagogical (or project's) aim too often begins *and ends* with the demand for confession of white privilege. "In other words, the confession becomes the entire antiracist project itself" (Applebaum, 2016, para. 41). French Philosopher Michel Foucault (1976/1990) has brought forth the overdetermined nature of the confessional in his work, and much of the postmodern landscape fantasizes that speech acts alone are enough for transformation and redemption. When there is not outright denial, evasion, or resistance concerning white people's complicity in racism, it can seem like the only thing left is performances of confession or virtue signaling. This is the environment and set of conditions that brought us slacktivism (activism reduced to "liking" and reposting online) and dangerous vacuums of real antiracist white political formation. It also makes many smaller predominately white civic groups (and some social justice groups) anemic at best at dealing with race substantively. Many of the conversations that do occur about race are largely dominated by whites trying to prove some legitimacy to People of Color while trying to "best" other whites with their understanding and know-how. Meanwhile, something like direct action remains an unrealized and faraway horizon, and People of Color are hardly ever impressed.

Black folks and People of Color are profoundly astute observers of white people. Why, then, would white people imagine that saying a few sentences in a particular way would quickly dislodge all that hard-won discernment and subsequent distrust that People of Color have of us? Such imagining, itself, betrays the ignorance and arrogance of most white people. Perhaps the masterwork of looking at relations between races is a 1992 essay by bell hooks (1998) entitled *Representations of Whiteness in the Black Imagination.* In it, she exposes this pernicious and grandiose fantasy thus: "They think they are seen by black folks only as they want to appear" (hooks, 1998, p. 42). The attempt to maintain this fantasy of control, even against "looking," seeing, and perceiving themselves, is the reason well-meaning whites (consciously or unconsciously) block increased participation by many, or by too many, Black people or People of Color. I think, to put it simply, white folks just do not want and cannot stand that much scrutiny. This is the outcropping and logical conclusion to what DiAngelo (2018) has coined *white fragility.* (This also applies, of course, when just one African American or Person of Color is too vocal and outspoken about race. That scrutiny and feedback is usually most unwelcome.) If an organization is overwhelmingly white (in a setting where People of Color are available and exist, which includes pretty much everywhere except some select areas of the country), or the few People of Color there are quiet and subdued, it is a pretty safe assumption that that organization has what I might call structural white fragility. By this I mean the culture of the group and its norms have not been able to sustain the full participation, or even presence, of many People of Color *because* it cannot yet welcome this diversity given its current level of capacity around race and racism. When in a stage of growth, such a group may attempt to invite and include more People of Color. This can go badly and traumatically for the People of Color who come in first unless and until the structural white fragility of the group is addressed. I will turn now to how I think these organizations might go about rectifying this critical deficit.

Certainly, there are a few structural moves that can work, like adding enough People of Color to dilute the group dynamic, pairing them with knowledgeable and seasoned white comrades, and/or ousting racist leadership. Part of my interest in focusing on smaller voluntary types of organizations is because they are indeed more malleable than large institutions or companies with more formal bureaucratic structures. While I've seen such structural maneuvers work a few times—and it is very gratifying and powerful when they do—more often, they are fraught, unreliable, and ineffective. These types of maneuvers, like ousting leadership, also run a risk of disrupting or destroying the good work that a group is performing even as it remains white supremacist. (People who disagree can quit to follow their preferred leader, for example.) For these reasons, I commit to elucidating ideas for addressing and dismantling the pervasive and structural group white fragility that undergirds the operation and commitment, however paradoxical or unnamed, to white supremacy.

I began this chapter talking about how many of the grand narratives of American life are, in often unseen ways, rooted in white supremacy and racism. So, my first suggestion is one that is probably already the most engaged in by groups that are taking the first steps to address their racism: Read, study, and reflect! Many of the books now available are accessible to lay audiences, and, as I remind my students, you can read more difficult and scholarly arguments and books with time. (Somehow, my students have always been clear that you can grow to lift more weight or to run farther but not that you can grow to read more difficult scholarly texts with effort, time, and experience.) As psychotherapists and clinicians know, the narratives in our brains are deeply constitutive of who we are and how we will be and become. This includes larger social narratives, which the mental health profession has finally begun to acknowledge with the help of the world-wide narrative therapy movement and other important US contributors, such as this volume's editor, Dr. Kenneth V. Hardy. In my city, many groups have regular readings of antiracist texts (films, too, are texts), including a mayor-sponsored one for the entire city, the very afternoon that I am writing, on the book *White Fragility* (DiAngelo, 2018).

An additional, less explored, and very powerful step is for a group to do a bit more formal self-study of its practices and norms around race and racism. I know the United Church of Christ developed such a study template that they have made available to their myriad local churches in the denomination. This template is also available to the public for adaptation (https://www.nhcucc.org/uploads/documents/conference-ministries/justice-witness-ministry/Racial%20Justice/Process%20for%20Becoming%20a%20 Racial%20Justice%20Church.pdf). Other of the many resources from the United Church of Christ website are helpful in this endeavor. Many racial justice organizations have relevant materials, and other groups have provided public accounts of their engagement in such processes. An obvious advantage to this approach is that it is proactive and is less attached to actual persons or specific processes of conflict. Also, those more personal issues can be discussed at a more fruitful time and through the particular lens of the group's goal for greater racial equity, wherein the issue or problem is named and diagnosed more precisely.

There is a great amount of writing on the modern notion of white identity and its important links to terror to Blacks and property theft and control for whites. I am of the view that knowing the stories and examples of how some white people have attempted to act and live out an antiracist white identity in solidarity and sacrifice is an important part of the decolonization of white people from white supremacy. I believe these stories and accounts should be read (and heard) by whites, but with the particular practice of critically noticing how most white lives are *not* reflected in these stories. A rigorous honesty demands that these stories do not get co-opted into any justification or minimization of the destructive history of *the vast majority* of white behavior toward Blacks and other Persons of Color. I'm taken with David Roediger's (1998) notion of being "initiated into whiteness" (p. 16) when millions of white people heard stories of lynchings. Regretfully, Roediger did not fully explicate what he meant by this where I encountered it. Still, it makes intuitive sense to me. A complicit bystander to heinous crimes and destructiveness is the moral definition of passive whiteness. Whites can also be initiated into antiracist whiteness when we hear real stories of great solidarity, action, and sacrifice of whites who helped preserve the very existence of their fellow Humans of Color. As important as I think ideas and narratives are, it is ultimately what we *do* that counts. When I hear the story of Carol Thomas, beloved elder and white activist in our community, and how, because of her activism and solidarity with Black residents, she had to leave the county for a time for her safety, my main takeaway is that, though I have done things—many things—to enact my antiracist values, I have NEVER done enough nor the type of thing to put myself or my family in that kind of danger. Talk is indeed cheap. Everyone has their own ethic and practice of how they evaluate their own moral actions. But "keeping it real," first and foremost to oneself but ultimately also to a community of accountability, is the necessary foundation of any such practice. There are big problems in activist communities of wildly flung and often public criticism levied at one another that is in fact movement-destroying (and beyond the scope of this work). Loretta Ross and others are leading critically important conversations about the judicious execution of critique; how to "call in the calling out culture." (I also believe folks should be extra cautious, if not sparing, with their criticism of people who are putting themselves on the line in ways that they are not. This is my personal ethic that I would like to promote.)

Still, where would we be without examples of people who more fully embody the values to which we aspire? So, we white folks must read the stories and, more importantly, put ourselves into circles where we might actually meet and work with white people who are universes apart from us in enacting a different, less oppressive, and more truly helpful version of typical whiteness. (Fortunately, these are parallel universes, so we can easily find one another.) During the writing of this chapter, I found W. Kamau Bell's (2019) *United Shades of America* "Not all White People" episode, which explores anti–white supremacist whites. I was delighted by its content and how Bell is representing the diversity within these antiracist white groups and people. I hope many white people, young and old, will see the show. It is yet another established ignorance that we white people do not need to be *aware* that such people and groups exist. It is likewise not in our best interest to be unacquainted with the many historic collaborations between white people and People of Color in many justice contexts. (It clearly and potently serves the perpetuation of white supremacy to suppress knowledge of such alliances.) The existence of racial conflicts and problematic dynamics in these interracial collaborations does not dim our need to know about the people who did try to work in cross-racial solidarity, including whatever lessons they might have to teach that could help us to avoid similar problems in the future.

A brief word about holding and processing guilt and shame as a white person: Since I came to this work before much had been formally written about guilt and shame, I worked it out either within myself or by using other psychological and moral tools (especially and profoundly helpful is practicing meditation). I do not have intimate knowledge of the newer work coming out on this. I do know that I'm very uncomfortable with calling what white people experience when encountering the horrors of white supremacy and the role of white people in the deaths and destructions of Black and Brown people *trauma*. That said, I would highly recommend reading the dialogue about trauma and race between theologians Serene Jones and Kelly Brown Douglas, found in Jones's (2019) text *Trauma and Grace: Theology in a Ruptured World*. And while I can technically see how it may be a form of *moral injury* to contemplate one's complicity in racial atrocities and social death, I would also reserve use of the critically important and descriptive concept for the important milieus in which it is currently being employed, namely war. Why not let us just call it what it is: guilt, shame, embarrassment, and even disgust with ourselves and our ancestors? I do know for certain that almost everything we might do constructively as white people to combat racism rests on our building a capacity to hold, process, and contain these emotions within ourselves. White people, in our civic and social justice groups, can absolutely set time and meetings aside to do this crucial processing of our "white stuff." Such attention to capacity building of nonreactivity *together* can build group coherence along truly antiracist lines. Many people have found Resmaa Menakem's (2017) work on racially informed trauma helpful in this endeavor to reflect our truest ideals more authentically.

In my academic studies of Afrofuturism and utopia (Bloch, 1959; Womack, 2013), I theorize and write about ideals and social visions for the possible future. Afrofuturism and utopia are two intellectual concepts, or rather umbrella conceptual rubrics, to bring attention to what is desired and wished for. It is profoundly insufficient to focus merely on what has been experienced and what must be recovered from. (Foucault's similar insight was developed by Michael White and David Epston to create the wildly transformational form of therapy known as narrative therapy.) As the great African American scholar-activist W. E. B. Du Bois (1998) reminds us in his 1920 essay, "A true and worthy ideal frees and uplifts a people; a false ideal imprisons and lowers" (p. 187). My own interest in ideals coupled with Du Bois's wise summation drew me decidedly to the following definition of white supremacy by Christian ethicist Reggie Williams (2020): "White supremacy is the manufacture and maintenance of systems and structure for whites only. Hatred and harm are always secondary effects of this primary thing: a longing for an idealized community populated by a fetishized, white ideal" (para. 10). He also warned that "no amount of hugging will eliminate" (para. 9) white supremacy. (Sorry huggers.) Yet I thought this definition might more aptly apply to readers of *The Turner Diaries* (Pierce, 1978) than the white people I have been attempting to reflect on here. The white people of our inquiry have other ideals, such as "the beloved community" or "liberal multiethnic democracy," and yet I have also been noting how white supremacy is also, always, already *in the soup*. But just as I seek the hidden signs of this pernicious white supremacy in order to transform it, I also choose to focus my gaze on the longings of our white people for something different than white-only spaces. (It is a utopian reading practice to look for longings and wishes inside the texts one is exploring, the word "text" here having extremely broad application to all types of cultural productions and artifacts as well as to living relations.) So even as I name profound white resistance to inclusion of People of Color into predominantly white spaces, there is a counterpoint to this, a paradox, that just might lead to Dr. King's dream of a profound recognition of the shared destiny of white people and People of Color.

I am alluding to the semiregular occurrence of us white folk starting to express our longing for the presence of People of Color (after our white exclusion of Black people and of ideas that would make Black people and other People of Color come around and feel at home). I wonder if People of Color have also borne witness to this occurrence. I recognize this longing by its typical contours: It is when we say, "I wish we had more People of Color. We need more People of Color in our group." Another version is, "I wish I knew more People of Color," or "I wish my life was more integrated with People of Color." One time when I was on a bus trip to Montgomery, Alabama, to visit the critically important national memorial to lynching victims in America, I was seated with a white person who desperately wanted to be seated with my African American friend, Venetia, whom I was shouting at and texting with from across the bus. Now, my friend Venetia is crazy sharp and engaging and downright fun, so, maybe the word was out. I also recognize that the trip was promoted as an encounter with this profound American memorial and accompanying museum *together as white and Black Americans*, but the woman next to me said she wanted to be seated with my friend so many times that it was past the point of politeness! I finally said, lamely, "We just have to be in the present," to address her disappointment. I also know that, in general, white folks have a profound longing to be made whole by being reconciled with the entirety of humanity and that no matter what else has happened, that longing never really goes away. I know this from living among white people. I see it in a million manifestations. It's also visible in white ideals such as unity, brotherhood, even The United States of America, even as these ideals tragically fail to address the hideous and horrific history of white supremacy and its lasting and current death-dealing effects. This longing to fulfill our ideals even as we don't yet fully know what such ideals might mean without white supremacy is our great contradiction, but it is also our great hope and opportunity for real transformation. I believe this is true for many (if not most) privileged, too often obstinate, and in many ways dangerous, white people. When these potentials are clouded and obscured, such seeing becomes a matter of faith.

When I am in these moments of longing for fuller and more inclusive community with other white people (inclusive community that *truly reflects* humanity's rich diversity), I always wonder, "Are we willing to do the work to create what we say we want?" "Are we willing to be committed forever and always to the ideals we hold most dear, no matter the difficulties, pain, and sometimes *intense* loneliness of this path?" Because as James Baldwin (as cited in Williams, 2020) reminds us,

> White people remain trapped within a history that they do not understand, one from which they need release—but they must act, must be committed. To act in response to this history, however, is terrifying. It requires engaging a complete recalibration of identity. Short of that, there is no exit. (para. 2)

I don't know what else to say now, in conclusion, except that I can't, I won't, I refuse to choose "no exit." Instead, I hold to striving for the deep, deep, and completing joy that I am certain is on the other side, and I *fully commit* to the lifelong path to getting there.

**ROBIN NUZUM, MDIV, AM, MA,** proudly born and raised in central West Virginia, began her clinical training and study in the great city of Chicago, where she encountered the rich tradition of social work, Kohut's self-psychology and family systems theory, and the revolutionary praxis of liberation theology. In Florida, she completed a postgraduate marriage and family certificate, focusing on oppression sensitive therapy and narrative therapy ideas. She has been working in private practice as a marriage and family therapist and clinical social worker for many years in Gainesville, Florida. She has taught literature, culture, and writing at the University of Florida and is a doctoral candidate there in the English Department, specializing in Afrofuturism and Utopia. Her activism and advocacy work has focused in large part on racial and criminal justice and human trafficking.

## References

*Applebaum, B. (2016, June 9).* Critical whiteness studies. *Oxford Research Encyclopedia of Education. Retrieved July 21, 2020, from https://oxfordre.com/education/view/10.1093/acrefore/9780190264093.001.0001/acrefore-9780190264093-e-5*

*Bell, W. K. (Writer & Director). (2019, May 15). Not all white people (Season 4, Episode 2) [TV series episode]. In W. K. Bell, A. Entelis, J. Fox, L. Fox, T. Pastore, L. Smith, & J. Yungfleisch (Executive Producers),* United shades of America. *Cable News Network; Objective Productions.*

*Bloch, E. (1959).* The principle of hope: Vol. 1 *(N. Plaice, S. Plaice, & P. Knight, Trans.). MIT Press. (Original work published 1959)*

*Bouie, J. (2018, June 5).* The enlightenment's dark side: How the Enlightenment created modern race thinking, and why we should confront it. *Slate. https://slate.com/news-and-politics/2018/06/taking-the-enlightenment-seriously-requires-talking-about-race.html*

*Cone, J. H. (2011).* The cross and the lynching tree. *Orbis.*

*DiAngelo, R. (2018).* White fragility: Why it's so hard for white people to talk about racism. *Beacon Press.*

*Du Bois, W. E. B. (1998). The souls of white folks. In D. Roediger (Ed.),* Black on white: Black writers on what it means to be white *(pp. 184–199). Schocken Books.*

*Eddo-Lodge, R. (2018).* Why I'm no longer talking to white people about race. *Bloomsbury Publishing.*

*Foucault, M. (1990).* The history of sexuality, Vol. 1: An introduction *(R. Hurley, Trans.). Vintage Books. (Original work published 1976)*

*Hodges, B. (2020, July 9). As mayor of Minneapolis, I saw how white liberals block change.*

New York Times. *https://www.nytimes.com/2020/07/09/opinion/minneapolis-hodges-racism.html?fbclid=lwAR2xKMBH90QJFsbW6G79Y6JwSigGNQPWLq*

*hooks, b. (1998). Representations of whiteness in the black imagination. In D. Roediger (Ed.),* Black on white: Black writers on what it means to be white *(pp. 38–53). Schocken Books.*

*Jones, S. (2019).* Trauma and grace: Theology in a ruptured world. *Westminster John Knox Press.*

*Kendi, I. X. (2018, January 13). The heartbeat of racism is denial.* New York Times. *https://www.nytimes.com/2018/01/13/opinion/sunday/heartbeat-of-racism-denial.html*

*King, M. L., Jr. (1963).* Letter from a Birmingham Jail [King, Jr.]. *African Studies Center, University of Pennsylvania. https://www.africa.upenn.edu/Articles_Gen/Letter_Birmingham.html*

*Menakem, R. (2017).* My grandmother's hands: Racialized trauma and the pathway to mending our hearts and bodies. *Central Recovery Press.*

*Nottingham Contemporary. (2015, May 20).* Critical whiteness: US and UK perspectives *[Video]. Youtube. https://www.youtube.com/watch?v=pCBoEQc5sSU*

*Pierce, W. L. (1978).* The Turner diaries. *National Vanguard Books.*

*Rabaka, R. (2006). The souls of white folk: W.E.B. Du Bois's critique of white supremacy and contributions to critical white studies.* Ethnic Studies Review, 29*(2), 1–19. https://scholarscompass.vcu.edu/cgi/viewcontent.cgi?article=1259&context=esr*

*Roediger, D. R. (Ed.). (1998).* Black on white: Black writers on what it means to be white. *Schocken Books.*

*Williams, R. (2020, September 15).* White supremacy is a script we're given at birth. *The Christian Century. https://www.christiancentury.org/article/critical-essay/white-supremacy-script-we-re-given-birth*

*Womack, Y. (2013).* Afrofuturism: The world of black sci-fi and fantasy culture. *Lawrence Hill Books.*

CHAPTER 18

# Whiteness in Community Mental Health

## Engagement, Service Provision, and Clinical Supervision

NIKI BERKOWITZ, MA, LMFT

As William Shakespeare (1599/1992) wrote in Hamlet: "*This above all: to thine own self be true*" (1.3.84–86). I am a white woman. I was raised in an upper-middle-class Jewish family in a small city in Central Canada. My late father's family strongly believed in the importance of diversity. As a result, my parents chose to send my sister and me to a public French immersion school across town, as opposed to the local private Jewish school. This choice was a privilege. My classmates and teachers at the public school were very diverse in race, religion, and class. We were not religious; we were secular, cultural Jews, and the values of *Tikkun Olam* and *Tzedakah* permeated our family tapestry.

> Tikkun Olam is the action of repairing the world through tzedakah. Tzedakah is defined throughout the Jewish community by one of two terms: charity or social justice. While the word itself translates to "charity" (which typically tends to separate the wealthy from the poor), it can be thought of as giving, justice, or assistance. Most importantly, tzedakah is giving because you can, not because you have to. (Anonymous, 2011, para. 1)

These values resonated with me beginning at a very young age. As a child, I accompanied my dad on various volunteer activities and fundraisers and then followed in his footsteps with community volunteer work and a dedication to activism.

In university, I studied theater and became very active in social justice issues, particularly in the antiapartheid movement in the early 1990s. My mother was extremely progressive for her time, and she exposed me to alternative perspectives and gave me the courage to make my own choices and to challenge norms. I pursued a Bachelor of Fine Arts in Theater. This alternative theater program included courses in critical art theory and women's studies. In these various classes, I woke up to the impact of power and privilege: the power that men and whites need to give up in order for change to begin. And so began my journey to deconstruct my whiteness while learning about feminism and racism.

> Privilege is the ability to ignore things that other people have no choice but to struggle with every day. White privilege is the taken-for-granted power we, who successfully assume a white identity, exercise when we act as if the status and comfort that whiteness gives us is something that we have earned, or that we deserve as an inherent right. (Combs, 2018, p. 1)

My lens broadened as I asked deep questions of myself and examined my positionality as a young white woman.

After graduation, I had the opportunity to travel widely during my mid-twenties, and then I moved to Toronto, a very diverse city, where I continued to explore the impact of my privilege within my diverse artists' community. My activism continued; "simply because you have a white body, you automatically benefit from white-body supremacy, whether you want to or no. . . . That alone provides you with a big advantage" (Menakem, 2017, p. 205). In those early years, I wrestled with my sense of white guilt; guilt regarding the unearned privilege afforded to me by my race and class. And still, my commitment to unpacking my privilege deepened. I was devoted to making an impact and serving humanity. Living as a conscious artist was not enough to fulfill this sense of purpose, so I decided to pursue a master's degree in psychology, and I moved to San Francisco, California.

During graduate school in the early 2000s, the focus in the field of psychology was on developing "cultural competence." This concept seemed simplistic; however, "possessing a comprehensive understanding of all the nuances of every cultural group with whom we might possibly interact is often a desirable but unfortunately impossible and improbable feat to accomplish" (Hardy, 2016b, p. 3). The concept of whiteness was not prioritized nor really named at that point. Fortunately, this focus has shifted over the years to the notion of "cultural humility." Melanie Tervalon and Jann Murray-García (1998) published a groundbreaking article that challenged the concept of cultural competency with cultural humility. Cultural humility was defined as

> committing to lifelong learning, critical self-reflection, and personal and institutional transformation. Accepting cultural humility means accepting that we can never be fully culturally competent. Cultural humility is the foundation for establishing trust and respectful relationships and for managing differences and conflict. (Tervalon & Murray-García, 1998, p. 120)

As a white woman, I will never know what it is like to navigate the world as a Person of Color. Additionally, all people and their experiences are unique. It is crucial to be curious, patient, humble, willing to make mistakes, and willing to have difficult conversations.

> When we are willing to check our privilege, we are not only identifying areas where we are perpetuating oppression in order to stop personally perpetuating that oppression, but we are also identifying where we have the power and access to change the system as a whole. (Oluo, 2018, pp. 64–65)

My work with social justice in the clinical realm includes a lifelong commitment to unpacking my whiteness and using it to make change.

My graduate training at a private school was primarily geared toward providing individual therapy in a private practice setting. Although it was very progressive, it was rooted in Western psychology with a white orientation. We had a few Teachers of Color. One of the most influential courses that I enrolled in was entitled Cross Cultural Counseling. Our professor was an amazing African American man named John Prowell, who, on the first day, provided a list of class agreements including: "safety does not equal comfort" (J. Prowell, personal communication, Spring 2001). He warned us that we would start to examine and deconstruct race, individually and collectively as a group, and how the examination of race impacts the clinical realm. He warned us that we would not always be comfortable throughout the process. The concept and experience of being uncomfortable and yet safe was new to me. Until then, I had not been confronted with or pushed to examine my privilege as a white person in a group context. But Mr. Prowell and this process dramatically shifted my paradigm.

> The key to moving forward is what we do with our discomfort. We can use it as a door out—blame the messenger and disregard the message. Or we can use it as a door in by asking, why does this unsettle me? What would it mean for me if this were true? (DiAngelo, 2018, p. 14)

Mr. Prowell provided a safe space for us to push our boundaries and forced us to look at our privilege; for me this meant naming and owning my whiteness. He introduced us to the necessary considerations and implications of clinical services across race and class lines. As a white woman and an immigrant, I had, and still have, a great deal to learn and was grateful for the opportunity to broaden my lens both personally and professionally. As Bobes (2016) says, "Humility and transparency are requisite skills for promoting cultural sensitivity" (p. 133). These values continue to be priorities for me both personally and professionally.

As Rick Warren (2012) stated, "Humility is not thinking less of yourself but thinking of yourself less" (p. 190). As clinicians, of course we are thinking primarily of our clients, and yet the therapeutic relationship requires us to also consider ourselves. In all clinical relationships, we therapists must consider similarities and differences, particularly those attributable to race. We must always consider the impact of cross-racial treatment. We cannot be ignorant to, or avoid, the elephant in the room; instead we must model our willingness and openness to engage in conversations of race. To know ourselves in clinical settings, we must pay attention to our bodies, our triggers, our reactions, our attitudes, and our beliefs. Paying attention to transference and countertransference are crucial and intrinsically related to the concept of humility. White clinicians in particular must be willing to pay attention, to not make assumptions or generalizations about clients, particularly Clients of Color, and to maintain a stance of curiosity. The important task of remaining curious must be an integral part of an ongoing practice. "Whiteness can mean taking responsibility" (Menakem, 2017, p. 271). In all contexts, we clinicians must repeatedly look at the impact of race, power, and privilege and where our responsibility lies.

From my first position as a therapy trainee and throughout my various internships and my many years as a licensed clinician, I have worked in community mental health (CMH) with youth and families. I provided outpatient treatment both in schools and in clinics, and I later worked in a residential group home for youth on juvenile probation. I served a diverse population with histories of extensive adverse childhood experiences. White clients were the minority; white clinical staff were the majority.

> When working with people who do not share in our whiteness, we can acknowledge our privilege (either directly or indirectly, depending on the particularities of the moment), taking it into account rather than acting as if we are inhabiting equivalent experiential worlds. (Combs, 2018, p. 11)

Racial humility is essential, and it is a practice that requires active attention and intention.

As white service providers in CMH settings, including therapists, supervisors, case managers, leaders, etc., we must be willing to examine the role of whiteness in our professional and clinical relationships, both in how we conceptualize cases and how our whiteness shows up in the room. Tierney (2013) highlights some crucial points to be considered in this area of mental health. He notes:

> The active partners in the new community mental health system must engage those who for reasons of race, ethnicity, language, age,

> sexual orientation, and gender identification have not had access to appropriate treatment and services delivered by culturally proficient, clinically competent, and qualified caregivers. . . . Community mental health can play a critical role in improving the lives of these and other individuals and communities. It cannot do this by reorganizing existing systems. It does this first by working directly with individuals and communities and not on behalf of them. Community mental health must do this by being willing to create new paradigms that are built on inclusion, respect, dignity and true collaboration and partnership. (p. xiii)

As Tierney (2013) indicates, in order to make systemic change within CMH organizations, collaboration, starting from the top down, must be an ongoing process. It must continue to prioritize collaborative partnership, dialogue, and action from leadership, boards of directors, management, and frontline staff.

During my early internships, I received strong training and supervision regarding cultural and racial humility. Still, the early message to young therapists in CMH was that it was our job as clinicians to name and recognize racial differences with our clients at the beginning of treatment. This implied that we completed the task and could move forward with the intimate, therapeutic work. Yet this approach was extremely simplistic and threatened to bypass the essential ongoing process that unfolds with time, trust, healing, and rapport. Trust must be earned. As Dr. Hardy (2013) discusses, it is the clinician's responsibility to "create space for race. . . . Conveying a sense of openness and curiosity, we take a very proactive role in encouraging conversations about race. An effort must be made to identify race as a significant variable" (p. 27). My naïve assumption that simply providing the space for the discussion will create safety for Blacks and Indigenous and People of Color (BIPOC) is incorrect. There is much complexity in a white outsider providing services to a family, given that CMH is offered primarily through state funding, which involves in-depth assessments that are very personal and potentially provocative. Most service provision models are inherently based on white supremacy and are exclusive of alternate forms of healing, making it difficult to interrupt negative cycles. Many families are extremely private and have a legacy of privacy and mistrust.

The foundations of CMH and psychotherapy are systems that were primarily created through a white lens. Historically, many mental health-focused programs stemmed from medical models that prioritized services for white people and created treatment protocols based on the current values, beliefs, and social models of white people and the white supremacist culture. These treatment models, based in an approach of power over others and of "experts" making decisions for the client and rarely in collaboration with the client, have often done an undeniable disservice to BIPOC. Through such treatment approaches, many BIPOC clients have been exploited, violated, harmed, and have suffered a great deal of trauma as their values, cultures, and beliefs were disregarded and/or forced to be examined through the lens of white supremacist culture. As a result, a legacy of mistrust in mental health treatment continues. Social service systems are organized in ways that expect BIPOC clients to unquestionably trust the disproportionately white service providers who have been assigned to them.

Over the years, there have been attempts to change these systems, including the consideration of alternative family systems, of different communication styles, and of healing models as well as by hiring and promoting more BIPOC mental health staff. This field can be extremely stressful and demanding. Staff are usually underpaid and under-supported, and as a result, there is a great deal of turnover. Some effort has been devoted to strengthening providers' capacity to build cross-racial awareness and trust via cultural humility training. Tokenistic trainings are not enough. Many organizations need to put work into broadening racial awareness so it becomes part of the tapestry of their organization. Despite the efforts that have been made, there is still much work to do, and many providers as well as the organizations that employ them continue to have racial blind spots. Interventions and suggestions that white providers offer to their clients must take into account the clients' values, history, race, religion, etc., and often their clients' contemporary and generational trauma histories and previous experiences, including those of navigating the various "systems," such as schools, medical services, courts, and probation—all systems created by and for white people. These complexities become particularly apparent when it comes to making Child Protective Services (CPS) reports.

The impact of power and privilege must be considered and explored in all clinical and professional relationships. In her book *Post Traumatic Slave*

*Syndrome*, Dr. Joy DeGruy (2017) emphasizes the generational impact of trauma:

> Post Traumatic Slave Syndrome is a condition that exists when a population has experienced multigenerational trauma resulting from centuries of slavery and continues to experience oppression and institutional racism today. Added to this condition is a belief (real or imagined) that the benefits of the society in which they live are not accessible to them. (p. 105)

This dynamic manifests clearly when a therapist who has been assigned/suggested/mandated by the system (e.g., schools, juvenile probation) makes a mandated report or even suggests alternative parenting interventions. Parenting styles vary greatly based on culture, religion, race, etc. Despite these variations, when Families of Color are mandated to engage a system based on the system's definitions, values, and requirements, they have very little choice other than to stringently cooperate. And yet, it remains unspoken that, due to the impact of white supremacy as it manifests via generational trauma and/or vulnerable immigration status, clients often feel forced to cooperate. Yet, that does not mean they are truly engaged in the relationship and/or the process or that they agree with a therapist's suggestions. For many Black and Brown families, it is not safe to question white authority. It is safer to acquiesce or comply, and as Dr. DeGruy (2017) stated, this is often connected with generational trauma.

I worked for many years with an older single African American father who was raising his second family. I'll call him "Mr. Harris." He was a military veteran. He had several very young children when we started working together. His other children were adults, and he had several grandchildren. His children had a variety of behavioral issues and were placed in special education soon after they started preschool. I was referred to support two of the children and their father. During our work together, I suggested various interventions, including creating clear boundaries and implementing consequences and rewards as well as praise for their progress and strengths. He was often stern and critical, even in public. On one occasion, I called him to inform him that I was making yet another CPS report for physical abuse/corporal punishment, and he replied, "Miss Niki, you do what you have to do. I was raised with whoopings and when they act up, I'm gonna whoop 'em." Initially he was very angry with me and refused to engage or respond for several weeks. "For hundreds of years, enslaved mothers and fathers had been belittling their children in an effort to protect them. Yet what originally began as an appropriate adaptation to an oppressive and danger-filled environment has been transmitted through subsequent generations" (DeGruy, 2017, p. 9). Over time, "Mr. Harris" and I were able to explore the use of corporal punishment together and identified alternative ways to set limits and to discipline his children. I don't think he stopped whooping or criticizing his children altogether, but the incidents may have declined in frequency and/or the children reported it less often.

It was important to validate "Mr. Harris's" challenges regarding his children's behavior, his inherent desire to provide for and keep them safe, and his overwhelmed state, especially when one chance encounter with law enforcement can have deadly results. Most often, we had brief collateral sessions and analyzed the costs and benefits of corporal punishment, particularly as this related to generational and learned parenting habits. Unfortunately, our time was limited due to his schedule (often working overnight shifts), his willingness, and the Medi-Cal billing structure, which limits individual therapy with caregivers. I did work with the family for several years, first as a therapist and then as a supervisor of staff performing the direct service. "Mr. Harris" was able to temper his reactivity at times and to try alternative measures. During family therapy, he was often open to learning and practicing alternative interventions, such as adding verbal praise, setting limits, and communicating differently. Other times he would agree in person and then not follow through. Over time, we had a more honest and trusting relationship. As the white female clinician, it was my responsibility to continue to bring race into our discussions. This process was new and uncomfortable and perhaps I worried I would offend him or not have the "right" words. Clinicians must be willing to make mistakes while deepening our commitment to the process.

Early during treatment with the Harris family, I suggested that we create a behavior chart including clear rewards and consequences (an intervention that was influenced by my white paradigm). The children were always very excited when I came over and Dad complied. Together, we created a basic chart. When I returned for the following home session, I saw the chart was untouched. I soon realized that "Mr. Harris" was illiterate. Because of decades of adaptation, some shame, and a desire to be agreeable, he did not tell me, and I did not even think to ask. This was a big learning moment for me about my assumptions and how I imposed my agenda. As Tierney (2013) wrote, the work must be based on "true collaboration" (p. xiii). Cultural and racial humility must also address different styles of communication; in this case, I needed to be clearer and more direct and to be sure that I had buy-in from the client. I had to check my ignorance and my blind spots and pay more attention to what I took for granted from my white, upper-middle-class perspective. I had to be mindful that he was impacted by his slavery legacy and his experience in the military: being told what to do without dissent. Often I wondered about the impact of my whiteness. Following this incident, "Mr. Harris" did avoid me for a time; there needed to be repair. I needed to lean in. I apologized for assuming he was amenable and that this was an intervention he was really willing and able to try. I owned my assumption and my blind spot. In time we were able to move forward. My intention was to continue to openly meet him where he was at, to collaborate, to actively assess his willingness, and to establish shared goals that we would review regularly.

As I reflect on my work with this father, I am reminded of Watts Jones's (2016) cautionary message to clinicians like me. She noted:

> There are concerns that I wish whites to have as they embark on therapy with people of color. Not whether people of color will trust them or feel free to share issues of racism, but whether they as therapists, can provide people of color the assurance that they have some understanding that racism impacts people of color, that they are aligned with defeating and healing from oppression, and that they know that because of their whiteness, there are limits to their experience of that oppression and other ways of knowing. . . . I wish white therapists to want to know. (p. 16)

"Mr. Harris" and I continued to work together and have discussions about race, and I was paying more attention to the nuances of the impact of our cross-racial relationship and my whiteness. "Regardless of race, we must all concern ourselves with both intent and impact" (King, 2018, p. 57). Good intentions are not enough, we must pay attention and take responsibility when our words and/or actions have a harmful impact. During the first year, "Mr. Harris" insisted on calling me "Miss Berkowitz"; eventually he called me "Miss Niki" even though I encouraged him to just use "Niki." In turn, I always called him "Mr. Harris." I wanted him to feel comfortable enough with me to use my first name. Yet I was unaware of the complex impact of race, class, and history on this "simple" invitation. I needed to be more respectful and patient without imposing my definition of "comfort." I actively sought support from and consultation with my colleagues to unpack the role of race, whiteness, privilege, and oppression in the clinical relationship. After I was promoted to clinical supervisor and then clinical manager, I reassigned this case to one of my clinical staff.

Working in CMH involves navigating multiple systems. The clients I served rarely volunteered for or requested mental health support. They were referred and/or mandated by a person in power through the school system, human services, and/or probation. As I was learning to navigate the waters of this profession and gaining confidence as a clinician, I would often assert myself and speak for my clients. "Voicelessness is a learned and adaptive response to domination and subjugation" (Hardy, 2016a, p. 141). I was not aware of the layers of complexity related to race, whiteness, and power that were at play in human services settings and in various meetings in which the work took place. I would encourage, boost, and even role-play with clients, primarily parents and caregivers, about how to ask for what they wanted and needed, and I encouraged them not to blindly agree or acquiesce to demands imposed by these systems. I was very naïve, and I often became frustrated with clients' lack of follow through. As Hardy (2016a) states, *voicelessness* is a survival skill that has been passed down for generations. This exemplifies my blind spot as a white woman, in that I did not have the lived experience of the impact of systemic oppression to fully comprehend all the subtle but potent racially based dynamics that were involved in these interactions. In retrospect, I also realize that though I tried to support my clients' emerging voices, I was remiss in that I did not directly work with these systems to invite them to explore the impact of systemic racism, the implicit biases embedded in the work, and how our whiteness was a critical intervening variable that affected the delivery of racially sensitive therapeutic services.

Advocating for clients and addressing the role of whiteness in such meetings involves slowing down the pace, checking in with caregivers and clients to be sure they understand, and making space for their voices to be heard. As a white person, it is safer for me to use my voice, whereas this is not the case for many BIPOC clients. There are moments in which I choose to assert my privilege to speak up, interrupt, disagree, and advocate for them. It is a delicate balance, knowing when to make space for and/or empower our clients' voices to be heard and when to use our own to challenge the system. I have encountered much resistance from those in positions of power, that is, principals, probation officers, and CPS workers. Even for a white woman, there are still dynamics of power over and hierarchy at play. Watching the power dynamics of systemic racism unfold over and over again can be very frustrating.

Personally, I am an extrovert and I am persistent. In many Western Jewish families, there are those of us who can be very demanding of the services we feel we deserve, and we push for the best. This does stem from a position of white privilege and entitlement that many BIPOC do not have. I had to learn that freedom to use my pushiness was a privilege, an entitlement that many BIPOC do not have, as they would be seen as aggressive, disrespectful, or rude. This power and privilege are not to be taken for granted. As clinicians in CMH, we usually play various roles, including advocate for our clients and their families. Wearing various hats in CMH settings, I continue to learn and to teach supervisees about when and how to assert oneself, when to push forward for themselves or on behalf of their clients, and when to step back. Learning the balance requires humility. White clinicians must pay attention to "the way that white privilege blinds" us (Combs, 2018, p. 13). This includes owning, naming, and addressing microaggressions.

When staff from a CMH agency participate, host, or facilitate a multi-system meeting, our roles are not clear, nor are there clear rules or expectations about appropriate levels of participation. As a white member of a team, I feel that it is part of my responsibility and my commitment to *Tikkun Olam* (Anonymous, 2011) and social justice to speak up in these settings regarding the perpetuation of white supremacy. And yet, these waters are tricky to navigate. In the clinical role, we are also balancing our commitment to the client's confidentiality and our desire to support and advocate for them. As a clinical supervisor, program manager, or director, we have greater flexibility and yet also more privilege and power. Discernment and communication skills are crucial as we assess whether our actions are empowering or disempowering to our clients and how/when we want to challenge the larger system.

Through trials and errors and experience, my attention to spoken and unspoken racism, prejudice, and negative assumptions and the diverse ways they manifest grew. This was particularly apparent in special education meetings, such as for IEPs (Individual Education Plans), and in Human Service and Juvenile Probation hearings, formally called TDMs (Team Decision Meetings), but which are now called CFTs (Child & Family Team Meetings) in Northern California. Many participants (e.g., CPS workers, school staff) are burnt out, overwhelmed, and managing their own vicarious trauma. Yet, many Black and Brown youth are negatively stereotyped and not given a chance to succeed. As a white provider, I always remind myself and my staff how to question and deconstruct our participation in and perpetuation of white supremacy at such meetings. As Ruth King (2018) wrote in her book *Mindful of Race*, "Understanding how we have been conditioned as racial beings to relate to others and ourselves is fundamental to transforming racism" (p. 69). Therefore, we must continue to advocate for and support our clients so they may receive fair and just treatment, accessibility to all resources, and inclusive, equal opportunities to prosper. We must commit to finding ways to ensure that they are given space and time to ask questions, to gain clarification, and to assert themselves. It is important for white providers to try to name and/or interrupt the conditioned patterns instead of blindly agreeing to an agenda to appease white superiors and an inherently racist system. We must repeatedly challenge the white system and hold it accountable so our clients have the space to heal and grow. And we still have a long road ahead.

While I was working at one nonprofit and providing outpatient treatment, administrative roles changed abruptly. We suddenly had a new director with next to no experience with children and youth—a white man who decided that we should immediately start providing family therapy in the clients' homes. Our team consisted of a small group of young, thoughtful, and committed white therapists who requested training to bridge this gap. His advice was "just bring a bucket of fried chicken and you'll be fine. . . . food helps." His comment was offensive, dismissive, and racist and certainly not *helpful*. It was hard to address because he was our new boss: a white man in a position of power with no one holding him accountable. I regret that we did not challenge him or the system itself. By remaining silent, I/we were complicit in the racist system. In this situation, and as Combs (2018) addressed in his article, my choice to avoid/ignore was, in itself, a privilege. This example has always stuck with me like a bad taste and reminds me to take risks, to speak up, even if it's uncomfortable and/or risky navigating the complex hierarchies within an agency. I do not want to make excuses from my white position, and I reflect on this moment as yet another big growth opportunity.

In my work as a clinical supervisor supporting my supervisees' growth as therapists in CMH, I experienced the additional complexity of simultaneously teaching case management and documentation skills and how to navigate various systems: schools, probation, CPS, etc. For example, what I learned from my work with "Mr. Harris" and many other cases allowed me to apply my knowledge and understanding about race as I supervised new white therapists. Although I was committed to raising the topic of race in both individual and group supervision settings, complexities ensued, particularly with my Supervisees of Color. Initially, I was hesitant and uncomfortable; I did not want this to be my white agenda, and yet I knew it was crucial to include race in our discussions about cases. Dr. Hardy had taught me the importance of asking supervisees early in the relationship, "How do you identify your race, and what is your experience of race in the clinical context?" (K. Hardy, personal communication, Spring 2017). Over the years, I worked with a few female supervisees who were BIPOC and who said, "I don't see race," and they were not very open to exploring the topic any further. My impulse was to avoid the issue. I noticed my triggers and pushed myself to lean in and deepen the exploration. Over time, I learned to identify my own discomfort with being a white woman in a position of power, I learned how to ask better questions and to respect their pace. "Color-blind statements insist that people do not see race, or if they see it, it has no meaning to them" (DiAngelo, 2018, p. 77). DiAngelo (2018) described an exchange with a Black cofacilitator who asked, in response to claims that one does not see race, "Then how will you see racism?" (pp. 41–42). As a white supervisor in positions of power as both supervisor and boss, this was a delicate situation to navigate. These particular supervisees were more comfortable addressing concerns about gender and sex than about race. Difficult as it was, my job was to bring the focus back to race. As a supervisor and administrator who trains new interns, I was committed to providing trainings and to having ongoing discussions about the complex implications of race and class, in both individual and group supervision, as it relates to home- and community-based treatment.

Throughout my work, I continually invite clients and families to explore racial dynamics, and I encourage my supervisees to do the same. Perhaps I am too keen and enthusiastic, and yet I am aware that I am a white provider with my own agenda. I continue to question my agenda and to work on being more patient and respectful. This is also part of the supervision process. Most of the families I have worked with had a long history of navigating white supremacy in all its many layers, and many of these families were dealing with extensive trauma histories related to racism and/or vulnerable immigration status. Dr. Hardy (2016a) stresses the importance of learning and applying crucial therapeutic skills and "developing a communication style that imbues intimacy, intensity, congruency, authenticity and transparency" (p. 138). In this article, he stresses how important it is to admit when we have made mistakes, to sit with our discomfort, to take risks in dialogues, and to "stretch beyond one's normal zone of comfort" (Hardy, 2016a, p. 138).

Deconstructing whiteness also requires unpacking our assumptions, and as Watts Jones (2016) implies, we must stay curious. Our curiosity will enable us to genuinely unpack our assumptions so that we are doing more than paying lip service to our commitment to diversity, equity, and inclusion. This also means that we must activate our own racial and cultural humility; we must be willing to continue the dialogue, to constantly check ourselves, to discuss the work with our colleagues, mentors, and supervisors, and, most importantly, to admit when we make mistakes, as we are bound to do. This position is applicable in all sectors of CMH, including therapy, supervision, and leadership. Interpersonally and on systemic levels, we need to be sure to be authentic and comprehensive and to not implement token policies. Always allow the heart and compassion to lead.

I would like to include some succinct recommendations for what CMH systems can do to effectively challenge and dismantle white supremacy as a mechanism for improving the quality of racially sensitive care to Clients of Color. Good intentions are not enough. As King (2018) wrote, "training programs build awareness; accountability changes culture" (p. 207).

- Diversify funding or amend contracts with funders to allow for more ongoing trainings, both internally and externally, to address racial humility. Expand from the common models that include one training during onboarding and/or one offered annually.
- Create job descriptions that are manageable and not measured by productivity of services; quality, not quantity.
- Provide longer, more thorough onboarding/new-hire training.
- Increase staff retention by paying higher salaries.
- Offer more regular team building activities/retreats at which race is addressed.
- Diversify staff, including supervisors and leadership, and promote internally when applicable—avoid simple token hires/promotions.
- Learn and implement methods to collaborate on goal identification and goal setting with intention, including what clients are willing to do.
- Provide ongoing training and groups, not singular token events, to hold people accountable on all levels of the organization, including group supervision and weekly/monthly staff meetings. Support ongoing accountability groups for different races.
- Incorporate mindfulness practices.
- Cocreate new standards/norms that are not based on whiteness.
- Offer communication trainings, provided by qualified trainers, on how to have difficult cross-racial discussions. Offer mediation (not facilitated by human resources or management) for coworkers who come into conflict over race/privilege.
- Expand the definition of what is "healing" to include different religious/spiritual perspectives.

In conclusion, there are many questions we must continue to ask ourselves in our roles as white therapists, supervisors, and administrators. We must continue to show up genuinely with commitment, persistence, curiosity, and humility. We must keep risking having the hard conversations, admit when we make errors, and speak up about injustice and oppression. As white people, we must be vigilant when we are complicit in racism and work toward catching our mistakes, gracefully receiving difficult feedback, and making growth toward change. We must make space to sit in our discomfort and to navigate the unknown, while nurturing safety and trust in the relationships. We must be both patient and persistent. I believe that we have a profound responsibility as white providers for *Tikkun Olam,* to repair the world as we know it.

**NIKI BERKOWITZ, MA, LMFT,** has been working in the San Francisco Bay Area, California, in community mental health for over 15 years. She began working as a school-based therapist and has worked with youth in various other settings, such as intensive wraparound and residential treatment. She has worked at various agencies as a trainer, clinical supervisor, program manager, and clinical director. She has been dedicated to antiracist work both personally and professionally since college. She also served as a board member with Hunters Point Family in San Francisco for a decade.

## References

*Anonymous. (2011, August 15).* Judaism: Tzedakah and Tikkun Olam. *The modern social worker. http://modernsocialworker.blogspot.com/2011/08/judaism-tzedakah-and-tikkun-olam.html*

*Bobes, T. (2016). Dialogues about power, privilege, and difference. In K. V. Hardy & T. Bobes (Eds.),* Culturally sensitive supervision and training: Diverse perspectives and practical applications *(pp. 127–135). Routledge.*

*Combs, G. (2018). White privilege: What's a white therapist to do?* Journal of Marital and Family Therapy, 45*(3), 1–15. https://doi.org/10.1111/jmft.12330*

*DeGruy, J. (2017).* Post traumatic slave syndrome: America's legacy of enduring injury & healing. *Uptone Press.*

*DiAngelo, R. (2018).* White fragility: Why it's so hard for white people to talk about racism. *Beacon Press.*

*Hardy, K. V. (2013). Healing the hidden wounds of racial trauma.* Reclaiming Children and Youth, 22*(1), 24–28.*

*Hardy, K. V. (2016a). Mastering context talk: Practical skills for effective engagement. In K. V. Hardy & T. Bobes (Eds.),* Culturally sensitive supervision and training: Diverse perspectives and practical applications *(pp. 136–145). Routledge.*

*Hardy, K. V. (2016b). Toward the development of a multicultural relational perspective in training and supervision. In K. V. Hardy & T. Bobes (Eds.),* Culturally sensitive supervision and training: Diverse perspectives and practical applications *(pp. 3–10). Routledge.*

*King, R. (2018).* Mindful of race: Transforming racism from the inside out. *Sounds True.*

*Menakem, R. (2017).* My grandmother's hands: Racialized trauma and the pathway to mending our hearts and bodies. *Central Recovery Press.*

*Oluo, I. (2018).* So you want to talk about race. *Seal Press.*

*Shakespeare, W. (1992).* Hamlet, prince of Denmark *(C. Watts & K. Carabine, Eds.). Wordsworth Editions. (Original work published 1599)*

*Tervalon, M., & Murray-García, J. (1998). Cultural humility versus cultural competence: A critical distinction in defining physician training outcomes in multicultural education.* Journal of Health Care for the Poor and Underserved, *9(2),117–125. https://doi.org/10.1353/hpu.2010.0233*

*Tierney, S. (2013). Foreword. In D. Maller & K. Langsam (Eds.),* The Praeger handbook of community mental health practice. Working in the local community *(Vol. 1, pp. xii–xvii). Praeger.*

*Warren, R. (2012).* The purpose driven life: What on Earth am I here for? *Zondervan.*

*Watts Jones, T. D. (2016). Location of self in training and supervision. In K. V. Hardy & T. Bobes (Eds.),* Culturally sensitive supervision and training: Diverse perspectives and practical applications *(pp. 16–24). Routledge.*

## CHAPTER 19

# Funhouse Mirror of Whiteness

## The Multidimensional, Complex, and Liberatory Practice of Challenging Whiteness

JEN LELAND, LMFT

Making whiteness visible is often declared a first task in antiracism work. This position implies that the task of seeing whiteness is simple (beginner's work) and fixed rather than complex and dynamic. It suggests that if one sees, one cannot unsee. I would offer that neither is true. Seeing whiteness is not rudimentary, even if it is fundamental. Far from being a single step on an antiracist journey, I've come to appreciate it as *the* path—demanding, transformative, and liberatory. For the purposes of this chapter, I use Ruth Frankenberg's (1993) definition of whiteness as multidimensional, complex, systemic, and systematic. She also says,

> whiteness has a set of linked dimensions. First, whiteness is a location of structural advantage, of race privilege. Second, it is a "standpoint," a place from which white people look at ourselves, at others, and at society. Third, "whiteness" refers to a set of cultural practices that are usually unmarked and unnamed. (p. 1)

Seeing whiteness requires a multidirectional lens to interrogate both who we are, absent whiteness, and the ways in which we are defined and distorted in the funhouse mirror of whiteness. This multidimensional lens asks us to see our internalized mechanics of white superiority that both advantages us (as white people) and distorts our perceptions and cuts us off from our humanity. It demands we see the structural engineering of whiteness, the cages of whiteness we trap others in, and the bars of whiteness that entrap us. Examining and interrogating whiteness function as more than a first step, but can also be a liberating practice for us as white people, a way of reclaiming stolen and sold off parts of ourselves and our humanity.

Interrogating whiteness in our health and behavioral health systems is essential in this time of multiple pandemics—COVID-19, racial uprising, and climate crisis—that are highlighting the deep racial inequities and divisions in the United States. Black and Brown communities are getting sicker and dying at higher rates from COVID-19. We see whose work is deemed "essential" but deny them health care; we see who is provided essential services and who is burdened with the risks of their provision. We can see racial inequities in data points but fail to see the point that drives the data. Whiteness disappears in the national discourse even as it is named and marked. This is the nature of whiteness, to conceal itself even as it reveals its deadly consequences.

As many of us march for Black lives, aspire to be antiracist allies or clinicians, and work toward racial justice, our internal (self-examination) and external (activism) actions are similarly compartmentalized and caught up in this dynamic of "othering" racism and whiteness as an act without an actor. We compartmentalize this work as somehow distant from our own healing. These threads of whiteness, distancing ourselves, othering, or disavowing our own white supremacy then embroider our clinical and antiracism approaches. We attend workshops to learn how racism impacts the other. We get certified in culturally competent therapy to become (or be perceived to be) more effective clinicians with other races. We protest, we march, and join white accountability groups largely with unconscious beliefs that we are doing this for or on behalf of others. These distancing defenses allow us to remain separate and superior (white saviorism) and reinforce dehumanization. When asked to examine how race impacts our own identities, our own location in organizations and power structures, and whether whiteness privileges us and at what cost, we balk. How often do we rigorously examine how whiteness is centering and dominating the discourses with other white therapists or white clients if no Person of Color is present? How do we understand this antiracism journey to be not just fundamental to our clinical efficacy but as central to our own personal healing ? If we look, but fail to see, and if we perform, but fail to feel and interrogate the ways we have both benefited from and been harmed by whiteness, we risk not only centering but reifying whiteness even as we intend to de-center and dismantle whiteness.

Far from being a passive, fixed ideology, this norming (and hiding in plain sight) of white superiority is dynamic, scheming, agile, and adaptive. Strategies to first make whiteness visible and to then decenter whiteness must also be adaptive, dynamic, tenacious, and rigorous. The work to see and unsee whiteness can also be loving and liberating work for us. Alternatively, it can persist as rote academic discourse that over-focuses on structural racism, but not the racist ideologies that organize our psyches and behaviors.

Examining whiteness multidimensionally demands much and affords much, not only for others, but for white people who have the stamina to see how whiteness contorts our relationships with others and especially ourselves, to feel our complicity with its dehumanization, and resulting loss of authentic belonging in humanity. Decentering whiteness demands we risk giving up the ways in which whiteness, even if we didn't ask for it or may not like it, still uplifts and protects us.

## Part I: Seeing Whiteness as a Multidimensional and Liberatory Practice

Recently, I facilitated a white accountability foundations workshop in which a (Zoom) room full of white clinicians and social workers were asked to share defenses we commonly employ when talking about racism and white supremacy. Our defenses mirrored those illustrated by Saad (2018) and ranged from color blindness, "I don't see color," to white exceptionalism, "I'm not like other white racists, I'm one of the good ones" (p. 70). When prompted to share how each of us specifically employs these defenses in our relationships or clinical care, the room fell silent. As a white facilitator, I understand these silences. Fear of naming our complicity, fear of being seen as a "bad" person, lifelong conditioning to *not see* ourselves as racialized beings, and disassociation from the parts of ourselves that act as racist aggressors all conspire to fill this swollen silence. Video screens go dim. The chat goes quiet. Then, something predictable happens: Commonly, a white woman (ciswomen are typically overrepresented in these workshops) breaks the silence and shares with growing outrage that her white supervisor really needs to be in this workshop as it is the supervisor that refuses to discuss issues of racism, forever reminding the clinician "these issues" fall outside of the "billable" presenting problem and interventions. This outrage toward the supervisor, regardless how righteous, serves an important defense for the clinician. Namely, she is moving the conversation away from the internal work (avoiding the prompt) toward seeing defenses enacted outside herself. This dynamic of examining whiteness in others versus ourselves is so predictable that it merits some scrutiny. What is being made visible, and what invisibility is being maintained?

By turning the gaze toward "organizational othering," we maintain our individual innocence or virtue, our standing as a good white person/antiracist who is focused on fighting the good fight. Whiteness conditions us to not see our own whiteness. We do not have to reckon with our complicity. Too often we use other white people to distance and disavow our own complicity with whiteness, the ways we are shaped by internalized white superiority and how whiteness shapes and is shaping every aspect of our life. Essential to seeing whiteness is becoming aware of how we *don't* see whiteness, how harmful that is to our best aspirations in antiracism work, and how we might start becoming aware by focusing on our blindness. What are the conditions that maintain invisibility? What conditions are necessary for us to reveal whiteness and its invisibility cloak? Many discourses privilege the structural conditions that maintain invisibility, and here I will explore the internal, psychological conditions that we must reveal, see, feel, reckon, and resist in order to heal.

"We see what we look for and thus are only capable of seeing what we want to see. Invariably, the 'what' we see is so often dictated by the 'who' that is looking" (K. V. Hardy, personal communication, March 10, 2020).

### *Starting with Self: Interrogating Whiteness in Self*

What does my white racial identity mean for me in my life? How have I been shaped by white supremacy? What are the costs of my contortions to whiteness? What are the advantages I have availed myself of? Who am I without whiteness? How has whiteness shaped my relationships, my imagination, my resilience, my psychological capacities? In my early discourses on the subject, I lacked what Hardy (2020) refers to as both the will and the skill to see myself in these terms and to interrogate the seeing. I spent large parts of my life not seeing myself as white nor as having been socialized by race nor as having a racialized identity. In the rare instances when I did, I often saw whiteness and racialized identity as distant from or outside of myself. I did not *see* myself as white nor how my whiteness organized my daily experiences, even though I checked the "white" boxes in depersonalized and/or begrudging ways. At other times, I acknowledged my white privilege with unspoken resentments that this privilege didn't come to me easily as a woman, queer person, or during periods of my life that were defined by poverty or institutionalization. I remained indignant about being "lumped into" a racial group, I did not want to see the ways I easily relax into whiteness, availing myself of its privileges and entitlements while also devising ways of disavowing it when convenient or when it benefited me to do so. It is not easy for me to see my whiteness, even harder to see my blindness. These days, I realize, through imperfect commitment to racial self-interrogation, that my white racial identity means everything. Everything. My white identity shapes every experience, every failure, every success, every relationship, and absolutely every way in which I perceive and organize every single one of my experiences. Every single one.

I remember going to get food stamps as a child in the early 1980s. We, along with our Mexican neighbor and her daughter of about my age, took our monthly bus sojourn to the social service agency, easily spending the entire day in lines that coiled through laminated hallways before reaching the women at the windows, most of whom were white, who doled out books of food coupons. Whenever it was her turn at the counter, my mom asked for, and often received, from the white agents (white solidarity) extra books of food stamps. Those agents, shaking their head with pity as they looked at us, consistently slid us extra books—extra books that our neighbor neither asked for nor ever received. Even in poverty, the privileges of being white afforded me these extra resources through white solidarity (who to ask) and a sense of entitlement to resources and care (the ask itself).

Though I may not have used this language then, I learned that whiteness is also relational and exists in relation to othering, particularly

Black but in this case Brown, skin color. To be advantaged, to be given more than, also requires subjugation: that someone else is given less. Whiteness is relationally bound. My mom did not ask for extra resources from non-white counter agents. On the bus ride home, we didn't mention that we got more coupons to our neighbor who received less. Neither did we share the bounty. I learned early that my entitlement to care is scaffolded and reinforced by white solidarity and subjugation. I learned how to play the white race card. Unspoken. Unwritten. I learned that when we get extra, we must hoard it. I learned to be misanthropic.

As a child, did I feel the injustice of getting more than others? Yes, I did feel that deep unfairness the way children feel injustice with their entire bodies, though I don't remember this feeling being persistent. I do remember feeling *better than*, special, and this feeling of superiority, reinforced by white supremacy, functioned as salve for the humiliation I felt about our poverty. My mom was more worthy than my neighbor (superiority). She used strategy to get more resources, not racial privilege (meritocracy). We got more resources because we deserved more. Perhaps the most powerful "more" we received from this dynamic was the psychological fortification that comes with conflating getting *more* with being *more* than.

If feeling worthy, valuable, and a sense of belonging is the salve, the toxins of this salve lay in the chemicals of who is made to be less than, less deserving than, less worthy than. Dehumanization is one of the more toxic chemicals. By this I mean to say that I came to see my neighbor, who had been like family to me, as less worthy, less deserving of basic human needs, less human.

Who am I without whiteness? Dehumanization is a blade that cuts both ways. To quote Toni Morrison in a PBS interview with Charlie Rose (Morrison, 1998), "If you can only be tall because someone else is on their knees, then you have a serious problem. And white people have a very, very serious problem."

It is no wonder that I, like many others, choose to dip in and out of these efforts at seeing. This, too, is a privilege and an advantage. It is difficult to sustain gazing at oneself in the funhouse mirror of whiteness. I am *not* conflating this more existential threat with the actual threats, violence, and brutality that whiteness—especially unexamined, triggered, projected, weaponized, and dispensed whiteness—confers to People of Color. I'm suggesting that, for white people, a part of our journey to examine whiteness must include both the seeing and the feeling: seeing the distortions of self, feeling the emotions we have been both protected from and unwilling to feel—vulnerable, uncertain, weak, unworthy, shameful. Disrobing whiteness requires reckoning with these disavowed parts of ourselves so that we resist projecting them onto others.

A close friend once told me that the sight of white skin triggers racialized trauma for her. I didn't know what to do with this. She sensed my unease. "You can't do anything," she informed me, "but as my friend, it is important for you to know this." We cannot extricate ourselves from racial advantages and legacies of trauma embodied in our skin. We cannot wake up tomorrow, and choose to emancipate ourselves from whiteness, but we can take small actions to dissent and divest.

Internalized and externalized white superiority is toxic, not only to BIPOC but to white people too. But the more proximity one has to subjugation in other places, the harder it is to abstain from using this "white salve" as a "drug." I needed to see my privilege, but more importantly, I needed to see how my investments in maintaining this lie protected me. To see how I was racially socialized to be white, I also had to feel into a deeper question: Who am I without racism? Who am I without whiteness?

### *Self-Interrogating Whiteness as Liberatory Work*

In a trauma-informed training last year, I facilitated a breakout session on practices that integrate trauma-informed approaches with strategies for racial justice. Most of the examples given were ones that, while important, focused exclusively on how to benefit People of Color. A Black nurse illuminated a blind spot at the center of our inquiry, "I'm tired of this being about what you all do for Black people. Don't do this (racial justice work) for us. We don't need you to do it for us. Do it for you. When will you do this for you?"

Unexamined whiteness often produces more devastating costs for white people than what unfolds through examining it. Whiteness is a learned behavior. It is socially and politically constructed. Learned behaviors can also be unlearned, but we cannot unlearn what we cannot see. The payoff for self-interrogation, for excavating whiteness, can be liberatory, giving us a consciousness for how we might free ourselves from our

TABLE 19.1: Personal Effects of Revealing Whiteness

| PERSONAL | CLINICAL |
|---|---|
| Increased capacity to listen instead of debate, defend, and distance | Increased ability to initiate conversations about race in both humble and confident ways that acknowledges my complicity and engenders more trust in therapeutic alliance to hold vulnerability |
| Increased skill at regulating my own distress | Increased ability to initiate ongoing conversations about my own social location with clients in meaningful ways that allows for more exploration of how their location impacts their mental well-being |
| Increased capacity to be vulnerable in ways that enhance the quality of all my relationships | Increased ability to tolerate discomfort around being challenged in conversations about race and racism and to affirm and hold pain of these experiences with others |
| Increased ability to organize other white people in antiracism work by naming my own racism and internalized white superiority | Increased ability to prioritize race as significant in the assessment and treatment process |
| Increased capacity for more interdependent and more deeply loving relationships versus shallow relationships organized by invulnerability | Increased ability to feel, to develop the coping skills to navigate the emotional intensity of this work, and to hold and honor the emotional experiences, and not just the cognitive understanding, of racialized trauma |

contortions. Seeing whiteness allows the greater consciousness a choice to consent or dissent, to invest or divest. We cannot fully emancipate ourselves from the advantages conferred upon us, regardless of our dissent; however, it is our connectedness, our authentic belonging, and our full humanity that gets expanded the more we consciously take action to see, dissent, and divest.

Self-interrogation work to define and see how whiteness has organized and shaped my early and ongoing experiences not only informs my antiracism work but reliably enhances the quality of all my relationships and moves the work from performative (centering whiteness) to transformational. Furthermore, it improves my efficacy as a clinician. These ways of seeing, feeling, dissenting, and divesting then translate into new ways of being. Self-interrogation and *seeing* whiteness change our *being* and how we show up in clinical practice. Table 19.1 is just a partial list of how my clinical and relational capacity *to be* has been enlivened by this practice of revealing whiteness.

Self-interrogation has increased my skills and capacity for self-soothing and self-regulating when the right to comfort is triggered in me, so I am more easily able to authentically join with clients in discomfort and am less likely to enact compliance or control interventions. Most profoundly, the practice of self-interrogation and the privilege of being in cross-racial spaces where others loved me enough to interrogate how whiteness shapes the ways I engage in the work have enabled me to be responsible for, to repair, and to redress ways that I have misused power and created harm; and in these acts of decentering whiteness, I work toward a more embodied stance that decenters whiteness.

## Part II: Seeing and Challenging Structural Whiteness

The master's tools will never dismantle the master's house.

—AUDRE LORDE (1984)

In Alcoholics Anonymous literature, there is a passage in the Big Book that promises the "infinite value of our painful past" (Alcoholics Anonymous, 1976, p. 124) that results from the self-searching process codified in the 4th and 12th steps. In this spirit, I offer the following cautionary tale of how my unexamined whiteness led to my centering whiteness, in painful and harmful ways, even as I led change intended to be trauma-informed and antiracist and to dismantle structural whiteness. To see structural whiteness is to see the mechanics of the funhouse mirror, to see how it situates white people in structural advantage, to see what gets amplified as normal, universally good, and right, and what becomes disfigured, blurred, or concealed.

Like many white clinicians, I quickly moved up the ranks of nonprofits (that served predominantly Black and Brown children and families) into leadership positions, despite any evidence of my being qualified to work with predominantly Black and Brown communities. About four years after obtaining my clinical licensure, I was hired as Director of Clinical Services at an Oakland-based nonprofit, managing clinical day treatment and special school settings for children diagnosed as severely emotionally disturbed (SED). As part of some of the children's individualized education plans (IEP), they were placed into small settings outside of mainstream elementary schools. Behind the disproportionate numbers of Black children in these settings, especially Black male children, lie structures (clinical and evidence-based practices) that maintain this disparity; assessments, diagnoses, behavior assessments and modification plans, and the metrics of normative whiteness are used to describe, diagnose, and problematize child behaviors that do not conform: students who requested different learning supports were labeled as defiant, oppositional, and inattentive; students who yelled whether due to hunger, distress, or irritability were labled as disruptive, aggressive, and unsafe.

During my first few months overseeing these programs, several organizations published investigative reports that exposed the dehumanizing and traumatizing practices of placing children into seclusion rooms (US Department of Education, 2012), often euphemistically referred to as "quiet rooms." Even the term "placing" children into seclusion rooms betrays the brutal reality of how we (educators and clinicians) wrestled and threw children into quiet rooms, often following prolonged physical restraint. Our quiet rooms resembled the descriptions in the investigative reports: concrete, windowless, padded walls, jail cell–like. The practice in our school included widespread misuses of these spaces and injurious outcomes for both students and staff. The year I moved into this position, school programs such as ours underwent a mandate to reduce and eliminate the use of restraints and seclusion. At the time, the relatively new framework of trauma-informed care was offered as a potential alternative and set of interventions that advocates for less trauma-inducing interventions and for reconceptualizing aggressive behaviors as adaptations to fear and stress arousal. Interventions rely on promoting internal control (self-regulation and self-soothing skills) versus an overreliance on external behavior modification or punitive controls (point systems, seclusion, and suspensions).

In our school, mental health counselors and educators restrained students almost daily as a response to a continuum of behaviors we defined as unsafe. These behaviors often included punching other students or teachers, self-injurious behaviors (headbanging, cutting oneself, etc.), running out into street traffic, climbing onto the roof of the school, or throwing objects at others. By understanding these behaviors as responses to internal stress and fear that require soothing rather than control, we hoped we might replace the escalating responses we once used with more de-escalating and humane strategies, such as assisting students with self-soothing, teaching skills to calm the body and to self-regulate, and lending students the calm neurobiology of adults in order to regulate their automatic stress response (coregulation).

Eager to adopt any support that might address the dehumanizing tactics of control in these settings, I brought forth a trauma-informed care set of interventions to our weekly team meetings. I crafted an impressive PowerPoint deck and a mandate that we would be "taking the doors to the seclusion rooms off their hinges" by the coming December winter recess, only two months away. A newly minted white director, I waltzed into these meetings, populated predominantly with Black counselors and a handful of white educators and clinicians, to unleash a new mandate to be implemented, with great urgency and no resources. At the end of my presentation, I passed out workflow protocols and accountability metrics to guide our progress for eliminating incidents of restraints and seclusion.

If I had seen whiteness at the center of these interventions, I would not have been so surprised at the expressions of distrust, anger, and exhaustion that met my newly minted PowerPoint and handouts, but I hadn't and I was. Responses, accompanied by eyerolls, came quickly:

"Sounds good and nice but won't work."
"So now we are supposed to take the hits, so the agency doesn't get sued?"
"This won't keep anyone safe and just teaches the kids they can do anything they want."
"We like you Jen, but we don't like this one bit." (*One can see the care taken to reassure me of my goodness even while challenging me.*)
"What happens if we take the doors off and a kid gets hurt?"
"Is the agency going to pay our hospital bills?"

My efforts and plans, though I worked hard on them and with good intentions, lacked any analysis of the structural legacies of violence and white supremacy that first installed the seclusion rooms in our schools. When we consider the legacies of white domination and violence and brutality in our psychiatric and mental health systems, we begin to see that the problem is not how to manage the unsafe behaviors of students, but how to manage the brutal interventions in our mental health systems. Consider how American psychiatrists pathologized enslaved people who attempted to risk their lives by running away or by refusing to work, diagnosing them with illnesses such as drapetomania or dysesthesia aethiopica, respectively. The prescribed treatment was whipping. In the 1960s, psychiatrists characterized angry Black Civil Rights movement activists as having a reactive psychosis. Antipsychotic advertisements from that era sometimes featured angry, threatening cartoons of Black men (Myers, 2014).

By not looking, I didn't have to see that we were using equally violent and brutal practices, justified by our pathologizing the emotional and behavioral experiences of the students rather than seeing the context of their stress arousal as adaptations to the more macrolevel racist policies and practices.

Furthermore, the set of trauma-informed interventions I extolled for our use focused exclusively on how to regulate stress responses of the "other" without any acknowledgment that we, the providers, ran around the school in chronic states of dysregulation. In fact, a primary trauma-informed intervention, that of coregulation, presumes that we providers walk around with "calm neurobiology" that the children can borrow in their moments of acute distress.

My plan also lacked any acknowledgment of the legacies of white managers, researchers, and clinical directors like me repeatedly offering white salve to fix or heal the trauma-inducing effects of last year's toxic white salve. Even this trauma-informed approach to understanding, studying, treating, intervening, and healing behaviors of both staff and students was absent of any strategies for how we might also understand, study, treat, intervene, and heal the toxins in the white salve. Finally, I disseminated this plan from a compliance framework that required the counselors, most of whom were Black, to fix the structures that white people and whiteness had put into place. I came in with an ahistorical solution wrapped up in the latest products branded with the white savior logo.

Teju Cole (2012) produced seven popular tweets about the white American savior industrial complex that describe the explicitly damaging effects of white saviorism that prioritizes a "big emotional experience" (para. 6), achieved through minor acts of charity or activism, over tackling larger issues like systematic oppression and corruption that create the "need for the need" (para. 17). The last of the seven influential tweets reads, "I deeply respect American sentimentality, the way one respects a wounded hippo. You must keep an eye on it, for you know its deadly" (para. 8). He goes on to describe the white saviorism/wounded hippo dynamic,

> His good heart does not always allow him to think constellationally. He does not connect the dots or see the patterns of power behind the isolated "disasters." All he sees are hungry mouths, and he, in his own advocacy-by-journalism way, is putting food in those mouths as fast as he can. All he sees is need, and he sees no need to reason out the need for the need. (para. 17)

This is a painfully accurate description of how I came to implement trauma-informed care in our clinical, day-treatment settings. I had good intentions and a developed understanding of antiracism work. I was working for justice and to reduce harm on Black bodies. I understood systems of white supremacy and the fallacies of white saviorism.

I had learned to always consult those most impacted by our solutions as we design them. And yet, here I was blindly enacting these patterns of whiteness, centering but not naming whiteness, fortified with positionality and power. I engaged in the *doing of decentering whiteness* without the *seeing* or *feeling*.

I walked away from that initial meeting feeling resentment, despair, and a profound urge to throw in the white towel. I had worked hard on a plan that would ultimately keep "them" (staff and students) safer. It wasn't perfect, but it was something. I chalked up their reactions and concerns to years of indoctrination of dehumanizing systems, again failing to see my blindness. Yes, there may have been a kernel of truth to my perspective at the time, but it lacked the wisdom of the larger truth being shown to me, a truth I could not hear through my defensiveness and refusal to be challenged to do the deeper work of seeing how whiteness organized that moment, the mandate, the problem, and the solution. In that moment, I failed to apply the same self-regulation skills I was mandating that others use.

## Part III: Lessons Learned and Key Strategies for Challenging Whiteness in Self and Structures

Eventually, our team succeeded in taking the seclusion doors off the hinges and eliminated seclusion rooms; however, the journey to get there required the interrogation of whiteness in both myself, in our institutional structures, and of the impediments to decentering and challenging whiteness. The impediments to seeing and challenging whiteness, especially in our institutions (e.g., schools, mental health), are numerous and complex in scope. These impediments are intrapersonal, relational, and structural, and so my efforts challenge that whiteness must also be internal, relational, and structural. The following section explores the structural and relational challenges that often interfere with challenging whiteness. After each artifact of whiteness I describe, I will share key learnings and strategies our team employed to decenter whiteness in our work to eliminate seclusion rooms and embed more relationship-centered and antiracist interventions.

*White Saviorism*

White saviorism is the first artifact of whiteness that I failed to see in myself and consequently came to embody. Decisions made by white people on behalf of Communities of Color, as though they are incapable of making their own decisions, is about control: by eagerly searching for solutions as an individual and as a white leader without consulting those who I expected to carry out the "solution" (BIPOC staff) or those most impacted by the harm (primarily Black children), I placed the "problem" to be solved (seclusion) at the feet of People of Color and advanced the "optimal," most efficient "solution" designed by white researchers and white leaders in trauma-informed care.

**Impediments to Seeing**

This saviorism, a function of white entitlement to control, allowed me to not see the racism and white superiority I was reinforcing by how I described the problem, the solutions, the interventions, and who was regulated and not regulated. I did not have to feel the horror of this practice, its legacies of harm, nor my own collusion with the brutality of this intervention that I enacted and normalized. By not naming my own complicity, I did not have to feel the implications of my own dehumanizing actions. I situated (and absolved) myself as part of the solution rather than recognizing myself as a purveyor of the problem.

*White Exceptionalism*

White exceptionalism refers to the stance that this work doesn't really apply to me, that "I am exempt because I . . . [fill-in-the-blank: voted for Obama; marched for Black Lives; serve marginalized communities; etc.]." It is another form of othering that allows us to distance and disconnect from the horrors and painful truths.

**Impediments to Seeing**

Seeing myself as distanced and doing this work to benefit the children protected me from my own memories of being in seclusion and restraints in an adolescent psychiatric unit and of the horrors of being strapped to a bed with leather belts at age 13. The savior/fixer role protected me from recognizing and feeling how I was both perpetrating this practice and reliving my own memories of its horrors.

*Right to Comfort; Exhaustion/Despair and the White Towel*

My immediate reaction to being challenged by my colleagues was to personalize it (center myself), to be distressed, angry, and resentful for not getting kudos for all my hard work (right to comfort and care). This entitlement to comfort trumped the focus on the profound discomfort and brutality of restraints and seclusion. With my comfort challenged, exhaustion gave way to what I would call a tantrum of whiteness or *throwing in the white towel.*

**Impediments to Seeing**

Centering my comfort allowed me to not feel my own uncertainty, vulnerability, and anger. Ultimately, this impoverished ability to feel led to more dehumanization. I prioritized my dignity and safety over the rights to care and to the dignity of children I claimed to care so much for. The right to comfort defends against feeling discomfort and/or feeling exposed. Throwing in the white towel protects me from feeling helplessness, uncertainty, incompetence, and provides an escape from exhaustion and developing the stamina necessary for sustained antiracism actions.

*Ahistorical Isolationist*

This aspect of whiteness seeks to address issues as specific incidents outside of their context or history in general. I isolated a particular problem (use of traumatizing restraints and seclusion rooms on children) from the larger context and sociocultural conditions related to structural whiteness (cultures of white supremacy, compliance and domination baked into our school site protocols, language, and policies). Taking an ahistorical stance toward the violent legacies associated with seclusion and restraints allowed our mental health care systems to preserve the "benefit of the doubt" or racial innocence. It separated the sin from the sinner and, in doing so, absolved the sinner and made the people who had been harmed responsible for making amends.

**Impediments to Seeing**

Not seeing the context shielded me from feeling responsible for this (or blamed), but this also prevented me from taking steps toward true accountability. Ironically, in trying to dismantle practices of control, my original plan centered quantitative accountability metrics rather than measurements of progress and accountability in our relationships with students, around our alignment with our values, and to create cultures of safety and well-being. Focusing on the reduction rates we could achieve (i.e., a goal of reducing our seclusion rates by 50% in two months) easily leads to using metrics of compliance against individual staff members and applying disciplinary interventions. These metrics kept us accountable to measuring the reduction of risk and harm but not to the presence of well-being or to building school cultures of safety and belonging.

*Four Key Lessons and Strategies for Challenging Structural Whiteness*

**Contribute, Don't Control**

I sought to control the solution, in its conception and dissemination, rather than seeing my role as one that contributes, interdependently with my team, to the solution and its implementation. I centered the white "fixing" instead of seeking to understand and listen. When I eventually sought to listen more, to take the time to understand the layers of the problem and the emotional wounds, rather than narrowly defining the problem, I began to see the burdens that I and others carried in perpetuating this problem. A more complex and shared understanding emerged. This was a collective trauma and it required an approach rooted in collective action and healing.

**Feel, Especially Feel into the Discomfort**

When we allow ourselves to feel into the outrage, the pain, the moral injuries, the guilt, the shame, and the discomfort of racism without drowning in it, we can bring our full humanity to the struggle of decentering whiteness and dismantling systems of white supremacy and the root causes of this pain. When I began to show vulnerability and expose that I felt both complicit and helpless, others felt more comfortable enough to share their own experiences, similar and different. What emerged was a collectively held tension, a reframing of our shared struggle and shared fates, that motivated us to take the risks necessary to redefine safety and transform this practice. No PowerPoint presentation, no matter how skilled, could have yielded this.

### Contextualize and Complicate

Restraints and seclusion took place within a context. Through collective critical inquiry, our team surfaced the contexts and larger structures of whiteness, of conflating safety with compliance, that increased intervention of seclusion rooms. We were able to acknowledge the lost legacies of safety practices that centered cultures of safety, including psychological safety. We began to adopt a prevention framework rather than an intervention framework. We began to address the work as collective rather than from a top-down mandate. We redefined safety as collectively held and not behaviorally managed. *We* keep each other safe—not systems nor quiet rooms. We began to measure safety by the strength of our relationships rather than by the surveillance and measures of harm.

### Center Metrics of Accountability, Not of Compliance to Whiteness

When we moved away from measuring safety by the reduction of harm (numbers of incidents to track in incident reports), we ended up feeling less afraid. We emphasized and measured more incidents of connection and playfulness as indicators of safety. Yes, a student may have kicked a rock too close to a staff on the way in the door, but he also just spent the night in his third foster home this year, woke up at 5 a.m. to take a two-hour bus ride in stop and go traffic, and likely has still not eaten when he arrives, sleepy, and kicking a stone that comes a little too close. Most metrics are solely focused on documenting noncompliance and risk. Examining whiteness in our metrics led to inquiry around what we are asking compliance to and whose risk we are assessing and mitigating. As we began measuring increases in connection, students requested opportunities to give out "kindness tickets" to one another. Upon reaching 1,000 tickets (collectively held), we celebrated by renting a bouncy house.

This process of weaving different metrics (e.g., kindness tickets, degree of playfulness) into our school culture improved our relational accountability with one another. It led to ideas of how we could center incidents of love and kindness, not just those of harm and risk. Students joined us in this process to reimagine how to measure safety by how loved students felt even during their hardest moments and by how much agency and personhood they felt even in moments of distress and dysregulation. Examining and decentering whiteness resulted in new accountability metrics that centered relationships more than fidelity to interventions.

### *Seeing and Challenging Structural Whiteness as a Liberatory Practice*

Seeing whiteness requires us to use a multidirectional lens to examine the internalized mechanics of white superiority that both advantage us, as white people, and distort and cut us off from our humanity. It demands seeing the structural engineering of whiteness, the cages of whiteness we trap others in, and the bars of whiteness that entrap us.

We will do this work imperfectly, and that we will fail often is a given. However, if we fail to *do* the work or fail to interrogate whiteness while we protest in the streets or hold tender truths offered in clinical practice, we rob ourselves of the opportunity for self-healing, for liberating ourselves from the anesthetizing and isolating artifacts of whiteness.

In *Me and White Supremacy*, Layla Saad (2020) warns that "systems do not change unless the people who uphold them change, and each person is responsible for upholding the system" (p. 209). Seeing whiteness, examining my internalized white superiority and the scars of dehumanization, is both a painful labor and a practice of unburdening from whiteness. This unburdening involves transforming my belief that my only worth is in my productivity or performance, being in a constant state of urgency and perfectionism, conditioning to suppress feelings and to devalue relationships and community, and extracting comfort from outside myself.

Though recent focus to racial equity training, plans, and audits in our mental health organizations has increased, we largely resist the deeper transformational work necessary to heal a mental health field where whiteness is a signifier for mental health and well-being. It is our responsibility and ethical duty as white clinicians to challenge whiteness and racialized re-traumatization in clinical care.

I deeply crave to live in a world where mental health care and systems extend all the resources we need for healing to all people and where the need for such resources is significantly diminished from current magnitude, rather than controlled through gatekeeping measures. I tell my five-year-old self that it's not the extra coupon books that makes her worthy, but her ability to see and hold her own worthiness with the innate worthiness of others. Looking in the funhouse mirror of whiteness is not fun, simple, nor a "first step" to any larger goal or deeper work. In my experience, examining and challenging whiteness, its conditions and conditioning, its harms and advantages, is more like the continuous Penrose staircase, steps that lead only to more, unending, steps. My experience shows me that, while this is not a linear path, it is the most durable path toward more liberatory and loving futures for all peoples, including white people, who carry both the positional power and the responsibility to challenge and transform white supremacy in mental health systems.

**JEN LELAND (SHE/HER/HERS), LMFT,** is a white, cisgender, queer woman who works as a licensed marriage and family therapist in California and serves as director of Trauma Transformed (www.traumatransformed.org) and clinical director for Ceremony Health. Her work strives to serve at the nexus of healing, justice, and public systems transformation. As someone who was partially raised in these systems while also structurally protected within them, she is committed to both the critical inquiry and the movement to reimagine how our systems and those who work within them can produce more stories of healing and liberation and fewer stories of harm and trauma.

## References

*Alcoholics anonymous: The story of how many thousands of men and women have recovered from alcoholism. (1976). Alcoholics Anonymous World Service.*

*Cole, T. (2012, March 21). The white-savior industrial complex.* The Atlantic. *https://www.theatlantic.com/international/archive/2012/03/the-white-savior-industrial-complex/254843/*

*Frankenberg, R. (1993).* White women, race matters: The social construction of whiteness. *University of Minnesota Press.*

*Hardy, K. V. (2020).* Critical relational factors for promoting and sustaining difficult conversations. *Eikenberg Institute for Relationships.*

*Lorde, A. (1984). The master's tools will never dismantle the master's house. In* Sister outsider: Essays and speeches *(pp. 110–114). Crossing Press.*

*Myers, B. E., II (2014).* "Drapetomania": Rebellion, defiance and free black insanity in the antebellum United States *[Doctoral dissertation, University of California, Los Angeles]. ProQuest.*

*Saad, L. (2018).* Me and white supremacy workbook. *Layla F. Saad.*

*Saad, L. (2020).* Me and white supremacy: How to recognise your privilege, combat racism and change the world. *Sourcebooks.*

*US Department of Education. (2012).* Restraint and seclusion: Resource document. *https://www2.ed.gov/policy/seclusion/index.html*

# SECTION VI

# ANTIRACISM AND ON BECOMING WHITE ANTIRACISTS

# CHAPTER 20

# Becoming an Antiracist Leader

## From the View of a Black Female Clinician and Consultant

MARY PENDER GREENE, LCSW-R, CGP

I'm a Black female therapist, executive coach, organizational consultant, and the President and CEO of a company that is committed to eliminating bias and structural racism in the workspace. I have supervised, taught, trained, and coached thousands of individuals and gained detailed knowledge of hundreds of organizations in my many years of practice—including tenure at three major mental health social service organizations, and years of private practice and organizational consultation.

Black, Indigenous, People of Color (BIPOC) often comprise more than half of the clients being serviced by our organizations, and yet, a 2019 study by Building Movement Project stated that "the percentage of people of color in the executive director/CEO role has remained under 20% for the last 15 years" (Kunreuther & Thomas-Breitfeld, 2020). Who better to articulate the depth, intensity, and perspective of diverse groups than a leader from a group who has lived the experience? This is not to say that other leaders cannot provide credible leadership. Rather, it is to suggest that knowledge based on lived experience in a culture creates the potential for bringing a unique perspective to leadership. Their presence also adds credibility to the organization and is extremely valuable to the community, the staff, and clients.

While some doors have been opened for BIPOC to attain senior level executive positions, those opportunities are in a predominantly White* leadership environment that too often celebrates a centrality of Whiteness. Despite the obvious need for and the unique contributions that BIPOC leaders can make to our organizations, why are there so few in leadership roles? One factor is that the mental model for leadership is a charismatic, heroic White male, which is deeply embedded in our collective mindset.

> Whereas White women frequently reference the "glass ceiling" as blocking their advancement up the career ladder, women of color often characterize the barriers they encounter as comprising a "concrete ceiling"—one that is denser and less easily shattered. The underpinnings of these barriers include stereotypes, visibility, and scrutiny; questioning of authority and credibility; lack of "fit" in the workplace; double outsider status; and exclusion from informal networks. (Catalyst, 2004, p. 12)

Though all leaders are vulnerable to criticisms and attacks, this tendency is exacerbated for BIPOC. Since BIPOC are underrepresented in leadership, they become much more visible and receive more scrutiny.

There is intense inspection under "the White gaze," the assumption that the observer is coming from a perspective of someone who identifies as White or the phenomenon in which BIPOC sometimes feel the need to consider the White observer's reaction (White Gaze, 2021). The White gaze can add pressure on BIPOC to assimilate into White institutional culture since they are evaluated by its norms. As a result, the credibility and authority of BIPOC leaders are constantly in dispute, which causes them to have to prove themselves endlessly. Receiving and internalizing intense criticism not only enhances this vulnerability, but also discourages these leaders from bringing their individuality and uniqueness to the role.

My work is guided by the principles of The People's Institute for Survival and Beyond (see Contact Information at end of chapter), who are recognized internationally for their Undoing Racism™ Workshop. If the comfortable

---

* Note: In the Racial Justice movement, the uppercase "W" is used in reference to White people.

red leather couch in my office could talk, it would tell personal stories of White-induced racial stress in the workspace. These tales include tears and fears where dreams and ambitions were murdered, confidence was slaughtered, dignity was brutally assaulted, and hope was crushed. In other words, unrestrained bias and structural racism operate almost like silent assassins, and the examples far exceed the pages allotted for this chapter.

Our organizations are being denied the benefits of the fresh perspectives and change that are so desperately needed in serving BIPOC communities. These issues form the basis of my work. As a therapist, a coach, and a consultant, I diligently offer validation and insights, help to develop strategies, feed spirits, and join in triumphant celebrations.

While workspace diversity is important, organizational culture is equally important, and often it is not hospitable to BIPOC in leadership roles. This is the reason so many women and BIPOC are overlooked, opt out of leadership paths, or simply leave after a few years. Many who leave claim publicly that it was for a better opportunity, but privately and on my couch, they admit to not feeling valued for who they were and to being denied the opportunity to fully contribute.

Unexamined and unimpeded bias and structural racism are a different way of placing a knee on the necks, voices, and contributions of BIPOC. This bias and racism destroy the uniqueness and nullifies the experience, inspiration, and vision that could be offered by Staff and Board Members of Color. Because the number of BIPOC in leadership positions is low, their influence in shaping organizational culture in mostly White-led workspaces is minimal, therefore bringing their full selves is extremely difficult at best, but more likely, unfeasible. The major reasons for the lack of influence of BIPOC leaders are deeply ingrained in White institutional culture. White culture causes organizations to proclaim that they want diversity and inclusion, yet what they really want is to see difference at the table but not hear or value the lived experience, contributions, or different approaches offered by BIPOC. The organization's failure to accept difference makes it extremely challenging for these BIPOC to be authentic, to thrive, or to influence organizational culture.

Therefore, the ultimate role of a leader on an antiracist institutional journey is to create an atmosphere of inclusiveness and belonging, which tends to produce an environment of collaboration. "Prohibition is not the only way to exclude" (McLachlin, 2003, para. 54). There are subtle, yet effective, methods in our midst that can cause BIPOC to be devalued. For instance, exclusion from work that matters, treating someone as though they are invisible when they're present, marginalizing their input, or requiring their contributions be cosigned by a White person (e.g., a point made by a woman or BIPOC is ignored or rejected, but when the same point is made by a White man, it's welcomed) (Pender Greene, 2017).

Belonging goes beyond the concepts of Diversity, Equity, and Inclusion (DEI) to a feeling of being fully accepted. Belongingness is "the sense of psychological and emotional well-being . . . that enables people to perform at their best" and to feel appreciated, respected, and motivated (Horizon Health Services, 2021, para. 7). People can contribute their unique views and ideas. Belongingness is also about representation. It is about being seen and seeing yourself reflected in leadership and decision-making roles. It's essential that Belonging be added as an integral part of DEI initiatives so that it becomes Diversity, Equity, Inclusion, and Belonging (DEIB).

> If we want people to fully show up, to bring their whole selves including their unarmored, whole hearts—so that we can innovate, solve problems, and serve people—we have to be vigilant about creating a culture in which people feel safe, seen, heard, and respected. (Brown, 2020, para. 1)

As an organizational consultant, I support executive leadership as my clients' antiracist journey begins, starting with leaders, managers, supervisors, and the board being clear and publicly acknowledging the organization's commitment to the antiracist journey. Since attitude change cannot be mandated, leaders often need much support in the form of executive coaching and consultation, coupled with the ability to have honest dialogue, in order to create and sustain an understanding that antiracist work is a messy process.

Blowback must be expected as some White leaders begin to take issue with the decision to place so much time and resources into antiracist work. Other White staff may feel neglected and unclear about their roles in the antiracist journey. They may be suspicious and fearful about the impact of antiracist work on their position, access, and power.

As an antiracist leader, one must set the tone for honest dialogue and embrace the need to acknowledge tensions. Conflict must be publicly recognized and resolved promptly and respectfully. The entire organization must be helped to increase its tolerance for discomfort and uncertainty.

As a consultant, one of my roles is to help leaders learn to listen deeply and to create brave spaces for differing views and concerns about issues of race, racism, and systemic change. A brave space provides an environment for difficult dialogue where participants are urged to speak authentically, be open to growth and lean into discomfort. It is important to explore how microaggressions and bias impact the workspace by helping leaders and their staff to engage in meaningful, courageous, and authentic conversations across differences in an atmosphere that is non-shaming, non-blameful, and nonjudgmental. Most importantly, I help leaders to ask and to face hard questions such as:

- Are Black, Indigenous, and People of Color thriving in our institution?
- Are there Black, Indigenous, and People of Color in decision-making positions?
- Is there congruence between those in decision-making positions and those being served?
- When there is a change in client demographics, are the decision makers actively seeking to be more closely aligned with and responsive to the new group?

## Barriers to Becoming and/or Transitioning to an Antiracist Organization

There are several predictable and recurring barriers that impede many organizations' growth and development toward becoming or transitioning into an antiracist organization. Here are a few of the common barriers:

### *"Check the Box" Mentality*

When an organization is dishonest about the racial makeup of the work environment and where it is with the race work, it attempts to take shortcuts rather than make meaningful and long-lasting changes. In other words, the organization has a "check the box" mentality:

- If they have a board of thirty that has one or two Members of Color
- If they have online diversity training
- If they have a chief diversity officer (extra points if that person is BIPOC, which also frees the rest of the organization from further accountability)
- If they have an all-White executive leadership team only because they have not found any BIPOC Leaders who are qualified and the right fit

Due to the lack of psychological safety, when only small numbers of BIPOC are in leadership roles, they cannot sufficiently influence organizational culture. Therefore, many White leaders are unaware of the true lived experience of BIPOC within their organization. As a result, they can check all the boxes and have the illusion of doing the antiracist work while issues of bias, White-body privilege, and structural racism all remain invisible, free of scrutiny, and unexamined.

*Favoritism*

In a particular presentation, Dr. Nancy DiTomaso (Cornell University, 2014) states that racial inequality in our organizations is driven by Whites' preferential treatment of people in their network. She goes on to point out that favoritism of Whites toward other Whites leads to unequal opportunities, resulting from group-based exchange of social and cultural capital.

Favoritism of Whites toward other Whites is often hidden, unconscious, and unacknowledged because many Whites hold the belief "I did it on my own" while pursuing group-based advantage. "The ultimate White privilege is the privilege not to be a racist and still benefit from racial inequality," says Dr. DiTomaso (Cornell University, 2014, min. 11:55).

*"Fit" (Cultural Similarities)*

"Fit" can be a code word for someone who reflects the dominant culture in body type, presentation style, and lived experience. In her research, sociologist Lauren Rivera (2012) found that fit often referred to cultural match, common hobbies, and shared alma maters (usually those where BIPOC are underrepresented), which were highly salient to employers and were often more valued than applicants' skills, potential, or ambitions.

Focus on fit within an all-White or predominantly White leadership team or board can cause BIPOC leaders to be excluded from leadership roles, thus creating a lack of congruence between those in decision-making positions and those being served.

*Pipeline Problem*

The pipeline problem is not a real problem, but a fallacy. You just must know where to look. If you want to find outstanding BIPOC leaders and board members, ask BIPOC leaders; they know where to find them. Also, sometimes, they are already within the reach and view of White organizational leaders; just learn to see, value, and develop them.

*Diverse Teams*

Working across differences is hard. Though working across differences triggers the expectation that there will be different ideas and perspectives and that it will produce better outcomes, there are pitfalls of having a diverse team. People don't necessarily like it. According to Katherine W. Phillips (NYU School of Law, 2019), it's harder to work with people who are different from you. This is due to several factors:

- Discomfort
- Rougher interactions
- Lack of trust
- Less cohesion
- More concerns about disrespect and other problems
- Complicated communication
- Greater perceived interpersonal conflict

When people work with others who are different from them, it changes how they work, which leads to better outcomes. Benefiting from a racially mixed team takes intentionality, tenacity, strong leadership, and diligent management. Doing the work is necessary to reap the rewards of a truly diverse team. Much thought, support, and cross-racial team-building is often needed, along with constant reminders about the organization's commitment to antiracist work. Leadership must consistently motivate, incentivize, and hold all staff accountable for them to embrace new ways of working together harmoniously through value-creating collaborative activities to meet the organization's antiracist goals.

### *Lack of Psychological Safety*

Originally coined by Dr. Amy Edmondson (1999), a professor at Harvard Business School, *psychological safety* refers to "a shared belief that the team is safe for interpersonal risk taking" (p. 354). There is a climate in which people feel free to express relevant thoughts and feelings without fear of being penalized. These risks can take many different forms, including:

- Speaking up in a meeting to share an opposing idea
- Admitting publicly that you made a mistake and sharing lessons learned in the process
- Disagreeing with your boss and proposing a different solution
- Speaking up on behalf of a teammate who is under attack
- Being authentic even though you're under pressure or stressed out

These decisions take courage because they require that you rely on your team members to grant you the benefit of the doubt. Lack of psychological safety prevents BIPOC from bringing their full selves and their full potential to the workspace. While all leaders are vulnerable to criticisms and attacks, this is exacerbated for BIPOC because they are underrepresented in leadership, thus they become much more visible and receive more scrutiny under the White gaze. This constant scrutiny often compels BIPOC leaders to conform to the status quo rather than offering their authentic and diverse viewpoint.

## Pockets of Staff Who Are Working Against an Antiracist Journey

Pockets of resistance by staff with positional power is the greatest threat to an organization's antiracist work. Everyone in the organization knows who they are, they hold the power to define what and who is good and valued, and yet they are tacitly permitted to opt out of the antiracist work even though they have the authority to limit the advancement and exposure of BIPOC talent. When these pockets of resistance are not held accountable, it allows for unchecked White-body privilege, bias, and structural racism, which is a different way of "taking a knee" on the voices and contributions of BIPOC. According to Dolly Chugh (Chugh & Bock, 2018) in her book, *The Person You Mean to Be: How Good People Fight Bias,* bias impacts:

- Who is hired
- Who is promoted
- Whose ideas are valued
- Whose potential is bet on
- Who is viewed as leadership material
- Whose emotional responses are reliable (p. 48)

In addition, bias impacts:

- Who is trusted, supported, rewarded
- Who is favored and given the benefit of the doubt when a mistake is made
- Who is oppressed by supervisory criticism and suspicion
- Who is burdened by conscious and unconscious racial biases, stereotypes, and judgments

When there is a pandemic of invisibility, the biases, White-body privileges, and White institutional culture remain unseen and thus free of examination, inspection, scrutiny, or evaluation. This murders the spirits, aspirations, and careers of BIPOC.

## Lydia's Story

Lydia is a hard-working, 36-year-old, Latinx social work administrative supervisor at a mental health agency in New York City that serves large numbers of BIPOC patients, many of whom are Spanish-speaking. She has been with the organization for six years. She works a second job because, as the first person in her family to go to college, she has crushing student debt and she helps her family back home in the Dominican Republic. Lydia came to me for therapy with a weary mind and a wounded heart, feeling frustrated, despondent, and depressed because she was overlooked for a promotion to director.

During our initial meeting, Lydia tearfully complained about microaggressions, microinequities, her racially toxic office environment, and discriminatory promotions for senior-level positions. Throughout our sessions, she describes that her White colleagues, who create the toxicity, are unaware that she feels helpless, muffled, lonely, and demoralized. Further, what's most difficult for Lydia is how oblivious they are to their access and opportunities. They are offered senior-level positions even when they are less-than-qualified. They don't have to be concerned about fit, a perpetual concern for Lydia and her BIPOC colleagues.

Lydia is an excellent therapist, supervisor, and administrator, and she believed that she had been performing well as the acting director for the prior six months. She felt very hopeful that she would be given the permanent position. She loved the organization and felt especially pleased to be working for an agency that serviced so many clients with whom she shared a common history, culture, and language. However, the greatest perk was that the job was only a few blocks from her home, and she knew many of the clients from the neighborhood. While she remained the only BIPOC in a leadership role, she was guardedly encouraged that the number of BIPOC clinicians in lower-level positions were increasing because of their diversity efforts.

As a result, Lydia was devastated and totally blindsided when Ellen, a 34-year-old White female from Connecticut, got the job as director, even though she had two less years of experience than Lydia. Ellen's previous role was similar to Lydia's at a smaller agency in Westchester County, NY. While Ellen had no prior experience with the culture of the clients nor knowledge of the community, she was personable, interviewed well, and exuded confidence. Ellen's father, a human resources executive, knew the agency's CEO. He referred Ellen as a sure fit for the position. Lydia was to orient Ellen to the job.

Therefore, Ellen entered her role without any feelings of benefiting from racial inequity. According to Dr. DiTomaso (Cornell University, 2014), when the focus is on *racists* and *discriminators,* it provides validity to Whites who profit from unfair advantage without having to have hostile feelings or discriminating against BIPOC. Since the processes of advantages is completely legal, routine, and accrues over one's career, it leads White people to believe that they did it on their own. There is no moral dilemma because they can benefit from White favoritism and good things that happen to them without doing bad things to BIPOC to gain these advantages.

Most White people get help throughout their careers, and personal/social connections are extremely helpful to this process. Since Lydia was the first person in her family to obtain a degree, her professional family network was limited. According to Dr. DiTomaso (Cornell University, 2014), "Many jobs are not on the market, but rather are hoarded for people in the same networks" (min. 52:50). Lydia experienced this when her new boss's social connections granted her access and the director position, even though Ellen was from outside of the organization and had less experience.

The advantages of access afforded by favoritism are accumulative, so receiving these rewards early in one's career can last a lifetime. The new role propelled Ellen's career beyond Lydia's, despite having less experience. Ellen believes that she did it on her own, even though she received group-based advantage. Despite having less experience than Lydia, she was likely given the benefit of the doubt due to her father's connection to the CEO. Ellen does not face any moral dilemma regarding racial inequality because from her perspective, she did not do anything bad to Lydia to gain advantage, she simply got help from her network and thus totally discounts the benefits of the group-based exchange of social and cultural capital.

Privilege is often invisible to those who have it and painfully obvious to those who don't. The Lydia/Ellen scenario follows Dr. DiTomaso's (Cornell University, 2014) findings that the "consequences of favoritism will accumulate over time" (min. 57:25–58:19) through opportunity hoarding. Since the benefits are likely to be subtle, invisible, and not publicly named nor commonly challenged, one of the major tasks of an antiracist leader is to pay close attention to the favoritism that Whites extend to other Whites throughout the organization. It pained Lydia deeply as leadership created a more forgiving and supportive work environment for Ellen and other White staff while denying her equal treatment.

Lydia's ambitious dream of becoming the organization's first BIPOC director was crushed because her beloved organization had publicly committed to diversity and inclusion but had failed to follow through again on their commitment. Therefore, yet another less experienced White person was allowed to advance their career because they were given the benefit of the doubt due to their White-body privilege and access.

Favoritism of Whites leads to unequal opportunity in hiring, promotion, and recognition. These micro-inequities diminish the value of and demoralize BIPOC staff.

> Micro-inequity is a theory regarding ways in which individuals are either singled out, overlooked, ignored, or otherwise discounted based on an unchangeable characteristic such as race or gender. Micro-inequities, micro-affirmations, and micro-advantages all fall within the broader category of micro-messaging. All represent the three ways we send subtle messages negatively or positively. Micro-inequities are subtle, often unconscious, messages that devalue, discourage, and impair workplace performance. They are conveyed through facial expressions, gestures, tone of voice, choice of words, nuance, and syntax. Repeated sending or receiving of micro-inequities can erode commitment and loyalty and have the cumulative effect of diminishing overall workforce performance. (Wikipedia, 2021, para. 1–2)

Lauren Rivera (2012) discusses culture as a vehicle of labor market sorting and provides a case study of hiring in elite professional service firms. Drawing from 120 interviews with employers as well as participant observation of a hiring committee, Rivera argues that hiring is more than just a process of skills sorting, but also a process of cultural matching between candidates, evaluators, and firms. According to the study, employers sought candidates who were not only competent but also culturally like themselves in terms of leisure pursuits, experiences, and self-presentation styles. Concerns about shared culture were highly meaningful to employers and often outweighed concerns about absolute productivity.

In seeking a candidate for the director job, Lydia was overlooked despite her performance in that very role, her knowledge of the director job, and her history with the organization simply because the CEO was focused on fit. According to Rivera (2020), "When you prioritize candidates you 'click with,' you run the risk of discriminating against candidates from different backgrounds" (para. 1). She also goes on to say that if the hiring manager is male, White, or wealthy, then a lack of diversity may be perpetuated in that organization. "What you're going to get is a copy of your existing employees. . . . In many instances, it is a form of discrimination" (para. 6).

As an antiracist leader, it is key to develop strategies for de-biasing your hiring process. The goal is to develop and support diverse hiring panels in practicing equity skills and interventions within job hiring and interviewing processes. This requires training to create a shared language, analyze situations, and develop skills so that the panel members can conduct job interviews with prospective candidates through an anti-oppressive/antiracist framework.

Dr. Ken Hardy (2008) offers tips to BIPOC on how they are expected to handle hidden race-related struggles that they will encounter in organizations that falsely claim to embrace diversity and on the invisible criteria that are required for their survival. While Dr. Hardy offers these tips in a "sardonic manner with a tinge of levity" (p. 468), they deeply speak to the issues facing BIPOC in predominantly White spaces.

> Smile! No matter how many racial slights or microaggressions you must endure, stay pleasant, smile, and remain mannerly and polite. Having a "bad" attitude can stifle your progress. Smile when you feel humiliated, when you feel misunderstood, when you feel the sting of discrimination. As a GEMM therapist, it is essential to maintain and exhibit a good, positive, GEMM-like attitude no matter what. Remember, there is no room in the field or in society for the inexplicably angry, belligerent, enraged person of color with an attitude problem. As a person of color, your attitude dictates your altitude! (Hardy, 2008, p. 464)

Lydia has student loans to pay and family to support, so she feels the need to orient her new boss and smile!

As you go forward toward antiracist leadership, you can do better! You must! We must!

## Sylvia's Story

Sylvia is a 46-year-old, Black director at a philanthropic organization. She sought my services as an executive coach because her credibility and authority were constantly in question, and she hopes to become CEO within the next year when Helen, her boss, retires.

She is constantly worried about mistakes that she fears will derail her goals. Since the organization has never had a BIPOC CEO, Sylvia is anxious, often works tirelessly, and sometimes focuses on minutiae to prove that she is the best candidate and deserves to be the next CEO.

Rosette and Livingston (2012) assert that deeply embedded in our society is the unconscious assumption that White men are typical and effective leaders.

> Since Black women are members of two marginalized groups (Black and female), they might experience greater discrimination, a "double jeopardy," compared to the discrimination faced by individuals that hold one marginalized identity (i.e., White women or Black men). In organizational settings, leaders are often judged based on the performance of the whole organization. Biases about race and gender could impact judgments of how much a leader is given credit for organizational success or judged harshly for organizational failure. (p. 1162)

According to Cheeks (2018),

> for black women, it's not just a pipeline issue. Once they are in the door, they need to feel supported in ways that are specific to being a woman of color. So that even if they are alone on their team, they will realize they're not alone at all. (para. 27)

Bias can have significant career consequences for Black women. Sesko and Biernat (2010) found that when a group of White people were shown random photos of different people, Black women's faces were least likely to be recalled out of a group of White men and White women. "Statements said by a black woman in a group discussion were also least likely to be correctly attributed compared to black men, White women, and White men" (Sesko & Biernat, 2010, p. 356). "Black women in leadership positions are also **more likely to be criticized or punished** [emphasis added] when making mistakes on the job" (Cheeks, 2018, para. 25).

Sylvia is concerned because while Helen and the board have given lip service to their DEIB work, she has often had to struggle for resources to support the initiative. Helen has even suggested that Sylvia gives too much importance to the DEIB work. As her role has expanded, Sylvia has spoken out more openly about the experiences of BIPOC staff and leaders, both within and outside the organization. She now inspires the BIPOC on her team and in her external network, providing helpful tips on more than facing and beating tough challenges, but for success.

Since Sylvia is of a darker hue, she is painfully aware that "the darker the hue, the thicker the concrete ceiling"; therefore, the criticism is fierce, and the barriers have been higher for her. "The good news is that even concrete can be cracked, but it won't be easy. Our biggest sledgehammer is making sure that women of color have a voice" (Babers, 2016, para. 8).

With the help of coaching and her Virtual Personal Board of Directors (VPBOD), Sylvia is strengthening her voice and is cautiously optimistic that the traditionally very White world of philanthropy will expand its focus on DEIB to make it truly inclusive, a significant tenet to true antiracist organizational change.

A VPBOD (Pender Greene, 2015) is a select group of trusted, respected advisors who can offer creative solutions to complex work challenges. It is your own "professional posse"— people that you turn to when you need to hear the unbiased truth in times of career changes, advancements, crises, transitions, difficult choices, and ethical dilemmas. Calling on this group takes some of the fear out of making difficult decisions and allows you to climb the learning curve faster than if you were on your own. The personal board is a virtual one; it does not meet, members do not know each other, there is no invitation to join, and the only common thread is you. It is also fluid; you will be seeking and adding new members all the time. You will call on subsets of them depending on which skill set you need to address a specific issue. Other members will fade without any need for dialogue.

According to Catalyst (2006), Women of Color face extensive barriers that include stereotypes, visibility, and scrutiny. Their authority and credibility are constantly questioned, and there's a lack of fit within their organization. They experience double outsider status, which leads to isolation and exclusion from informal networks. Catalyst (2006) likens the professional journey of Women of Color to a labyrinth, defined by Dictionary.com (2020) as an intricate, confusing combination of paths in which it is difficult to find one's way; or "a complicated or tortuous arrangement" (para. 3). Women of Color face negative race-based stereotypes consistently, which causes them to have to prove themselves incessantly.

During our coaching sessions, Sylvia often complains about having to work twice as hard, a circumstance her staff shares. She feels especially guilty for her staff as she and her department are under constant scrutiny. Although she has learned to live under an omnipresent White gaze, Sylvia has been successful in building a racially mixed team. Many of her younger BIPOC staff have complained about the challenges posed by increased visibility and vulnerability. Being one of very few BIPOC leaders working in White institutional spaces adds intense emotional labor and drains energy.

Sylvia laments how so few of her White coworkers have cross-racial relationships that support, mentor, or sponsor BIPOC staff. Unseen, unexamined, and unaddressed bias and microaggressions block both the BIPOC's and the organization's ability to benefit from a diverse team.

These subtle indignities are hard-hitting, a part of the daily lives of BIPOC staff, and are not confined to the workspace. Since microaggressions strike at the core of one's identity, an emotional response can be expected. Therefore, as an antiracist leader, it is crucial to first acknowledge that microaggressions exist and to become familiar with the various forms they take so that you can address the issues and hold offenders accountable.

These repeated invalidating insults can eventually begin to destroy the BIPOC's self-esteem and sense of competency. This battle can consume an enormous amount of energy. The recipients of these insults need validation, emotional support, and direction. Some BIPOC may be so well defended against race-related insults that they tune out the insult and do not explore their own affective experience, especially their vulnerability and pain.

At the other extreme, some may believe that all conflict is race related and tend to use racism as a reason for not exploring personal and professional areas that may need improvement. This could cause them to deny even substantive concerns that are raised and therefore find it difficult to grow and develop in their work. Some White supervisors may worry about appearing as racist, thus denying BIPOC vital feedback rather than confronting and dealing with difficult situations.

Since BIPOC leaders are deeply aware of these issues, they often take on the never ending, often invisible role of helping BIPOC staff to sort out what is legitimate race bias and what are professional development issues that may need improvement. They help BIPOC staff to focus on selecting realistic alternatives and strategies for coping using questions such as: *Is this a battle worth fighting? Is now the best time to focus on this issue? What do you hope for by choosing to fight this battle now? Does another matter require your attention?* In other words, BIPOC leaders often remind other BIPOC colleagues that some situations are unworthy of a response and that not every battle deserves to be fought.

While this work is "unpaid emotional labor," many BIPOC leaders see the value of this work to support the next generation of BIPOC leaders and as a part of their organization's solution to the pipeline issue. BIPOC in predominately White organizations often experience a unique type of stress—racial trauma—which ultimately affects their health and emotional well-being. Research on race-related stressors that can affect the mental health of socially disadvantaged racial and ethnic populations revealed that although discrimination is the most studied aspect of racism, racism can also affect mental health through structural/institutional mechanisms and racism that is deeply embedded in the larger culture (Williams, 2018).

According to the Coronary Artery Risk Development in Young Adults (CARDIA) study (Forrester et al., 2019), biological age is a construct that captures accelerated biological aging attributable to wear and tear from various exposures. The study reveals that Blacks show accelerated biological aging (weathering) compared to Whites; that psychosocial factors are associated with weathering; and that psychosocial factors are more strongly associated with weathering among Blacks. Data from the Study of Women's Health Across the Nation (SWAN) (Geronimus et al., 2010) estimates that at ages 49 to 55, Black women are biologically 7.5 years "older" than White women of the same chronological age.

As an antiracist leader, it is critical to be aware that the constant pressure of the White gaze, increased visibility, and the emotional labor that is often taken on by BIPOC leaders can lead to added racialized trauma, health issues, and burnout. It is vital to intentionally promote a culture of inclusion and belonging by encouraging the development of White co-conspirators, which plays an important role in the support and success of BIPOC leaders. Additionally, it addresses the pipeline issue for future leaders and lessens the emotional labor of BIPOC staff.

Since this is a slow process, it is important to strategically develop and retain young BIPOC millennials who are joining the workforce, boldly demanding more and refusing to constantly walk on eggshells. It is imperative to support and encourage them to actively expand their network, both inside and outside the organization, by developing a VPBOD.

Sylvia's scenario is far too common for BIPOC. She has been left out of informal networking gatherings due to a lack of connections and sponsors. Helen, her White boss, is nearing retirement and is not fond of networking. She does not see the value of networking and neglects to share opportunities that would be tremendously helpful to BIPOC leaders. Helen is oblivious to the lived experience of BIPOC in the foundation community and believes that Sylvia is too sensitive and hypervigilant regarding race-related issues. Many invitations never made it to Sylvia, which caused her to miss out on access to information and a seat at other industry tables. These critical connections are essential for success and are often a challenge for Women of Color due to their double outsider status. Most of my coaching time with Sylvia is devoted to handling her boss, strategizing for her promotion, managing her frustration, and planning to expand her VPBOD to give her greater support and networking access.

It is important to be aware that being the first BIPOC CEO is a stretch because many organizations, and the philanthropy sector as a whole, are profoundly steeped in White institutional values and norms. Women of

Color experience a more complicated leadership journey than their White counterparts due to White-body privilege and stereotyping. Sylvia, like other BIPOC leaders, witnesses infuriating injustice daily in White spaces within and outside of her organization. Yet, she, like other Black women, must manage the pent-up rage, burdened by the expectation that she'll be regarded by her colleagues as an "angry Black woman," destroying her chances for promotion. It's not yet the norm for a Black woman to be a CEO; additionally, society deems it unusual for BIPOC leaders to seek senior-level positions and demand competitive salaries. A confident and successful BIPOC leader continues to remain uncommon. Philanthropy and many other prestigious sectors tend to prefer individuals who have attended Ivy League schools. Like many other BIPOC leaders, Sylvia attended a city university. She is the most qualified of all the directors, is deeply committed to the organization, and is more than capable of doing the job. However, she and other BIPOC leaders combat the hurdles of White favoritism, bias, White-body privilege, and structural racism daily.

## Harold's Story

Harold is a 52-year-old Black executive director of a midsize social service agency that primarily serves BIPOC. He began his career there 25 years ago, right after college. He is married and has two young adult sons in college. Harold is deeply committed to the organization and feels especially grateful because they supported him during his pursuit of an MBA.

Michael, his recently retired White boss and former CEO, strongly advocated for Harold to replace him as the organization's first Black CEO. Harold was aware that there was some hesitancy to his selection from various board members because they had envisioned that the grandson of one of the founding board members would become the next CEO when Michael retired. Harold was extremely appreciative and delighted that he was chosen for the role and has worked tirelessly to strengthen his relationships with his board chair, Irving, the executive committee, and with the other board members. He has received "diligent oversight" since his appointment two years ago and is keenly aware that this type of surveillance sharply differs from the pattern of oversight that Michael received during his tenure.

Anxious and perplexed, Harold engaged my services as an organizational consultant when he began receiving strong pushback and suspicion regarding his robust DEIB initiative, especially when he began encouraging antiracist training for the board because the only BIPOC board member resigned after only three months, citing an overextended workload. Harold credits much of his success and upward mobility to the early and consistent support of Michael. Their cross-racial supervisory relationship was awkward and anxiety producing in the beginning. At Michael's suggestion, they began having walking supervisory meetings.

A walking meeting is a working meeting that takes place while walking (Clayton et al., 2015). It can be held outside or inside the building as an alternative to meeting in traditional offices or conference rooms. Walking meetings are often credited with developing and strengthening interpersonal relationships since walking side by side means the conversation is more peer-to-peer than when in an office and across a desk. They are credited with reducing hierarchical status distinctions and with helping to reduce tension during discussions.

Clayton et al. (2015) reported on walking meetings and the work of Ted Eytan, MD, the Medical Director of the Kaiser Permanente Center for Total Health and a vocal advocate, who believes that walking meetings produce positive benefits in the workplace by leading to "better employee engagement and breaking down barriers between supervisor and subordinate or between coworkers" (para. 7). He sees the bonding achieved through walking meetings as a micro version of the bonding that can be experienced when coworkers travel together on business trips. These meetings ultimately lead to an authentic relationship, where the discussions lead to conversations about race, racism, microaggressions, bias, and belongingness. Michael attended The People's Institute's Undoing Racism™ Workshop, read books, watched Ted Talks, joined other White leaders outside of his organization on their shared antiracist journey, and became fluent in his ability to see, discuss, and interrupt bias and structural racism.

Michael was vigilant in seeking out and eliminating bias throughout the organization. He made sure to publicly share credit with Harold, the deputy director, for organizational accomplishments whenever there was an opportunity, and often did so in meetings. He recognized that meetings were important to success and that many BIPOC leaders often struggle during meetings due to bias and favoritism of White bodies and White organizational norms. Therefore, he was conscious about making his meeting more inclusive to increase the psychological safety of his entire team.

Michael paid close attention at meetings to who was invited and who wasn't. Those who spoke up versus those who didn't. Voices that were valued versus voices that were ignored. Which voices were disruptive? Which voices were interrupted? Michael was aware of a pattern that certain individuals' ideas always received positive regard from the group while others' ideas were often disregarded until the same idea was presented by a valued team member and miraculously became an awesome contribution.

BIPOC are often reluctant to speak up at meetings especially because they are more likely to be interrupted than their White counterparts. This atmosphere diminishes or silences BIPOC voices and suppresses their contributions. People thrive at work when they can connect their ideas to those of the organization. When bias and favoritism for White bodies and voices remain invisible and go unexamined, uninterrupted, and unchecked, BIPOC cannot bring their whole selves to work.

It is your responsibility to recruit, develop, and set up your diverse team for success, which requires the practice of inclusion in meetings. This necessitates a meeting that is intentionally inclusive, where BIPOC contributors can have an equal impact. Since our eyes have not been trained to see this often-invisible epidemic of White favoritism, these subtle indignities can sink the careers of BIPOC staff. Therefore, we must first train our eyes to see and then actively and purposefully give BIPOC staff opportunities to offer their unique contributions by creating and modeling an inclusive meeting culture that is characterized by emotional safety, open communication, and a sense of belonging. While there is a pandemic of invisibility, we see what we look for; the goal is to speak out against inequities and create meeting spaces where there is zero tolerance for racist or oppressive behavior, and where everyone is held accountable.

According to an article by Heath and Wensil (2019), "Most organizations have already put a stake in the ground on diversity in hiring practices and creating diverse teams. The same needs to happen for inclusion—we need to insist that it is the standard in meetings and beyond" (p. 3). Leaders should begin with themselves:

- Clearly define inclusion.
- Communicate the definition of inclusion in meetings with clarity and transparency.
- Model inclusive behavior and decisions for staff.
- Hold teams accountable for being consistently committed to inclusion.

Michael was always conscious about including BIPOC staff, and he learned that looking and listening are essential to antiracist leadership. If you can't truly see BIPOC, you can't successfully lead or develop them. It's important to pay close attention to the organizational dynamics, the personal relationships, and how people interact with each other.

Michael and Harold had successfully built a diverse team. Harold is tenacious and diligent about supporting his racially mixed team, and the organization is reaping the benefits of their collaborative work and his leadership. Additionally, their vigorous DEIB initiative is moving toward their antiracist goals. Harold enjoys the respect of his team, even though he is not surprised that there remain a limited number of complaints about "how Michael used to do it." However, he was confused and surprised by the responses from his board since Michael's retirement, because as the deputy director, his interactions with Irving and the board had been limited, and he had experienced them as cordial.

Harold is acutely aware that his board, like most others, exists within a larger culture that promotes, protects, and supports White dominant culture. He also knows that White norms of wealth, similar education, and experience influence the selection of board candidates, board governance, and how the board itself operates—all of which cause them to struggle to identify, include, and retain diverse voices and to create an environment that supports these goals. As a result, there has been extreme pushback about the need for any discussion regarding antiracist training for the board.

Yes, Harold knows that racism is forever present, but he is hopeful that his successful long history with the agency, his hard work, and his dedication will count for something. He works tirelessly seven days a week, witnesses much unexamined bias from his board chair, and swallows many indignities. In addition to his long hours, Harold is also concerned about his two sons, who are both attending predominately White Ivy League schools. While they are both wonderful young men, he and his wife are always concerned about their well-being in mostly White spaces. Following the brutal murder of George Floyd, Harold became preoccupied with the safety of his sons.

According to DeSilver et al. (2020), most Black and White Americans say Black people are treated less fairly than Whites in dealings with the police and by the criminal justice system. DeSilver et al. (2020) state that a 2019 Pew Research Center survey reported that 84% of Black adults noted that, in dealing with police, Blacks are generally treated less fairly than Whites; 63% of Whites said the same. Similarly, 87% of Blacks and 61% of Whites said the US criminal justice system treats Black people less fairly.

Harold was also becoming concerned about his health, because his own father died at his desk at age 55. Working under the constant White gaze of the board and with Irving's lack of trust has added additional racialized trauma. Harold has high blood pressure and is prediabetic. He is painfully aware of how the life expectancy of Black men is far below average while the rates of those dying from diabetes, heart disease, cancer, and COVID-19 are astronomical.

Much of the research strongly links these deaths, and poor physical and mental health outcomes in general, to racism. According to Assari (2020), for Black men in the United States, "racism is a daily experience that harms their health and leads to chronic disease and poor health" (para. 4). About 66% of Blacks report high levels of day-to-day racial discrimination.

There are also blocked opportunities for Black men and other types of discrimination that are less frequent but very consequential. Combined, these discriminatory experiences make living harder and the life span shorter for Black men. While discrimination is known to be a risk factor for premature death, heart disease, depression, and suicide, we know that Black men experience discrimination more frequently than other groups, including Black women.

These discriminatory encounters marginalize Black men in US society and harm their health. Only a small proportion of Black men successfully climb the social ladder. And when they do, society discriminates against them more, which puts them at high risk of depression and depressive symptoms.

Although Black men and Black women are both affected by racism and bias, discrimination is more consequential for Black men. And this is partially because anti-Black bias is higher in the most socially powerful and privileged group in the United States: White men (Assari, 2018, para. 19).

Appointing and accepting Harold as the new CEO were especially challenging for Irving and some of the long-term board members because they firmly believed that Jason, the grandson of one of the founders, was the natural replacement for Michael because of his family connection and the years of support and generous donations the family gave to the agency. Harold was privately informed by several board members that Irving was secretly disappointed that Harold was not more grateful for his position as deputy director and that Michael had pushed hard for Harold's appointment to CEO, citing his credentials, long successful history at the organization, and value to the community—more than 80% of the clients were from Communities of Color.

While Irving halfheartedly consented, he strongly believed that Harold was fine as the deputy director but not quite the "right image" to best represent the organization as the CEO. Despite the obvious need and research confirming the value that diversity and inclusion can add to our organizations, a compelling, valiant, White male leader remains in our collective mindset. Change is hard for everyone, but especially hard for Irving and many of the board members. Being a Black man, Harold wasn't quite the right fit in their minds, which translates into the unexamined and unchecked biases, stereotyping, microaggressions, and distrust that impact Harold's racial trauma, sense of value, confidence, and contribution; even though he is performing well in his role, it takes a great personal toll.

As an antiracist leader, it is imperative that you are aware that unquestioned White organizational norms promote decision makers, leaders, and board members with no connection to the communities they serve. Because CEOs are most often chosen by boards, bias, preference, and favoritism for White leaders greatly impact the selection. These predominately White governing officers often ignore or underestimate the value and experience of BIPOC leaders who join their board. They are oblivious of the fact that, while a board needs members with wealth and financial-driven expertise, there is an equal need for members with mission-related competence and expertise.

These members with lived experience are an enormous value. They speak with the authority and proof of authentic experience and connections with the community. Since they don't know what they don't know, Irving and the board are offended by the suggestion of antiracist training because they view themselves as caring and generous, the product of generations of philanthropists. Therefore, they see the request as a personal affront.

Most of us have what Aquino and Reed (2003) call a central *moral identity,* which is a measure of whether one cares about being a good person, not whether one is a good person. Their research reveals that most of us want to feel like good people. This is an identity we claim and want granted.

Psychologist Dolly Chugh (2018) states that

> even when we fall short, our reflex is to claim an identity as a good person. Evidence to the contrary is a self-threat. It is difficult to overstate just how quickly and seamlessly we deal with self-threats. Our bodies are built to fight off bacteria and our minds are built to fight off self-threat. Through it all, we cling to an illusion of being a perfectly ethical and unbiased person and to the idea that such a "good person" can exist. This illusion is problematic. (para. 30)

Chugh (as quoted in Forsey, 2019) suggests trying our best to be *good-ish* and "let go of being a good person and embrace being a good-ish person. Good-ish people actively look for their blind spots and mistakes. So, if someone helps us notice a blind spot, it is actually doing us a favor" (para. 32). "Our need for affirmation overrides our genuine desire to be a good colleague, friend, and ally" (Chugh, 2018, para. 19). We value boosts to our self-esteem, like compliments, even more than sex and food. Chugh (2018) goes on to say that

> we all fall into this pattern. We fish for affirmation. We center our needs, nudging away the needs of others. We seek what activists call "cookies," acknowledgments of our good intentions, even when the impact is costly to the cookie giver. (para. 20)

One could assume that Irving and the board members are fighting off self-threat to claim their identity as good people. Pockets of resistance with positional power are the greatest threat to an organization's antiracist work. Since Irving and the board have the authority to define what and who is good and valued, they can suppress Harold's professional development and damage his career despite his successful job performance and his value to the community. Their treatment of Harold illustrates unchecked White-body privilege, bias, lack of appreciation of mission-related expertise, and structural racism, which often persist when predominantly White boards maintain control and oversight of organizations serving Communities of Color.

Board diversity and board culture require awareness, effort, and tenacity. Change beyond a token effort at increasing diversity includes conducting a board assessment and developing antiracist strategies for board structure, recruitment, retention, education, training, and board culture development.

## What White Leaders Need to Know and Do to Promote Organizational Change

### *Train Your Eyes to See*

White leaders' eyes must be trained to see White institutional culture and the types of subtle bias that can impede performance and success as well as reduce the morale, motivation, and spirits of BIPOC. You see what you look for! The eyes of most White leaders have not been trained to see, name, examine, or evaluate White favoritism or White-body privilege and how it impacts the aspirations and careers of BIPOC.

### *Hold Offenders Accountable*

It is the antiracist leader's role to boldly state and ensure that antiracist work is not elective. To become an antiracist organization, it is mandatory to include every single person working within your organization—leadership, *all* full- and part-time staff, students, board members, independent contractors, volunteers, and anyone else who is affiliated with your institution.

Staff with positional power who resist the antiracist goals and mission especially must be held accountable. It is important that leaders conduct private meetings with offenders and clearly state their unwavering commitment to the organization's antiracist journey and the importance of the offender's buy-in. However, if they continue to resist, leaders must hold them privately and publicly accountable. When certain staff are tacitly allowed to opt out of the antiracist work, it is another form of favoritism. A leader's silence will be viewed as a lack of genuine dedication to the antiracist mission. This inaction is the number one threat to an organization's antiracist mission because it causes people, both within and outside of the organization, to distrust the commitment of leadership.

Both "will and skill" (Hardy, 2017, para. 11) are needed to be an antiracist leader. Therefore, you may need coaching or other support to hold people accountable. Certain team members may be unfairly advantaged, and others disadvantaged, due to conscious and unconscious judgments, racial biases, and preconceptions from people who can opt out, as they often determine which voices are denied, silenced, and muffled or nurtured, encouraged, and elevated. This frequently leads to the lack of support and development of BIPOC.

Repeated microaggressions, subtle insults, witnessing White favoritism, and feeling unvalued can consume an enormous amount of energy. The amount of time and energy that BIPOC are forced to spend on addressing these issues, fighting for job survival, and proving themselves repeatedly causes racial trauma, which kills their aspirations and their ability to bring their best selves to their roles and to the organization. All of this leads to less-than-optimal success and retention, to burnout, and to low morale. Supervisory and all leadership evaluations should stress the ability to recruit, develop, and maintain a diverse team. Supervisory sessions must include consistent conversations about the status of cross-racial relationships.

Take a bold step: request walking meetings with select BIPOC to learn about their experience at the organization, and ask if their BIPOC colleagues are thriving. You must be patient with this process because it will take time to build trust in these relationships. You can also track the hiring, retention, and promotions of BIPOC staff and check for departmental or supervisory patterns regarding turnover or complaints. Think outside the box. You must have no tolerance (nada, nil, zilch, zero!) for racist or oppressive behavior from anyone in the organization. Holding everyone accountable is key to the success of your antiracist initiative.

*Expand Your Network*

Develop authentic cross-racial relationships. If you have BIPOC in your life and race is not a part of the conversation, the relationship is shallow and inauthentic. Creating a diverse leadership team and board is directly connected to the diversity of your network. It is important to expand your network to include BIPOC. Remaining in a silo of White voices limits your ability to meet BIPOC and to have meaningful cross-racial relationships.

Purposefully interact with BIPOC professionals beyond the workspace. You must consciously identify and reach out to people who are of interest to you to expand your network. Join networks and attend events where you are in the minority. On social media, follow and connect with BIPOC while deliberately seeking to develop cross-racial relationships. When you interact regularly with BIPOC beyond your work life, it will expand your worldview, help you to understand different perspectives, and enable you to begin to truly see, understand, and value BIPOC. Developing these cross-racial relationships will take commitment, time for trust to build, and consistency.

Keep in mind that BIPOC usually suppress their authentic thoughts and feelings to survive in White spaces. Don't get turned off or give up; anticipate discomfort; avoid being the tone police; be prepared to stay present, deeply listen, and hear what most BIPOC hold back from White people. Keep in mind that growth begins where comfort ends! Developing authentic cross-racial relationships is challenging because of the initial lack of trust and familiarity with the process from all parties. While a diverse workforce can be created through deliberate hiring practices, when BIPOC are hired, often they do not feel a sense of belonging because of their lack of authentic relationships within the organization. Also, if BIPOC do not see anyone who looks like them in leadership roles, it is harder for them to feel a sense of trust or belonging.

*Be Honest*

As a developing antiracist leader, it is important to set the tone from the top by being honest about where you are as an organization. Don't pretend that you have a diverse leadership team or board by adding one or two BIPOC (although a good start), as it leads to the illusion that the diversity issue is solved and lessens the urgency of the antiracist work. Due to deeply ingrained White institutional culture, small numbers of BIPOC leaders have very little influence in shaping organizational culture in mostly White-led workspaces because bringing their full selves is at best extremely challenging to do, and more likely impossible.

Be mindful that assigning all race-related matters to the one or two BIPOC board/leadership team members frees the rest of the team from the accountability of antiracist work. In addition, this saddles these members with the responsibility of addressing the organization's unwavering systemic racial and bias issues and increases their racial emotional labor. Since these roles are often given to those without authority, resources, or extra compensation, it signals to constituents both within and outside the organization of the roles and value of BIPOC. The success of your initiative lies in holding yourself and the entire organization accountable for the antiracist mission, learning to see the value of each team member, and eliminating barriers to the honest and unique contribution of BIPOC staff. You must become racially literate to be able to see, discuss, and interrupt bias and structural racism.

## Resources to Increase Racial Literacy

Here are some suggested resources to help you increase your racial literacy:

*Take: The Undoing Racism™ Workshop*

The Undoing Racism™ Workshop is a unique two-and-a-half-day workshop offered by The People's Institute for Survival and Beyond, a national, multiracial, antiracist network from New Orleans, dedicated to ending racism and other forms of institutional oppression. Now in its 40th year, the Institute has provided training, consultation, and leadership development to hundreds of thousands of people in organizations nationally and internationally. (It changed my life and my practice.)

The People's Institute for Survival and Beyond—www.pisab.org | 504.301.9292

*Attend: What White People Can Do About Racism (Workshop Series)*

The Center for the Study of White American Culture (CSWAC) – contact@euroamerican.org | 908.245.4972

*Take: Specialized Training in Anti-Racist Work for White People and White Helping Professionals*

Irene Greene, MSED Coaching, Counseling, and Consultation—www.irenegreene.com | irene@irenegreene.com | 612.874.6442

*Join: The Undoing Racism™ Executive Collective Meeting*

This group is designed for people in senior leadership roles in their organizations, particularly executive directors and their senior leadership teams, who have substantial decision-making authority and are invested in nurturing the organizations they lead to become more equitable, just, and antiracist institutions. The Executive Collective offers the opportunity to learn from speakers, to obtain resources, and to gather with peers to grapple collectively and honestly with the challenges leaders encounter as well as to build strategies and support for overcoming those challenges in your personal and organizational antiracist journey. Others are also welcome.

First Monday of Every Month, 9am–11am | Zoom Meeting (No Cost)

To be added to email list, contact: mpgconsultingnyc@gmail.com | 212.245.2510

*Read:* The Person You Mean to Be: How Good People Fight Bias *(Chugh & Bock, 2018)*

The antiracist journey requires a baseline of knowledge that none of us received, regardless of the type or level of education or how good or kind we are as people. Therefore, personally investing time, resources, and antiracist education is the only way to become an antiracist leader. Racial inequities are so deeply baked into our systems that the journey is never ending. We must be prepared to work on these issues forever. There is no such thing as done! The work is ETERNAL, but we can do it together!

**MARY PENDER GREENE, LCSW-R, CGP,** is the President & CEO of MPG Consulting (MPGC), a NYC-based company committed to eliminating bias and structural racism in the workspace. She is a career/executive coach, consultant, trainer, and psychotherapist. Mary is recognized by her peers for her novel ideas on leadership and antiracist organizational change.

She supports the growth of equity-fluent leaders in their pursuit of creating an inclusive, fair, and respectful work environment that values all individuals and embraces difference—with the goal of removing barriers to success. Through coaching and leadership development, she also works with senior leaders in enhancing their antiracist/anti-oppressive leadership style.

MPGC's multiracial diverse team has significant experience in providing antiracist capacity building with justice and dignity. MPGC understands the constructs and intersections of race and racism with gender (including gender fluidity), LGBTQIA+, class, religious (including anti-Semitism and Islamophobia), intellectual, emotional, and physical bias, as well as other systemic forms of oppression based on social identity.

Publications:

- *Strategies for Deconstructing Racism in the Health and Human Services*
- *Racism and Racial Identity*

## References

*Aquino, K., & Reed, A. (2003). The self-importance moral identity.* Journal of Personality and Social Psychology, 83*(6), 1423–1440. https://doi.org/10.1037/0022-3514.83.6.1423*

*Assari, S. (2018, November 15).* How anti-black bias in White men hurts black men's health. *The conversation. https://theconversation.com/how-anti-black-bias-in-White-men-hurts-black-mens-health-99005*

*Assari, S. (2020, July 2).* This is the toll that everyday racism takes on black men in America. *World economic forum. https://www.weforum.org/agenda/2020/07/george-floyd-racism-opportunities-life-expectancy/*

*Babers, J. (2016, April 19).* For women of color, the glass ceiling is actually made of concrete. *Aspen Institute. https://www.aspeninstitute.org/blog-posts/for-women-of-color-the-glass-ceiling-is-actually-made-of-concrete/*

*Brown, B. (2020, September 29).* If we want people to fully show up and to bring their whole selves including their unarmored, whole hearts so *[Tweet]. Twitter. https://twitter.com/brenebrown/status/1311061975393337345*

*Catalyst. (2004).* Advancing African-American women in the workplace: What managers need to know. *https://www.catalyst.org/wp-content/uploads/2019/01/Advancing_African_American_Women_in_the_Workplace_What_Managers_Need_to_Know.pdf*

*Catalyst. (2006, May 31). Report: Connections that count: The informal networks of women of color in the United States. https://www.catalyst.org/research/connections-that-count-the-informal-networks-of-women-of-color-in-the-united-states/*

*Cheeks, M. (2018, March 26).* How black women describe navigating race and gender in the workplace. *Harvard Business Review. https://hbr.org/2018/03/how-black-women-describe-navigating-race-and-gender-in-the-workplace*

*Chugh, D. (2018, November 5).* Being a "good" person is overrated. "Good-ish" is much better. *Next big idea club. https://nextbigideaclub.com/magazine/good-person-overrated-good-ish-much-better/19435/*

*Chugh, D., & Bock, L. (2018).* The person you mean to be: How good people fight bias. *HarperCollins.*

*Clayton, R., Thomas, C., and Smothers, J. (2015, August 5).* How to do walking meetings right. *Harvard Business Review. https://hbr.org/2015/08/how-to-do-walking-meetings-right*

*Cornell University. (2014, March 20).* The American non-dilemma: Racial inequality without racism *[Video]. YouTube. https://www.youtube.com/watch?v=U_NeqTjz13Q*

*DeSilver, D., Lipka, M., & Fahmy, D. (2020, June 3).* 10 things we know about race and policing in the US. *Pew Research Center. https://www.pewresearch.org/fact-tank/2020/06/03/10-things-we-know-about-race-and-policing-in-the-u-s/*

*Dictionary.com, LLC. (2020).* Labyrinth. *Retrieved on November 11, 2020 from https://www.dictionary.com/browse/labyrinth*

*Edmondson, A. (1999). Psychological safety and learning behavior in work teams.* Administrative Science Quarterly, 44*(2), 350–383. https://doi.org/10.2307/2666999*

*Forrester, S., Jacobs, D., Zmora, R., Schreiner, P., Roger, V., & Kiefe, C. I. (2019). Racial differences in weathering and its associations with psychosocial stress: The CARDIA study.* SSM - Population Health, 7, *1–8. https://doi.org/10.1016/j.ssmph.2018.11.003*

*Forsey, C. (2019, April 11).* How being 'good-ish' can make you a better leader. *Hubspot. https://blog.hubspot.com/marketing/how-being-good-ish-can-make-you-a-better-leader*

*Geronimus, A. T., Hicken, M. T., Pearson, J. A., Seashols, S. J., Brown, K. L., & Cruz, T. D. (2010). Do US black women experience stress-related accelerated biological aging?* Human Nature, 21*(1), 19–38. https://doi.org/10.1007/s12110-010-9078-0*

*Hardy, K. V. (2008). On becoming a GEMM therapist. In M. McGoldrick & K. V. Hardy (Eds.),* Re-visioning family therapy: Race, culture, and gender in clinical practice *(2nd ed., pp. 461–468). Guilford Press.*

*Hardy, K. V. (2017, January/February).* Race matters: How far have we come? Ken Hardy weighs in. *Psychotherapy Networker. https://www.psychotherapynetworker.org/blog/details/1114/race-matters*

*Heath, K., & Wensil, B. F. (2019, September 6).* To build an inclusive culture, start with inclusive meetings. *Harvard Business Review. https://hbr.org/2019/09/to-build-an-inclusive-culture-start-with-inclusive-meetings*

*Horizon Health Services. (2021, March 31).* Horizon's stronger together action plan. *https://www.horizon-health.org/blog/2021/03/horizons-stronger-together-action-plan/*

*Kunreuther, F., & Thomas-Breitfeld, S. (2020). Race to lead revisited: Obstacles and opportunities in addressing the nonprofit racial leadership gap. Race to lead. https://racetolead.org/race-to-lead-revisited/*

*McLachlin, Beverley. (2003, March 7). The civilization of difference. LaFontaine-Baldwin Symposium [Symposium remarks]. Halifax, Nova Scotia, Canada. https://www.scc-csc.ca/judges-juges/spe-dis/bm-2003-03-07-eng.aspx*

*Micro-inequity. (2021, June 3). In Wikipedia. https://en.wikipedia.org/wiki/Micro-inequity*

*North, A. (2010). "Bias Effects." Performance Appraisal. http://www.performance-appraisal.com/bias.htm*

*NYU School of Law. (2019, November 18).* Katherine W. Phillips on understanding the value of diversity *[Video]. YouTube. https://www.youtube.com/watch?v=gHFwoBQB5i4*

*Pender Greene, M. (Summer 2020). Becoming an Anti-Racist Organization: An Anti-Racist Model for Organizational Change.* Summer Edition of Currents- National Association of Social Workers (NASW-NYC). *https://cdn.ymaws.com/www.naswnyc.org/resource/resmgr/currents/2020/MPG_Full_Article_-_Summer202.pdf*

*Pender Greene, M. (2015).* Creative mentorship and career-building strategies: How to build your virtual personal board of directors. *Oxford University Press.*

*Pender Greene, M. (2017, October 1). Vulnerable populations: People of color in leadership roles. Behavioral health news. https://behavioralhealthnews.org/vulnerable-populations-people-of-color-in-leadership-roles-2/*

*Race, Racism, and Black Men's Health. Men's Health. Men's Health. Accessed July 22, 2021. https://www.menshealth.com/racism-black-mens-health/.*

*Rivera, L. A. (2012). Hiring as cultural matching: The case of elite professional service firms.* American Sociological Review, *77(6), 999–1022. https://doi.org/10.1177/0003122412463213*

*Rivera, L. A. (2020, August 4).* Stop hiring for "cultural fit." *KelloggInsight. https://insight.kellogg.northwestern.edu/article/cultural-fit-discrimination*

*Rosette, A. S., & Livingston, R. W. (2012). Failure is not an option for black women: Effects of organizational performance on leaders with single versus dual-subordinate identities.* Journal of Experimental Social Psychology, 48*(5), 1162–1167. https://doi.org/10.1016/j.jesp.2012.05.002*

*Sesko, A. K., & Biernat, M. (2010). Prototypes of race and gender: The invisibility of black women.* Journal of Social Psychology, 46*(2), 356–360. https://doi.org/10.1016/j.jesp.2009.10.016*

*White gaze. (2021, July 6). In Wikipedia. https://en.wikipedia.org/wiki/White_gaze*

*Williams, D. R. (2018). Stress and the mental health of populations of color: Advancing our*

*understanding of race-related stressors*. Journal of Health and Social Behavior, 59*(4)*, *466–485. https://doi.org/10.1177/0022146518814251*
*Yuan, K. (2020, June 16)*. Working while black: Stories from black corporate America. *Fortune. https://fortune.com/longform/working-while-black-in-corporate-america-racism-microaggressions-stories//*

## CHAPTER 21

# How I Was Taught "Unseeing"[1] to Internalize White Supremacy

## Understanding and Undoing, a Personal Narrative

HINDA WINAWER, MSW, LCSW

To be white was to be forced to digest a delusion called white supremacy.

—JAMES BALDWIN (1998A, P. 788), DARK DAYS

I was not raised by my family alone. I was raised by my country. I was taught to unsee racism around me. My own white racial identity was invisible to me. As part of this learning process, I unconsciously also learned to value whiteness. In other words, my internalization of white supremacy was an ongoing insidious and elusive process that was not cognitively or emotionally *visible* until later in life. As a child, I put my hand on my heart every weekday and pledged "liberty and justice for all." I had to learn on my own about the inaccessibility of justice for "all." The learning process has been both unconscious and deliberate, complex and generally flawed. Undoing racism, for me, is an ongoing undertaking, characterized alternatively or simultaneously by guilt, ignorance, insensitivity, complicity, credentialing myself as the "good white" (DiAngelo, 2018), insecurity, humility, accountability, and gratitude. These experiences will be illustrated in vignettes and then reflected upon throughout this narrative.

## Defining Terms as a Framework for Self-Examination

As this essay is personal, it seems essential to examine certain concepts in terms of how they apply to my self-examination.

### *White Supremacy*

Discourses about racism in the United States can be misleading. The phrase "white supremacy" evokes images of rifle-toting burly white men or of other terrorists, including abusive police officers or politicians who utter veiled or blatant violent racist rhetoric. But violence alone does not sustain white supremacy. Nonviolent systemic white supremacy can legitimize racist violence. We need a "grammar," or an approach to language, therefore, that contextually structures cognition to help us deconstruct the meaning of commonly used language (Bonilla-Silva, 2012, p. 174). We must widen the historical lens to fully examine white supremacy to see that it is the organizing social, political, and financial paradigm on which this country was founded and is, today, maintained by people in power (DiAngelo, 2018; Oluo, 2019; Wilkerson, 2020; Billings, 2016). Therefore, discourse that limits attributing white supremacy solely to terrorists is complicit in maintaining its hegemony and its invisibility in virtually all aspects of US life (Newkirk, 2017). The collective unconscious or conscious collusion to keep white supremacy invisible renders it difficult to challenge. We cannot fight or cure what we are rigorously taught not to see. Unsurprisingly, many white people do not own our unintentional acts of racism (Winawer, 2017; DiAngelo, 2018; Kliman et al., 2019). In the 1990s, for example, I was a member of a racially diverse committee of community members that addressed racial profiling in Princeton, New Jersey. The New Jersey Office of Bias Crime began offering free "undoing racism" workshops. Only one other white person and I from among the members of the community group attended. Other whites on that committee, who were self-identified as liberals, didn't see a need to attend the workshop. They claimed that because they had marched during the Civil Rights movement, such a workshop was not necessary for them. Their denial of a need to examine their possible racism illustrates the power and invisibility of white supremacy in the United States. This nation's systemic racism is comparable to the caste system in India; however, hierarchy in the United States is designated by skin color. Nonwhites, especially African Americans, and also Latinx and Native Americans, are relegated to a lower rank in society—a society that is structured to maintain an order to assure the stronghold on power and privilege of the dominant group: whites (Wilkerson, 2020).

After attending that undoing racism workshop I began to unconsciously consider myself a "good white." That self-perception was well-intended, but naïve; I needed to do more personal work. Being the good white is for me a complex phenomenon that I must subject to examination, lest it seduce me into claiming it as a complacent illusionary status that can impede the work of antiracism.

Language that references discrimination, microaggressions, implicit bias, and other similar descriptions of racist acts is not useful for me; embracing *them* as the problem to be addressed distracts from addressing the power of white supremacy. The more we understand that race was invented by racism (Coates, 2015), the more we see the intentionality of white supremacy. Moreover, race is not merely a social construct; it is a power construct (Kendi, 2019) through which the advantages of structural racism cannot endure in an equitable society. Overcoming this power requires persistent effort.

### *Thoughts About Being an Ally*

I am honored that Colleagues and Friends of Color and whites committed to antiracism generously refer to me as an ally. Alliance connotes mutuality and solidarity. Mutuality is relevant because whites participating in a racist society are affected by an oppressive system that poisons all of us (Baldwin, 1998b; King, 1963). Of course, the consequences for whites are unequivocally never comparable to the bodily, social, and economic assaults on African Americans, Native Americans, Latinx, and others.

However, I question the appropriateness of the title "ally" because it can imply reciprocal responsibility. People of Color are not accountable for my well-being. Other suggested titles have been *coconspirator* (Hackman, 2015; Love, 2019) or *accomplices*, which are more activism-related words (Powell & Kelly, 2017). If I am truly in solidarity, it is essential that I review and assess my thoughts and actions with a rigor commensurate with the power of racism on my thinking and being. Therefore, "being an antiracist requires persistent self-awareness, constant self-criticism, and regular self-examination" (Kendi, 2019, p. 22). I protest for Black Lives Matter. But I cannot delude myself. I do not put myself at risk as abolitionists did for the Underground Railroad (Love, 2019), nor as those in my generation did during Freedom Summer, when Chaney, Goodman, and Schwerner were murdered. Therefore, "antiracist/coconspirator" as an identity may be a possible designation for me, albeit limited by the degree of risk to my personal safety. An ideal self-designated categorization is illusive, as will be discussed later. My internalization of white supremacy is, of course, no accident. This chapter provides examples of my internalization process through various phases and aspects of my life. I will also include attempts to deconstruct how white supremacy inadvertently influenced my perceptions and behaviors.

## Social Location, Childhood, and Youth: Secure, Loving, and Awash in White Supremacist Images and Behaviors

I emphasize self-examination when working with families or students of all backgrounds. I locate myself socially so that our cultural borderlands and differences are a spoken aspect of a collaborative relationship (Watts-Jones, 2016).

I am a cisgender white woman; I was born in Brooklyn, New York, to white[2] Polish-Jewish working-class immigrant parents. My father and uncle immigrated alone as teens. My older brother went to medical school when there were quotas that severely limited the admission of Jews. However, I did not think about anti-Semitism, even though I noticed tattooed (concentration camp) numbers on the forearms of some visitors to our home. I did not see us as privileged; however, being white invisibly paved the way for my brother, sister, and me to access higher education, to receive quality health care, and to expect a good life. Our neighborhood was segregated, although no one used that word. White Jews predominated. African Americans, then called Negroes, were usually housecleaners. Everyone else was white: police, the ice-cream man, shopkeepers, the letter carrier. My teachers were white. The first-grade reader was *Dick and Jane*, about an idealized white family with yellow-haired girls in a world that looked nothing like mine. The only Child of Color I knew of was *Little Black Sambo*. I loved that he fooled the tigers; I was not taught that the illustrations were insulting caricatures. Among the great lies (Loewen, 2007) of my elementary school education, beside the myths of Columbus and Thanksgiving, was the celebration of Eli Whitney, inventor of the cotton gin. The suffering that invention inflicted on Black men, women, and children was no part of the lesson.

My mother, like many immigrants, embraced the United States. She would hold up a glass of New York City water and playfully proclaim, "The champagne of America." I didn't question whether other children in America had champagne water. The water in New York City was safe. My mother's mother had lost five of the ten children she birthed, perhaps from impure water. No killer-water in the United States. Mother didn't know unsafe drinking water was (and still is) a danger for People of Color in the United States (VanDerslice, 2011). But her Jewish family was safe in the United States. They had left Poland in the first quarter of the twentieth century. Poland had a population of 3.3 million Jews before World War II, and 380,000 after. My mother's gratitude for US citizenship filled her, yet made her "unseeing."

My mother, an attractive, outgoing, friendly, brown-haired, shapely, white woman, was always attractively, but not lavishly, dressed when she took me on the subway to downtown Brooklyn. Not knowing how they might have felt, she flirted with Black babies and greeted their mothers. The only other African American with whom my mother interacted, Ella, came twice monthly to clean our apartment in Brooklyn, as James Baldwin's mother had done for white families in the Bronx (Baldwin, 1998c). My father used the derogatory Yiddish term *schvartze* to refer to Black people, but never said it directly to them. I didn't challenge him until adolescence. My mother didn't use that language, nor do I remember her correcting him. She was not afraid of him. Perhaps she was sensitive to his insecurities or she tacitly agreed with him. My father, a warm, rotund, white, medium-height man, provided basic needs for the family. He accepted assistance from my mother's oldest sister, Aunt Malka, the wealthy, childless family matriarch who paid the woman to clean our house (and for other luxuries). It was a source of shame for him, but he accepted the subsidy because he wanted his wife to have household help. His one business venture failed, leaving him the least financially viable man in the extended family. He drove a taxi, which was not a respected vocation among our relatives; it humiliated him. In hindsight, I think his reduced self-worth, exacerbated by his perceived failure to save their first child (who died at eight years old), made him a likely candidate for racist attitudes. He defensively said, often, that even wealthy (white) Andrew Carnegie could not save his own child from the same illness. My dad's adoration of my mother was his greatest gift to me. That love, his pride in his children, and his gifted folk harmonica playing sustained him through his unspoken, underlying sadness.

My mother prepared and served Ella hot lunch, and they chatted in the kitchen. Sometimes she gave Ella food to take home or a garment that might fit her larger body. Ella was a tall, heavy-set, light-complexioned, often laughing African American woman. Her sleeveless blouses exposed the cellulite on her large upper arms, on which she had multiple bruises. I had no thoughts about her discolored arms, whether she had been injured or if she had diabetes and bruised easily. Ella was friendly, sometimes mumbling words I couldn't understand interspersed with her laughs. I vaguely remember her gently teasing me, without malice, using the word "bad," telling me to obey my mother. A shy child, I was hurt by being characterized as "bad," but I must have felt she had no power. She was the first Person of Color in my life, but I didn't have much of a relationship with her. My mother, who was much older, worked alongside Ella, who seemed to do the heavier work. My mother didn't shirk housework. The relationship, nonetheless, exemplified *occupational hierarchy*, one of eight pillars—structural principles—that determine and maintain white supremacy as described in *Caste* (Wilkerson, 2020). For example, a nineteenth-century politician stated that "there must be a class to do the menial duties, to perform the drudgery of life" (Wilkerson, 2020, p. 131). Such was Ella's role in relationship to my racist father as well as to my charitable mother, who, regardless of intention, were both elevated above her as they inevitably behaved in accordance with the grand design of the caste system, "an artificial construction, a fixed and embedded ranking of human value that sets the presumed supremacy of one group against the presumed inferiority of other groups" (Wilkerson, 2020, p. 17).

It is personally troubling to describe my parents as racist. According to my cultural and religious tradition, I fear I have dishonored their memories. However, because of my familiarity with the importance of justice (*tzedek*) in Jewish teaching and my confidence in the unconditional love of my family, I am comforted knowing: (1) that in the search for relational truth, I have obeyed the injunction to serve the greater good (justice); and (2) that were my parents alive, I am now sufficiently emotionally, spiritually, and socially mature to have this conversation with them and they would listen. Looking back, seeing how my white supremacist development enabled me to treat Ella as invisible has taught me to better "see" and respect the humanity of people in service positions.

For religious observance, I attended all-white conservative and orthodox Jewish congregations. Today I am unaffiliated and attend two Jewish study and worship groups where racial injustice in the United States and Israel is addressed. I have also begun to participate in prayer services of Jews of Color. The deep Christian and Muslim faiths of many African American clients, colleagues, and friends have influenced me. Fifteen years ago, a friend invited me to join the choir of an African American church in Princeton. The church was once pastored by singer/actor Paul Robeson's father.[3] The current Pastor, Rev. Lukata Mjumbe, a scholar, community activist, and inspirational preacher, has deepened my faith in my own tradition.

The 1953 execution of Julius and Ethel Rosenberg, a Jewish couple, reverberated among US Jews. At the time, I sensed my Jewish parents' vulnerability to persecution. I now understand how that vulnerability could easily have made them even more susceptible to internalized white supremacy. They "had to enter into a silent, unspoken pact of separating and distancing themselves from the established lowest caste" (Wilkerson, 2020, p. 50), perhaps to reassure themselves about their security as Americans, which I do not excuse but must understand if I am to pursue antiracism.

### *Adolescence: Two African American Men, Connecting Without Seeing*

When I was twelve years old, Aunt Malka took me to an orthodox Jewish hotel in the Catskills for the summer to engineer a match between me and the owners' sweet, but uninteresting, thirteen-year-old son. My aunt, a very proper-looking, buxom woman whose attire was tailored, was distant. We had no emotional connection. I was bored. As no business was conducted on Saturday (the Jewish sabbath), on those days I would visit for an hour or two with two African American men, bellhops, in the empty reception area. The older of the two, Jim, was an avuncular, middle-aged man, who was warm, friendly, and wise. The younger man, Michael, was a City College of New York student who often humored me with the riddle: "Why are fire engines red?" His answer was a witty string of phrases that ended with "the Finns fought the Russians, and the Russians are red." The day I departed for home, I left a good-bye note at the reception desk. I later received a reply. Michael's note was written in a small, neat script on the reverse side of the hotel stationery, and was a bit formal, ending with wishes "for success in all your future endeavors." On the front page, under the hotel letterhead, was Jim's message, written in light blue fountain pen ink, in a beautiful, calligraphic script. The salutation to his note of kindness was "Dearest little one."

The Catskill experience was my first substantive contact with Black men. The conversations had a familial quality. But I don't know if these men wanted my presence. I trust my memory of Jim's warmth. However, as a white, paying guest, I did not see my privilege nor the white supremacy I was performing. Did I ask their permission to join them? Did they feel entitled to dismiss me? I certainly invaded their downtime. I referred to them by their first names, not realizing it was disrespectful, an example of "occupational hierarchy," in which by virtue of their position, I did not address them more formally (Wilkerson, 2020). My presence could have created a problem: I was a white girl with Black men. At home, I showed the note to my mother, who was always interested in my experiences. I was proud that these men had written to me. They taught me something different from my sheltered experience. They allowed me relationship, perhaps at their expense. I felt seen by them and, perhaps deluding myself, thought I knew them a bit. However, I did not see that I had enacted white supremacy. Even as an otherwise respectful kid, even with appreciation for their congeniality, I may have exploited them to relieve my boredom, an example of the social narcissism of my unrecognized white supremacy.

During this period, I had no Teachers of Color or clear understanding of racism in my country. Curricula in schools inaccurately represented the history of racism in the United States, as they still do today (Vasquez Heilig et al., 2012). With regard to images of People of Color, in the influential realm of public pedagogy (Sandlin et al., 2011), TV limited African Americans to specific kinds of roles (Sewell, 2013). In the 1950s and '60s, I was exposed to negative stereotypes of People of Color. Beulah, for example, (played by Ethel Waters) was a warm, kind, and wise housekeeper, perhaps like Jim, and was portrayed working for *kind* whites, a deceitful reification of the caste system. Similarly, Eddie Anderson was a highly successful actor who portrayed the irreverent, albeit stereotyped, Rochester, valet to the popular comedian, Mr. (Jack) Benny. Rochester was addressed by first name. Additionally, Native Americans were stereotyped in many films of that era, and beyond, as either violent aggressors, or as sympathetic victims who were rescued by a white protagonist savior.

At the end of my Catskills summer, in August, a Black child, just a few years older than I, Emmet Till, was tortured and murdered in Mississippi because of a white woman's false, despicable accusation. I was not aware of the event at the time. I now wonder if Mr. Jim and Mr. Michael had that news in their consciousness. Acts of white supremacy occur along a spectrum from hurtful, ignorant, or intentional disrespect to brutality. Those two men certainly understood acts of white supremacy, performed, albeit without violence, by me. And although I later learned that Rosa Parks, that December, dared to sit in the front of a bus, I was not yet fully cognizant of the developing Civil Rights movement. The following spring, I attended a rock and roll show at the Brooklyn Paramount theatre, where I cheered Black musicians. Despite the pervasive violence against Black people in my country, in my sheltered white supremacist early teenage existence, I was still oblivious to the racist system in which they and I lived.

### *The College Years: Getting Out*

When I was sixteen, my Aunt Malka said, "Forget college. Stay home, marry a nice Jewish boy." To the contrary, I took it upon myself to enroll at Brooklyn College (for free) that fall, and I commuted there from home. My world opened: I developed a love of foreign languages. I met (white) Christians and joined a choir and performed masses in the classical music tradition. I attended a summer semester in Paris, which Aunt Malka subsidized because I promised I would visit our religious relatives in Zurich, which I did. However, I was more interested in the European, African, and Middle Eastern students. I wrote to my mother about my Iranian boyfriend. When I returned, my mother sighed, "I thought you were going to come off the plane with a handsome dark prince." Her romanticism about Persia allowed an imagined princely status to eclipse color. My mother, in her wistful comment, had implicitly legitimized the notion that exotic adventure might supersede racism. Though not yet seeing, the boundaries of my white world started to blur.

Later, I attended the March on Washington on August 28, 1963, which I do not claim as an indication of my antiracist identity, but which I mention because it was part of the beginning of my greater awareness and activism. There were 250,000 marchers, a peaceful, diverse assembly of people from all across the country. We walked from the Washington Monument to the US Capitol building, chanting and singing. People listened to the speakers while sitting on the grass; kids climbed the trees to get a view of Dr. King and others. As Dr. King spoke, everyone listened intently in the oppressive August heat. I felt I was part of something right, something bigger than myself. Afterward I became more attuned to the national news, to the murder of four little Black girls in a Birmingham church. And later, I understood the eloquent rage against "moderates" in the letter from Birmingham Jail (King, 1963) that Dr. King wrote the following spring. A year after the march, the murdered bodies of antiracists Chaney, Goodman, and Schwerner were discovered. I was becoming aware, but did not yet see, that the conspiracy was *nationwide*. I have attended many protests over the years, including the 50th anniversary of the march and, most recently, as part of the Black Lives Matter movement. Two potentially contradictory phenomena explain my testimony here: I am both presenting myself as the good white protester and attesting to activist accountability. Apparently, disparate phenomena can coexist in the continuing evolution of an aspiring antiracist (Kendi, 2019).

## The Post College Years, My Early 20s in the 1960s: Opening the Lens of Experience as a Benevolent Oppressor

I began working in various positions for the New York City Department of Welfare after college. I was increasingly exposed to the lives of People of Color but in an unearned, unseen (by me), elevated position in the racial hierarchy. On a required home visit, for example, an African American mother feared I would report her television—which welfare recipients were not allowed to have back then. I didn't report it and now wonder how she felt in that conversation with a 23-year-old white worker who had *power* over her. "Every day is a new little hurt, a new little dehumanization" (Oluo, 2019, p. 19). Unseeing, I did not grasp assaults on Blacks regardless of economic status, an illustration of Wilkerson's (2020) *heritability principle*, by which one's place in society is determined by how you were born, regardless of wealth or achievement. Similarly, I was assigned to teach infant care to young Women of Color, even though I had no training in early childhood development. I undoubtedly performed *cultural imperialism*, a form of oppression (Young, 1990), as I imparted views that were insufficiently sensitive to culture and context. My whiteness, at least in part, allowed me to be easily elevated, and regardless of how much I cared about the women, I was still an oppressor. I was part of a design that Wilkerson (2020) compares to the invisible power of social control, described in the film, *The Matrix*. Unseeing, I did not know that I was performing acts of injustice that look like justice (Wilkerson, 2020).

Subsequently, as a graduate social work student, I had no Professors of Color. In one internship, I was assigned to work with African American and Latinx middle school students, who were considered having "behavior problems," in a special guidance department program called "G classes." One of the students said to me: "Do you know what 'G' stands for? Garbage." Working through these feelings with the students, I became more attuned to how schools were disproportionately concerned with compliance (Coates, 2015) and how their actions could damage a child's sense of self. I began to meet with these students' white teachers as a group. A male teacher was able to reveal his fear of Black male students, reflecting the frequent theme of preoccupation with *the body* of Black men (Coates, 2015; Wilkerson, 2020). I saw how helping whites address their racism could have a place in my work.

## Entering the Mental Health Field: Abandon All Racism Consciousness, Ye Who Enter Here

As a second-year graduate social work student, I was assigned a field placement to work in a psychiatric hospital; I was later hired by that institution and became immersed in mainstream mental health culture. Whiteness was the norm and was invisible. Indeed, unnamed white supremacy characterized my experience of the mental health field in the mid 1970s and beyond: in the hospitals, in my post degree family therapy training, in training videos in and in professional organizations. As I have noted elsewhere, professional journals frequently mention race only when the articles are specifically about People of Color. Indeed, racism, and other forms of oppression, are, today, often inadequately challenged, or disregarded, much-less deconstructed, in mental health practice (Dolan-Del Vecchio, 2019).

### *A Hint of Conspiratorial Action: Covert Racism, Elucidated by Luz*

In another psychiatric institution in which I worked, Luz,[4] a young Puerto Rican Catholic woman, exhibited symptoms of catatonia.[5] It was her first psychiatric hospitalization, and after a scant course of antipsychotic medication, the white psychiatrist recommended electroshock therapy (ECT). He directed me to secure family consent. Luz's husband, Edmundo, a recent Ecuadorian immigrant, was dealing with work, three small children, and a profoundly unreachable wife, and he was overwhelmed. With Edmundo's agreement, I invited the rest of Luz's family. The psychiatrist off-handedly agreed that I could expand the conversation to the larger family group, but reiterated authoritatively, that I needed to procure ECT consent. The meeting included Edmundo, Luz's mother, Luz's sister, and her brother, who was the family spokesperson.

I had privately thought Luz was being prematurely tracked into aggressive treatment. I was relieved when the family refused ECT. The psychiatrist expressed surprise when I described the family's thoughtful deliberation. Luz recovered with medication. The psychiatrist's discharge summary, a brief paragraph that omitted most details of the consultation, confirmed my impression of his indifference; and I couldn't think of any explanation for that indifference other than the fact that Luz was a woman of color.

After her discharge, I saw Luz and Edmundo as outpatients. Another white psychiatrist and I collaborated to decrease her medication as soon as safely possible. As the couple's therapist, psychopathology receded in my thinking. When Luz reported that she had taken the children to a department store on her own, I was impressed. I asked her to change seats to teach me how to do that, as I had young children, too. This was the beginning of the end of therapy. Thanks to Luz, I would never see anyone of any background as unidimensional. Luz returned to her work and sent me photos of each child's holy communion. My seeing what seemed to be racism had helped us all profoundly. I had become conspiratorial, implicitly with Luz's family, and with the second psychiatrist. My veiled disobedience to the original psychiatrist was "unprofessional" in the mental health culture. I now realize, however, that I was part of a system which obscures a person's complexity and humanity, especially a Person of Color. I was conspiring against an invisible enemy, —again, reminiscent of The Matrix—white supremacy, but now seeing a bit more. Furthermore, Luz exemplified the lesson of the miners' canary (Guinier & Torres, 2009), alerting me not only to potential individual racist disparities of care, but also to overall potential systemic problems in mental health treatment (McGoldrick & Hardy, 2019). However, I was essentially alone in these discoveries. I did not have a community of professionals who could see the racism.

## Collegial Interactions in a White Supremacist Culture

### *White Liberal Professionals*

Later in my evolution as a family therapist, I was learning to be curious about what was missing in therapeutic encounters. In a collegial group, an experienced white clinician, who self-identified as liberal, presented her work with an Afro-Caribbean family. The presentation did not address the Black–white encounter. Invited, I commented that precisely because of the excellence of the work, it provided an opportunity to consider cross-racial factors. Several people in the group immediately rebuffed me as though I had devalued the presentation. One person later apologized but did so outside of the group. I had "threatened the hum of the Matrix" (Wilkerson, 2020, p. 33); in other words, I had challenged the unspoken but known rules in this institutional context—which were in the service of those in power. I had raised the possibility of racism where those in power denied their racism. I was treated like a rabble-rouser.

White liberal professionals often surprise me. In private conversations, some erroneously expected me to collude with them in their views. Like the white moderates in Birmingham referenced by Dr. King (1963), these professionals saw the assertions of Colleagues of Color as too insistent on addressing racism. As in the caste system, those at the higher levels, the more privileged in the power hierarchy, block incursions by those deemed inferior (Wilkerson, 2020). Shocked, I witnessed mistreatment of accomplished Colleagues of Color through veiled racist acts, by white professionals who, denying their racism, acted to maintain power. This insidious white supremacy is another example of the *heritability pillar* (Wilkerson, 2020, p. 108), which dictates that no matter what people's achievements, they are not afforded legitimacy by those more elevated in the hierarchy. Colleagues of Color have shared their painful experiences with me. My deep respect for and connection to them continues. When I work to counter white supremacy in professional contexts, I, too, have been dismissed, even when in positions of leadership. My discomfort is infinitesimal compared to the suffering inflicted by a system that privileges me.

*Compañeros/Colleagues*

Fortunately, I was eventually buoyed by others engaged in antiracism work: Colleagues and Friends of Color and whites committed to racial justice. They have provided a well-spring of support. The Multicultural Family Institute, under the leadership of Monica McGoldrick, has for many years supported the integration of ethnicity and racial justice in the practice and teaching of family therapy. The institute's conferences were designed specifically to address racial and other injustices. Monica McGoldrick and Kenneth V. Hardy, and now many others, have convened, published, and presented work that supports and informs a community of antiracist psychotherapists. A more recent forum for this community is the annual Soul Work conference. Additionally, the American Family Therapy Academy, though struggling with racial hierarchy, has convened regularly occurring forums to address racism and other forms of oppression. I am indebted to a leader and mentor beloved by many, Dr. Elaine Pinderhughes, whose encouragement led me to the study of whiteness.

## Oppressed Communities: Lessons in Learning

For approximately twenty years, I was executive director of a nonprofit I will refer to as the Center[6] that had programs in up to twenty schools in economically disadvantaged New Jersey communities. Since its inception, the Center had been intentionally racially diverse at every level: staff, faculty, supervisors, community partners, and board. The founders were white but were later succeeded by a Person of Color as executive director. The schools serviced by the Center practiced retributive justice. Nationally, Students of Color are disproportionately disciplined (US Department of Education, 2018). Annual assessments by an independent evaluator revealed that approximately 90% of high school students in the Center's programs showed improvement and either remained in school or graduated, far surpassing the performance for students in the general population of those schools. However, no systems in the schools were changed during the time of the Center's involvement in those schools. In 2006, staff, faculty, supervisors, community partners, and representatives of client families participated in a two-day training by the People's Institute and Beyond, and the Center officially became an undoing racism organization.

### *Ms. S: Antagonist as Teacher*

I went to a meeting in Camden, New Jersey. The site director, Ms. S, an African American woman, was considering partnering with the Center at Camden High School. Within the group of ten people, another woman sat across the table from me and interrogated me for two hours. I was the only white. I was entering their community, as had many whites in the past, without trust or racial credibility. Why should anyone trust me? Moreover, I was from Princeton, town of the southernmost Ivy League school, where southern white male students had brought enslaved men to serve them and where white supremacist Woodrow Wilson was university president and denied admission to African American Paul Robeson, even though the popular Rev. William Drew Robeson implored Wilson to admit his son. It is the university where First Lady Michelle Obama struggled with Blackness as a student (Obama, 2018), where Black Princeton professor Rev. Dr. Cornell West was stopped in his own neighborhood for essentially driving while Black (West, 2017). Furthermore, Princeton was the last Ivy League university to admit Students of Color (Bradley, 2010). The town is currently considered elitist. As a native New Yorker, I felt, on arrival, that the dominant interactional style was Anglo-Saxon white. The ambience there was in sharp contrast to the openly ethnic communities that characterized New York, despite racial inequities, even though Princeton has a rich African American history (Watterson, 2017).

The Center's program was eventually accepted. Ms. S and I collaborated in hiring and programming; clinical supervision and family therapy training were provided by the Center. Years later, I asked Ms. S why she had decided to partner with us. "Because you came back," she responded. I inferred that I had not overtly exhibited fragility (DiAngelo, 2018). Our relationship, however, was initially difficult. At official meetings, whenever I commented, she rolled her eyes. By this point in my life, I had known powerful Black women, some colleagues, some friends; some have challenged me. Ms. S was different. She was a forceful, imposing figure, a large woman, whose attractive attire and grooming seemed to herald her physical presence when she entered a room. I was intimidated. I didn't think I judged her negatively as an angry Black woman. On the contrary, in clinical supervision, I encouraged and supported counselors to try to understand why a Black mother expressed anger toward school personnel. We taught staff to understand those mothers' frustration and their anxiety about their children. Ms. S was different; her staff feared her, but they also loved her. I didn't love her. She was angry with me. It felt personal. During the first year, Ms. S called me "honey" and exhibited impatience with me at meetings. I felt a dismissive rage undergirded her pronounced gestures. She made me feel like the "bad white." She didn't trust me. She didn't see me as I wanted to be seen. I wanted to *help*, but to her my motivation was suspect. The work of the Center's staff, who were People of Color, working at her site were effective, but inside I regressed into the failed savior mode. Bad white. Can't be trusted.

Ms. S and I worked together, and I learned from her. Her assessment of every proposal was based on: "How is it good for the kids?" Eventually we had joint programs at more than five sites. I began to appreciate her combination of Ivy League education, political savvy, clear leadership, and compassion for the children she served. She, in turn, respected our clinical supervision and training, and she particularly appreciated that we did not blame struggling families but rather saw them as resources for their children. She helped me progress in my white identity development as I learned to learn from a Person of Color (Helms, 1990). I turned to her for advice at times. Within about a year, we were on a first name basis. Eventually she referred to me as "baby." Over the ensuing years we lunched together and talked about our personal lives, about our clothes, about her joy with her newly found partner. We also commented on child protective services' racist treatment of Black families. Additionally, she encouraged me to challenge a situation I considered racist in another school district.

On a warm sunny day in May 2012, as I was leaving another site, my phone rang. Ms. S had died suddenly. I stopped the car in the parking lot and sobbed. Ms. S had taught me how to work with her kids and how to follow her leadership in what had begun as an adversarial relationship. Her trust was not a privilege; I had to work for it in a metaphorical dance that many Black people have had to do to be accepted or even tolerated by whites, much less respected. I learned from her to stay the course, to be open. I learned humility and that I didn't have to be in charge of the process. She taught me how to be more accountable for my whiteness, especially in Black spaces. She forced me to deal with my whiteness in a way that no one had before. I went through the discomfort and humiliation that I imagine many People of Color experience when attempting relationships with whites. My loving friends have probably not taught me as much. The outpouring of love and admiration at her homegoing service and the celebratory repast showed me further that I had been privileged to learn from a powerful, brilliant, and widely loved and admired woman.

### *Compromised, Complicit, Corrupt*

In another site in a northern New Jersey urban setting, a white male site director, Angelo, retired after many years of service. An often-smiling man, he was dedicated to the students and fostered a respectful congenial relationship with the diverse group of men and women whom he supervised. The sponsoring agency replaced him with a white woman, Elaine, who instituted operational and physical changes upon assuming her new position.

Almost immediately, she complained about the Center's employee, Darweshi, an Afro-centric male, who dressed in stunning African attire with his hair in dreadlocks. He gave inspirational presentations about African and African American heritage to the students and to the Center's training meetings. Elaine disapproved of almost everything he did, although he was a gifted counselor. He accompanied students to court, and developed relationships with prosecutors on the teens' behalf. He formed and conducted groups of teens and taught them to peacefully mediate conflict within the school context. He had a large following in this effort, contradicting the negative stereotypical white assumptions that African American and Latinx kids don't think it's "cool" to promote peace. His students gave a presentation of their work at one of our trainings in Princeton. Furthermore, with his guidance, Latinx students dropped their (gang) colors. If he couldn't locate students in school, he found them on the streets of the neighborhood. He was a model of ideal practice.

Despite his clear gift as a counselor, Darweshi's entries into the site's files were not satisfactory according to Elaine. This was due to his learning disability; writing was not his strong suit. He was a Center employee, partly accountable to Elaine as task supervisor. I had meetings with Elaine and Darweshi, to support their relationship. I helped him improve recording skills so that his entries met all the applicable criteria.

Nonetheless, Elaine began to push for his dismissal. I secured support from the head of the Board of Education for that district. He was a white man who valued Darweshi's work. I asked for a meeting with the school Superintendent, a white man. She included the director of the sponsoring agency, another white woman, Elaine's employer. Another Center clinical supervisor, a Woman of Color, came with me to that meeting to support and advise me. Elaine, the Superintendent and Elaine's local agency employer were in alliance with one another. They all minimized Darweshi's talents as a counselor, his long history of dedication to the community, and his popularity among the students. His improved recording skills were not even taken into consideration.

I advocated for Darweshi's talents and value to the students, but sensed my entreaties were futile. Finally, I met with a representative of the state government in a department which had authority over funding for that aspect of our programming. That person, a man of color, stated that our overall funding was contingent upon our cooperation with local agencies where the Center's staff was placed. He, therefore, would not support my entreaties to retain Darweshi. Without his foreknowledge, Darweshi was banned from school property within a day or two of my meeting with the superintendent. As his employer, I had no option but to dismiss Darweshi from the work on that site where he had been highly valued by people in the community.

Shortly after Darweshi was let go, a pastor from that community called me. He asked me if the ordeal was racist. I said that was my feeling even though no one had uttered a racist word or made a comment that could objectively be characterized as racist during the process. I felt personally responsible: I had given up, afraid to involve the Center in litigation. We were a few dozen employees and consultants serving many children and families. I deeply admired Darweshi, professionally and personally. I had met his wife and son and attended his mother's funeral. Yet, I failed him. He and I have talked. He is too kind and too spiritual a person to blame me. I did not enact justice effectively. The programs on that particular contract alone served at least 960 students and their families each year in eight high schools. As one who aims to be an antiracist, I made a racist choice and obeyed the authorities, oppressed a highly talented counselor and deprived the youth he served.

The episode is reminiscent of the collusive network of individuals of diverse backgrounds who captured people escaping enslavement in Song Yet Sung (McBride, 2008). Applying the principles of Caste (Wilkerson, 2020) to this situation, in hindsight, I think that Darweshi's dismissal shows the following: in the fixed ranking of human value, Darweshi was devalued (p. 17); the heritability concept, regardless of accomplishment, ranked him as inferior (p. 107); the pillar purity versus pollution (p. 115) was relevant as he was banned from the district because his visible Afro-Centrism "polluted" the dominant white view of counselors; he was not seen as belonging as a counselor in their perceived ranking of the occupational hierarchy; and he was the target of dehumanization and stigma (p. 142) because his individuality (his talents) was not seen because of his skin color and (for them) his too visible pride in his African heritage. The situation reeked of racism and conspiracy. Despite my efforts, I allowed myself to be corrupted in order to save the program, the Center, the employees and the many students it served. Of course, I saved myself as well, in succumbing to white supremacy. I did not risk. I am reminded that I "can be a racist one minute and an antiracist the next" (Kendi, 2019, p. 10).

*Staying in the Fight as a White*

My narrative reveals that I have been indoctrinated into and have intermittently hobbled against the force of white supremacy. The following are reminders to myself, which may or may not be useful for others:

1. Learn. When I have all the answers, I am lost.

2. Expect mistakes. Discomfort is in the cards, infinitesimal compared to oppression.

3. Be open to other whites, without judgment. See the transformative experience of a white nationalist (Saslow, 2018).

4. We are not to blame for internalized white supremacy, but we *are* accountable.

5. Learn from People of Color, without burdening them with teaching me. Practice humility. Listen. Relinquish control of the process.

6. Increase antiracist action and risk on the micro and the macro level: march, vote, donate, lobby, challenge racist policies.

7. Be mindful that, as a white person, I will inevitably be hurtful, consciously or unconsciously, to People of Color.

8. Never stop "seeing" the paradox: that I am a participant in a powerful system that is fueled by apparent invisibility and the denial of its existence.

9. Be aware that as a white person, I can have a dual consciousness, not the same, but reminiscent of life behind the veil, the double life for

African Americans described by Du Bois (1903). While the elements of choice and involuntary suffering involved in Dubois' construct compared with my dilemma are, of course, vastly different, both involve conflict, which I see as just. I, as a white person, have a dual existence: that of the accountable antiracist and that of the good white, which is a seductive illusion that can distract me from the just role of accountable antiracist. Both identities are participants in a system of oppression. For me, the good white identity, while never denying systemic racism, can be vulnerable to a self-congratulatory mindset, similar to the concept of "color celebrate" (DiAngelo, 2018, p. 79), related to my presence in Communities of Color and to my deep, enduring relationships with People of Color. My antiracist self has to occasionally poke me to prevent slippage into the complacency of the good white identity. For me, the force of the good white identity may be the confluence or alternation of a number of factors: a manifestation of my overall insecurity and need to be accepted; my wish to reassure People of Color that I can be trusted to be respectful; my desire to be compassionate and loving; or my denial of the unearned privilege afforded by my skin color. Keeping these *dueling consciousnesses* (Kendi, 2019) in mind, I must keep in the forefront of my thinking the *pull* of the good white fallacy, which can have the power to eclipse antiracist white. Living with this contradiction is an essential and inevitable condition. My accountable white actions can also delude me into the unseeing complacency of good white me. The accountable white cannot congratulate itself, lest it succumb to seeing itself as good, because I am inevitably and concurrently in the oppressor class of the caste system (Wilkerson, 2020; DiAngelo, 2018), which is where the work is to be done.

10. Practice gratitude: for my privilege, for the knowledge, and for all the people, my many teachers and friends, to whom I am connected in the work.

## Epilogue

Our country has been conspiratorially racist since 1619, when white men stole land belonging to others and stole the lives and freedom of others, who have since risen up to fight for our democracy (Hannah-Jones, 2019). The most fitting role for me, therefore, is antiracist co-conspirator. Imperfect as my path has been, and will be, the work is a lifelong learning and action process. A colleague committed to justice, psychologist Jodie Kliman,[7] reminded me of a scriptural phrase: "You are not required to complete the task [of healing the world], yet you are not free to desist from it"—*Pirkei Avot,* Ethics of Our Fathers 2:21 (Yanklowitz, 2018, p. 183).

**HINDA WINAWER, MSW, LCSW,** is cofounder of the Princeton Family Institute, LLC, Princeton, New Jersey. Hinda is a faculty emerita at the Ackerman Institute for the Family in New York, New York, and a former adjunct faculty at Rutgers University Graduate School of Social Work in New Brunswick, New Jersey. She is the founder and former executive director of the Center for Family, Community, & Social Justice, Inc., in Princeton, New Jersey. Hinda is also the past president of the American Family Therapy Academy.

## Notes

1. I have sometimes used the term *white blindness* (Kliman, Winawer, & Trimble, 2019) to describe whites' inability to see our privilege, but this negative term may be experienced as disrespectful to physically unsighted people. It is my view that a blind person, as exemplified by Tiresias—the blind prophet—in Sophocles' (429/2011) tragedy, *Oedipus the King,* can reveal Truth; it is "unseeing" that renders Truth invisible.
2. A common misconception is that Jews in the United States are exclusively white. For more information about Jews of Color, see Gordon (2016) and visit jewishmultiracialnetwork.org.
3. Rev. William D. Robeson, Pastor of the Witherspoon Street Presbyterian Church for approximately twenty years. The church was officially established in 1840, but Princeton's African American community has a longer history (Watterson, 2017).
4. Names and identifying details are fictitious to maintain confidentiality.
5. Luz's official psychiatric diagnosis of catatonic schizophrenia was ignorant of cultural, religious, and contextual data. Very soon before hospitalization, Luz, a devout Catholic, had birthed a third, unplanned, unwanted child. Severe post- or peripartum depression could be relevant if her experience had to be reduced to psychiatric nomenclature.
6. The Center for Family, Community, & Social Justice, Inc., now defunct.

7. Jodie Kliman, PhD, Clinical Psychology Department, William James College, Newton Massachusetts; Boston Institute for Culturally Affirming Practices.

## References

*Baldwin, J. (1998a). Dark days. In T. E. Morrison (Ed.),* James Baldwin: Collected essays *(pp. 788–798). The Library of America.*

*Baldwin, J. (1998b). The price of the ticket. In T. E. Morrison (Ed.),* James Baldwin: Collected essays *(pp. 830–842). The Library of America.*

*Baldwin, J. (1998c). The white man's guilt. In T. E. Morrison (Ed.),* James Baldwin: Collected essays *(pp. 722–727). The Library of America.*

*Billings, D. (2016).* Deep denial: The persistence of white supremacy in United States history and life. *Crandall, Dostie & Douglass Books.*

*Bonilla-Silva, E. (2012). The invisible weight of whiteness: The racial grammar of everyday life in contemporary America.* Ethnic and racial studies, 35*(2), 173–194.*

*Bradley, S. M. (2010). The southern-most ivy: Princeton university from Jim Crow admissions to anti-apartheid protests, 1794–1969.* American Studies, 51*(3/4), 109–130.*

*Coates, T. N. (2015).* Between the world and me. *Spiegel and Grau.*

*DiAngelo, R. (2018).* White fragility: Why it's so hard for white people to talk about racism. *Beacon Press.*

*Dolan-Del Vecchio, K. (2019). Dismantling white male privilege within family therapy. In M. McGoldrick & K. V. Hardy (Eds.),* Re-visioning family therapy: Addressing diversity in clinical practice *(pp. 226–235). Guilford Press.*

*Du Bois, W. E. B. (1903).* The souls of black folk. *A. C. McClurg & Co.*

*Gordon, L. R. (2016). Rarely kosher: Studying Jews of color in North America.* American Jewish History, 100*(1), 105–116.*

*Guinier, L., & Torres, G. (2009).* The miner's canary: Enlisting race, resisting power, transforming democracy. *Harvard University Press.*

*Hackman, R. (2015, June 26).* 'We need co-conspirators, not allies': How white Americans can fight racism. *The Guardian. https://www.theguardian.com/world/2015/jun/26/how-white-americans-can-fight-racism*

*Hannah-Jones, N. (2019, August 14). The 1619 Project.* The New York Times. *https://www.nytimes.com/interactive/2019/08/14/magazine/black-history-american-democracy.html?mtrref=www.google.com&gwh=74CF85EA1C76B4EBDA2A8F0138655FAF&gwt=regi&assetType=REGIWALL*

*Helms, J. E. (1990).* Black and white racial identity: Theory, research and practice. *Praeger.*

*Kendi, I. X. (2019).* How to be an antiracist. *One World.*

*King, Jr., M. L. (1963, August). Letter from Birmingham jail (published as: The negro is your brother).* The Atlantic, 212*(2), 78–88.*

*Kliman, J., Winawer, H., & Trimble, D. (2019). The inevitable whiteness of being (white): Whiteness and intersectionality in family therapy practice and training. In M. McGoldrick & K. V. Hardy (Eds.),* Re-visioning family therapy: Addressing diversity in clinical practice *(3rd ed., pp. 236–250). Guilford Press.*

*Loewen, J. W. (2007).* Lies my teacher told me: Everything your American history textbook got wrong. *Touchstone.*

*Love, B. L. (2019).* We want to do more than survive: Abolitionist teaching and the pursuit of educational freedom. *Beacon Press.*

*McBride, J. (2008).* Song yet sung. *Riverhead Books.*

*McGoldrick, M., & Hardy, K. V. (2019). The power of naming. In M. McGoldrick and K. V. Hardy (Eds.),* Re-visioning family therapy: Addressing diversity in clinical practice *(pp. 3–27). Guilford Press.*

*Newkirk, V. R., II. (2017, October 6). The language of white supremacy.* The Atlantic. *https://www.theatlantic.com/politics/archive/2017/10/the-language-of-white-supremacy/542148/*

*Newkirk, V. R., II. (2017). The language of white supremacy.* The Atlantic, October, 6, *2017.*

*Obama, M. (2018).* Becoming. *Crown Publishing Group.*

*Oluo, I. (2019).* So you want to talk about race. *Hachette.*

*Powell, J., & Kelly, A. (2017). Accomplices in the academy in the age of Black Lives Matter.* Journal of Critical Thought and Praxis, 6*(2), 42–65. https://doi.org/10.31274/jctp-180810-73*

*Sandlin, J. A., O'Malley, M. P., & Burdick, J. (2011). Mapping the complexity of public pedagogy scholarship: 1894–2010.* Review of Educational Research, 81*(3), 338–375.*

*Saslow, E. (2018).* Rising out of hatred: The awakening of a former white nationalist. *Anchor.*

*Sewell, C. J. (2013). Mammies and matriarchs: Tracing images of the black female in popular culture 1950s to present.* Journal of African American Studies, 17*(3), 308–326.*

*Sophocles. (2011). Oedipus the king. In R. Bagg & J. Scully (Trans./Eds.),* The complete plays of Sophocles: A new translation *(pp. 388–490). Harper Collins. (Original work published ca. 429 BCE)*

*US Department of Education. (2018).* 2015–2016 civil rights data collection: School climate and safety. *https://www2.ed.gov/about/offices/list/ocr/docs/school-climate-and-safety.pdf*

*VanDerslice, J. (2011). Drinking water infrastructure and environmental disparities: Evidence and methodological considerations.* American Journal of Public Health, 101*(S1), S109–S114. https://doi.org/10.2105/AJPH.2011.300189*

*Vasquez Heilig, J., Brown, K., & Brown, A. (2012). The illusion of inclusion: A critical race theory textual analysis of race and standards.* Harvard Educational Review, 82*(3), 403–424.*

*Watterson, K. (2017).* I hear my people singing: Voices of African American Princeton. *Princeton University Press.*

*Watts-Jones, D. T. (2016). Location of self in training and supervision. In K. V. Hardy & T. Bobes (Eds.),* Culturally sensitive supervision and training: Diverse perspectives and practical applications *(pp. 16–24). Routledge.*

*West, C. (2017).* Race matters *(25th anniv. ed.). Beacon Press.*

*Wilkerson, I. (2020).* Caste: The origins of our discontents. *Random House.*

*Winawer, H. (2017). White racial identity in therapy with couples and families. In S. Kelly (Ed.),* Diversity in couple and family therapy *(pp. 121–150). Praeger.*

*Yanklowitz, R. D. S. (2018).* Pirkei Avot: A social justice commentary. *CCAR Press.*

*Young, I. M. (1990).* Justice and the politics of difference. *Princeton University Press.*

# CHAPTER 22

# From Illness Toward Wellness

## Transmuting Individual Consciousness

BONNIE BERMAN CUSHING, LCSW

If I am not for myself, who will be for me?
But if I am only for myself, what am I?
*And if not now, when?*

—RABBI HILLEL THE ELDER, PIRKE AVOT 1:14 (BERKSON, 2011, P. 41)

Healing does not occur in a vacuum. We also need to begin mending our collective body. This mending takes place in connections with other bodies—in groups, neighborhoods, and communities.

—RESMAA MENAKEM (2017, P. 132)

Throughout my life I have moved between defining my identity as unique and separate from my tribe and race and recognizing tribe and race as integral to my identity and my life. At times, I have distanced myself from the collective history and present reality of these categories, and at other times, I have individually and collectively embraced the work of healing the dehumanizing and confining impact of their borders. I have worked with and witnessed these impacts within myself and others from the micro through the macro level. To conceive of myself as either an individual or part of a collective is a false dichotomy. There can be no white without a Black to compare itself to, no "superior" without an "inferior." There is no "I" without a "we." *Everything* is interconnected and interdependent.

As I write this, I have a view through my window of the falling leaves. We are in the heart of autumn where I am, and the trees are shedding their cover to reveal their bare branches and trunks. The parallel between this shedding of nature's cover and what is occurring in our nation right now is undeniable. The centuries-old, intentionally engineered division between us is being more clearly unveiled. To build border walls or not; to wear masks or not; to see our Earth solely as a resource to own/extract from or to see it as a partner; to finally engage in a reckoning with structural and systemic racism or to continue to deny its reality. Is it that our society has fallen so deeply into the illusion of "*I*" that the "*We*" is now beyond our grasp? COVID-19, continued ecological degradation, demographic shifts, and uprisings protesting racial and economic violence have, together, uncovered just how perilous our inability to see our interconnectedness has become. The definition of freedom itself is currently wrestling in the streets and political halls of our land. In his recent article in *The Atlantic,* Dr. Ibram X. Kendi (2020) makes the parallels crystal clear:

> Slaveholders desired a state that wholly secured their individual freedom to enslave, not to mention their freedom to disenfranchise, to exploit, to impoverish, to demean, and to silence and kill the demeaned. *The freedom to.* The freedom to harm. Which is to say, in coronavirus terms, the freedom to infect. Slaveholders disavowed a state that secured any form of communal freedom—the freedom of the community *from* slavery, from disenfranchisement, from exploitation, from poverty, from all the demeaning and silencing and killing. *The freedom from.* The freedom from harm. Which is to say, in coronavirus terms, the freedom from infection. (para. 4)

Individualism, a foundational attribute of white dominant culture, is threatening our very sustainability as a species. And yet, even in the face of this existential ultimatum, white supremacy doubles down.

At 4 o'clock on a Friday afternoon in the fall of 1958, a three-year-old white girl with cornsilk blonde hair dangles her feet from a vinyl kitchen chair while she reads a children's book. At the stove stands a stout, dark-skinned woman peering over a pan of boiling eggs. With a large wooden spoon, she scoops the eggs out of the water and places them on the counter to cool. The woman peels the soft-boiled eggs, puts them in a bowl and, as she places them before the girl, she whispers in her ear, "Eat up, sweetie. It's a long time 'til Monday."

I was that little girl and Lizzie was that woman, caretaking me since I was one while my parents worked at the store. Her advice was well warranted—she knew I would eat little of what my mother or father prepared for me over the weekend. Lizzie was my safe harbor in the tumultuous sea of my family. She was the calm counterpoint to my mother's ubiquitous anxiety and my father's frequent absence. With Lizzie I felt safe and seen. With Lizzie I felt both grounded and carefree.

One Monday Lizzie didn't return to our house. When I asked why, my mother told me that Lizzie wasn't going to come anymore because I was old enough to go to school. I became hysterical with panic and grief. I didn't even get to say goodbye to her, this woman who had been so important, so instrumental to me. This formative loss in my life—this unnatural tear in the *We* I shared with Lizzie—parallels the historical tear in the fabric of our country's society when the solidarity between African and European indentured laborers was torn apart by the false construct called race. And that experience has been replicated time and again over the course of my life, as so many of my cross-racial relationships, made tenuous by racism, were—and remain—frail and floundering, or they failed.

Reflecting on my relationship between my *I* and my *We*, I turn back even farther to my immigrant grandparents and their pilgrimage from the Shtetls of Eastern Europe to America at the turn of the twentieth century. They crossed the sea to escape the Jewish pogroms and find a better life in the United States. Facing discrimination, they clung to the old ways in a reconstituted ghetto of fellow Ashkenazim. In this way, they resisted assimilation into US culture and sustained a modicum of continuity and safety. My parents, being first generation natives, were hybrid "probationary" whites, navigating the gains and losses that resulted from their Americanization. I continued this progression, distancing myself even further from my Jewish heritage, by marrying "out" to an Anglo-Saxon Protestant. Of course, there were many reasons I married him (love certainly being one), but knowing what I know now, I can't help but wonder if it was also a subconscious attempt at moving ever closer to the "normality" I had been programmed and conditioned to believe that I, and mine, fell short of.

Much like the biblical metaphor, I placed my two children in reed baskets and sent them down the Nile to be rescued and raised in Pharaoh's palace.

In my late twenties, after a series of unfulfilling jobs, I pursued a career as a clinical social worker. There was no exploration of the history of movements of resistance and no connection to community organizing in the clinical track of the master's program I enrolled in. There was much discussion about the underprivileged, but not even a mention of the privileged (much less the overprivileged). I didn't even notice these omissions. I embraced, without question, that my professionalism depended solely on my objectivity and therapeutic techniques. Not too long after, nearly everything I understood to be true would one by one be challenged.

When I was 34 years old, I was the upper-middle-class mother of a one-year-old toddler. I had been licensed as a clinical social worker for all of two years and—with just one year of counseling experience at a community mental health center in a white suburb under my belt—I returned to part-time work. There I sat, in a cramped and airless room, facing a 20-year-old African American man who, despite all my attempts to engage him, refused to respond beyond monosyllabic answers. Everything I had learned in school and my brief tenure at the community clinic fell flat in the face of his relative silence. And who could blame him? He was doing nine months for selling marijuana, and we were on a floating barge in the Hudson River that held overflow prisoners from the City of New York. This makeshift jail was designated as a work-release facility, where inmates went out five days a week to work for two dollars an hour. It was a sweet deal for those who qualified. And I was the qualifier. My job was to assess whether candidates were psychologically appropriate for the placement. If I found that a prisoner was not, he was sent to the psychiatric ward at Riker's Island, a snake pit of rampant abuse. In my inexcusable ignorance and inadequate training, I referred numerous people there. The ghost of that job and the damage I did while I was there still haunt me—yet it stands as one of the most potent motivations for my commitment to racial justice.

As I sat uneasily across from this young man, his file on the desk beside me, a cognitive and moral dissonance began to grow within me. This dissonance was replicated time and again as I faced subsequent candidates. What became, over time, impossible to reconcile was the truth that I, too, had done most of the things that resulted in their incarceration—

shoplifting as a teenager and using and dealing drugs in college, to cite a couple of examples—yet I had done them with impunity. What could explain this stark difference in the present realities of our lives?

Over the course of my three interviews for the job, there was not even a mention of race or poverty, despite the fact that 99% of the incarcerated people were Black and Brown and the great majority indigent. I thought nothing of that at the time, but looking back, I am amazed that I was not asked about my perceptions and attitudes regarding both. I was, however, grilled on my understanding of sociopathic, manipulative, and defiant behaviors. And at each of these interviews I was assured that there would be sufficient security at the facility to counter the dangerous nature of the people I would be working with. Looking back I can clearly see that, given who I am and how much I didn't understand, I was profoundly unqualified to serve these men righteously.

I wish I could say that my worldview was forever transformed by the dissonance I experienced in that job, but it wasn't. While I did manage to move almost immediately from assessor to HIV test counselor, I know I continued to do harm. I left this job just before the birth of my second child. But the job has never left me.

During the ensuing years, I studied at a family therapy institute that specialized in multicultural issues and took numerous racial sensitivity and implicit bias workshops. This education was, at times, extremely uncomfortable. I understood I was white yet resisted interrogating and accepting what that really meant. Besides, I was Jewish and a woman—surely, I knew how it felt to be subjugated and marginalized. I was challenged by both faculty and colleagues, particularly Faculty and Colleagues of Color, when I disavowed my privilege and sense of superiority. I remain challenged by this as, under stress, I continue to prove capable of default defensiveness.

A major turning point in my journey was when I participated in the two-and-a-half-day Undoing Racism and Community Organizing Workshop led by the People's Institute for Survival and Beyond (PISAB) in 1999. Their workshop provided me an analysis of what racism is, how and why it was constructed and continues to be perpetuated, and how it has profoundly affected the way people in our country experience ourselves and function as a society. Perhaps most importantly, it was through the People's Institute that I began to see the imperative of coming together collectively to build multiracial community. Racial healing requires both internal (*I*) and external (*We*) work. In addition to my private practice, I began organizing in my community with other mental health practitioners, whites and fellow Jews. In 2006, I became a trainer with the People's Institute, and I later became a trainer with other institutes and organizations devoted to racial justice and equity. Cofacilitating as part of multiracial training teams in venues countrywide continues to deepen my consciousness and practice of *I* and *We*.

Two powerful tools from the People's Institute that strengthen this practice are the Covenant and Antiracist Organizing Principles presented in their Undoing Racism/Community Organizing Workshop (PISAB, established in 1980). The Covenant, offered early in each workshop's process, sets mutual agreements for our behavior over the course of our time together. Among the agreements that challenge our individualistic and competitive socialization are (PISAB, personal communication, 1999):

- *Struggle Together*—Everyone has valid experiences and unique contributions to make and is worthy of respect. No one is expendable (although in certain circumstances they may be temporarily sidelined).
- *Lean into the Growing Edge*—It is imperative to bravely venture out of one's comfort zone to grow and change. This is a particular challenge for those of us who are white, as we have come to feel entitled to comfort 24/7. Greet discomfort with gratitude and curiosity.
- *Take Literacy Moments*—Stop fronting. Risk being vulnerable about what you don't know. This is counter to a culture that worships expertise and, in social justice spaces, where people compete for the status of the "most woke."

PISAB's Antiracist Organizing Principles facilitate informed and humanistic practices, which are applicable not only in the domain of racial justice but in all social environments—including clinical work. Here are a few of these foundational precepts (PISAB, 2018):

- *Learning from History*—We live in an ahistorical culture, one that practices the selective amnesia and revisionism necessary to preserve the myth of America's exceptionalism. This principle calls us to learn the history of our people(s), neighborhood, community, country, and world. Knowing history allows us to trace the roots of our present reality and to strategically plan a way forward, knowing who we are and to whom we belong. Learning from history underscores the truth that we never get anywhere all by ourselves and that we stand on the shoulders of those that came before us. History instantaneously transforms our *I*'s into *We*'s.

- *Networking*—Relational networking is starkly different from transactional networking. Our culture commodifies everything—especially people—resulting in a person's value being tied to their usefulness. Antiracist networking is based on the humanistic belief that everyone has value simply because they are human. It asks us to build a "Net That Works"—for everyone. Networking in an antiracist way requires us to see the *person* before we see their *purpose.*
- *Developing Leadership*—This is about power and an alternative way of managing it. It is about sharing power—not accumulating and protecting it for oneself. It is about preparing others to challenge leadership and sharing the credit and spotlight. It is also about a different kind of leader—one who leads with transparency and vulnerability *alongside* others. Most of all, it is about seeing our work as part of a movement that began long before us and continues long after we are gone.
- *Maintaining Accountability*—Central to white culture's reverence for individualism is the belief that one need only be accountable to and for oneself. Yet, to work for racial justice (or any other of the interlocking oppressions) with integrity, one must follow the collective leadership and guidance of the communities most affected by that oppression. Everything that white indoctrination teaches rubs against this, so this principle demands constant vigilance. Accountability has as much to do with how one amends harm as it does to avoid enacting it.
- *Undoing Internalized Racial Oppression*—Racism is an airborne virus we inhale every moment of every day. Even with awareness, we are bound to cough it up now and again. Recognizing, interrogating, and circumventing the manifestations of internalized racial superiority (these learned behaviors include, but are not limited to, silence, denial, defensiveness, entitlement, domination, paternalism, and appropriation) is a major obligation of an antiracist white person.

Doing antiracist work and trying to live a righteous life presents daily dilemmas for me and for the *We*'s to which I belong. I cite some of these dilemmas here, in hopes that this can help others in their struggle to balance personal agency with collective responsibility.

## Navigating the Dilemmas of Whiteness

### *Speak Up or Remain Silent*

Being white, I am unaccustomed to having to *think* about my racial status, which is one of its most precious advantages. I need to ask, "In this moment and situation, do I stand up or do I step back? Will my voice be helpful or harmful to the BIPOC involved? Am I acting performatively or in genuine solidarity? Is my speaking up motivated by paternalism? Is my silence protecting me and white supremacy?"

### *Be Accountable to Antiracist BIPOC*

This requires I check my discernment process. Am I selecting people that are easier to be accountable to? Those who, through friendship or colleagueship, I feel will give me a pass? BIPOC that deliver the message in a manner I deem appropriate? How can I know whether my disagreement with feedback, even after much deliberation, is me acting out my racism? And, if accountability need be reciprocal, do I have the audacity to challenge a BIPOC when it comes to issues of race?

### *To Center or Not to Center Whiteness?*

Building an equitable multiracial society requires confronting the historical and current centrality of whiteness. Paradoxically, my experience has taught me that the way to decenter whiteness is to first reveal, expose, and examine it in all its complexity and nuance. Centering whiteness in this way serves the purpose of decentering it. But I need to be keenly sensitive to when and how this is done.

*Getting Paid for Racial Justice Work*

There is an intrinsic irony in being white and earning money through racial justice training and facilitation. It is comparable to being both arsonist and firefighter. To do this work with some integrity, I have to devote a portion of my earnings to BIPOC-led businesses and racial justice organizations.

*Accepting That a Dedication to Antiracism Doesn't Exempt Me*

Regardless of what is in my mind, heart, and soul, I am still a part of the white collective. I wear the same skin as every white person who has ever launched assaults on the dignity and the bodies of BIPOCs or stood silent in the presence of that violence. Despite all the work I've done and continue to do, I carry the distortions of my socialization. I am fated to do harm from time to time, despite my best intentions and vigilance.

*I'm Also Jewish and a Woman*

I've found myself in many a racial justice space where only my white identity was relevant. The implicit and explicit message was that our work was focused on our racial identities and none other, and when I brought other identities up, I was practicing escapism. Escaping my whiteness was, and continues to be, a possibility to consider each time, and yet, I have come to recognize that I need all the parts of myself to do this work and to live the life I was meant to live. As Penny Rosenwasser (2012) writes in *Hope into Practice: Jewish Women Choosing Justice Despite Our Fears,*

> Part of my wrestling: how to hold the suffering of so many in our world who are daily impoverished, ignored, brutalized—and also to hold the validity of Jewish pain, whether directly from genocide or pogroms, or indirectly from self-disdain, *without exaggerating, without diminishing.* (p. 13)

I must live out of all my *Is*, both privileged and subjugated, to authentically be part of the *We.*

*Acknowledging the Need for White People to Heal*

Resmaa Menakem (2017), a Black therapist and expert on cultural somatics, states:

> Throughout the United States' history as a nation, white bodies have colonized, oppressed, brutalized and murdered Black and Native ones. But well before the United States began, powerful white bodies colonized, oppressed, brutalized and murdered other, less powerful white ones. The carnage perpetrated on Blacks and Native Americans in the New World began, on the same soil, as an adaptation of long-standing white-on-white practices. This brutalization created trauma that has yet to be healed among white bodies today. (p. 62)

Later, he prescribes "white Americans need to imagine themselves in Black, red and brown bodies and *experience* what those bodies had to endure. They also need to do the same with the bodies of their own white ancestors" (Menakem, 2017, p. 65). I consider what Resmaa describes as *white* trauma to be *European* trauma. Yet, over the years I have witnessed in myself and in other white people two other forms of trauma that I believe *are* related to our whiteness. One has to do with the toll that was exacted from "ethnic" whites to be fully accepted as whites in the race construct—the hiding, minimizing, or sacrificing of their ancestral culture and ways of being to assimilate into the white Protestant standard. This severing, this ripping up of one's roots, is a trauma that has been passed down from generation to generation. To heal from this requires some form of intentional reckoning—perhaps something akin to Kübler-Ross's (1969) stages of grief, a forgiveness and/or a reclaiming.

The second kind of trauma involves our response upon realizing the truth about racism—and *our role in it*. This trauma, bringing with it shame and fear, must in some way be metabolized, or we are likely to fight, flee, or freeze instead of stay, reflect, and move into meaningful action.

Also of great import is the need for a thorough examination of the ways that racism has, and does, harm us. I've been asked countless times what could possibly move white people to want to give up their racial privilege. As an organizer, I have come to understand that it is imperative to locate the ways that ending racism serves *our* best interests. Those of us racialized as white need to recognize and *feel* what we have traded in for the advantages we've been given as well as what we gain by dismantling white supremacy. Some of the price paid for these "wages of whiteness" are rigid roles and patterns of behavior, diminished capacity for empathy and emotional expressiveness, distorted sense of self, fear of difference and of retaliation from marginalized groups, disembodiment and despiritualization, barriers to authenticity and intimacy, moral ambivalence, and disconnection from nature (Du Bois, 1998). Although this list of barriers to wholeness and relational health is not limited to white people, they reach epidemic levels in the white collective. I am convinced that race has something to do with it.

### *To Caucus or Not to Caucus*

I have always been drawn to the sense of community, humor, and joy I experience in Cultures of Color—a sense of connection that is sorely lacking in white spaces—even white antiracist spaces. I do not look forward to struggling together with other white people. But white people have been told that is where our focus needs to be by Leaders of Color, Malcolm X and Stokely Carmichael among them. As Michael Eric Dyson (2017) unequivocally states:

> You must ***school*** your white brothers and sisters, your cousins and uncles, your loved ones and friends, and all who will listen to you, about the white elephant in the room—white privilege. Share with them what you learn about us, but share as well what you learn about yourself, about how whiteness works. . . . They may not be as defensive with you, so you must be an ambassador of truth to your own tribes. (p. 203)

So, I try to be an antiracist ambassador to the white *We* through my work with the Center for the Study of White American Culture and by facilitating white affinity spaces and doing presentations and workshops with other whites. It is the most difficult and, often, the least gratifying work I do, but I have come to believe it is a good way to put my white skin to use.

White affinity or caucus spaces are controversial because they are intentionally segregated, but over years I have come to view them as necessary for more effective cross-racial organizing. Whites must practice tolerating racial anxiety and thickening our individual and collective skin together, learn how to build loving and noncompetitive community, and constructively challenge ourselves and each other. As Gulati-Partee and Potapchuk (2014) articulate,

> The value of caucusing is so both white people and people of color have intentional space and time to focus on their respective work to dismantle racism and advance racial equity. Caucusing does not happen instead of integrated groups; rather, caucusing can lead to more authentic and powerful integrated groups. Caucusing not only respects the choice of marginalized groups to be together, it also makes the dominant culture visible—an important step in making intentional changes to the culture. (pp. 35–36)

White affinity gatherings also serve as places to do our grieving outside of the sight of BIPOC so as not to further traumatize or enrage them. We need to see—and deeply feel—how racism has compromised our humanity. For this reason, I have stopped using the term "ally." It implies that I and other white people are helping BIPOC with *their* problem, when racism is *our* problem. Currently I've been using the terms "racial justice collaborator" or "coconspirator." This language serves to remind me of my broader and deeper stake in this work. In addition to ending the oppression of others, I need to end my collusion with white supremacy, to end it for my white children and for the generations that follow. This reframing serves several purposes: helping to heal what ails me, ensuring I don't give up when the work gets too difficult, and guarding against toxic paternalism.

Through my process of learning and unlearning, I have developed a clinical "third eye." Inside my office, I can better assess power and its misuse. I notice who is in control and where injustice is operating. I can recognize where history may be repeating itself, who gets to be comfortable, who gets to be uncomfortable, and whose story is missing.

This enhanced vision has powerfully infiltrated my approach and treatment strategies. Initially it was far easier to employ when working with

Clients of Color and biracial couples, even those who didn't bring up race as an issue themselves. Bringing up race—and the connection between racism and their presenting troubles—with just us white folks in the room proved, and continues to prove, far more formidable.

White supremacist culture has invisibly and profoundly informed the way all of us relate to one another, raise our children, and work. I usually begin the naming and unpacking of its ubiquitous influence by tracing certain themes in clients' families and cultures of origin. Slowly (or quickly) our conversation expands to include the dominating culture and how it relates to their family's story. While investigating their immigration stories, for instance, we wonder: When did your people come to the United States? Why did they come, and where did they settle? How were they treated when they arrived, and how did they adjust? What traumas did they experience and how did they survive them? *When did your people become white?*

The benefits of whiteness are routinely made invisible to us, appearing as either universal (everyone has it, and if they don't it is their own fault) or as earned solely as a result of personal talent and effort. Compassionately exposing the unearned power that whiteness confers is an important step in helping white clients gain a realistic, "rightsized" view of themselves. Highlighting the impact of internal racial superiority as well as the values and standards of our larger society locates the struggles and suffering of each of us, not only within, but also outside of ourselves. Perhaps most importantly, this exposure reaches for the spiritual unrest that accompanies knowing, deep within, that we are beneficiaries of an unjust arrangement.

What distortions to our humanity have occurred by being placed in this inflated position in our society, one that is dependent on and sustained by the devaluation of others? What have been the costs to us and to society as a whole? Engaging together in an exploration of the ways we have been acculturated into whiteness can begin to externalize the distortions and the costs enough to begin, or continue, our deprogramming. We start a dialogue between our whiteness and the uncontaminated soul that entered the world.

My thinking and feeling, as both an *I* and part of my various *We*'s, continue to evolve. I must continue to let go of dearly held beliefs and to struggle with coexisting contradictions. If I am on the right path, I hope soon to wince at some of the words I have written here. Right now, my focus is shifting from *struggling against* racism and white supremacy to *creating* a world without it. I am unapologetically against racism, of course, and still use the term antiracist to describe myself and our movement, but I have begun to feel that framing my purpose as "anti" limits my imagination and effectiveness in making change.

In closing, I would be woefully remiss if I didn't acknowledge some of the *We* that has provided me with much needed companionship and grace on this pilgrimage. My heartfelt gratitude goes out to Dr. Kenneth V. Hardy of the Eikenberg Academy for Social Justice[1]; to everyone, past and present, at the People's Institute for Survival and Beyond[2]; to everyone associated with the Center for the Study of White American Culture[3] and the Center for Racial Justice in Education[4]; to my family at the Soul Focused Group[5]; to my comrades in the Antiracist Alliance Northeast[6]; to my kin in European Dissent, New Jersey and New York; and to all the teachers, heroes, and sheroes, both living and dead, who have shared their wisdom along the way. Lastly, I want to thank my children, Molly and Jerome, for remaining the two most compelling reasons I walk this road.

**BONNIE BERMAN CUSHING, LCSW,** is white, Jewish, and a licensed clinical social worker and antiracist organizer/educator. She has worked in the mental health field for 30 years as a family-systems therapist and for over 25 years has been engaged in the movement for racial and social justice. Bonnie has been a core trainer with the People's Institute for Survival and Beyond since 2006 and, in addition, has trained for the Center for Racial Justice in Education, the Eikenberg Institute for Relationships, the Soul Focused Group, and the Center for the Study of white American Culture. She is a cofounder and member of both the Antiracist Alliance-North Jersey and its white affinity group, European Dissent. Bonnie was editor of *Accountability and White Antiracist Organizing* and *Living in the Tension: The Quest for a Spiritualized Racial Justice* (both CDD Books). In 2016, she authored the article "Decolonizing Therapy" for *VOICES magazine.*

## Notes

1. Eikenberg Academy for Social Justice, https://www.eikenbergacademyforsocialjustice.com
2. People's Institute for Survival and Beyond, http://www.pisab.org
3. Center for the Study of White American Culture, https://www.euroamerican.org
4. Center for Racial Justice in Education, https://centerracialjustice.org
5. Soul Focused Group, https://soulfocusedgroup.com
6. Antiracist Alliance Northeast, https://antiracistalliance.com

## References

*Berkson, W. (2011).* Pirke avot: Timeless wisdom for modern life. *Jewish Publication Society.*

*Du Bois, W. E. B. (1998).* Black reconstruction in America 1860–1880. *Free Press.*

*Dyson, M. E. (2017).* Tears we cannot stop: A sermon to white America. *St. Martin's Press.*

*Gulati-Partee, G., & Potapchuk, M. (2014). Paying attention to white culture and privilege: A missing link to advancing racial equity.* The Foundation Review, 6*(1), 25–38.*

*Kendi, I. X. (2020, May 4). We're still living and dying in the slaveholders' republic.* The Atlantic. *ttps://www.theatlantic.com/ideas/archive/2020/05/what-freedom-means-trump/611083/*

*Kübler-Ross, E. (1969).* On death and dying. *Macmillan.*

*Menakem, R. (2017).* My grandmother's hands: Racialized trauma and the pathway to mending hearts and bodies. *Central Recovery Press.*

*People's Institute for Survival and Beyond. (2018).* Our principles. *http://www.pisab.org/our-principles/*

*Rosenwasser, P. (2012).* Hope into practice: Jewish women choosing justice despite our fears.

# SECTION VII

# STRATEGIES FOR DECONSTRUCTING, DECENTERING, AND DISMANTLING WHITENESS IN CLINICAL PRACTICE AND BEYOND

## CHAPTER 23

# On Being Black in White Places

## A Therapist's Journey from Margin to Center

KENNETH V. HARDY, PHD

Long before I knew exactly what a therapist was, I knew I wanted to be one. From the time I was in elementary school I was intrigued by the complexity of the human condition. I was perpetually curious about why certain things were the way they were. My parents and grandparents often attempted to provide me with satisfying answers but seldom did they, or did the insights they offered, succeed in soothing the soul of my incessant sense of curiosity. I always seemed to have had an endless stream of "why" questions that ranged from the absurd to the profound, from micro- to macro-related issues; from questions about the here-and-now to those about the afterlife . . . assuming that such a phenomenon even existed. Beneath all of the questions was a blaze of curiosity, intrigue, and dogged determinism to gain a firmer grasp of the nuances that help to elucidate what made us tick as human beings. I wondered how twin brothers, David and Donald Watkins, family friends, could share the same parents, grow up in the same family, and yet be so fundamentally different. I had the same query about my family: how did my brother and I grow up to be so different, although we shared the same parents, were just two years apart in age, and did virtually everything together as children? I also wondered why my first cousin Johnny had no siblings and why his father was alive but not present in his life. Although these curiosities were persistent, they were fairly benign compared to the ones that constituted the major "haunt" in my life.

The haunting curiosities were almost always reserved for and related to the phenomenon of race. My questions about race and race relationships were recurring, disturbing, and emotionally disruptive. They felt very personal. Through the eyes of a young child it was always difficult to understand the many whys associated with the phenomenon of race. For instance, why did white men who were often 10–15 years my father's junior insist that he address them by using the term "Mister" while they routinely and consistently addressed him by his first name? Why? Why did they insist? And why did my Dad so willingly acquiesce? I wondered why my father, who often seemed so omnipotent and sturdy under some circumstances, especially within our family, seemed so small, fragile, and frazzled outside of the family, especially when in the presence of whites? Why? Why were my mother, and other Black women like her, constantly treated as if they were servants? Why was she and other Black women like her never afforded the respect, deference, or regal treatment that was commonplace for their white female counterparts? Why did she often behave as if it were her duty to care for the very whites who seemed to care little about her? The rules of race relationships in the world in which I was socialized supplied me with a multitude of phenomenological/existential questions—among those were questions about the meaning of Blackness in general and what did it mean for me specifically.

My great grandmother, Anna, the granddaughter of a slave, lived with my family until I was a junior in college and tried feverishly to help me answer all of my emerging questions regarding what it meant to be Black. She was one of the first and few people in my earlier life to talk to me so openly and candidly about race with the uncensored rawness befitting the topic. She recalled countless stories, devoid of any detectable emotion, of women she knew who had been raped at the hands of white men. Stories of young innocent Black men who were hanged, castrated, and terrorized for merely looking at a white female. She witnessed firsthand the brutality and inhumanity of the segregated South in this country; yet she neither harbored nor displayed any discernible expressions of hostility, rage, or hatred. Her sense of humanity and undying faith in God would not allow her to harbor ill feelings, she often noted. She was a deeply religiously devout person who believed in God and His capacity to rid the world of evil and sin. As her first-born great grandson, she made two requests of me: (1) "Make sure you get an education!"—an experience she had been denied by law—and (2) "Put your faith in the Lord." Because education, both in my biological and ancestral family, was considered the key to liberation, honoring this dimension of my grandmother's request was simple. The second request was far more challenging.

At that point in my life, I had already developed an ambivalent relationship with religion. In fact, I couldn't understand why the white, blond-hair portrait of Jesus Christ that was so prominently displayed in our home and the homes of virtually every Black person I knew were so revered. It was painfully difficult for me to differentiate between "the image" in the portrait and the picture etched in my young psyche of those who routinely belittled, humiliated, and disrespected my parents. My introduction and exposure to church, God, and religion only intensified my sense of curiosity. The more I learned of God and His holiness, the more I began to question life as I knew it and the harsh cold world of mean-spiritedness that I got a glimpse of on a daily basis. The set of questions and curiosities that I was left with were complex and even more difficult to discuss without high affect. Why, I wondered and asked on numerous occasions, was there so much hatred in the world if God was so good? Why so much suffering? What did it mean that Blacks were slaves and whites their "masters"? Why did God allow slavery to last for nearly 300 years without intervening? Were I and other Blacks like me cursed, as some religious doctrines would assert? My incessant questions often left my parents, grandmother, and even some teachers and clergy worried and frustrated. Admittedly, I had a very difficult time reconciling the matter of race and all of its intricacies and complexities. At a very early and impressionable age, the plight of Black people had tremendous resonance for me. It was personal and quite intimately interwoven in my life. It lived robustly in the house I grew up in. It loomed large over the street where I resided. It permeated not just the school I attended, the church where families like mine congregated, but also every corner of the world in which I inhabited. My walks to school and church were rude reminders of a world divided, the impenetrable chasm that existed between the haves and the have-nots, those who were valued and devalued, and those who were spiritually alive as well as those who had been cast aside to die a slow and irreversible spiritual death. Put my faith in the Lord? How did Great Grandmother Anna? How could I do so without feeling betrayed? Why didn't she feel betrayed? After being harshly reprimanded by several powerful and influential adults in my life for expressing such disrespectful and sacrilegious sentiments, I learned to conceal my thoughts and feelings about race and religion. In spite of it all, the questions remained.

## The Pre-College Years

By the time I reached high school, I was certain of what I wanted to do in life, although I still didn't have a name for it. Full of adolescent naivete, blind ambition, and race-related rage, I wanted to change the world! I was sickened by the absurdity and hypocrisy of the world in which I lived. My daily walk to high school was "inconvenienced" by the omnipresence of homelessness and people sleeping on the streets because they had nowhere else to go; yet houses seemed in abundance. Arriving at high school where most of the students were Black and most of the teachers and virtually all of the administrators were white was fraught with racially based complications. My school, like so many others, was one where well-intentioned teachers attempted to educate students without understanding or being educated about the complexities of their conditions. It was the place where the students saw race with impeccable clarity and felt the pangs of it with an undeniable sting, while the teachers denied seeing it at all. There was no space for common ground or any plausible possibilities for traversing the divide. The teachers were often considered right in their self-righteous and self-declared view that they were color-blind. They promulgated the notion in every possible way that race didn't matter, while the students were accused of using it as a crutch or excuse for their academic ineptitude, lack of interest, drive, and ambition. My high school then, like many urban schools now, was a type of slaughterhouse. It was a place where the hopes, dreams, and spirits of young children of color were routinely and systematically destroyed. There were two dominant educational tracks: one that prepared the precious few for future careers at prestigious colleges and universities like Harvard, University of Pennsylvania, and Yale; the other that prepared the critical masses for a future inextricably tied to the juvenile justice system, detention facilities, and ultimately jail. One of the most egregious offenses that could ever be exacted against young curious minds took place as a matter of routine at my school: well-meaning school personnel routinely placed expiration dates on the dreams and ambitions of young curious minds. Children's dreams, in my view, no matter how far-fetched, preposterous, or seemingly unattainable should never be discouraged or taken away.

Unfortunately, African Americans, and other students of color, were routinely discouraged from pursuing college by academic advisors and guidance counselors. The common and general belief was that "we were not college material." Several decades later I still have vivid memories of conversations that I had with my guidance counselor about going to college and my desire to pursue a psychology degree. The advice and "guidance" I received was to pursue trade school so that I would be equipped to pursue a career where I could use my hands. I received this "encouragement" on more than one occasion, which was extremely odd given that I was enrolled in a college preparatory curriculum and had no demonstrated skills "in using my hands." This is what it looks like to have your dreams, hopes, and ambitions eclipsed by the subtleties of race. It is a process that is akin to what educator and activist Jonathan Kozel (1967) referred to decades ago as a type of "death at an early age." Having dreams decimated, destroyed, and/or deferred has been a common experience for many African Americans both individually and collectively. It is in part, I believe, what inspired the poet Langston Hughes (1958/1994, p.268, emphasis in original) to pen his inspirational poem, "Harlem (2)."[1] Hughes asks:

> What happens to a dream deferred?
> Does it dry up like a raisin in the sun?
> Or fester like a sore—
> And then run?
> Does it stink like rotten meat? Or crust and sugar over— like a syrupy sweet?
> Maybe it just sags
> like a heavy load.
> *Or does it explode?*

## The College Years

My life in college greatly enhanced my understanding, awareness, and sensitivity to what it meant to be Black and especially, to be Black in white places. No longer embedded within the familiar surroundings and security of Blackness that my family and community had afforded me in the mostly racially segregated margins of society I called home, college represented a new and sometimes harsh cold world. My life in college not only provided a jaundiced view of Blackness but of whiteness, as well. I learned very quickly that virtually everything associated with being Black was framed as bad, pathological, demonic, and even dirty in some instances while "pure, wholesome, normal, and superior" often characterized whiteness. These proracist notions about Blackness and whiteness were present virtually everywhere from private peer interactions to the classroom and lecture halls. Even the living quarters on campus perpetuated the broader cultural narrative that Black was inferior and white was superior. The dormitories that "coincidentally" housed students of color were without fail less aesthetically attractive, poorly maintained with tiles missing from the floor, cracked windows, water-stained walls, a scarcity of toilet paper, and washers and dryers that were frequently inoperable. On the other hand, the dormitories that were inhabited by white students were very well maintained and adequately furnished with all necessary paper products and supplies. The floors were spotless and cleaned routinely, and not just during parents' week. The appliances were state of the art, and the ambience that permeated all of these dorms was one that invited, perhaps even demanded, honor, dignity, and respect. This is what it means to be Black in white places. According to Hardy and Laszloffy (2005, p. 149), "devaluation refers to a process by which an individual or group is stripped of the essentials of their humanity." At its core, devaluation assaults one's sense of dignity, while heightening sensitivity to disrespect, and elevating the demand (need) for respect. Devaluation is a driving and central force in the experience of Blackness. It is virtually impossible to feel respected in a context of devaluation.

Any effort to bring attention to the obvious inequities that existed based on race was pointless and perilous. The push-back by the white establishment— administrators, faculty, and students—expressed a familiar sentiment. Thus any claims of racial bias were considered unfair and unfounded allegations advanced by those who were "hypersensitive" about race and merely trying to "play the race card."

My journey to becoming a therapist involved attending three different large state universities, and completing two post-doctoral training programs in five different regions of the country. My professional journey mirrored that of many African Americans and other people of color of my generation and beyond: I never had a single classmate, professor, or mentor of color. While I had the pleasure of working with several supportive white mentors, and had some white classmates who became lifelong acquaintances, race was always the unspoken and unacknowledged dimension of these relationships. It was rarely, if ever, discussed. In our relationships, we understood intuitively that open discussions about race were off limits. We colluded in pretending, acting "as if" it didn't matter or that we had transcended it. Yet it mattered so much that we could never discuss it. In the rare instances when race was acknowledged, it was usually introduced by a white professor or student assuring me that they did not think of me, nor see me, as Black.

I have vivid memories of sitting in classes and wondering how many of my self-assured, confident, brilliant, eloquent, and articulate white classmates could do what I was doing? How many of them, I wondered, would be willing to submerge themselves into a context where they would automatically be relegated to a non-negotiable, irrevocable *world of otherness*? How many of them would be willing to leave their sanctuaries of sameness to explore and experience the world of otherness . . . where the rules of engagement were not their rules, where their core values and values of the system were replete with tension and incongruity, where a sense of safety was not ensured by the familiarity of the surroundings? I wondered how many of them would be able to show up every day as *the only one*, and tolerate being the someone who was obviously noticed but never acknowledged? Would they be able and willing to endure the many microaggressive racial slights that occur almost daily (see Sue et al., 2007) or to bear the innocent acts of ignorance that were *never intended* to do harm but somehow always managed to do so? These were often the thoughts, self-reflections, and feelings of resentment that invaded and interrupted my thinking while sitting in class very visible but unseen.

## On Becoming a Therapist (Who Happens to Be Black)

For many Blacks, and other people of color, on the path to becoming therapists, the journey is a rather emotionally tumultuous one that requires a constant sorting through the intricate entanglements of race and racial oppression. The process and experience demand so much more than mastery of an academic curriculum, successful completion of an internship, scholarly work, and licensure. It also involves managing the emotional burdens of being Black in white places . . . having to cope on a daily basis with the often painful and emotionally laden experience of managing the dilemmas of race. Black and other people of color understand that the process of becoming a therapist, unlike with their white counterparts, requires mastery of two curricula—one explicit, one implicit; one for all trainees, and one for "minorities only."

### *The Dilemmas of Race*

The *implicit, for minorities' only* curriculum requires Blacks and other people of color to effectively deal with a myriad of racially charged issues and dilemmas that occur on a regular basis. Unfortunately, many of us are often confined to dealing with these matters in private, alone, and devoid of support. It is often this dimension of the process of becoming a therapist that leaves many therapists of color questioning their sanity, mental stability, and appropriateness for the field. After all, there is something potentially "crazy-making" about seeing and feeling racial slights, whether intentional or not, so potently while they are simultaneously denied and remain invisible by everyone around you. The *implicit, for minorities' only* curriculum requires that Blacks and other people of color continue to remain sane even while operating in the midst of (seemingly) insane places. We must always demonstrate the proper decorum, stay polite, remain a team player, and take the "high road" in response to racial slights and abuses regardless of how much pain we have to endure. The following vignette provides a brief example of the type of restraint, stamina, and internal fortitude that being Black in white places often requires.

## CASE OF "THE ULTIMATE PATHOLOGY"

In a doctoral seminar entitled "Dynamics of Family Processes," one of my white classmates asked the professor: "Does illegitimacy or female-headed households constitute the ultimate pathology in Black families?" The professor received the question and after a few pensive moments said, "Well, I am not sure what you mean by ultimate pathology . . . pathology is pathology." The ensuing class discussion was devoted to how one measures degrees of pathology and the topic of race was never mentioned.

Unfortunately, neither the professor nor the students advanced a single comment devoted to the incendiary racial premise of the question. Several class members did glance at me as if anticipating a reaction, but experience had taught me to remain still and silent, no matter the emotional cost. The dilemmas of race are such that African Americans, as well as other people of color, are often expected to be the resident experts on a host of race-related issues (see Kirkland, 2011). The positions they posit, however, must be self-deprecating, affirm the views of the dominant racial discourse, and never implicate whites. Any deviation from the aforementioned prescription for executing one's race-related expertise deems the African American an angry, polarizing, hypersensitive, self-proclaimed victim. Although I was overcome with emotions during the remainder of the class, for these reasons, I "chose" to remain silent.

As I recall the details of the class, I am still not sure, even as I commit these words to writing, what was more personally painful and disappointing: (a) the premise of the question; (b) the absence of any racial critique by a professor I admired and respected professionally; or (c) the utter silence of all my classmates. More importantly, the collective silence of the class made it clear that it was incumbent upon me to understand that the pain, agony, disappointment, and furor that the experience generated, belonged to me. There was no processing it in class, there was no discussion to be had regarding the inherent racism threaded in the question, or consideration of what the experience was like for me as the only one in the class who had grown up in a Black family. As is often the case, I, like many other people of color in similar situations, had to stay centered, not take it personally, don't play the race card, and "choose" whether I should speak up and be punished publicly—but allow my soul to thrive—or whether I should remain silent, thus allowing my physical self to be embraced and have my soul assaulted. Every conceivable effort you expend to extricate yourself from the cycle of "being defined" only serves to intensify and reinforce the dynamic. Blackness as an experience means standing in the midst of a double bind, where both one's passivity and assertion in response to being defined, for example, often renders the same outcome. Essentially, you are double-bound, "damned if you do, and damned if you don't." Demonstrating the ability to effectively confront and manage dilemmas of race, even when it is virtually impossible to do so, is a salient feature of the *implicit, for minorities' only* curriculum. Early in my clinical career, during a family therapy session (reported in Kottler & Carlson, 2005, pp. 123–128) in which I was confronted with the overt racism ("I ain't goin' to see no nigger doctor") of a 9-year-old white boy and his parents, I was distressed by the intransigence of the patients, of course, but was even more angered by the response of my white colleagues who were observing through a one-way mirror when they advised, during a consultation break, "You can't allow this racialized interaction to distract you from the real issues operating here" and "You just gotta hang in there."

Ironically, I was recently contacted by a large university located on the West Coast to assist with a racial issue that was quite similar to the ones described above. According to the dean of the college, "The situation started out as a benign misunderstanding that has since become racialized by a few. Now it simply won't go away as it continues to spread like an untreated cancer." Consider the following summary of the major events.

## CASE OF "THE FACTS"

The program in question is a doctoral clinical training program that prides itself on its commitment to diversity and social justice. Several African American students were outraged regarding a dynamic that occurred in one of their classes. During a class lecture devoted to HIV and AIDS, the professor noted, according to

> one of the students, that one out of every five Black women suffers with AIDS. Ironically, there were five Black females in the class who immediately drew scrutiny in the form of stares from the class as well as some scattered and intermittent laughter. Feeling overexposed, embarrassed, and humiliated, one of the students immediately left the classroom in tears, while the others stared at the professor with disbelief. The professor responded by stating: "What do you all want me to do . . . these are the facts, I'm giving you the facts here. I can't change the facts in deference to political correctness. In all due respect, this is the type of hypersensitivity to race that makes it impossible for all of us to move forward. I'm counting on all of you here to make a difference in the world out there and you can't do that if you overreact every time someone makes a statement about race that you disagree with or think shouldn't be stated."

The professor, a licensed therapist, seemed oblivious to the process of the class dynamics and how it was profoundly shaped by the nuances of race.

In these vignettes and countless others that have been omitted but could have been included, the African American students were left to deal with the racially charged, emotionally laden burden of being Black in white places. It was their task, burden, and responsibility to stay present, not overreact, or personalize the issue at hand, regardless of how personal it was or felt. They must accomplish this feat while simultaneously managing deeply seated feelings of hurt and shame for which there were no invitations or avenues to open and honest discussion. Regardless of the depths of the emotions experienced, the rules of race and racial oppression dictated that it was imperative that silence be the expression of choice.

## The World of Work and "Coming Home"

In many ways my graduate and post-doctoral training prepared me well for my work as a clinician in the "real world." My first full-time permanent position as a clinician was in an outpatient mental health facility in Brooklyn, New York, where I also served as Director of Group and Family Treatment. My clients were largely lower-income and poor African Americans and Latinos whose mental health difficulties were compounded by the intersections of race, class, and the everyday social, psychological, and emotional hardships of life in the inner city. From a distance, and based on what was typically documented on referral sheets, my clients' presenting problems were similar to those one would expect to find in any behavioral health treatment center: anxiety and other affective disorders; psychoses; and a myriad of child-centered family dysfunctions, all compounded by trauma. However, in treatment, clients routinely discussed problems that were never taught throughout my graduate school training or treated in the many university-based clinics where I had worked. Their "problems" had no *DSM* diagnostic categories and often centered on a recurring list of social problems that seemed beyond the reach of the *psychological solutions* that constituted our preferred treatment protocol. So much of their reported suffering was rooted in what they reported as maltreatment by the police, teachers who preferred to punish and discipline their children rather than educate them, landlords who refused to repair the dilapidated, often rodent-infested buildings where many lived, and politicians who only saw them when it was in the politicians' best interest to do so. I heard the painful human cry of those who wondered why dialing 911, for example, was of no consequence while the blood of their children and other loved ones saturated the streets of East New York. Many of the clients, who frequented the Center were obviously depressed, both those who expressed a frightening sense of unbridled rage, as well as those who appeared sunken in a sea of sullenness. It was a detail that was too stark and keenly obvious to overlook. Yet, the clients' incessant experiences with oppression and the ways it was so intricately intertwined into every fiber of their daily existence was much harder for many clinicians to see. Efforts to uncover the roots of depression, rage, or other serious mental-health issues repeatedly focused on the clients' biology, psychology, and family-of-origin experiences, but almost never their *ecology*, that is, the impact of their environment and the sociological-cultural context in which they and their behaviors were deeply embedded.

Although I had never treated clients of color prior to accepting this position, there was something familiar about their experiences that extended beyond words or conscious recognition. For the first time as a practicing clinician, I was able to breathe a little more freely. There was suddenly no more anxiety about greeting a client in the waiting room and watching the shock on their faces and the temporary paralysis-like state they exhibited when discovering that "their doctor" was not white. Gone were the anxieties and awkwardness about having to hear denigrating references to Blacks and/or other minorities in sessions that subsequently exempted me because I "was different." I relished the idea of finally being able to practice in a context, as I assumed was commonplace for my white counterparts, where race didn't matter; where my anxieties and insecurities could be considered relative to my clinical competencies and not the color of my skin. In many respects, this job was a godsend. It was a kind of homecoming. It was what I believed I was called to do. It was exactly what, I believe, my great grandmother had in mind when she demanded that I "make something of my life." No, she wasn't referring to objects, things, or material wealth, she was speaking of giving back to the dispirited, the silenced, and the disenfranchised while never forgetting upon whose shoulders I climbed and stood to elevate and escape the walls of oppression. Furthermore, this job was exactly what I believed I needed to help repair the many wounds to my soul that were sustained from many years of training as a Black person in predominantly white settings.

The treatment population served, the essence of the work at the Center, and the neighborhood in which it was embedded was central to the early life curiosities that initially sparked my interest in the profession without a name. My life had come full circle. The questions, curiosities, and musings that I had about the world, particularly in regards to race, that had been such a catalyst for my chosen profession was now the centerpiece of my work as a therapist. I could not imagine another job for which I was more aptly suited.

Unfortunately, the seemingly intuitive understanding that I believed I had of my clients and their experiences did not easily translate into them understanding me or feeling understood by me. In a relatively short period of time several of my clients expressed apprehension, skepticism, and even suspicion about me. Both privately and publicly they wondered if I were "Black enough." After over 10 years of being "educated" in white places, this was a question I had privately asked of myself on numerous occasions, breathlessly fearing the answer. One Latino client eventually confirmed one of my greatest fears as he stated wryly: "Hey Doc, I don't really get you, man. You look Black but everything else about you tells me you're white . . . I really can't trust someone like you who has the complexion but not the connection . . . I feel I'm Blacker than you and technically I'm not Black!" A day earlier, my secretary, Janie, who was African American and a single parent, also confronted me regarding what she perceived as my lack of racial connection. Her words were carefully chosen, expressed with the utmost respect and sensitivity but cut liked a knife nonetheless. She noted that she was offended by the language and descriptions that I had used in a Psychosocial Assessment that I had written. She stated that she felt that I had equated single parenthood with "being dysfunctional" and that everything I had written about the family in question was what she thought white people thought, wanted to believe, and would be delighted that "I" had written it. "Somehow I, as well as the others, here expected something different from you," she stated disappointedly. Both my eyes and my heart began to weep. She went on to say: "We were so proud of you and thought you would be different but you seem lost . . . you seem like all that book knowledge has ruined you." In many ways Janie reminded me of my great grandmother, Anna, not in terms of physical appearance or age but with regard to her centeredness, wisdom, and seemingly unflappable demeanor. She had a hearty wisdom and unshakeable clarity that all of my "book knowledge" had not equipped me with during my process of miseducation. Her words resonated with me intellectually and jarred me emotionally. Janie, as well as other clients and colleagues, were voicing externally what I already knew internally but found too painful to fully embrace. They were absolutely correct: I had been trained to be a good white therapist!

## A Well-Trained White Therapist

I was once again reminded of the inescapability of race. In the world of work I was much too white to earn the trust of many people of color, and among whites, I was always too Black to be taken too seriously. Janie was absolutely right, I had lost my self. After all, this was a precondition for successfully navigating and completing graduate school. How could someone like me, who was completely educated and trained by whites, who was fully indoctrinated in Eurocentric ideology, whose clinical exposure was primarily to white clients, and who was consistently and systematically discouraged from paying too much attention to race throughout his training, be anything but a good white therapist? I was tremendously skilled at writing "great" case notes exactly the way I was trained to do. Unfortunately, so much of what I looked for, what I wrote, and what I was unable to see because of what I had been trained to look for, unwittingly maligned many of the clients of color that I endeavored to help. To my white colleagues, my notes were excellent, "professional," and "objective." To my clients of color, my notes, case summaries, and assessments were essays of betrayal, written by a good white therapist.

As a good white therapist, I had become what I now refer to as a GEMM (Hardy, 2010), a Good Effective Mainstream Minority therapist. To accomplish this feat, therapists of color, like me, must commit to never discussing or acknowledging race. We must understand that "being professional" and "being objective" are sacred virtues that should never be violated or compromised even when our souls are being murdered. Being "professional" means never discussing or reacting to personal issues like race. It means always having the unshakable ability to stay calm, composed, and centered especially in the face of egregious racial slights, microaggressions, and insults. "Being objective" often means not seeing what I believe I see but rather seeing what whites believe I should see. Along the way, I have had numerous opportunities to demonstrate my sense of professionalism and objectivity, such as in the following scenario.

While employed as a senior-level executive for a professional association representing therapists, it was an integral part of my responsibility to attend the Board of Directors meetings. The association president, serving as Chairman of the Board, became visibly irate during a rather spirited discussion at a Board of Directors' meeting regarding whether rehabilitated ex-felons should be allowed to join the association. The President made it unambiguously clear to the board that he was a strong advocate for the proposal in question.

When the motion to adopt a policy to grant ex-felons admittance to the organization received little support, the President assertively pursued his argument with the Board even further. When the Board appeared unimpressed and unfazed by his impassioned plea, the

> President stated to the Board in a frustrated and tersc manner: "Damn it, I feel like the nigger in this group." After a brief and silent pause, he turned to me and said: "Oh, excuse me, Ken! I guess I'm frustrated because all of you have stated that you want to increase our minority membership base and how in the world are we ever going to do that if we make it impossible for (rehabilitated) ex-felons to join our organization."

Not surprisingly, not one of the eleven remaining Board members or any of the three staff in attendance said a word or even acknowledged the inherent racism contained in the President's heartfelt plea. After all, he was using "nigger" as a metaphor not a vitriolic racial slur. "His intention," I was later encouraged to consider, "was not to insult or malign Blacks . . . he is just a passionate guy." I was once again told what I have often been told in situations such as this one: "Ken, you are too emotional—you can't afford to personalize these issues, they are not personal. You have to look at the big picture, stay professional, and be objective." While the commitment of the President—who was a well-educated, powerful, white, heterosexual male—to increase the "African American membership" was laudable, it was never questioned why his proposed strategy was relegated to admitting ex-felons and not targeting for recruitment the wealth of Historically Black Colleges and Universities located throughout the country, at least five of which were located within driving distance of the national headquarters of the Association. This interaction and all of its intricacies was a potent example of what it means to be Black, feel Black, and be in a "white place."

"White places" are those "places" where "normal, healthy, the standard" are code words and synonyms for whiteness. In white places "white" and "right" are interchangeable. It is where it is commonplace and acceptable practice to negatively define the experience of others, deny their realities, and impose meaning on the lives of others regardless of how little is actually known about them. Both privilege and the privileges of privilege are strongly sanctioned in white places, including the privilege to: speak or not speak; to be seen or not seen; to define others' in accordance with one's image; to deny and/or dictate the length of others' suffering; to ignore history; to obfuscate the critical distinctions that exist between excuses and reasons, explanations, and justifications; and to remain righteous about the rightness of one's position. Finally, "white places" negatively affect the lives of white people who are poor, gay/lesbian/transgender, women, as well as countless others who are marginalized due to social location, stigma, or experience with trauma.

Over the years many of these experiences have become increasingly less toxic and painful. In a perverse way, I am grateful to have had all of these experiences. While being Black in white places has certainly been the epicenter of considerable pain, disappointment, hopelessness, and despair in my life, it has also contributed to my growth and development as a therapist and as a human being. It has provided me with a perspective that enables me to be in the world as it is and simultaneously aspire to help mold it into what it quite possibly could become. Perhaps this is why I see my role as a therapist in broad terms. It is not just a process that can or should be limited to the small, intimate, sanctuary known as the consulting room. There is a global imperative as well contained in this work, and that is for those of us aspiring to be healers, to be wherever human suffering is, and to recognize that healing the world is and has to be a fundamental aspect of the work that we do.

## Lessons Learned

My great grandmother often encouraged me, sometimes while on the brink of tears, to "Do something with your life . . . make a difference in the world, even if it's a small one. Too many people along the way died for us for you or any of us to squander a precious life away." My great grandmother's words and the complex experiences of being Black in white places have profoundly shaped my worldview and how I practice as a therapist. The lessons I have learned along the way have been many and the contributions they have made to my evolution as a therapist have been extraordinary. The salient lessons I have learned have been: (a) the meaning of what it means to be Black; (b) the meaning of white places; (c) the meaning of what it means to be Black in white places; and (d) the meaning of what it means to be a therapist as healer.

### *Implications for Therapy and Beyond*

*Being Black in white places* has had a profound impact on my life and how I view the human spirit and the process of therapy. It has underscored the importance of embracing positions of both/and in and outside of therapy. This perspective was a welcome relief from the segregated thinking that often left me, and especially those who had been entrusted to train me, feeling bleak about my future. It was the segregated thinking that made it difficult for many whites in my life to see me as Black and a good student, friend, or colleague. Too often the visibility and recognition of my Black being was denied to create space for some other role, e.g., "Ken, I don't see you as Black, I see you as just another student!" It seemed near impossible to have both positions simultaneously honored.

Embracing both/and enabled me to continue to respect many of my professors for their wisdom and faith in me as a developing therapist, while having virtually no faith in their abilities to see the inherent struggles underpinning being Black in white places. It was essential that I had the ability to see them more complexly than they were able to see me. They were professors and white, and in this regard they were simultaneously trustworthy and untrustworthy. The most powerful lesson I learned was from interactions with the relatively small, albeit significant, number of whites with whom I interacted over the years who did make a concerted effort to understand race and themselves as white people. These were the whites who stood up, spoke up, and stretched themselves to reach beyond racial stereotypes to be allies to people of color while their white colleagues remained paralyzed by racial polarization and holding onto claims of color blindness. As whites, they listened and refrained from labeling; and they worked earnestly and assiduously to show respect while acknowledging their emotional reactivity. These whites and my experiences with them taught me an invaluable lesson about the relevancy of embracing both/and and appreciating that there are always exceptions to dominant stories. The life lesson is that there is good contained in bad and bad embedded in good.

### *Therapist as Healer*

Being Black in white places has also aided me in developing a rather sophisticated understanding of the human condition and how to work with it in therapy, and why it is imperative to work beyond the four walls of the therapy office. It has taught me in the most raw and brutal ways what it feels like to be locked out, stepped over, and at times stepped on. *In the spirit of my great grandmother Anna, I now understand how she could endure so much injustice and harbor so little anger or hatred. Perhaps like my great grandmother, I see absolutely no value in engaging in ways of being that relegate others to the margins of society, especially knowing what I know about life along the margins.* It is a place that can crush the spirit, puncture hope, and destroy dreams if those who are entrapped are ignored, deemed invisible, or stripped of inspiration. Hope and inspiration are essential keys to transforming and transcending life along the margins. Inspiration and hope can be derived from multiple sources and forces, but it has to be harnessed. My parents, grandparents, the teachers who believed in me as well as those who didn't, the professors, guidance counselors, and others who suggested implicitly and/or explicitly that I wasn't smart enough, good enough, white enough, or even Black enough provided me an unwavering inspiration that became a life force unto itself. There is something uniquely transformative and transcendent in instilling a sense of inspiration and hope in someone for whom it has been denied and/or destroyed. It has a way of lighting the internal fire of our souls in a way that suddenly makes the impossible possible and the unimaginable imaginable.

Consequently, I have learned the healing and transformative potential of inspiration, hope, and the restoration of dignity. I regard the resurrection of hope a major task of the therapeutic process and it has become a focal point of my work as a therapist regardless of the presenting problem. I believe as therapists we are actually stockholders in the *hope manufacturing business*. Our job as therapists is to help create a sense of hopefulness for those who are in places where inspiration has been placed among the deceased and hope has long since ceased to exist. The igniting of inspiration and restoration of hope cannot be achieved through acts of placation or the extension of platitudinous remarks and gestures but instead by looking for, and hence having the ability to see, the redeemable parts of all human beings no matter how egregious their transgressions or inferior we consider them to be. It is the insatiable hunger I believe each of us has to be validated and deemed worthy that unites all of us in our humanity, regardless of race, class, gender, or sexual orientation. It is through the recognition of one's inherent worth that we as therapists get to the deeply protected places where hope and inspiration reside within those we serve. For this reason, I believe therapy must essentially involve processes of healing and transformation. Healing is what we must do to bring comfort; to soothe; and to repair that which has been disrupted, fractured, and even broken. Transformation is what we do to help forge a new way and to alter the sociocultural conditions that nurture the lethal forces of racism, sexism, homophobia, elitism and all other conditions that devalue. It is my view that when therapy fails to address systems of domination and the multitudinous ways in which people's lives are significantly hindered and devalued by them, the process falls short of one of its greatest potentials—to uplift the human spirit and transform the human condition.

Therapy as I conceptualize it is not limited to a focus on emotions, cognition, and one's psychology, but on political and contextual variables as well. Thus, attending to issues of social justice is integral to my view of therapy. I can no longer sit with women, gay/lesbians/transgendered, or poor clients without thinking critically about sexism, heteronormativity, and classism. I look earnestly for the possible linkages between the manifestation of individual suffering and the sociocultural circumstances in which the individual (and their problems) are embedded. I am now able to better understand that these clients, even when they are white or hold privilege in other ways, exist in "white places" and suffer the symptoms of "Blackness," although they are not Black. While I think it is crucial to create space for both the naming and honoring of these untold stories, talking is simply not enough. I believe it is crucial for us to take socially just positions in and outside of therapy that help to give voice to the voiceless and uplift those who have fallen or been pushed from society's grace because of the color of their skin, shape of their eyes, or whom they happen to love. The tensions between the ideals of my professional training and the practical realities of everyday life where I practice have invited me to reconsider some sacred truths of therapy.

I have spent years in recovery from many of the ways I was trained to do therapy. As a result, I no longer strive to achieve objectivity. I recognize that I am hopelessly biased. In fact, I am as biased as those who taught and trained me how to be objective. I am not a tabula rasa. I wear the human stain. The prism through which I see the world, both mine and the client's, is heavily jaded by who I am: African American, male, middle class, heterosexual, and so forth. Being Black in white places has taught me all too well about the perils of unacknowledged subjectivity disguised as objectivity. It is a misguided truth that often leads us down a path to prejudgment, righteousness, and a foreclosure of possibilities. My experiences along the way have taught me the importance of locating myself in all human interactions, because it is my location that dictates my perceptions. What I look for invariably dictates what I see. *Self-location* also enables each of us to engage in a process of self-interrogation and ultimately helps to deconstruct the *manufacturing of other*. This important concept has been crystallized and reinforced for me repeatedly over the years. Every time I have been asked incredulously and disdainfully by a white colleague, professor, student, etc., "Ken, why do you always have to bring up race?" I am reminded why it is important to locate ourselves. If the questioner were to engage in such a process, the answer would be profoundly simple: "Oh, maybe he always brings up race because I as a white person never do!" Unfortunately, it appears more expedient and righteous to ignore the influences and dislocation of the self while demanding accountability from the so-called Other.

## Coming Full Circle

My journey as therapist and civilian has provided a sense of purpose to my life, work, and my life's work. It also has imbued me with an acute clarity regarding where I fit into the process. I, like many therapists, have had to make a critical choice regarding *who it is* and *how it is* I want to be not only in my role as therapist but as a citizen in the world as well. The choices are somewhat finite in scope: Helper, Jailer, and/or Healer. The role of the *Helper* is to meet those who suffer where they are and to provide comfort and a context for healing and recovery. It is usually outside of the self-proclaimed scope of practice of a Helper to get involved in applying one's work to the larger social order. The main role of the Helper is to be present and provide assistance to those in need. The principle role of the *Jailer*, by contrast, is to establish and maintain order; to promote personal responsibility and accountability, often using punishment, the establishment of firm boundaries, and control as the primary tools. The world of the Jailer is comprised of *Us* versus *Them*. There is a clear line of demarcation between those who are "good" and "right" and those who are "bad" and "wrong." Those who are wrong or bad, according to the ideology of the Jailer, should be punished. Those who are good can do no wrong. The *Healer*, on the other hand, like the Helper, provides comfort and the essence of one's being to those who are served, but is also vigilant in addressing the larger sociocultural forces that are interwoven into the everyday pain and suffering of those who are trapped in white places. The Healer recognizes that both the focus and force of our work must be directed toward both the micro- and macro-systems. The Healer recognizes the inherent challenges involved in continuously attempting to treat social problems with psychological solutions. The Healer never assumes that the way things are is the way that things have to be. The Healer recognizes and operates from the premise, as Martin Luther King, Jr. said in his 1963 "Letter from Birmingham Jail," that we are all "entangled in a web of mutuality" in which none of us can truly be what we wish or ought to be until each of us is. Thus if we have compassion for the poor, although we ourselves may not be poor, we must also have an undying resolve to address poverty and greed. It must become a part of our work even when it is not within the scope of our job. As a therapist I believe it is incumbent upon me to overtly give voice to these issues and not retreat behind the masks of neutrality, and objectivity. I owe it to myself, my ancestors, and especially to my great grandmother.

**Catch the Fire**[2]

BY SONIA SANCHEZ (1995)

(Sometimes I wonder:
What to say to you now
in the soft afternoon air as you hold us all in a single death?)
I say—
Where is your fire?
I say—
Where is your fire?

You got to find it and pass it on.

You got to find it and pass it on
from you to me from me to her from her to him from the son to the father from the brother to the sister from the daughter to the mother from the mother to the child.
Where is your fire? I say where is your fire? Can't you smell it coming out of our past? The fire of living . . . not dying
The fire of loving . . . not killing
The fire of Blackness . . . not gangster shadows.
Where is our beautiful fire that gave light to the world?
The fire of pyramids;
The fire that burned through the holes of slaveships and made us breathe;

The fire that made guts into chitterlings; The fire that took rhythms and made jazz;

The fire of sit-ins and marches that made us jump boundaries and barriers;

The fire that took street talk sounds
and made righteous imhotep raps.
Where is your fire, the torch of life
full of Nzingha and Nat Turner and Garvey and DuBois and Fannie Lou Hamer and Martin and Malcolm and Mandela.
Sister/Sistah Brother/Brotha Come/Come

CATCH YOUR FIRE . . . DON'T KILL HOLD YOUR FIRE . . . DON'T KILL LEARN YOUR FIRE . . . DON'T KILL BE THE FIRE . . . DON'T KILL
Catch the fire and burn with eyes that see our souls:
WALKING.
SINGING.
BUILDING.
LAUGHING.
LEARNING.

LOVING.
TEACHING.
BEING.
Hey. Brother/Brotha. Sister/Sista. Here is my hand.
Catch the fire . . . and live. live.
livelivelive. livelivelive. live.
live.

**KENNETH V. HARDY, PHD,** is a Clinical and Organizational Consultant at the Eikenberg Institute for Relationships in New York, New York, where he also serves as director. He provides racially focused trauma informed training, executive coaching, and consultation to a diverse network of individuals and organizations throughout the United States and abroad. He is a former professor of family therapy at both Drexel University in Philadelphia, Pennsylvania, and Syracuse University in Syracuse, New York, and has also served as the director of Children, Families, and Trauma at the Ackerman Institute for the Family in New York, New York. He is the author of: *Culturally Sensitive Supervision: Diverse Perspectives and Practical Applications*; *Promoting Culturally Sensitive Supervision: A Manual for Practitioners*; *Revisioning Family Therapy: Addressing Diversity in Clinical Practice*; and *Teens Who Hurt: Clinical Interventions to Break the Cycle of Adolescent Violence*. In addition to his consultation work, Dr. Hardy is a frequent conference speaker and has also appeared on ABC's 20/20, NBC's Dateline, PBS, and the Oprah Winfrey Show.

## Notes

1. "Harlem [2]" from THE COLLECTED POEMS OF LANGSTON HUGES by Langston Hughes edited by Arnold Rampersad with David Roessel, Associate Editor, copyright © 1994 by the Estate of Langston Hughes. Used by permission of Alfred A. Knopf, an imprint of the Knopf Doubleday Publishing Group, a division of Penguin Random House LLC. All rights reserved. For electronic edition: Reprinted by permission of Harold Ober Associates. Copyright 1951 by the Langston Hughes Estate

2. "Catch the Fire" from *Wounded in the House of a Friend* by Sonia Sanchez. Copyright © 1995 by Sonia Sanchez. Reprinted with permission from Beacon Press, Boston Massachusetts

# References

*Hardy , K. V., & Laszloffy, T. A. (2005).* Teens who hurt: Clinical interventions for breaking the cycle of adolescent violence. *New York: Guilford Press.*

*Hughes, L. (1994). "Harlem 2." In* The Collected Poems of Langston Hughes *(p. 268). New York: Knopf/Random House. (Original work published 1958)*

*Kirkland, S.L. (2011, September/October). The new face of racism.* Psychotherapy Networker, 35*(5), 17–18.*

*Kottler, J., & Carlson, J. (2005). Ken Hardy: Mister Black Doctor. In* The Client Who Changed Me: Stories of Therapist Personal Transformation *(pp. 123–128). New York: Routledge.*

*Kozel, J. (1967).* Death at an early age. *Boston: Houghton Mifflin.*

*Sanchez, S. (1995). "Catch the Fire." In* Wounded in the House of a Friend *(pp. 15–17). Boston: Beacon Press.*

*Sue, D. W., Capodilupo, C.M., Torino, G.C., Bucceri, J.M., Holder, A.M.B., Nadal, K.L., & Esquilin, M. (2007). Racial microaggressions in everyday life: Implications for clinical practice.* American Psychologist, 62*(4), 271–286.*

## CHAPTER 24

# The Uphill Climb of Black Men

## Therapeutic Treatment and Educational Considerations for Mental Health Engagement

KEITH A. ALFORD, PHD

UNIVERSITY AT BUFFALO, SCHOOL OF SOCIAL WORK

Familiarity with the maxim that we are all members of the human race may pleasantly resonate for many individuals in American society. This declaration offers the comfort of homogeneity of purpose, thought, and even demeanor. It also represents satisfaction with a prescribed way of being that operates as the standard bearer for a "sovereign nation." In essence, this is what is meant by whiteness. While the notion of a compliant behavioral and attitudinal ordering offers a pseudo semblance of solidarity, it simply does not speak for the true diversity of American society—nor should it. Disavowing lived experiences correlated with the mosaic of diversity in our society is not the humanitarian way. In the case of Black Americans, these experiences encompass a historical salience that is made up of struggle and triumph; pain and reprieve; degradation and uplift; as well as distress and amity.

There is, for an abundance of Black males, a culture-coping bond in trying to understand, as well as survive, the lived experiences of systemic racism and debilitating subjugation (Hardina et al., 2007; Simpson, 1990). In this chapter, I will explore the ramifications and address the regularity of what many denote as living under a state of surveillance. There is a labeling of what is considered acceptable comportment for Blacks in American society—specifically concentrating on the subjugated role of Black males in twenty-first century America; Black males who routinely face the comparison equation in terms of what constitutes satisfactory social norms for all. Nonetheless, Black men from varying socioeconomic conditions possess a tie that binds them to each other. Their inherent Blackness, regardless of the degree to which they embrace it, is a solidifying factor. This culture-coping bond is one that touts survival over defeat, chiefly in the face of white intolerance. However, the blow of being on bigotry's receiving end is humiliating and is mentally and emotionally draining. Being measured by standards of whiteness is an unscrupulous ethnocentric practice that largely knows no bounds. What is the appropriate deportment of a Black man such as me—an academician, mental health professional, father of a disabled son, man of faith, and one who was born in the South? This multilayered question will be discussed as it pertains to my personal story. In the paragraphs that follow, I will delineate and reveal the uphill climb for Black men, who regularly are unjustly and unfairly scrutinized. Practice tenets for mental health providers and those studying clinical work with Black men will be discussed. The far-reaching treatment and educational value of these tenets will be presented as both pragmatic considerations and keen techniques, worthy of application.

## My Story

There is an emancipatory consciousness for me in being afforded the opportunity to share my story. I am grateful for this opening and understand the responsibility attached to it. I will offer a compressed version because one's story is not usually generalizable. However, my accounts, offered here, could be viewed as transferable in ways that shed light on other Black men who have similar backgrounds or who find certain parts relatable. Suffice it to say, not a day passes that I do not recognize that I am a Black man. The distinction is immediate when I look into the mirror and see my Black identity. It is one filled with pride, but it is also one that I must frequently navigate with precision. I live with the knowledge that simply because I am a Black man, I will be judged by a white-dominated society that does not always incorporate or appreciate my racial and cultural underpinnings. I have been judged in stereotypical ways by white people and have found myself immediately shifting my behavioral stance or posture so as to not be viewed as a stereotypical threat (Steele & Aronson, 1995). For example, I found myself carefully informing a white police officer that I needed to reach over to my side glove compartment to search for my driver's license. This occurred during the immediate aftermath of a minor automobile accident in which no injuries occurred. At the time, my driver's license was not in my wallet. The revelation for me is that I felt the need to explain my every move to the officer so he would not jump to erroneous conclusions and, frankly, so that I would not become another victim of excessive force. It was about life preservation for me. The other driver involved was a white man, and I would venture to say that he did not share my angst nor feel the need to explain his actions. The exchanges were not abrupt nor combustible. My offering here is to share a glimpse of what was occurring internally for me: my anxiety. Even after years of teaching others about survival habits for Black males and of providing therapeutic support to Black males in this area, when in the midst of an incident, I return to a place of distress. This is a by-product of living while Black and realizing that whiteness is still viewed as a standard for all to follow. I still worry about members of my own race who grapple with internalized racism and who have been victimized by oppression. The manifestations of racism are unfortunately numerous and still exist in internalized ways for Black men.

I have enjoyed a long career in the human service practice arena and academe. I have learned lessons from the Black male mental health consumers I once served, engaged in fruitful projects with fellow academicians, and reaped enormous benefits from sage dialogues with students. These experiences have been invaluable; I have decided to work hard to let go of negative experiences that were seemingly steeped in racism. I believe that therein lies the quagmire of not being able to see beyond that which one has knowledge of, and which requires an inquisitive bandwidth. My steps have been to work hard and push for an atmosphere where that kind of bandwidth is second nature.

Moreover, I have worked to expand the circumference of knowledge-building in academe to see beyond positivist or postpositivist thinking and to be inclusive of new paradigms that bring diverse points of view to the forefront (Troka & Adedoja, 2016). I mention this because going the extra mile (when it is not required but is needed) can be exhausting work for Men of Color. We know this push has befallen us, but we also need to fulfill the regular duties of our assigned roles. Essentially, as a Black academician and administrator, my plate often overflows, and it is lonely being one of so few minority voices conferencing with others. In many circles, this is referred to as the "Black tax." To clarify, the "Black tax" refers to the emotional tax that Black people may experience as they deal with the impact of microaggressions and racism. There are countless numbers of us who are willing to pay it because we believe we are doing so to help those who will follow, and we will not give up the opportunity to mentor any Black student that comes knocking at our door. We pay it forward in hopes that someone, somewhere, who is of minority status, will not have such a laborious road to travel because we, hopefully, made it somewhat easier.

A personal concern in greater ways for me is when I think about the love and admiration I have for my son. "Teflon man," as I will dub him for this narrative work, was given 48 hours to live when he was born. His prematurity was severe, and yes, he was not expected to survive beyond two days. After nearly a year in neonatal intensive care, he survives. As the product Teflon is known to be "insoluble" and "sturdy," so is my son. My use of the term *Teflon man* is both in salute of him choosing life over death and his insoluble strength to persevere. His Teflon mystique is one that deserves his father's meritorious recognition. He is now in his early twenties and has disabilities, but these challenges have not halted his will to live and thrive. While I see Teflon man as my proud Black son with special needs, will others see him that way as well? Will others see him and watch out for him when I am not around, or will they only see another young Black man whose life is disposable? I share these thoughts from a place of racial concern that is omnipresent for me and so many Black fathers who want their sons, typical or disabled, to live happy, productive, and safe lives, free of prejudice and discrimination.

My faith experience is one that I hold dear. It has been a part of my life and journey as a Black man for as long as I can remember. There was, and remains, a sense that I have a refuge from the trials and tribulations of the world. From a racial point of view, finding solace in something other than earthly presence is reassuring to me. In fact, my faith experience is a part of my support base, a virtual support system that is accessible all the time. Some of the difficulty I have endured is the poking from others that I have received in professional circles. These comments or assertions are fortunately not habitual, but they have happened enough to leave a sour impression. For example, "Oh, I know you are talking your church talk when you make that claim," or "I suspect you will not be able to join us on Sunday for our discussion, Keith, given your church duties." The challenge for me—and it was difficult—was deciding how to react to these comments. Should I take what was being said at face value or denounce it, given how deeply rooted my faith is in my soul? My faith is the very apparatus that allows me to stay the course through turbulent academic waters. I have found myself second-guessing my choice to forgo the opportunity to educate my white colleagues about what faith meant to me as a Black man. On the other hand, is it my responsibility to educate them, or theirs to educate themselves? The sheer weight of addressing these issues is overwhelming.

The Black Church, as it is called, is a spiritual infirmary for all who are heavily ladened (Boyd-Franklin, 2010; Williams, 2008). Living through constant subjugation requires resuscitation from time to time. My faith experience, by way of the Black Church, has provided such and deserves to be respected, not abused. I would venture to say that this is the case for other Black men who have similar beliefs. One's faith experience is often a personalized meaning that it is unique to the individual. My Black faith experience should not be generalized. My belief patterns may be different from those of others who share the same religious domination. My personal faith walk is one that I either choose to share, or not. Do not treat it as fodder for pointed comments, because it is for me a deep and refreshing wellspring of strength in a racialized society.

This personal walk for me was borne out of my Southern upbringing. With all the racial concerns that still resonate in the South, it remains home to me, decades after my departure. For many Black Southerners who migrated to the Northeast or the Midwest, denouncing one's Southern rearing is not a thing to do. My character and value base were formed, in part, by my faith tradition, the many community members that I held in high regard, my extended kinship, my fictive (nonrelative) kin, and my immediate family members. My Southern roots are still with me today in my speech, actions, and way of being. While I sobbed several years ago in disbelief over the murder of nine courageous souls at the Mother Emanuel A.M.E. Church in Charleston, South Carolina, by a white supremacist who joined them for bible study, I also released a sigh of relief at the decision to take down the confederate battle flag that flew in front of South Carolina's state house. Nine lives, Black lives, innocent lives, productive lives, had to be lost in order for this symbol, and what it represents to People of Color, to be removed. This scenario of disregard and death has been repeated too often throughout history. No race of people should feel demeaned in a place they call home by a symbol that constantly reminds them "to stay in their place."

Who am I? I am more than what anyone can physically see or know me to be. Principled significance must be afforded to my social and ecological dimensions. Living while Black for me encompasses my triangulation of multiple spheres. This is a reality that white men of my age and accomplishments do not have to face. What's more, living while Black also comprises my unyielding determination to not let the racial disdain cast upon my race hold me back.

## Setting the Stage for Mental Health Treatment

Having shared my abridged story, I will now build on it and devote—from a mental health perspective—the remainder of this chapter to ways of reversing the uphill climb. I know my journey has influenced my ideas about Black men in general, as well as the clinical implications for working with them. Real and nonperformative change requires those of us who have the noble calling to serve in helping capacities to do so with an accentuation on decentering whiteness in therapeutic services with Black men. The Black experience, a phrase that continues to resonate historically and in modern times, denotes a historical significance that begins with the heinous racial injustice of enslavement. The devaluation and near annihilation of the Black family during that era of our nation's history remains one of our country's original sins, as noted by Ponds (2013). Scholars who have written extensively about the contextual realities of the Black experience also note that phenotype matters (West, 1995; Parmer et al., 2004). To assert that the human race is the gold standard of coexistence and not give credence to the impact of racism linked to a person's skin color negates blatant social and structural realities.

The term *African American men* is an appropriate designation to use when speaking about that population—particularly in reference to those who trace their origin back to the continent of Africa. My preference is to use the term *Black men*, a choice based on the ethnohistory of Black people in American society and the contemporary social movement of Black Lives Matter. In this regard, an elevation of the term *Black* as a focal point of reference is fitting.

### *Theoretical Focus*

The role of theory as a guiding force in clinical practice is crucial (Polansky, 1986). Theory is viewed metaphorically as a road map, akin to a Global Positioning System (GPS) for clinicians. There needs to be an ongoing understanding of the devaluing impact of bias and its propensity, if unchecked, to develop into racism against minoritized groups (Cummins, 2015). Adopting a theoretical focus and utilizing it proactively is paramount. Theory is the guidepost for pinpointing environmental impediments that result in the debilitation of living while Black. Context is central, and the realities of not being given the benefit of the doubt cry out "subjugation." This is particularly so when considering typical stressors of life associated with self-preservation, familial care, relationship blues, job security, or joblessness. When one couples these vicissitudes with the race differential of being Black in a society dominated by whiteness, the proverbial bar for affirmability over suitability becomes steeper. Additionally, whether others' actions are perceived to have racist intent, are perceived to be racist or are deemed to be outright stressful overt acts of racism, the end result of a devalued status remains. Practitioners who tap into their "theory-driven GPS" will be in the best shape to help Black men unload and to discern the best course of treatment.

The ecological systems theory (Bronfenbrenner, 2005; Darling, 2007), a theoretical model with origins in the natural sciences, has been routinely accessed by mental health professionals. It has a compelling emphasis on the person-in-the-environment. This emphasis positions Black men in treatment well with respect to obstacles and strengths that must be navigated on multiple levels of relational activity (Darling, 2007; Bronfenbrenner, 2005). Attention to the ebb and flow of homeostasis is borne out of the ecological systems model. Competent practice would also emphasize the need to expand our thinking to include appropriate utility of theoretical integration (Denby & Curtis, 2013; Plagerson, 2015). I am a proponent of the Africentric perspective and see curative value in employing it as a second model of choice, thereby blending the best of both when providing mental health services to Black men (see Figure 24.1).

Africentricity or Afrocentricity—both spellings are correct; the preference is within the purview of the user—is a theoretical framework that builds on themes steeped in Black traditions (Schiele, 1996; Stewart, 2004). Interconnectedness or survival of the tribe is a primary assumption of Africentricity (Asante, 1988; Alford, 2003; Borum, 2007; Schiele, 1996). The Eurocentric worldview endorses a spirit of individualism, which is largely opposite to a more collectivistic frame of reference (Asante, 1988; Montón-Subías & Hernando, 2018; Schiele, 1996; Stewart, 2004). An emphasis in Africentricity advances the importance of mutual aid as a cord that binds. This is a strengths-based orientation. It is a stronghold from yesteryear and one that has ancestral ties. "Self," from an Africentric perspective, is not differentiated from nor devoid of others who make up one's immediate and extended circles (Alford, 2003; Borum, 2007; Schiele, 1996). This appreciation of "self and family" or "self and the collective" is central to understanding the dissonance felt by Black mental health consumers when treatment approaches are not immersed in mores and traditions that parallel the Black experience (Curtis-Boles, 2017).

The assertion that the spiritual or nonmaterial component of human beings is just as important and valid as the material component is a second assumption postulated by Schiele (1996). This position confirms the vast nature of spirituality and its connectivity to the universe, not just with a deity (Boyd-Franklin, 2010). A third primary assumption of the Africentric model promotes the epistemological validity of the affective approach to knowledge. We should not negate affect, nor should it be viewed as pathological (Borum, 2007; Schiele, 1996). From an Africentric perspective, healthy expression of one's affect should be encouraged. Black men need to be able to let down their guard, even if their expressions are peppered with expletives. This type of truth-telling is liberating on levels that have not been touched. Engaging Black men in the moment with authenticity and a genuine desire to comprehend will make a notable difference in the therapeutic relationship.

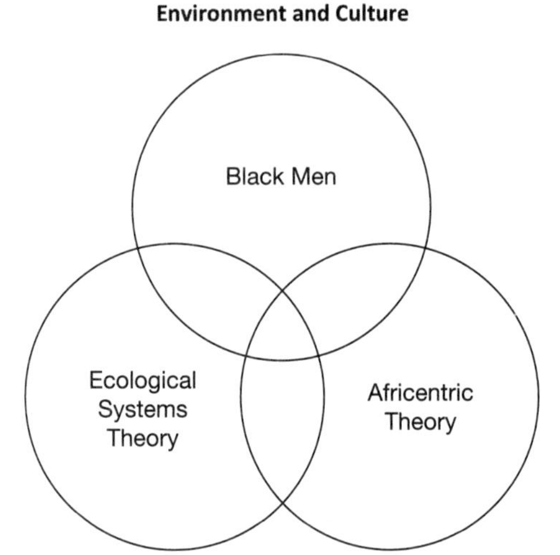


Figure 24.1: An integration of ecological systems theory and Africentric theory for mental health treatment with Black men.

## Central Tenets for Elevating Black Men

Targeted therapeutic treatments and educational considerations that encompass ecological systems theory and Africentricity can positively facilitate healthy mental functioning for Black men. The ability to effectively cope with what life has dealt you—both positive and negative—is the ultimate challenge of human existence. Black men who fervently try to meet this challenge often find themselves battling the winds of subjugation. There are five central tenets that must be unpacked and nurtured during the process of helping Black men win in this sociocultural warfare. Below, each tenet is explained in narrative form, interwoven with practice implications (see Figure 24.2 for a full illustration).

### *Create Spaces for Cathartic Release*

Peters and Massey (1983) wrote a germinal publication that illuminated the regularity with which Black Americans face stressors due to explicit bias. In this paper, they suggest that the daily external sociopolitical environmental stimuli that degrades the dignity of one's rightful existence has a name.

It is *mundane extreme environmental stress* (MEES), which includes such microaggressions as when at the end of a transaction, a merchant places the change on the counter, as opposed to putting it in the hand of the Black customer. This is particularly true when the previous customer, who was white, was given their money in hand. Even though this could be perceived as a microaggression, perception in cases like this become reality. Another example occurs in work settings, when a Black staff member's idea is overlooked during a group meeting, and the same idea, shared moments later by their white counterpart, is acknowledged and the white staff is given credit for the "new concept." For Black men, these types of experiences are emasculating and have become predictable due to their regularity over the years (DeFreitas, 2019).

The traumatic nature of these occurrences has been noted with respect to the development of physiological concerns. Hypertension, heart disease, and even the common cold can be tied to one's mental capacity to cope with unrelieved suffering. Are Jamal, Kwame, Tyson, and Jake (fictitious names for the purposes of this chapter) angry Black men if they openly express their disgust about the daily grind of MEES? In a therapeutic sense, these are men in need of a haven to discharge their emotions. Africentric theory denotes the importance of opening channels or spaces for affect to be authentically and boldly expressed. The need for this often exists in greater measure for Black men, due to the shocks and waves of white-dominated society. Rage is compounded in these instances, and sometimes, when men are not afforded proper venues for venting their anger, it can be expressed in destructive ways. The price of disenfranchisement is astronomical. Rage that is not appropriately redirected and discussed could manifest itself in the form of violence and even self-inflicted harm. The creation and fortifying of safe and racially affirming spaces remains vital to restorative measures needed for Black men who are mental health consumers. The encouragement and planful outlining of productive ways to channel rage is a key treatment maneuver.

### *Rehumanize Loss*

Loss, from a relational standpoint, is frankly one of the hardest life hurdles to overcome. One could easily make the argument that "overcoming" loss of a relational kind is arduous when the cause is death, separation, familial cutoff, divorce, or emotional impairment. The added pressure of being assessed by a rule of democratic sanity, as Akbar (1991) put it, in which social measurement and acceptability are tacitly approved by white European standards, is unfair. We in American society are a mosaic of diversity. Our differentness should be elevated as a strength as we respect each other and affirm our humanity. Sadly, loss—and this is acutely so in various areas of major cities—is tied to urban unrest.

Hardy and Laszloffy (2007) purport that rage is due to the devaluation of People of Color. This devaluation has impacted how Black youth measure their self-worth. These youth, many of them Black males, may have witnessed a murder or may be living in communities where killings happen far too often. Given such frequencies, Hardy and Laszloffy (2007) propose that a dehumanization of loss is occurring. Assisting young Black males who have experienced multiple losses to grieve is serious, while simultaneously helping these males embrace the sanctity of human life is essential. Treatment professionals supporting an ecological systems and Africentric approach to treatment would be wise to enlist, as needed, contemporary rites of passage (CROP) programming, which undergirds psychoeducational engagement of Black male youth. Goals of CROP center around development of life skills through a lens of Africentricity (Alford, 2003; Blumenkrantz, 2016; Mazama, 2001). Proracial identity development and self-esteem enhancement are also cornerstones of this initiative.

Because of classism, racism, heterosexism, ablism, and more, the world has taught young Black males to believe that they are underlings. The streets have taught them to be tough and to never show any vulnerability. They follow a code as a way of protecting themselves from societal backlash and from turning on each other (Alford, 2003; Rich & Grey, 2005). Some younger Black males either do not know or do not choose to partake in code switching, which involves ascribing to a set of behaviors that would be considered suitable by white standards of conduct. These behaviors, of which authority figures would approve, are viewed as survival techniques. But not every young Black male will adapt his behavior accordingly or is even aware of what behavior is deemed acceptable. Code switching is not automatic. For some Black male fathers, it is a matter of educating their sons on how to communicate properly or how to dress a certain way (Curtis-Boles, 2017; Rich & Grey, 2005).

For the older guard of Black men, dual socialization has been a mainstay for quite some time. They believe that while it is not ideal, it is for real, and for them, being able to apply one set of user-friendly behaviors in white society and another set with one's posse on the collective home front is routine. This phenomenon is directly tied to racialized existence and is a way to be "acceptable" or "tolerable" in the depths of white dominance. In the face of these competing worlds, the other "-ism" that deserves to be promoted with Black men is "optim-ism," that is, optimism. Rehumanizing loss for Black males who are caught in the desolation of street life is a huge feat. Facilitating the restoration of hope, sometimes in the midst of despair, is a daunting task. However, reclaiming the interconnectedness that has sustained People of Color over time remains the clarion call for all human service educators and providers.

We must help Black men who are seeking treatment to believe in their worthiness, despite the negative environmental stimuli, such as racial bias, microaggressions, and profiling, that say otherwise. There is a period of emotional excursion that one must take for loss to be rehumanized. Inoculating a sense of hope again may be as simple as the treating professional believing the Black male in front of them is worthy and has promise. Conveying validating messages may very well be the relief needed, giving rise to induction of concrete action steps that will lead to healthy emotional liberation. Africentric theory asserts that aloofness on the part of the treating practitioner is undesirable (Mazama, 2001; Schiele, 1996). Practitioners should actively engage with Black men in a way that encourages them to increase cohesion in the therapeutic relationship.

Because of adverse capitalistic structures in our society that maintain unequal and inequitable distributions of wealth and resources—also known as the underbelly of systemic racism—a significant contingent of Black men experience depression (Baker, 2001; Lowery & Stankiewicz, 2016). Depression, no matter how severe, has a domino effect in other parts of Black men's lives. Yet again, loss surfaces due to unaddressed areas of functioning, and loss is often at the root of depression. The loss of not being treated or validated as a bonafide member of humanity is enough to bring about depressive episodes. We must give credence to the impact and stigma of this type of life trauma in relation to Black men's mental health (Lindsey et al., 2018).

### *Look Beyond Appearance*

Every opportunity to form a communal bond with someone is a gift. The next steps reside with each of us in terms of what to make of building new comradeships. Greater attention must be given to the multidimensional aspects of the Black man. His social and ecological dimensions could quite easily encompass his personal habits and hobbies, his family and relationship formations, his athletic prowess and exercise regimen, and much more. There may be biased thoughts that he is only of a certain sort so he would not be able to converge and connect within social circles. The focal point here is Black manhood and if one presumes to know him before any attempts are made to truly know who he is and what he is about (DeFreitas, 2019). In this instance, the whole, meaning the disposition of Black men, is indeed greater than the sum of "his" parts.

While each of the previously listed dimensions may exist in Black men, there are countless others I have not listed that should be given equal credibility. Socioeconomic status should be considered because Black men doing their best to make ends meet may have another set of dimensions or the same ones, but some dimensions may be rendered unavailable if strongholds linked with economic deprivation are present. Once again, adding the race differential makes a case more complex.

Conventional beliefs assert that Black men are reluctant to share and are mistrustful of therapeutic help (Bennett, 2020; Simpson, 1990). Quite frankly, therapeutic engagement has never been a "one size fits all" approach. This is doubly true for Black men who seek treatment. I contend that the treating party has the added responsibility of exhausting all possibilities in their efforts to retain Black male consumers. The toils of living in a racialized society have sent messages, subtle and pronounced, of disregard to Black males. As mental health providers and educators, we must overcompensate for those messages and take up robust efforts to solidify a nexus with each Black man who seeks services.

Bonner (2010) says the term *intersectionality* does not adequately encompass the dimensional actualities that Black men possess. Crenshaw

(2017) has introduced the meaning of intersectionality for women with respect to their varied dimensional aspects. Bonner (2010) believes that the definition of the term lacks critical elements for defining and operationalizing masculinity. The nomenclature allied with the dimensional elements of Black people, in general, needs a closer inspection. Any detailed discussion of masculinity must involve a comprehensive accounting of the term's extended definition and where it resides on the continuum of sexuality for people in the Black community (Allen, 2016; Keene et al., 2021). For example, are voices raised strongly enough in solidarity with Black men who identify as gay as they are for their white counterparts? The helping process should explore and assess this question with Black sexual minority men in treatment from an emancipatory space of inquiry. Treatment professionals should also assess for the presence of conflict between sexual identity and racial identity. Of late, myriad sexual identities within the Black community have gained the community's support, but the Black community is far from fully accepting all Black sexual identities (Darling, 2007; Keene et al., 2021).

*Respect Dignity and Worth*

While some progress has been made toward racial and gender equality in American society, the struggle for equality is not nearly over. Structural systems where white is viewed as right and privilege is not evenly shared continue to stifle progress toward a more optimal and equitable coexistence. The conditions that Peggy McIntosh (1989) wrote about and published in her groundbreaking article "White Privilege: Unpacking the Invisible Knapsack" are still, sadly and frankly, the despicable circumstances that Black men and women face today. At the time, Peggy McIntosh was associate director of the Wellesley College Center for Research on Women. She noted that her education did not train her to see herself as an oppressor nor as an unfairly advantaged person (McIntosh, 1989). She thought of her life as normative. Below are 3 of the 26 conditions she posited. These conditions, if encountered, would not hinder nor adversely impact her as a white woman. In fact, they are conditions that rang true for her lived experience. Conversely (and disturbingly), decades after McIntosh's publication date, these same conditions still ring false for Black people today.

- I can do well in a challenging situation without being called a credit to my race.
- I can speak in public to a powerful male group without putting my race on trial.
- If my day, week, or year is going badly, I need not ask of each negative episode or situation whether it has racial overtones. (McIntosh, 1989, p. 2)

Is there a proverbial ordering that occurs? Black men are compared to white men in terms of standards of behavior, ability, knowledge, style, and more. No one group is a monolith, and this fact is certainly apropos for Black men. However, all Black men are subject to experience in our society what it feels like to be devalued and unworthy. The hashtag #saytheirname is a mega refrain that has flooded social media and stimulated racial justice rallies in 2020. In fact, the devastation of the COVID-19 pandemic was exacerbated by a racial pandemic in relation to the horrific murders of George Floyd, Ahmaud Arbery, and Breonna Taylor.

These heinous killings ignited a racial reckoning in America that spread across the world. In fact, for Black people, and Black males in particular, the exhortation of "Say their name!" gives voice to 400 years of degradation and atrocious brutality inclusive of enslavement, Jim Crow, and the rampant lynching that took the innocent Black lives of so many men who were fathers, brothers, and sons. The gut-wrenching pain that I feel, as do so many Black men I call my brothers, is exhausting. Am I tired? Yes, but I am not crushed. All lives matter, without question, but because Black lives have not mattered throughout history and the current status quo, transformation at micro, mezzo, and macro levels must commence with haste (Anderson-Carpenter, 2020; Troka & Adedoja, 2016). To effectively engage Black men in mental health treatment, practitioners must appreciate the urgency of this transition (Bean et al., 2002; Bennett, 2020).

### *Foster Resilience and Support*

Black men experience burnout. There is a concern that working oneself to the bone, as the adage goes, is not just a metaphor for Black men. This concept takes on many forms. For Black men, all of life's upheavals come with the added dimension of being Black. The race differential is a foundational component in every rite of passage and life transition. Accentuating the positive in these instances, relative to bolstering coping skills for Black men, is essential. When others believe in and uplift Black men, such as by being an active listener or a positive thinker, it feeds their resilience.

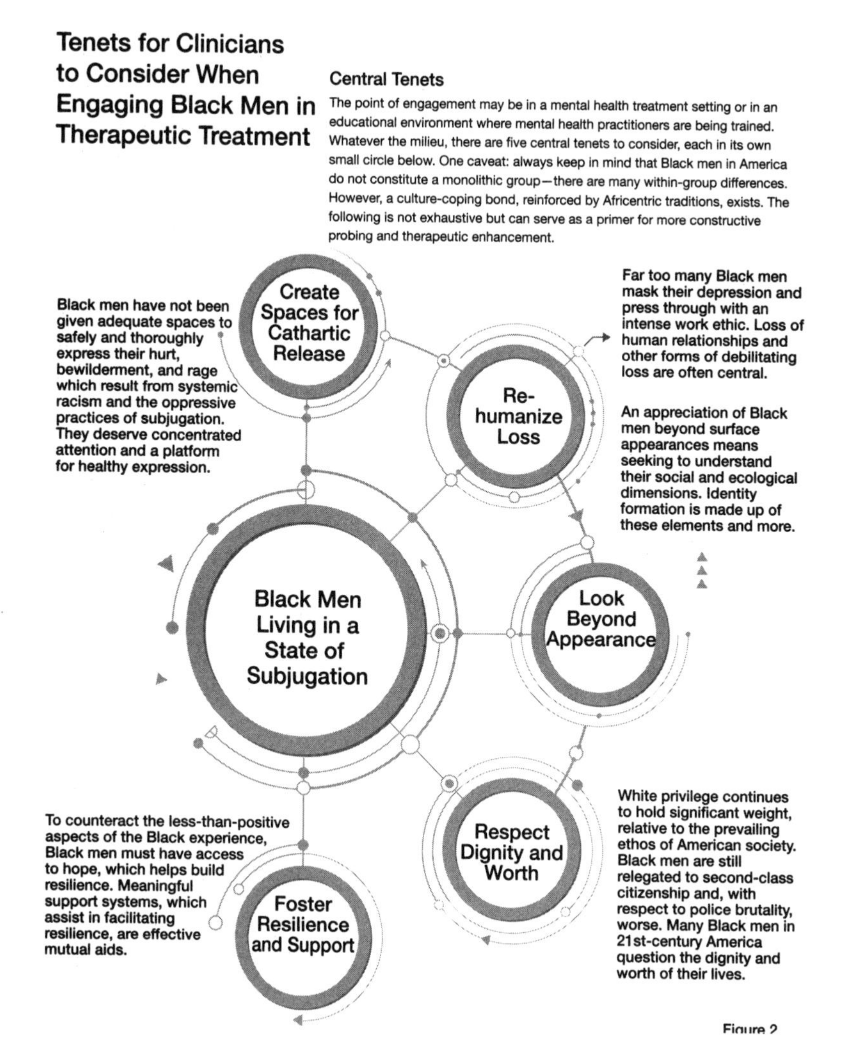


Figure 24.2: A depiction of central tenets germane to therapeutic treatment and educational considerations associated with Black men's mental health.

There is an internal locus of control that can and should be tapped for its redeeming value. Nonetheless, identifying trusted support systems is imperative to mitigating the hard times that befall daily functioning. For example, Black men who are rebuilding their lives after serving a prison sentence may find that a harsh social environment awaits them, such as with respect to applying for jobs. While some employers and institutions of higher education have chosen to incorporate "ban the box," removing the check box or question on job applications that asks about criminal history, there are still employers that continue to ask for this information. And then what? Helping Black men work through stark issues of social justice and sort through numerous inequities are necessary components of the therapeutic process.

Assessing the social supports of Black men in treatment is imperative. Bennett (2020) posits that a general definition of social support is: the sense that one is cared for in meaningful ways. He further states that there is a dearth of research on social support and its capacity to buffer the effects of racism in lived experiences of African American males (Bennett, 2020). Nonetheless, determining whether the man has a supportive network of comrades available to vent and replay frustrations and triumphs of the day is an essential ingredient of any helping process that aims to bolster Black men. Suffice it to say, clinicians should not assume that these networks already exist. Black men, who are in denial of their subjugated state, could balk at needing a support network because it is not in keeping with what some have called rugged independence. This train of thought often indicates that a man needs therapeutic services, but he may, as a result of these beliefs, resist them.

## Conclusion

It is up to the reader to determine which takeaways of this chapter speak confidently to their knowledge acquisition. I want to invite you to absorb the breadth of what has been conveyed. Bringing the mental health needs of Black men to the fore during these unprecedented times in our transforming world is the order of the day. Being intentional in our outreach and service delivery to Black men honors the potential meaning and opportunities that can be found in their crisis or life altering moment (Alford & Lantz, 2002; Baker, 2001; Bennett, 2020). Subjugation can camouflage feelings of dismay. Utilizing our conceptual GPS, we must continue to support and encourage Black men while always listening intently to their stories. Some tellings will be similar to another, and others will be completely unique, but all exchanges are cardinal. Our assessments must go beyond the immediate and include the ecological environment of Black men. This is imperative if we are to truly decenter whiteness in therapeutic realms and in halls of learning. The right and just thing to do is reverse the grossly hindering designation of Black men as subjugated and instead create a new classification for them to inhabit: truly empowered. Continuous affirmation of Black men's valued status must prevail. Meeting Black men who are seeking mental health services where they are and cultivating a safe milieu, free of normative white judgment, is the best prescription for early therapeutic success.

**KEITH A. ALFORD, PHD,** is a professor of social work. Professor Alford has previously served as a Chief Diversity and Inclusion Officer and as a social work practitioner, providing mental health treatment services to children, families, and adults. He received his PhD and MA degrees from Ohio State University and his BA from Coker University. Dr. Alford has published in the areas of child welfare, culturally specific human service interventions, contemporary rites of passage programming, and family mental health. He is a member of the National Association of Social Workers and the Council on Social Work Education. Previously, in the central New York area, he served as a board of directors' member for AccessCNY and InterFaith Works (IFW). He also served as a founding contributor and facilitator of IFW's Community Wide Dialogue Circles to End Racism. A former human services administrator, Dr. Alford has conducted workshops across the country and internationally associated with diversity, equity, and inclusion. He espouses the African proverb, "I am because we are, and because we are, therefore I am."

## References

*Akbar, N. (1991). Mental disorder among African Americans. In R. Jones (Ed.),* Black psychology *(pp. 339–352). Cobb & Henry.*

*Alford, K. (2003). Cultural themes in rites of passage: Voices of young African American males.* Journal of African American Studies, 7*(1), 3–26. DOI: 10.1007/s12111-003-1000-y*

*Alford, K., & Lantz, J. (2002). Existential crisis intervention.* Journal of Brief Therapy, 2*(1), 43–51.*

*Allen, Q. (2016). 'Tell your own story': Manhood, masculinity and racial socialization among black fathers and their sons.* Ethnic and Racial Studies, 39*(10), 1831–1848. doi:10.1080/01419870.2015.1110608*

*Anderson-Carpenter, K. D. (2020). Black lives matter principles as an Africentric approach to improving black American health.* Racial and Ethnic Health Disparities. *doi:https://doi.org/10.1007/s40615-020-00845-0*

*Asante, M. (1988).* Afrocentricity. *Africa World Press.*

*Baker, F. (2001). Diagnosing depression in African Americans.* Community Health Journal, 37, *31–38. doi:https://doi.org/10.1023/A:1026540321366*

*Bean, R., Perry, B., & Bedell, T. (2002). Developing culturally competent marriage and family therapists: Treatment guidelines for non-African-American therapists working with African-American families.* Journal of Marital and Family Therapy, 28*(2), 153–164. doi:10.1111/j.1752-0606. 2002.tb00353.x*

*Bennett, M. (2020). So much trouble on my mind: African American males coping with mental health issues and racism.* Urban Social Work, 4*(2), 152–172.*

*Blumenkrantz, D. G. (2016).* Coming of age the RITE way: Youth and community development through rites of passage. *Oxford University Press.*

*Bonner, F. A., II. (2010). Focusing on achievement: African American student persistence in the academy. In T. L. Strayhorn & M. C. Terrell (Eds.),* The evolving challenges of Black college students: New insights for practice and research *(pp. 66–84). Stylus Publishing.*

*Borum, V. (2007). Why we can't wait! An Afrocentric approach in working with African American families.* Journal of Human Behavior in the Social Environment, 15, *117–135. doi:https://doi.org/10.1300/J137v15n02_08*

*Boyd-Franklin, N. (2010). Incorporating spirituality and religion into the treatment of African American clients.* The Counseling Psychologist, 38*(7), 976–1000. doi:10.1177/0011000010374881*

*Bronfenbrenner, U. (Ed.). (2005).* Making human beings human: Bioecological perspectives on human development. *Sage Publications, Inc.*

*Crenshaw, K. (2017).* On intersectionality: Essential Writings. *The New Press.*

*Cummins, I. (2015). Discussing race, racism, and mental health: Two mental health inquiries reconsidered.* International Journal of Human Rights in Healthcare, 8*(3), 160–172. http://dx.doi.org/10.1108/IJHRH-08-2014-0017*

*Curtis-Boles, H. (2017). Clinical strategies for working with clients of African descent.* Best Practices in Mental Health, 13*(2), 61–72.*

*Darling, N. (2007). Ecological systems theory: The person in the center of the circles.* Research in Human Development, 4*(3–4), 203-217. doi:10.1080/15427600701663023*

*DeFreitas, S. C. (2019).* African American psychology: A positive psychology perspective. *Springer Publishing Company, LLC. doi:10.1891/9780826150066*

*Denby, R. W., & Curtis, C. M. (2013).* African American children and families in child welfare: Cultural adaptation of services. *Columbia University Press.*

*Hardina, D., Middleton, J., Montana, S., & Simpson, R. A. (2007).* An empowering approach to managing social service organizations. *Springer Publishing Company.*

*Hardy, K. V., & Laszloffy, T. A. (2007).* Teens who hurt: Clinical interventions to break the cycle of adolescent violence. *The Guilford Press.*

*Keene, L. C., Heath, R. D., & Bouris, A. (2021). Disclosure of sexual identities across social-relational contexts: Findings from a national sample of black sexual minority men.* Journal of Racial and Ethnic Health Disparities. *https://doi.org/10.1007/s40615-020-00944-y*

*Lindsey, M. A., Banks, A., Cota, C. F., Scott, M. L., & Joe, S. (2018). A review of treatments for young black males experiencing depression.* Research on Social Work Practice, 28*(3), 320–329. doi:10.1177/1049731517703747*

*Lowery, W., & Stankiewicz, K. (2016, February 15). 'My demons won today': Ohio activist's suicide spotlights depression among black lives matter leaders.* The Washington Post. *https://www.washingtonpost.com/news/post-nation/wp/2016/02/15/my-demons-won-today-ohio-activists-suicide-spotlights-depression-among-black-lives-matter-leaders/*

*Mazama, A. (2001). The Afrocentric paradigm: Contours and definitions.* Journal of Black Studies, 31*(4), 387–405. doi:https://doi.org/10.1177/002193470103100401*

*McIntosh, P. (1989, July/August). White privilege: Unpacking the invisible knapsack.* Peace and Freedom Magazine, *10–11.*

*Montón-Subías, S., & Hernando, A. (2018). Modern colonialism, Eurocentrism and historical archaeology: Some engendered thoughts.* European Journal of Archaeology, 21*(3), 455–471. doi:10.1017/eaa.2017.83*

*Parmer, T., Arnold, M. S., Natt, T., & Janson, C. (2004). Physical attractiveness as a process of internalized oppression and multigenerational transmission in African American families.* The Family Journal, 12*(3), 230–242. doi:10.1177/1066480704264931*

*Peters, M. F., & Massey, G. (1983). Mundane extreme environmental stress in family stress theories: The case of black families in white America.* Marriage & Family Review, 6*(1–2), 193–218. https://doi.org/10.1300/J002v06n01_10*

*Plagerson, S. (2015). Integrating mental health and social development in theory and practice.* Health Policy and Planning, 30*(2), 163–170.*

*Polansky, N. (1986). There is nothing so practical as a good theory.* Child Welfare, LXV*(1), 3–15.*

*Ponds, K. T. (2013). The trauma of racism: America's original sin.* Reclaiming Children and Youth, 22*(2), 22–24.*

*Rich, J., & Grey, C. (2005). Pathways to recurrent trauma among black men: Traumatic stress, substance use, and the "code of the street".* Public Health Matters, 95*(5), 816–824. doi:10.2105/AJPH.2004.044560*

*Schiele, J. H. (1996). Afrocentricity: An emerging paradigm in social work practice.* Social Work, 41*(3), 284–294. doi:10.1093/sw/41.3.284*

*Simpson, R. A. (1990).* Conflict styles and social network relations as predictors of marital happiness: A comparison of black and white spouses *[Doctoral dissertation, University of Michigan].*

*Steele, C. M., & Aronson, J. (1995). Stereotype threat and the intellectual test performance of African Americans.* Journal of Personality and Social Psychology, 69*(5), 797–811. https://doi.org/10.1037/0022-3514.69.5.797*

*Stewart, P. E. (2004). Afrocentric approaches to working with African American families.* Families in Society, 85*(2), 221–228. doi:10.1606/1044-3894.326*

*Troka, D., & Adedoja, D. (2016). The challenges of teaching about the black lives matter movement: A dialogue.* Radical Teacher: A Socialist, Feminist, and Anti-Racist Journal on the Theory and Practice of Teaching, 106, *47–56. http://dx.doi.org/10.5195/rt.2016.311*
*West, C. M. (1995). Mammy, Sapphire, and Jezebel: Historical images of black women and their implications for psychotherapy.* Psychotherapy: Theory, Research, Practice, Training, 32*(3), 458–466. https://doi.org/10.1037/0033-3204.32.3.458*
*Williams, T. M. (2008).* Black pain: It just looks like we're not hurting. *Scribner.*

# CHAPTER 25

## Behavior Modification

### Experiments in Resisting White Supremacy in Clinical Practice

MICHAEL BOUCHER, MSW

At best, current models of clinical practice marginally address the deep impacts of racism and white supremacy in the lives of clinician and client or in the process of counseling itself. At worst, these models are dangerous to People of Color and reproduce serious harm at psychological, emotional, and physical levels. As a white clinician, my understanding of this has grown over the years, and I have worked to decenter whiteness at both the personal and professional levels. This chapter will focus on some of that journey and explore steps that I took along the way in order to find new ways of working with people, ways that are more consistent with my values of liberation, community, healing, and accountability.

* * *

It was probably 6 months into our counseling relationship that Ms. Pamela told me, "You know, I watched you."

Having no idea what she meant, I said, "What?"

"I watched you . . . before we started meeting," she said. "I needed to see if you were OK." Ms. Pamela, then a 60-year-old African American woman, recounted to me how she had heard my name from a friend and that I might be a "good counselor" for her. She had had other counselors before, particularly white male counselors. Things had not always gone so well for her in these encounters. So for a few weeks prior to our first meeting, Ms. Pamela sat in our waiting area and watched how I interacted with people—clients, walk-ins, other staff. This was the level of research that she needed to do to try to protect herself. I don't know for sure, but perhaps if she were white, such scrutiny would have never happened, nor would it likely have been necessary. This is one small example of white privilege and of what it means to be Black living in a white world.

I started to cry when she told me this story, partly because I was honored that she decided I was worth the risk. And I cried, in part, because I knew that for her and for every other Person of Color who consults a white therapist and engages in the project of what is considered counseling or therapy (regardless of modality), there is significant risk that the therapeutic encounter will replicate (in some form and to some extent) colonization, enslavement, and oppression.

Erica Woodland (quoted in Babu, 2017), a queer Black clinician and healing practitioner, says that "there have been countless stories of racial trauma happening in the therapeutic relationship" (para. 10) because most clinicians, especially white clinicians, have done little in the way of racial analysis beyond superficial understandings. Woodland goes on to say that clinicians do "not have a deep understanding of white supremacy, period, and then to be doing clinical work and not understanding how that plays out [in therapy] is really damaging" (para. 11).

In the ten or so years since that exchange with Ms. Pamela, I have grown in my awareness of the potential harm that is present in the therapeutic encounter between a white therapist and a Client of Color. While I am glad that I am now aware of these things, I regret that I didn't think about them sooner.

The possibility of harm in clinical relationships is always present due to the power differential. But the potential for inflicting racial harm is so much higher for white clinicians because we lack a fundamental awareness of how racial oppression works. And while I do not believe that "it takes one to help one," I now have a deeper appreciation for the work and reflection that white clinicians need to do in order to show up in these relationships in ways that make them safer for Clients of Color (acknowledging that there is probably no such thing as a totally "safe" encounter for People of Color with respect to white folks).

I come to this work as a 52-year-old, white, heterosexual, cisgender male with advanced degrees and economic privilege, living in a suburb of Rochester, New York, and my primary work is as a counselor and community worker at a health center for people who have no insurance or are underinsured. It is in this context that I have come to learn a great deal about what privileges I hold and the assumptions I can make about the world I move through that so many others cannot. I have had a deep commitment to doing justice work since I was young, but it has really been in the past few decades that I have deepened and sharpened that commitment, in part because I have become more acutely aware of the violence inflicted by past and current realities of colonization and white supremacy at so many levels. While I have so much to unlearn and account for (given my privileges and the histories that I am located in), my hope is to be a stronger ally and accomplice in the work of undoing oppressive legacies and in catalyzing healing at the individual and collective levels. At least that's what I strive to do every day.

This chapter is intended to provide a snapshot of what it might look like if we white clinicians were able to move beyond our usual color blind reactions, efforts, and clinical initiatives to more urgently disrupt and interrupt racially oppressive practices that result in deadly consequences for People of Color.

What this interrupting and disrupting work looks like in your life and context may look different than what it looks like in mine, so I am cautious about being too proscriptive or of offering a "this is what you do list." I offer what I have learned, questions I am continually asking, and things I am trying to remain mindful of in my practice. My hope is that my story prompts you, especially white clinicians, to do the same.

## Our Training Is Steeped in Whiteness

My friend Liz and I recently copresented a workshop at a local college on decentering whiteness in therapy. Liz is a Black Haitian-American workers' rights attorney and antiracism consultant, and she has her share of painful stories of racism playing out in therapy and in wider society. Because she is not a therapist, Liz asked me to send along my prep materials so she could get a sense of what I was exploring. When I sent her my PowerPoint and a few articles, she responded emphatically, "My God, the counseling world is so white!" (personal communication, December 2019).

I would submit that if you are trained as a clinician, then you have been trained in how to be a *white* clinician. The major theorists we study are white. The textbooks are written predominantly by white people. The training videos we watch are almost all of white people doing therapy. And the intended audience for therapy is generally white people.

Whether we wanted it or not, that's what our training gave us. No one ever taught us that this was "white psychology" or "white social work" or "white mental health," and they didn't have to, because whiteness was the assumed norm. What's more, we were also probably taught that our training, skills, and knowledge had universal applicability, were essentially "neutral," and were generally beneficial/helpful to all people.

Clausen (2015) says that most psychological theories "remain Eurocentric, yet are largely assumed to be universal" and that the racism that is baked into those assessment and diagnostic systems goes on to become the "guideposts in courts of law, prison, schools, and medical venues." Furthermore, psychological research largely "makes assumptions of universality without qualification that population samples are overwhelmingly white; and [the] delivery of services, even the 'culture' of psychotherapy itself, remains white-centric" (para. 2).

### *Tools of the Oppressor*

I was also never taught in social work school, and I am guessing most clinicians are never taught (regardless of race), that the fields of mental health, psychiatry, psychology, clinical social work are, as Erica Woodland (quoted in Babu, 2017) says, "rooted in the degradation of indigenous people, black people, women, queer people," and that the "entire system is set up to uphold the systems of oppression we live in" (para. 16).

This may be harder to see and feel if we are white, but the fields of psychology and psychiatry were used to support the racial status quo and were part of the much larger machinery of racist socialization—even as they purported to help and heal.[1]

Indigenous therapist and social work professor Nicole Penak (quoted in Donato, 2019) would even say that "our offices are not a sanctuary from capitalism, neoliberalism, or colonialism. They're actually an expression of it" (para. 30). For me, this raises a series of crucial questions—particularly for white clinicians.

- How would we even know if white supremacy were operating in our clinical practice (or in our agencies and organizations)?[2]
- What does colonialism look like in our modern context?
- In what ways might my practice, my methods, my thinking, and my lived experience reinforce and replicate racial oppression?
- What sources would help me understand the answers to these questions?

Not knowing history—especially as told by those who have been (and continue to be) victimized and marginalized by the very systems we work in—makes white clinicians potentially dangerous to Clients of Color and at risk of replicating dominance models of practice. It doesn't matter if we are good people, what our intentions are, or what our self-image is.

If you are white, then you, like me, have been steeped in relatively uninterrogated white dominant values, authors, traditions, and power structures that benefit us, affirm us, support us, and encourage us.[3] These same structures have told us for generations that how we think, what we think, how we organize, what we do, and how we do it are good and even are the ideal. Franz Fanon (1963) was a Black psychiatrist who was one of the first clinicians to name the profound connections between oppression and mental illness as well as naming psychiatry as an extension of the colonial project. And researchers like Hall and Malony (1983) submit that majority (white) clinicians are far more likely to influence people from minority groups toward the dominant values and behaviors—exerting pressure to conform. We may not be purposefully trying to steer clients toward whiteness, but we likely do if we don't understand it and actively resist it.

## The First Step in Healing

One of the more profound experiences of my clinical training has been attending workshops with Dr. Joy DeGruy, who writes about and presents on post traumatic slave syndrome. In her trainings, Dr. DeGruy spends significant amounts of time unveiling the racist history of medicine and psychiatry in this country. The history is brutal and shocking, and most of it has been either hidden from us or sanitized. Dr. DeGruy knows that this history is hard to engage, but she tells people in her study guide that the foundation of health is to "tell the truth" (DeGruy, 2009, p. 41).

When I first started to learn about the hidden history of our profession and began coming to grips with just how white my training was, it was depressing and overwhelming. As time has gone on, however, it has been such a liberating move because I no longer have to defend something that I don't think I ever believed in.

In a recent study, Baima and Sude (2020) outlined what white mental health professionals need to understand about their own whiteness. Most of us won't be shocked at their top findings:

- White people need to "learn about the historical and contemporary implications of whiteness in society and in the mental health profession, specifically highlighting the problem of asserting whiteness as the 'norm' in clinical practice" (p. 66).
- White therapists need to explore their own oppressive tendencies, explore their judgements/attitudes about People of Color, and acknowledge their own social location.
- "Self of the therapist work," which has often focused on areas of therapist victimization, needs to focus on perpetration (especially as it pertains to racial trauma).

The authors are cautious to say that there is no "how to avoid whiteness checklist" that white people can get through and then feel good that they have arrived at some enlightened state of wokeness. Rather, our journey is going to be messy, confusing, and even contradictory—and that's when it is going well!

In his poignant article "When Black People Are in Pain, White People Just Join Book Clubs," Tre Johnson (2020) reminds white folks:

> The confusing, perhaps contradictory advice on what white people should do probably feels maddening. To be told to step up, no step back, read, no listen, protest, don't protest, check on black friends,

> leave us alone, ask for help or do the work—it probably feels contradictory at times. And yet, you'll figure it out. (para. 13)

White people can figure it out, but only if we stick with it. Clausen (2015) says that white people "can dip in and out of this work, and we can choose what aspects in which we want to participate" (para. 32). To counteract that, one of our primary tasks, then, is to keep increasing our capacity to engage race more fully and more often.

### *So How Do We Engage the Work?*

What often amazes me about white folks—including myself—is how easily we become paralyzed when it comes to antiracism work. In almost every other area of life, if we faced some kind of problem, we'd talk to others and make a plan to try to address it. In antiracism work, however, we seem to freeze and get easily confused. Yet so much is available to us.

What I have found to be critically important to my efforts to decenter my whiteness in therapeutic contexts is to study it. For quite a few years now, I have tried to read all I can about whiteness and how it works. Standard books like Robin DiAngelo's (2018) *White Fragility* and *What it Means to Be White* (2012), Debby Irving's (2014) *Waking Up White* and Tim Wise's (2005) *White Like Me* have been foundational to increasing my racial literacy in the therapy room. Reading a list like *The Characteristics of White Supremacy Culture* (Jones & Okun, 2001) also helps me to understand some of my own behavior and how others might be perceiving me. Recently I also came across Lisa Savage and Kim Knight's (2020) *White Therapists, Here's What Your Black Colleagues Want You to Know* as well as Zencare's (2020) *10 Ways White Therapists Can Address Racism in Therapy with Black Clients.* Articles like these are incredibly useful in giving me a peek into what People of Color are thinking without ever having to burden them with direct conversation.

Another concept that has been really helpful to me is the idea of "pretransference." Therapists like Lennox Thomas (quoted in Jackson, 2018) describe it as the "racism, projections and prejudices" (para. 13) that the therapist brings even *before* the encounter begins. This means getting real (in the company of another white person to whom we can be accountable) about our racial programming, our guilt and shame, our stereotypes, our ignorance, and all of the racist history we have been fed. Some of this racial programming may be in the form of presence—from things that happened or were taught to us, etc. But it may also come in the form of absence—things that we didn't experience or weren't taught to us, etc.

My antiracism work has me diving into my own racial identity development to understand where I am on the journey and where I might need to move to. I highly recommend the work of Janet Helms (2019) on racial identity development; I have found her work incredibly useful for understanding my own reactions and development as a white person in a racist society. Her work has also helped me to understand and to work with other white people, who may be at different points on the journey, as I work to stay engaged with them as well.

In my individual supervision and in my peer supervision groups, we regularly take up issues of race and real-time dilemmas that we face in our practice. We grapple with the questions that help us to critically assess our thinking and practice from a racial equity lens, and we work to remain honest and accountable to one another around our own racism.

*Behavioral Modification*

While it is crucial to do a *lot* of self-study about our whiteness, it's also really important to change our practices. Tre Johnson (2020), who I mentioned earlier, has some harsh words for white liberals (which probably describes a lot of white clinicians like me). He says that when we are confronted with "really murderous, really tragic, really violent or aggressive" actions against People of Color, white folks "read. And talk about their reading. [Then they] listen. And talk about how they listened" (para. 3).

It would hurt less if it weren't so true. If we're going to do less harm through our profession, we will need to do more than read and listen. *10 Ways White Therapists Can Address Racism in Therapy With Black Clients* (Zencare, 2020) offers specific actions clinicians can take. Most of them probably sound simple enough:

- Commit to an ongoing practice of readings and trainings
- Focus your learning about race outside of your practice (so your clients can focus on their healing and not on your education)

- Develop a personalized education plan for yourself
- Cultivate an awareness of the ways you commit microaggressions
- Validate the reality of racial trauma
- Be curious about clients' specific experiences versus relying on stereotypes

While I label these as "simple" steps, I do not think that they are easy.

For example, take curiosity. What does it mean to develop curiosity with Clients of Color? In my practice, it starts by asking if I can ask some questions. I often say to clients (and especially Clients of Color), "Do you mind if I ask you more about what you just said?" Seeking permission, for me, is a small way to counteract the historical colonization and oppression that disregard boundaries and preferences. Then it moves into understanding the specific ways that race and culture may be operating in this person's life. Earlier in my journey to understand race, I relied heavily on stereotypes or my limited knowledge about People of Color. I failed to see the incredible diversity within the experiences of People of Color (among all the similarities). My understandings were superficial, at best, until I started to ask more specific questions that revealed my ignorance and made me vulnerable.

I remember talking to a Black client a few years back about her depression. I realized that, given her racial identity (as well as her low socioeconomic status), I knew quite little about what she faced beyond what I could guess. After a bit of exploring how her depression showed itself, I asked if she thought that the depression that Black people faced was similar to and/or different from the depression that white people faced. I said that I was more familiar with the depression of white people and admitted that my professional training had not spoken much of other depressions. I also went on to ask if and how her depression was similar or different from what she witnessed in other Black people. My client appreciated my questions and recommended that I read *Black Pain*, by Terrie Williams (2008). I did, and this opened me up not only to an increased understanding of my client but to a lot of other resources and conversations with People of Color about depression and what it looked like for them.

For the past 15 years, my therapeutic work has been deeply informed by narrative approaches to counseling and community work as developed by

Michael White and David Epston. Their work has been transformational for me in so many ways. In narrative approaches, the clinician is thought of as an appreciative audience to the "performance" of a client's preferred story, which is being enacted in the clinical encounter (White & Epston, 1990). Rob Rice (2015) even describes the narrative therapist as an "appreciative ally" (p. 697) in the process.

But what if we have very little basis for understanding what is being performed in front of us? What if we have limited ability to appreciate the story we are hearing? How would we even know if we are being a meaningful ally in the process?

In a wonderful article entitled "Why I Left My White Therapist," contributor Erica Woodland (quoted in Babu, 2017) says that "ultimately the therapeutic process is about being witnessed" (para. 14). The systems that we operate in, however, were not originally designed to bear witness to what People of Color go through, and we can't assume that our training will somehow prepare us for this without intentional and concerted effort.

In fact, many of the forms of resistance to oppression embodied by Clients and Communities of Color have been pathologized, dehumanized, and discouraged because they do not fit with, or may even directly challenge, white hegemony and white power. Mukungu Akinyela (2002) says that when therapists—especially white therapists—"can become curious about these acts of resistance and the meanings people give to them, opportunities for reclaiming dignity and humanity may be provided" (p. 39).

That's the kind of curiosity that we need to develop.

Trying to be a partner with our clients requires us to be more honest about what we know and what we don't know. It means that we acknowledge that we have some training and skill and that what we know may have limited use to the person in front of us who might have very different experiences in the world, assumptions about how it works, and what is required for healing. It might mean that we have to work harder than our clients (which I was taught never to do) because *we* are the ones catching up.

### *Staying Present*

A big part of being curious is staying present. I know that I find it hard to stay present as a white person when People of Color challenge me on race—especially clients. My heart beats faster, I get red in the face, and I don't know what to say.

A few years ago, I was in a session with a Black man named Larry whom I had worked with for a long time (and perceived myself doing a lot for over the years). He told me, "All you white people are the same. You don't care about Black people. You just sit there and listen, but you're not helping me with the things that I need help with. You people just don't fucking care" (personal communication, Spring 2018). His words stung.

Not really knowing what to say, I said (with all sincerity), "If you think it may be time for you to meet with someone else who is able to do more for you . . ." This made things even worse. Instead of leaning into the relationship, I offered to sever it—which is what so many People of Color critique white folks for doing whenever the heat gets turned up!

In hindsight, I wish I had said, "Thank you for saying that. I had no idea that you have been carrying that and I am sorry that I didn't even notice or ask." This would have at least acknowledged what he had just shared with me. But many white people—and white clinicians—move so quickly to shame, guilt, or defensiveness (like I did) that we cannot even hear the message coming our way. In Larry's case, I heard what he was saying about me personally without listening to what he was saying about the collective as well. Thinking back, I know that he was frustrated with me personally, but he was also tired of the collective "white people" who behave just as he says. In general, white people hear the pain of People of Color and effectively do nothing. And when this is brought to our attention, we generally disengage. Which is what I did.

Research shows that the strength of the therapeutic relationship is one of the biggest predictors of the success of therapy (Norcross & Lambert, 2018). My experience has taught me that many of my Clients of Color raise issues of race with me precisely because they are *trying* to connect with me more deeply. But more often than not, white clinicians are unprepared for this, might frame it as threatening, might not know what to do with it, or might miss it all together. Staying open to race in our therapeutic work—even (and maybe especially) when it is hard and painful—has the potential to strengthen our relationships. And, mind you, staying open this way doesn't make us incapable of doing harm. It does, however, make it more likely that we will recognize, take responsibility for, and work to repair what

Derald Wing Sue (2010) calls the microaggressions, microassaults, microinvalidations, and microinjuries that we will inevitably commit.

*Addressing White-Body Supremacy*

One of the actions that I consider essential for white clinicians to take is to further explore our white bodies. My Black friend Lisa always brings this to my attention when she imitates white people—especially the white, male lawyers that she works with. She flattens her voice a bit, tightens her jaw and upper body and usually starts her sentences with, "Well . . ." It is both funny and true.

Resmaa Menakem's book, *My Grandmother's Hands* (2017), has been a profound resource for me in this body-recovery process, and his book is both theory and practice for people to reconnect with their bodies and affect. Menakem (2017) contends that white supremacy—which he calls white-body supremacy—has resulted not only in the terrorizing of "bodies of culture" (as he calls them) but in the physical and emotional constriction of white people. He says that for years we have "earnestly tried to address white body supremacy . . . with reason, principles and ideas" (p. 4). As clinicians, we have tried to similarly address it through workshops and trainings. Yet he asks, "Why is there such a chasm between our well-intentioned attempts to heal and the ever-growing number of dark-skinned bodies who are killed, injured?" (p. 4). Reason, ideas, workshops, and trainings for white folks have clearly not addressed white-body supremacy.

Something else is needed.

Menakem (2017) says that this white-body supremacy that has become the default operating system of the wider culture has

> allowed many white Americans to avoid developing the full range of necessary skills for navigating adulthood. Instead of building resilience and accepting the full pain and grief and disappointment of human existence, [white people] outsourced some of that pain, grief and disappointment to dark-skinned bodies. (p. 211)

When Clients of Color ask white clinicians, "Do you feel me?", this is not just rhetorical. Can we really feel in our bodies what Clients of Color are saying to us? Do we believe their narration of reality—especially when it is not our experience? Can we feel our own fears and racialized programming? Are we prepared to change how and what we do based on what is said to us? Menakem (2017) says that "the body is where we live" (p. 7), and if we do not do the necessary healing of our bodies from white-body supremacy, we cannot move forward in any meaningful ways.

### *Which Side Are You On?*

In the summer of 2020 in Rochester, New York, we had protests in response to the police killings of unarmed Black people like George Floyd, Breonna Taylor, and, locally, Daniel Prude. As part of the street protests, the crowd chanted, "Which side are you on, my people, which side are you on?" While I usually am not a person who subscribes to binaries, in this case, I think we need to take sides.

Paul Kivel has influenced a lot of my work and is a mentor for me in antioppression work. Ever since I read his article "Social Service or Social Change?" a decade ago, I haven't been able to stop thinking about his challenge. Kivel (2000) asks human service professionals to reflect on two questions. The first is, "What do you value?" This helps us name and identify the professional values we strive to uphold in our work. But then he asks, "And who do you stand with?"[4] Many of us, while saying we uphold values like equity and justice, do not find ourselves alongside those most affected by racist systems.

If we are going to position ourselves against white-body supremacy, it must cost us something. I can't tell you exactly what that will look like in your context. But author Tre Johnson (2020) tells us that the

> right acknowledgment of . . . justice, humanity, freedom and happiness [for people of color] . . . will be found in your earnest willingness to dismantle systems that stand in our way—be they at your job, in your social network, your neighborhood associations, your family or your home. (para. 11)

Which systems are we "earnestly willing" to dismantle these days, and how are we going about that work? What wider social freedom movements is our work connected to? How would anyone—especially our clients—know that we're doing this work? These need to be frequent questions we ask ourselves and one another.

*Reconnecting with Our Humanity*

Through her work related to decolonizing therapy,[5] Jennifer Mullan (quoted in Chary, 2020) invites clinicians to reconnect with the humanity of the therapeutic encounter. She says that "to decolonize therapy is to reconnect [and] reclaim therapy, to include [critical analysis of] systems and oppression into our therapy practices . . . and to re-humanize therapists . . . as well as to center the person and their cultural and political identities back into the work" (para. 8).

To center the identities of People of Color, white clinicians have much to do to understand ourselves, our politics, our racial socialization, and our histories. White-body supremacy has taken part of our humanity away from us as it has used us to enact oppression. Defecting from our place in that system is required for us to reclaim our humanity.

But the great Indigenous activist Lila Watson (2004) states that if we are white and engaging in this work "for our clients," we are "wasting our time." She goes on to say, "but if you have come because your liberation is bound up with mine, then let us work together" (sent. 2).

We're in a serious struggle for the souls of white folks, the soul of our profession, and the soul of this nation. May we let that urgency move us into great awareness and action.

**MICHAEL BOUCHER (HE/HIM/HIS), MSW,** currently lives on the traditional territory of the Seneca Nation in what is now known as Rochester, New York. He works as a social worker and counselor at St. Joseph's Neighborhood Center (a health center for people without adequate insurance). He strives to explore the intersections of poverty, racism, oppression, resistance, and resiliency through his work. He also works on the pastoral team of Spiritus Christi Church. He is married to his wife, Lynne, and has two adult children.

## Notes

1. For starters, you may want to read *Creating Racism: Psychiatry's Betrayal* published by the Citizens Commission on Human Rights (2008), which can be downloaded at https://www.cchr.org/cchr-reports/creating-racism/introduction.html
2. Robin DiAngelo (2017) reminds us that white supremacy does not mean the KKK. She says that "white supremacy is a highly descriptive term for the culture we live in; a culture which positions white people and all that is associated with them (whiteness) as ideal. White supremacy captures the all-encompassing centrality and assumed superiority of people defined and perceived as white, and the practices based upon that assumption. White supremacy is not simply the idea that whites are superior to people of color (although it certainly is that), but a deeper premise that supports this idea—the definition of whites as the norm or standard for human, and people of color as an inherent deviation from that norm." (para. 4–5)
3. I recommend readers check out Natasha Stovall's *Whiteness on the Couch* (https://longreads.com/2019/08/12/whiteness-on-the-couch/), which takes a deeper and more substantive dive into why white people don't talk about race in therapy and what we can do about it as clinicians.
4. I recognize that this is ableist language but am trying to honor the words he used in framing the question.
5. Be sure to check out Mullan's amazing Instagram account @DecolonizingTherapy

## References

*Akinyela, M. (2002). De-colonizing our lives: Divining a post-colonial therapy.* The International Journal of Narrative Therapy and Community Work, 2*, 32–43.*

*Babu, C. (2017, January 18).* Why I left my white therapist. *VICE. https://www.vice.com/en/article/d7pa5j/why-i-left-my-white-therapist 1/18/2017*

*Baima, T., & Sude, M. E. (2020). What white mental health professionals need to understand about whiteness: A Delphi study.* Journal of Marital and Family Therapy, 46*(1), 62–80. https://doi.org/10.1111/jmft.12385*

*Chary. (2020, April 16).* Dr. Jennifer Mullan, decolonizing therapy. *Thecnnekt. https://www.thecnnekt.com/spotlight/2020/4/8/dr-jennifer-mullan-decolonizing-therapy*

*Citizens Commission on Human Rights. (2008).* Creating racism: Psychiatry's betrayal. *https://www.cchr.org/cchr-reports/creating-racism/introduction.html*

*Clausen, M. (2015).* Whiteness matters: Exploring white privilege, color blindness and racism in psychotherapy. *Psychotherapy.net. https://www.psychotherapy.net/article/racism-white-privilege-psychotherapy*

*DeGruy, J. (2005).* Post traumatic slave syndrome: America's legacy of enduring injury and healing. *Uptone Press.*

*DeGruy, J. (2009).* Post traumatic slave syndrome: America's legacy of enduring injury and Healing. The study guide. *Joy DeGruy Publications, Inc.*

*DiAngelo, R. J. (2012).* What does it mean to be white?: Developing white racial literacy. *Peter Lang.*

*DiAngelo, R. J. (2017, June 30).* No, I won't stop saying 'white supremacy'. *Yes!. https://www.yesmagazine.org/democracy/2017/06/30/no-i-wont-stop-saying-white-supremacy/*

*DiAngelo, R. J. (2018).* White fragility: Why it's so hard to talk to white people about racism. *Beacon Press.*

*Donato, A. (2019, September 9).* What therapy looks like when it acknowledges people of colour's experiences: Racism, colonialism, and stigma are common issues. *HUFFPOST. https://www.huffingtonpost.ca/entry/therapy-people-of-colour-racism_ca_5d72b392e4b0fde50c262fcb*

*Fanon, F. (1963).* The wretched of the earth. *Grove Press.*

*Hall, G. C. N., & Malony, H. N. (1983). Cultural control in psychotherapy with minority clients.* Psychotherapy: Theory, Research & Practice, 20*(2), 131–142. https://doi.org/10.1037/h0088484*

*Helms, J. (2019).* A race is a nice thing to have: A guide to being a white person or understanding the white persons in your life *(3rd ed.). American Psychological Association.*

*Irving, D. (2014).* Waking up white, and finding myself in the story of race. *Elephant Room Press.*

*Jackson, C. (2018, October).* Why we need to talk about race. *bacp. https://www.bacp.co.uk/bacp-journals/therapy-today/2018/october-2018/why-we-need-to-talk-about-race/*

*Johnson, T. (2020, June 11). When black people are in pain, white people just join book clubs.* The Washington Post. *https://www.washingtonpost.com/outlook/white-antiracist-allyship-book-clubs/2020/06/11/9edcc766-abf5-11ea-94d2-d7bc43b26bf9_story.html*

*Jones, K., & Okun, T. (2001).* The Characteristics of white Supremacy Culture. *DRWORKSBOOK. https://www.dismantlingracism.org/white-supremacy-culture.html*

*Kivel, P. (2000).* Social service or social change? *Paul Kivel: Educator, Writer, Activist. http://paulkivel.com/resource/social-service-or-social-change/*

*Menakem, R. (2017).* My grandmother's hands: Racialized trauma and the pathway to mending our hearts and bodies. *Central Recovery Press.*

*Norcross, J. C., & Lambert, M. J. (2018). Psychotherapy relationships that work III.* Psychotherapy, 55*(4), 303–315. http://dx.doi.org/10.1037/pst0000193*

*Rice, R. H. (2015). Narrative therapy.* The SAGE Encyclopedia of Theory in Counseling and Psychology, 2, *695–700. http://dx.doi.org/10.4135/9781483346502.n250*

*Savage, L., & Knight, K. (2020).* White therapists, here's what your Black colleagues want you to know. *Psychotherapy Networker. https://www.psychotherapynetworker.org/blog/details/1775/white-therapists-heres-what-your-black-colleagues-want*

*Sue, D. W. (2010).* Microaggressions in everyday life: Race, gender, and sexual orientation. *John Wiley and Sons.*

*Watson, L. (2004, September 21–24).* Let us work together *[Keynote Address]. A Contribution to Change: Cooperation Out of Conflict Conference: Celebrating Difference, Embracing Equality, Hobart, Tasmania, Australia. https://uniting.church/lilla-watson-let-us-work-together/*

*White, M., & Epston, D. (1990).* Narrative means to therapeutic ends. *W. W. Norton & Company.*

*Williams, T. M. (2008).* Black pain: It just looks like we're not hurting. *Scribner.*

*Wise, T. J. (2005).* White like me. *Soft Skull Press.*

*Zencare Group, Inc. (2020).* 10 ways white therapists can address racism in therapy with Black clients. *ZENCARE. https://blog.zencare.co/how-white-therapists-address-racism-black-clients/*

## CHAPTER 26

# Recovery from White Conditioning

## Building Antiracist Practice and Community

CRISTINA COMBS, MSW, LICSW

> We talk about race a lot, we do. I don't think we talk about it in depth as much as we should. When we start recognizing that there's something congenital: it's as if I had a problem with alcohol. That's a different conversation in that I have to confess that there's something in me. That I will always have to cope with that. That I will always have to deal with that. The honesty that takes, the courage that takes, the strength that takes is pretty profound. (Coates, 2014, min. 13:38–14:38)

As a white woman and clinical social worker, my formal education demanded less honesty, courage, and strength than is necessary for antiracist clinical practice. My coursework included one diversity class, in which I learned about "other" cultures. I was rarely challenged to understand my own racial identity and to examine the role and presence of whiteness in my work. After years of seeking training and consultation to deepen my skill and understanding in this area, I was profoundly moved by Mr. Coates's words. Upon hearing them, I proceeded to develop the model of recovery from white conditioning (RWC), gather feedback from Black, Indigenous, and People of Color (BIPOC) mentors, and launch RWC groups to create a container for lifelong self-reflection and change in my community.

The RWC model, a derivative work based on the twelve steps of Alcoholics Anonymous (AA), is rooted in accountability and love. It involves white people working, within our community, to transform violent legacies of whiteness into healthier, white, antiracist community . . . and it requires having the courage to start with ourselves.

In this chapter, I will review the literature on white supremacy and clinical practice and then the twelve steps of recovery from white conditioning; implementation lessons learned will be discussed; and inherent tensions that exist for white people on this lifelong journey will be explored. "We," "our," and "us" will be used to refer to white people in order to center the responsibility for dismantling racism with the community responsible for creating and perpetuating it.

## Literature Review

> Throughout history, POCI [People of Color and Indigenous] communities have shown collective resistance to colonization and racism—resistance that required radicalism. We believe that we are currently in critical and radical times, which necessitate a radical response to injustice—one that moves beyond individual Eurocentric symptom reduction and toward collective multisystemic resistance and new realities. (French et al., 2019, p. 19)

As we fight for social justice and multisystemic change, the literature review that follows may guide us as we seek the following personal goals: (1) understand the journey of becoming antiracist, (2) embrace accountability practices, and (3) do our part to transform our ways of being as well as our clinical work.

In *White Habits, Anti-Racism, and Philosophy as a Way of Life*, Noe (2020) describes the importance of self-examination regarding "one's own complicity in the socially engineered and by-design hidden (to whites) sources of one's *white* thoughts, feelings, attitudes, and default responses to raced perceptual stimuli" (p. 289). In short, the goal is to make one's socialized habits of whiteness transparent to oneself. Values rooted in whiteness, transmitted through complex socialization processes, are also reflected in clinical discourse models. In a 2018 study on racial microaggressions in therapeutic encounters, Lee et al. (2018) found that therapists' approaches persistently centered "on 'Eurocentric Western values as the norm' including: individual focus around self-care, self-experience, and self-merit; a turbulent and independent adolescence; and a system that is rational and fair" (p. 231). This centering of Eurocentric values—and the microaggressions that emerge from it—interferes with white clinicians' ability to connect with BIPOC clients in culturally relevant ways and perpetuates harmful practices that invalidate their experiences.

Beyond the centering of white values and understandings, claims of color blindness in clinical work are another major problem that compromises the integrity and efficacy of the services delivered to Clients of Color. Adams et al. (2015) argue that when white clinicians claim that they "don't see color," they are engaging in epistemic violence. They elaborate further to explain:

> The primary goal of the denaturalization approach to decolonization is to disrupt these forms of epistemic violence and to illuminate alternative ways of being—critical consciousness of racism versus colorblind ignorance, sustainable relationality versus the pursuit of growth—that reflect epistemological perspectives of the oppressed and resonate with Fanon's call to develop new concepts as a foundation for a more human(e) psychology. (p. 230)

To build a more human(e) psychology, some of the core values and principles of our work as healers can prove helpful. Across clinical disciplines, groups like the National Association of Social Workers, the American Association for Marriage and Family Therapy, and the American Psychological Association offer various essential guidelines for clinical practice: ethical codes require clinicians to promote social justice and protect diversity; principles of nonmaleficence, beneficence, and justice are expected to be endorsed by therapists; and formal position statements have been issued, denouncing racism and acknowledging its harmful impact on human development. In "Know history, know self: Art therapists' responsibility to dismantle white supremacy," Hamrick and Byma (2017) posit that white therapists "must first acknowledge the fact that they, as white people, benefit from the systemic oppression of People of Color and the continued dominance of white (therapist) subjectivity in the field" (p. 109). This acknowledgment can serve as a grounding force for developing antiracist practices and an antiracist identity.

Beyond these acknowledgments, many clinical recommendations for advancing antiracist change have been offered for decades and continue to develop today. In their work on treating race-based traumatic stress (RBTS), Carter et al. (2017) assert that clinicians must understand the implications of race in their lives. "One difficulty that practitioners may face is their own confusion about the various forms racism can take in the United States, causing them to miss signs of RBTS when it enters the therapy room" (Carter et al., 2017, p. 36). Beyond simply resolving this confusion, white clinicians are also encouraged to develop a healthy sense of self as a racial being. Per Drustrup (2020):

> For people who are white, a sense of self is unstable when it is founded on an understanding of an idealized history about their country and ancestors or on a false sense of conscious or unconscious superiority. . . . Effective therapy can happen only when the white therapist is aware of self as a racial and cultural being with various biases and assumptions that influence the therapist's worldviews and therapeutic work. (pp. 185–186)

Additionally, Tummala-Narra (2016) expressed concern with white clinicians' struggle to name social oppression with their BIPOC clients, describing it as "an unfortunate and problematic consequence of the denial of the impact of social conditions on people's lives in the history of psychoanalytic theory and practice" (p. 665).

As white clinicians embark on a journey of self-examination related to their whiteness, it can be helpful to consider the benefits of antiracist practices and ways of being. In a 2010 qualitative study among eighteen white antiracists, participants reported:

> "sense of integrity," "peace of mind," "joyful feeling of connection to humanity," and sense of "moral fulfillment" as part of their journey toward antiracism. They also reported feeling hope for future generations, for a better world with less racism, and greater humanity for all. (Smith & Redington, 2010, p. 546)

As white clinicians consider these benefits, alongside ethical principles of nonmaleficence and justice, Case (2012) recommends conceptualizing the journey of becoming a white antiracist "as a personal striving rather than a goal with a definitive ending because unraveling one's racism never stops" (p. 91). Grzanka et al. (2019) made recommendations for advancing antiracist practice, including "identifying the structural dimensions of racism in institutions and practices that are not obviously racialized *or* generally perceived as relevant to counseling psychology" (p. 503).

## Recovery from White Conditioning

The RWC model offers one pathway for identifying, resisting, and transforming multifaceted dimensions of racism in our clinical practices and lives. Derived from the 12-Step model of Alcoholics Anonymous (AA), each step is designed to provide a vision and task that is considered critical for white people who are striving to recover from toxic patterns of white conditioning. Like other recovery programs, these steps are written in the past tense to remind us of the legacy of white antiracists who have gone before us, reassuring us that we are not alone in our present journey. The 12 steps of RWC are as follows:

Step 1: We admitted that we had been socially conditioned by the ideology of white supremacy and that our minds were subject to racial biases, often unconsciously so.
Step 2: We came to believe that we could embrace our ignorance as an invitation to learn.
Step 3: We developed support systems to keep us engaged in this work.
Step 4: We journeyed boldly inward, exploring and acknowledging ways in which white supremacist teachings have been integrated into our minds and spirits.
Step 5: We confessed our mistakes to ourselves and to others.
Step 6: We were entirely ready to deconstruct previous ways of knowing, as they had been developed through the lens of white supremacy.
Step 7: We humbly explored new ways of understanding, proactively seeking out new learning and reconstructing a more inclusive sense of reality.
Step 8: We committed ourselves to ongoing study of our racial biases,

conscious or unconscious, and our maladaptive patterns of white supremacist thinking.

Step 9: We developed strategies to counteract our racial biases.

Step 10: We embraced the responsibility of focusing more on our impact than our intentions in interactions with People of Color.

Step 11: We engaged in daily practices of self-reflection.

Step 12: We committed ourselves to sharing this message with our fellow white people in order to build a supportive recovery community and to encourage personal accountability within our culture.

## Implementation Lessons Learned to Date

In every RWC training, this 12-step model is carefully positioned within the movement for racial justice. It is one tool, among the many needed, to advance a more just and liberated world. It is centered on asking white people to work, as Dr. Kenneth V. Hardy (personal communication, January 27, 2017) has expressed, to "see and be different so we can do differently." At this intrapersonal level of change-making, this model also assists with building white, antiracist community: authentic relationships, shared values, rituals, and accountability practices.

Since the development of the RWC model in 2015, various RWC groups have been launched across the United States. Some are open, community-based groups that host weekly meetings, in-person or online, for anyone willing to join this lifelong effort. Other RWC meetings are closed (formal or informal) agency-based groups. To date, RWC groups have been launched in mental health centers, schools, universities, social service organizations, places of worship, and one county probation department. In many settings, white staff attend RWC group meetings while BIPOC staff concurrently participate in affinity or healing group spaces. Some program directors, across many disciplines, have built learning about RWC into their standard training efforts, compelling staff to participate. In other settings, employees (e.g., staff at the county probation department mentioned above) were motivated to use this model together, informally, on their lunch breaks.

All materials needed to facilitate RWC groups, including the meeting outline and the RWC book, are available for free as a download on the website: www.recoveryfromwhiteconditioning.com. Within meetings, members volunteer to facilitate on a rotating basis. The facilitator reads the meeting outline, which includes guiding members through welcoming and closing statements; reading of the 12 steps and the step of the day chapter; and holding space for each member to have an uninterrupted chance to share (or pass). During their uninterrupted turns, members share reflections about the identified step; back and forth dialogue may happen after the meeting.

Groups proceed through the 12 steps, one step per week. Community-based open groups repeat the 12-step cycle time after time, welcoming newcomers at any step. Because of the lifelong nature of this work, newcomers are encouraged to attend whenever they're able, to read the RWC literature on their own, and to trust that, no matter when or how often they join, they've found a community that will hold and encourage them on their journey. Proceeding sequentially from step 1 is not required because the focus is on creating a welcoming container that is strong enough to hold its members' varying scheduling and developmental needs. The lifelong invitation reminds us that, no matter when or how we start the journey, there is always more work to do and more understanding we can acquire.

Alongside the current and potential benefits of implementing this model, some risks also exist. As in other recovery models, individuals and groups may use the literature and community in varying ways: many faithfully commit to honest self-exploration to drive action for racial justice, while others engage at a superficial level of working the steps or refute them altogether. Additionally, some have asked how white people can evolve their understandings about racism without a teacher (BIPOC or white) to guide the group. Our response has been that the RWC materials (book and meeting outline) ground us in creating a container to pursue inner truth—and to drive commitment for external learning. We also believe that individuals who are farther along on their antiracism journey can positively impact individuals who are newer to the work through modeling and sharing lessons they've learned. Many of these members linger after meetings to hold space for questions that emerge from newcomers.

## Exploring the Value and Tension in Each Step

Beyond the value and risk involved in the RWC model at a conceptual level, each step holds power for transformation in its focus area, alongside limitations. Reviewing the steps while simultaneously uplifting the value and tension in them reminds us of the many layers of nuance and complexity required to embrace an antiracist life.

For white people new to learning about white privilege and systemic racism, I encourage you to hold this complexity with care: trust in the power of important questions and tensions to guide you, knowing that simple, prescriptive answers rarely exist to complex, multilayered challenges.

### *Step 1*

***We admitted that we had been socially conditioned by the ideology of white supremacy and that our minds were subject to racial biases, often unconsciously so.***

The first step to any kind of recovery is admitting that we have a problem. Individuals not ready to acknowledge a problem may be unable to pursue and receive the help they need. Becoming aware of a problem—and admitting it to others—can be challenging, but it is a fundamental step on the recovery journey.

#### Value

Stepping out of denial is a liberatory, daunting, and essential step toward building an antiracist life. It can be a significant step forward on the recovery journey and a helpful way to ground oneself daily, holding close Mr. Coates's (2014) wisdom: "There's something in us, it will always be there. We'll always have to deal with that" (min. 14:24–14:31).

Recently, a young white therapist explained: "Two years ago, when I first learned about this model, I was convinced that it didn't apply to me because I was a 'good white person.' Hearing it [the model] now, two years later, I receive it differently. I see how I'm complicit in injustice, and I want to do the work to change." Step 1's focus on moving past denial allows members a pathway forward into doing antiracism work; repeated rounds of working the steps allow group members to deepen their level of accepting that there is always work to do within us and around us.

**Tension**

Unlike individuals in other recovery journeys, who are accepting powerlessness over addiction, white people, living in a society built and sustained by white supremacy, are *not* powerless. While we cannot control the social conditions into which we were born, we can ground ourselves in a commitment to act differently now. The decision to do so, however, rests with the individual. As in other recovery groups, newcomers may be ambivalent or reluctant to invest in this lifelong journey. To support newcomers in stepping out of denial, group members who are farther along on their journey model their commitment to antiracist practice and change; many of these members will also reach out, after the meeting or using the phone list, to new members who have expressed their struggle to understand systemic racism in order to build supportive relationships and motivate continued engagement.

*Step 2*

***We came to believe that we could embrace our ignorance as an invitation to learn.***

We acknowledge that we, as white people, will *never know* what it feels like to walk in the world as a Person of Color. We embrace our *not knowing* as a powerful reminder of our ongoing need for new learning, and we abandon white supremacist traditions of *"knowing"* how others should feel, think, and act.

**Value**

This step directs us, white people, to consistently practice humility. We work to stop toxic patterns of "knowing" other people's answers, stories, or experiences. One RWC member and clinician expressed that Step 2 helps him stay focused on listening to others' stories. It helps him to watch for times in which he pontificates in session, imposing his views instead of staying open to the wisdom of the people he serves, especially when serving BIPOC clients.

**Tension**

There exists a challenge in naming ignorance without glorifying it. While disrupting a pattern of thinking we know everything and of asserting our ignorance can be a helpful step forward, we must also commit to active knowledge-seeking in order to humbly and consistently advance our understanding of racial justice.

*Step 3*

***We developed support systems to keep us engaged in this work.***

We are aware that facing and recovering from the effects of white supremacist conditioning will involve difficult, sometimes painful, moments. We commit to developing practices that facilitate self-care to ensure that we are gentle with ourselves, while also bravely confronting the dehumanizing ideology of white supremacy.

**Value**

This step promotes radical self-love: holding our humanity sacred while insisting on a path of transformation forward. As it has been said, the journey toward inner truth can be too overwhelming to be made alone. In countless ways and settings, relationships serve as powerful vessels to support growth. Many recovery group members say that their family or friends are not on this journey with them. Step 3 reminds us of the value of weekly meetings, of *partnership* (similar to sponsorship), and of the use of a phone list to stay connected to a community of people who are striving to embrace antiracist ways of being.

**Tension**

"To keep us engaged in this work" is the essential message in this step. As racial disparities and violence against BIPOC communities persist, it can be challenging to center the need for white people to pursue support for our antiracism work. Yet, without supportive practices and relationships, we often retreat: we try, we fail, and we give up. Step 3 serves to counter that unacceptable pattern.

*Step 4*

***We journeyed boldly inward, exploring and acknowledging ways in which white supremacist teachings have been integrated into our minds and spirits.***

After acknowledging the problem, we must also acknowledge that it has impacted *many* areas of our lives, consciously and unconsciously. Each of us must explore ways, past and present, in which the ideology of white supremacy has negatively impacted us: our understanding of history, our social networks, and our patterns of interacting with People of Color, with an emphasized focus on microaggressions.

**Value**

As Ta-Nehisi Coates (2014) suggested, the strength it takes to face oneself is "pretty profound" (min. 14:36–14:38). Step 4 affords us a proactive opportunity to look within and uncover parts of ourselves—and our upbringing as it relates to race—that often have been hidden from view. Recently, a probation officer expressed in an RWC meeting, "The more I work Step 4, the more I realize how deeply my views are shaped by race. I've started sharing that new learning with judges, encouraging us to think differently about sentencing recommendations."

**Tension**

Journeying inward to explore the role and presence of whiteness in various areas of our lives requires fortitude. Some individuals who haven't invested much time in the first three steps have regressed or suspended their recovery journey. Additionally, as we look within, we remember that we have blind spots related to matters of racial justice, which necessitates lifelong learning *outside* of ourselves as well.

*Step 5*

***We confessed our mistakes to ourselves and to others.***

Beyond identifying ways in which our thinking, feeling, and relating have been impacted by white supremacist conditioning, honestly addressing the *actions* that have emerged from that conditioning is a separate, necessary step. Confessing past (and ongoing) microaggressions to a group and receiving support is an essential part of recovery.

**Value**

During an online presentation of this model, white audience members were sharing many books and resources in the chat section. One white person responded with the important observation and question: "Everyone shares resources; how many of us share our mistakes?" Her comment disrupted the common pattern of white people wanting to appear to be the superior antiracist in a space. It also reflected the spirit of Step 5, which guides us to name our missteps—and the learning and repair work that follows—as a model for others.

**Tension**

While accepting that we will make mistakes can be helpful to promote engagement with antiracism work—freeing us from the illusion that we could do everything "right"—we must never lose sight of the actual harm that our mistakes cause in the lives of BIPOC individuals and communities. By naming our mistakes, we can then focus on strategies for repair and practicing accountability with our fellow humans.

*Step 6*

***We were entirely ready to deconstruct previous ways of** knowing, **as they had been developed through the lens of white supremacy.***

After admitting these problems (white supremacist conditioning and related actions), it is then time to let go of "knowledge" developed in isolation from People of Color.

**Value**

A member recently shared her personal reflections on the idea of what we "know" and "don't know." She spoke about an uncle in her family of origin who had had an affair for twenty years; as she described it, "No one in the family 'knew,' but everyone knew." As a parallel to white conditioning, she described the ultimate freedom in moving, as a family, into greater honesty, letting go of patterns of hiding the truth from themselves and each other.

**Tension**

One RWC member explains that Step 6 is, in her experience, a grief step. Letting go of much of what we've learned in life can be difficult; saying so aloud can sound terribly self-centered when BIPOC are grieving the loss of loved ones, homelands, languages, etc.

*Step 7*

***We humbly explored new ways of understanding, proactively seeking out new learning and reconstructing a more inclusive sense of reality.***

This step involves mindfully and intentionally learning to more deeply understand the experience of People of Color in a white supremacist society. This type of learning can take place in a variety of ways, including reading books and articles from BIPOC authors, patronizing BIPOC-owned businesses, actively listening to BIPOC individuals, etc.

**Value**

In each Step 7 meeting, a quiet group member says, "This is my favorite step!" Members value this opportunity to share resources, as Step 7 focuses on centering wisdom from BIPOC voices.

**Tension**

During a Step 7 meeting, one group member explained: "I read and read, but I'm alone, and that new knowledge doesn't always move beyond me into action." Seeking new learning alone won't guarantee that we show up courageously in the fight for racial justice, but it is an important step on the path.

*Step 8*

***We committed ourselves to ongoing study of our racial biases, conscious or unconscious, and our maladaptive patterns of white supremacist thinking.***

This step is about identifying our triggers to negative thoughts (or other stereotypes, positive or negative) about People of Color. We remain curious about the source of our thoughts, fears, and assumptions and become perpetually aware of their existence.

**Value**

This step allows us to uncover the remaining intrapersonal work we need to do—and to encourage others to do. As James Baldwin said: "Not everything that is faced can be changed, but nothing can be changed until it is faced" (Baldwin, 1962, p. 38). In this spirit, Step 8 invites raw honesty that, if thoughtfully and consistently faced, can support identification and transformation of toxic dynamics that live inside us and shape our actions.

**Tension**

As one recovery group member explains, Step 8 is a "slimy" step. When white people are socialized to not speak about race, honestly naming the racial biases and related patterns that continue to show up in our lives can be a complicated undertaking. Hearing our voices say aloud the racist messages that continue to affect how we see and treat our BIPOC brothers, sisters, and siblings can provoke feelings of shame.

*Step 9*

***We developed strategies to counteract our racial biases.***

Developing positive associations to counter negative thoughts is an important, proactive strategy in our recovery from white supremacy. We believe that a powerful way to develop positive associations is to develop authentic relationships with People of Color. In lieu of such relationships, we can still engage in daily, proactive practices to retrain our brain from the ill effects of white supremacist conditioning.

**Value**

Promoting daily practices to retrain our brain can feel like a powerful step after our "slimy" experience with Step 8. Step 9 reminds us that, thanks to our ever-evolving understanding of neuroplasticity (the brain's ability to grow and change throughout our lives), we can create new neural pathways; for example, meditating, as one member does, on phrases such as "Black Lives Matter" or "*In La'Kech*" (you are my other me).

**Tension**

While this step suggests that *authentic* relationships with People of Color can help us shift understandings of individuals and communities who are deemed "different" from us, it is unfair to ask BIPOC folks to expose themselves to us for the purpose of our growth, evolution, and working through biases. Self-examination of our motivations—in cultivating relationships and in all facets of our recovery—is essential for navigating this complexity and for promoting mutual respect.

### *Step 10*

***We embraced the responsibility of focusing more on our impact than our intentions in interactions with People of Color.***

Taking responsibility for the *impact* of our actions is an ongoing part of recovery. If we fall back into perpetuating white supremacist ideology—or defending actions that have caused hurt to People of Color—it's important to stop and admit it. Prioritizing impact over explaining the intent of our behavior (e.g., "I didn't mean to offend you") is essential for attending to the human being in front of us.

#### Value

Many of us have heard that we should focus on impact more than intentions, and we understand the responsibility at an intellectual level. Walking the talk can be challenging, however; many group members report that their instinct to revert to explaining their intentions persists. Elevating this reminder to commit to focusing on impact is a core component of recovery from white conditioning.

#### Tension

When we think of the impact of white supremacy in our world in Step 10, macrolevel changes (e.g., LandBack initiatives[1] and reparations[2]) should be considered. Because this model is designed in a way that calls for personal and communal changes, yet doesn't explicitly focus on macrolevel shifts, there is a risk that readers may focus on microlevel impacts to the exclusion of broad organizing efforts to effect structural change.

### *Step 11*

***We engaged in daily practices of self-reflection.***

Reflecting on the day—on moments in which we confronted our own white supremacist conditioning and on moments in which we were still bound by its limiting beliefs—is an investment in our recovery.

**Value**

In presenting this model to a wide range of audiences, varying levels of comfort and skill appear in regard to self-reflection. Some professionals dive in to their first meeting with ease while others sit in awkward silence. Pushing all of us, no matter our profession or comfort level, to practice daily self-examination can be a powerful tool in deepening our commitment to antiracist practices.

**Tension**

Self-reflection lives at an individual, intrapersonal level. While powerful, there remains a need to seek feedback from outside ourselves as well, especially from BIPOC voices, to drive action for racial justice.

*Step 12*

***We committed ourselves to sharing this message with our fellow white people in order to build a supportive recovery community and to encourage personal accountability within our culture.***

Assisting others to seek help in recovering from white conditioning and in becoming an ally with People of Color is a core component of recovery. Committing to work with future RWC groups is a common choice for this step.

**Value**

This step calls us to build antiracist community with other white people—those who are similarly committed to antiracist practice *and* those who may not understand white privilege or agree that it exists. This step offers us an opportunity to think about *calling in* other white people in thoughtful and humble ways. Specifically, as in other recovery circles, new members are welcomed in a spirit of "We're so glad you're here. I've been where you've been. Let's keep growing together." This call-in approach can also be applied when responding to a variety of challenges in other settings, including colleagues using racial stereotypes to describe their clients or white friends expressing problematic beliefs while trying to better understand systemic racism. By grounding ourselves in awareness of our own lifelong journey, Step 12 encourages us to share what we've learned with as many white people as possible, focusing on effectiveness and relationship as we do.

**Tension**

There exist many debates about "calling in" versus "calling out" as strategies for promoting social change. When active interpersonal or institutional abuse or harm is happening, we must intervene in ways focused on stopping the harm, often using calling-out as a tool to protect BIPOC victims. Many times, however, we white people have opportunities to invite conversation and corrective action with our community members, but remain silent. Step 12 calls us to use our voices and our access to white people in the fight for racial justice.

## Closing

It has been suggested that in striving to live an antiracist life, we need both will and skill. By committing to a lifelong recovery journey of looking within, changing habits, seeking knowledge, and building community with others to drive action for racial justice, I believe we can embody and pass on new legacies of whiteness.

As Paulo Freire (2000) said: "No one can be authentically human while he prevents others from being so" (p. 85). May we fight, alone and together, to (as our RWC slogan reads) "reclaim our full humanity."

**CRISTINA COMBS, MSW,** works as an in-home family therapist, outpatient therapist, and clinical supervisor of a school-based mental health program in Minneapolis, Minnesota. As a white, female clinical social worker, Cristina strives to provide culturally affirming services that honor personal and communal strengths, and she attends to issues of social justice as essential components of clinical practice. In 2015, after years of struggling to navigate the role and presence of whiteness in her personal, academic, and professional journeys, Cristina sought consultation from BIPOC mentors and developed the Model of Recovery from white Conditioning. She is grateful for all the thought leaders, healers, mentors, and humans who have shared their authentic selves with her and nurtured and challenged her pursuit of lifelong learning, innovation, and growth.

## Notes

1. LandBack initiatives: Land repatriation to Indigenous people in the ongoing struggle against colonization. https://landback.org
2. Reparations: Repairing harm, including material compensation, to African descendants of American slavery. https://www.theatlantic.com/magazine/archive/2014/06/the-case-for-reparations/361631/

## References

*Adams, G., Dobles, I., Gómez, L. H., Kurtiş, T., & Molina, L. E. (2015). Decolonizing psychological science: Introduction to the special thematic section.* Journal of Social and Political Psychology, 3*(1), 213–238. https://doi.org/10.5964/jspp.v3i1.564*

*Baldwin, J. (1962, January 14). As much of the truth as one can bear.* The New York Times. *pp. 38.*

*Carter, R. T., Johnson, V., Roberson, K., Mazzula, S. M., Kirkinis, K., & Sant-Barket, S. (2017). Race-based traumatic stress, racial identity status, and psychological functioning: An exploratory investigation.* Professional Psychology: Research and Practice, 48*(1), 20–37. https://doi.org/10.1037/pro0000116*

*Case, K. (2012). Discovering the privilege of whiteness: white women's reflections on antiracist identity and ally behavior.* Journal of Social Issues, 68*(1), 78–96.*

*Coates, T. (2014, May 23).* Facing the truth: The case for reparations *[Video]. Youtube. https://www.youtube.com/watch?v=Pm9DJuTrO8Q (13:38–14:38)*

*Drustrup, D. (2020). White therapists addressing racism in psychotherapy: An ethical and clinical model for practice.* Ethics & Behavior, 30*(3), 181–196. https://doi.org/10.1080/10508422.2019.1588732*

*Freire, P. (2000).* Pedagogy of the oppressed *(30th anniversary ed.). Continuum.*

*French, B. H., Lewis, J. A., Mosely, D., Adames, H. Y., Chaves-Dueñas, N. Y., Chen, G. A., & Neville, H. A. (2019). Toward a psychological framework of radical healing in communities of color.* The Counseling Psychologist, 48*(1), 14–46. https://doi.org/10.1177/0011000019843506*

*Grzanka, P. R., Gonzalez, K. A., & Spanierman, L. B. (2019). White supremacy and counseling psychology: A critical-conceptual framework.* The Counseling Psychologist, 47*(4), 478–529. https://doi.org/10.1177/0011000019880843*

*Hamrick, C., & Byma, C. (2017). Know history, know self: Art therapists' responsibility to dismantle white supremacy.* Art Therapy, 34*(3), 106–111. https://doi.org/10.1080/07421656.2017.1353332*

*Lee, E., Ka Tat Tsang, A., Bogo, M., Johnstone, M., & Herschman, J. (2018). Enactments of racial microaggression in everyday therapeutic encounters.* Smith College Studies in Social Work, 88*(3), 211–236. https://doi.org/10.1080/00377317.2018.1476646*

*Noe, K. (2020). White habits, anti-racism, and philosophy as a way of life.* The Southern Journal of Philosophy, 58*(2), 279–301.*

*Recovery from white Conditioning. (n.d.). https://www.recoveryfromwhiteconditioning.com*

*Smith, L., & Redington, R. M. (2010). Lessons from the experiences of white antiracist activists.* Professional Psychology: Research and Practice, 41*(6), 541–549. https://doi.org/10.1037/a0021793*

*Tummala-Narra, P. (2016). Discussion of "culturally imposed trauma: The sleeping dog has awakened. Will psychoanalysis take heed?": Commentary on the paper by Dorothy Evans Holmes.* Psychoanalytic Dialogues, 26*(6), 664–672. https://doi.org/10.1080/10481885.2016.1235946*

## CHAPTER 27

# Transforming the Shame of Whiteness for Collective Healing

ROBIN SCHLENGER, MSW, LCSW &
ALANA TAPPIN, PSYD

As two women, one Black and one white, we bear witness to lives being destroyed by the racially based denial and silence of white people. It has been our experience that the shame that is evoked as many whites come to terms with their complicity with white supremacy is often a paralyzing and debilitating condition for well-intentioned white people who desire, but seem unable to, deeply explore their whiteness in an honest and transparent way. Understanding that real change and transformation can only happen through compassion and connection, we have searched for a way to create opportunities for white people to be truly accountable by practicing shame resilience. We have created a training specifically designed to help white people stay actively engaged in meaningful racial conversations and cross-racial relationships without surrendering to the white shame that often stifles and smothers racially just behaviors.

* * *

In March 2018, Robin Schlenger and I (Alana Tappin) met at a conference in Washington, DC. We had both come to see Dr. Kenneth Hardy, but he was ill. I expressed my disappointment and Robin generously told me about *Soul Work: Unmasking Internalized Superiority and Overcoming Internalized Inferiority*—an event hosted by the Eikenberg Academy for Social Justice, an organization led by Dr. Hardy. At that powerful conference, something stirred in me. As a clinician, I began to realize that the powerful and complicated emotion of shame, when not appropriately addressed, elicits significant and complex defense mechanisms that often take us away from our core emotional or relational experience (Fosha, 2000), which then cuts us off from healthy relational connection and associated healthy and responsible behavior. At the conference, we spoke about our ancestors. Racially, there were both People of Color and white people at the conference. As white people spoke about their ancestors, I noticed that most were struggling to find ancestors they were proud of. The People of Color had a much easier time naming and connecting with ancestors who had many positive and inspirational traits. This triggered a flood of thoughts and feelings. I was proud that I could easily name several of my ancestors who served as guides and motivation for my own journey. What if I didn't have this? What if I didn't have a legacy of fierce, brave, and brilliant Black people fighting for our liberation? I knew I would be flooded with shame and a sense of inner badness if I didn't have it. I would likely shut down, dissociate from the experience, or engage in appeasing behaviors.

In some ways, the interaction started to feel like "good us" and "bad them." I do believe that unmasking internalized racial superiority in white bodies is a vital part of dismantling white supremacy. White bodies need to wrestle with the consequences of their ancestors' actions and with how they benefit from and act out inherited and unearned advantages that maintain white supremacy. I was conflicted though. On the one hand, white people need to wrestle with white supremacy. On the other hand, if they have too much shame in response to being appropriately challenged in their complicity, they are not able to take responsibility for the situation at hand. If they can't take responsibility for their racist actions, then white supremacy continues to destroy all of our lives. And just like that, an idea was born. White people need to take *much* more responsibility for racial justice. *They also need to be helped to manage their shame in response to their complicity in whiteness, white privilege, and racism so they can take more responsibility and cause less harm.* Without this support, they react and act out a myriad of sophisticated defensive strategies that prevent accountability and cause damage to us all. As a Black woman watching my people experience and experiencing myself the "torture and brainwashing" (P. Gianotti, personal communication, February 7, 2020) of white supremacy, I was, and am, only interested in strategies that work to effectively facilitate accountability in racial justice. As a therapist and consumer of the ideas of researchers and clinicians in the field, I knew deep in my bones that if we do not have the tools to respond well to our shame, it will trap us in our problematic and damaging behaviors.

I (Robin Schlenger) clearly remember the moment that Alana shared her developing theory about using empathy to transform white shame and increase white accountability in racial justice work. Everything in me resonated with what she was saying, and all I could think were, "YES! I'm in, if you'll have me," and "What can I do to help get it out there?" It has been, and continues to be, a powerful journey of love and healing. I am honored and blessed to be partnering with Alana. Together we have witnessed deep connection, empathy, growth, and transformation through our workshops and ongoing connections with participants. Our relationship continues to deepen from doing this work together. This has become our life work.

## White Supremacy and Its Impact

Dr. Derald Wing Sue is a psychology professor at Columbia University in New York. I (Alana Tappin) was struck by an open letter he wrote to and about his fellow Black, Indigenous, and People of Color (BIPOC), outlining the historical and current challenges we have encountered in our everyday lives (Sue, 2016). In the letter, Dr. Sue indicated that throughout our histories, we have encountered invalidation, oppression, injustice, torture, terrorism, and genocide. He further claimed that racism is a constant *everyday* reality in our lives that has sought to strip us of our identities, to take away our dignity, to make us second-class citizens, to destroy our people, cultures, and communities, to steal our land and property, and to torture, rape, and murder us. It imprisons us on reservations, in concentration camps, in inferior schools, in segregated neighborhoods, in prisons; it uses us as guinea pigs in medical experiments and blames our victimization on the faults of our own people. When we express our reality, we are met with disbelief (Sue, 2016). Despite a massive amount of empirical evidence supporting the impact of racism on BIPOC, we are not believed; we are accused of being too sensitive, being dishonest, "playing the race card," and suppressing free speech.

> Our daily stressors can include: poverty, high unemployment rates, lower standards of living, conflicting values imposed by whiteness, a history of broad governmental actions that have led to the enslavement of Black Americans, the internment of Japanese Americans, the genocide and colonization of Native Americans and the constant microinvalidations and microaggressions on all BIPOC. (Sue, 2016, p. 96)

Bodies of Color must justify our existence, and as a result of all this, we are *so* tired, and *so* angry. We are trauma survivors that are still being traumatized. And we are also extremely resilient in the face of this adversity. We persevere.

We (Alana and Robin) believe that white supremacy is destroying the lives of BIPOC *and* has eroded the humanity of white people. We also believe that white people created white supremacy, benefit from it, maintain it, and need to take an active role in dismantling it. We also know that we cannot force people to make positive changes "by putting them down, threatening them with rejection, humiliating them in front of others or belittling [or shaming] them" (Brown, 2007, p. 1). Conclusion: *We cannot dismantle white supremacy by rejecting, humiliating, or belittling those who are complicit. We cannot dismantle white supremacy through shaming.* This brings up the importance of distinguishing between the experience of *shame* and the act of *shaming*. Facing one's racist beliefs or actions will likely elicit feelings of shame, which is considered an embodied belief (B. Lyon, personal communication, May 2019). It is "the piercing awareness of ourselves as fundamentally deficient in some vital way as a human being" (Kaufman, 1992, p. 9). The experience of being shamed, that is, being on the receiving end of "an act of diminishing, reducing, or the conscious or unconscious act of retaliation" (P. Gianotti, personal communication, September 25, 2020) compounds and reinforces the shame that already exists. This can lead to more entrenched defensive behaviors. However, white bodies *feeling shame* about their racist beliefs or behaviors is not the same as being *shamed*.

We decided to create a training based on the foundation that overwhelming shame about whiteness does *not* lead to accountable antiracist behavior. In fact, the inability of white bodies to manage shame that comes up around their complicity in white supremacy *maintains* the very system many of them claim they do not want to be a part of. White bodies need to deeply understand how their shame about their whiteness and their role in white supremacy show up as well as ways they can begin to process or metabolize that shame in order to clear some of the ways for authentic, accountable, racially just behavior. In our training, we help participants develop an understanding of white supremacy and its impact on white people and on BIPOC. We would ultimately help them to begin or continue to build an active and lifelong antiracist, antioppressive perspective and practice. We realized that to do this, we would need to facilitate change from the bottom up. This would mean targeting unconscious and disavowed emotions and beliefs about white superiority that are deeply intertwined with everyday life and making them explicit (Fosha, 2000).

According to Sensoy and DiAngelo (2017), whiteness "refers to the specific dimensions of racism that elevates white people over all people of Color. Basic rights, resources, and experiences that are assumed to be shared by all, are actually only available to white people" (p. 142). These authors explain that white people often feel as if being white has no meaning and that they often say that they are "just human." The authors further state that the ability to experience whiteness as not having meaning or to be able to state that one is just human is itself a powerful manifestation of whiteness (Sensoy & DiAngelo, 2017). Whiteness studies focus on the cultural, historical, and sociological aspects of being white and how these factors are tied to power and privilege. *White supremacy* refers to the "pervasiveness, magnitude, and normalcy of white privilege, dominance, and assumed superiority in mainstream society" (Sensoy & DiAngelo, 2017, p. 142). Ultimately, "white supremacy is [also] a powerful ideology that promotes the idea of whiteness as the ideal for humanity" (Sensoy & DiAngelo, 2017, p. 143).

Kenneth Jones and Tema Okun (2001) outlined the characteristics of white supremacy culture in organizations. We believe that these characteristics are not limited to organizations but are manifest in virtually all areas of human interaction in our society including, but not limited to, family/friend/loved-one interactions, education, Western science, criminal justice, and religious organizations. Jones and Okun (2001) define white supremacy culture as the ideology that espouses that white people and the ideas, thoughts, beliefs, and actions they possess are superior to those possessed by all other racial groups. White supremacy can manifest as a sense of urgency, defensiveness, and valuing quantity over quality. Valuing quantity over quality involves seeing "things that can be measured [as] more highly valued than things that cannot . . . little or no value attached to process; if it can't be measured, it has no value" (Jones & Okun, 2001, para. 8). White supremacy can be further manifested as: the elevation of the written word over other forms of expression, belief in only one right way, paternalism, either/or thinking, power hoarding, fear of open conflict, *individualism*, the belief that progress should look bigger and more, a belief that one can be fully objective, and entitlement to comfort. In white supremacy, too, is a tendency to point out the inadequacies of another's work. These inadequacies are often discussed with others and not directly with the person whose work is being evaluated. Jones and Okun (2001) further point out that mistakes are seen as personal and a reflection of the inherent value of a person. As a result, little energy is spent on learning from mistakes and there is an associated tendency to easily identify what's wrong and to have trouble identifying and appreciating what's right. These tendencies are also internalized. These characteristics "are damaging because they are used as norms and standards without being proactively named or chosen by the group" (Jones & Okun, 2001, para. 1). Persons who display behaviors outside of these norms and standards are often excluded, devalued, and punished for standards they did not consent to be evaluated by. This can result in social exclusion, chronic disconnection and isolation, loss of opportunities for advancement, internalized oppression, unjust hiring practices, devaluation of cultural norms that lie outside of these standards, and appropriation, to name a few impacts.

Another important concept is internalized racial oppression (IRO). IRO manifests itself in two forms: internalized racial superiority (IRS) and internalized racial inferiority (IRI; Pender Greene et al., 2016). We are all racialized beings, and this impacts every aspect of our lives.

> Internalized racial oppression is a multigenerational process of accepting social messaging about one's standing in society and one's comparative value. Unless there are conscious, rigorous, and well-informed efforts to challenge them, social messages become internalized and, thus, invisible. Once invisible, the legacies of privilege and oppression become part of what is handed down through generations as social, cultural, and institutional norms and practices. Therefore, to understand structural racism, we must understand internalized racial oppression. (Pender Greene et al., 2016, para. 2)

For our purposes, we will focus on IRS. We believe that some of the manifestations of IRS and characteristics of white supremacy culture represent individual and collective defense mechanisms against shame and other painful emotion states, such as powerlessness, terror, anguish, aloneness, helplessness, deep grief, regret, and remorse.

## The Dynamics and Psychology of Shame

One of the emotions that often operate unconsciously, but powerfully, is *shame*, which Dr. Brené Brown (2007) defines as "the intensely painful feeling or experience of believing we are flawed and therefore unworthy of acceptance and belonging" (p. 30). As mentioned before, Kaufman (1992) says:

> Contained in the experience of shame is the piercing awareness of ourselves as fundamentally deficient in some vital way as a human being. To live with shame is to experience the very essence or heart of the self as wanting. (p. 9)

Shame is a unique, powerful, and impactful emotion. Lyon & Rubin (2021) talk about shame being an *embodied belief.* When triggered, it involves strong automatic bodily responses, with powerful and overwhelming thoughts about our worthlessness; feelings of danger and threat; and a deep sense of helplessness and hopelessness that viscerally communicate that we will never be able to change our inner defectiveness. This emotion is excruciating and deeply isolating. When we experience it, we are disconnected from others and drowning in our aloneness. Not belonging causes unbearable pain and unspeakable terror. As a result of this intensely horrifying feeling, we develop defense mechanisms or coping strategies to *not feel shame*. While it is completely understandable that we do this, moving too far away from our shame, not being able to sit with and hold ourselves in the discomfort of it in order to process it effectively, can eventually result in harm to others. If a white person does something racist, shame about this harmful behavior is likely the first thing that gets triggered. If they immediately move into a defensive place to escape the shame, then they will be unable to be truly accountable for the racist behavior, which then *maintains* white supremacy, whether that is their intention or not.

Some theorists, researchers, and practitioners believe that, despite the agonizing experience of shame, there are healthy *and* unhealthy aspects (Kaufman, 2004). A more debilitating or toxic aspect of shame sends a powerful and clear message of one's absolute and permanent defectiveness. Any messaging or meaning that says the self is utterly defective and worthless is a toxic aspect of a shame experience. Healthier aspects of a shame experience would be connected to behaviors that are potentially or actually hurtful and that are a violation of another's dignity (Amodeo, 2016). When we have acted in a way that has broken trust or wounded a relationship, "shame grabs our attention" (Amodeo, 2016, para. 9) and gives us an opportunity to correct our behavior and repair the relationship. Thus, Kaufman (2004) explains, shame plays an important role in the development of one's conscience. Shame resilience skills help an individual to move through the overwhelming and toxic messages of shame in a way that minimizes the crippling parts that communicate utter worthlessness. These skills allow increased awareness of one's participation in harming another and open the ways to repair and to making it right. The goal of shame resilience for white bodies is to increase their capacity and tolerance of shame, pain, and anguish connected to their harmful actions so that they become more effective at responding from a truly authentic and reparative place.

Our bodies respond to shame as if it is a threat to our survival. It signals our brains to go into fight, flight, freeze, or submit/fawn mode. Shame lives with other powerful emotions that are connected to a deeper level of generational harm and trauma. Menakem (2017) speaks of the origins of white body supremacy. He cites Janice Barbee who says, "What white bodies did to Black bodies [and red bodies] they did to other white bodies first" (Menakem, 2017, p. 57). He believes that, prior to Europeans coming to the land that is now referred to as the Americas, European bodies held incredible trauma from the everyday torture and brutality of the Middle Ages and many eras before this. Menakem (2017) goes on to describe the ways Europeans "murdered, butchered, tortured, oppressed, abused, conquered, enslaved, and colonized one another" (p. 59). Torture was wildly popular and an embedded part of everyday life. This, in addition to events such as the Great Plague of the seventeenth century, created a desperate situation for many English across class. Menakem (2017) asks: "Isn't it likely that many of them were traumatized by the time they arrived here? Did over 10 centuries of medieval brutality, which was inflicted on white bodies by other white bodies, *begin to look like culture*?" (p. 61).

We believe that this enormous trauma was never processed or metabolized but was instead blown through the bodies of African and Indigenous peoples. This unprocessed and unmetabolized trauma continues to be passed down, generation after generation, through white bodies. This deeply rooted and unprocessed trauma, if not unpacked and processed, continues to unconsciously drive behavior and responses to trauma triggers. Shame is a part of this trauma response. This means white bodies are also holding many generations of shame, pain, and anguish, which compounds the present-day shame white people hold when exposed to the reality of their participation in the system of white supremacy.

For many decades, mental health practitioners and researchers have debated and presented findings about the differences between guilt and shame. Some have said that shame is about who we are, and guilt is about our behaviors (Brown, 2007). Guilt is seen as a reaction to something one has done or not done that fails to live up to one's personal values. It is seen as an appropriate motivator and precursor to accountable actions and is set against shame, which is painted as only destructive (Brown, 2007). Kaufman (2004) challenges some parts of this view of guilt and presents more nuance and complexity. He believes that guilt is not inherently different from shame per se but is one of multiple manifestations of it. For example, he considers discouragement, self-consciousness, embarrassment, and shyness as different experiences of the same emotion of shame. Discouragement is seen as shame about a temporary defeat; self-consciousness is the self scrutinizing the self; embarrassment is shame before any type of audience; and shyness is shame in the presence of a stranger (Kaufman, 2004). Guilt "is shame about moral transgression, [*immorality shame*]" (Kaufman, 2004, p. 47). Guilt can be experienced as self-disgust or contempt against the self by the self for moral infraction; and/or a combination of anger at, distress with, and fear of the self for moral infractions. The commonality in these different experiences of guilt is the presence of the ethical judgement of immorality (Kaufman, 2004). We believe that the shame that is elicited when white bodies have to face their complicity in white supremacy is this form of guilt: *immorality shame*. The pathway to authentic and accountable action is not just the simple presence of guilt, as suggested by some researchers (e.g., Brown, 2007). The mere presence of shame is not what prevents accountable behavior. Like anything else, the amount of shame someone holds at any given point in time is on a continuum from mild to severe. What prevents authentic and accountable action by white bodies is *overwhelming* immorality shame when faced with their complicity in white supremacy.

## The Relational Impact of Shame

Feelings of shame are virtually always generated when whites interact with each other about race and white supremacy. When speaking with other white people about racism, there seems to be a confusing and highly reactive process that occurs. In some situations, it seems as if there are massive amounts of shame, guilt, fear, anger, and disappointment, much of it unconscious. Other white people behaving in racist ways likely trigger shame about complicity in white supremacy in a way that feels closer to home. Generally speaking, the closer or more intimate a relationship, the more likely the powerful vortex of feelings that comes up is to be extremely complicated. When a white loved one expresses a racist idea or engages in racist behavior, it can create deep confusion, shame, and disorientation. How can this person I love so much believe or do something so harmful? What does it mean about me and my identity that someone this close to me holds these views? Powerful defense mechanisms are usually evoked, such as projection (putting your shame and sense of inadequacy onto someone else so you don't have to deal with it), splitting ("I'm nothing like those racist white people over there"), and competition ("I'm a better white ally than you are"). Below is an example of how shame can show up with other white people and how it can sever empathic connection when not recognized and managed.

The following is a personal story that I (Robin) share in our workshop. We find that it helps to decrease defensiveness, so that participants can feel open to sharing and unpacking their own stories. It also cultivates empathy, compassion, and connection among the participants. People hear their own stories in mine, and it dissolves feelings of isolation and aloneness. When people feel more connected and less ashamed, they are better equipped to look more squarely at the truth of their harmful ideas and behaviors. Only then can we begin to move toward healing and real accountability.

I (Robin) was asked to collaborate on and facilitate a five-week virtual course with a friend and colleague who identifies as a Black man. The course was based on his theory of mindfulness-based racism reduction. The first virtual course we did together just happened to be with a group of about eighteen white women. This group of women was intentionally organized into this course by my colleague's white, cisgender female friend, who was trying to build a coalition of antiracist women in her community. This particular evening, we were running behind schedule, and I was feeling anxious about having enough time to get through the agenda. Needless to say, my perfectionism and the need to control were pumped up and already triggered when it was time to start my piece on internalized racial oppression and the manifestations of internalized racial superiority. I named what was happening in me and used it as an example of my manifestations of internalized racial superiority. This released some of the anxiety and seemed to ground me at first. However, about halfway through my presentation, with time ticking away, one of the participants, who had already challenged my cofacilitator several times, interrupted to tell me that she felt that I was making huge generalizations about white people. My response was to tell her that this is what happens all the time to BIPOC and that it was a moment for her to reflect on what it might be like to feel like this all the time. She proceeded to tell me that as a woman she was put in a box all the time. Time was ticking away; I could feel my control over the agenda slipping. I felt a rush of emotions and then went into attack mode. For the sake of brevity for this piece, I will spare the full details here. I believe I put my hand out and said, "STOP! You are not going to compare your experience as a white woman to being a Black person!" Unfortunately, my cofacilitator, a Black man, had to come in and break it up and get us back on track (more heavy lifting for him due to my acting out). The day after the session, the same participant emailed the cofacilitator, telling him that I was very unprofessional and that she didn't feel safe in the space and was going to drop out of the course. He asked me what I thought. Thankfully, I had already started to explore and investigate what happened in me. It was a perfect storm. Her comments triggered my feelings of inadequacy and, in a split second, I reacted with an attack on her. I was already anxious about time and desperately trying to hold on to some control over the agenda. I didn't feel as if I had the skill to "adequately" speak to her comment without totally letting go of the agenda. This is when my all-too-familiar shame narrative loudly proclaimed, "You're not good enough." (According to my narrative, being inadequate means I am flawed, and if I am flawed, I am not good enough, and if I am not good enough, then I will be abandoned.) This "inadequacy" narrative is connected to my family of origin story and is not new to me. In fact, it has been a focus of my own therapy throughout the years. However, when you compound this deeply rooted narrative with unprocessed (and in many cases, unconscious) shame connected to whiteness, it can create a powder keg.

We want to acknowledge that if there is a history of untreated trauma or a history of struggling with chronic shame, participants might need additional therapeutic support. We often facilitate appropriate referrals to address this need as it comes up. In this example, the fire that ignited the powder keg was what I (Robin) perceived as a challenge to my identity. My embodied beliefs were "I am not good enough," "I am a bad and worthless antiracist," and "I will be thrown away!" My nervous system registered this as a threat to my existence. My defenses jumped automatically into protection mode and activated a fight/attack response. After the incident, I used the skills I've learned in our work with shame, resilience, and transformation. I was able to recognize my thoughts, feelings, body sensations, and behavioral urges and just let them be, with as little judgment as possible. Then, I explored what beliefs were coming up and what the vulnerable parts in me were saying. I processed this experience with a trusted fellow white antiracist so that I could increase my awareness of what might have been happening for me. I also processed it with Alana. What I discovered was, at the root of it all was my shame narrative that keeps telling me that I'm not good enough, and beneath that is the deeper terror of abandonment and being thrown away for good. This was not happening on a conscious level, but this was to what my nervous system was responding.

Following my attack came shame about the way I lashed out, which was later compounded by the participant calling me unprofessional. There were many people who felt that my response to her was warranted and that she had "hijacked" the session. However, after going through some of the processes I described above, I realized that even if that were so, I came at her from a place of retaliation, not from a place of curiosity. I was not regulated enough to try to understand what was happening for her. I was hijacked by my own nervous system. A few days later, after these realizations, I was able to apologize to her and to the group in a way that felt authentic. If given a chance to do it over again (with the awareness this processing has given me), I would have validated the participant's concern and acknowledged that she was probably not the only person who was having this reaction. Due to the nature of her multiple interruptions and to our limited time, I would then have set a boundary; taking more time to address her comments when there wasn't space would have actually facilitated her acting out of her internalized racial superiority (entitlement to monopolize and disrupt the conversation).

If this came up in one of our Shame, Resilience, and Transformation workshops, we would take her through a mindfulness and compassion exercise (Brach, 2019), where we would ask her to acknowledge and allow her thoughts, feelings, urges, and body sensations in the moment. We would continue to explore the beliefs, meanings, and underlying vulnerability that are likely underneath her shame defenses and manifestations of internalized racial superiority. Then we would look for the underlying shame story and unwanted white identity(ies) that were being triggered. From here, we could explore her shame defenses and how they were manifesting. We would use self-disclosure and empathy from ourselves and from the group to normalize her shame and its defenses. We would also affirm and show understanding for her vulnerable parts. This would likely facilitate her ability to respond more effectively to her own vulnerable parts. In general, once participants are able to feel deep grief, anguish, and genuine remorse, they often begin to experience increased clarity about their harmful behavior. In the end, the participant from this example accepted my apology and actually admitted that she was purposefully being provocative. She stayed with the course and the experience allowed us all to be more vulnerable and to experience increased intimacy. I have been able to heal most of the toxic aspects of the shame from that experience. I was able to name my shame, seek connection and care for my vulnerable parts (e.g., the terror of abandonment), feel genuine remorse for acting out, and make a repair.

## Coming to Terms With White Supremacy: Roadblocks and Impediments

### *White Fragility*

DiAngelo (2018) coined the phrase *white fragility* to describe one of the main impediments to white bodies addressing their complicity in white supremacy. She says:

> White people in North America live in a society that is deeply separate and unequal by race, and white people are the beneficiaries of that separation and inequality. As a result, we are insulated from racial stress, at the same time that we come to feel entitled to and deserving of our advantage. Given how seldom we experience racial discomfort in a society we dominate, we haven't had to build our racial stamina. Socialized into a deeply internalized sense of superiority that we either are unaware of or can never admit to ourselves, we become highly fragile [reactive] in conversations about race. We consider a challenge to our racial worldviews as a challenge to our very identity as good, moral people. Thus, we perceive any attempt to connect us to the system of racism as an unsettling and unfair moral offense. The smallest amount of racial stress is intolerable—the mere suggestion that being white has meaning triggers a range of defensive responses. . . . These responses serve to reinstate white equilibrium as they repel the challenge, return our racial comfort, and maintain our dominance within the racial hierarchy. . . . Though white fragility is triggered by discomfort and anxiety, it is

> born of superiority and entitlement. White fragility is not weakness per se. In fact, it is a powerful means of white social control and the protection of white advantage. (DiAngelo, 2018, pp. 1–2)

Our hypothesis is that a huge part of what triggers white fragility and its various defense maneuvers is in fact immorality shame that erupts in the face of one's complicity in whiteness. We believe the *fragility* in white fragility refers to the inability to tolerate the shame and pain associated with the harm one has committed or participated in. Our work is centered on helping white bodies build the tolerance and stamina for this shame in order to minimize their defensive, and ultimately harmful, reactions to their complicity. We will examine these defenses in more detail below.

### *Shame*

The manifestations and the characteristics of white supremacy are powerful, automatic, and enduring. They represent a collective attempt to bypass, avoid, and act out generations of pain, shame, grief, anguish, horror, powerlessness, and helplessness. White bodies experience these states as intolerable and develop coping strategies or defensive styles to avoid what feels like tormenting pain. The manifestations of white supremacy and the characteristics of internalized racial superiority are part of these defenses or coping styles. Defenses against shame and trauma can be broken down into several categories [influenced by B. Lyon & S. Rubin's diagram, "Reactions to Shame" (personal communication, May 4, 2019) and Danielian & Gianotti (2013)].

1. *Withdrawal* involves moving away from situations that cause shame. This can involve a compulsive preference for solo activities, isolating, emotional avoidance, silence, not asking for help when needed, attempting to care for all of one's needs without help, and refusing to speak publicly. Some examples of this are white silence, distancing, indifference, and *individualism*.

2. *Denial and avoidance,* in their various forms, are attempts to remove intense feelings of shame from conscious awareness. Denial of any

awareness of inferiority or weakness can be found in persons utilizing this strategy. They also tend to have difficulty admitting that they are wrong as a result. Some examples of this defensive style are intellectualizing, rationalization, color blindness, minimizing, denial of white supremacy, denial of white privilege, numbness, dismissiveness, and credentialing (DiAngelo, 2021).

3. *Moving toward* (Danielian & Gianotti, 2013) is a type of denial defensive style that says "Look at me, I'm good, please love me" as a way to cope with shame. With this class of defense, the body is seeking to please and appease to minimize or avoid shame. There is an effort to diminish the threat of further criticism and rejection by being excessively compliant. The body recognizes others as potential resources who can support the self and help reduce its distress (Danielian & Gianotti, 2013). Examples of this tendency are: the investment in being seen as the "good white person"; being excessively nice to People of Color (in ways you would not be to a white person); white savior behavior; tokenism; self-congratulations; paternalism; diminishing the self's importance; and keeping connection no matter what (even in the face of abuse or mistreatment). It may be hard to tell if a white body in this state is in a purely defensive place or is trying to be accountable. In many instances, it is usually a combination. One way of further exploring what might be happening in this defensive state is to notice any feelings of superiority, judgement, and criticism of another white person's antiracism journey. Any kind of harsh judgement of another's journey suggests that there are similar aspects of your own journey that you may be holding shame about (Brown, 2007). When you have acknowledged and increased tolerance for your own shame, you are more likely to experience remorse, regret, grief/deep sadness, and anguish about the way someone else experiences that shame than you are to feel a sense of superiority.

4. *Attack other* is the use of aggression to avoid feeling shame or to discharge feelings of shame on others. This can involve blaming others for one's feelings of shame (more severe forms involve projection—completely attributing your shame to someone else); seeking to control,

dominate, or intimidate; seeking power over, exploitation of others; dehumanization; and subtle and overt acts of retaliation against anyone who challenges one's complicity in white supremacy. Some examples of attack-other reactions are overt racist behaviors (displays of white superiority); insulting others who challenge racist behavior; trying to harm others who challenge racist behavior; insulting and looking down on others deemed less "woke"; white centering; white exceptionalism; entitlement; expectation of comfort; appropriation/theft; white tears (weaponized distress and helplessness); the expectation and need to be in control; belief in absolutes; promoting white = normal; arrogance; and "professionalism."

5. *Attack self* is blaming oneself when exposed to the reality of racism and white supremacy. There can be an attack on the self physically and/or mentally, such as "I only cause harm as a white person—I'm worthless. I'm toxic." There is a distinct presence of an inner critic that communicates powerfully that "there's something wrong with me," "I deserved it," "They were right," "I'm bad," and "I'm a toxic white person." Attacking the self can often look like an attempt at accountability. It is problematic, though, because a person in this state is usually fixated on punishing themself and is not able to address the problematic or harmful behavior in question. Once a white body is better able to tolerate their shame, genuine remorse, grief, and regret for enacting harm often becomes possible. These genuine states are more likely to motivate authentic repair and accountable action. Self-blame around racial harm results in white centering.

## A Framework for Addressing Shame as a Pathway to Racial Justice Work

In general, shame is a taboo emotion. It is something we avoid addressing due to massive pain and discomfort when we feel it; but we do so to our peril. Shame is a complex part of our experience that plays a huge part in the development of our conscience and identity. While the experience of it makes an individual feel utterly worthless, it is adaptive in its origin and purpose. In general, "Our emotions mobilize and guide us to deal with life and the different situations that come our way in a positive, life-enhancing manner" (Frederick, 2020, para. 9). One of the adaptive or life-enhancing purposes of shame is to keep us connected to the ones we love and depend on the most. When we hurt each other, shame is our conscience and barometer that guides us back to connection. Shame and the wish to be loved are different sides of the same coin. Kaufman (2004) writes,

> In the midst of shame there is an ambivalent longing for reunion with [the person you harmed]. We feel divided and secretly yearn to feel *one*, whole . . . shame feels like a rupture either in self, in a particular relationship, or both. (p. 37)

In many ways, the presence of shame when you commit harm is a kind of mobilization for repair and reconciliation.

In our work, we start with building stamina and increased capacity in the face of shame connected to whiteness. We start by building shame resilience (Brown, 2006), which is the ability to recognize shame when we experience it and to move through it in a constructive way that allows us to maintain our authenticity and to grow from our experiences. Courage, empathy, and connection are vital aspects of shame resilience. Brown (2006), in her extensive research on shame and shame resilience, has found that empathy is an *antidote* to shame! Empathy is the ability to put ourselves in someone else's shoes, to understand what someone is experiencing, and to reflect back that understanding. Importantly, Brown (2007) stated that unearned privilege kills empathy, and shame diminishes our capacity to practice empathy. If we are compromised in our ability to practice empathy in our privileged identities, then we are less likely to effectively process our shame about those identities. This means unmetabolized or disavowed shame about privilege ends up contributing to the perpetuation of white supremacy and other systems of power. Mindfulness and compassion become the foundation for increasing awareness of how shame shows up in our bodies and for learning ways to respond to what shows up that allow it to be felt at within a manageable range. Compassion for self in the moment of committing a harmful behavior can feel counterintuitive. However, empathy neutralizes the parts of shame that communicate worthlessness and allows one's remorse, regret, grief, healthy anger, and pain to take up more space and to exert more influence.

Another important aspect of shame resilience is connection and community. Menakem (2017) believes that healing white-body supremacy must involve body-centered collective action that heals. This means that white bodies need to build community with other white bodies as they all build their tolerance for their immorality shame. As they do this work together, emergent responses clear the way for more and more motivation, creativity, and innovation to repair the harm they have caused and to create a cohesiveness and a sense of belonging. As bodies are engaged in collective action, there must be a focus on working toward "settled bodies," or bodies that are emotionally regulated and socially connected as they fight for racial justice. Strategies and interventions are aimed at repeatedly calming the nervous system so as to minimize reactive and defensive behavior; this is a huge part of what will keep our bodies regulated and connected (Menakem, 2017). Overall, these different principles and strategies will eventually create a culture that dismantles white-body supremacy. Menakem (2017) says:

> Culture is how our bodies retain and re-enact history—through the foods we eat (or refuse to eat); the stories we tell; the things that hold meaning for us; the images that move us; what we are able (and unable) to sense or feel or process; the way we see the world; and a thousand other aspects of life. (p. 245)

Culture lives in our bodies and has a stronger influence on us than cognitive approaches to antiracism. Culture provides a profound sense of belonging that creates a deep sense of safety in human bodies. This sense of soothing and harmony with other bodies provides a sense that life has value and meaning. Menakem (2017) believes that a culture that calls out, rejects, and undermines white-body supremacy must be formed. "If enough people do the same thing over and over, or if they share something with each other enough times, eventually it becomes culture" (Menakem, 2017, p. 247). The collective white body needs to heal from engrained patterns of avoiding their immorality shame and other forms of anguish passed down from multiple generations. Creating this culture is a powerful way to do this. There will need to be "new stories, symbols, rituals, role models, and elders" (Menakem, 2017, p. 251). It is through relationships built in this culture that individual and collective transformation will happen.

### *The Shame Resilience Training for White Bodies (or Bodies with White Privilege)*

Our core training provides 16 hours of instruction. It includes a focus on white supremacy, the psychology of shame, mindfulness, compassion, and dealing with the racial harm committed in relationships with others. Additionally, we rely on a series of experiential exercises, while also devoting attention to the cultivation of connection. The training begins with a history of the creation of the category of whiteness and of the racial caste system in the United States (Wilkerson, 2020). We then talk about the biological, psychological, spiritual, and cultural impact of white supremacy on white bodies and Bodies of Color. After each segment of information is presented, we ask participants to notice body sensations, images, and emotional reactions and then we invite sharing. While cognitive and intellectual responses are welcomed, visceral experiences to the material are given priority (Fosha, 2000). We instruct participants to notice their shame triggers associated with whiteness. We give them an exercise, based on an aspect of Brené Brown's (2006) model of shame resilience, in which we ask participants to name three unwanted racial identities, for example, "racist," "Karen," "colonizer," or "settler." Then participants are taught about the various ways they defend against the experience of shame and other painful emotions. We often have participants split into small groups to practice an exercise aimed at helping them apply their understanding of shame triggers and the defenses that usually come up quickly after being triggered.

The second half of the training is focused on ways to respond to shame triggers and defenses connected to whiteness. The interventions are focused mainly on using the regulating functions of mindfulness, empathy, and connection from group leaders, other members of the group, and from the self. There is a short lesson on empathy and its role in regulating shame. Participants are then exposed to multiple interventions aimed at deepening their awareness of their inner states and deepening their empathy for self and others. One such intervention (e.g., Brach, 2019) gives participants a structure that helps them increasingly pause, recognize, and allow their inner (often painful) states to emerge. As they allow these states to emerge, they are asked to explore in more depth their beliefs or meanings and their more vulnerable states or needs. Participants are then asked to explore ways to meet the needs of these vulnerable states with explicit acts of self-compassion. What often emerges here is a sense of deep regret, grief, anger, and clarity about some aspect of whiteness and their behavior. Participants are then taken through a lesson on racial microaggressions to continue building their awareness of how racist behavior is deeply embedded in our everyday lives and how People of Color are affected by it. They are then given exercises on how to acknowledge and repair the harm caused by microaggressions and how to intervene when they are committed. While the focus of the lesson is on helping white bodies take responsibility for racist behaviors committed interpersonally, there are also reminders and lessons on how to consistently speak truth to power. Participants are also introduced to the patterns and dynamics that play out between white bodies when discussing white supremacy. Interventions focus on helping white bodies explore their own triggers and vulnerability when loved ones in white bodies enact racist behavior so that they can more effectively confront this behavior. Overall, this training is aimed at helping white bodies build tolerance for their shame as they build a community of white antiracists.

The *relationship* is the centerpiece of this work. Continual focus and effort are made at every step of the training to help participants feel understood and less alone in their shame. There are explicit instructions and requests we make from participants to share what resonates in them from what they have heard. In our facilitation, we use strategies to normalize vulnerability and increase compassionate and truthful responses from participants. Dr. Gabor Maté (Braden-Foxx, 2020) put forward a way of working with emotional pain called compassionate inquiry. He stresses the importance of using our curiosity to pursue an understanding of why someone is suffering with questions like "Why is this person suffering?" or "What happened to them?" He also speaks about holding the value that the person in front of you is no better or worse than you. Dr. Maté highlights what he calls the compassion of possibility, which is holding, even in the face of their dysfunctional behaviors, the belief that the person in front of you is a *whole, complex person* while also focusing on every moment as a possibility for change. Dr. Maté stresses *compassionate truth.* This is the display of fearlessness in the face of another's pain. It is allowing whatever is there to emerge without trying to take it away. Only when compassion is present will a person allow themselves to face the truth and see the truth. These are fundamental principles that drive the interventions we take as facilitators throughout the course. As participants see the truth, feel less alone in their pain, and feel their own goodness, the door for transformation opens wide.

As stated before, if participants have a history of untreated trauma or a history of struggling with chronic shame, they might need additional therapeutic support to help build their shame tolerance. We give these warnings regularly throughout the training to ensure that trauma survivors pace themselves in this work. We regularly provide referrals for extra therapeutic work as needed and as requested. If therapeutic needs are identified, participants are asked to work with their therapeutic support while they go through the training. The training is for people who identify as white or who hold a great deal of white privilege as a Person of Color (often called white presenting). It is currently held in a variety of formats: 2-day (back-to-back days, 8 hours each day), 4-week (once a week, 4 hours each session), and 9-week (once a week, 2 hours each session). The first two formats consist of a total of 16 hours. The 4-week and 9-week formats also include assignments, which we call *lifework,* that are to be done between sessions in assigned accountability groups. The different formats are offered according to the need of the group. The 2-day training is for participants who want an immersive and intense experience. The 4-week trainings are for larger groups who also want an immersive experience but are not able to accommodate a 2-day training. The 9-week training (which is 18 hours in total) is for those persons who need a slower pace due to their trauma history or due to multiple demands on their resources. It contains the same information as the other formats but accommodates adjustments to the flow of the curriculum. Below is some of the feedback we have received on the training:

> *I can't thank you enough for this workshop. I have been thinking about it constantly for the last two days. It has changed the way I think about my teaching, my relationships, my speech, and my willingness to risk and take action. The more I think about it, the more I realize how shame*

*separates and hardens us, and the more I realize the specific ways it manifests in me and keeps me from conversations/ways of being that would be more engaged and authentic.*

*The accountability groups and the opportunity to apply the learnings in a safe space with white partners. The insight and shared experiences by Alana were also extremely helpful in challenging perceptions and preconceived notions or assumptions. Finally, the way in which both Robin and Alana embodied and modelled—whether intentional or not—empathetic supportive listening while holding a place for accountability was so valuable. I will forever have an inner Robin and inner Alana voice that pops in! Somehow you created a class that moved mind and the heart.*

## Personal Reflections

It has been a little over two years since we started to organize and facilitate trainings on shame resilience and transformational skills for white people. In every single one so far, we have witnessed vulnerability and shared pain and empathy and a deep desire to get unstuck from harmful patterns. At the request of participants, we created ongoing monthly consultation groups where we continue to build our understanding, empathy, and window of tolerance for discomfort around shame and trauma. We do this by speaking our shame, sharing the places where we are feeling growth, and using the skills we've learned to recognize when shame triggers come up and working through them and metabolizing the shame into accountability. The best part is that we do this in community.

As a Black woman doing this work (Alana), I was surprised at how deeply moving and hopeful it has been for me. I have also realized that I regularly suppress my rage toward white bodies that continually perpetuate the harm of white supremacy. Through my own therapeutic work, I realized that my own internalized racial inferiority shows up in my taking care of white bodies so as to decrease their threat to me and thus my suppressing rage at my own mistreatment. This has been a powerful revelation that is still hazy, even as I write about it. The suppression of this rage cost me in ways I hadn't recognized. My physical health was compromised, and a part of my heart was closed off from Robin and even some of the participants whom I have grown to love and feel deep affection for. There is a distrust that still exists; some of it from my unacknowledged rage and some of it from living in a body still under daily threat. While I am deeply inspired by this work and softened by the perseverance of Robin and our participants, I'm still somewhat closed off. At first, I was critical of myself for being closed off. Robin's behavior toward me and our work has shown me someone authentically committed to doing real powerful transformational work. Why am I still closed off? Now, I see it a bit differently. I'm still somewhat closed off because white supremacy still dominates globally. As we speak, it is actively destroying the lives of my people and shortening my own from the strain of living in a hated body. My body is protecting me because I still need protection from the torture and brainwashing of a system that sees me only as an object to be used. I am endangered. Until that changes, my body will protect my heart. I have faith that good things will continue to emerge, and healing will continue. Until then I will guard my heart.

I (Robin) continue to learn and grow with each new facilitation. I use the skills we teach in my own life (i.e., continued interrogation of the ways I have internalized and normalized white supremacy culture; understanding my shame triggers and the narratives that go with them—especially around unwanted racial identities; cultivating awareness of and empathy for my shame defenses; practicing managing my shame responses; and making authentic and accountable repairs). I share my strengths and growing edges as a way to heal my own shame so that I can better show up for racial equity. When I speak about my shame, it helps others by melting defensiveness and aloneness. This invites us into a deeper relationship and stronger sense of interdependence where my well-being is intimately tied in with theirs. This slowly metabolizes the shame and allows me to use it in a healthy way. It also allows me to have compassion and empathy for myself while still being accountable for my thoughts and actions. I have left every workshop feeling a sense of community, love, and hope. Feedback from participants continues to humble me and remind me that this is indeed the work I am supposed to be doing.

Robin said: "This invites us into a deeper relationship and stronger sense of interdependence where my well-being is intimately tied in with theirs." This sentence summarizes exactly why I (Alana) do this. I didn't realize this at first. I came into this work to help white people deal with their internalized racial superiority and its manifestations in maintaining white dominance. White supremacy is destroying the lives of my people and I wanted to do everything in my power to interrupt and dismantle it. I didn't realize that, in addition to this, the well-being of these beautiful human beings was deeply intertwined with my own. This powerful and life-altering realization has forever changed how I show up to do racial justice work. This is not just about teaching people how to do something they don't yet know how to do; this is about *building transformational relationships that heal us all.*

**ROBIN SCHLENGER, MSW, LCSW,** is an antiracist therapist, supervisor, consultant, coach, and organizer. She specializes in facilitating presentations and trainings that are rooted in restorative and antiracist principles. She speaks extensively on white privilege from an individual and organizational perspective and what it means to partner with People of Color in antiracist work. Robin is a current member of The People's Institute of Survival and Beyond's (PISAB) North East Leadership team and a member of The European Dissent (ED) leadership team, which is an Affinity Group of PISAB. ED is a group of people of European Decent who "dissent" from the ideology of white supremacy and organize together with other whites and People of Color to undo racism. She received her Master of Social Work from New York University and continues to study and utilize Psychodrama, Drama Therapy, and Playback Theater. Robin wants to acknowledge and lift up the BIPOC in her life whose generosity and patience have made it possible to be doing this work. Without them, she would not be where she is today.

**ALANA TAPPIN, PSYD,** Dr. Alana Tappin is a clinical psychologist and the owner of a psychology clinic that specializes in psychological support for marginalized and racialized people, based in Toronto, Ontario, Canada. Dr. Tappin earned her doctorate degree from Long Island University, C. W. Post Campus in 2012 (specialization in family violence). She has a book chapter (in press) aimed at exploring the Black female identity and mental health. Dr. Tappin developed the idea of applying shame resilience theory (by Dr. Brené Brown) to racial justice. She and her colleague Robin Schlenger, LCSW, codeveloped a training series based on this idea entitled *Shame Resilience and Transformational Skills for White People*. She has developed a new training series entitled *Addressing the Pain of Internalized Anti-Blackness* and does antioppression and antiracism trainings for mental health professionals. Dr. Tappin is a faculty member at The Institute for Advanced Psychotherapy at Loyola University in Chicago. She teaches about the intersection of systems of power, oppression, and the therapeutic process and leads weekly case consultations for students pursuing a postgraduate training in advanced psychotherapy.

## References

*Amodeo, J. (2016, August 18). The power of healthy shame: How shame can attune us to others.* Psychology Today. *https://www.psychologytoday.com/ca/blog/intimacy-path-toward-spirituality/201608/the-power-healthy-shame*

*Brach, T. (2019).* Radical compassion: Learning to love yourself and your world with the practice of RAIN. *Penguin Life.*

*Braden-Foxx, A. J. (Producer & Director). (2020, March 1).* A masterclass for healers *[Web series]. Wholehearted. https://www.wholehearted.org/title/a-masterclass-for-healers/*

*Brown, B. (2006). Shame resilience theory: A grounded theory study on women and shame.* Families in Society, *87(1), 43–52. https://doi.org/10.1606/1044-3894.3483*

*Brown, B. (2007).* I thought it was just me (but it isn't): Making the journey from "what will people think?" to "I am enough". *Avery.*

*Brown, B. (2018).* Dare to lead: Brave work. Tough conversations. Whole hearts. *Random House.*

*Danielian, J., & Gianotti, P. (2013).* Listening with purpose: Entry points into shame and narcissistic vulnerability. *Jason Aronson, Inc.*

*DiAngelo, R. (2018).* White fragility: Why it's so hard for white people to talk about racism *Beacon Press.*

*DiAngelo, R. (2021).* Nice racism: How progressive white people perpetuate racial harm. *Beacon Press.*

*Fosha, D. (2000).* The transforming power of affect. *Basic Books.*

*Frederick, R. (2020, November 24).* Why we need to treat anger as an emotion, not a behavior. *The Center for Courageous Living. https://www.cfcliving.com/anger-is-an-emotion-not-a-behavior/*

*Jones, K., & Okun, T. (2001).* The characteristics of white supremacy culture. *Showing up for racial justice. https://www.showingupforracialjustice.org/white-supremacy-culture-characteristics.html*

*Kaufman, G. (1992).* Shame: The power of caring *(3rd ed.). Schenkman Books, Inc.*

*Kaufman, G. (2004).* The psychology of shame: Theory and treatment of shame-based syndromes *(2nd ed.). Springer Publishing Company.*

*Lyon, B. (2020, September 11).* Advanced 1: Giving back the shame *[Online workshop week 1]. Center for Healing Shame.*

*Lyon, B., & Rubin, S. (2021).* Healing shame: How to work with this powerful, mysterious emotion--and transform it into an ally *(B. Lyon & S. Rubin, Narrs.) [Audiobook]. Sounds True.*

*Menakem, R. (2017).* My grandmother's hands: Racialized trauma and the pathway to mending our hearts and bodies. *Central Recovery Press.*

*Pender Greene, M., Blitz, L. V., & Bernabei, S. (2016, October 13). Achieving racial equity through social work: Internalized racial oppression.* The New Social Worker. *https://www.socialworker.com/feature-articles/practice/internalized-racial-oppression/*

*Sensoy, Ö., & DiAngelo, R. (2017).* Is everyone really equal?: An introduction to key concepts in social justice education *(J. A. Banks, Ed., 2nd ed.). Teachers College Press.*

*Sue, D. W. (2016).* Race talk and the conspiracy of silence: Understanding and facilitating difficult dialogues on race. *Wiley.*

*Wilkerson, I. (2020).* Caste: The origins of our discontents. *Random House.*

## CHAPTER 28

# Transformative Love

## An Antidote to White Domination Disorder

TIMOTHY BAIMA, PHD

PALO ALTO UNIVERSITY

I am a 48-year-old, straight, white, cisgender man who has been searching for spiritual wholeness and love for as long as I can remember. Less than ten years ago, I found a therapist who was able to help me begin to heal from long-standing wounds and trauma and to learn to love myself. I had always balked at the notion of loving oneself. To me it conjured up images of superficial affirmations and cotton candy emotions. I could not have been more wrong. The work of loving myself has proven to be one of the most challenging endeavors of my life. Instead of merely cultivating positive feelings, I have been working to develop something that aligns with bell hooks's (2000a) definition of love: committed action dedicated to nurturing spiritual growth. "Spiritual" does not refer only to religion. While spirituality is the life breath of religion, it is also our life breath, that aspect of self that feels core to us. Spiritual growth involves the essence of our being and transcends the limitations of our being to connect us with that which is greater than our self (hooks, 2000a; Walsh, 2019). Self-love involves intimacy with that core aspect of self and a tenacious dedication to nurture the wholeness of one's being.

It wasn't until I started to practice self-love that I gradually became aware of my dependence on domination. Loving myself has required me to draw near to parts of myself that I have feared and hated. I suppressed these parts of myself so thoroughly that I came to believe they didn't exist. This was especially true of my own racism and internalized racial superiority. For many years I understood, cognitively, that everyone who lives in a white supremacist society internalizes white supremacy to some degree, especially white people. I acknowledged that this was also true of me, but only to the degree that it was an inevitable circumstance of socialization (DiAngelo, 2016). I was too afraid to honestly examine my heart for racism. It is no surprise that many white people share my experience (DiAngelo, 2016). We tend to think of racism in a binary and totalizing manner, that one either is or is not a racist. This way of thinking makes it very difficult to honestly acknowledge our own racism without feeling as if we are losing our identity as a good person (Hardy & Laszloffy, 2008). But even if we resist this binary conceptualization of racism, it is extremely difficult to be present with the fear, shame, and heartache of recognizing racism within ourselves, especially if we have not learned to be present with ourselves in a nurturing manner. Without a capacity for self-love, we are not likely to know what to do with the intense feelings that emerge when we learn about ourselves as white people. Consequently, we tend to unconsciously and unintentionally draw upon our power to shut down interactions we could learn from (Hardy, 2016a, 2016b) or suppress the very thoughts and feelings that need our attention if we are to nurture growth that goes right to the core of our being. These reflexive and compulsive behaviors are examples of the ways in which white people use domination and control to cope with discomfort. When people have access to unearned power, they can draw upon that power to take control of inherently vulnerable situations that call upon them to grow (Hardy, 2016a; Menakem, 2017). Consequently, those of us with great social privilege and power, such as white people, may develop an addiction to domination without even realizing it (McGoldrick & Hardy, 2019). As long as we remain driven by an addiction to domination, it will be very difficult to cultivate love that nurtures spiritual growth.

Only through practices of self-love have I begun to find the courage to intimately examine my own internalized white supremacy. Cultivating practices of self-love includes learning to care for myself. When I can trust myself to recognize my need for care and give it to myself when needed, I am best positioned to self-reflect honestly. When my self-reflection reveals racist thoughts and feelings, I am better equipped to be present with myself in a way that nurtures deep emotional growth. Each step of this process could be considered an act of self-love, and each step can only occur when I resist the constant lure to exercise domination and escape. In this chapter, I reflect on some of the ways domination undermines our capacity, as white people, to practice the love that nurtures spiritual growth, and I also offer a perspective on how self-love can help us to let go of our addiction to domination. I believe that this internal work is critical to healing the spiritual depravity in our hearts caused by internalized white supremacy and that engaging in a process of personal transformation is fundamental to developing racial sensitivity as a white therapist (Baima & Sude, 2020; Hardy, 2016b).

For most of my life, I would have dismissed the notion that I had any relationship with domination at all, let alone consider that I was addicted to it. This is because I had a very narrow understanding of what domination meant. I thought of it as intentional. I associated it with mean-spiritedness, greed, narcissism, and tyranny. People who practiced domination were willfully corrupt, violent, and arrogantly self-assured. I felt nothing like this. My working-class background and the lack of education in my family have fostered a deep sense of imposter syndrome since my first days in college. Additionally, I had untreated experiences of childhood trauma that manifested in feelings of anxiety, inferiority, and an insatiable need for acceptance and affirmation from others. The pain and shame of these repressed experiences exacerbated a good–bad binary (DiAngelo, 2016) within me. My drive to be a "good" person was directly proportional to a deep sense of being "bad," and I dared not acknowledge "badness" in myself, since doing so would cause me to lose my sense of being good. Being white provided me with the opportunity to deny my badness and project it onto People of Color.

I rationalized that I could not practice domination because I felt insignificant and emotionally fragile. I now realize that I am *most* likely to exercise domination not when I feel powerful, but when I feel vulnerable (Hardy, 2016a). Exercises of domination are often free of intention or feelings of personal strength. They can be impulsive reactions to naïveté, fear, insecurity, and pain in anyone who has access to power (Hardy, 2016a). For me, this is especially true when my sense of self is so fragile that I cannot tolerate authentic self-reflection about my faults or the harm I have caused. In these moments, my self-absorption with my own sense of vulnerability leads me to react with impulsive defensiveness. It is the unearned social power I hold as a white man that affords me the ability to react impulsively without concern for the consequences of my actions or sensitivity to the People of Color I harm. Indeed, white privilege has taught me that I can anticipate care rather than consequences when I react with impulsive defensiveness (Hardy, 2016a; Hardy, 2016b). Because People of Color are socialized to take care of the privileged (Hardy, 2019), I am probably unaware of the vast majority of times my racism has harmed People of Color. I find it deeply troubling and painful to recognize that People of Color have felt compelled to take care of me when my racism has harmed them. I also find it troubling to recognize a common reaction I have had to People of Color who are courageous enough to be honest with me instead of taking care of me. My response has often been to feel like a misunderstood victim, to become defensive, and to recruit care from the very person I have harmed. I have done this even when the Person of Color has been honest with me in an effort to strengthen our relationship. Instead of appreciating their effort and vulnerability, I have been consumed with my own vulnerability and with regaining a sense of comfort and control.

My experiences of expecting care when my racism causes harm and feeling like a victim when that care is not offered are common among white people (DiAngelo, 2018; Hardy, 2016a; Menakem, 2017). White supremacy cultivates a perverse form of narcissism in which white people insist on superiority to compensate for a lack of self-knowledge and feelings of inferiority. Our racism harms People of Color, and when they have natural human responses such as pain, rage, self-advocacy, or withdrawal, we insist that we are the victims of the natural consequences of *our actions*. White privilege has gotten us so accustomed to an entitlement to feel good and right that an accurate challenge to our need to grow, even when offered supportively, feels unfair, unsafe, and sometimes assaultive to us. This is especially true when these challenges come from People of Color to whom we see ourselves as superior (DiAngelo, 2018). Therefore, to us, using domination to safeguard our privilege tends to feel fair rather than oppressive. I am convinced that we white people simply cannot nurture our own spiritual growth, nor the spiritual growth of other people in our role as therapists, when we stubbornly cling to our addiction to domination, our entitlement to privilege, and our delusional narcissistic stance of being perpetually misunderstood victims.

## Domination and Whiteness

Fundamentally, domination is a form of control. But unlike a healthy sense of control or mastery, which may be rooted in personal empowerment or power in community, domination exercises power over others, requiring their submission (Pinderhughes, 2017). The resulting power inequity tends to be rationalized by creating myths about the inherent inferiority of the subjugated groups and the inherent superiority of the dominant groups (DiAngelo, 2016). As mental health professionals, we are likely to hypothesize that an individual who requires a sense of superiority is compensating for a sense of inferiority. However, we seem reluctant to apply this insight when social structures of domination dictate a group's inherent right to superiority, namely, white people and men. As bell hooks (2000b) says:

> Cultures of domination attack self-esteem, replacing it with a notion that we derive our sense of being from dominion over another. Patriarchal masculinity teaches men that their sense of self and identity, their reason for being, resides in their capacity to dominate others. (p. 70)

To maintain this dominance, patriarchy requires men to sacrifice all parts of themselves that are affiliated with anything that would render us feminine, childish, or gay, such as tender emotions, softness, vulnerability, and uncertainty (hooks, 2004). hooks (2004) further asserts that a boy's first act of violence is likely to be against himself, as he tries to kill any part of his humanity that would give the slightest indication of weakness or vulnerability.

Whiteness has always operated in a similar fashion to patriarchy, providing white people with a sense of identity through the myths of superiority and of a right to dominate over People of Color (Billings, 2016; Menakem, 2017). The concept of "whiteness" was created in the American Colonies toward the end of the seventeenth century for the purpose of tyrannical rule (Billings, 2016). Whiteness ensured that Indigenous people and people of African descent would not be granted rights and privileges under the laws that were intended to benefit Anglo settlers. Whiteness was also used strategically, giving poor whites a false sense of superiority via their identification with the ruling class, in order to ensure poor whites would not ban together with Indigenous people and enslaved Africans to overthrow the ruling class (Billings, 2016). Jobs were created to reinforce poor whites' sense of superiority by tasking them with overseeing and policing People of Color with every form of genocide, torture, and physical and psychological terrorism imaginable (Billings, 2016; Muhammad, 2019). The narrative about the superiority of whites and their inherent right to domination has been maintained for centuries. The violent methods used to assert and maintain dominance have changed, but the physical and psychological terrorism that maintains this power differential is so deeply embedded in our cultural identity that protests for racial equality are commonly viewed as anti-American.

Whiteness does not only cultivate an addiction to domination, it is the essence of it. Just as patriarchy requires men to assault anything within themselves associated with femininity in order to maintain dominance, whiteness requires that we white people assault vital parts of our own human spirit in order to dehumanize People of Color (Menakem, 2017). At times, it even requires white people to cut with their own ethnic ties to become white (Billings, 2016). The history of whiteness as domination is clear. What is often less clear to those of us who are white is why we continue to get hooked on the myth of racial superiority and to replicate whiteness as a structure of domination.

In *I Am Not Your Negro*, James Baldwin (2017) writes:

> What white people have to do is try and find out in their own hearts why it was necessary to have a "nigger" in the first place, because I'm not a nigger. I'm a man. But if you think I'm a nigger, it means you need him. (pp. 108–109)

Baldwin's charge is a powerful call for us white people to examine our own internalized white supremacy and to try to understand what has made us so susceptible to the myth of racial superiority. But as I read these words, I do not immediately pause and examine myself. Instead, my defenses spring into action. My first inclination is to think about other white people; the white people I consider to be the "real racists," and I celebrate Baldwin's power as he calls on *them* to be accountable. I don't want this quote to apply to me. I don't want the horrors of racism to be about me. I want to be an exception, a good white person. But the part of myself that I often suppress knows that Baldwin is also speaking to me.

I ask myself, "Why not try to answer Baldwin's charge for this chapter? Wouldn't that embody the kind of love I am aspiring to write about?" This thought floods me with fear. I know this fear. It is the same fear that has often flooded me when I have been challenged to examine myself racially. I have often responded to it with domination, either by using my power to silence People of Color or to shame other white people to make myself look better, or by suppressing thoughts and feelings that would reveal my own racism and racial superiority. I have often chosen domination and maintaining my illusion of being a "good white man" over cultivating the type of love that would nurture my spirit and help me actually become a better white man.

My illusion of myself as a good white man who was free of any "real racism" came crashing down when I had a mental health crisis several years ago. A friend gave me two referrals for therapists, one a white woman and one a Black man. When I saw the referrals, I instantly knew I would choose the white woman. I remember having a simultaneous thought and feeling flash through me: "I need someone I can trust—someone who will help me instead of challenge me on racial privilege." I knew this was racist, but even so, I never called the Black therapist. At a time when there was no one to try to look good for and I was confronted with a moment of great need, my racial superiority was self-evident. I viewed white people as more competent than Black people. I saw white people as better—plain and simple.

So, while I desperately want Baldwin's charge to apply only to other white people, it most certainly applies to me. If I see white people as superior, I simply cannot say that I have not had a need for People of Color to be inferior. When I stop resisting and simply look in my heart with the question, "Why have I needed a 'nigger'?", I find that the answer comes to me quite clearly. I have clung to the notion of my inherent superiority, and the inherent inferiority of People of Color, to compensate for the insecurity, shame, guilt, and inferiority I have carried my whole life. I have leaned on racial superiority to avoid my own pain and to bolster a superficial sense of worth. I have used it to avoid racial stress and pain and the discomfort of being emotionally present with People of Color who are speaking truthfully about race and challenging my power and privilege. I have used racial superiority to further elevate my status to a white person who cares about race, feeding my own sense of superiority not only to People of Color, but also to other white people who I perceive as not caring as much about racial justice as I do.

Racial superiority is a myth and a tactic for avoiding our internalized inferiority and pain. Domination is the behavior we engage in to avoid the hard work of dismantling white supremacy and of healing the underlying pain and inferiority that cause us to cling to this myth. It seems that our dependency on racial superiority is so great that dominating behaviors become not only impulsive but compulsive. We white people seem compelled to exercise domination to protect our unearned power and our illusion of racial superiority. Next, I share five of the primary ways I have exercised domination to that end.

*Defensive Denial*

In my early days of engaging in racial sensitivity training, I felt entitled to being seen and accepted as an ally, especially by People of Color. I also considered my intentions to have more validity and importance than another person's experience of me (Hardy, 2016a/2016b). If a Person of Color was hurt or offended by me, I considered the issue to lie within them, not in me. Moreover, I viewed the responses to the hurt caused by my racist actions to be acts of aggression toward me. Often feeling like a misunderstood victim, I used my power to silence People of Color with defensive arguments and deadly glares. Essentially, I was afraid of losing my perceived status as a good person. I also believed that if I had any racism at all, I would be a "bad person" and lose my relationships with People of Color. My binary thinking allowed no space for honest self-reflection or awareness or sensitivity in my relationships with People of Color.

Over time, the way I practiced defensive denial shifted. I gradually began to accept the inevitability of internalizing racist views, but I only allowed myself to acknowledge this at an abstract intellectual level (DiAngelo, 2016). I also recognized that overt defensive denial was only digging me deeper into disconnection from People of Color. I began to *genuinely* care about undoing racism in my own life. I *genuinely* ached over the stories

I heard about racial oppression. I *genuinely* worked hard to improve myself. But the thing I needed most was an ability to *genuinely* look at my own racism, and I was too afraid and insecure to do that. Instead, I exercised defensive denial over myself, suppressing the racist thoughts and feelings that needed my attention in order for me to nurture deep spiritual growth. I also practiced the other exercises of domination that follow in this section. Each one is essentially a form of defensive denial, in that each has been a tactic for avoiding the vulnerable self-examination of my own racism.

### *Shame*

When challenged on racism, I expressed intense shame. I cried. I made declarations of how awful I was. I apologized profusely. I took up a lot of space and made myself the center of attention. While this was never an intentional exercise of manipulation, the message I was attempting to communicate through all my shame was, "That racist thing I did does not reflect who I truly am; my intentions and miserable feelings do, and I deserve your acceptance because of them." When I expressed shame, I felt intense emotion that I assumed was repentance, passion for justice, and love for the Friends and Colleagues of Color I harmed. I do not doubt the authentic presence of these emotions. However, I suspect that what I actually felt most intensely was fear. My inability to love myself and nurture my own worth left me dependent on external validation. I feared what was in my own heart. I feared losing control of how my mentors and peers viewed me, especially my Mentors and Peers of Color. I feared losing control of how I viewed myself. Although challenges on my racism were usually offered to me in order to develop more honest, trustworthy, and intimate relationships with People of Color, I was haunted by fear that once my true self was revealed, everyone would see how unlovable I was, and I would be left alone. My fears were intensified by my inability to love and care for myself when I felt vulnerable. My shame was the desperate defense of a cornered animal warding off the call to honestly examine myself, rooted in the delusions that this would preserve rather than harm my relationships with People of Color.

When I coupled shame with expressions of my sincere desire to learn and grow, I was often able to successfully recruit compassion and care, which I had not yet learned to give myself. Recruiting care and compassion from People of Color became a way for me to elicit a superficial sense of redemption for my own racism and internalized white supremacy that I was too afraid to intimately confront myself.

### *Intellectualization*

When I was a child, I used intellectualization as a coping strategy to manage trauma and family distress. Intellectualization numbed me to vulnerable emotions and offered me a sense of control. As is the case with so many coping strategies, that which served me well at one time later became a hindrance to my growth. When challenges to examine my own racial superiority triggered my sense of being a bad person, I used intellectualization as a way to remain engaged with ideas while obfuscating my personal relationships with white supremacy and racism. Because intellectualization has long been a favorite coping mechanism of mine, I convinced myself that intellectual understanding of race and white supremacy was the same thing as doing the hard work of nurturing emotional and spiritual growth. It wasn't. Information is not the same as transformation. Intellectualization distanced me from my own vulnerable emotions and fed my internal good–bad binary as I convinced myself that only a good person would take time to understand racism. I also used intellectualization to exercise control over People of Color in conversations about race. Derailing dialogues from emotional engagements to intellectual exchanges made interactions safer and more comfortable for me, while creating frustrating and painful interactions for the People of Color who tried to engage my heart.

### *Perfectionistic Performance*

When a sense of inherent entitled superiority is foundational to self-worth, the unconscious prideful arrogance that positions us as *better than* becomes reflexive and powerfully addictive. My dependence on a sense of superiority did not suddenly disappear when I began to learn about racism and whiteness. Instead, I began to also assume superiority over other white people whom I judged to care less about racial justice than I did. Perfectionistic performances have been my way of feeding this sense of superiority.

White people do not stop being white when there are no People of Color around. Instead, superiority and domination become central to how we exist and operate in our relationships with each other. Therefore, perfectionistic performance often takes the form of shaming and intimidating other white people when they are racially insensitive. Perfectionistic performances are often filled with good intentions. In my case, perfectionistic performances are often born out of a sincere desire to act as an ally and use my privilege to hold other white people accountable. However, the notion that accountability must include shaming and intimidation further reveals my addiction to domination. Furthermore, when I have used shame and intimidation to hold white people accountable, I have often had a hidden agenda to look good in the eyes of People of Color.

When People of Color have expressed pain or held me accountable, I often have not been emotionally attuned and engaged with them. Instead, my focus has been on assessing how well I am acting as an ally. Therefore, even my validating conversations with white colleagues and tearful apologies to People of Color were perfectionistic performances whenever what I cared most about at the time was how people were perceiving me.

One of the ways perfectionistic performance has been most salient in my life is through my acts of service to People of Color. In my adolescence and early 20s, I joined my church on several missionary trips to economically disadvantaged areas of Mexico to provide simple construction and to lead Bible camp activities for children. I never bothered to pause and ask why the people in these villages, who were already predominately Christian, would want or need large groups of mostly white non-Spanish-speaking teenagers to pray for them or teach their children about Jesus through translators. It was our race and US citizenship that allowed me to feel special for being willing to spend a week with Brown people that I obviously felt were inferior enough to be grateful for our presence among them. My sense of racial superiority had not changed 15 years later when I started working as a home-based therapist in economically disadvantaged African American and Latino urban communities. I continued to view my service to People of Color as something that made me exceptional, and I expected praise for my efforts.

Once again, the driving force of my perfectionistic performances has been my fear of confronting my spiritual depravity, immaturity, and pain in a way that might nurture authentic growth. Fear of confronting my authentic self has only maintained the very condescending attitudes toward People of Color that are the antithesis of the image I have wished to uphold, and my white savior complex has only further distanced me from an awareness of my own need for growth.

*Self-Domination*

When all else has failed, I have directed domination toward myself. Any indication of racism or white supremacy that surfaces in my consciousness has been swiftly met with suppression. When I have been confronted with my racism and internalized white supremacy and suppression has failed, I have harshly punished myself with a cruel and abusive internal dialogue. I have engaged in enough verbal self-abuse to refine my perfectionistic performances, but abuse cannot nurture growth. My abusive self-talk has only served to intensify my fear of looking inward and nurturing authentic growth. Ultimately, I have found it easier to punish myself with abusive self-talk than to do the work of examining myself and nurturing growth.

*Choosing Love Over Domination*

In *The Fire Next Time*, Baldwin (1993) writes:

> There appears to be a vast amount of confusion on this point, but I do not know many Negroes who are eager to be "accepted" by white people, still less to be loved by them; they, the blacks, simply don't wish to be beaten over the head by the whites every instant of our brief passage on this planet. White people in this country will have quite enough to do in learning how to accept and love themselves and each other, and when they have achieved this—which will not be tomorrow and may very well be never—the Negro problem will no longer exist, for it will no longer be needed. (pp. 21–22)

As white people, we struggle to know ourselves racially, and we cannot love ourselves when we do not know ourselves. Our inability to know ourselves as racial beings makes it even more difficult for us to know and love ourselves as a group. This seems particularly true of white liberals, such as me, who aspire to be antiracists. We often seem more prone to project our own racism onto other white people and to attempt to forage allyships with People of Color by distancing ourselves from the white people we deem to be the "real racists" than we are to dedicate ourselves to helping white people work through their racial superiority. Knowing ourselves racially requires us to be present with the guilt, shame, and despair that inevitably come with an awareness of the atrocious history of white supremacy, the ways in which we have personally benefited from the oppression of People of Color, and the harm we have each individually caused. It is very difficult to accept and be present with these uncomfortable emotions, so we avoid them. Since we do not know ourselves racially, we are not likely to be aware of our dependency on domination.

Furthermore, as white people, we tend to conceptualize race in a disembodied way and think of it as something separate from all other aspects of ourselves. Each and every aspect of the white person's self is infused with whiteness. Therefore, our dependency on domination is likely to interact with all parts of our self, including how we respond to our subjugated and wounded parts. We may rely on domination to avoid the painful work of healing and nurturing vulnerable aspects of our self, which only intensifies our dependency on a sense of superiority and dominance. In this way, the tension between the unearned power embedded in our privileged selves and the suppressed pain of our subjugated selves generates a powerful feedback loop in which the more we feel inferior, the more we lean on racial superiority, and the more we enact racial superiority, the more we suppress the pain and insecurity that underlie our internalized inferiority. Endowed with social power that we have little to no awareness of, we develop a racial narcissism and continue our legacy of centuries of unimaginable horrors against People of Color, all the while feeling that we are the real victims. Furthermore, we insist that the atrocities we commit be ignored and our insatiable appetite for adoration and exultation as good moral people be continuously fed. Domination drives this feedback loop. Therefore, enacting more domination will only perpetuate it, whether it be directed toward People of Color, toward other white people, or toward ourselves. As Baldwin (1993) insists, it is only through learning to love ourselves that we can begin to overcome racism and internalized white supremacy.

Love nurtures growth. Domination restricts and undermines love. hooks (2000a) references Carl Jung's teaching that domination cannot exist in love. As Jung (1972) explains:

> Logically the opposite of love is hate, and of Eros, Phobos, (fear); but psychologically it is the will to power. Where love reigns, there is no will to power; and where the will to power is paramount, love is lacking. (p. 53)

When we understand love as action, we see that the mechanisms of domination—abuse, shame, intimidation, manipulation, disassociation, and suppression—cannot coexist with love (hooks, 2000a). Even when these mechanisms elicit desired behaviors, they do so out of fear. hooks (2004) reminds us that many spiritual traditions teach us that there is no fear in love. Committing to love that nurtures spiritual growth requires us to learn to let go of domination and to embrace the uncertainty and vulnerability that is central to authentic love.

A commitment to love can be relentless in the face of hardship. Spiritual growth has never been confined to the comfort of pleasant feelings and favorable conditions. In fact, suffering often intensifies the commitment of love and fortifies spiritual growth. Caring for ourselves through experiences of suffering may be an essential component to growing up (Menakem, 2017). Love is power, tenacious in its efforts and stubborn in its commitments. Therefore, love is an enactment of hope. Cornel West (2004) explains that hope is not an objective optimistic evaluation of possible outcomes, but the enduring dedicated stance we take even as we wrestle with despair. In this way, love as action and hope as action are inseparable.

## Learning to Love Myself

It wasn't until I was nearly 40 years old that I found a therapist who helped me begin to learn to love myself. During a session, I flashed on an image of myself at five years old—the age I can first remember experiences of trauma. Seeing my five-year-old self in my mind's eye filled me with repulsion. I hated that kid and wanted to keep him as far away as possible, just as I had wanted to keep the racism in my heart as far away as possible. I had suppressed any memory of him, just as I had so effectively suppressed awareness of my racism and internalized white supremacy. I was afraid to get close to him because of what I might feel if I did, just as I had been afraid of what I would feel if I drew close to my own racism and white supremacy. I had tried to heal from trauma by exercising control, just as I had tried to use control to overcome my own sense of racial superiority.

My work of self-love began by finding a photo of myself at five years old and putting it on my refrigerator to remind myself that little Timmy needed a lot of help and a lot of love. Each meditation and ritual I performed to love my five-year-old self was interrupted by impulses to regain control through denial, suppression, intellectualization, self-abusive talk, or perfectionistic performance for my therapist. All the defenses I learned from whiteness and patriarchy were pulling on me to take back control and abandon love. I think I kept going only because I had such an insatiable craving for spiritual wholeness, healing, and authentic love.

As I learned to love my traumatized inner child, I began to experience deep emotional healing and growth that was raw, vulnerable, and all-consuming. This growth felt entirely different from the ways I had previously tried to grow, when I had focused more on what I could perform than on being present with what was in my heart. This was especially true in the ways I had tried to nurture my racial development. I realized that much of the work I had done on myself as a white man was a house of cards constructed to support my preferred image of myself. Conversely, the work of loving myself to heal from childhood trauma was not driven by anxiety or a compulsive need for superiority, but rather a slowly growing ember of self-respect, self-forgiveness, and hope. While healing happened slowly, each step felt like a step on solid ground. I wanted that kind of authentic growth in addressing my privilege and racial superiority as well. Beginning to heal from wounds that fed my sense of inferiority gave me hope of overcoming my dependency on racial superiority. The self-nurturance that helped me move through the intense pain and shame of my childhood trauma helped me trust myself to be present with intense pain and shame related to my racism. I began to apply self-loving practices in my work to examine myself racially and felt a significant shift from anxious intellectualization and perfectionistic performances to a much more emotionally engaged heart.

To this day, I feel like a small child in my work of uprooting racism and racial superiority. I continue to catch myself compulsively using domination to avoid addressing my whiteness. I believe that recognizing this is an important part of self-love. I don't know if it is possible for me, or any white person, to ever be completely free from a sense of racial superiority or from exercising domination. Because of this, I don't know if we can ever be completely spiritually whole. However, loving myself in a way that helps me confront my own racism and dismantle racial superiority seems to facilitate healing and transformation, and it feels spiritually fulfilling. It is an enactment of hope (West, 2004) despite the difficulty of the work to be done. Below I share a few self-love practices that have helped me confront my racism and nurture my spiritual growth.

*Being Present with Self in a Nurturing, Affirming Manner*

When white people are engaged in conversations about race, we often recruit affirmation from People of Color (Hardy, 2016b). There is nothing wrong with needing nurturing affirmation, but there is something quite insidious about relying on People of Color to give it to us, especially during interactions that are likely to be far more taxing and emotionally exhausting for them than they are for us (DiAngelo, 2018). When privileged people recruit this affirmation from subjugated people, we do not learn to nurture and affirm ourselves. Because men tend to recruit care from women, and white people tend to recruit care from People of Color, we white men may have an especially hard time learning to nurture and affirm ourselves. Consequently, the charge to stop recruiting care from People of Color (Hardy, 2016b) can become conflated with a notion that we should not require this kind of care at all.

Rather than excusing bad behavior or distancing from vulnerable emotions, nurturing self-affirmation enables us to stay engaged with the intensely uncomfortable emotions that come when we confront our own racism. Affirmation can support us to work through the reactivity and pain attached to whatever we find within ourselves (Menakem, 2017). Without a means to stay engaged with intense emotion, we are likely to retreat to dominating behaviors that pull us away from growth.

I needed to learn to provide self-affirmation to keep myself emotionally engaged with healing from childhood trauma, and I gradually began to provide myself with similar affirming messages to keep myself engaged with confronting whiteness. For example, I might say something like, "I am feeling so much shame right now for saying that hurtful racist thing to my friend, and I am so embarrassed about being challenged in front of everyone. It's OK to feel this way and it is OK to take some time to care for myself. I feel awful because I want to be a racially sensitive, trustworthy friend. I can do that by making sure I learn from this experience and being more mindful in the future."

It is important to note that nurturing self-affirmation could easily be used to distance oneself from vulnerable thoughts and feelings (Hardy, 2016a), but this would be another act of domination, not love. The purpose of nurturing self-talk is to remain engaged, not to disengage. It is also important that we don't become dogmatic about refusing affirmation from others. Indeed, it is often through affirmation freely given by others that we learn to affirm ourselves.

### *Develop a Capacity for Honest Self-Reflection*

Nurturing self-affirmation creates a context for honest self-reflection. It can be difficult for white people to practice honest self-reflection because we can draw on our unearned power to deflect attention from our vulnerable thoughts and feelings. On the rare occasion that someone is courageous enough to challenge us to take a deeper look at ourselves, we tend to be well equipped to dismiss them.

We simply cannot nurture any part of ourselves that we cannot confront. We cannot love ourselves without being honest with ourselves. As hooks (2000a) puts it:

> Widespread cultural acceptance of lying is a primary reason many of us will never know love. It is impossible to nurture one's own or another's spiritual growth when the core of one's being and identity is shrouded in secrecy and lies. . . . A core foundation of loving practice, cannot exist within a context of deception. . . . Lying has become so much the accepted norm that people lie even when it would be simpler to tell the truth. (p. 46)

I believe honesty with self is the best way for us white people to get disentangled from perfectionistic performances. Honesty about our racism, our self-proclaimed racial superiority, and our addiction to domination (as well as the insecurities or pain that cause us to cling so tightly to these things) positions us to know ourselves and give ourselves what we need to grow. However, for me, honesty can be the most fear-inducing part of loving myself in a way that nurtures spiritual growth. Honesty feels vulnerable, and vulnerability is scary. When I am honest about my racism and internalized white supremacy, I see that I am still far from being as racially sensitive as I would like to be. It is so tempting to escape vulnerability that I sometimes suppress my racial attitudes or enact perfectionistic performances without even realizing I am doing so.

I recently attended an online workshop on race. At the end of the day, a request was made for a white man to share what he plans to do with the information he heard. After an awkward pause, I decided to comment. I said I would use the stories people told to reflect on how I enact expectations of whiteness from Students and Clients of Color. I meant it, but after the meeting, my comments ate at me. I took some time to reflect and realized that my words were primarily rooted in a desire to look good to the people present. A more honest response would have been that I was moved by the stories that had been shared, but I wasn't sure what I was going to do with them. I then asked myself what it would have been like to share my honest response. Simply asking that question filled me with fear, illuminating how deeply dependent I still am on receiving affirmation from peers, especially People of Color, in order to feel comfortable with myself. I then wondered what might have led me to be so dependent on affirmation in that particular moment. I realized that, in addition to my pervasive entitlement to superiority, I was feeling lonely and depressed in the midst of isolation during COVID-19. It felt good to see colleagues and friends online, and I wanted to end the meeting with positive feelings. Finally, I was able to remind myself that honesty, instead of nice words, would likely have led to the more authentic connection I craved.

My self-reflection was painful. It was frustrating and demoralizing to recognize how dependent I still am on a superficial superiority. My self-reflection was also an exercise of self-love. It was only through honesty that I was able to nurture a bit more growth and become aware of the underlying vulnerabilities that led me to compulsively act out domination instead of telling the truth.

*Deepen Emotional Engagement*

Heartfelt emotional engagement is fundamental to spiritual growth. Many spiritual traditions teach that we are best positioned to grow when we are intimately in touch with sincere humility, interdependency, and even pain. The Sufi poet Rumi (as cited in Siddiq, 2017) writes, “You have to keep breaking your heart until it opens” (para. 16). A heart broken open is open to love. Authentic self-love and spiritual growth are characterized by messiness, vulnerability, pain, and so many other emotions that we white people tend to insist make us *unsafe* when we feel *uncomfortable* (DiAngelo, 2018). No wonder our insistence on the emotional comfort of our privilege leads us to be so developmentally stunted when it comes to race.

Like spiritual growth, relational growth requires vulnerable emotional engagement. Attachment theory continues to provide evidence that secure relational bonds are nurtured in interactions that are attuned, responsive, and *emotionally engaged* (Johnson, 2019). Despite how well we white people think we understand this, in conversations about race, we tend to stay in an emotionally disengaged cerebral place when People of Color are trying to engage us at an emotional level (Hardy, 2016a). White entitlement and racial superiority convince us white people that we deserve trust and friendship from People of Color without having to do the relational work to earn it. Emotional disengagement in our interactions with People of Color is a tactic to safeguard our privilege.

It is no surprise that it is challenging for white people to be emotionally engaged with race and our own racism. For centuries, People of Color have been dehumanized by us (DeGruy, 2017), and we have been systematically desensitized to the trauma we have inflicted upon them (Menakem, 2017). We have clung to the myth of our inherent superiority and to our addiction to domination (Hardy, 2016a; McGoldrick & Hardy, 2019), which closes us off to love (hooks, 2000a). Because People of Color have been so profoundly dehumanized by us, working through our own racism must be nothing less than a process through which People of Color are rehumanized to us—that is, we learn to see them as fully human. Rehumanizing People of Color calls upon our own humanity, especially those parts we have sacrificed in order to be numb to and to justify the atrocities committed against People of Color throughout history and the injurious behaviors we ourselves have committed (Menakem, 2017).

I believe there are at least two ways in which we white people must work on becoming more emotionally engaged with race and our own racial superiority. First, it is essential to engage with People of Color at an emotional level when they are sharing experiences of race with us. This is particularly vital when they are telling us about harm we have caused through our own racism (Hardy, 2016b). We white people can build security, trust, and intimacy with People of Color when we engage in conversations about race in a vulnerable, heartfelt manner and practice accountability and responsible action (DiAngelo, 2018; Hardy & Laszloffy, 2002).

Second, I believe it is important for us to regularly set aside time for self-reflective meditation on our own racism and whatever insecurities or pain lead us to cling so tightly to racial superiority and domination. Our spiritual growth as white people depends on our ability to get out of our heads and into our hearts. However, I have often found it difficult to soften my heart to racial injustice and my own racism. My brain can be quick to make meaning, and my mouth, even quicker, to speak, but my heart often remains stubbornly calloused. After all, it seems naïve to assume that my heart would suddenly break wide open, after a lifetime of being hardened against racial injustice, simply because I willed it to do so. Instead of heaping more shame on myself or dogmatically working to will emotions into existence, I have found it helpful to develop a discipline of self-reflective meditation to engage my heart around race. In these meditations, I strive to get as honest as possible with myself about what I am thinking and feeling. I work to resist all forms of suppression. I try to be present with any emotions I experience and to be curious about what I can learn from them. When my heart is calloused, I focus on the experiences of People of Color and wait for compassion to come. When I am impatient with myself, I get curious about underlying insecurities that I may be unconsciously trying to protect. Sometimes I don't sense much change. Other times my heart breaks open and I feel that I have regained some of my humanity. But it is the discipline of regularly reflecting this way that seems to be softening my heart overall.

### *Embrace Connectedness with Whiteness and White People*

Love can provide us with the courage to understand how we white people are intimately connected to white supremacy, historically and currently. Just as we can heal only the parts of ourselves that we can draw close to, our hope to uproot white supremacy in individuals and institutions lies in our ability to recognize our own complicit actions and inactions that reinforce and benefit from white supremacy. Supportive and collaborative endeavors executed in a communal spirit of humility have the power to uproot racial superiority and dismantle structures of domination. There are certainly places and times for strong advocacy and speaking truth powerfully. There are times for white people who enact white supremacy to be exposed, fired from jobs, and put in prison. However, if we embrace a love ethic, we must be cautious that our righteous indignation not become simply another way for us to bolster our own sense of superiority or to project our own racism onto easy targets. All too often, our target is not an alt-right white supremacist, but our colleague, student, client, friend, or family member who is actually not in such a developmentally different place than we are. Calling people out is often an act of domination that allows us to project our own sense of badness and feed our own sense of superiority.

Love can imbue us with the humility to see our own version of the struggles we see in our white peers. Love guides us to hold each other accountable in the humble spirit of a brother or sister who is on the same path. We can answer the call to support one another in this work so that the burden does not continuously fall on People of Color, but our efforts will likely be effective only when we commit ourselves to mutual vulnerability, honesty, and compassion, as well as accountability. In this space, we can build and nurture white affinity groups that support our own ongoing growth.

### *Seek Healing for All Wounded Parts of Self*

The more unearned social power we have to draw upon, the easier it becomes to avoid vulnerable self-reflection and the difficult work of self-love and healing. It is especially important for us white people who endeavor to be healers to carefully examine how we may use our power to avoid our own healing. We white people tend to believe that our racial identity and consciousness can develop independently from other parts of the self. I believe that whiteness is too intricately entangled with all that we are and that the wounded aspects of the self are too seamlessly entwined with our whiteness for us to successfully address one while neglecting the other. It is very difficult to nurture spiritual growth related to whiteness if we neglect wounded parts of ourselves. Alternatively, working on healing all parts of ourselves strengthens our capacity to confront and to work through racism and racial superiority.

## Application to Teaching, Supervision, and Therapy

I believe that we can only guide our students, supervisees, and clients as far as we have gone in our own work (Hardy, 2016b). As we white therapists, supervisors, and educators begin to choose love over domination, we are better positioned to help the white people we work with to learn to confront their internalized racial superiority in ways that foster spiritual growth. As we do this work, it is extremely important for us to be vigilant about the temptation to misuse the inherent power of our positions to feed a superficial sense of superiority. It is not uncommon to find ourselves wielding the tools of domination even as we endeavor to support personal growth and promote equity and justice. Alternately, we can facilitate this work with humility and in a spirit of mutual support.

The vast majority of white people I have worked with have never learned to be self-nurturing while also being honest with themselves about their own racism. Instead, they tend to swing between defensiveness and shameful self-abuse. Even when they are trying to grow, they often do so by exercising domination and control. I am reminded of my own struggles when I see these processes in the white people I work with. Sometimes I see that, like me, their dependency on domination is rooted in deep insecurities and pain. I remember how the patient and loving investments of my teachers, supervisors, and therapists helped me learn that love, not domination, nurtures growth and healing.

Therefore, as I challenge white people to examine whiteness, it is extremely important to me to help them develop processes to lovingly nurture their own holistic growth. I strive to speak in ways that model positive nurturing self-talk. I rely heavily on Hardy's (2016b) Validate, Challenge, Request (VCR) model, rooting challenges in genuine validation. To facilitate self-exploration, I attempt to act as a broker of permission to get honest about race and racism (Hardy & Bobes, 2016). For me, self-disclosure about my own struggle to overcome racial superiority has been the most effective way to deepen explorations of whiteness in therapy and training. Additionally, transparency about my struggle with whiteness can demonstrate that I have at least some awareness of myself racially. This can be particularly important to People of Color who are gauging how much of a risk they are willing to take in groups that are facilitated by a white man.

I strive to facilitate interactions around race that are as emotionally engaged as possible. My work on becoming more emotionally engaged in issues related to race is fundamental to my efforts. When I am emotionally engaged with Students, Supervisees, and Clients of Color, they seem to feel safer and thus more likely to risk disclosure about their experiences of race and racism with white people in the group as well as with me. When I am emotionally engaged with white students, supervisees, and clients, they seem to experience challenges more supportively, instead of feeling called out. Since white people tend to be emotionally disengaged around race, I tend to devote a great deal of energy helping them to get more connected to their feelings. This is not only for their benefit, it is also an effort to create a safer and more respectful atmosphere for People of Color. In my efforts to help white people deepen their emotional engagement, I invite them to accept the presence of whatever feelings come to them and to be curious about what these emotions might have to teach them. When it seems that a white person is stuck in a cerebral space, I sometimes ask them to stop and notice what is happening emotionally for them before they continue talking. I may also ask a short series of questions such as: "What are you feeling? What might you be feeling if you were more engaged with your heart? What would it be like for you to allow yourself to feel that deeper emotion?" When someone consistently has difficultly becoming emotionally engaged, I might ask them to consider how emotional distance benefits them. When I sense that People of Color may be restricting their authentic expression, I often reflect on what the other white people present and I may be able to do to increase their sense of safety and respect. When working individually with white supervisees and clients, I sometimes draw upon experiential activities, such as art, sand trays, or somatic exercises, to help them connect emotionally to race.

As white students, supervisees, and clients begin to examine their racism, I like to ask about their internal self-talk as they sit with their thoughts and feelings. When their self-talk seems harsh and self-abusive, I often facilitate a guided visualization. I ask them to imagine themselves in the role of a parent whose child has said or done something racist. I invite them to consider how they could be both firm and loving, asking something like, "What would you need to do to ensure the power of your message was communicated while also maintaining a loving connection?" I then invite them to adopt a similar stance with themselves as they examine their own whiteness.

The further I guide a white student, supervisee, or client to become emotionally engaged with their whiteness, the more responsibility I assume in helping them develop the self-loving practices necessary to stay engaged in this work. When participants seem emotionally flooded, Menakem's (2017) somatic exercises can be helpful in learning to discharge and metabolize difficult emotion constructively. It can be very empowering to experience the effectiveness of simple exercises such as humming, moving one's body, or putting our hands over the part of the body that is holding painful emotion (Menakem, 2017). These exercises can teach us white people that we are capable of caring for ourselves when we feel intense emotion as we examine race. As we white people learn to do this, we are less likely to pressure People of Color to take care of us, thereby leaving more space for them to express themselves authentically (Hardy, 2016a).

## Conclusion

White therapists who care about racial justice must be committed to advocating for racial equity in every part of their lives (Baima & Sude, 2020). However, when we remain addicted to domination, we frequently end up relying on this instrument of oppression, even in our efforts to advance healing and justice. It is my hope that we white therapists will relinquish our dependency on domination and learn to trust in the power of love (hooks, 2000a).

**TIMOTHY BAIMA, PHD,** is an associate professor in the Master of Arts in Counseling program at Palo Alto University, California, where he serves as the coordinator for the marriage, family, and child counseling emphasis area. He is also a licensed marriage and family therapist with a private practice in San Mateo, California, and serves on the board of the American Family Therapy Academy. Dr. Baima received his PhD in marriage and family therapy from Syracuse University in 2009. There, issues related to social privilege and power became central to his understanding of relational health. His current research interests center on whiteness and training the "self" of the therapist.

## References

*Baima, T., & Sude, M. E. (2020). What white mental health professionals need to understand about whiteness: A Delphi study.* Journal of Marital and Family Therapy, 46*(1), 62–80. https://doi.org/10.1111/jmft.12385*

*Baldwin, J. (1993).* The fire next time. *Vintage Books.*

*Baldwin, J. (2017).* I am not your negro. *Vintage Books.*

*Billings, D. (2016).* Deep denial: The persistence of white supremacy in United States history and life. *Crandall, Dostie & Douglass Books, Inc.*

*DiAngelo, R. (2016).* What does it mean to be white? Developing white racial literacy. *Peter Lang Publishing, Inc.*

*DiAngelo, R. (2018). White fragility: Why it's so hard for white people to talk about racism. Beacon Press.*

*DeGruy, J. (2017). Post traumatic slave syndrome: America's legacy of enduring injury and healing. Joy DeGruy Publications, Inc.*

*Hardy, K. V. (2016a). Anti-racist approaches for shaping theoretical and practice paradigms. In M. Pender-Greene & A. Siskin (Eds.),* Anti-racist strategies for the health and human services *(pp. 125–139). Oxford University Press.*

*Hardy, K. V. (2016b). Mastering context talk: Practical skills for effective engagement. In K. V. Hardy & T. Bobes (Eds.),* Culturally sensitive supervision and training: Diverse perspectives and practical applications *(pp. 136–145). Routledge.*

*Hardy, K. V. (2019). Towards a psychology of the oppressed: Understanding the invisible wounds of trauma. In M. McGoldrick & K. V. Hardy (Eds.),* Re-visioning family therapy: Addressing diversity in clinical practice *(3rd ed., pp. 133–148). Guilford Press.*

*Hardy, K. V., & Bobes, T. (2016). Core competencies for executing culturally sensitive supervision and training. In K. V. Hardy & T. Bobes (Eds.),* Culturally sensitive supervision and training: Diverse perspectives and practical applications *(pp. 11–15). Routledge.*

*Hardy, K. V., & Laszloffy, T. A. (2002). Couple therapy using a multicultural perspective. In A. Gurman & N. Jacobson (Eds.),* Clinical handbook of couple therapy *(3rd ed., pp. 569–593). Guilford Press.*

Hardy, K. V., & Laszloffy, T. A. (2008). The dynamics of a pro racist ideology: Implications for family therapists. In M. McGoldrick & K. V. Hardy (Eds.), Re-visioning family Therapy: Race, culture, and gender in clinical practice (2nd ed., pp. 225–237). Guilford Press.

hooks, b. (2000a). All about love: New visions. HarperCollins.

hooks, b. (2000b). Feminism is for everybody: Passionate politics. South End Press.

hooks, b. (2004). The will to change: Men, masculinity, and love. Washington Square Press.

Johnson, S. (2019). Attachment theory in practice: Emotionally focused therapy (EFT) with individuals, couples, and families. Guilford Press.

Jung, C. G. (1972). The collected works of C. G. Jung: Two essays in analytical psychology (2nd ed., Vol. 7). Princeton University Press.

McGoldrick, M., & Hardy, K. V. (2019). The power of naming. In M. McGoldrick & K. V. Hardy (Eds.), Re-visioning family therapy: Addressing diversity in clinical practice (3rd ed., pp. 3–27). Guilford Press.

Menakem, R. (2017). My grandmother's hands: Racialized trauma and the pathway to mending our hearts and bodies. Central Recovery Press.

Muhammad, K. G. (2019). The condemnation of blackness: Race, crime, and the making of modern urban America. Harvard University Press.

Pinderhughes, E. (1989). Understanding race, ethnicity, & power: The key to efficacy in clinical practice. The Free Press.

Pinderhughes, E. (2017). Conceptualization of how power operates in human functioning. In E. Pinderhughes, V. Jackson, & P. A. Romney (Eds.), Understanding power: An imperative for human services (pp. 1–23). NASW Press.

Siddiq, A. (2017, October 9). How Rumi inspired me to live soulfully: A journey of gratitude and love for the mystery of life. ThriveGlobal. https://thriveglobal.com/stories/how-rumi-inspired-me-to-live-soulfully/

Walsh, F. (2019). Spirituality, suffering, and resilience. In M. McGoldrick & K. V. Hardy (Eds.), Re-visioning family therapy: Addressing diversity in clinical practice (3rd ed., pp. 73–90). Guilford Press.

West, C. (2004). Prisoners of hope. In P. R. Loeb (Ed.), The impossible will take a little while: A citizen's guide to hope in a time of fear (pp. 293–297). Basic Books.

# Index